Roger,

With warm regards and appreci[illegible] have done and continue to do, as well as for your support of me during my career. Congrats on the Leona Tyler Award -- I was so pleased to learn that you were chosen.

I hope you like the book.

Charlie

Counseling Psychology

WILLIAM
JAMES
CENTENNIAL SERIES

COUNSELING PSYCHOLOGY

Charles J. Gelso, Ph.D.
Bruce R. Fretz, Ph.D.

University of Maryland

Harcourt Brace Jovanovich College Publishers
Fort Worth Philadelphia San Diego New York Orlando Austin San Antonio
Toronto Montreal London Sydney Tokyo

Publisher Ted Buchholz
Acquisitions Editor Eve Howard
Project Editor Clifford Crouch
Production Manager Annette Dudley Wiggins
Art & Design Supervisors Pat Bracken, Serena Barnett Manning
Text Designer Rita Naughton
Cover Designer Margaret Unruh

Library of Congress Cataloging-in-Publication Data

Gelso, Charles J., 1941–
Counseling psychology / Charles J. Gelso and Bruce R. Fretz.
p. cm. — (William James centennial series)
Includes bibliographical references and indexes.
ISBN 0-03-027858-9
1. Counseling. 2. Counseling—Vocational guidance. I. Fretz, Bruce R., 1939– . II. Title. III. Series.
BF637.C6G414 1991
158'.3'023—dc20 91-13805
CIP

Address editorial correspondence to: 301 Commerce Street, Suite 3700, Fort Worth, TX 76102

Address orders to: 6277 Sea Harbor Drive, Orlando, FL 32887
1-800-782-4479, or 1-800-433-0001 (in Florida)

Printed in the United States of America

1 2 3 4 016 9 8 7 6 5 4 3 2 1

To our wives, Jean and Barbara. Although it is conceivable that we could have written this book without the wonderful support and stimulation they have provided over the years and throughout the life of this project, the writing would have been immeasurably harder and our lives a lot less joyful.

Contents in Brief

Preface

Since our graduate school days in the 1960s, we have been troubled by the absence of a beginning textbook in counseling psychology. It appears that every field within psychology has specialized books for students being introduced to the science and practice of that field—except the field that we study, practice, teach, and care most about, counseling psychology. To be sure, there are many books on the activity of counseling, and such books are often used as the texts in beginning courses in counseling psychology. As a result, in fact, not only students but many professionals have mistakenly confused counseling, the activity, with counseling psychology, the profession, (which includes counseling among many other interventions), considering them synonymous.

As the field of counseling psychology expanded in the 1970s and 1980s, the need for a beginning text also grew, but it was not until we personally felt the need for a book that we could begin the arduous task of writing it. Our felt need deepened as we taught introductory courses in counseling psychology at the advanced undergraduate level (Gelso) and the beginning graduate level (Fretz). Improvising with materials from a wide range of sources took us only so far; what we lacked was a beginning text that broadly covered the science and the profession of counseling psychology. By the mid-1980s, we felt moved to action.

This book is about the speciality of counseling psychology—its professional practices and issues, its interventions, its science and research, and its basic concepts. We have sought to furnish a broad overview and at the same time incorporate enough depth to make the material intellectually stimulating. Although the text should prove useful to experienced counseling psychologists, our basic focus is the student commencing his or her study of counseling psychology, be that student at the beginning graduate or the advanced undergraduate level. For usage at the undergraduate level, the book is suitable for the upperclass student who has already completed a number of psychology courses.

The book is divided into four parts. In Part I, we introduce the reader to counseling psychology per se—discuss its defining features and relationship to other specialties and fields within and outside of psychology; its historical background; the ethical and professional issues faced by the specialty; and its scientific and research bases. In Part II, we focus on individual counseling and psychotherapy. After examining the essential ingredients of counseling (the counselor-client relationship and counseling techniques), we provide overviews of the three primary theoretical perspectives in the field (psychoanalytic, cognitive-behavioral, humanistic). We then examine diagnosis and assessment, with an eye toward how assessment uniquely relates to counseling psychology. Part II concludes with a discussion of what has become a vital area within counseling psychology in recent years: cultural diversity and cross-cultural interventions, which relate to all aspects of the profession.

Part III reviews theory, research, and practice in several key intervention areas: career counseling and psychology; couples and family interventions; therapeutic groupwork; prevention and outreach; and consultation. Part IV includes a single chapter that addresses career issues for the student contemplating a future as a counseling psychologist, for the graduate student already steeped in the field, and for the practicing counseling psychologist negotiating the early part of his or her career.

Despite the book's fundamental purpose as a useful comprehensive text, portions of *Counseling Psychology* are also applicable to other courses in the field. For example, the four introductory chapters composing Part I; Chapter 11, which addresses cultural and cross-cultural questions; and Chapter 18, which discusses graduate school and the early postgraduate years, may be combined into a package suitable for courses on professional issues in counseling psychology. Likewise, outside the field proper, Part II and much of Part III could be incorporated into courses covering topics such as theories of counseling and therapy; techniques of counseling; or, simply, introduction to counseling. Thus the inherent value of the text lies in the range of topics covered, which makes the book a useful source at all levels of study and which, at the same time, can be exploited to suit particular aims and needs.

We have been aided in this endeavor by so many people that we could not come close to naming all of them. To begin with, we are grateful to the people at Holt, Rinehart and Winston for their enthusiasm for our idea of a counseling psychology text right from the beginning, and for their guidance throughout. Drs. Jean A. Carter and Jeffrey A. Hayes read many of the chapters and offered numerous helpful suggestions. We are indebted to them. We are also very grateful to those who offered helpful comments on individual chapters: Ms. Roberta Diemer, Dr. Ruth Fassinger, Ms. Cara Forrest, Dr. Clara Hill, Ms. Mollie Jaschik, Ms. Mara Latts, Dr. Mary Leonard, Mr. Richard Lightsey, Dr. James Mahalik, Dr. Thomas Magoon, Mr. Paul McCusker, Dr. Naomi Meara, and Ms. Anne Regan. We are also very appreciative of the large number of graduate and undergraduate students who read chapters as part of their course work and offered valuable comments. Finally, we would like to acknowledge the assistance of the following fellow academics who reviewed our work for Holt, Rinehart and Winston: Dr. Terence Tracey of the University of Illinois; Dr. Roger Myers of Columbia University; Dr. Elizabeth Altmaier of the University of Iowa; Dr. Samuel Osipow of Ohio State University; Dr. Lawrence Schneider of the University of North Texas; Dr. Linda Brooks of the University of North Carolina; Dr. C. Edward Watkins, Jr., of the University of North Texas; Dr. Kathleen Davis of the University of Tennessee; Dr. James Lichtenberg of the University of Kansas; Dr. Mark Hector of the University of Tennessee; and Dr. Thomas Dowd of Kent State University.

We have tried to offer an overview of counseling psychology that is even-handed, accurate, and "objective." Because of our personal interest in the field, however, the reader does not get a completely unbiased perspective; but we think our biases appear controlled and up-front. You, the reader, will of course be the ultimate judge of that.

C. J. G.

B. R. F.

Contents

Counseling Psychology

Part I

An Introduction to Counseling Psychology

Chapter 1

Counseling Psychology: A Growing Profession

This book is devoted to counseling psychology, a specialty within the science and profession of psychology that has shown considerable growth within recent years. In the book we shall delve into what the specialty of counseling psychology is about—its central interventions and practices, the practicing professionals, and the job arenas in which counseling is practiced. We shall examine both the scientific and the professional aspects of counseling psychology, while maintaining the view that science and research are, have always been, and always will be vital and necessary elements of this growing field. Finally, we shall take an in-depth look at the professional issues, problems, and beliefs that characterize the specialty.

On a personal note, this book has been written by two counseling psychologists who have practiced counseling psychology throughout their professional careers. You will not get a wholly impartial picture of the specialty and its issues and practices, simply because we, the authors, are steeped in the field, value it, and are strongly committed to its growth and development. We believe that counseling psychology has something special to offer to both its practitioners and the public, and you will certainly detect this viewpoint in the pages to come. Nonetheless, we have done our best to present the facts of the specialty in a clear, precise, and unbiased way.

STRUGGLE, GROWTH, AND DIVERSITY

In providing a general introduction to the specialty of counseling psychology and its development, three concepts are highly pertinent: struggle, growth, and diversity. The field has labored to clarify its identity, to distinguish itself from other specialties and fields within and outside of psychology, and indeed to maintain itself as a separate and independent specialty within psychology.

There have been times in the life span of counseling psychology in which the specialty seemed to flag. For example, one indication of the health of a professional field is the number of accredited training programs it offers and the changes in this number over the years. Within the first decade of the specialty's life (in the 1950s), there were approximately two dozen doctoral training programs accredited by the American Psychological Association (APA). These programs provided training at the doctoral level and offered degrees such as doctor of philosophy (Ph.D.) and doctor of education (Ed.D.). Following the first decade, however, the growth appeared to stop as the number of programs remained stable for several years and those in other, related specialties such as clinical psychology increased markedly. In the early 1970s, the number of accredited programs even diminished slightly (dropping to 19 in 1972). During this time, the specialty was showing signs of stress and strain: was it really distinctive enough to maintain itself as a separate entity? Did it have broad enough appeal to attract a sufficient number of the best students to its doctoral programs? Was it viewed in sufficient esteem within the psychological community that its graduates could compete successfully in the job markets of their choice?

Any field, specialty, or profession must endure constant flux if it is to avoid stagnation and must struggle with issues involved in defining and enhancing itself. Countering these difficulties, counseling psychology has managed to resolve some of its most serious problems and in recent years has grown substantially. Over fifty doctoral training programs are now accredited by the APA, a figure that has more than doubled within less than a decade (a time when other specialties are growing much more slowly). The third and most recent national training conference, called the Georgia Conference (see the July 1988 issue of *The Counseling Psychologist* for summaries of the conference), reports many other signs of growth and optimism for counseling psychology, its prospects and contributions.

One aspect of the specialty that has been a part of it since its beginnings, and has, if anything, increased in recent times, is its diversity. Counseling psychologists can be found working in a wide range of job settings and performing an even wider range of activities within them. In fact, some have suggested that counseling psychology is the most diverse of all of the specialties in psychology. Ivey (1979), for example, contends that:

> Counseling psychology needs to declare itself for what it is—*the most broadly-based applied specialty of the American Psychological Association.* Our practitioners focus on the broadest array of professional psychological activities of any specialty. The counseling psychologist has the greatest array of possible interventions to assist client development and works with populations from infants through seniors in an almost infinite array of settings. (p. 3)

In a recent textbook Fretz (1985) begins a chapter on counseling psychology by presenting a wide range of job activities and settings for psychologists and asking his reader to guess what kind of psychologist performed all the jobs in each of the settings. Interestingly, all of the jobs have been filled by counseling psychologists and are seen as highly appropriate for these professionals. (We shall present information on job functions and settings later in this chapter.)

Clearly counseling psychology is diverse and diversity is one of its major assets. However, clear and easy self-definitions and rich heterogeneity do not go hand in hand. It is not surprising that counseling psychology has had difficulty defining itself over the years.

At this point it is important to note that, within the diversity we have discussed, there have always existed several general roles and unifying themes in counseling psychology. Although it may seem at times that the specialty is so broad as to have no boundaries, and thus no identity, we believe that the general roles and unifying themes to be discussed below have always served to lend coherence and identity to the field.

DEFINING FEATURES OF COUNSELING PSYCHOLOGY

Throughout the history of counseling psychology, three roles have been central: the remedial, the preventive, and the developmental. (Probably the first to articulate these systematically were Jordaan, Myers, Layton, & Morgan, 1968). The individual importance of the roles has varied over time, yet all three have been significant in lending counseling psychology self-definition.

The *remedial* role entails working with individuals or groups, to assist them in remedying problems of one kind or another. As noted by Kagan et al. (1988), remedial interventions may include personal-social counseling or psychotherapy at an individual, couples (e.g., marriage counseling), or group level. Crisis intervention and various therapeutic services for students requiring assistance with unresolved life events, are additional examples of work at the remedial level.

In remedial work, we take the view that something is awry, something needs to be "fixed," or some problem needs to be solved in the individual, couple, or group. The problem(s) may be specific or general, at the surface level of personality or more deep-seated, and/or current or long-standing. As will be discussed later in this chapter, more counseling psychologists devote more time to this role than to the others; the frequency and popularity of individual counseling and psychotherapy are evidence of the role's prominence (Watkins, Lopez, Campbell, & Himmell, 1986). Nevertheless, the two remaining roles are viewed as vital to the specialty.

The *preventive* role is one in which the counseling psychologist seeks to "anticipate, circumvent, and, if possible, forestall difficulties that may arise in the future" (Jordaan, 1968, p. 1). Preventive interventions may focus on what are called psychoeducational programs aiming to forestall the development of problems or events.

In a university counseling center, one of the principal employers of counseling psychologists, preventive interventions may entail classes or workshops designed to impact a large number of students, for example, drug prevention programs, date-rape seminars for students, or suicide prevention programs for residence hall counselors and university personnel (Kagan et al., 1988). In a business or industrial setting, the preventive role is exemplified by consultations held with the company on matters such as team building, supervisor-staff relationships, management assessment and development, communication enhancement across departments, and so forth. As you can see from these examples, the specific form of the preventive activity is different for various settings. The key feature is to help clients make changes in their personal and interpersonal environments to minimize the occurrence of problems (Fretz, 1985) and forestall remedial work.

The third general role of the counseling psychologist is referred to as the *educative and developmental* role, the purpose of which is to "help individuals to plan, obtain, and derive maximum benefits from the kinds of experiences which will enable them to discover and develop their potentialities" (Jordaan et al., 1968, p. 1). Examples of the educative-developmental role might include various skill training interventions, couples groups formed to enhance relationships, growth groups, various workshops or seminars, and so forth. Another example might be a study skills class for college students aimed at making good students even more effective (rather than remedying ineffective academic behavior).

In the developmental role, the focus is on enhancement. We teach skills or enhance attitudes that facilitate dealing with inevitable, everyday problems and that maximize effectiveness or satisfaction. Obviously, the distinction between the developmental and preventive roles is often subtle—a matter of degree rather than kind. The key feature of the developmental role is that when performing it we are going beyond prevention, and are involved in enhancement.

We have been addressing the three general roles of the counseling psychologist as if each activity involved only one of the roles. Thus, the reader might now think, for example, that individual therapy or counseling is remedial, consultation with residence hall counselors is preventive, and couples' enhancement workshops are developmental. This is far from the truth. Most or perhaps all activities combine the three roles in one way or another. The difference is the point of emphasis. For example, when working in individual counseling with a client suffering from anxiety that interferes with job performance, the primary role of the counseling psychologist may be remedial, but the preventive and developmental roles will also be present. Indeed, one of the distinguishing features of the counseling psychologist is his or her consistent attention to the three roles, and to the preventive and developmental, even when working with clients suffering from severe problems.

Unifying Themes

Although the three roles discussed above help to clarify what counseling psychology is and does, they do not show how it is distinguished from other fields. However, there have always existed certain themes that serve to bring together the diverse and sometimes disparate elements and activities of the profession and to differentiate it from related fields and specialties within and outside of psychology.

The first theme is the focus on intact, as opposed to severely disturbed, personalities. Thus, the specialty and its practitioners devote much of their energies to working with persons within a relatively normal range of problems and with personalities that are not emotionally fragmented. The central thrust of the specialty has always been on clients who are within or closer to the "normal" range—for example: clients who have problems in living; ordinary people with everyday psychological concerns; individuals in the normal-neurotic rather than psychotic range; and clients who function well but would like to improve still further. Considering these focal points, it is easy to see how the preventive and developmental roles discussed earlier fit quite naturally into the work of the counseling psychologist.

As one examines the history of counseling psychology, a subtle but definite change is apparent in what counseling psychologists view as appropriate clientele and problems (see the historical review by Whiteley, 1984). In the earlier years of the specialty, it was most often stated that counseling psychologists worked with "normal" people. In more recent times, however, the range of problems (in terms of severity) with which counseling psychologists work has been extended. Although present-day counseling psychologists continue to be vitally interested in the concept of normality, some do most of their work with the severely disturbed, and most spend at least some of their time working with such persons.

The second unifying theme is the focus on people's assets and strengths and on positive mental health *regardless* of the degree of disturbance. Many years ago, in a classic paper by Super (1955), this emphasis on assets was referred to as a focus on hygiology, or health, rather than psychopathology, or sickness. Super noted that even when working with the severely disturbed, the counseling psychologist tended to look for strengths and build on them. The underlying assumption is that even profoundly disturbed persons have strengths, assets, and coping abilities and that it is valuable to work with these.

Tied to this emphasis on the positive is a "point of view" characterized by hopefulness and optimism, based on the belief that

> individuals can change, can lead satisfying lives, can be self-directing, and can find ways of using their resources, even though these may have been impaired by incapacitating attitudes and feelings, slow maturation, cultural deprivation, lack of opportunity, illness, injury, or old age. (Jordaan et al., 1968, p. 2)

How is this philosophical emphasis on the positive, and on assets and strengths, put into practice? In part, it is an assumption and attitude that we carry with us and convey to our clientele. In addition, the focus on strengths is operationalized in numerous ways. When counseling psychologists do career counseling with very disturbed clients, they are expressing the belief that the client has coping abilities that can be built upon and will allow him or her to make use of the counseling. When counseling psychologists work in an in-patient setting and develop an empathy training program for disturbed patients, they are building on these patients' resources. The reader is encouraged to think of other examples of how this emphasis on strengths may be manifested. Suffice it to say for now that, whenever the counseling psychologist is functioning in the educative/developmental role, she or he is focusing on strengths and assets.

The third unifying theme of counseling psychology is an emphasis on relatively brief interventions. Thus, counseling psychologists typically view counseling as one of their primary activities, and this intervention is, by definition, relatively brief. To clarify what we mean by the term *brief*, it will help to contrast what we call *counseling* with a closely related term, *psychotherapy*. Some psychologists view these two terms as representing the same process, but we think the terms can be differentiated at least in the extreme, and that it is useful to do so.

Although exact numbers (e.g., numbers of counseling sessions) are of course arbitrary, we think of interventions up to about 12–15 sessions as constituting counseling, whereas interventions beyond that point are psychotherapy, or "therapy" as it is commonly called. In further differentiating counseling and therapy, we subscribe to the model suggested by Brammer and Shostrom (1982). In that model, at the extreme ends of the continuum, the two activities differ. At one extreme, work that is supportive, seeks to educate, and focuses on situational problems and problem solving at a conscious level, with normal individuals, is aptly called counseling. At the other end of the continuum, interventions that seek to reconstruct personality, include depth analysis, and analytically focus on unconscious processes with more troubled individuals, are best labeled psychotherapy. In the broad middle-range of this continuum, when the interventions contain a mixture of the factors just described, the terms *counseling* and *psychotherapy* imply one and the same process.

Having discussed the terms, counseling and psychotherapy, let us now return to the issue of duration of treatment. We have said that counseling psychologists view counseling as defined above as a central part of their work (cf. Fitzgerald & Osipow, 1986). Furthermore, although counseling psychologists certainly conduct psychotherapy, the kind of psychotherapy that has been seen as central to the counseling psychology tends to be short-term. Again, although exact figures would be arbitrary, generally interventions of up to six months in duration would be considered short-term therapy.

It should be noted that counseling and therapy are not the only interventions and activities of counseling psychologists. Although they are clearly very important activities, there are many others, for example, consultation, teaching, guidance, supervision, research, administration, training, and so forth. Many of these will be examined in various parts of this book.

The fourth unifying theme of counseling psychology is an emphasis on person-environment interactions, rather than an exclusive focus on either the person or the environment. Although the specialty has been criticized for not paying enough attention to the environment portion of the person-environment interaction in actual practice (as opposed to writing about practice; see Ivey, 1979), counseling psychology has since its inception carefully considered the impact and role of the situation in the client's life (whether the client is an individual, group, organization, etc.). Consequently, theories that have placed an extreme emphasis on *intrapsychic* explanations of behavior have not on the whole been attractive to counseling psychologists. The interest in person-environment transactions is also evident in the attention paid in recent times to activities such as consultation, outreach, and environmental modification (Ivey, 1979; Meade, Hamilton, & Ka-Wai-Yuen, 1982; see also Chapter 13 of this text).

The fifth and final unifying theme is an emphasis on educational and career development of individuals and on educational and vocational environments. Along with educational psychologists, counseling psychologists have contributed significantly to the study of academic performance and problems. An early example of this is the work of Robinson and his students on the development of effective study methods and treatments (Robinson, 1970). In the career development area, counseling psychologists both study vocational choice and development and provide services to enhance career development and treat vocational problems. For some counseling psychologists, career counseling and development is the heart of counseling psychology and is its most distinctive area of research and practice (e.g., in contrast to personal counseling or therapy, an activity counseling psychologists share with many other professionals). These psychologists are concerned that practitioners are no longer making career counseling a central enough part of their work and are not as interested in it as they ought to be or used to be (Fitzgerald & Osipow, 1986; Watkins et al., 1986).

Although counseling in the career development area does represent less of the worktime of counseling psychologists than, for example, counseling in the area of personal problems, counseling training has been strong in the vocational area (Birk & Brooks, 1986) and has remained as strong as it was a number of years ago (Schneider, Watkins, & Gelso, 1988). Also, practicing counseling psychologists continue to devote time to career and educational interventions, particularly when they work in educational settings, such as counseling centers.

A Perspective on Definition and Identity

From what we have presented thus far in this chapter, it can be seen that counseling psychology is that specialty within psychology that focuses on research, assessment, and interventions on and with relatively intact personalities, i.e., people who are usually not severely disturbed and might be considered in the "normal range," but who want psychological assistance of one type or another. Also, the specialty tends to focus on people's assets or psychological strengths—even when those people are severely disturbed. The central interventions of the specialty tend to be relatively brief and varied, e.g., counseling, therapy, guidance, training, consultation and outreach, teaching, etc. Throughout the life of the specialty, particular attention has been paid to person-environment interactions and to educational and vocational development and environment.

It is important to stress that the roles and themes discussed in the preceding sections represent central tendencies. Among individual practitioners, there exists a great deal of variability, each differing with respect to modes of practice and areas of emphasis. A given practitioner may do primarily long-term therapy but still consider herself a counseling psychologist, because she focuses on assets, does a good deal of career counseling within the context of her psychotherapy, and tends to focus on her clients' coping abilities. Another counseling psychologist-practitioner may do little counseling or therapy. Instead, he conducts workshops on a variety of issues and works with emotionally healthy individuals in a developmental-educative role.

Given the above complexity, what determines whether one is a counseling psychologist and whether one is doing counseling psychology? Just as in any field or profession, the answer to such a question must be complex. We would offer that whether one is a counseling psychologist and does counseling psychology is determined by the interaction of all of the variables discussed so far. Given that the practitioner is properly credentialed in the specialty (discussed in the next section), that practitioner may perform a wide range of activities and be legitimately considered a counseling psychologist doing the work of counseling psychology.

TRAINING, JOB SETTINGS, AND ACTIVITIES

In this section, we shall look at the kind of graduate training required to be a counseling psychologist, where counseling psychologists work, and the typical job activities in which they are involved.

How and Where Are Counseling Psychologists Trained?

Unlike numerous psychological and educational-vocational counselors who work with a master's degree, the counseling psychologist is trained at the doctoral level. It is strongly recommended that the doctorate (usually a Ph.D.) be earned from a university training program accredited by the APA. Such accreditation influences several factors that are typically quite important to the professional life of the counseling psychologist: how readily he or she can become licensed as a psychologist in the state in which he or she practices; the range of psychologist positions in which he or she is employable; whether or not he or she can become a member of several important organizations, for example, the National Register of Health Service Providers in Psychology; how likely his or her clients are to obtain insurance payments when being treated on a private basis. Although many present-day counseling psychologists were not trained in APA-accredited programs, the importance of graduating from an accredited program has increased markedly in recent years and may well continue to increase in the future.

As of this writing, there are some 55 counseling psychology doctoral training programs that are APA-accredited. Although the number of accredited programs has increased dramatically during the past decade, the number of programs seeking accreditation in the last few years has leveled off. Accreditation patterns suggest that the list of accredited programs will, as in other areas of professional psychology, continue to grow at a slow but steady rate.

Characteristics of Training in Counseling Psychology. We have been focusing thus far on the question of APA accreditation for doctoral programs. But what are the main features of these programs? And what is the nature of training in counseling psychology?

To begin with, most doctoral programs are organized so that students will need about five years to complete graduate study. Also, in most programs students either earn a master's degree on the way to the doctorate or have already earned the master's prior to admission to the doctoral program.

Doctoral training programs in counseling psychology are located in either colleges of education or departments of psychology, and these two settings often differ with respect to whether or not the master's degree is required or expected before admission to the doctoral program. In departments of psychology, students are typically admitted to the doctoral program regardless of whether they have a master's. If they do not already have that degree, they usually earn it on the way to the doctorate. In many programs located in colleges of education, on the other hand, students must first get a master's degree and then apply for admission to the doctoral program. Some of these programs also consider it desirable for the student to gain work experience in the counseling field before being admitted to a doctoral program. These issues (experience, master's before admission) being somewhat controversial, students contemplating a career in counseling psychology should think through the pros and cons in deciding about what programs to apply to.

Counseling psychology programs in colleges of education and those in departments of psychology are extremely similar in nearly all other important respects. Most significantly, the overall quality of training in psychology generally and counseling psychology specifically is equivalent in the two settings (see Birk & Brooks, 1986). Furthermore, in the most recent national conference on graduate education in psychology, it was resolved unequivocally that where graduate programs were administratively housed was essentially unimportant (Resolutions Approved by the National Conference, 1987).

Another main feature of training in counseling psychology is that the scientist-practitioner or scientist-professional model is seen as the basic training model in the field. (Note that the terms *practitioner* and *professional* are used interchangeably.) Thus, counseling psychology training at the doctoral level seeks to prepare students both to practice psychology (e.g., conduct counseling) and to perform research. Although the scientist-practitioner model may be somewhat less prominent in applied fields of psychology in general than it has been in the past (see

Resolutions Approved by the National Conference, 1987), in counseling psychology this model of training is probably more prominent than ever. Thus, at the aforementioned Georgia Conference (counseling psychology's third national conference), the following statement on training was approved:

> We acknowledge the balance of science and practice will vary across programs, their faculty and students. Some counseling psychologists may not publish research, some may never consult or evaluate programs, and others may neither teach nor offer direct therapeutic services; but all are expected to have education and training which will provide them with entry level professional competencies in research, therapeutic practice, teaching and other skills of our discipline. (Meara et al., 1988, p. 369)

In Chapters 2 and 4, we shall take a further look at the scientist-practitioner model of training in counseling psychology. In terms of the main features of training that we have been discussing, the point to be made here is that throughout graduate education, counseling psychology students are expected to learn about and conduct both scientific research and counseling practice. Three or four years of coursework are followed by an internship, ordinarily a full-time one-year experience in which the student receives in-depth supervised training in a service setting such as a university counseling center, community mental health center, or medical hospital. During the last phase of training, and what for many is the end point of their program, the student completes a doctoral dissertation. This is a major piece of scientific research aimed at advancing knowledge in the field. The student works closely with a research advisor, typically a faculty member in his or her counseling psychology program, in developing the project.

Where Do Counseling Psychologists Work?

Over the years, a number of surveys have been conducted on counseling psychologists, examining where they work and what they do. Of the recent ones, the largest and most adequately conducted has been by Watkins et al. (1986). These researchers randomly sampled 980 members of the Division of Counseling Psychology (Division 17) of the APA. They obtained usable returns from 716 participants, over one-fourth of the total division membership. Table 1-1 presents data on job settings of counseling psychologists, adapted from Watkins et al.

As you can see, over a third of the participants in the Watkins et al. survey had their primary employment in college and university departments, undoubtedly mostly as faculty members, although some were probably administrators (the researchers were not clear on this point). Approximately 18 percent were employed at college and university

Table 1–1
PERCENTAGE OF COUNSELING PSYCHOLOGISTS IN VARIOUS JOB SETTINGS

Setting	Percentage
College or University Department (includes departments of psychology, counseling psychology, educational psychology, etc.)	33.9
Independent Practice	21.5
University Counseling Center	17.8
Community Mental Health Center	3.3
General Hospital	2.7
Mental Hospital	2.7
Outpatient Clinic	1.5
Medical School	1.4
None	.6
Other	14.6

Source: Adapted from Watkins, Lopez, Campbell, and Himmell (1986).

counseling centers, and when this figure is combined with the percentage employed in departments, it can be seen that over half the counseling psychologists had their primary employment in a higher-education setting.

Of the remaining job settings, the only one that stands out in terms of the size of the percentages is private practice. Over a fifth of the sample (21.5%) had their primary employment in independent practice. The remainder of the participants were spread across a wide range of settings. Watkins et al. listed five of these—community mental health centers, general hospitals, mental hospitals, outpatient clinics, and medical schools. Other recent surveys, such as that by Banikiotes (1980) and the large-scale occupational analysis by Fitzgerald and Osipow (1986), indicate an even wider range of settings. Counseling psychologists are shown to be working in Veterans Administration (VA) hospitals (probably included in Watkins et al.'s general and mental hospitals); rehabilitation centers; substance abuse centers; business and industry; government agencies; public and private school systems; the correctional system; and state, county, and local agencies.

When we compared the recent surveys with earlier ones, several trends become apparent. First and perhaps foremost is the great diversity of employment settings demonstrated in each and every survey.

Throughout, a few settings are shown to employ the majority of counseling psychologists, while the remaining professionals are spread out among the rest.

Second, over the years a remarkably stable proportion of counseling psychologists have been employed in higher-education settings. From the time of the first analysis by Dreese (1949), one half or more of the participants sampled have found their primary employment in this setting, either as a faculty member, counseling center practitioner, or administrator. Within the higher-education setting, the percentages filling such jobs have also appeared to remain stable; for example, the 17.8 percent figure for those working at counseling centers is similar to the findings of the other studies.

Over the years, some transient patterns have appeared in employment for counseling psychologists. For example, when community mental health centers (CMHCs) were receiving sound federal support in the 1970s, the percentage of Ph.D. graduates who sought employment there increased dramatically. By the time of Banikiotes' 1979 survey (Banikiotes, 1980), nearly one-fifth of the new graduates were obtaining their first jobs at CMHCs. As federal funding dwindled, however, so did the attractiveness of CMHCs; in the most recent occupational analyses, the percentages are markedly smaller.

Two additional changes in employment patterns deserve comment here. The first of these represents a trend over many years, whereas the second is much more recent. Regarding the first trend, a steady decline has occurred over the years in the percentage of counseling psychologists who have their primary employment in VA medical centers. Historically the VA has been a primary employer of counseling psychologists. In fact, as shall be discussed in Chapter 2, the VA was instrumental in the development of counseling psychology as an independent and separate specialty in psychology. In the first occupational analysis of counseling psychology, Dreese (1949) found that 19 percent of his sample worked at VA centers. In Samler's analysis in the early 1960s, however (Samler, 1963), this number dropped to 9 percent, and in Fitzgerald and Osipow's recent analysis (1986), the number declined further, to less than 3 percent.

On the other side of the ledger, the percentage of counseling psychologists who are employed primarily as independent practitioners has increased markedly in recent years. For many years, the number of counseling psychologists who chose private practice as their primary career hovered around 5 percent. In the late 1970s and early 1980s this began to change. The two most recent analyses (Fitzgerald & Osipow, 1986; Watkins et al., 1986) both make clear that independent practice is second only to higher education as a primary employment setting for counseling psychologists. Importantly, more counseling psychologists are now in independent practice than in university counseling centers, the traditional practice setting for this specialty.

This pattern appears to be intensifying. When classed by age, the percentage of younger counseling psychologists who are selecting private practice as a primary employment setting is notably greater than that for the older counseling psychologists (Fitzgerald & Osipow, 1986). Finally, the two recent surveys suggest that many of the counseling psychologists who are not primarily in independent practice are involved in it on part-time basis, more than two-thirds of the current professionals doing at least some private work. It appears that the percentage of counseling psychologists who are involved primarily or secondarily in private practice will remain high in the foreseeable future. It is important that beginning students in the field and experienced professionals alike recognize this pattern, and that the Division of Counseling Psychology (Division 17) of the APA, as well as doctoral training programs in the specialty, incorporate these data into their thinking about counseling psychology training. Based on pertinent reports from the Georgia Conference (see Kagan et al., 1988), awareness of current trends is growing within the field.

What Do Counseling Psychologists Do?

Probably the most fundamental and clear finding from recent job analyses (Fitzgerald & Osipow, 1986; Watkins et al., 1986) is that counseling psychologists are involved in performing an extensive range of jobs. Just as their job settings are highly diverse, so are their actual job activities. For example, sizeable numbers of counseling psychologists devote at least a portion of their work time to each of the following: counseling and psychotherapy (individual, group, couples/family); consultation; psychological testing, assessment, and evaluation; research and writing; teaching, training, and supervision; and administration. When one considers the specific activities incorporated under each of these general job categories, as well as the various job settings in which the activities are carried out, one can appreciate the rich diversity of activities within counseling psychology.

Within the context of this diversity, the activity performed by the greatest number of counseling psychologists for the greatest amount of time is counseling in general and individual counseling in particular. (Here we include psychotherapy under the general category "counseling.") Despite certain puzzling differences between the findings of the two major surveys discussed earlier (Fitzgerald & Osipow, 1986; Watkins et al., 1986) both are entirely clear and consistent on this point.

Table 1-2 presents the percentage of counseling psychologists in Fitzgerald and Osipow's large sample who indicated involvement in six

Table 1-2
PERCENTAGE OF COUNSELING PSYCHOLOGISTS PERFORMING VARIOUS COUNSELING ACTIVITIES

Job Activity	Percentage Performing
Personal Adjustment Counseling	80.1
Vocational Counseling	70.9
Long-Term Psychotherapy	69.2
Couple and Family Counseling	58.4
Group Counseling	49.3
Group Vocational Counseling	36.2

Source: Adapted from Fitzgerald and Osipow (1986).

different counseling modes. As can be seen in the table, personal adjustment counseling and vocational counseling are the activities engaged in by the greatest numbers of counseling psychologists. As group counseling and group vocational counseling are separate items, it is likely that Fitzgerald and Osipow's respondents viewed the personal adjustment and career counseling items as pertaining to individual interventions. That being so, their findings are fully consistent with those of Watkins et al., which indicated that individual treatments were the most frequently performed of the counseling activities and virtually all other activities.

In addition to the numbers of counseling psychologists who perform various activities, Watkins et al. and Fitzgerald and Osipow both looked at the percentage of respondents' work time devoted to the different job functions. Both research teams found that counseling psychologists typically devote about 25 percent of their time to counseling activities, more time than is devoted to any other single activity or cluster of activities.

Fitzgerald and Osipow also found that the majority of their respondents were involved in: research (67% of the respondents), the supervision of counseling (70%), teaching and training (75%), administration (68%), consultation (71%), and writing/editing (65%). Of these activities, the median percentage of work time devoted to them was greatest for teaching/training (19%), followed closely by research combined with writing and editing. The total percentage of time devoted to these two sets of activities is 15 percent. (Note that Fitzgerald and Osipow separated research from writing and editing, whereas we believe they are better placed into one broad category, research.) The percentages of work time devoted to the remaining activities are as follows: consultation, 10 percent, administration, 10 percent, and supervision 9 percent.

Given the job activities of counseling psychologists, one might ask, as did Watkins et al. (1986), how professionals in this specialty

Table 1-3
PRIMARY AND SECONDARY SELF-VIEWS OF COUNSELING PSYCHOLOGISTS

	Primary		Secondary	
Self-View	**n**	**%**	**n**	**%**
Clinical Practitioner	330	47.7	131	19.2
Academician	197	28.4	103	15.1
Administrator	79	11.4	100	14.7
Consultant	40	5.8	136	19.9
None	25	3.6	34	5.0
Researcher	17	2.5	68	10.0
Other	2	0.3	36	5.3
Supervisor	2	0.3	74	10.8
Total	692	100.0	682	100.0

Reprinted from Watkins et al. (1986).

view themselves. For example, what percentage of counseling psychologists view themselves primarily as practitioners? What percent view themselves secondarily as clinical practitioners? What percent view themselves primarily or secondarily as consultants? academicians? researchers? administrators? and so forth.

As seen in Table 1-3, in the Watkins et al. sample of over seven hundred members of the Division of Counseling Psychology of APA, most respondents viewed themselves as either clinical practitioners (47.7%) or academicians (28.4%). Few claimed as *primary* roles any of the other roles listed by Watkins et al. The respondents' *secondary* self-views, however, seemed more spread out, with 10 percent or more seeing their secondary self-view as either that of clinical practitioner, academician, administrator, consultant, supervisor, or researcher. Thus, although most counseling psychologists see themselves primarily as either practitioners or academics, most also have secondary self-views, and these reflect the variety of roles that are played.

Changes in Job Activities over the Years. Have things changed in terms of what counseling psychologists do? Is the specialty different in this way from when it emerged as an independent specialty nearly forty years ago? The answer must inevitably be "yes and no." Let us try to clarify why.

Just as has always been true, counseling and related activities (therapy, assessment, interviewing, etc.) are engaged in by a sizeable proportion of counseling psychologists. Things have changed, however, in that when one compares the review by Samler (1964) with analyses by Watkins et al.

and Fitzgerald and Osipow, it is clear that a greater percentage of counseling psychologists appear to be involved in a wider variety of counseling interventions than ever before. For example, in 1962 Super noted that more than a quarter of the counseling psychologists at that time did counseling as their main activity. In looking at the figures from Watkins et al. and Fitzgerald and Osipow, although these are not directly comparable, it appears clear that significantly more than 25 percent of the current counseling psychologists do counseling as their main activity. Remember, well over 50 percent are in practice settings (Table 1-1) and for nearly 50 percent the primary self-view is as clinical practitioner (Table 3-1).

In contrast to Fitzgerald and Osipow, however, we do not interpret these changes as indicating that the specialty is becoming increasingly service-oriented and decreasingly research-oriented. To begin with, it is inevitable that as the specialty graduates more and more counseling psychologists, the percentage holding service positions will increase. After all, we cannot simply train counseling psychologists to be academicians because of the finite number of academic posts available, and because the training, by definition, focuses on teaching students to *practice* counseling psychology, not just to study it.

When comparing earlier with more recent studies, there does appear to be a substantial increase in the numbers of counseling psychologists who call what they do "psychotherapy." In earlier times, that activity appeared to be the sole province of clinical psychologists (within psychology). In more recent times, counseling psychologists have joined the large number of professionals from several fields (psychiatry, psychiatric social work, clinical psychology, etc.) who perform therapy as a part of their clinical practice. Although not fully documented, it does appear to us that, given the specialty's historical and current emphasis on brevity, the psychotherapy performed by counseling psychologists tends to be short-term. Such an interpretation is consistent with the emergence of time-limited counseling and psychotherapy during the past decade (Gelso & Johnson, 1983; Robbins & Zunni, 1988).

As increased numbers of counseling psychologists have become focused on personal counseling and psychotherapy in recent years, some observers have suggested that the centrality of the vocational side (e.g., vocational psychology and career counseling) has been eroding simultaneously. Samler's (1964) earlier review, however, indicates this was also the case twenty-five or so years ago. It seems to us that if vocational psychology and vocational counseling were ever *the* foundation of counseling psychology, that may have been in the earliest days of the specialty; soon after a host of other activities were added to form the core of the field.

Moreover, training in career counseling currently appears to be effective and substantial (Birk & Brooks, 1986). Furthermore, such training has not declined in quality or amount, at least over the last 15 years (Schneider et al., 1988). It does appear that, when forced to state a preference, counseling psychologists prefer to do personal counseling or therapy more than career counseling. But it appears equally true that career counseling continues to be engaged in by most practitioners, and that practitioners view this activity as important to their identity as counseling psychologists (see specific percentages and ratings in Fitzgerald & Osipow, 1986).

Finally, rather than seeing the specialty as becoming less oriented toward research and science, as do Fitzgerald and Osipow, we see the research emphasis being a major thread of continuity in the specialty from its beginnings to the current time. Furthermore, the data suggest that, if anything, there appears to be a greater emphasis today on the research role of the counseling psychologist. That role has been stressed by a number of authors (see Whiteley) and has been reasserted in major papers based on the Georgia Conference (Gelso et al., 1988; Meara et al., 1988; Rude, Weissberg, & Gazda, 1988). Most counseling psychologists are involved in research, even if their primary job activity involves counseling practice. And, as noted by Watkins et al., most counseling psychologists publish several articles based on their research over the course of their careers.

COUNSELING PSYCHOLOGY AND OTHER SPECIALTIES AND FIELDS: DISTINCTIVENESS AND OVERLAP

Within the broader discipline of psychology, there are a number of applied specialties that overlap considerably with each other and thus with counseling psychology. The specialties most closely related to counseling psychology are clinical psychology, industrial/organizational psychology, school psychology, and community psychology. These specialties are referred to as "applied" because each seeks, in its own ways, to apply principles of psychology to the solution of human problems. The lack of clear and concise boundaries among these specialties is inevitable because they rely essentially on the same training and education in basic, core areas of psychology. Furthermore, all employ similar assessment and intervention procedures in their attempts to solve human problems. At the same time, each specialty has some distinctive foci.

In comparing counseling psychology to other fields and specialties within and outside of psychology, it is useful to keep in mind the unifying themes of counseling psychology as discussed earlier: (1) the focus on intact personalities, or more "normal" problems and people; (2) attention to assets and strengths, even when working with the severely disturbed; (3) implementation of relatively brief interventions; (4) emphasis on person-environment interactions; and (5) emphasis on educational and career development of individuals and on educational and vocational environments.

The specialty most often compared to counseling psychology is that of clinical psychology. The latter is the largest of the applied specialties in psychology. Despite much overlap in training, job activities, and job settings of counseling and clinical psychologists, there are notable differences. Historically as well as currently, clinical psychology has concerned itself with the study and treatment of abnormal or maladaptive behavior (Garfield, 1985). Although clinical psychologists do not ignore people's assets or strengths, relatively greater attention has typically been paid to underlying pathology rather than health. Perhaps as a consequence, clinical psychologists have tended to implement treatments of longer duration, more often called psychotherapy (of a longer-term, more intensive nature) than counseling. Attention to educational and vocational development and environments has not been a central part of the clinical psychologist's work. Because of the focus on psychopathology, clinical psychologists are much more likely than counseling psychologists to be found in work settings that focus on the severely disturbed, for example, in-patient psychiatric settings and mental hospitals; they are much less likely to be found in educational settings, for example, university counseling centers.

However, the two specialties appear to have moved closer together in recent years. Garfield (1985) notes that present-day clinical psychologists are more likely than in the past to work with the less disturbed and focus on assets. Likewise, as noted earlier, counseling psychologists increasingly conduct psychotherapy, and much of the therapy is long term. The differences, however, do persist.

In attempting to define themselves and their specialty, counseling psychologists have most often focused on the similarities and differences between themselves and clinical psychologists. Perhaps that is because of the major overlap in the area of counseling/psychotherapy, an activity that holds broad appeal to both specialities (as well as to other fields). In fact, though, there are similarities with other specialties that seem about as great.

The specialty of *community psychology* focuses on person-environment interactions as they promote psychological health and cause disturbances. Although this specialty is more difficult to cleanly and neatly define than perhaps any in psychology, its general goal is "broadly . . . concern . . . with clarifying the complex interrelationships between individuals and their social environment, and with the discovery and implementation of more effective ways of coping with the stresses of modern life" (Spielberger & Stenmark, 1985). Through a wide variety of interventions, community psychologists seek to help broader systems, institutions, communities, and so forth, change so that they facilitate psychological well-being.

In contrast to either counseling or clinical psychologists, community psychologists are more likely to be involved in consulting on issues of organizational development, on community development and social change, with school systems, on community mental health planning and administration, on social policy analysis, and so forth. (See Bachman, Smith, & Jason, 1981; Skotko, 1980.) They are indeed concerned with clinical and counseling activities but not nearly as much as clinical and counseling psychologists.

Counseling psychology and community psychology overlap considerably in their attention to the environment side of person-environment interaction. This is most clearly seen in the counseling psychologist's role in consultation and outreach (see Chapters 16 and 17). Also, both fields emphasize preventive and developmental roles in intervention. The counseling psychologist, however, is more likely to be concerned with direct counseling or psychotherapeutic interventions and with problems of educational and vocational development and choice.

A third specialty that overlaps with counseling psychology is *school psychology*. This specialty has been defined by Bennett as "the application of knowledge and skills to the prevention or solution of problems children face in learning what society deems essential for success" (1985, p. 129). Bennett goes on to note the overlap between school psychology on the one hand and counseling, clinical, and industrial/organizational psychology on the other but stresses that their key difference lies in the concern of school psychologists for children, adolescents, and college students "in their world of work, the school setting." School psychologists do consultation, counseling, and assessment with students, parents, and teachers, with the aim of furthering the educational process, for example, helping children learn more effectively and enhancing emotional adjustment.

The overlap between counseling and school psychologists is especially great when counseling psychologists work in elementary and secondary schools (more typically the setting for the school psychologist) and when school psychologists work in higher education (more typically the setting for the counseling psychologist). Even in these settings, it appears that the school psychologist is more likely to be involved in educational and psychological assessment of students (e.g., to determine what factors are impeding effective learning), whereas the counseling psychologist is more often involved in counseling efforts with students and their families. Essentially, though, the major differences between these two specialties is in work setting and all of what that leads to. The school psychologist is primarily employed in elementary and secondary schools; the counseling psychologist is found in the variety of settings discussed earlier.

The final applied specialty within psychology that will be contrasted with counseling psychology is industrial/organizational (I/O) psychology. Siegel (1985) defines I/O psychology as "the science of behavior applied to persons in industrial and other organizations. Its objective is to enhance organizational effectiveness" (p. 207). Moreover, I/O psychologists, as Siegel notes, are centrally involved, in one way or another, in the assessment and enhancement of employee, supervisory, and managerial performance. They empirically study and assess the problems of organizations and workers within those organizations and then devise treatments aimed at solving those problems. Although the assessment and enhancement of performance are key overall activities, Siegel notes that if there is a single pervasive goal of these activities it is that of helping create work environments that are physically and psychologically safe and healthy. I/O psychologists are not simply concerned with helping organizations be more productive, they are also invested in encouraging persons within organizations to "make the most effective use of their abilities, to develop new ones, and to do work that is intellectually and emotionally satisfying" (Siegel, 1985, p. 238). In accomplishing these goals, psychologists in this specialty organize training programs, consult with management and with individuals, counsel workers to improve job and personal adjustment, and construct instruments aimed at assessing all aspects of organizational functioning and individual functioning within organizations.

In comparing I/O and counseling psychology, a major area of overlap becomes evident: the concern with career and vocational development and environments. Counseling psychologists study career development in all settings and have sought to develop theories of what makes people gravitate toward certain fields, what interferes with their deciding on a suitable career path, and what treatments facilitate career development. I/O psychologists are more interested in the work and worker-performance aspect of career functioning. When working within business and industrial settings, both types of psychologists perform similar functions. The differences are a matter of degree rather than kind. Overall, the counseling psychologist is more likely to work with individuals in a counseling context, whereas the I/O psychologist is more inclined to study and intervene at a broader organizational level. The counseling psychologist is probably more invested in overall individual emotional adjustment; the I/O psychologist in organizational as well as individual work performance and its impediments.

Like the counseling psychologist, I/O psychologists deal with relatively intact personalities and are concerned in a very basic way with person-environment interactions. Both specialties are involved in organizational consulting. The counseling psychologist, on the whole, however, is basically more involved in therapeutic interventions, again at the level of the individual.

A Perspective on Similarities and Distinctiveness

Counseling psychology has struggled to define itself and the ways in which its identity is unique. It has sought to clarify its distinctiveness within applied-psychology specialties. At times critics, especially from within counseling psychology, have lamented the lack of clear differences, and have even suggested that, because of the lack of distinctiveness of its own, counseling psychology should be merged with other fields.

However, arguments about the lack of distinctiveness of the specialty seriously overlook the fact that virtually all of the applied specialties in psychology overlap with each other. The in-depth descriptions of applied specialties in psychology by Altmaier and Meyer (1985) substantiate that each specialty overlaps considerably with every other one. Counseling psychology is by no means unique in that way.

At the same time, each specialty is different from every other one in certain ways. To be sure, no specialty in applied psychology can lay exclusive claim to a given activity (e.g., counseling, consulting) or setting. Yet each has its particular areas of emphasis, its particular foci, and settings in which it is more often found than are other specialties. To reiterate, the unifying themes of counseling psychology lend this specialty its distinctiveness, although not in some simple, linear way. Counseling psychology may differ from one specialty, e.g., clinical psychology, in relation to certain of these themes, but differ from another specialty, e.g., school psychology, in relation to others of the five themes.

Counseling Psychology vs. Fields Outside of Psychology

Although there are a number of fields outside of psychology that are involved in similar activities to those of counseling psychology, there is a fundamental difference between these fields and counseling psychology. Counseling psychologists, from the beginnings of the specialty, have been psychologists first and "counselors" second. That is, professionals in this specialty are trained in basic areas of psychology and seek to apply theories and principles of psychology to their professional activities and interventions. The three fields outside of psychology proper that are most closely related to counseling psychology are psychiatric social work, psychiatry, and the general counseling profession (often referred to as counselor education, guidance, counseling and guidance, or counseling). Let us briefly discuss each of these.

Psychiatric social workers generally complete a two-year master's degree, referred to as Master of Social Work (MSW) degree. Ordinarily one year of their program is academic and the second entails closely supervised work in an agency. Many psychiatric social workers, like counseling psychologists and others, conduct counseling and psychotherapy and are often found in private practice settings. In hospital and clinic settings, psychiatric social workers work on health-care teams. They may specialize in the intake process, consult with other agencies, do family counseling, and develop social histories on patients (Brammer & Shostrom, 1982). Professionals with MSWs rarely conduct research, do not perform psychological testing, and do little educational and vocational counseling.

Psychiatrists are physicians who have gone on to specialize in psychiatry. This medical specialty is concerned with the diagnosis and treatment of severe emotional disorders and in this way is probably most closely related to clinical psychology among the applied psychology specialties. As MDs, psychiatrists are responsible for medical-psychological interventions, such as the prescription of drugs. They overlap with counseling psychologists, and a number of other specialists, in conducting counseling and psychotherapy. The brand of therapy they conduct is often the same or similar to counseling psychologists, although psychiatrists are more likely to take a psychodynamic and psychoanalytic perspective in their work than are counseling psychologists.

The final field we shall cover is perhaps the most similar of all to counseling psychology. The counseling profession, or counselor education, probably adheres to the same unifying themes as counseling psychology. Counselors are found in a wide range of job settings and may function as school counselors, rehabilitation counselors, employment counselors, college counselors, community counselors, and so forth. Many counseling positions require a master's degree rather than a doctorate.

In addition to differences in the level of training, counseling psychology, to a greater extent than the general counseling profession, subscribes to the scientist-practitioner model of training and practice. Because of this, the counseling psychologist receives more training in research and the scientific aspects of psychology.

Also, the counseling psychologist is extensively trained as a psychologist, with required graduate-level coursework in several core areas (e.g., biopsychology, learning) of the discipline of psychology. In contrast, although students who pursue degrees in counseling may take many psychology courses, expectations about what psychology courses they take, as well as how many, vary greatly from training program to training program. The combination of extensive study in the discipline of psychology with acquisition of the skills needed to be both a psychological practitioner and a scholarly investigator provides counseling psychologists with a broader array of competencies and career choices.

SUMMARY

A specialty within the science and profession of psychology, counseling psychology has struggled to establish itself firmly as a distinct profession and in recent years has shown notable growth. Diversity is a key aspect of this field, which encompasses an extensive range of activities and positions.

Throughout the history of counseling psychology three roles have been most central: the remedial, the preventive, and the developmental. Carried out in various settings, the three roles are combined in most activities performed by counseling psychologists.

One can distinguish five unifying themes in counseling psychology: (1) a focus on intact as opposed to severely disturbed personalities, (2) attention to people's assets and strengths regardless of degree of disturbance, (3) emphasis on relatively brief interventions, (4) attention to person-environment interactions rather than an exclusive focus on either the person or the environment, and (5) emphasis on educational and career development and environments. These themes help bring together the diverse aspects of the specialty and clarify how counseling psychology is differentiated from other specialties within and outside of psychology. Despite their defining character, the five themes represent no more than central tendencies. Counseling psychology practitioners differ considerably in the extent to which they subscribe to each particular theme.

Counseling psychologists are trained at the doctoral level, usually earning a Ph.D. from a counseling psychology training program accredited by the American Psychological Association. Their training typically adheres to the scientist-practitioner model, whereby the student is educated to be a scientist and researcher as well as a counseling practitioner.

Counseling psychologists work in a wide range of job settings, the most frequent being higher education (in academic departments and counseling centers) and independent practice. Likewise, counseling psychologists perform a wide array of professional activities. Individual personal and vocational counseling and therapy are the most commonly conducted, but a sizeable percentage of counseling psychologists also frequently perform many additional activities and interventions. In terms of self-views, most counseling psychologists see themselves as either practitioners or academicians.

Comparing and contrasting counseling psychology with other applied specialties within psychology, such as clinical psychology, community psychology, industrial/organizational psychology, and school psychology, serves to delineate the unique characteristics of each. Likewise, common ground can be found between counseling psychology and fields outside of psychology, such as social work, psychiatry, and the general counseling profession, though substantial differences exist.

References

Altmaier, E. M., & Meyer, M. E. (1985). *Applied specialties in psychology.* New York: Random House.

Bachman, S., Smith, T., & Jason, L. A. (1981). Characteristics of community psychologists in 1974 and 1978. *American Journal of Community Psychology, 9,* 283–291.

Banikiotes, P. G. (1980). Counseling psychology training: Data on perceptions. *The Counseling Psychologist, 8(4),* 73–74.

Bennett, V. C. (1985). School psychology. In E. M. Altmaier & M. E. Meyer (Eds.), *Applied specialties in psychology* (pp. 129–154). New York: Random House.

Birk, J. M., & Brooks, L. (1986). Required skills and training needs of recent counseling psychology graduates. *Journal of Counseling Psychology, 33,* 320–325.

Brammer, L. M., & Shostrom, E. L. (1982). *Therapeutic psychology* (4th ed.). Englewood Cliffs, NJ: Prentice-Hall.

Dreese, M. A. (1949). A personnel study of the Division of Counseling and Guidance of the American Psychological Association. *Occupations, 27,* 307–310.

Fitzgerald, L. F., & Osipow, S. H. (1986). An occupational analysis of counseling psychology: How special is the specialty? *American Psychologist, 41,* 535–544.

Fretz, B. R. (1985). Counseling psychology. In E. M. Altmaier & M. E. Meyer (Eds.), *Applied specialties in psychology* (pp. 45–74). New York: Random House.

Garfield, S. L. (1985). Clinical psychology. In E. M. Altmaier & M. E. Meyer (Eds.), *Applied specialties in psychology* (pp. 19–44). New York: Random House.

Gelso, C. J., & Johnson, D. H. (1983). *Explorations in time-limited counseling and psychotherapy.* New York: Columbia University, Teachers College Press.

Gelso, C. J., Betz, N. E., Friedlander, M. L., Helms, J. E., Hill, C. E., Patton, M. J., Super, D. E., & Wampold, B. E. (1988). Research in counseling psychology: Prospects and recommendations. *The Counseling Psychologist, 16,* 385–406.

Ivey, A. E. (1979). Counseling psychology—The most broadly-based applied psychology specialty. *The Counseling Psychologist, 8(3),* 3–6.

Jordaan, J. E., Myers, R. A., Layton, W. C., & Morgan, H. H. (1968). *The counseling psychologist.* Washington, DC: American Psychological Association.

Kagan, N., Armsworth, M. W., Altmaier, E. M., Dowd, E. T., Hansen, J. C., Mills, D. E., Schlossberg, N., Sprinthall, N. A., Tanney, M. F., & Vasquez, M. J. T. (1988). Professional practice of counseling psychology in various settings. *The Counseling Psychologist, 16,* 347–365.

Meade, C. J., Hamilton, M. K., & Ka-Wai-Yuen, R. (1982). Consultation research: The time has come, the walrus said. *The Counseling Psychologist, 10(4),* 39–52.

Meara, N. M., Schmidt, L., Carrington, C., Davis, K., Dixon, D., Fretz, B., Myers, R., Ridley, C., & Suinn, R. (1988). Training and accreditation in counseling psychology. *The Counseling Psychologist, 16,* 366–384.

Resolutions Approved by the National Conference (1987). *American Psychologist, 42,* 1070–1084.

Robbins, S. B., & Zunni, V. R. (1988). Implementing a time-limited treatment model: Issues and solutions. *Professional Psychology: Research and Practice, 19,* 53–58.

Robinson, F. P. (1970). *Effective study* (4th ed.). New York: Harper & Row.

Rude, S. S., Weissberg, M., & Gazda, G. M. (1988). Looking to the future: Themes from the Third National Conference for Counseling Psychology. *The Counseling Psychologist, 16,* 423–430.

Samler, J. (1964). Where do counseling psychologists work? What do they do? What should they do? In A. S. Thompson & D. E. Super (Eds.), *The professional preparation of counseling psychologists: Report of the 1964 Greyston Conference.* New York: Columbia University, Teachers College Press.

Schneider, L. J., Watkins, C. E., & Gelso, C. J. (1988). Counseling psychology from 1971 to 1986: Perspective on and appraisal of current training emphases. *Professional Psychology: Research and Practice, 19,* 584–588.

Siegel, L. (1985). Industrial and organizational psychology. In E. M. Altmaier & M. E. Meyer (Eds.), *Applied specialties in psychology* (pp. 207–238). New York: Random House.

Skotko, V. P. (1980). Professional activities and the perceptions of and opportunities for community psychologists. *American Journal of Community Psychology, 8,* 709–714.

Spielberger, C. D., & Stenmark, D. E. (1985). Community psychology. In E. M. Altmaier & M. E. Meyer (Eds.), *Applied specialties in psychology* (pp. 75–98). New York: Random House.

Super, D. E. (1955). Transition from vocational guidance to counseling psychology. *Journal of Counseling Psychology, 2,* 3–9.

Watkins, C. E., Lopez, F. G., Campbell, V. L., & Himmell, C. D. (1986). Contemporary counseling psychology: Results of a national survey. *Journal of Counseling Psychology, 33,* 301–309.

Whiteley, J. M. (1984). A historical perspective on the development of counseling psychology as a profession. In S. D. Brown & R. W. Lent (Eds.), *Handbook of counseling psychology* (pp. 3–55). New York: Wiley.

Chapter 2

Development of the Profession

This chapter describes the emergence of counseling psychology as a profession. We shall first examine the roots of the profession as found in changes in both American society and in the discipline of psychology during the late 1800s and early 1900s. Then, within a broad developmental framework, we shall look at how the profession of counseling psychology has matured since its formal establishment in the 1940s. Finally, we shall describe how these developments explain why counseling psychology has remained firmly committed to the scientist-practitioner model through all three of its major conferences (1951, 1964, 1987) despite pressures from many sources to provide alternatives to this demanding model.

ROOTS OF THE FIVE UNIFYING THEMES

An interesting exercise for a beginning counseling psychologist is to trace the academic heritage of his or her instructor or advisor. The profession is sufficiently young that it is usually possible to find out who one's advisor's advisor was, his or her advisor, and so forth, back at least to the formal beginnings of the profession in the 1940s (and in many cases, to trace the lineage back to some of the progenitors in the first half of the century, and in a few cases, back even to the 19th century). As Alex Haley illustrated in his work on the African roots of black Americans (1976), understanding heritage gives deeper and even new meaning to life in the present. Themes and traditions that link past and present can also help make sense out of what, at times, may seem scattered and chaotic. We shall explore the roots of counseling psychology by examining how the five unifying themes reviewed in Chapter 1 (assets and strengths, person-environment interactions, educational and career development, brief interactions, and intact personalities) grew out of distinctive social movements, historical events, and disciplinary developments in the late 19th and early 20th centuries.

Assets and Strengths

It is now only a little more than a century since persons with mental illness were seen as possessed by demons and hopelessly incurable. Insane asylums were the best life could offer to those who became mentally ill. Then, in the mid-19th century, what is now known as the "mental health movement" became well-established. Under the leadership of Dorothea Dix (1802–1887) in 1848, New Jersey built a hospital (rather than an asylum) for the mentally ill. At this point in history, the mental health movement sought to provide more humanitarian custodial care for the mentally ill; there was still little expectation for cures. Several decades later, a new level of understanding concerning the role of assets and strengths in working with mental problems was reached via the work of Clifford Beers (1876–1943). His book *A Mind That Found Itself* (1908) represents a critical turning point in the public's awareness that people with mental problems could recover and that, even in the depths of depression or other problems, they had strengths that could be utilized to help them make that recovery. Freud's significant contributions to therapeutic treatment served to further enhance the viewpoint that many persons with mental health problems had the potential for moving beyond their difficulties, that is, they were not incurable.

Another major step forward in mental health ideology was the establishment of a psychological clinic by Lightner Witmer at the University of Pennsylvania early in this century. His clinic was devoted to working with children who had learning or behavioral problems in contrast to those yet described as insane or mentally disturbed. Such a clinic helped the public understand that persons other than those identified as mentally ill could be helped by therapeutic interventions. In one sense, his clinic is the precursor of thousands of mental health clinics and counseling centers that now exist throughout this country. Although the clinic's operations were largely remedial, the concept that children could be helped to function more effectively served to lead counseling psychology to focus more on potential development of the individual rather than on deficits that must be overcome.

Person-Environment Interactions

To understand the theme of person-environment interactions in counseling psychology, we must first explore the roots of psychology's measurement of persons, then the "discovery" of the critical role of environment, and then, finally, how the two are interactively bound in the creation of human behavior.

Essential to the approach of psychologists in understanding behavior (in contrast, for example, to the approaches of philosophers and theologians) is the incorporation of the methods of empirical science as developed in the physical and natural sciences in the 18th and 19th centuries. According to these methods, psychological phenomena can and must be measured.

Thus, one of the first tasks of early psychologists (and still a major task of all psychologists today) was to develop means of measuring psychological processes and behaviors—now referred to as *psychometrics.* Psychology's roots in the area of measurement may be traced back to the work of Galton (1822–1911) and his quest for understanding differences among people by applying quantitative methods. J. M. Cattel (1860–1944) continued this study of individual differences, using much of what he had learned in Wilhelm Wundt's (1832–1920) laboratory, established in Leipzig in 1879. Shortly thereafter, Binet (1857–1911), in France, established the first intelligence test, further expanding the measurement of differences in persons.

The combination of these psychometric developments with the vocational guidance movement, described in the next section, helped launch psychology as a profession in the first half of this century. The mass use of tests for occupational selection in World Wars I and II provided further stimulus. By the late 1920s, leading psychologists of the day expressed hopes that aptitude testing would soon be the answer to many of the educational and vocational problems faced by a society (Hull, 1928).

Even in those halcyon days of aptitude/intelligence testing during World War I and the postwar boom years of the 1920s, there were those who were beginning to see that limits existed to what could be accomplished through measurement of differences only in persons. In 1935 Lewin provided his now (but mostly not well-recognized until the 1960s) classic explication of the concept that behavior is a function of both the person and the environment. In his view, predictions of what persons will do, no matter how much information one has about aptitudes or skills, will always be limited unless information about the environments in which persons function is also considered.

Psychologists have increasingly come to understand that they cannot simply ask the question "What kind of person will succeed as a dentist?"

or "Which kind of client problem will benefit from psychotherapy?" outside of an environmental context. One type of person may be an effective leader of one kind of organization (environment) but not of another. The critical factor is the *interaction* of the person and the environment. Not only do environments affect persons but persons affect environments. Claiborn and Lichtenberg (1989) have elaborated the history of interactional thought in psychology, and more specifically within counseling psychology.

Even in one-to-one counseling, "environments" will differ, and will change, according to who constitutes a dyad (similar vs. different gender, race, etc., of client and counselor) and how the counseling progresses. Clients who change their behaviors produce variable environments. Organizational psychologists have become increasingly aware that environments do not exist in a vacuum but rather are defined by the sum of the people who compose them (Schneider, 1983). Unlike the predominantly person-oriented strategies developed in the middle decades of this century, the research and counseling interaction strategies of the 21st century will be heavily influenced by interactional and systems approaches.

Educational and Career Development

The transition from the 19th to the 20th centuries also saw the beginnings of the vocational guidance movement, one of the profession's most visible roots (and, in the view of many, the taproot of counseling psychology). In today's technological age, with literally thousands of jobs to choose from, many requiring highly specialized training, it may be difficult to realize that just over one hundred years ago the majority of young people did not really consider career choices. Most followed in their parents' occupational footsteps, whether that be farmer, bootmaker, or seamstress. With the many new and different jobs created by the Industrial Revolution, it became increasingly clear that not only were there career choices to be made but also that certain kinds of work required specific skills and training.

The social reformer Frank Parsons saw the need to develop what would today be called a career counseling service. In 1908 he established his vocations bureau in Boston to guide individuals through a three-step process he developed, which still serves as the foundation of most current career counseling. His three steps involve acquisition of "(1) a clear understanding of [oneself], [one's] aptitudes, abilities, interests, ambitions, resources, limitations and their causes; (2) a knowledge of the requirements and conditions of success, advantages and disadvantages, compensation, opportunities, and prospects in different lines of work; (3) true reasoning on the relations of these two groups of facts" (1909, p. 5).

The vocational guidance movement quickly incorporated much of the psychometric tradition as a way of providing information about individual aptitudes, abilities, and interests. In subsequent years, the need for occupational classification of literally millions of men in World Wars I and II was answered in large part by the methods of the vocational guidance and the psychometric movements.

Of even greater significance for the development of counseling psychology was the response of these movements to the American Depression in the 1930s:

> The economic depression of the 1930's added a new current to the stream of history. Large scale unemployment highlighted vocational guidance as a job placement activity as well as educational function. The Minnesota Employment Stabilization Research Institute experimented with psychological tests, occupational information, and retraining as methods of getting adult workers back into the labor force. Then many private and public vocational counseling centers, together with the United States Employment Service, quickly took over the research and counseling methods developed in this pioneer project. (Super, 1955, p. 4)

In Chapters 12 and 13 we shall see how the vocational guidance movement continues to foster some of the major unique research and theoretical and practical contributions of counseling psychologists.

Brief Interactions

Until the 1930s, treatments based on humanitarian (not to be confused with humanistic) viewpoints emanating from the late 19th century mental health movement were limited largely to the psychoanalytic perspective and were lengthy and intensive. Then E. G. Williamson and Carl Rogers each developed very different perspectives on counseling and psychotherapy. As a leading figure in the development of college student personnel services, Williamson dealt with the full range of problems of personal living and other nonacademic problems that students bring to large universities. He developed a process of focused, goal-oriented counseling to help students adjust to their environment. In addition to his own writings (see *How to Counsel Students* [1939]), he was the mentor for several generations of counseling psychologists who further researched and developed his brief, active, focused counseling in the various university counseling centers established all across the country after World War II to meet the educational, vocational, and personal counseling needs of the thousands of veterans then returning to college.

During the same time period, mostly as a reaction against his psychodynamic training in child clinical psychology, Carl Rogers developed his phenomenological, client-centered approach to counseling. His now classic book on counseling and psychotherapy (1942) had a tremendous impact on shifting the focus of the then emerging specialty of counseling psychology from assessment and diagnosis to counseling and psychotherapy. Evidence that such a shift had taken place was clearly manifested in the decade after Rogers' book was published: "[The] early 1950's saw the publication of ten books on counseling methods and only three had retained their exclusive diagnostic and assessment emphases" (Whiteley, 1984b, p. 5).

Intact Personalities

It was only in the 1960s and afterward that the profession of counseling psychology, and indeed psychology at large, began to fully recognize the distinctive importance and relevance of developmental-stage models produced by Piaget (1952), Erikson (1959), Perry (1970), and Kohlberg (1984). During the last 30 years, counseling psychologists have given increasing attention to these developmental models for the understanding they provide about normal developmental crises and transitions, all of which are accompanied by threats to well-being as well as opportunities for growth.

The "translation" of these theoretical concepts into the work of counseling psychologists may be seen in two distinctive bodies of literature in contemporary counseling psychology. The first describes the movement known as *deliberate psychological education*, and includes the major work by Mosher and Sprinthall (1971). These researchers outline the many ways in which counseling psychology can promote psychological development of all adolescents, not just those seeking personal counseling. As teachers, consultants, and counselors, counseling psychologists can create conditions that reduce the number of psychological casualties likely to occur during the adolescent years.

The second body of literature based on developmental aspects of intact, normal persons focuses on human adaptation to transition (Schlossberg, 1981) as well as intervention strategies for coping with transitions (Brammer & Abrego, 1981). Later work (Matheny et al., 1986) analyzes coping with stress. All these studies discuss interventions for persons acknowledging need for help in coping with both everyday and transitional situations but who are not sufficiently distressed to require counseling or therapy.

In these five brief sections, we hope we have shown how each of the five unifying themes of counseling psychology is clearly linked to developments in the early 20th century (or even before) in both psychology as a discipline (e.g., psychoanalysis, developmental theory) and in society at large, such as the Industrial Revolution, war, and depression. We now turn to an exploration of the formal organizational steps of the psychological specialty that came to be identified as counseling psychology.

COMING OF AGE: STAGES IN THE DEVELOPMENT OF THE PROFESSION

In this section we shall see how, and most importantly from our perspective, why counseling psychology became an identifiable profession in the years immediately following World War II. Some of the factors leading to the creation of the profession during that time continue to contribute to its present vitality.

In elaborating the events of each of the past five decades, we shall use a broad developmental model, including the terms *infancy, childhood, adolescence, young adulthood,* and *maturity.* The use of this framework is clearly one of personal interpretation. Some counseling psychologists would not agree with the meanings we attribute to certain historical events. In fact, in each counseling psychologist's own professional development, a phenomenon may occur akin to "ontogeny recapitulating phylogeny." That is, each individual may pass through the developmental stages of the profession even when the profession is mature. For example, younger counseling psychologists are often concerned with issues of autonomy and identity; as we grow older in our careers, however, these issues seem less significant.

Albeit provocative, our categorizations are intended as a way of gaining meaningful chronologic perspective.

(Note that, from this point forward, the terms *profession* and *specialty* will be used interchangeably. The term *specialty* usually denotes a specific discipline within the profession of psychology. Yet, in most ways, the level of autonomy and organization of the various specialties allows them to be classified as professions.)

Infancy: The 1940s

Sociologists studying professions specify that for a group of workers to constitute a profession they must form governing organizations that establish educational and service standards and thereby create the conditions necessary for autonomous functioning. The psychologist Erikson (1959) emphasized autonomy as a major task for the period of infancy. The beginning autonomous organizational steps for counseling psychology were set in motion during the 1940s, even though the official written record of many of these initial steps did not appear until the early 1950s.

The beginnings of organized counseling psychology can be found in the "psychological foxholes" (Scott, 1980) of World War II. During that time, almost every person with any training as a psychologist became involved in some way with assessment activities, either for selection and training of military personnel or for psychological diagnosis of military casualties. Thus there were collections of psychologists in every major military installation throughout the country and even sometimes abroad. During the war years, an increasing number of psychologists who were involved in selection and training began to see the need for an organization that would respond to their specific interests, outside the realm of psychiatric hospitals.

In the rapidly expanding divisional structure of the American Psychological Association (APA) immediately following World War II, these interests became represented by a new division, that of the Division of Counseling and Guidance. Founded in 1946 by E. G. Williamson and John Darley, it joined the increasing number of applied divisions then being added to APA, for example, those of clinical psychology, consulting psychology, industrial psychology, educational psychology, and school psychology. Whiteley has provided extensive original source material (1980) and descriptions (1984a, 1984b) of the details of these early organizational developments, including meeting places, agenda, persons involved, and so forth.

Let us raise a twofold question not often addressed in these historical descriptions: Why did persons interested in counseling choose to affiliate with psychology and why did psychology choose to include counseling? Many prospective counselors still choose to practice outside the profession of psychology. Others have felt the need for connections to the empirical and psychometric traditions of psychology. It is this grafting of counseling onto empirical roots that helps explain the greater commitment of counseling psychologists, as compared to counselors in general, to the scientist-practitioner model of training and functioning.

On the other side of the coin, why did psychology include counseling as a division? As already noted, in the beginning, clinical psychologists concentrated on assessment and diagnosis primarily in psychiatric hospitals; the focus on counseling and therapy did not develop for *any* psychologists until the 1950s. Industrial psychology began as the study of what is known today as human factors and engineering psychology. (The emphasis on organizational behavior now seen in industrial/organizational psychology was largely a development in the 1960s.) The emergence of counseling psychology filled a perceived vacuum within psychology between industrial psychology and clinical psychology: the study and treatment of normal personality functioning and development, which was not yet represented by any applied division.

Despite the overlaps and shared heritage with generic counseling on the one hand and other applied psychology fields on the other, in the nearly fifty years of its history counseling psychology has continued to be linked to both. During that time, probably more than half of those who identify themselves as counseling psychologists have also maintained membership in either a major counseling organization (e.g., American Association of Counseling and Development, formerly known as the American Personnel and Guidance Association) or a more clinically oriented psychology division (e.g., the APA Division 12, Division of Clinical Psychology or Division 29, Psychotherapy). Although these dual associations have sometimes caused tensions, the maintenance of breadth of perspectives is one of the sources of the profession's vitality. As suggested in Moore's (1970) sociological study of professions: "The plight of the professional is that extreme specialization radically narrows those significant others with whom he can carry on job-centered social discourse. Here, once more, the importance of identification with a broader calling is apparent, even if common interests are in some measure nostalgic rather than strictly contemporary" (p. 83).

Another perspective on this post–World War II emergence of counseling psychology has been provided by Schmidt (1977) in his examination of why the specialty developed and has remained strongest in the United States. Schmidt draws a parallel between our society's commitment to change—specifically change wrought through scientific technology—and counseling psychology as a process of change that builds on the empirical findings of the science of psychology. Schmidt also notes the high degree of mobility in our culture coupled with the emphasis on achieving self-improvement. Counseling psychologists have provided both the social support needed to cope with changed environments as well as the technical assistance for launching personal careers. After World War II, millions of veterans, who had been dislocated for several years from their home communities, were expected to forge ahead in new careers for which they typically had little or no preparation. From this perspective, in 1945–1950, counseling psychology was a profession "waiting to happen."

Childhood: The 1950s

If the 1940s are counseling psychology's infancy, where it began to take the steps toward autonomy, the 1950s encompass the stages of childhood when it had to demonstrate its ability to stand and be recognized as an independent entity. The exciting times of "let's get organized" had to give way to a period of sustained development that would establish the foundation of systematic knowledge needed to maintain a profession. The first of these major steps was addressed by the Northwestern Conference in 1951, the first major conference for the profession of counseling psychology. Key leaders of the Division of Counseling and Guidance met at Northwestern University August 29–30, 1951; they prepared formal definitions of the roles and functions of counseling psychologists. They proposed standards for practicum training, research training, and the content of core psychology courses. Final versions of these statements were originally published in the *American Psychologist* (APA, 1952) and were reprinted in Whiteley's (1980) *History of Counseling Psychology.*

Although there have been two subsequent conferences addressing many of the same definitional and curriculum issues, and innumerable position papers published about these topics, it is of interest to reread many of those original statements for their timelessness. Although surveys of the actual training practices and employment locations of counseling psychologists have documented a number of changes over the years, the applicability of many of the initial statements is truly remarkable. Consider the following definition of roles and functions: "The professional goal of the counseling psychologist is to foster the psychological development of the individual. This includes all people on the adjustment continuum from those who function at tolerable levels of adequacy to those suffering more severe psychological disturbances" (APA, 1952, p. 176).

The impetus for setting training standards right at the beginning of the specialty derived mostly from the interests of the Veterans Administration in employing counseling psychologists. The VA had created the job title of counseling psychologist to function in the Division of Medicine and Neurology, outside of the psychiatric division where clinical psychologists normally practiced, in order to provide counseling services for the full range of general medical and surgical patients. The standards of training and practice established at the Northwestern Conference were used to set VA employment standards. The VA has remained, throughout the history of counseling psychology, a major employer of counseling psychologists. These same training standards also served as the foundation for the creation of a diplomate in counseling psychology from the then newly created American Board of Examiners in Professional Psychology and in the establishment of program accreditation procedures by the APA Doctoral Education Committee.

Hammering out these position statements also led the pioneers of counseling psychology to realize their increasing connections to the discipline of psychology; in 1952 the decision was made to change the discipline's title from "counseling and guidance" to "counseling psychology."

Through the wisdom and initiative (though some colleagues of the time probably thought foolhardiness) of four young counseling psychologists, Milton E. Hahn, Harold G. Seashore, Donald E. Super, and C. Gilbert Wrenn, in the 1950s a major new empirical journal was launched to address publication needs in the same areas which the division of counseling and guidance had been established to fill—the *Journal of Counseling Psychology.* The idea of putting a journal into practice, of course, required considerable funds. Wrenn describes the journal's economic origins as follows:

> We established a list of probable stockholders who would represent various dimensions in counseling, each to be asked to buy a limited number of shares at $50 a share. None was to have over ten shares even if he was foolish enough to want to risk that much money . . . for it was clearly stated that this was a risk investment. . . . The response was remarkable. I found an early list of 28 prospects . . . there were 19 of the 28 who had become stockholders—and I am not even sure that we invited all on this particular list!" (p. 486)

The first volume of the *Journal of Counseling Psychology* was published in 1954; it has become the most important empirical journal in counseling psychology. Because of the excellence it achieved over its first decade of publication, it was actively sought by the APA for inclusion in its set of journals and has been published by them since 1967. The journal today is one of the most selective of the APA publications and is one of those most widely read by students (Carskadon, 1978). A fascinating perspective on the journal's first 25 years, including its antecedent social and political conditions (1946–1956) as well as its subsequent impact on the profession of counseling psychology, has been prepared by Pepinsky, Hill-Frederick, and Epperson (1978).

Adolescence: The 1960s and 1970s

Perhaps it is fitting, because counseling psychologists work with adolescents who have significant and prolonged identity problems, that the profession itself seems to have had to endure a long period of self-searching with regard to its identity. Barely before the ink was dry on some of the documents of the 1950s that created counseling psychology as an organized and autonomous profession, some writers were raising questions about the identity of the specialty. The 1960s and early 1970s were a time of significant self-doubt among the leadership in the profession. Growth leveled off in both membership of the division and number of accredited programs.

Whiteley (1980) brought to light previously unpublished papers that had been written in the early 1960s regarding the "decline" of counseling psychology (Berg, Pepinsky, & Shoben, 1980), and another concluding that counseling psychology "presently has only a weak potential for growth" (Tiedeman, 1980, p. 126). Other articles during this period cited the low-level prestige of counseling psychologists as compared to clinical psychologists. The strains were not just around declining growth but also about future directions. Because the 1950s had seen an increase in the counseling and psychotherapy activities of both counseling and clinical psychologists (based on much of the work of Rogers), some counseling psychologists were proposing that it was time for a merger of these specialties. Others, vehemently opposed to the remedial therapeutic emphasis in clinical psychology, identified more with the emergence of community psychology and its emphasis on prevention and developmental activities. For almost every paper that criticized the profession, others in the profession arose to prepare counterarguments (e.g., Tyler, Tiedeman, & Wrenn, 1980).

The division responded by organizing a second conference to reexamine its self-definition and the standards it had originally set at the Northwestern Conference. In the Greyston Conference of 1964, many concerns were aired extensively. The majority of participants endorsed the Northwestern statements. Recognizing changing times and contexts, the conference included in the introduction to its specific recommendations (Thompson & Super, 1964) the following statement:

> The conferees further recognize that counseling psychologists have significant overlapping interests with the related specialties of clinical, educational, industrial or personnel, and school psychology. The great majority, but not all, subscribe to the statement that counseling psychology has a special substance and emphases requiring preparation in a number of didactic as well as practicum courses that are not necessarily included in the preparation of other psychologists. This special substance consists of the educational and vocational and, less distinctively, the familial and community environments of the individual, of the psychology of normal development, and of the psychology of the physically, emotionally, and mentally handicapped; the special emphases are on the appraisal and use of assets for furthering individual development in the existing or changing environment. (pp. 3–4)

Perhaps as is true in the developmental phase of adolescence, these publicly manifested aspects of self-doubt and confusion were hiding, or at least overshadowing, the ongoing accomplishments of counseling psychologists that were building upon the foundations established in previous decades. Both theoretical and empirical developments in the area of career psychology were expanding and growing with considerable practical impact, for example, new assessment instruments and new types of interventions. Research on how to train counselors to provide the necessary and sufficient conditions in psychotherapy was building so rapidly that, by the end of the 1960s, counseling psychology researchers were among the ones most often identified (Bergin & Garfield, 1971) for research on training.

Continuing the linkage with mainstream psychology, developments in experimental analysis of behavior were being translated into counseling theory and practice most notably by Krumboltz and Thoresen (1969). Perhaps the clearest manifestation of the continued growth of the conceptual as well as empirical expertise of the profession was the establishment, at the end of the 1960s, of *The Counseling Psychologist,* a journal dedicated to stimulating professional dialogue about important theoretical and conceptual issues of the day. John Whiteley, founder and first editor (1969–1984), developed the format of having each issue dedicated to one or sometimes several major conceptual articles on a single topic, followed by a set of reactions from other counseling psychologists and professionals. This "dialogue" format has clearly withstood the test of time—more than 20 years later, it remains the primary format of the journal. The topics of the journal serve as a quick survey of the major controversial issues of each decade, from early issues on client-centered, behavioral and vocational counseling to more recent issues on nigrescence, victimization, and paradoxical approaches to counseling.

By the 1970s, although the identity problem of counseling psychology was still not fully resolved (are any of us absolutely sure of who we are?), the character of the identity issue shifted from pessimism about whether the field should exist to how it should be defined in relationship to others. The task of the seventies seems to have been to find out how it would relate to all of those other professions with which it shares so many aspects.

In terms of the number of APA-approved training programs, the beginning of the 1970s saw the nadir of the profession. However, since that time, the growth in number of accredited programs has been phenomenal by any standard—an over 150 percent increase in little over a decade. Significant developments in the setting of standards for credentials in professional psychology were a major factor in this growth. With an increasing number of states developing procedures for the licensing of psychologists in the 1960s, plus the more widespread inclusion of mental health benefits in health insurance policies, there were a series of questions raised, for all of psychology, about what kinds of training qualified persons for licensure as psychologists as well as for providing health-care service. Conferences sponsored by the National Register of Health Services Providers in Psychology and the APA, attended by psychologists from all specialties, resulted in greater specifications regarding the curriculum and the identity of the programs (see Chapter 3 for further details).

Most importantly for counseling psychology, these standards recognized that psychological training might take place in a variety of settings other than psychology departments, for example, colleges of education, colleges of business and management, colleges of medicine, or free-standing schools of psychology. The formal recognition that psychology programs could exist in colleges of education (long the home of many programs in counseling and guidance), coupled with the new requirement for identification of the programs as *psychology* programs (if the graduates were to be eligible for licensing as psychologists), had an immediate impact on many programs that were formerly identified as "counseling and guidance" but that had for years graduated persons who considered themselves trained as counseling psychologists.

Many programs moved as expeditiously as possible to make whatever changes were necessary to their curriculum, faculty, and resources to receive accreditation by the APA. This rapid growth brought new political strength and, at the end of the seventies, counseling psychology was regaining, within the APA, some of the representation and leadership roles that it had had in the fifties but that had waned over the sixties and early seventies. The leadership of the Division of Counseling Psychology and the newer organization of the Council of Counseling Psychology Training Program Directors found itself, for the first time in the profession's history, in continual dialogue with the leaders of clinical, school, and I/O psychology, as well as professional leaders in the American Personnel and Guidance Association for the purpose of developing an understanding of both overlapping and distinctive roles.

Young Adulthood: The 1980s

The decade of the 1980s began with the publication of two collections of papers, one set looking to the year 2000 (Whiteley and Fretz, 1980), the other to "The Coming Decade" (Whiteley, Kagan, Harmon, Fretz, & Tanney, 1984). Both sets of papers addressed how the profession would develop for coming generations of counseling psychologists.

The most tangible indicators of the emerging maturity of counseling psychology were the publication of the profession's first comprehensive handbooks, *Handbook of Counseling Psychology* (Brown & Lent, 1984) and *Handbook of Vocational Psychology* (Walsh & Osipow, 1983), and the beginning of two book series, *Advances in Vocational Psychology,* edited by Walsh and Osipow, and the Brooks/Cole series in *Counseling Psychology,* edited by Whiteley and Resnikoff.

Also during this decade, three reviews of counseling psychology, published in the *Annual Review of Psychology* (Borgen, 1984; Osipow, 1987; Gelso & Fassinger, 1990) covered a broad array of topics, indicating the growing diversity of the field. Borgen (1984) noted that "the discipline teems with vitality and resolve" (p. 597). Osipow (1987) examined its strengths, especially in the areas of career counseling and vocational developments. Gelso and Fassinger (1990) applauded the accomplishments of the eighties; observing that many of the methodological and conceptual recommendations of earlier reviewers and critics had been incorporated by researchers.

Two "firsts," again reflecting the confidence that comes with maturity, enabled the profession to look at some nontraditional research methodologies. For the first time ever, the *Journal of Counseling Psychology* published a special issue dedicated entirely to the topic of research design (October 1987). *The Counseling Psychologist* also published a special issue on alternative research paradigms, with special attention to the teaching of them, in January 1989.

The emerging maturity of the profession was also indicated in the recognition accorded counseling psychology by other specialties and organizations. At some time during the 1980s, almost every major board and committee in the APA was chaired by a counseling psychologist, as were the boards of related credentialing organizations, for example, the National Register of Health Service Providers in Psychology, the American Board of Professional Psychology, and the American Association of State Psychology Boards.

Responding to long-standing calls for a third national conference on Counseling Psychology, the Georgia Conference was held in April of 1987. Despite having less governmental and foundation support than either of the prior conferences, over 180 psychologists attended this working conference. They formed five different task groups to prepare recommendations in the areas of training and accreditation, research, organizational and political structures, public image, and professional practice in various settings. Each group's recommendations for the development of the profession may be found in the July 1988 *Counseling Psychologist.*

Rudd, Weissberg, and Gazda (1988) summarized the common themes of the conference discussions as follows:

> First, we are scientist-practitioners. . . . Discussion[s] of identity . . . include counseling psychology's emphasis on "positive mental health . . . adaptive strategies . . . empowerment of individuals.". . . Also mentioned was what might be termed the counseling psychologist's *scope of vision,* the attention to promotion of mental health at the level of groups and systems as well as individuals, to development across the entire life span, to adjustment and satisfaction in vocational as well as personal spheres, and to prevention and enhancement as well as remediation. (pp. 425–426)

Their closing observation was the reaffirmation, seen in all the task groups, of the importance of viewing people and behavior in the context of cultural variables such as ethnicity, gender, age, and sexual orientation. The conference participants promoted a diversity of roles but remained passionately committed to the viability of the unifying themes.

Maturity: The 1990s and Beyond

By the end of the 1980s there was a sense of meaningfulness in what had been accomplished that permitted greater receptivity to diversification within the profession in terms of work setting, theoretical orientation, gender, race, lifestyle, and so forth. Rather than fighting the problems of diversity and feeling compelled to choose to go one way or the other (e.g., remedial/therapeutic versus developmental/educational), professionals were embracing diversity and finding strength in it. Naomi Meara, president of the Division of Counseling Psychology for 1989, chose the theme "unified diversity" for the annual convention (Meara, 1990). Even though counseling psychologists engage in many different roles in many different settings, they share a unity of perspective and ideology. James Hurst, a recent president of the Division of Counseling Psychology, titled his presidential address "Counseling Psychology—a source of strength and pride in the ties that bind." We print his conclusions for their succinct summary of what the profession encompassed as it entered the final decade of the 20th century.

> In general, I came away with the following conclusions:
> (1) The focus on preventive and developmental intervention with persons in environments is alive and well.
> (2) The intolerance of mediocrity prevails in education and training, practice and research.
> (3) Our diversity of theory, work settings, special interest in ethnicity, lifestyles and interventions is a source of pride, is intentional and celebrated.
> (4) Organizational and personal authenticity is dominant.
> (5) We have the security and courage to say who we are *not* as well as who we are.
> (6) Our internal locus of control has defied the tyranny of marketplace and other environmental presses and has assured our being the captain of our own ship.
> (7) Our uncommon interests in ethics and morals persist.
> *And most important:*
> (1) There prevails a deep sense of respect of persons—for each other. People really do matter and are targets of dignity.
> (2) The scientists and practitioners among us like each other—they have a healthy interdependence.
> (3) We celebrate our diversity within our core of inner sameness.
> (4) We rally around the common cause of facilitating growth processes in persons and environments. (1989, p. 158)

THE SCIENTIST-PRACTITIONER MODEL: AN ENDURING THEME

From the initial founding conference at Northwestern in 1951 through the third conference in Atlanta, Georgia, in 1987, the training model that has been endorsed by counseling psychologists is the scientist-practitioner model. From the earliest days this choice has been and continues to be controversial. We hope it is clear to the reader, by this point, that keeping the "scientist" part of counseling psychology is *the* central reason for some counselors to have a home in psychology.

What is the scientist-practitioner (also known as scientist-professional) model? Stated simply, it is a model of training requiring that professionals master both the helping, practitioner roles and the methods of investigative science. Such professionals can ask the questions that will help establish, maintain, and enhance the body of specialized knowledge needed to make contributions to the welfare of all individuals and society.

As one often finds out in interdisciplinary staff meetings, many persons trained to do counseling in psychiatry, social work, and other counselor training programs typically do not know how to design investigations for questions like "Is what we are doing effective?" or "How does counseling work?" or "Can counseling be made more effective for these kinds of clients?" Similarly, persons trained exclusively in research methodology, who may have tremendous sophistication in terms of research design but lack training and experience in actually conducting counseling, may have extraordinary difficulties in asking and answering the questions in ways that are meaningful to practitioners. As recognized in the inaugural definition of the profession, "counseling psychologists can make unique contributions to psychological knowledge *because* [italics added] their counseling experience provides an especially fruitful opportunity to formulate hypotheses. It is therefore essential to maximize their research training" (American Psychological Association, 1952, p. 180).

Throughout the years, there have been at least three challenges to the continuation of the scientist-professional model of training in applied psychology, especially in clinical, school, and counseling psychology. The first of these challenges relates to the time needed to provide quality training in both research and counseling techniques. As more models and courses for training have been developed, course work requirements have increased. These competing time demands were a major factor in the development of professional schools of psychology and the doctor of psychology (Psy.D.) degree. In these programs, the number and rigor of the research and statistics courses is often (but not always) less than in scientist-practitioner training programs; more typically, it is the level of independent research expected that differs. In many professional psychology programs, works of a conceptual nature are accepted for meeting thesis and dissertation requirements as compared to the empirically based work often required in scientific-practitioner programs.

The second challenge to the scientist-practitioner model is related to issues of self-selection. The majority of graduate students entering counseling, clinical, and school psychology graduate programs are motivated primarily by their interest in becoming professional helpers. Only a small percentage of students enter these specialties with the primary motivation of becoming scientists. Limited interest in research is often coupled with little or no background in doing research. However, the assertion "I don't like to do research" may be a way of saying "I don't know how to do research." One of the ways to cope with a sense of inadequacy in an area is to express no interest in it and avoid it. Without adequate scientific training, investigators will be unable to use their practical counseling experience to formulate new hypotheses. Scientist-practitioner training programs enable bright, help-oriented students to develop counseling theories and techniques. Programs emphasizing practice provide mainly "skilled laborers" who will repeat mostly what they have been taught rather than extend it to new frontiers.

A third challenge to the scientist-practitioner model has been the criticism that few graduates of scientist-practitioner programs (or even strictly scientist programs) go on to produce new research. However, as will be elaborated in Chapter 4, there are many ways in which counseling psychologists can be scientists in how they think and conduct their practice of psychology. It is an error of judgment to exclude any model of training on the basis of publication only.

A second response to this challenge is related to the self-selection factors discussed above. Training and employment patterns have often interfered with motivation and skill in scientific research. Magoon and Holland (1984) provide detailed descriptions of some of the deficiencies in training conditions for scientific emphases, including neglect of individual differences in styles of developing and conducting research, faculty modeling and supervision, and "mismanagement" (our term) of the dissertation process. They also review deterrents to the conduct of research and other scientific endeavors in the work settings of many counseling psychologists. Science, like counseling, requires time commitments and environmental supports, that is, tangible resources plus colleagues' positive evaluations and feedback for scientific accomplishments. If "agency accountability" is limited to counting the number of clients seen, there will be almost no investigative activity possible on the part of the agency, which would include evaluating whether the services being delivered are efficacious or cost-effective. Royalty, Gelso, Mallinckrodt and Garrett (1986) have provided data on environments that foster the attitudes and skills necessary for counseling psychologists to become accomplished scientist-practitioners. The challenge in the coming decades is to incorporate the critical components of those environments into both training and employment settings.

Indeed, expensive resources are needed to support the scientist-practitioner model—faculty time, students' time, research facilities. Of the myriad ways to become a counselor or a psychologist, this model is unique in producing a full-fledged counseling psychologist: "First, we are scientist-practitioners" (Rudd, Weissberg & Gazda, 1988, p. 424).

SUMMARY

Although the formal, written history of counseling psychology is just approaching the half-century mark, the roots of the profession lie in sociocultural and disciplinary developments of the late

19th and early 20th century. Changes in lifestyles and work, two world wars, and the Great Depression created the need for a new helping profession—counseling psychology was a profession "waiting to happen." Conceptual developments in psychology and mental health care formed the foundation for the research and practice of the emerging profession and served to delineate its five unifying themes.

The mental health movement of the 19th century led to changes in society's perspective on mental illness, revealing that not only could "insanity" be cured but also that the problems of daily living can be alleviated by drawing on the unique set of assets and strengths each individual possesses.

Psychology's long and distinguished history on measurement of human behavior laid the foundation for counseling psychology's emphasis on person-environment interaction. Without measurement there can be no science. Equally important to the development of this emphasis was the much slower recognition, and subsequent measurement, of the effects of environment on human behavior. Within the various disciplines of psychology, too often those assessing personality have ignored the work of those studying environmental influences, and vice versa. Psychologists in applied practice have gradually realized, perhaps sooner than basic researchers, that behavior is not only a function of individual differences and environment but that the two have a reciprocal relationship. Persons affect environments just as environments affect persons. Only now are research and intervention strategies being developed that truly incorporate this interactive thinking.

The profession's emphasis on educational and career development has perhaps the clearest lineage—the vocational guidance movement, established at the beginning of this century to assist persons in the transition from the world of agriculture to the world of work created by the Industrial Revolution. This movement continues as counseling psychologists assist workers in the changing work world resulting from today's technological revolutions.

Because counseling psychology was created to respond to the psychological needs of persons that did not have to be hospitalized, primary emphasis was given to theoretical developments advocating brief treatment. Both directive (Williamson) and nondirective (Rogers) models of counseling, developed in the late 1930s and 1940s, provided a springboard for the development of myriad time-limited strategies during the second half of the 20th century. Finally, conceptualizations of cognitive developmental theorists complemented the work of personality theorists on how humans process interpersonal and environmental experiences, promoting research and interventions for prevention of psychological adjustment problems and for helping persons move through transitions with a minimum of disruption and a maximum of new opportunities.

The formal steps of establishing an autonomous specialty within psychology occurred in the 1940s. The 1950s saw the profession through the "childhood" stages, with the establishment of sets of standards, accredited programs, employment designations, and a major research journal. The "adolescence" of counseling psychology coincided with the turbulent 1960s and 1970s, during which American society itself struggled with identity problems in relation to sociopolitical issues like the Vietnam War and the civil-rights movement. Counseling psychology wrestled with its own increasingly diffused identity, encompassing remedial counseling and therapy, prevention, career psychology, and so forth. Despite efforts toward mergers and hostile takeovers (to borrow the language of today's business world), in the 1970s the profession was ready to build on its foundation and to define itself. Though sharing interests with other specialties and professions, it possessed a unique core of emphases. A journal, numerous accredited programs, and affiliation with professional organizations all helped propel the profession toward the highly productive 1980s—impressive years in terms of highly visible accomplishments—handbooks, book series, taskforces, and conferences, all representing increased vitality and promising continued growth and development.

Throughout the profession's history, a constant theme has been the reliance on the scientist-practitioner model. While training and practice according to this model are highly demanding and have been challenged on several grounds, it is the very essence of counseling psychology.

References

American Psychological Association, Division of Counseling and Guidance (1952). Recommended standards for training counseling psychologists at the doctoral level. *American Psychologist, 7,* 175–181.

Beers, C. W. (1908). *A mind that found itself.* Garden City, NY: Longman, Green.

Berg, I. A., Pepinsky, H. B., & Shoben, E. J. (1980). The status of counseling psychology: 1960. In J. Whiteley (Ed.), *The history of counseling psychology* (pp. 105–113). Monterey, CA: Brooks/Cole.

Bergin, A. E., & Garfield, S. L. (1971). *Handbook of psychotherapy and behavior change.* New York: Wiley.

Borgen, F. (1984). Counseling Psychology. *Annual Review of Psychology, 28,* 257–278.

Brammer, L. M., & Abrego, P. J. (1981). Intervention strategy for coping with transitions. *The Counseling Psychologist,* 9(2), 19–35.

Brown, S. D., & Lent, R. W. (Eds.) (1984). *Handbook of counseling psychology.* New York: Wiley.

Carskadon, T. G. (1978). Thrillers among the journals: A technique to increase graduate students' reading of research. *Professional Psychology, 9,* 83–86.

Claiborn, C. D., & Lichtenberg, J. W. (1989). Interactional counseling. *The Counseling Psychologist, 17,* 355–453.

Erikson, E. H. (1959). Identity and the life cycle. *Psychological Issues, 1,* Monograph 1.

Fretz, B. R., & Mills, D. H. (1980). *Licensing and certification of psychologists and counselors.* San Francisco: Jossey-Bass.

Gelso, C., & Fassinger, R. (1990). Counseling psychology. *Annual Review of Psychology, 41,* 355–386.

Haley, A. (1976). *Roots.* Garden City, NY: Doubleday.

Hull, C. L. (1928). *Aptitude testing.* Yonkers: World Book Co.

Hurst, J. C. (1989). Counseling Psychology—A source of strength and pride in the ties that bind. *The Counseling Psychologist, 17,* 147–160.

Kohlberg, L. (1984). *Essays in moral development.* New York: Harper & Row.

Krumboltz, J. D., & Thoresen, C. E. (1969). *Behavioral counseling.* New York: Holt, Rinehart and Winston.

Lewin, K. (1935). *A dynamic theory of personality: Selected papers.* New York: McGraw-Hill.

Matheny, K. B., Aycock, D. W., Pugh, J. L., Curlette, W. L., & Cannella, K. A. S. (1986). Stress coping: A qualitative and quantitative synthesis with implications for treatment, *The Counseling Psychologist, 14,* 439–549.

Meara, N. (1990). Science, practice and politics. *The Counseling Psychologist, 18,* 144–167.

Mischel, W. (1968). *Personality and assessment.* New York: Wiley.

Magoon, T. M., & Holland, J. L. (1984). Research training and supervision. In S. D. Brown & R. W. Lent (Eds.), *Handbook of counseling psychology* (pp. 628–715). New York: Wiley.

Moore, W. E. (1970). *The professions: Roles and rules.* New York: Sage.

Mosher, R. L., & Sprinthall, N. A. (1971). Psychological education: A means to promote personal development during adolescence. *The Counseling Psychologist,* 2(4), 3–84.

Osipow, S. H. (1987). Counseling psychology: Theory, research and practice in career counseling. *Annual Review of Psychology, 28,* 257–278.

Parsons, F. (1909). *Choosing a vocation.* Boston: Houghton Mifflin.

Pepinsky, H. B., Hill-Frederick, K., & Epperson, D. L. (1978). The *Journal of Counseling Psychology* as a matter of policies. *Journal of Counseling Psychology, 25,* 483–498.

Perry, W. (1970). *Forms of intellectual and ethical development during the college years.* New York: Holt, Rinehart and Winston.

Piaget, J. (1952). *The language and thought of the child.* London: Routledge and Kegan.

Rogers, C. R. (1942). *Counseling and psychotherapy.* Boston: Houghton Mifflin.

Royalty, G. N., Gelso, C. J., Mallinckrodt, B., & Garrett, K. D. (1986). The environment and the student in counseling psychology. *The Counseling Psychologist, 14,* 9-30.

Rudd, S. S., Weissberg, N., & Gazda, G. M. (1988). Looking to the future: Themes from the third national conference for counseling psychology. *The Counseling Psychologist, 16,* 423–430.

Schlossberg, N. K. (1981). A model for analyzing human adaptation to transition. *The Counseling Psychologist, 9*(2), 2–18.

Schmidt, L. (1977). Why has the professional practice of psychological counseling developed in the United States? *The Counseling Psychologist, 7*(2), 19–20.

Schneider, B. (1983). On the etiology of climates. *Personnel Psychology, 36,* 19–39.

Scott, C. W. (1980). History of the division of counseling psychology: 1945–1963. In J. M. Whiteley (Ed.), *The History of Counseling Psychology* (pp. 25–40). Monterey, CA: Brooks/Cole.

Super, D. E. (1955). Transition: From vocational guidance to counseling psychology. *Journal of Counseling Psychology, 2,* 3–9.

Tiedeman, D. B. (1980). Status and prospect in counseling psychology: 1962. In J. M. Whiteley (Ed.), *The history of counseling psychology* (pp. 125–132). Monterey, CA: Brooks/Cole.

Thompson, A. S., & Super, D. E. (Eds.) (1964). *The professional preparation of counseling psychologists. Report of the 1964 Greyston Conference.* New York: Bureau of Publications, Teacher's College, Columbia University.

Tyler, L., Tiedeman, D., & Wrenn, C. G. (1980). The current status of counseling psychology: 1961. In J. M. Whiteley (Ed.), *The history of counseling psychology* (pp. 114–124). Monterey, CA: Brooks/Cole.

Walsh, W. B., & Osipow, S. H. (Eds.) (1983). *Handbook of Vocational Psychology* (Vols. 1–2). Hillsdale, NJ: Erlbaum.

Walsh, W. B., & Osipow, S. H. (Eds.) (1983). *Advances in Vocational Psychology* (Vol. 1). Hillsdale, NJ: Erlbaum.

Whiteley, J. N. (Ed.) (1980). *The history of counseling psychology.* Monterey, CA: Brooks/Cole.

Whiteley (1984a). Counseling psychology: A historical perspective. *The Counseling Psychologist, 12*(1), 3–109.

Whiteley (1984b). A historical perspective on the development of counseling psychology as a profession. In S. G. Brown & R. W. Lent (Eds.), *Handbook of counseling psychology* (pp. 3–55). New York: Wiley.

Whiteley, J. N., & Fretz, B. R. (Eds.) (1980). *The present and future of counseling psychology.* Monterey, CA: Brooks/Cole.

Whiteley, J. N., Kagan, N., Harmon, L. W., Fretz, B. R., & Tanney, F. (Eds.) (1984). *The coming decade in counseling psychology.* Alexandria, VA: American Association for Counseling and Development.

Williamson, E. G. (1939). *How to counsel students.* New York: McGraw-Hill.

Wrenn, C. G. (1966). Birth and early childhood of a journal. *Journal of Counseling Psychology, 13,* 485–488.

Chapter 3

Ethical and Professional Issues

Psychologists respect the dignity and worth of the individual and strive for the preservation and protection of fundamental human rights. They are committed to increasing knowledge of human behavior and of people's understanding of themselves and others and to the utilization of such knowledge for the promotion of human welfare.

—*Preamble to* Ethical Principles of Psychologists, *American Psychological Association (1990b)*

What does it require to be an ethical counseling psychologist?

The primary goal of the first half of this chapter is to provide a broad perspective on ethics. Note that we examine ethics before presenting the principles of counseling psychology. There are in fact many complex ethical issues one must consider before seeing any clients: "Thus it appears that effective self-regulation entails more than clearly written, widely disseminated, frequently taught and strictly enforced ethical codes. What appears to be necessary is a membership capable of making sophisticated judgments about which course of action may be ethical in situations in which no one behavior seems entirely ethical or unethical" (Welfel & Lipsitz, 1984, p. 31). In our illustration of ethical principles, we make a distinction between unethical behavior and ethical dilemmas. The former is far more visible because of sensational articles in the mass media; the latter is more problematic in that ethical dilemmas may necessitate the violation of one principle so that another can be upheld. We then review the components for becoming an ethical counseling psychologist.

The second half of this chapter is devoted to four current controversial professional issues in psychology that affect the training and practice of all psychologists, but especially those who practice psychology (e.g., counseling, clinical) as compared to those who are exclusively teachers and researchers. These issues have developed as the profession seeks to meet its goal of promoting human welfare in the most effective ways: (1) the protection of consumers through the licensing and credentialing of psychologists, (2) the ambivalence of the discipline of psychology regarding master's degree practitioners, (3) emerging developments in accreditation and specialization in psychology to ensure quality control, and (4) conflicts between health service providers and other psychologists as the practice of psychology becomes more prevalent. These issues are controversial, in part, because the various professional actions that have been taken and new ones that are being considered can be seen either as selfish ways to promote the profession or as appropriate altruistic action to protect the public welfare, that is, as extensions of our ethical obligations. The exploration of these issues also highlights some critical issues that graduate students in counseling psychology need to consider concerning their own career possibilities.

THE DEVELOPMENT OF PROFESSIONAL ETHICS

In a society strongly predicated on observance of individual rights, the very fact that a profession develops a code of ethical standards that mandates some behaviors and forbids others may seem "un-American." Yet most of the major service professions in our society have developed codes of ethics in the 20th century. Since a profession is by definition a group that has "expertise and competence not readily available to the general public" (Biggs & Blocher, 1987, p. 3), the public is not usually very knowledgeable about what constitutes competent professional behavior. The concept of being professional thus includes a trust that members will monitor their own and other members' professional behavior so that competent services are provided to the public. Notice both elements—professionals are to be competent in their services, and it is their responsibility to see that fellow professionals provide competent services. When persons contact a physician, attorney, or psychologist, they typically do not know what is best for them (other than that they need help); otherwise they would not be contacting a professional. It can be argued that the marketplace principle *caveat emptor* (let the buyer beware) does not apply to human services, as it does to products like clothes or refrigerators. Counseling psychologists, like all mental health professionals, have supreme responsibility to the public trust. Persons seeking help from them are troubled and vulnerable and, consequently, are especially subject to exploitation and manipulation. Client trust is one of the most valuable commodities of the profession, but too often ethics are considered only after a problem arises.

Although the need for professional ethics has been widely recognized by most professionals, developing specific codes of ethics has been a controversial issue. At the most basic level, ethics have been a part of philosophy, asking such questions as "What rules do people in a given society decide constitute justice?" When such rules are clearly stated and written, they are, of course, laws; other, broader, less explicit standards of a society, such as those regarding sexual relationships, are not written down as laws but are referred to as *morals.* As Kitchener (1984a) notes, ethics intersect both morals and law; she argues that attempts to distinguish between morals and ethics have proven relatively futile.

This interchangeability raises considerable concern because many persons think of morals as religious or parental commandments. Yet ethics, too, are a kind of consensual professional commandments. What determines those shared by a profession? Both Biggs and Blocher (1987) and Beauchamp and Childress (1983) describe a variety of philosophical positions that underlie the development and evolution of ethical codes, ranging from divine authority to the authority of duty to various utilitarian theories; that is, a behavior's ethical status is to be determined by the usefulness of its consequences. At this level of discussion, the development of ethics links with such fundamental philosophical issues as the basic nature of humans, free will vs. determinism, and the theory of social contracts.

However, any collection of professionals will disagree about these issues, which helps explain the complexity of ethical issues. Few behaviors seem entirely ethical or unethical. Many ethical problems will elicit as many different proposals for resolution as there are persons looking at the problem. Similarly, all ethical codes seem transitory. The APA revised its code of ethics at least three times in the last 30 years. The revisions reflect certain changes in society but mostly they are the result of testing experience against an inadequate set of ethical principles.

Recent authors (Kitchener, 1984, Biggs & Blocher, 1987) think that too much attention has been given to issues of ethical standards and not enough to ethical decision-making. Interestingly enough, it is psychologists themselves, especially developmental and social psychologists, who have provided some of the most descriptive data in this area. Rest (1984) provides the most succinct summary of social psychology and developmental psychology research in suggesting that there are four components of moral behavior: "Component 1 . . . to interpret the situation in terms of how one's actions affect the welfare of others. . . . component 2 . . . to formulate what a moral course of action would be; to identify the ideal in a specific situation. . . . component 3 . . . to select among competing value outcomes of ideals, the one to act upon; deciding whether or not to try to fulfill one's moral ideal. . . . component 4 . . . to execute and implement what one intends to do" (p. 20).

Note that the use of a code of ethics is mostly related to component 2, that is, identifying the moral ideal of a specific situation. All the other components involve individuals' perceptions and responsibilities outside of a specific code. Component 3 recognizes that there is always the choice to act in a moral way or in ways that typically serve self-interests as compared to the values of others. As Rest (1984) notes, one uses various perceptual distortions and other social-psychological processes to justify decisions to act in a way that serves oneself more than one's moral ideals. Regarding the ethical implications of a behavior (component 1), Rest is also a keen observer: "Typically, professional education is so focused on the technical aspects of the job that students in graduate programs in most professions are 'professionally socialized' not to look for moral problems or to recognize moral issues in their work. The students who complete professional programs . . . often have a mind set not to look for moral issues, do not expect that they are an inevitable part of professional life, and are usually ill prepared to know how to approach a moral problem when one does smack them in the face" (Rest, 1984, p. 21).

The purpose of the following sections, which describe and illustrate the APA code of ethics, is to sensitize the reader to a number of situations that involve ethical issues and to afford a better understanding of ethical principles and decision-making processes.

ETHICAL PRINCIPLES, WITH ILLUSTRATIONS OF UNETHICAL BEHAVIOR

In this section, nine of the ten ethical principles of the APA (1990) will each be illustrated by abbreviated quotations and by at least one example of a violation of the principle. The comment that follows each violation typically includes quotations from pertinent elaborations of the ethical principle. Of the 65 subsections of the ten principles, only 12 are illustrated. We have tried to choose a part of each principle that captures its essence as well as allows an exploration of some of its nuances. (We urge readers to order a copy of the *Ethical Principles of Psychologists* and a copy of the *Guidelines for Providers of Psychological Services,* to be discussed later in this chapter. Copies of each may be obtained without charge by writing to: The American Psychological Association, 1200 17th Street, N.W., Washington, DC 20036.)

Many of the ethical violations cited include acts that were carried out with good intentions or that seemed reasonable at the time. "Violators" were simply not giving full consideration to the ethical implications of their behavior. More blatant violations of each principle, as it is described, should readily come to mind. After reading each principle, but before reading the violation example, try to think of appropriate examples of violations you have heard or read about.

"*Principle 1:* Responsibility. . . . Psychologists maintain the highest standards, they accept responsibility for their acts and make every effort to ensure that their services are used appropriately" (APA, 1990, p. 390).

Ethical Violation: In an interview published in the campus newspaper, Professor A, a psychologist, questions the mental competency of a candidate for the presidency of the United States, based on some of the candidate's recommended foreign policy statements.

Comment: "1-f. As practitioners, psychologists know that they bear a heavy social responsibility because their recommendations and professional actions may alter the lives of others. They are alert to personal, social, organizational, financial, or political situations and pressures that might lead to the misuse of their influence" (APA, 1990, p. 390). Professor A is entitled to his views about political candidates, but, in accordance with the responsibility principle, should not make public statements about a candidate's *mental competence.*

"*Principle 2:* Competence. [. . .] Psychologists . . . provide services and only use techniques for which they are qualified by training and experience" (APA, 1990, p. 390).

Ethical Violation: Psychologist B accepts and begins working in a position at a mental health clinic where many of her clientele are children in an American Indian community. Psychologist B has had no prior experience or training in working with American Indians or with children.

Comment: "2-d. Psychologists recognize differences among people, such as those that may be associated with age, sex, socioeconomic, and ethnic backgrounds. When necessary, they obtain training, experience, or counsel to assure competent service or research relating to such persons" (APA, 1990, p. 391). Psychologist B, when deciding to accept the position, should have agreed to seek appropriate training and supervision in preparation for seeing the clients she was expected to handle at the center.

"*Principle 3:* Moral and legal standards. Psychologists' moral and ethical standards of behavior are a personal matter . . . except as these may compromise the fulfillment of their professional responsibilities or reduce the public trust in psychology" (APA, 1990, p. 391).

Ethical violation: Psychologist C is asked by the Chief Executive Officer (CEO) of the company that employs him to provide psychological evaluations of several candidates being considered for promotion to a vice-presidency. The CEO indicates that the only persons he wants evaluated, from among those nominated, are the men, since he will not consider any females as vice-presidential candidates. Psychologist C agrees to conduct the evaluations.

Comment: "3-b. As employees or employers, psychologists do not engage in or condone practices that are inhumane or result in illegal or unjustifiable actions. Such practices include, but are not limited to, those based on consideration of race, handicap, age, gender, sexual preference, religion, or national origin in hiring, promotion, or training" (APA, 1990, p. 391). Psychologist C, by agreeing to test only the male nominees, colluded in discriminatory actions against women. What alternatives might the psychologist have explored with the CEO to avoid this violation?

"*Principle 4:* Public statements. . . . Psychologists represent accurately and objectively their professional qualifications, affiliations, and functions. . . . Psychologists base their statements on scientifically acceptable psychological findings and techniques with full recognition of the limits and uncertainties of such evidence" (APA, 1990, p. 392).

Ethical Violation: Psychologist D agrees to write a short statement describing the virtues of a book designed for parents dealing with teenagers in exchange for receiving $200 in credits toward book purchases from the publisher.

Comment: "4-f. Psychologists do not participate for personal gain in commercial announcements or advertisements recommending to the public the purchase or use of proprietary or single-source products or services when that participation is based solely upon their identification as psychologists" (APA, 1990, p. 392). Psychologist D could possibly have maintained her objectivity in writing the statement, but remunerative arrangements, such as the book order credits, increase the possibility of distortions. This illustration applies to the "conflict of interest" concept now so prevalent in ethical charges against government employees. This concept refers to someone benefiting personally from action taken on behalf of another without clear acknowledgment of the potential benefit—for example, when a city council member votes to approve a zoning change that, if approved, will benefit him or her by significantly increasing the value of the land he or she owns.

"*Principle 5:* Confidentiality. Psychologists . . . reveal . . . information [obtained from persons in their work as psychologists] to others only with the consent of the person or the person's legal representative, except in those unusual circumstances in which not to do so would result in clear danger to the person or to others" (APA, 1990, p. 392).

Ethical Violation: Psychologist E shows the counseling center receptionist the results of an IQ test he has recently given to one of his clients, noting that the client has obtained the highest IQ scores he had ever seen.

Comment: "5-a. Information obtained in clinical or consulting relationships, or evaluative data concerning children, students, employees, and others, is discussed only for professional purposes and only with persons clearly concerned with the case" (APA, 1990, p. 393). Though Psychologist E was not sharing anything she thought was damaging, *any* information obtained in professional relationships is to be treated confidentially.

"*Principle 6:* Welfare of the Consumer. Psychologists respect the integrity and protect the welfare of the people and groups with whom they work" (APA, 1990, p. 393).

Ethical Violation 1: Psychologist F, a professor and counselor at a university, is approached by one of her students who wants to get counseling from her about a personal problem. The course includes a term paper and essay exams that Psychologist F will be grading later in the semester. Psychologist F agrees to provide the counseling.

Comment: "6-a. Psychologists are continually cognizant of their own needs and of their potentially influential position vis-à-vis persons such as clients, students, and subordinates. . . . Psychologists make every effort to avoid dual relationships that could impair their professional judgment or increase the risk of exploitation. Examples of such dual relationships include, but are not limited to, research with and treatment of employees, students, supervisees, close friends, and relatives. Sexual intimacies with clients are unethical" (APA, 1990, p. 393). The appropriate behavior for the teacher would have been to refer the student to another psychologist. As Psychologist F would be evaluating the academic work of the student at some point in the semester, she is clearly forming an inappropriate dual relationship by agreeing to provide counseling to the student.

(Highly publicized incidents of sexual intimacies in psychotherapy relationships, discussed later, are also dual relationships that have led to the development of a most important set of guidelines for those who encounter these situations. See "If Sex Enters into the Psychotherapy Relationship" [Committee of Women in Psychology, 1989].)

The following is another illustration of a violation of the principle concerning welfare of the consumer that goes beyond the all-too-common sexual intimacies violation.

Ethical Violation 2: Psychologist G is asked by the president of the company that employs him to provide employee Jones with some counseling to "get him out of his plateau." Psychologist G invites employee Jones to have coffee with him in his office and subsequently continues to invite him in for "coffee," during which time the psychologist shapes the sessions into ever more personal counseling sessions.

Comment: "6-b. When a psychologist agrees to provide services to a client at the request of a third party, the psychologist assumes the responsibility of clarifying the nature of the relationships to all parties concerned" (APA, 1990, p. 393). By not making clear to employee Jones that he, the psychologist, had been requested to be of assistance to him, the psychologist, no matter how well-intentioned in his approach to the employee, violated this ethical principle.

"*Principle 7:* Professional relationships. Psychologists act with due regard for the needs, special competencies, and obligations of their colleagues in psychology and other professions." (APA, 1990, p. 393).

Ethical Violation 1: Psychologist H at a university counseling center is approached by a client wanting treatment for some bouts of depression.

She indicates that her family physician has prescribed some antidepressants, but they are not helping. Psychologist H begins seeing her for counseling without consulting her physician and without further discussion of the issues in receiving treatment for the same problem from two professionals.

Comment: "7-b. Psychologists know and take into account the traditions and practices of other professional groups with whom they work and cooperate fully with such groups. If a psychologist is contacted by a person who is already receiving similar services from another professional, the psychologist carefully considers that professional relationship and proceeds with caution and sensitivity to the therapeutic issues as well as the client's welfare. The psychologist discusses these issues with the client so as to minimize the risk of confusion and conflict" (APA, 1990, p. 393). Psychologist H would not have been in violation if he or she had contacted the physician with the client's permission or had discussed with the client the need for *her* to consult her physician regarding her desire for counseling. Such consultation may be extremely complex if the two professionals have widely divergent views on what treatment the client needs. On the other hand, not to consult can lead to dangerous consequences for clients who might receive incompatible medical and psychological treatments.

Two other illustrations of the principle on professional relationships:

Ethical Violation 2: Professor J asks a graduate student to work with him on developing a research project, to collect the data and run the analyses. When he prepares the article for submission, the professor lists himself as sole author and acknowledges the contributions of the graduate student only in a footnote.

Comment: "7-f. Publication credit is assigned to those who have contributed to a publication in proportion to their professional contributions. Major contributions of a professional character made by several persons to a common project are recognized by joint authorship, with the individual who made the principal contribution listed first. Minor contribution of a professional character and extensive clerical or similar non-professional assistance may be acknowledged in footnotes or an introductory statement" (APA, 1990, p. 393). The involvement of the graduate student in designing the study, collecting the data, and conducting all the statistical analyses clearly constitutes more than clerical or non-professional assistance. These contributions should be recognized through joint authorship rather than a footnote.

Ethical Violation 3: Psychologist Z becomes aware that his colleague, Psychologist K, frequently invites his clients to go out to dinner with him and, on several occasions, has invited them to go on weekend trips with him. Psychologist Z speaks with Psychologist K and indicates his concern about K's violation of dual relationships (see Principle 6). Psychologist K argues that taking these clients out is part of the treatment they need for learning how to develop effective friendships. Subsequently, Z hears from several different sources that K engages in sexual relationships with some of these clients. As he has already expressed his concerns to K, Psychologist Z takes no further action.

Comment: "7-g. When psychologists know of an ethical violation by another psychologist, and it seems appropriate, they informally attempt to resolve the issue by bringing the behavior to the attention of the psychologist. If the misconduct is of a minor nature and/or appears to be due to lack of sensitivity, knowledge, or experience, such an informal solution is usually appropriate. Such informal corrective efforts are made with sensitivity to any rights of confidentiality involved. If the violation does not seem amendable to an informal solution, or is of a more serious nature, psychologists bring it to the attention of the appropriate local, state, and/or national committee on professional ethics or conduct" (APA, 1990, p. 394). Psychologist Z, by not taking any further action, has committed an ethical violation himself; it is his responsibility to take further action given his colleague's continued violation of the ethical principle of dual relationships.

"*Principle 8:* Assessment techniques. Psychologists guard against the misuse of assessment" (APA, 1990, p. 394).

Ethical Violation: Psychology Professor L, who teaches career development at a community college with 60 percent minority students, 30 percent of whom have English as a second language, offers them the opportunity to come in and use his personal computer to take a computer-assisted assessment battery developed for university students. The students receive a sheet interpreting their results which, the professor tells them, can be of use in helping them to decide whether or not they have the ability to consider going beyond the community college level. They do not have any further contact with Professor L to discuss the results.

Comment: "8-c. In reporting assessment results, psychologists indicate any reservations that exist regarding validity or reliability because of the circumstances of the assessment or the inappropriateness of the norms for the person tested. . . . 8-e. Psychologists offering scoring and interpretation services are able to produce appropriate evidence for the validity of the programs and procedures used in arriving at interpretations" (APA, 1990, p. 394). Psychologist L, by offering an assessment battery that was normed for typical four-year college students, who are an extremely different population from that attending his junior college, and by not meeting with the students to discuss possible inappropriateness of the norms and other factors in their backgrounds, for example, language differences that could affect the interpretation of the results, violated both sections c and e of the principle on assessment.

"*Principle 9:* Research with Human Participants. . . . The psychologist carries out the investigation with respect and concern for the dignity and welfare of the people who participate and with cognizance of federal and state regulations and professional standards governing the conduct of research with human participants" (APA, 1990, p. 394).

Ethical Violation: Psychology Professor M invites students to take part in an experiment she describes as an investigation of various models of group discussion. Once students have begun participating in the experiment, they are asked, in some of the groups, to reveal their most pressing personal problem.

Comment: "9-d. . . . The investigator informs the participants of all aspects of the research that might reasonably be expected to influence willingness to participate and explains all other aspects of the research about which the participants inquire. Failure to make full disclosure prior to obtaining informed consent requires additional safeguards to protect the welfare and dignity of the research participants" (APA, 1990, p. 394). Professor M neither fully informed students nor took safeguards to protect their welfare when they were essentially manipulated into revealing personal problems.

The final APA principle, on the care and use of animals, is not illustrated here because it seldom involves counseling psychologists. Moreover, as of 1988, no official complaints had ever been received by the APA concerning noncompliance with this principle. As those authors (Ethics Committee of the American Psychological Association, 1988) note, institutional committees reviewing both human-participant and animal research minimize the number of problems in these areas.

We have now presented essentially the ten ethical principles of the APA and have provided illustrations for nine of them. It is important to note that the number of violations reported for each of these principles varies widely. In a most informative article about changing trends in ethics through the 1980s, the Ethics Committee of the APA (1988) indicated that the largest number of violations were related to the welfare of the consumer; specifically, these involved dual relationships.

Three types of dual-relationship violations are prominent. One is the often publicized issue of therapist-client sexual relationships. Two states (Wisconsin and Minnesota) have now passed laws criminalizing sexual intimacy with clients. (Furthermore, over one-third of all psychologists' liability insurance fees goes for payment of settlements with such clients.) The second most common complaint under this principle concerns therapists entering into sexual intimacies with ex-clients, that is, after therapy has ended. Numerous legal cases were documented in the 1980s, and ethical changes brought about, as a result of legal action taken by clients who felt that their therapists had exploited their prior therapy relationship by entering into a subsequent sexual relationship.

Difficult questions have been raised about how long one must be an "ex-patient" before entering into a relationship. There are no set guidelines so one is always potentially at risk, even many years later, when engaging in sexual intimacies with former clients.

The third type of dual-relationship violation involves psychologists' providing therapy to their employees, students, supervisees, friends, or relatives. Although arguments are sometimes made for the "practical" reasons supporting such arrangements, for example, doing it for lower fees, in a geographic area where not many other alternatives are present, the pertinent literature suggests high risks for such arrangements and the principle of dual relationships firmly advises against these practices. The ethics committee notes that committees' and courts' past permissiveness regarding such arrangements are now being reversed and sanctions are being applied to those who continue such dual relationships—especially when the dual relationship is not part of an ethical dilemma such as described in the next section.

Although the preponderance of violations may relate to dual relationships, there are typically more discussions in the literature on ethics regarding the principle of confidentiality. Reported violations here may be fewer, but the dilemmas that result in seeking to maintain confidentiality are almost countless for every practitioner. In the next section, we focus on some of the most frequently occurring dilemmas and present a framework that can be used to realize Rest's (1984) fourth component of moral behavior, that of selecting among competing value outcomes.

ETHICAL DILEMMAS

In ethical dilemmas, the professional is in a situation where, no matter which choice is made, one or more ethical principles are being violated. Consider the following situations, which occur quite frequently in professional practice.

A. A client tells the counselor that he wants to commit suicide, and has a plan to do it, but does not want the counselor to tell anyone. The client has thought about it carefully and has decided this is his "best" choice. He refuses all the counselor's attempts to have him consider alternatives. Sensing the counselor's concern and suspecting that she might commit him, he threatens to sue for breach of confidentiality if she tells anyone about his plans. (This scenario assumes that the counselor and the client have not previously discussed limits to confidentiality. See Ethics and Law section below.)

B. The only female counselor in a rural county's mental health center has a list of eight persons who have been waiting up to three months for counseling. A new client comes to the clinic in a highly agitated state of depression and insists on seeing a female counselor because "no men are to be trusted." The female counselor suspects that if this client is not treated promptly, she is at risk for either a psychotic break or possible suicide. Yet if the counselor begins seeing her at this time, she would be making other clients, who were referred earlier though are less disturbed, wait several more weeks or months. There are no practical referral resources available, as the next nearest female counselor is 125 miles away.

C. "The counseling psychologist concerned with the increase in cases of bulimia reported in university counseling centers decides to compare the effects of a cognitive-behavioral intervention with a pharmacological treatment in a controlled study. He considers using a wait-list control group and a placebo group but is aware that the use of the placebo group will involve deceiving subjects and the use of a wait-list group will involve refusing some individuals treatment for several months" (Kitchener, 1984, p. 43).

In both counseling and research settings, counseling psychologists often find themselves "between a rock and a hard place." Although such situations typically get far less media attention than ethical violations such as dual relationships, misrepresentation of credentials, and inappropriate public statements, it is the dilemmas, rather than the violations, that help us most clearly understand the limitations of ethical codes in solving ethical problems. The APA ethical principles, each related to a specific area such as competence or professional relationships, give psychologists little guidance on how to proceed. "The dilemma exists because there are good, but contradictory ethical reasons to take conflicting and incompatible courses of action" (Kitchener, 1984, p. 43).

Four authors—Kitchener (1984), Fitting (1984), Powell (1984), and Lindsey (1984)—have made a valuable contribution to all counseling psychologists in their "translation" of the fundamental principles of biomedical ethics developed by Beauchamp and Childress (1983). These four authors use the basic ethical principles of autonomy, beneficence, nonmaleficence, fidelity, and justice to provide a reasoning process that can be used to resolve ethical dilemmas. Still, choices are never easy, and one principle may be violated to honor another. It is beyond the scope of this chapter to develop the conceptual bases for all these principles or even to provide illustrations of all of them, but applying the five basic principles helps create a greater awareness of the rationale needed for the decision to be made. Our intention here is to show how these principles can help counseling psychologists make choices in dealing with the three situations presented at the beginning of this section. The five principles are thus defined:

> Autonomy . . . includes the right to act as an autonomous agent, to make one's own decision, to develop one's own values . . . [and] includes

respecting the rights of others to make autonomous choices, even when we believe they are mistaken, as long as their choices do not infringe on the rights of others. . . .

Nonmaleficence . . . not causing harm to others, includes both not inflicting intentional harm nor engaging in actions which risk harming others. . . . seeing nonmaleficence as fundamental suggests that if we must choose between harming someone and benefiting that person, another, or society, our stronger obligation, other things being equal, would be to avoid harm. . . .

Beneficence . . . doing good to others is critical to ethical issues in psychology and especially counseling psychology. . . . the term "helping profession" underlines this obligation. . . .

Justice . . . in order to live together with minimal strife, people must develop rules and procedures for adjudicating claims and services in a fair manner. . . . considerations of equal need are particularly relevant to the issue of how to distribute scarce psychological services. . . .

Fidelity . . . involves questions of "faithfulness," promise-keeping, and loyalty. Issues of fidelity arise when individuals enter into some kind of a voluntary relationship (e.g., counselor-client, husband-wife, supervisor-supervisee). . . . the issue of fidelity seems especially critical in psychology because issues like truthfulness and loyalty are basic to trust . . . it is particularly vital to client-counselor, research-participant, supervisor-supervisee, and/or consultant-consultee relationships. All are dependent on honest communication and the assumption that the contract on which the relationship was initiated, obliges both parties to fulfill certain functions" (Kitchener, 1984, pp. 46–51).

The example of the suicidal client at the beginning of this section represents a conflict between the principles of autonomy and beneficence. As Snipe (1988) nicely illustrates in her exploration of ethical issues in the treatment of a rational suicidal client, such a situation brings into question even parts of the preamble to the APA ethical principles. On the one hand, the preamble states that psychologists respect the dignity and worth of the individual, but on the other hand, it also states that psychologists make every effort to protect the welfare of those who seek services. In the case of the suicidal client, one cannot do both simultaneously. If interventions are made to protect him from harming himself, his dignity and worth as an autonomous person have been "violated": "The autonomous person determines his or her course of action in accordance with the plan chosen by himself or herself" (Beauchamp & Childress, 1983). On the other hand, if no effort is made to intervene, then there is great risk that the welfare of the client has not been protected, assuming "protecting the welfare" means keeping him from suicide. Beauchamp and Childress (1983) see "protecting the welfare" as meeting the basic principle of beneficence. In their conclusions to a discussion of the dilemma of clients planning suicide, those authors note that, in our society, principles of beneficence usually outweigh those of autonomy, the justification for this being that "beneficent treatment for such patients is to intervene directly to protect them against harms resulting from their illness, immaturity, psychological incapacitation, and the like" (p. 102).

In the example concerning the highly agitated, depressed woman, a conflict between the principles of justice and nonmaleficence is illustrated. As the principle of justice is based on the presumption that all people are equal, one could argue that treatment of them should be equal and presupposes a "first come, first served" basis. However, in this particular case, *not* to provide treatment to the agitated client seems to contribute to potential harm to the client, that is, to maleficence.

Ideally, in a just society, there would be adequate resources for all individuals. However, such availability of resources is all too rare, especially in rural settings, and this kind of issue is almost a daily ethical dilemma. University counseling centers oftentimes find themselves in similar situations when there are huge waiting lists at critical times during the semester. Beauchamp and Childress (1983) note that the tendency in the health professions has been to recognize that some needs are greater than others and that distribution of services then is based on this differential assessment of needs, thereby redefining the basis of justice.

In the third example concerning research on bulimia, the conflict is between the principle of nonmaleficence (do no harm by eliminating the waiting list and so avoid refusing some individuals treatment for several months) with the principle of beneficence (the research potentially could make significant contributions to determining what is the most effective treatment for bulimia). Making decisions about research projects, as well as whether to use treatments when there is little or no research to support its benefits, has to include, in the reasoning process, a careful consideration of whether or not the potential benefits of the research project outweigh the actual costs suffered by those treated with placebos or not treated at all (if on a waiting list).

We have now presented information on three components of Rest's (1984) ethical model, specifying ideals (APA principles), illustrating the effects of actions through examples of violations, and outlining fundamental principles to consider in selecting among competing values. Rest's last component of executing and implementing what one intends to do is, of course, a matter of practicing what one learns in applying the first three components of his model.

Regarding implementation, Jordan and Meara (1990) have presented a case for more careful consideration of *virtue ethics,* that is, focusing on "who shall I be" as much as on "what shall I do." Knowing what to do may be necessary but may not be sufficient for executing a decision: "The ideals of professional psychology must include conscientious decision making, but they also must include virtuous deciders, who emphasize not so much what is permitted as what is preferred" (Jordan & Meara, 1990, p. 112).

Ethics and Values

> Frequently, when we are faced with a difficult ethical decision, we are told we must fall back on our own values or sense of personal obligations. But the question arises: Which values should we rely on and are they equally acceptable?. . . Thus, when we say that we should decide an ethical dilemma on the basis of our personal values, we need to be clear that these are not just any values, rather they are ethical ones. . . . other values (e.g., money) frequently compete with and win against ethical concerns when people are faced with moral decisions. Perhaps part of the reason that this is so is that people are unclear about what ethical values they ought to hold or whether they ought to hold any at all. (Kitchener, 1984, p. 17)

The issues of values in counseling have been and continue to be widely discussed ones. Before ethics became as prominent a topic as it did in the 1980s, much more attention was given to values than to ethics. In earlier decades, from both traditional Freudian analytic and Rogerian client-centered perspectives, there were theorists who argued that counseling needed to be value-free. Since the 1960s, few psychologists have found this position tenable.

> Perhaps the most fundamental question we can raise about values in the therapy process is whether it is possible for counselors to keep their values out of their counseling sessions. In our view, it is neither possible nor desirable for counselors to be scrupulously neutral with respect to values in the counseling relationship. Although we don't see the counselor's function as persuading clients to accept a certain value system, we do think it is crucial for counselors to be clear about their own values and how they influence their work and the directions taken by their clients. Since we believe that counselors' values do inevitably affect the therapeutic process, we also think it's important for counselors to be willing to express their values openly when they are relevant to the questions that come up in their sessions with clients. (Corey, Corey, & Callanan, 1979, p. 85)

Reaching decisions in ethical dilemmas clearly calls upon psychologists' values and a consideration of how these values are to be dealt with in the counseling relationship.

Ethics and the Law

Slightly different issues and dilemmas arise because of the relationships of ethics and law. Although laws and ethics most often agree about a course of action, in certain critical cases, laws and ethical standards may directly contradict each other. Perhaps the best example of clear agreement between laws and ethics is licensing laws, which, in most states, specifically identify who can legitimately call himself or herself a psychologist. These regulations usually agree with APA ethical standards on public statements. Another example is laws forbidding sexual relations with clients, as in Wisconsin and Minnesota.

Of greatest concern in the relationship of laws and ethics are those cases in which they call for contradictory actions. Here it is not a matter of two ethical principles being in conflict, but rather a conflict between a legal principle and an ethical one. Perhaps the greatest discussion of such issues has been stimulated by what are now called "duty to warn" requirements based on the Tarasoff case: "On October 27, 1969, Prosenjit Poddar killed Tatiana Tarasoff. Plaintiffs, Tatiana's parents, allege that two months earlier Poddar confided his intention to kill Tatiana to Dr. Lawrence Moore, a psychologist employed by the Cowell Memorial Hospital at the University of California at Berkeley. . . . they further claim that Dr. Harvey Powelson, Moore's superior, then directed that no further action should be taken to detain Poddar. No one warned plaintiffs of Tatiana's peril" (Beauchamp & Childress, 1983, p. 281).

This particular case resulted in the establishment of laws stipulating that psychotherapists must warn individuals when they become aware of intentions to harm: "We conclude that the public policy favoring protection of the confidential character of patient-psychotherapist communication must yield to the extent that exposure is essential to avert danger to others. The protection privilege ends where the public peril begins" (Beauchamp & Childress, 1983, p. 283). Before such laws emerged, most standards on confidentiality indicated to psychotherapists that they should not initiate actions on the basis of what a client told them without the consent of the client to do so. Now standards on maintaining confidentiality and the laws were placed in direct conflict. Numerous articles have been written about the Tarasoff case; Fulero (1988) has noted many of these and described the pertinent legal developments in the ten years following the ruling. Most ethical standards, including those of the APA, have since been amended to recognize that confidentiality does not apply in situations where the duty to warn exists or therapists are legally bound to report actions to authorities, such as presence of substance abuse, intentions of minors to obtain abortions, and the abuse of family members. Similar concerns are now being raised about health and mental health professionals' duty to warn the sexual partners of clients with AIDS if the clients refuse to do so themselves (Lamb, Clark, Drumheller, Frizzell, & Surrey, 1989).

Because of the potential conflict of observing the law and maintaining confidentiality of clients' communications, it is recommended that clients be apprised of these limitations to confidentiality at the beginning of counseling. Dilemmas like the one described above concerning a suicidal client can be precluded by informing a client from the outset about the legal limits to confidentiality. On the other hand, many psychologists believe that therapeutic goals can be thwarted by too zealous a listing of all the conditions under which confidentiality would be broken. Throughout the 1990s, there will continue to be debates about what ethical courses of action to take when laws and ethical principles conflict (e.g., Ansell & Ross, 1990).

ON BEING ETHICAL

We now return to the question that we raised at the beginning of this chapter: "What does it require to be an ethical counseling psychologist?" Both Jordan and Meara (1990) and Beauchamp and Childress (1983) argue that a health profession needs virtuous persons. *Virtue* is, ironically, a term rarely heard in psychology. Beauchamps and Childress' description is both enlightening and succinct: Virtue "should not be confused with a principle or rule. . . . rather it is a habit, disposition, or trait that a person may possess or aspire to possess. A moral virtue is an acquired habit or disposition to do what is morally right or praiseworthy" (p. 261). This argument for a focus on the habit or trait of ethical decision making, as compared to the study of what ethical principles to have, is clearly supported by Welfel and Lipsitz (1984). However, Bernard and colleagues (1986, 1987) found that, at least among clinical psychology graduate students and clinical psychologists, approximately half of the former and a quarter to a third of the latter would do less than what they themselves believe they *should* do when encountering ethical violations. Pope and Bajt (1988) found 21 percent of their respondents withholding information from authorities about child abuse.

Are there certain professional characteristics that predict the occurrence of unethical behavior? From their review of the published research, Welfel and Lipsitz (1984) were able to conclude that therapists with a high need for love and positive regard and a low level of impulse control were particularly likely to become involved with their clients in sexually intimate ways. Haas, Malouf and Mayerson (1988) have looked at other professional characteristics and found, for example, that among the variables of theoretical orientation, gender, clinical setting, hours of formal ethics training, and years of experience, only the latter was consistently related to choices in reporting ethical violations. Therapists with greater levels of experience were *less* likely to deal actively with the issues.

In short, acquaintance with ethical principles is not enough to ensure ethical behavior. Probably too little has been written about the responsibilities of both students of psychology as well as psychologists themselves on how to cope with the unethical behavior of other psychologists even though ethical standards in this area are explicit, as previously noted. Many ethical situations are messy. The evidence of actual violations may be less than clear even if abundant in terms of number of complaints. Also, those who have been violated may not wish to press charges for a variety of personal reasons (e.g., risk of having one's own reputation impugned, fear of retaliation if one's employer or supervisor is the violator). Furthermore, there are other culturally based supports to staying uninvolved. Simply think of Ann Landers' use of the acronym MYOB (Mind Your Own Business)—a reflection of our country's emphasis on the individual. Social psychologists' work on "bystander interaction" (Darly & Latané 1968) is also relevant to an understanding of psychologists' reluctance to act. In perceiving the gravity of a situation, one must also, in the face of others, feel the responsibility to take effective action.

Finally, inaction may be the result of a lack of awareness about what can be done to help an offender beyond "punishing" him or her. In recent years increased attention has been given by the APA to the opportunities for remediation of impaired psychologists, especially those whose work has been affected by substance abuse. State and national ethics committees can offer valuable referral information as well as guidelines on how to enable such psychologists to recognize their problems and seek help. Lamb et al. (1987) have provided detailed suggestions for confronting professional impairment during trainees' internships.

Only if all psychologists recognize and take more responsibility for management of ethical issues will the profession of psychology demonstrate to the public that it can manage its own members. Otherwise new laws will continue to proliferate. Laws almost inevitably result in transforming what is really an ethical quality-control issue into an adversarial legal one, often resulting in increased concerns for both clients and practitioners rather than improved mental health services. To summarize, being ethical is a virtuous habit that is needed just as much as are heightened sensitivity to ethical principles and issues and a reasoning process for making choices when conflicts occur.

PROFESSIONAL ISSUES

In the remainder of this chapter we review four current controversial issues regarding the practice of psychology by applied psychologists in the various fields (school, clinical, I/O, counseling, etc.). Interestingly, in many ways counseling psychology, because of its allegiance to the scientist-professional model, is a microcosm of the discipline of psychology at large. Because of the conceptual support that both proponents and opponents have developed for each of these issues, it is unlikely that any of them will be finally resolved within the immediate future.

The first two issues to be discussed, licensing and master's degrees in psychology, each has a controversial history of nearly fifty years. The third issue, that of expanding specialized accreditation, became a major issue only in the 1980s. The final issue concerning "academic" and "applied" psychology has aroused passions since the founding of the APA in 1892! In one sense, each of these issues is an extension of the first half of this chapter in which we explored practitioners' and researchers' ethical responsibilities toward the public's trust. For almost all of the proponents of the various viewpoints, one could argue that their proposals are necessary to meet that trust. However, the same proposals could be viewed as selfish actions to gain new markets for services and to protect the profession from competition. To provide an adequate perspective for these issues, a brief history of each will be presented, followed by a description of its current status and an examination of the implications for the career development of psychologists, especially counseling psychologists.

Licensing

Psychologists, like lawyers, medical doctors, and many other professionals, are subject to a kind of licensure. Because professions, by definition, include high levels of training in a specific kind of expertise, it is a reasonable assumption that the public cannot readily make informed decisions about whether the services being offered are of adequate quality. Licensure enables a state to legally regulate the use of the title of the profession and legally define the activities that constitute its practice. Typically, psychology licensure laws include definitions of what training and supervised experience are necessary to be eligible for licensure and, for those eligible, what examination procedures may be required, what professional activities are included, and what sanctions apply to people who violate specifics of the licensing regulations. Also, in an increasing number of state licensing laws, the ethical standards of the APA are included as part of the legal responsibilities of the psychologist.

Most of the nearly fifty years of controversy surrounding licensing laws have focused on the definitional statements about what training is required and what activities psychologists can engage in. The controversies were especially heated in the late 1960s and 1970s, the first time period in which a majority of states were involved in the development and revision of licensing laws. Although a few psychologists were in independent practice from the beginnings of clinical and counseling psychology in the 1940s, the vast majority of such psychologists in those earlier decades were employed in hospital, clinic, and university settings. With the emergence in the 1960s of health insurance policy reimbursements for some counseling and psychotherapy, there was a rapid increase in the number of persons seeking to establish independent practice, a step that in many states required licensure. (Most states still do not require licensure for those who work in agencies, hospitals, and universities.) Moreover, health insurance reimbursements were often limited to, as in medicine, licensed professionals.

Critics of licensure surfaced as quickly as states developed licensing laws. Although it was acknowledged that licensing laws could protect the consumer, there was great concern that licensure was a way of monopolizing third-party insurance payments for a particular group of persons, in this case, doctoral-level psychologists. Both Hogan (1979) and Gross (1978) argued forcefully that the consumer was *not* better protected by licensing laws that restricted psychologists' training. Gross maintained that a better alternative was simply written self-disclosure by psychologists regarding information on their performance-related training and certification: "Accurate information about the service offered by a practitioner is a consumer's best chance of getting what he or she wants or needs and the best protection against harm and exploitation. In effect, it restricts the counselors to do what they will say they will do" (Gross, 1979, p. 588).

Extensive discussion of the pros and cons of licensing can be found in Fretz and Mills (1980). Licensing that sets minimal standards of training does increase the likelihood of protection of the consumer but at the same time is exclusionary. Some persons will not be eligible who have received other training that enables them to provide competent counseling services.

The psychology license laws of the 1950s and 1960s had very broad definitions about who could be considered a psychologist. Source papers for credentialing conferences held in the mid-1970s by the APA and the National Register for Health Service Providers in Psychology, then newly established, revealed that applicants for psychology licensure had received 35 different graduate degrees (for example, J. D., M. P. H.) from just as many different departments. It appeared that the term "primarily psychological in nature" contained in many psychology licensing laws could be construed as meaning "not psychology."

Ten recommendations emerged from this series of conferences and were subsequently adopted by the APA. These recommendations included a much more restrictive definition of the educational backgrounds that could be submitted to licensing boards for eligibility. Of major importance for counseling psychology was the recommendation that "the program, wherever it may be administratively housed, must be clearly identified and labeled as a psychology program. Such a program must specify in pertinent institutional catalogs and brochures its intent to educate and train professional psychologists" (Wellner, 1978, p. 33). Unless programs met both the standards of the recommendations and became publicly identified as strictly a psychology training program, its graduates would be ineligible for licensing. At that time, many applicants for licensure came from counselor education or guidance and counseling programs that were labeled as such. However, the recommendations also stated that psychology training could take place outside psychology departments, for example, colleges of education, colleges of business and management, and so forth. Thus, it became possible for many programs in counseling and guidance that trained counseling psychologists to make the curricular changes necessary for a formal transition to psychology training programs, even though they were housed in colleges of education, their typical location. In fact, the more than 100 percent increase in the number of APA-accredited programs in counseling psychology from the early 1970s to the late 1980s was directly related to this change. The majority of the newly approved programs were formerly counselor education or counseling and guidance programs in colleges of education.

Licensing laws are continually being challenged and revised in terms of what training requirements and activities define the role of a psychologist. In the late 1970s and early 1980s, "sunset legislation," phasing out many existing laws, including professional licensing laws, resulted in a few states' not licensing psychologists for a period of time. Subsequent media attention to the ability of anyone to use the title "psychologist," including a dog in the state of Florida (Blum, 1979) resulted in all states eventually reinstating some type of psychology licensing law. The APA provides a model psychology licensing law (1987b). The American Association of State Psychology Boards (AASPB) attempts to assist states in developing laws that are relatively consistent with one another, though each state varies slightly in what its laws require and include.

The variations within each state and the continual changes in licensing laws, usually as a result of legal challenges from someone or some group that has been excluded from eligibility, make it extremely difficult to advise a graduate student as to exactly what he or she will need to become licensed. Students in APA-approved counseling, clinical and school psychology programs who complete internships accredited by the APA clearly have the least difficulty meeting licensing eligibility requirements. Even graduates of these programs will have their transcripts evaluated to determine compliance with a given state's curriculum requirements. Those who wish to become practicing counseling psychologists are well advised to complete accredited doctoral programs. Although alternative routes exist, in that a couple of states will license, to some extent, master's degrees in psychology, and some other states will consider applicants from non-APA-approved programs, obtaining such degrees can pose problems for subsequent employment as well as licensure. (In Chapter 18 we provide more details on meeting eligibility requirements and on preparing for the Examination for Professional Practice in Psychology, a standardized examination used in most states.)

The worst of the controversies about licensing may be past. First, in our increasingly credential-oriented and litigious society, some form of licensing for professions seems almost essential to protect against the most blatant forms of misrepresentation and fraud. Second, strong reactions to the restrictions of the 1970s conferences (Wellner, 1978) have diminished as more and more programs and departments have complied with the stipulations. Finally, the emergence of licensing for master's degree counselors, as compared to master's degree psychologists, has reduced the heat of the debate about psychology's ambivalent treatment of master's-level training programs and pracititioners—the focus of the next controversy to be discussed.

The Master's Degree in Psychology

Numerous documents and articles in both clinical psychology (Albee, 1977; Perlman, 1985) and counseling psychology (Watkins, Campbell, & McGregor, 1989) have been written about psychology's ambivalent treatment of master's programs and master's degree recipients. Repeated calls for accreditation of master's training programs have so far been rebuffed by the major professional psychology organizations, which note that, since the beginnings of the organized specialties in applied psychology, the expectation was that the doctoral degree would be the entry, or journeyman, level for independent practice. Calls for licensing of master's-level psychologists have been rejected in the majority of states for at least the last 30 years. Yet, on the other hand, hundreds of universities, including many with doctoral programs, but especially those not sponsoring doctoral programs in psychology, offer master's-level training in clinical, school, and counseling psychology. Psychology master's programs in universities without doctoral psychology programs are usually referred to as "terminal" master's programs. Critics note that universities are pleased to collect the tuition money provided by those students in classes several times larger than doctoral-level classes, while the graduates themselves are doomed to permanent "second-class citizenship" in terms of career, licensing, and professional organizational membership within the profession of psychology.

Although as many as half or more of such master's degree recipients will eventually go on to doctoral programs (cf. Quereshi and Kuchan, 1988), the others will enter the professional marketplace. Such graduates typically find that there are few positions to be obtained where they may call themselves psychologists, and they quickly learn that in all but a few states they may not practice independently as psychologists unless they agree to be supervised by a psychiatrist or doctoral-level psychologist. Just as importantly, the job opportunities available to master's degree holders often have a very limited range of opportunities for advancement.

Although beginning salaries may be nearly the same as those for doctoral-level psychologists, such positions typically have very low ceilings; in some states, master's degree holders reach the highest salary they can earn after just a few years of service, even if they stay in these positions another 20 or 25 years.

From the beginning, many counseling psychologists have maintained professional involvement both with psychology organizations and with guidance and counseling organizations, which has made the dilemma all the more acute for counseling psychologists. On the one hand, their commitment to the scientific discipline of psychology has led to their strong support of scientific training as part of their preparation. Yet, as found by Watkins et al. (1989), master's-level students have much greater interest in individual and group personal counseling than in theory, test construction, or research. The lack of interest of master's-level students in this scientific-practice integration therefore exacerbates the "second-class citizenship" of master's level students. Although the APA is petitioned every few years to reconsider accrediting master's degree programs and/or upgrading the status of the recipients of such degrees, all current evidence seems to suggest that neither of these directions will be pursued (Master's graduates suffer identity crisis, 1990).

The emergence of licensure in an increasing number of states for mental health counselors has allowed some master's-level counseling programs to pursue that route. By the late 1980s, approximately one-third of the states provided licensing for professional counselors or mental health counselors at the master's level. Most of these licensure acts require the completion of a master's degree in a counseling program, but not necessarily counseling psychology, as they do not include the right to practice psychology per se. Even with a master's degree in counseling psychology, the licensed mental health counselor cannot refer to himself or herself as a psychologist. Some post-degree experience is also required for such a license. Nonetheless, many persons who hold master's degrees now have an alternative for licensure besides going on to complete a doctoral degree in psychology.

Accreditation and Specialization

In this section we first briefly describe what accreditation is and why it has been controversial. As a way of illustrating some of the controversies, the process of accreditation by the APA will be described. Further, the growing interest in both predoctoral and postdoctoral specialization beyond counseling and clinical psychology (e.g., neuropsychology, forensic psychology, and behavioral psychology) is examined along with its controversial implications for probable changes in accreditation. Of all of the issues addressed in this chapter, those of accreditation and specialization impact most directly the training options and career opportunities of applied psychologists, including counseling psychologists.

What is accreditation? "Accreditation . . . applies to educational institutions and to programs, not to individuals. It does not guarantee jobs and licensure for individuals, though being a graduate of an accredited program may facilitate placement or licensing. It does speak to the manner and quality by which an educational institution or program conducts its business. It speaks to a sense of public trust, as well as to professional quality, and does so through the development of national criteria and guidelines for assessing educational effectiveness, through the process of continuous self-study and review, and through a public commitment to excellence" (APA, 1986, pp. ii-iii). Accreditation is a voluntary process in psychology, at least to the extent that no organization or agency mandates that a program in school, counseling, or clinical psychology (the only kinds of programs currently accredited by APA) be accredited. How, then, has accreditation become so controversial?

One controversy has developed over the "development of national criteria and guidelines," as called for in the APA *Accreditation Handbook* cited above. Each university program develops according to the interests and standards of the participating faculty. One university faculty may have a viewpoint about quality education quite different from the faculty at another university. Obtaining a consensus on what standards *all* programs should be held to has always proved extremely difficult. At the beginning of the profession, when curriculum guidelines were established, they included only very general statements about goals and content. Each succeeding decade has specified these further. For example, after the credentialing conferences of the 1970s, accreditation standards included specific course requirements in four different areas of basic psychology as well as specification of a certain number of hours of practicum and supervision. University faculties, citing academic freedom so central to universities throughout their history, found the imposition of specific requirements from an outside agency particularly provocative. Indeed, the development of national criteria is inherently intrusive on academic freedom.

A more recent, different type of controversy has come about because of the increased use of accreditation as a prerequisite for licensing and employment opportunities. One can argue that if accreditation is truly a voluntary process, then students who graduate from nonaccredited programs should not automatically be discriminated against in terms of subsequent credentialing opportunities. However, the Veterans Administration, for example, now requires that applicants for psychology positions complete their degrees and internships in APA-accredited programs. Also, as already noted above, an increasing number of states specify that a degree from an APA program is the preferred standard for licensing eligibility. Even the highest-quality programs, some of which had never sought accreditation, found that their students were being denied opportunities to make use of their training. Such programs were put in the difficult situation of having to submit to the accreditation process even though they saw that it in no way contributed to the quality of their program. Not having accreditation left their students with a potential lifelong career handicap. Needless to say, such dilemmas led to many heated controversies about the "imposition" of accreditation.

For counseling psychologists, the most important kinds of accreditation are those provided by the APA graduate training programs and psychology internships. (Other kinds of accreditation of counselor training programs are primarily for master's-level programs outside of psychology, for example, accreditation provided by the Council for Accreditation of Counseling and Related Educational Programs, the Council on Rehabilitation Education, and the American Association for Marriage and Family Therapy. While all of these accrediting bodies may affect the career development of persons wanting to practice at the master's level, they have no direct impact on credentials, employment, and license eligibility of counseling psychologists. Fretz and Mills (1980) describe some of the basic components of accreditation in those areas as well as the particular advantages for master's-level counselors.) Some training programs in counseling psychology and psychology internships are not accredited. Does this mean that they are inadequate and inferior? Not necessarily, although, as we elaborate in Chapter 18, obtaining a degree or internship in such settings does entail certain risks to one's career development. Relatively new programs may not have been established long enough to apply for accreditation—training programs cannot receive full accreditation until they have a certain number of students complete the doctoral degree. Other programs may have quality training features but do not have sufficient resources to meet some of the major criteria. For example, accredited internships require that there be more than two intern positions; some internship agencies do not have sufficient supervisory personnel or financial resources to have more than one.

What is involved in the process of accreditation? Programs are asked to conduct a very thorough self-study to identify their specific intentions with regard to professional training in psychology and to demonstrate how they meet the criteria for accreditation. The APA specifies criteria in seven categories, including evidence of institutional support; attention to cultural diversity; a training sequence; practicum training; and qualities of students, of faculty, and environmental resources. These criteria are fully described in the *Accreditation Handbook* (APA, 1986). As part of the accreditation process, after a self-study has been completed, a program is visited by two or three site visitors to verify compliance with the criteria. Reports of the site visitors and the self-study are then examined by a special committee of the APA. A decision is made regarding whether the program merits full accreditation, provisional accreditation, or should be placed on probation. Provisional accreditation indicates that a relatively new program is not meeting all of the criteria but is in sufficient compliance to be given this initial form of accreditation. Programs that cease to meet a sufficient number of the criteria are placed on probation, and if sufficient changes are not made within two to three years, they lose their accreditation. Even fully accredited programs are site-visited at least once every five years, more often if significant changes in the program's resources or training program requirements warrant review.

Further controversy about accreditation may occur at the level of the individual program, especially when site visitors' observations do not agree with the program's self-study report. Sometimes the self-study describes what kind of training *can* be obtained rather than what typically *is* obtained. When there are significant discrepancies, the program may receive a list of specific deficiencies to correct before the next site visit. On the other hand, if site visitors find that students are receiving the kinds of training and enjoying the kinds of resources described in the self-study, the program typically receives a good review.

Psychological Specialties. A more recent controversy over accreditation relates to proposals to expand accreditation beyond clinical, counseling, and school psychology, the only areas accredited by APA since the beginning of accreditation some forty years ago. During the past two decades, an increasing number of programs in areas such as neuropsychology, applied developmental psychology, and forensic psychology have developed highly specialized curricula that lead to work in professional settings, yet, according to current APA policy, these programs cannot be accredited. For over ten years, various APA committees have been exploring whether and how recognition should be given to "new specialties." A major issue concerns how to define a separate specialty. For example, is child clinical psychology a separate specialty from clinical psychology?

Although the full extent of the controversy entailed in this issue is beyond the scope of this chapter, certain aspects must be discussed that affect training in the presently recognized specialties of clinical, school, and counseling psychology. Will new specializations that are recognized for accreditation be viewed as "co-equals" with established ones, or should they build on the foundations of the present service-providing specialties? In the latter case, some procedure is needed for accrediting postdoctoral training—at this point no accreditation exists beyond the predoctoral internship. In the former case of "co-equalship," multiple accredited programs will abound in each university, to account for the different specialties. What would such multiple specializations do to the integrity of core training in psychology and how would the costs of such multiple accreditation be met? Would additional specializations drain resources from the current specialties?

The pros and cons of the issue have been argued for the past ten years. At this point, based on observation of accreditation controversies for over twice that time, it is likely there will be increased recognition of new specialties, largely at the internship and postdoctoral level. Both the Association of Psychology Internship Centers and other educational leaders, especially those from professional schools of psychology, are calling for a mandatory second year of internship to be taken following receipt of the doctoral degree (Belar et al., 1987). This postdoctoral experience would be somewhat more like a physician's residency and would be more highly specialized than the first year of internship. It could focus on, for example, geropsychology, forensics, marriage, and family.

To ensure more homogeneous backgrounds for this degree of specialization at the advanced level, there is likely to be an increased specification of predoctoral requirements for any student who seeks to work in a professional capacity. The traditional specialties will still exist, but there may be greater specification of what courses, practica, and experiential requirements must be met by all students, regardless of specialty. The predoctoral graduate work in school, clinical, or counseling psychology will be seen, more than it currently is, as the generic foundation for preparation of health-service-providing psychologists. The internship will also be relatively broad, then followed by a postdoctoral internship, which would be highly specialized. This model is very much like traditional medical schools; it is not surprising that many of its strongest advocates are psychologists working in medical settings. (An additional advantage of developing one-year specialized postdoctoral training programs is that psychologists that have been out 5, 10, or 15 years who want to develop an additional specialization will have available a more formal one-year training program.)

A growing number of professionals are in fact willing to compromise on many aspects of the problems deriving from the emergence of new specialties. A much more extensive discussion of the pros and cons and complexity of these issues may be found in Bickman and Ellis (in press). Their work describes the results of a special conference on graduate education in psychology dealing with the themes of unity, diversity, quality, and humanity. Also see the *Taskforce Report of the Committee on Scope and Criteria for Accreditation* (APA Education and Training Board, 1987).

Psychology's Two Cultures

From the very beginning of organized psychology in the late 1800s, the relationship between psychologists with applied interests and those with basic research interests has been like a courtship between two strong personalities, each of whom wants to dominate the relationship. VandenBos (1988) recently reviewed the various "splits" that have been recurring since 1901 (less than a decade after the founding of the APA in 1892), when one group of applied psychologists, disenchanted with the organization they saw developing, decided to withdraw. In recent years, frictions have greatly increased and resulted in major new developments regarding psychology organizations. The professional interests and perceived needs of psychologists providing mental health services—especially given the challenges from psychiatrists regarding insurance reimbursements, hospital privileges, and so forth—are increasingly at odds with the needs of academic/research psychologists. The former see the need for a strong advocacy professional organization like the American Medical Association. The latter see little need for such a body and want an organization devoted primarily to promoting exchange of scientific ideas and research. In 1988, a large group of academic/research psychologists left the APA to form the American Psychological Society (APS). The society focuses on the scientific aspects of psychology. It intends "to preserve the scientific base of psychology, to promote public understanding of psychological science and its applications, to enhance the quality of graduate education, and to encourage the 'giving away' of psychology in the public interest" (APS, 1990, p. 77).

Counseling psychology, with both strong scientific and applied components, is, as noted before, a microcosm of the profession of psychology at large. Many counseling psychologists actively support the APS and count among its leadership. For nearly every such activist in the APS, there is another counseling psychologist that feels strongly that the split should not have occurred and that counseling psychologists owe full allegiance to the APA. A significant number of counseling psychologists maintain membership in both organizations, though because of current animosity between the two organizations, it is virtually impossible to have leadership roles in both organizations.

As of this writing, within counseling psychology, more "scientists" are talking to "practitioners" and vice versa than is true in the profession of psychology in general. Many years ago, C. P. Snow (1964) argued for the potential enrichment of society through increased dialogue and interaction between the humanistic and scientific cultures. A number of counseling psychologists have sought to facilitate such interaction between the research and practitioner groups. Counseling psychologists, who have decades of experience with the scientist-practitioner model, are perhaps better equipped to manage the ongoing tensions of the two cultures than are, for example, research psychologists, who have, up until recent times, been able to ignore practitioners' concerns. The long history of cross-purposes suggest that a consensus will not emerge. The ideal resolution would be that psychologists at both ends of the two cultures, as well as those sharing values with both, will be able to find ways to mutually respect and support each others' needs, values and goals. That is a challenge all contemporary psychologists face in the 1990s.

SUMMARY

As professionals serving persons in troubled and turbulent situations, counseling psychologists need to keep ethical considerations at the highest level of awareness. In the 1980s it was realized that not enough attention had been given to the *processes* of ethical behavior. Rest's (1984) four-component model of moral behavior serves as a foundation for exploring ethical issues.

In illustrating nine of the ten APA principles with one or more of the less publicized types of violations, our purpose was to sensitize readers to the frequent ethical implications of professional behavior. Many ethical violations include behaviors that are carried out with good intentions. Often "violators" simply do not give full consideration to the ethical implications of their behaviors.

Ethical dilemmas are situations in which honoring one ethical principle means violation of one or more others. For example, a counselor's wanting to maintain confidentiality about a client's communications might lead to significant bodily harm to another person. The basic concepts of *principle ethics* and *virtue ethics* can be used to help with the value-laden decision making called for by ethical dilemmas. There are no absolutely correct answers to these dilemmas; the *reasoning* one uses becomes even more important than the final decision itself.

The second half of the chapter explored four issues relevant to all professional psychologists, but special attention was given to how the issues affect counseling psychologists. First is the issue of licensing, whose 50-year history has been marked by controversy. Licensure protects the consumer by setting minimal standards of training, but at the same time can exclude competent professionals from practice. Licensing laws are constantly being challenged and revised, though the major problem they represented for counseling psychologists has been eliminated, with the emergence of licensing for counselors with master's degrees.

Next, the "terminal master's degree" is an issue with which all of psychology has struggled for over fifty years. Should students with only a master's degree in psychology be allowed to practice as psychologists? The emergence of licensing for mental health counselors in over one-third of the states has greatly reduced the controversial nature of this issue within counseling psychology even though it remains a broader issue for all of psychology yet today.

Third is the issue of training program accreditation and of emerging questions about specialization within psychology. As with the licensing of psychologists, there are both pros and cons for accreditation procedures. During the 1980s, the use of accreditation as a credential for obtaining internships and employment greatly increased, so more attention was given to the problems of accreditation. Currently numerous controversies are raging about the nature of accreditation, what specialists should be eligible for it, and what organization(s) should be granting it.

The chapter closed with an examination of the issues inherent in psychology's two "cultures," that of applied interests and that of basic research interests. Counseling psychology, as a scientist-practitioner specialty, is a microcosm of the controversies that led to many noted scientists' leaving the American Psychological Association in 1988 to form the American Psychological Society. All psychologists, from the traditional experimentalists to those in the new applied areas, will need to work together during the 1990s in achieving mutual respect and support for each other's needs, values and goals.

References

Albee, G. W. (1977). The uncertain future of the M. A. clinical psychologist, *Professional Psychology: Research and Practice, 8,* 122–124.

American Psychological Association (1981). Specialty guidelines for the delivery of services. *American Psychologist, 36,* 639–681.

American Psychological Association (1986). *Accreditation Handbook.* Washington, DC.

American Psychological Association (1987a). *General Guidelines for Providers of Psychological Services* (rev. ed.). Washington, DC.

American Psychological Association (1987b). Model act for state licensure of psychologists. *American Psychologist, 42,* 696–703.

American Psychological Association (1990). Ethical principles of psychologists. *American Psychologist, 45,* 390–395.

American Psychological Association and Training Board (1987). *Taskforce on the review of the scope and criteria for accreditation,* Report Number 4. Washington, DC.

American Psychological Society (1990). American Psychological Society. *Psychological Science, 1,* 77.

Ansell, C., & Ross, H. C. (1990). Reply to Pope and Bajt. *American Psychologist, 45,* 399.

Beauchamp, T. L., & Childress, J. S. (1983). *Principles of biomedical ethics* (2nd ed.). New York: Oxford University Press.

Belar, C. D., Biellauskas, L. A., Larson, K. G., Mensh, I. N., Poey, K., & Roehlke, H. J. (Eds.) (1987). *Proceedings: National Conference on Internship Training in Psychology: Gainesville Conference.* Baton Rouge, LA: Land and Land Printers, Inc.

Bernard, J. L., & Jara, C. S. (1986). The failure of clinical psychology graduate students to apply understood ethical principles. *Professional Psychology: Research and Practice, 17,* 313–315.

Bernard, J. L., Murphy, M., & Little, M. (1987). The failure of clinical psychologists to apply ethical principles. *Professional Psychology: Research and Practice, 18,* 489–491.

Bickman, L., & Ellis, H. C. (Eds.) (In press). *Proceedings of the Conference on Graduate Education: Utah Conference.* Hillsdale, NJ: Erlbaum.

Biggs, P., & Blocher, D. (1987). *Foundations of ethical counseling.* New York: Springer.

Blum, D. (1979). Clearwater okays tougher psychology standards. *St. Petersburg Times,* July 20, 1979, p. 3.

Brammer, L. M., & Shostrom, E. L. (1977). *Therapeutic psychology* (3rd ed.). Englewood Cliffs, NJ: Prentice-Hall.

Committee of Women in Psychology (1989). If sex enters into the psychotherapy relationship. *Professional Psychology: Research and Practice, 20,* 12–115.

Corey, G., Corey, M. S., & Callanan, P. (1979). *Professional and ethical issues in counseling and psychotherapy.* Monterey, CA: Brooks/Cole.

Darly, J., & Lantané, B. (1968). Bystander intervention in emergencies: Diffusion of responsibility. *Journal of Personality and Social Psychology, 8,* 377–383.

Ethics Committee of the American Psychological Association (1988). Trends in ethics cases, common pitfalls, and published resources. *American Psychologist, 43,* 564–572.

Fitting, M. D. (1984). Professional and ethical responsibilities for psychologists working with the elderly. *The Counseling Psychologist, 12*(3), 69–78.

Fretz, B. R., & Mills, D. H. (1980). *Licensing and certification of psychologists and counselors.* San Francisco: Jossey-Bass.

Fulero, S. M. (1988). Tarasoff: Ten years later. *Professional Psychology: Research and Practice, 19,* 184–190.

Gross, S. J. (1978). The myth of professional licensing. *American Psychologist, 33,* 1009–1016.

Gross, S. J. (1979). Professional disclosure: An alternative to licensing. *Personnel and Guidance Journal, 55,* 586–588.

Haas, L. J., Malouf, J. L., & Mayerson, L. H. (1986). Ethical dilemmas in psychological practice: Results of a national survey. *Professional Psychology: Research and Practice, 17,* 316–321.

Haas, L. J., Malouf, J. L., & Mayerson, L. H. (1988). Personal and professional characteristics as factors in psychologists' ethical decision making. *Professional Psychology: Research and Practice, 19,* 35–42.

Handelsman, M. M., & Galvin, M. D. (1988). Facilitating informed consent for outpatient psychotherapy: A suggested written format. *Professional Psychology: Research and Practice, 19,* 223–225.

Hogan, D. B. (1979). Licensing mental therapists. *The New York Times,* July 18, 1979, p. A-23.

Jordan, A. C., & Meara, N. M. (1990). Ethics and the professional practice of psychologists: The role of virtues and principles. *Professional Psychology: Research and Practice, 21,* 107–114.

Kestenbaum, J. D. (1986). Perceived impact on personnel counseling by counseling psychology graduate students. Dissertation Abstracts International, 48, 01B. (University Microfilms No. AAC8709088).

Kitchener, K. S. (1984a). Guest editor's introduction. *The Counseling Psychologist, 12*(3), 15–18.

Kitchener, K. S. (1984b). Intuition, critical evaluation and ethical principles: The foundation of ethical decisions in counseling psychology. *The Counseling Psychologist, 12*(3), 43–56.

Lamb, D. H., Presser, N. R., Pfost, K. S., Baum, M. C., Jackson, V. R., & Jarvis, P. A. (1987). Confronting professional impairment during the internship. *Professional Psychology: Research and Practice, 18,* 597–603.

Lamb, D. H., Clark, C., Drumheller, P., Frizzell, K., & Surrey, L. (1989). Applying Tarasoff to AIDS-related psychotherapy issues. *Professional Psychology: Research and Practice, 20,* 37–43.

Lindsey, R. D. (1984). Informed consent and deception in psychotherapy research: An ethical analysis. *The Counseling Psychologist, 12*(3), 79–86.

Master's graduates suffer identity crisis (August, 1990). *APA Monitor,* p. 28.

Muehlman, T., Pickens, B. K., & Robinson, F. (1985). Informing clients about the limits to confidentiality, risks, and their rights: Is self-disclosure inhibited? *Professional Psychology: Research and Practice, 16,* 385–397.

Perlman, B. (1985). Training and career issues of APA-affiliated master-level clinicians. *Professional Psychology: Research and Practice, 16,* 753–767.

Pope, K. S., & Bajt, T. (1988). When laws and values conflict: A dilemma for psychologists. *American Psychologist, 43,* 828–829.

Powell, C. D. (1984). Ethical principles and issues of competence in counseling adolescents. *The Counseling Psychologist, 12*(3), 57–68.

Quereshi, M. Y., & Kuchan, A. M. (1988). The master's degree in clinical psychology: Longitudinal program evaluation. *Professional Psychology: Research and Practice, 19,* 594–595.

Rest, J. R. (1984). Research on moral development: Implications for training counseling psychologists. *The Counseling Psychologist, 12*(3), 19–30.

Snipe, R. M. (1988). Ethical issues in the assessment and treatment of a rational suicidal client. *The Counseling Psychologist, 16,* 128–138.

Snow, C. P. (1964). *The two cultures: And a second look.* Cambridge: Cambridge University Press.

VandenBos, Gary R. (1988). Loosely organized "Organized Psychology." *American Psychologist, 44,* 979–986.

Watkins, C. E., Jr., Campbell, V. L., & McGregor, P. (1989). APA-affiliated master's-level counselors. *The Counseling Psychologist, 17,* 289–300.

Welfel, E. R., & Lipsitz, N. E. (1984). The ethical behavior of professional psychologists: A critical analysis of the research. *The Counseling Psychologist, 12*(3), 31–42.

Wellner, A. M. (Ed.) (1978). *Education and credentialing in psychology.* Washington, DC: American Psychological Association.

Chapter 4

Research and Science

In this chapter we focus on the topics of science and research in counseling psychology. This chapter is divided into three sections. In the first, further exploration is offered of the concept of "scientist" within the scientist-practitioner model. Here we seek to answer the question "What does the scientist part of the scientist-practitioner model really mean?" Different levels of "being a scientist" are explored.

Whereas the first section tends toward the philosophical, the second is more practical. The aim is to help the reader understand approaches to counseling psychology research. The typical survey of research issues and methods presented in other beginning texts is too superficial for, and not especially helpful to, the reader we hope to reach, that is, the student or professional with some background in psychological research but little background in counseling psychology research. With this in mind, we focus in the second section on four research strategies used in counseling psychology. These strategies have been labeled "investigative styles" by one of the authors (Gelso, 1979a).

After a discussion of the four strategies, the chapter concludes with a perspective on research in counseling psychology and a discussion of the relevance of research to practice. In this final section, Gelso's "bubble hypothesis" is suggested as a useful way of thinking about the advantages and disadvantages of different research strategies and of the many decisions the researcher must make about the methods used in any given study. We also explore the concept of research relevance, with an emphasis on what the counseling psychology practitioner should and should not expect from research. Finally, some often ignored complexities of the idea of relevance are explored, and ways in which research can be highly relevant to practice are discussed.

THE SCIENTIST PART OF THE SCIENTIST-PRACTITIONER MODEL: WHAT DOES IT MEAN?

In previous chapters, especially Chapter 2, the scientist-practitioner (or scientist-professional) model of training and practice in counseling psychology was discussed. We noted that from the beginnings of the specialty, this model has been seen as crucial to sound progress in our understanding of all of the activities in which counseling psychologists are involved (for example, counseling, assessment, consultation, etc.) and the phenomena that counseling psychologists study (for example, career development).

Within the scientist-practitioner model, students are trained (more precisely, educated) so that they will be scientists as well as professional practitioners. And a vital element of this scientific training is learning how to do scientific research. Because research is so vital in this model and in the field, before proceeding further, we shall offer answers to the questions "Why, in fact, is scientific research so important to counseling psychology?" and "Why not just practice what we believe to be true from our personal experiences with clients and human beings more generally?"

Without the benefits of scientific checks and rigorous scientific tests of our favorite hypotheses, we run the risk of creating magical solutions, of cures that are more products of our fantasies and personal needs than of reality. Along this same line, without scientific research and theory, we shall very likely develop treatment approaches that are simply products of our biases and prejudices. In the last analysis, counseling practice, in the absence of controlled tests of the efficacy of that practice, is doomed to limited effectiveness at best and inappropriate application at worst. Research allows us to check whether our beliefs and theories hold up under controlled conditions, and, just as important, whether we are in fact having the effects (e.g., on our clients) that we think and hope we are. In this way, science helps us continually improve practice.

Along with helping the counseling psychologist check and study his or her theories and treatments, scientific research can have a still more proactive effect. Not only can we find out if our research hypotheses hold up under controlled conditions, but we can also create new knowledge and theories through research. Research findings virtually always lead to new directions for the researchers, suggest new ideas and theories, and point to ways in which treatments may be modified so as to be more effective. In these ways, scientific research and the findings emanating from it are always exciting—at least a portion of what turns up is almost always new!

Do the above formulations imply that all counseling psychologists should be involved in science and research? Should the counseling psychologist who, for example, is working full time as a private practitioner, make empirical research a part of his or her workday? Is it enough for the practitioner to think scientifically? To be a consumer (i.e., reader of) rather than a producer of scientific theory and research? These important questions lead us to a discussion of what the scientist part of the scientist-practitioner model really means.

Although the scientist-practitioner model has been around for a long time, there has never been a great deal of agreement or clarity about what the terms of the model mean and how they are to be actualized, both in graduate education and in the worklives of counseling psychologists (or psychologists in other specialties). Defining just what is meant by being a scientist within this model is more complicated than might first appear. Thus, there are several meanings to the concept of "scientist" and several ways in which the concept is manifested in practice.

From the time of the Northwestern Conference in 1951, it has been suggested that, at a minimum, "being scientific" means having the "ability to review and make use of the results of research" (APA, 1952, p. 179). Thus, the counseling practitioner should be able to understand research and apply research findings to his or her practice. We might view this as the first level, or minimal level, of functioning as a scientist-practitioner.

A second way in which the counseling psychologist is to be a scientist is in the way he or she goes about thinking of practice as well as the manner in which he or she conducts counseling psychology practice. With respect to one's thinking, the practitioner follows what is perhaps the most fundamental tenet of the scientific attitude: think critically and be sufficiently skeptical. Thus, one is to think critically about theories, one's own and others, rather than just accepting them. Also, when one reads research studies, one is to think critically. When new approaches are suggested in the literature, the practitioner does not simply swallow them, he or she is duly skeptical. After careful examination, approaches may be tentatively tried out.

In terms of the manner in which the practitioner conducts his or her practice, for example, in his or her work with clients, a scientific process is followed. In counseling, the counselor sifts through material the client presents and forms hypotheses about (1) what the client's problem is, (2) how to best intervene, and (3) the ways in which the client might respond to various interventions. The counselor then puts these hypotheses to the test of practice, and the hypotheses are subsequently revised as a result of the client's response. These steps continually recycle throughout the therapeutic work.

This adherence to a critical thinking style and to a scientific process in one's work may be viewed as a second level of functioning within the scientist-practitioner model. The scientific process, as used in counseling, was first systematically articulated many years ago by Pepinsky and Pepinsky (1954) and has been an important part of the scientist-practitioner model since then. The reader is referred to Howard (1986) for a current and interesting version of the "counselor as personal scientist" model.

Many scholars in the specialty believe that the scientist part of the scientist-practitioner model means or ought to mean much more than being able to review research, apply research findings to practice, and carry out one's practice in a scientific way. In effect, they are calling for a third level of functioning within the scientist-practitioner model. Whiteley (1984), for example, is a leading spokesperson for a more demanding view of the scientist-professional model of training. He suggests that, at a minimum, training at the doctoral level in counseling psychology should teach students to "formulate hypotheses, and to conduct original inquiry" (p. 46), as well as to review and make use of research.

In fact, at the doctoral level, students are and have always been taught to "formulate hypotheses and conduct original inquiry." What Whiteley and others are implying is that, not only should students be taught this, but there should be an expectation that they actually do empirical research as part of their subsequent careers, regardless of whether they are in academic settings, independent practice settings, or others. In this sense, being a scientist-practitioner means being involved in research as well as counseling practice throughout one's career, although individual counseling psychologists will of course differ greatly in just how much of their work time is devoted to research.

In sum, the concept of "scientist" within the scientist-practitioner model refers to each of the three levels just discussed. Although the counseling psychologist functions as scientist at each and any level, we suggest that the field will benefit most if the individual actualizes all three levels. The counseling psychologist must be able to understand research and be able to apply it to practice, although as shall be proposed later in this chapter, the application of research to practice should rarely if ever be a direct one. The counseling psychologist should also think scientifically and carry out practice in a scientific fashion. Finally, if the field and our clients are to profit maximally, the counseling psychologist should conduct scholarly work as part of his or her career. Note that we here use the term *scholarly work* rather than *research, empirical research,* or *science.* Scholarly work is the broadest and most inclusive of these terms; and, as we shall see, expecting that counseling psychologists will do scholarly work is more realistic than expecting that they will do empirical research, regardless of their work settings. To make sense of this suggestion, we first need to clarify further our use of the terms *research, science,* and *scholarly work.*

Research, Science, and Scholarly Work

At the most recent national conference on counseling psychology, the Georgia Conference, the committee addressing issues and prospects in counseling psychology research (Gelso et al., 1988) grappled with the similarities and differences among three related concepts: research, science, and scholarly work. Too often these terms are used interchangeably, and without clarification, in the counseling psychology literature. In discussing the scientist-practitioner model and the role of research in counseling psychology, it is important to differentiate them.

As noted by Gelso et al. (1988), empirical research is done within the broader context of science. In such research, the investigator ordinarily imposes controls so that his or her observations will lead to nonbiased conclusions about the phenomena under study. Usually, but not always, there is a degree of quantification in counseling psychology research. The purpose of research, as discussed by Gelso et al. (1988), is to contribute to a body of knowledge that, together with theory, comprises the scientific endeavor.

Note here that theory, as well as research, is part of the scientific endeavor. Too often in counseling psychology, and other specialties and fields, the fact that theory and research go hand in hand in science is forgotten. In producing hypotheses, theories provide the subject matter that research studies seek to test (of course, theories themselves vary greatly in how formally, coherently, comprehensively, etc., they are stated). In turn, research results serve to revise and refine theoretical hypotheses.

Of the three concepts (research, science, and scholarly work), science is the hardest to define clearly and simply. That is because science is many things. Not only does science consist of theory and research, as discussed above, but it can be seen as an attitude, a method, and a set of techniques. (See Howard, 1985, and Rychlak, 1968, for clear and interesting elaborations.) For present purposes, science may be viewed as an attitude and method that places a premium on controlled observations, precise definitions, and repeatability or replicability. The scientist controls variables so as to rule out competing explanations; he or she clearly defines terms, operations, and procedures so that other scientists may understand what is meant. Finally, in order for a scientific theory or research finding to be accepted as valid, the events or phenomena being observed must be replicable. The value placed on control, precision, and replicability in science applies to both scientific theory and scientific research.

As indicated by Gelso et al. (1988), scholarly work or activity is the most general of the three concepts (research, science and scholarly work), including intellectual activities that may go well beyond what we ordinarily consider as science, for example, philosophical inquiry, historical analysis, and thoughtful but nonquantified and minimally controlled analyses of counseling cases. We may define scholarly work as a disciplined and thoughtful search for knowledge and understanding. Although it may not include the degree of control, precision, and replicability characteristic of science, the search for knowledge inherent in scholarly work is disciplined nonetheless.

Scholarly Work and the Counseling Psychologist

A key point to this discussion of research, science, and scholarly work is that when we discuss the scientist side of the scientist-practitioner model in counseling psychology (and other applied specialties in psychology), we are concerned first and foremost with training effective scholars—individuals who thoughtfully and creatively seek to understand phenomena in counseling psychology, who seek to understand deeply, and who communicate that understanding to others, for example, in written papers and articles. It is within this intellectual context, as Gelso et al. (1988) proposed, that we promote graduate students' functioning as scientists and empirical researchers.

Let us now return to the discussion of what ought to be expected from the scientist side of the scientist-practitioner model. To recapitulate, we looked at three ways in which being a scientist within the model is manifested: (a) reviewing and applying research findings to one's practice, (b) thinking scientifically and carrying out one's work scientifically, and (c) actually doing research as part of one's career—regardless of one's job setting.

The expectation that the counseling psychologist be able to review and apply research is the least demanding of the three courses, whereas the expectation that he or she actually do research is the most demanding. Is this latter expectation realistic and viable? Not really. On the one hand, as affirmed by Whiteley (1984), Magoon and Holland (1984), and Gelso (1979a, 1979b), it is undeniable that counseling psychology would profit from and in fact needs more and better research. Faculty who train counseling psychologists should do everything possible in the training situation to promote students' continuing their research after obtaining the doctorate. A sizeable minority of counseling psychologists do in fact carry out empirical research, even when they are not working in university settings (Gronsky, 1982).

Yet, on the other hand, it is also true that many counseling psychologists are in work settings (e.g., community mental health settings, private practice settings) in which carrying out empirical research is extraordinarily difficult. Also, some counseling psychologists (no matter how inspiring or competent their doctoral training) simply do not have the inclination or perhaps enough of the kinds of abilities needed to do empirical, quantitative research. Many of these people can do very effective scholarly work other than empirical research. Thus, for example, developing theories and treatment approaches, and publishing these in the professional literature, can be highly scholarly, and contribute significantly to science as well as good practice. One who writes conceptual articles that are not based on research—clinical theory papers, hypotheses developed from individual cases, and so forth—effectively satisfies the dictates of the scientist side of the scientist-professional model. Also, such activities are more viable than is empirical research in some settings.

In summary, scholarly work should be a part of the counseling psychologist's job activity, regardless of job setting. The particular kind of scholarly work that is done will depend on a host of factors, most notably, the job demands and facilities of the specific setting and the inclinations and abilities of the individual counseling psychologist.

In regard to setting, those who work in university settings, especially in academic departments, will have the most favorable climate and the most concretely facilitative environment for the conduct of empirical research. Those who work in private practice and other agency-type settings will typically have the fewest practical and psychological facilities for doing research. Unless they are exceptionally motivated and/or are able to collaborate with colleagues in more favorable settings (e.g., universities) research will not get done. But, again, scholarly work can and should be contributed by counseling psychologists in all settings.

INVESTIGATIVE STYLES: A TYPOLOGY FOR RESEARCH

Although we have been discussing scholarly activities that are viable options to empirical research within the scientist-practitioner model, it needs to be underscored that empirical research has always held a highly prominent place in counseling psychology. Because of its importance to the specialty, this second part of Chapter 4 is devoted to empirical research and to the presentation of a classification system that should aid the reader in understanding counseling psychology research generally. In line with earlier formulations of one of the authors (Gelso, 1979a, 1979b), it is suggested that there are basically four types of or approaches to counseling psychology research. Scherman and Doan (1985) suggest that virtually all empirical studies in the specialty can be placed into one of the four categories of this system. Each of the four types has its own set of advantages and disadvantages, and it is important for the student of counseling psychology research to understand these.

Before discussing categories of research, it should be reiterated what this chapter is and is not, and why. The student of research methodology knows that there are a great many key issues in counseling psychology research as well as in psychological research generally. One could devote many pages to topics such as the selection of criteria, the use of control groups, reliability and validity of measurements and instruments, and so on. Rather than cover topics such as these in a very superficial manner, as would be necessary in a book seeking to examine the entire specialty of counseling psychology, we have chosen to focus, instead, on types of research, which are fundamental to an understanding of counseling psychology research in general. In the course of the discussion, some of the most important issues in counseling psychology research should become apparent. Also, references to in-depth readings on some central issues in counseling research will enable the reader to pursue these topics more fully.

To arrive at the four types of research in question, it is useful to think of counseling research as existing along two basic dimensions. One of these dimensions reflects the degree to which the experimenter or researcher controls or manipulates the independent variable (the variable or variables that are considered to have the experimental effect). As you can see in Table 4-1, we can divide studies into those that are

Table 4-1
A SYSTEM FOR CATEGORIZING TYPES OF RESEARCH

		Degree of Control of Independent Variable (Internal-Validity Question)	
		A Manipulative (High Control)	B Nonmanipulative (Low Control)
Setting (External-Validity Question)	A Lab	Type AA Experimental Analogue	Type AB Correlational Analogue
	B Field	Type BA Experimental Field	Type BB Correlational Field

Source: Reprinted from Gelso (1979a).

manipulative (high control of the independent variable) or nonmanipulative (low control).

Note that in Table 4-1 this dimension of "degree of control" is termed an internal validity question. That is because the extent to which the researcher manipulates or controls the independent variable relates very closely to how internally valid the study is—how clearly we can say that the variable(s) we presume to be producing the experimental effect, and not other variables, are the ones that are in fact having that effect.

The second dimension of counseling psychology research is simply labeled "setting" in Table 4-1. As you can see, there are basically two different settings, one being the laboratory and the other the field. Laboratory studies are usually simulations of the activity they are studying, whereas in field studies, the researcher examines the actual activity (e.g., counseling) in its natural setting.

Whereas the first dimension, as discussed above, related directly to internal validity, this second dimension relates to external validity—the extent to which one can generalize the findings from this particular study and this particular sample to the actual activity and population of interest. For example, if one studied career counseling with a sample of college students, the question of external validity would ask to what extent the findings could be generalized to career counseling, as practiced outside of the experiment, for example, in actual college counseling centers. Generally, studies done in field settings are high on external validity (one can generalize from them), whereas those done in laboratory settings contain some problems with external validity. These issues shall be explored more fully as we examine the types of research below. (The reader is referred to Campbell & Stanley, 1963, and Cook & Campbell, 1979, for classic work on internal and external validity issues in research.)

As is evidenced in Table 4-1, when one combines the two levels of the "degree of control" dimension (manipulative and nonmanipulative) with the two levels of the setting dimension (laboratory and field), four types of research, or investigative styles, result. Before examining how each of these operates in counseling psychology research, it should be underscored that categorization systems such as these are inevitably simplifications. In the real world of counseling psychology research, studies usually vary in the extent to which they represent a given type, and often studies are mixtures of the four types. Yet such simplifications can be very useful in understanding the strengths and weaknesses of different approaches.

Research Strategy AA: The Experimental Analogue

The first investigative style, the experimental analogue, is considered experimental because the researcher has full control over the independent variable (in counseling, for example, the treatment, who gets it, and when). The researcher controls the independent variable (IV) ordinarily through randomly assigning subjects to different treatments and determining when the treatments are offered. Thus, for example, in a therapy study, the researcher may randomly assign clients who visit an agency to different types of treatments and perhaps to a control group for whom treatment is delayed. The groups receiving different therapies are compared with each other and with the delayed-treatment control group.

If assignment to groups was random, and if all treatments were offered at equivalent times, the researcher is in a good position to conclude that the experimental effects were due to the treatments and not to other, extraneous, variables. In other words, the experimental control allows for strong causal inferences. If you manipulate IVs in a highly controlled situation and find changes in the dependent variables (those being affected) that follow the manipulation, you can safely conclude that it was the IV that had the effect.

So far we have been discussing how the experimental analogue is experimental. These comments reflect general thinking in psychology and other fields about what constitutes an experiment and what kinds of conclusions an experiment permits. The experimental analogue, however, is also an analogue of something we are interested in studying. That is, the analogue does not study the activity directly in a real-life situation; rather it studies the activity by analogy—by, in one way or another, approximating or simulating the activity.

Analogue research within counseling psychology most often studies an intervention. This intervention may be any of a wide range of activities or treatments in which the counseling psychologist is involved. Some examples of these are counseling, psychotherapy, consultation, guidance, assessment, supervision, training, and teaching. Again, the intervention is not studied as it actually is or naturally occurs, but, instead, as it is approximated by the researcher. Also, it should be understood that the typical analogue examines some aspect of the intervention rather than the entire intervention.

In the context of a given intervention, the experimenter may study the effects of any of an almost infinite array of independent variables and an equally wide range of dependent variables. Among the manifold aspects of counseling, for example, one can study the effects of (1) counselor techniques, behavior, personality, appearance, intentions, or style; (2) numerous client characteristics; and (3) different kinds or characteristics of treatments. In a like manner, the researcher may examine the effects of such variables on various client and counselor behaviors, perceptions, reactions, and so on. Here we can look at how the independent variable(s) affects some aspect of the client's behavior, some aspect of the counselor's behavior, some aspect of their interaction, or all these.

Let us be more specific about how experimental analogues are carried out. Basically there are two kinds of analogues: the audiovisual (AV) analogue and the quasi-intervention (Q-I) analogue. In the AV analogue, to use an example from counseling, the subject typically is (a) presented with a stimulus tape or film (although at times only written stimuli are used); (b) asked to assume the role of counselor or client; and (c) asked for different responses at various points in time. Typically, the tape or film will display a client, a counselor, or both. The researcher has complete control over what transpires on the tape or film.

A recent example of an AV analogue was published by Jones and Gelso (1988). These experimenters wanted to find out if a particular class of counselor response (an interpretation) is preferred by clients when delivered in a tentative as compared to an absolute manner. College student-subjects, who were asked to psychologically place themselves in the role of the client, listened to audio tapes of a counselor making one or the other type of interpretation at three points in a session. Thus, the counselor noted to the taped client what she viewed as the causes of the client's problems (an interpretation), and she did this in either a tentative or an absolute manner. Unbeknownst to subjects, the roles of taped counselor and client were played by counseling graduate students.

The student-subjects were randomly assigned to listen to either the tentative or the absolute interpretations. After listening to three segments of an interview (each containing one counselor interpretation), the students then evaluated the counselor and counseling. Generally, the counselor and counseling were rated as more effective when counselor interpretations were tentative rather than absolute. Note that the study also looked at whether a particular client characteristic (labeled as "resistance") affected the kind of interpretations subjects preferred. This variable had no detectable effect.

How does the AV analogue, as exemplified above, compare to the second kind, the quasi-intervention (Q-I) analogue? In the Q-I analogue, one or more interviews are actually held, and the activities that transpire may vary greatly in how closely they approximate the actual intervention being studied. To continue our use of counseling as an example of the intervention being studied, in the Q-I analogue, characteristics such as the following are typically displayed: (a) one or more interviews are held in which (b) counseling is approximated to one degree or another, and (c) a confederate client or counselor exhibits behaviors or characteristics that are prearranged or predetermined by the experimenter and are (d) systematically varied in order to (e) assess their effects on certain behaviors of the client-subject, the counselor-subject, or their interaction.

We have noted that the interaction may closely or remotely approximate counseling. Many Q-I analogues have college student-subjects role-play a client, and the problem they discussed with the "counselor" may not be a real one. The counselor, in turn, does not do actual counseling but behaves according to some prearranged script. Thus, for example, the counselor may behave in a planfully expert or inexpert manner to assess the impact of expertness on the subject-client's perceptions of the counselor. The role-played counseling session in such situations is often much briefer than actual sessions, for example, 15–20 minutes as compared to the usual 50-minute session.

Because of concerns about the artificiality of certain analogue methods, many researchers have done analogues that are more realistic. An experiment by Hubble and Gelso (1978) exemplifies a Q-I analogue that closely approximates counseling. These researchers wanted to determine the effects of the counselor's attire on certain client reactions. Male counselors consequently dressed in either traditional (coat and tie), casual (sport shirt and casual pants), or highly casual (sweatshirt and jeans) attire. Female clients then participated in a 45-minute counseling session with a counselor sporting one of these attires. Clients, recruited from beginning psychology classes, were asked to "discuss real problems with a real counselor." The counselors were counseling graduate students and were told to do actual counseling for a 45-minute session.

Client-subjects experienced greater levels of anxiety when counseled by highly casually attired counselors than in other dress conditions. Also, the experimenters found that the client's typical attire affected how she reacted to the counselor's attire. Clients seemed to react most favorably to counselors whose attire was one level more formal than the client's typical attire; for example, casually attired client-subjects reacted most positively to traditionally attired counselors, whereas even more casually attired clients reacted most favorably to the casually attired counselors.

The counseling in this experiment was the "real thing." So what makes this an analogue? The client-subjects were recruited for an experiment and were not voluntarily seeking counseling. And even though they were asked to discuss real problems with a real counselor, who, in turn, did actual counseling, the counseling was artificially time-limited. That is, it did not have a natural ending or one that approximates the typical duration of counseling. The counseling lasted only for one meeting, for the purposes of the experiment. In these ways, actual, real-world counseling was only approximated, although the approximation was a close one, especially in terms of the first session of counseling.

Evaluation of the Experimental Analogue in Counseling Psychology Research. The laboratory analogue has a number of strengths and weaknesses that must be kept in mind when conducting and reviewing research. On the positive side, it permits precise control of variables in a tightly controlled setting. Relatedly, the researcher is able to isolate some very specific variables for study, as in the Jones and Gelso (1988) study of counselor interpretation.

Not only can specific variables be isolated and tightly controlled, but the experimenter can manipulate variables to an extent that is not possible in actual counseling. Thus, in actual counseling conducted in, for example, a counseling center, the researcher could not possibly have counselors limit or modify their behavior with clients in a way that prohibits them from doing the best job possible. Contrary to the Jones and Gelso (1988) experiment, for example, actual counselors could not be restricted to a certain number of interpretations and their interpretations limited to only certain kinds, even when that seemed ineffective or clinically unwise. The researcher cannot manipulate variables as freely in the real world of counseling because of ethical considerations. Ethics must of course always be an issue in considering experimental control.

Probably the most fundamental strength of the experimental analogue is that because it tightly controls and manipulates, it allows for strong causal inferences. If an experimental effect occurs, we can have a high degree of confidence that the effect was *a function of the independent variable(s)* and not due to some other extraneous factors.

As in all research strategies, though, all is not methodologically well with the experimental analogue. In a certain way, its very strengths are its weaknesses. In isolating specific variables, and in rigorously controlling them, we violate nature, so to speak. To isolate a variable, that variable must be pulled out of its natural context. Again using Jones and Gelso's (1988) experiment as an example, interpretation was essentially the only kind of response made by the counselor in the taped vignettes. This response was carefully isolated, and it was manipulated in that different subjects heard different kinds of interpretations.

By contrast, in the real world of counseling, counselor interpretations are offered in a broader context, which includes a range of other counselor responses, numerous client responses, and a client-counselor relationship that has developed. When we isolate variables in an analogue, the effects of that variable may be assessed in and of themselves, but we cannot know if they would occur in a like fashion in the real world. In this way, internal validity is enhanced at the expense of external validity.

To maximize experimental control, laboratory research inevitably simplifies the phenomena it studies. As implied above, the whole package is not studied, but only portions of its contents. The question about this is always, "Have we simplified too much—such that the findings are not really relevant to the treatment we sought to study?" In counseling psychology there is currently a great deal of sensitivity to this issue, and analogue researchers are seeking to develop simulations that are as realistic as possible.

Despite attempts to make analogues as realistic as possible, it should be clear that there will always be artificiality to them—by their very nature. Because of this artificiality, and the attendant problems of generalizing analogue results to real-life counseling, the ultimate usefulness of the laboratory analogue has come under close scrutiny in recent years. The merits of this investigative style have been debated, hotly at times (e.g., Forsyth & Strong, 1986; Goldman, 1979; Gelso, 1979a, 1979b, 1982; Stone, 1984). Some believe that research by analogy is not of particular value and might best be done away with or conducted only under very special circumstances.

Indeed, it is, above all, one's research question that should dictate the research approach taken. For many questions, an analogue experiment is the best approach, and for some it is the only viable method. Some studies, again because of the questions being asked, require the tight control and precision allowed for by the analogue. Also, for ethical reasons, there are many important questions that simply could not be studied in real-life counseling.

In a recent analysis (Scherman & Doan, 1985), it was found that over a five-year period, approximately 27 percent of the studies published in the *Journal of Counseling Psychology* (the specialty's primary research journal) were experimental analogues. Our impression is that analogues in general have declined somewhat in recent years. But, as long as their inherent limitations are appreciated and efforts are made to produce sound simulations, experimental analogues will continue to hold an important place in the counseling psychology research literature.

Research Strategy AB: The Correlational Analogue

The correlational analogue, our second investigative style, is similar to the experimental analogue in that it is an approximation or simulation of some intervention situation. Also, the correlational analogue does not ordinarily occur in a real-life intervention setting but, rather, in a laboratory setting that itself is a simulation of the natural intervention setting.

It should be noted that even when the correlational analogue (or the experimental one, for that matter) occurs in a natural setting, for example, a university counseling center office, it is still an analogue. That is because, although the actual physical setting may be naturalistic, real-life counseling as it typically occurs is not being investigated.

The correlational analogue is unlike the experimental analogue in that the design is correlational rather than experimental. It is correlational in nature because independent variables are not manipulated; random assignment (of subjects to treatments, for example) does not occur. Essentially, the researcher does not have full control of who receives which experimental condition at what time. What does happen in the correlational analogue is that the researcher examines how two or more variables are related to one another in a controlled context. An almost infinite array of variables may be studied in this manner, although it is important that the selection of variables be guided by some theory or sound reasoning (and preferably both).

It must be underscored here that the AB strategy's *correlational* aspect in no way relates to the type of statistics used to analyze the data in a study. One may use correlational statistics (e.g., correlation coefficients) in experiments; and, likewise, the researcher may examine the differences between means for different groups in a correlational study. Correlational and group difference statistics are essentially interchangeable mathematically. Our use of the terms *correlational* and *experimental* pertain strictly to the experimental operations used—to the extent to which variables are isolated, manipulated, and controlled.

The fact that the AB strategy is correlational has profound implications for what we may conclude about the findings. Specifically, we may conclude that variables are systematically interrelated, but we cannot make strong causal inferences. We cannot know what causes what. For example, if a researcher finds that, after a 30-minute interview, degree of counselor empathy is closely related to whether or not interviewees would want to be counseled by that person (should they desire counseling), we cannot know that empathy caused the wish to see the counselor. It is equally plausible that subjects who would want to be counseled possess qualities that counselors easily empathize with.

The axiom that "correlation does not imply causation" underlies an interesting paradox in psychological research. As a result of correlational findings, we cannot infer causality based on our methodology; yet we can, and in many cases should, *theorize* about what causes what, and, further, we can use correlational research to test theories about what causes what. In testing the theory, for example, that counselor empathy is causally related to clients' wish to be counseled by the counselor in question, a correlational study will support the theory in that, if we find the hypothesized relationship, the theory has *escaped disconfirmation* (a relationship was, in fact, found to exist).

Let us examine some examples of correlational analogues. In an early and fascinating set of studies, Bordin (1966a, 1966b) wanted to find out if, in a psychoanalytic situation, personality integration was related to the quality of free associations. He paid subjects to free-associate for 30 minutes while reclining on a couch. Generally, it was found that personality integration and quality of associations were positively related.

More recently, Tracey, Hays, Malone, and Herman (1988) studied whether counselors' experience levels were associated with the kinds of responses they made to simulated client statements. Counselors at three experience levels (those with doctorates, advanced graduate students, and beginning graduate students) were asked to imagine themselves in the middle stages of counseling and then to write their responses to the written statements of 21 clients. When the kinds of responses made by counselors were analyzed, the authors found that greater experience was associated with the more effective and flexible responses. Can we conclude that experience causes, for example, flexibility of responses? Based on this correlational design, certainly not. It is equally plausible that flexibility helps a counselor to complete a doctorate and continue in the field (flexibility causes experience). Also, some other variable may cause both experience and flexibility. On the other hand, from the results of this study, we can *theorize* that experience is a causal factor, and we can use the findings to support such a theory.

Evaluation of the Correlational Analogue in Counseling Psychology Research. The correlational analogue generally is not discussed as a research strategy or approach in itself. Writers often seem to mistakenly assume that analogues are by definition experimental. This assumption confuses control of the context of a study with control of the independent variables. As we have seen, the correlational analogue is indeed one of the approaches to counseling psychology research.

In terms of limitations, the correlational analogue, as an analogue of an intervention or situation, shares many of the problems of the experimental analogue, such as artificiality and external validity (generalizability). On the other hand, because we are not isolating and manipulating specific independent variables, the correlational analogue may be more realistic than the experimental one.

An example may help clarify how this increased realism is possible. Suppose you wanted to study in a laboratory context the relationship of counselor expertness to clients' self-exploration. In an experiment, you might arrange for counselor-confederates to behave in expert or inexpert ways. Client-subjects would be assigned randomly to the expert or inexpert condition and asked to discuss some role-played problem in a 30-minute interview. This study is low in realism because counselors are required to behave in arranged ways and clients are asked to role-play. In fact, in experiments such as this, the "inexpert" counselor has been required to behave so ineffectively that she or he was less expert than would be conceivable in the real world (even granting that some counseling can be pretty awful). Now, contrast this with a correlational analogue in which, during a 30-minute session, counselors behave naturally while students recruited to participate in a counseling study discuss a real problem (which is ethically permissible because the counselors are doing their best). Trained raters could evaluate expertness and these ratings could be related to subjects' self-exploration during the session (using whatever statistics best fit the specifics of the study). This approach is correlational in that the independent variable (counselor expertness) is not manipulated, and obviously what transpires is a more realistic approximation of counseling than in the experiment.

The trade-off for the increased realism that is permitted in the correlational analogue is the inability in this strategy to make strong causal inferences. The correlational analogue is ordinarily much more controlled than the correlational *field* study (discussed later), but it is correlational nonetheless.

According to Scherman and Doan's (1985) analysis, only 7 percent of the studies published in the *Journal of Counseling Psychology* over a five-year period were correlational analogues. Yet the AB strategy has some strengths that make it highly valuable. It allows for greater control (e.g., of the context) than the field study, greater realism than the experimental analogue, and perhaps greater convenience than any other strategy. In terms of convenience, for example, Tracey et al. (1988) would have had to put in an enormously greater amount of time and effort to study the effect of counselor experience level on type of responses in a comparable way in real-life counseling. At the same time, the lessened control that is possible in actual counseling would have increased the chances that the relationships uncovered by the researchers would have been masked by other, uncontrolled factors.

Finally, although correlational analogues are not frequently used in and of themselves, correlational components are very often incorporated into experiments. Thus, many studies have a correlational and an experimental component. Watkins and Terrell (1988), for example, did an interesting study on whether black college students' level of mistrust for whites related to their expectations of counseling with black or white counselors. The correlational component in this study was black students' level of mistrust, and the experimental component was whether the counselor was black or white. The black students imagined themselves being counseled by either a black or white counselor (randomly determined) and then completed a counseling expectations scale. Expectations were more favorable in general when the student was more trusting of whites. Also, as expected, the highly mistrustful black students had the least favorable expectations regarding white counselors. (In previously discussed experiments, correlational components were client resistance in Jones and Gelso, 1988, and client attire in Hubble and Gelso, 1978.)

Incorporating a correlational component into an experimental analogue can be a powerful way of taking advantage of the strengths of both approaches. The advantages of this procedure have been discussed by both authors in greater detail elsewhere (Fretz, 1981; Gelso, 1979a).

Research Strategy BA: The Field Experiment

The third type of investigative style is called the *field experiment.* As you can see in Table 4-1, the Type BA study is manipulative; the researcher has full control (or nearly so) over the independent variable—who gets what experimental treatment, when. Random assignment of subjects to groups or treatments occurs.

The term *field* implies that the intervention being observed is the real-life activity itself. For example, if one is interested in studying the effects of consultation, the field experiment would examine actual consultation. Typically, the term *field* also implies that the study occurs in the natural setting of the intervention. In counseling or therapy, that setting might be a counseling center, a community health center, or a psychology department clinic. The basic feature of the field experiment, as we use this term, though, is that the real-life activity under study is being carried out (rather than an approximation of it) in a context that is not artificial.

In counseling psychology research, the field experiment usually investigates the effects of some intervention(s). When the Type BA study does look at the effects of interventions it is called an *outcome study.* Such outcome studies will frequently compare the effects of an intervention on subjects randomly assigned to one or more treatment groups and a control group; to treatment groups and more than one control group; or to treatment groups without control groups.

There are many methodological and ethical issues surrounding the use of control groups in experimental field research in counseling psychology. To begin with, methodologically, control groups or modified controls are usually necessary in order to be sure that the treatment(s) had an effect. For example, if we compare two methods of training and find that one is superior to the other, without a control group we cannot know if both had a desirable effect, neither had such an effect, or, in fact if one or both had a deleterious effect.

On the other hand, if subjects or clients must wait for some extended time period in a control group before receiving treatment, the likelihood increases that they will either decide against professional help or seek help elsewhere. The latter, especially, presents the researcher with serious methodological concerns. But what about the ethics in such situations? Is it ethical to delay treatment? What about under conditions in which the evidence is substantial that a given treatment is effective? Or when the potential client experiences some urgency in terms of the need for the intervention?

These are complex and vexing questions that cannot be answered simply or in the abstract. Each study needs an assessment of the appropriateness of control groups; the liabilities must be weighed against the benefits, both of using and not using control groups. Because of some of the methodological and ethical issues in the use of traditional control groups, alternative methods of forming and carrying out controls have been suggested and deserve consideration: established treatments as quasi controls, time-abbreviated waiting periods as controls, and approximations of random assignments to control groups (see Gelso, 1979a).

Two different field experiments, again from the counseling literature, may help exemplify the BA research strategy. Oppenheimer (1984) studied the effects of a small-group intervention on the social adjustment of college freshmen. Based on several social and personal adjustment measures, freshmen were divided into (a) those who might be expected to be particularly vulnerable to the transition stress caused by being at college for the first time and (b) those who were not predicted to be especially vulnerable. All subjects were randomly assigned to one of three groups: regular group counseling; focused group counseling in which the counselors emphasized the universality of social adjustment stress among freshmen; and a control group that did not receive counseling. Freshmen in the two counseling groups received six weekly group counseling sessions during their first semester. Oppenheimer found that the counseling resulted in improved social adjustment during the remainder of students' freshman year, especially for those who were considered vulnerable to stress. The regular and focused groups improved equally, and both improved more than the control group.

In a second field experiment, Gelso, Spiegel, and Mills (1983) wanted to find out how time-abbreviated individual counseling compared to regular counseling (in which a time limit is not established). Clients seeking personal counseling at a university counseling center were randomly assigned to one of three conditions: 8-session time limit, 16-session time limit, no time limit. Clients were told of the time limit during their first session. Note that Gelso et al. (1983) did not use a control group. Instead they compared the time-limited treatments to the established, regular counseling done at the agency.

In this field experiment it was found that at 1 month and 18 months after counseling had ended, clients in the regular treatment reacted slightly more favorably than those in the time-limited treatments. This tendency to react more favorably to the regular counseling was especially notable for clients who were in the lower half of psychological adjustment when they began treatment. For those who were in the upper half, however, time-limited counseling was reacted to as positively as was time-unlimited counseling.

In comparing the two field experiments, we can see that in both there was random assignment of clients to treatment conditions. Oppenheimer's group intervention study compared two treatments and a control group. Gelso et al. (1983) did not use a traditional control group but, instead, compared two treatments with an established treatment. Both studies examined outcomes well after the end of the intervention, an important ingredient of outcome research. Also, both incorporated a *client factor* into their design. Thus, Oppenheimer looked at the effects of group intervention on clients rated as psychologically vulnerable or nonvulnerable; Gelso et al. (1983) compared time-limited and time-unlimited counseling for clients initially above and below the midpoint on psychological adjustment.

The inclusion of a client factor into these field experiments moved both studies a step toward what is perhaps the most prominent and by now established trend in counseling psychology research: going beyond asking, simply, if a given treatment is better than no treatment, toward finding out who the intervention works best with, under what conditions, at what times, and when offered by what types of interveners. The importance of going beyond the broad question of "Does it work?" and, in effect, looking at the conditions under which a given intervention succeeds was perhaps first pointed to in counseling psychology by Krumboltz (1966) over two decades ago. This more refined and complex set of questions has been referred to as the "who, what, when, and where" question by one of the authors (Gelso, 1979a). Fretz (1981) has discussed the need to address questions at this level in career intervention research.

An Evaluation of the Field Experiment in Counseling Psychology Research. Because it is a controlled experiment in a field setting, the BA research strategy combines scientific rigor with clinical relevance. Its rigor stems from the fact that, because of random assignment and the related ability to determine who gets what experimental condition, at what times, the field experiment can be well controlled. On the other side of the ledger, the clinical relevance is high, or at least is capable of being high, because the BA strategy investigates actual interventions or other phenomena in field settings in which these activities occur. As implied earlier, field experiments can be especially effective strategies if they incorporate additional independent variables, that is, additional to the primary treatment variable. These added variables, in practice, are often aspects of the client, the counselor, the intervention, the intervention situation, and so forth. No one experiment can look at more than a few factors; but the inclusion of one or more in addition to the main independent variable allows the experiment to move toward addressing the "who, what, when, where" questions that are so important.

Because of its many desirable features, a sizeable number of the studies appearing in counseling psychology research journals represent the BA strategy. For example, Scherman and Doan (1985) found that 31.2 percent of the research articles appearing in the *Journal of Counseling Psychology* over a five-year period were field experiments. Given the current emphasis on studying phenomena in their natural settings (Gelso et al., 1988), the percentage of field experiments in counseling psychology research should remain high.

Despite the positive features, the BA strategy is not without its limitations. A major difficulty is that field experiments are simply *very hard to do.* There are many practical problems in carrying out controlled experimentation in a field setting. For example, if a researcher plans to do an intervention study in a university counseling center, randomly assigning clients to different treatment groups, pretesting clients, posttesting clients, following them up later, and perhaps assigning clients to control group conditions—these all create concerns in the agency setting. Not only are ethics an ever-present issue, but if the experiment is not well organized, the research can create administrative difficulties in agency settings.

In addition to being difficult to accomplish in many applied settings, the field experiment is limited in that it tends to examine global variables. When offering actual interventions to recipients who are in an actual client role, it is often not possible to inspect specific variables that are elements of the treatment. For example, in the Jones and Gelso (1988) analogue experiment discussed earlier, the researchers could readily isolate one specific counseling technique (interpretation) for examination. In a field experiment, it would not be possible to offer counseling to clients, with the implicit promise that counselors are doing their very best, and then provide a treatment that was only a fraction of the promised intervention.

Because field experiments ordinarily examine global variables, and laboratory studies are able to inspect specific variables (in a more precise manner), it can be extremely valuable for researchers to use both approaches in studying particular phenomena. In this manner investigative styles can be combined in a way that most effectively advances knowledge.

We noted earlier that the field experiment in counseling psychology is usually an outcome study. Before concluding this discussion of the field experiment, a brief comment is in order about counseling outcomes. Over the years, there have been virtually hundreds of outcome studies on the effects of well-known psychological treatments, for example, individual personal and career counseling, psychotherapy, group counseling, and marital counseling with couples. During the past 15 years, sophisticated methods (called meta-analysis) have been developed to quantitatively integrate the findings from large groups of individual studies, so that we could get a picture of the overall effects of given treatments.

Throughout this book we shall point to the effects of the different treatments that are discussed. As an overall statement, it may be noted that the established psychological treatments have been found in general to be effective. For large-scale, integrative reviews of studies on the outcomes of different psychological treatments, the reader is referred to the following: individual counseling and therapy—Lambert, Shapiro and Bergin (1986); marital and family counseling—Gurman, Kniskern and

Pinsoff (1986); career counseling—Myers (1986); group therapy—Kaul and Bednar (1986). Just as it is clear that the established psychological treatments are beneficial on the whole, it is also true that not everyone benefits to a satisfactory extent from them. Thus, outcome researchers are now devoting their energies to the "who, what, when, where" question noted earlier.

Research Strategy BB: The Correlational Field Study

The last investigative style is the most commonly used of the four approaches. In Scherman and Doan's (1985) analysis of research articles appearing in the *Journal of Counseling Psychology* over a five-year period, more than a third (34.5%) of the studies employed Type BB strategies. As we shall see, the correlational field study is also the most varied and multifaceted of the investigative styles.

What are the defining features of the correlational field study? Its most basic elements are that it is nonmanipulative and occurs in a field setting. The researcher does not seek to control the "when" and "to whom" of exposure to experimental conditions—no random assignment to treatments is attempted. As regards setting, either the BB strategy takes place in the setting in which the phenomena being studied naturally occur or there is no attempt to simulate treatments or situations, or both. Overall, the correlational field study aims to look at relationships between and among variables as they naturally occur.

As noted in examining the correlational analogue strategy, the fact that the BB strategy is correlational has nothing whatsoever to do with the kinds of statistics used to analyze the data. The researcher conducting a correlational field study may analyze his or her data with correlational statistics (e.g., correlation coefficients), group difference statistics (e.g., analysis of variance), or in fact may not use statistics at all. As will be discussed further below, counseling psychology researchers are becoming increasingly interested in qualitative analyses, wherein data are analyzed linguistically and logically rather than statistically. Again, the key in the BB strategy is that the researcher studies the relationships between and among variables, as they naturally occur.

Whereas the three investigative styles discussed earlier typically (not always) examine the effects of some intervention (e.g., counseling, consultation, training, supervision), or elements of an intervention, the correlational field study may or may not focus on interventions. It may, and often does, study the interrelationships between and among characteristics of the person, for example, between personality and behavior, thoughts and feelings, interests and choices, and so forth.

An example of a central content area in counseling psychology in which the BB strategy is most frequently used is vocational psychology or what is called the "psychology of career development" (see Chapter 11). Some of the fundamental questions being addressed in this large and important area of study are: "What factors underlie the choice of a career? How do people develop career maturity? What factors influence some individuals to have satisfying, stable careers and others to have unhappy and unstable ones? What are the causes, effects, and correlates of career indecision?" As you can see, these questions do not directly involve interventions. Also, although the questions point to causes and effects, the research most often done to address the questions is correlational. This is because the research studies personal characteristics, usually as the independent variables, and one cannot ordinarily manipulate experimentally qualities that are an inherent part of a person.

In attempting to understand the BB research strategy, it is important to examine its connection to what is usually called *naturalistic research.* It is common for observers of the research scene to view correlational field research and naturalistic research as one and the same, almost by definition. This view is incorrect. Although naturalistic research is invariably correlational field research, the reverse may or may not be true. What are the characteristics of naturalistic research? In a classic paper, Tunnell (1977) clarifies that there are three independent dimensions of naturalness: natural behavior (part of the person's existing behavior and not instigated by the researcher), natural setting, and natural treatment (an event the subject would have experienced with or without the research).

Artificiality can occur along any of the three dimensions pointed to by Tunnell. Consider the fairly common practice in correlational field research of testing subjects at several points. To begin with, when we use a test of our making, we are imposing categories on the subject's responses, and that intrudes on naturalness (i.e., the categories prevent subjects from responding as they naturally would). The process of repeatedly testing subjects also intrudes on the natural flow of behavior. So a correlational field study may be very "nonnaturalistic" in certain ways—or it may be fully naturalistic.

As in the correlational analogue, the correlational aspect of the BB strategy has great consequences for what we may conclude about its findings. Namely, although we may conclude that the variables are systematically interrelated, we cannot conclude, *on methodological grounds,* that they are causally related. Also as noted earlier, however, we certainly may and should make causal interpretations on theoretical and subject-matter grounds. The reader is referred to a thoughtful piece by Neimeyer and Resnikoff (1982), in which these authors discuss a procedure, called "analytical induction," for making causal inferences from correlational data. In effect, the researcher using analytical induction searches for "control groups" in the natural world.

Let us now look at some examples of published studies using the Type BB strategy. A study by Hill, Carter, and O'Farrell (1983) is fast becoming a classic in the field because, unlike virtually all the empirical studies preceding it, this one examines counseling with a single client. The authors intensively study the case of a 20-year-old college senior who received 12 sessions of counseling for which a duration limit was established at the beginning of the work. The client, called Sue, was involved in extensive testing as part of the research. She took a battery of psychological tests before counseling; completed a session evaluation after each session; was tested again early in the treatment; and completed posttesting one week, two months, and seven months after ending counseling. Sue also kept a diary during the counseling. With her permission, sessions were audiotaped, and a small undergraduate honors class observed all sessions through a one-way mirror. The counselor also completed a number of evaluation measures. As you can see from this brief summary, this research could hardly be considered naturalistic, although it clearly was a correlational field study in that no variables were manipulated and real-life counseling was involved.

The researchers found that the client improved up to the two-month follow-up but relapsed at seven months. They suggested that the relapse was because counseling did not last long enough for this client. Also, as one part of the work, Hill and her colleagues found that counselor interpretations occurred more frequently in sessions rated as "the best" (vs. "the worst"). From this they made causal inferences; that is, interpretations had desirable effects on client self-exploration.

Given the correlational nature of the study, was it appropriate for the researchers to conclude that the relapse was because counseling did not last long enough? To conclude that interpretations have a desirable effect? On strictly methodological grounds, it clearly was not appropriate to assert or imply these causal inferences. Yet these researchers drew on a variety of data and theoretical sources to arrive at their causal statements. Thus, causal inferences were made on theoretical and subject-matter grounds, which we maintain is appropriate as long as it is clear that this is what is being done.

A second study demonstrates the variety of research included under the BB category. In recent years there has been much study of the social consequences of shyness. Phillips and Bruch (1988), however, wondered if shyness also has undesirable effects on behaviors essential to people's career development. They administered a battery of tests assessing shyness and vocationally relevant behaviors to 151 college students (81 women, 70 men), and found that for both genders shyness was associated with career indecision, with a preference for careers that were not interpersonally oriented, with less seeking of information that is important to making good choices, and with the belief that assertiveness is inappropriate in a job interview. Based on their knowledge of this area of study and on theory, the researchers concluded that shyness was causally related to these other variables. However, it is plausible that another variable may underlie both shyness and its correlates. Shyness, in itself, may or may not causally influence career-relevant behaviors.

Alternative Methodologies and the BB Research Strategy. At the beginning of this section, we noted that the correlational field study was at once the most commonly used strategy and the most varied and multifaceted. The vast differences between the single-case approach of Hill et al. (1983) and the large sample analysis by Phillips and Bruch (1988) on two vastly different topics give the reader a glimpse at the varied nature of research designs within the BB strategy. Indeed, these studies only hint at the multifaceted nature of correlational field research.

In recent years in counseling psychology, there has been increasing dissatisfaction with traditional approaches to research. The sense has been growing among a number of scholars that different approaches are needed if knowledge is to be advanced substantially (Borgen, 1984; Gelso, 1982), and this viewpoint has become widespread enough to be considered a movement in counseling psychology research. Virtually all of the approaches to research that have been suggested as a result of the so-called alternative methodologies movement fit squarely within the broad category of the correlational field study. Nearly all seek to study humans in their natural context and relationships among variables nonmanipulatively.

What approaches to research are being advocated? Which are being "reacted against"? Table 4-2 contains what appear to be the primary characteristics of the movement as well as the characteristics being opposed. The left-hand column presents and defines the terms that reflect the alternative-methodologies movement, whereas the right-hand column gives the terms characterizing traditional psychological research.

We want to emphasize two points about the material in Table 4-2. First, the concepts in the two categories, alternative and traditional, are presented to accentuate the differences. Few of the advocates of the alternative approaches suggest that traditional methods are not valuable. They say that different approaches are needed to supplement, not supplant, traditional methods. Second, few if any of the advocates of alternative methods promote all seven of them. The movement, in effect, is not very uniform. For example, Howard (1985), who is one of the leading spokespersons of the movement, promotes research that views the subject as an active agent whose goals and intentions, rather than external

Table 4–2
CHARACTERISTICS OF ALTERNATIVE RESEARCH METHODS COMPARED TO THOSE OF TRADITIONAL METHODS

Alternative Research Methods	Traditional Research Methods
1. *Qualitative:* Observations are made and interpreted in words, i.e., verbally and linguistically. Research seeks underlying, subjective meanings.	*Quantitative:* Observations are transformed into numbers and expressed mathematically. Results analyzed statistically.
2. *Molar:* Broad and general patterns studied.	*Molecular:* Specific and precise behavior studied.
3. *Naturalistic:* Research does not impose categories or disrupt natural behavior.	*Experimental:* Research isolates variables, imposes categories, disrupts natural behavior.
4. *Idiographic:* Focus on individual; N = 1, or small sample studies.	*Nomothetic:* Focus on general patterns; large sample studies.
5. *Field:* Research conducted in natural context.	*Laboratory:* Research is an analogue done in laboratory.
6. *Subjective:* Attention to internal processes and meanings for the individual person.	*Objective:* Attention to external processes and to outer behavior of persons.
7. *Nondeterministic:* Views subject as active agent who guides own behavior; has goals, intentions, etc., that cause actions.	*Deterministic:* Subject seen as passive recipient of stimuli; behavior caused by external stimuli.

stimuli, determine his or her behavior. Nowhere in Howard's extensive writing are there criticisms of laboratory research. Hill (1982), on the other hand, advocates case study (idiographic) research that is *partly* qualitative. She does not necessarily promote nondeterministic or naturalistic research (or criticize their traditional counterparts).

The movement is having an impact, as shown by current studies in counseling psychology that contain a number of the features listed in the left-hand column of Table 4-2. Also, although there certainly is disagreement between traditional and alternative-methods scholars, few if any scholars are defending the traditional approaches to research as uniquely viable. The report of the Research Group at the Georgia Conference (Gelso et al., 1988) sought to further this view that all methods (including traditional ones) be given a fair hearing. They indicated that their strongest recommendation was for diversity in research approaches and underscored that what ought to determine the appropriateness of a given method, more than anything else, is the research question being studied.

To further pursue issues and ideas within the alternative-methodologies movement, the reader may consult the following references. The *Journal of Counseling Psychology* published a special section on the philosophy of science and counseling research in its October 1984 issue (Vol. 31. no. 4). In that issue Polkinghorne (1984), Howard (1984), and Patton (1984) present philosophical premises of the alternative methodologies as well as their disagreements with the "received view." Five prominent scholars in the field respond to the papers in the same issue, and their responses give the reader a taste of the lively disagreements that exist among counseling psychologists. Other important papers on alternative methods have been published by Goldman (1976), Howard (1984, 1985), Hoshmand (1989), Hill (1982), Hill and Gronsky (1984), and Neimeyer and Resnikoff (1982).

An Evaluation of the Correlational Field Study. Given the movement toward alternative methodologies, which are carried out largely with correlational field strategies, the Type BB study may be more popular in counseling psychology today than ever before. Indeed, it has many strengths. More than any strategy, the correlational field study allows for the simultaneous study of many variables. At the same time, this strategy permits a relative lack of interference with natural processes of the phenomena being studied. By definition, also, the BB strategy occurs in the field rather than the laboratory. Kiesler (1971) sums up these strengths nicely when he states that this type of research "represents a more comprehensive strategy, potentially dealing with multiple variables, thus bowing toward the admitted complexity of real-life events" (p. 55).

From the perspective of alternative methodologies, correlational field research allows for the methods given in the left-hand column of Table 4-2: More than other strategies, it permits (and in certain ways facilitates) research that is qualitative, molar, naturalistic, idiographic, in the field, subjective, and nondeterministic. It should be noted that the BB strategy does not stipulate any of the alternative-methodology concepts (except that of the "field"). In other words, the BB strategy in no way *requires* the research to be idiographic and naturalistic, but it permits the research to be such.

Perhaps the main overall strength of the correlational field study is its external validity. This is especially true when the BB strategy moves toward the naturalistic side of the continuum. The more we study natural behavior and events in natural settings, the more clearly we can generalize the results to the real world, which is, after all, what our theories are about. On the negative side, external validity is gained at an expense, and that expense is *internal validity.* In the correlational field study, as indicated, we cannot determine what is causing what, on methodological grounds. Also, as the strategy moves more toward the naturalistic side, we have less assurance about what is causing what. In fact, as the correlational research strategy increasingly incorporates the concepts of the alternative-methodologies movement, causality becomes increasingly less clear. To reiterate, though, under appropriate conditions, causal inferences may be made on theoretical and subject-matter grounds.

THE BUBBLE HYPOTHESIS AND THE SEARCH FOR CLINICAL RELEVANCE

In this final section of the chapter, we offer a perspective on psychological research in general and counseling psychology research in particular. The aim is to clarify how each and every piece of research or, more broadly, approach to research possesses inevitable weaknesses and, especially, to demonstrate *the inevitable connection between the weaknesses and strengths of all studies and research approaches.* In addition to presenting this research perspective, the final section explores the issue of the relevance of research to counseling practice—the ways in which research may be relevant, the costs of relevance, and the consumer's role in making research relevant to practice. These issues are presented to show that the concept of relevance is a complex one and that the problem of perceived low relevance of research to practice does not have simple solutions.

One need only be involved in a tiny amount of research to begin to see what is so obvious to the experienced scientist—that each and every study is highly imperfect and that each contains some inevitable flaws. Each broad investigative style also has strengths and weaknesses. Although one begins to see the inevitability of this with a little experience, what may be less clear is that weaknesses cannot be eliminated and that each attempted solution to methodological problems and shortcomings *in itself* causes another set of problems.

As a way of illuminating the phenomena discussed in the above paragraph, Gelso (1979a, 1979b) coined the term *bubble hypothesis.* This concept likens the research process to a sticker on a car windshield. Once a bubble appears in the sticker, it is impossible to eliminate it. Pressing the bubble simply causes it to pop up in another place. Each attempted solution causes a problem to appear elsewhere.

In order to clarify how the bubble hypothesis operates in counseling research methodology, Gelso (1979b, p. 62) offers two propositions, as follows:

a. Immutable trade-offs exist with respect to the choices the researcher must make in each and every phase of the research process. These trade-offs are most apparent in critical general areas such as the basic selection of a design, the choice of criteria, sampling procedures, decisions about the scope of the project, etc.

b. Solutions to problems of design themselves create problems, such that the partially subjective, partially objective choices as regards matters of design need to be based on formulations about which problems are least (and most) injurious to the research endeavor, the generation of knowledge in which the investigator is most interested.

In effect, every choice we make with respect to how we design a study entails a trade-off; every decision we make to solve one or a set of methodological problems, in itself, causes another problem or set of problems. Consider how the bubble hypothesis might apply to the four investigative styles discussed in the last section, to the strengths and weaknesses of each.

As but one example of the application of the bubble hypothesis to the general area of research methodology, one can examine what has been called the "rigor-relevance issue" in counseling psychology research (Gelso, 1985). The term *rigor* usually implies that a study is tightly controlled—high on internal validity. That is, the design of the study allows a good degree of certainty that the independent variables, rather than other extraneous variables, are what produce the changes in the dependent variables. In other words, we have a good idea of what is causing what. Of the four research strategies discussed earlier, the one that is strongest in terms of internal validity is the AA strategy, the experimental analogue.

In the experimental analogue, the researcher attains rigorous control at the expense of relevance. The greater the control, the less the operations of the study reflect what happens in real life—the less natural the procedures. In other words, *we attain internal validity at the expense of external validity.*

To solve the problem of low external validity (low generalizability to the real world of whatever phenomenon we study) we can conduct a fully naturalistic version of the correlational field study. Obviously in this case we have the greatest possible external validity, since nothing is tampered with by the experimenter—he or she simply observes what is happening, for example, in counseling. As discussed earlier, this external validity is gained at a cost. We now have proportionately reduced the ability to make sound causal inferences and so to know what is causing what.

The reader is encouraged to think through how these trade-offs exist with respect to other aspects of methodology. In doing so, he or she may begin to wonder if we can ever advance knowledge and improve our research techniques. As all research is flawed, should we just give up and settle for inferior studies? How is knowledge advanced if problems are inevitable in every study and approach?

Our answers to the above questions are optimistic and positive. Despite the inevitable limitations, we can and should design studies to answer most effectively the questions being asked. Even in the face of the bubble hypothesis, knowledge may indeed be advanced by studying topics from a variety of vantage points, each with its own sets of problems. To use an example discussed earlier, in studying the effects of the counseling technique called *interpretation,* a number of different analogue studies (e.g., the Jones & Gelso 1988 analogue experiment) may be combined with various field studies (e.g., Hill et al.'s 1983 correlational field study of a single case), each with its own set of methodological problems. Convergent findings from these studies (again, each with its own set of weaknesses) allow us to have confidence that knowledge has been advanced reliably. The key concepts here are *continued study* (or programmatic research, as it is called), the use of *a variety of methods,* and the *convergence of findings under conditions of methodological diversity.*

In recent years in counseling psychology and other applied-psychology specialties, great concerns have been expressed that our research is not sufficiently relevant to our practice. Some critics have attacked research, especially experimental research, as being irrelevant because of an obsession with control and quantification (Goldman, 1978, 1979). Others have proposed that the problem of low relevance is due to the fact that traditional research models view humans as passive recipients of stimuli, whereas counseling practitioners see humans as active agents whose goals, plans, and intentions determine their behavior (see Howard, 1985). This profound difference in the image of humans held by scientists versus practitioners, according to Howard and others, makes for a poor fit between science and practice—thus the low relevance of research to practice.

The belief that research should be highly relevant to practice is perhaps most clearly expressed in what was called the "test of relevance" a number of years ago by one of the leading researchers in the field (Krumboltz, 1968). According to Krumboltz's test of relevance, for any piece of research to be worthwhile, it must have an effect on what counselors do in their practice. Research that does not affect what counselors do is seen as "academic calisthenics" (Krumboltz & Mitchell, 1979, p. 50), and, by implication, probably should not be published in counseling psychology journals.

Although there is debate within the field as to just how relevant research typically is to practice (see, for example, the more positive views of the Georgia Conference; Gelso et al., 1988; and Heppner & Anderson's 1985 discussion of the many areas in which counseling psychology research has aided practice), and how relevant it *ought* to be, most researchers and practitioners do believe we should continually work on relating research to practice.

In seeking to make research relevant to counseling psychology practice, however, we encounter certain difficulties that need to be understood. In fact, we may be faced with a dilemma in the search to enhance clinical relevance. The kind of research that is most clearly relevant has been discussed by Gelso (1985) as *experience-near* research. In experience-near research, the questions being studied closely approximate those raised in practice (e.g., in counseling); the theory from which the research originates closely approximates the counselor's experience of what goes on in counseling; the methodology of the research closely approximates counseling; and the constructs being studied closely approximate those used in practice. Examples of the most experience-near research are the uncontrolled and unquantified case study in counseling, and counseling itself as a research method (as is popular in psychoanalysis—where analysis itself is seen as a research model).

The problem with experience-near research, and the source of the dilemma noted above, is that as we move more in that direction we become increasingly less sure of what causes what in the research and of how the findings generalize to other samples. That is because of the lack of control and quantification, and because experience-near research tends to focus on the individual (as in the case study). *Experience-far* research, on the other hand, is better controlled, and does allow for clearer explanations about what causes what. (The tightly controlled experimental analogue tends to be the prototype of the experience-far study.) Yet, as we move in the direction of experience-far research, perceived relevance is diminished. The research tends to capture less of the fullness, richness, and vitality of the intervention experience. We again are faced with the bubble hypothesis; experience-near (relevant) and experience-far (rigorous) research both have costs. And we cannot optimally advance knowledge and improve practice by simply doing research that has the greatest perceived relevance (experience-near research).

Despite these inevitable limitations, research still can be profoundly important to practice. It can help the practitioner think more clearly and in a less biased way about his or her practice, and organize his or her ever-changing personal theory about whatever processes he or she is involved in (e.g., consultation, teaching, therapy). In this way research is relevant, but *indirectly rather than directly relevant to practice.* One should not expect to apply research findings, even those based on experience-near research, directly to one's practice. Rather, findings help one refine one's theory of practice and think more clearly about that practice. When the issue of relevance is considered in this way, experience-far research is seen as highly relevant (indirectly) to practice.

In addition to the issue of indirect relevance, research can be made relevant to practice only if the practitioner is an *active agent* in the process. All too frequently consumers of research expect to be able to read journals and have the relevance of the research strike them, without having to actively work at seeing the relevance. This passive approach is doomed to failure. If the reader is going to be able to use empirical research in practice, he or she must approach the reading with the notion of *finding what is relevant.* That is, the reader needs to take the attitude that he or she is going to look for what is relevant and actively think about how a given study may apply to practice. When one takes this active approach to reading research, it is striking to see just how many applications most pieces of research have.

SUMMARY

Scientific research is vitally important to counseling psychology. It allows us to test our theories and improve them. Without scientific research, we would simply be acting out our biases in counseling psychology practice, and in the final analysis such practice would be ineffective.

Within the scientist-practitioner model, three levels of being a scientist were explored: (1) reviewing and applying research findings to one's practice, (2) thinking and carrying out one's work scientifically, and (3) doing research as part of one's career. All three levels are important for the practicing counseling psychologist to be involved in, although many counseling psychologists have neither the physical facilities nor the inclination to do traditionally defined empirical research. Instead, these practice-oriented psychologists can and should do scholarly work, which is a broader concept than empirical research. Scholarly work may include research but also includes other intellectual activities aimed at advancing knowledge.

In terms of counseling psychology research strategies, four prominent *investigative styles* were explored in depth. These four styles or strategies result from combining two dimensions: setting (field or laboratory) and degree of control of the independent variable (high or low control). The resulting styles are labeled (1) the experimental analogue, (2) the correlational analogue, (3) the experimental field study, and (4) the correlational field study. Each of these four strategies has notable advantages and disadvantages. Combining strategies in certain ways may maximally advance knowledge in the field.

Within the strategy labeled "correlational field study," the *alternative methodology movement* was explored. This complex and important movement is being advanced by scholars who are opposed to what they view as an overuse of traditional experimental methods. Alternative approaches are advocated, for example: qualitative research, naturalistic approaches, and research focusing on the individual. This emphasis on alternative methodologies is benefiting the field and will continue to do so. As a bottom-line principle, the approach that should be taken in a given study is determined by the research questions the investigator seeks to answer.

Gelso's *bubble hypothesis* serves as a way of clarifying the inevitable advantages and disadvantages of every research strategy and of demonstrating how each decision the researcher makes about the design of a study contains a cost. The most basic features of this perspective on research are that inevitable trade-offs exist about choices the researcher must make at all stages of research and that solutions to problems of design create other problems. In effect, all studies are flawed to some extent. Knowledge is most powerfully advanced by the continuing study of a given topic through the use of a variety of methods, each with different methodological limitations.

Regarding the issue of *relevance,* counseling psychology researchers must continually work on connecting their research to practice. In keeping with the bubble hypothesis, however, a trade-off exists with respect to relevance. The most clearly relevant research, called *experience-near,* is also often the least rigorous and controlled. The field needs a balance of experience-near (relevant) and *experience-far* (controlled) research. It should be emphasized, though, that research is rarely directly relevant to practice. Rather, it is indirectly relevant and aids practitioners by helping them to think more clearly, reduce bias, and refine personal theories of practice. Finally, if research relevance is to be perceived by the consumer, he or she must take an active approach to discovering the relevance of a given piece of research.

References

American Psychological Association (1952). Recommended standards for training counseling psychologists at the doctorate level. *American Psychologist, 7,* 175–181.

Bordin, E. S. (1966a). Personality and free association. *Journal of Consulting Psychology, 30,* 30–38.

Bordin, E. S. (1966b). Free association: An experimental analogue of the psychoanalytic situation. In L. Gottschalk & A. Auerbach (Eds.), *Methods of research in psychotherapy.* New York: Appleton-Century-Crofts.

Borgen, F. H. (1984). Counseling psychology. *Annual Review of Psychology, 35,* 579–604.

Campbell, D. T., & Stanley, J. C. (1963). *Experimental and quasi-experimental designs for research.* Chicago, IL: Rand-McNally.

Cook, T. D., & Campbell, D. T. (1979). *Quasi-experimentation: Design and analysis for field settings.* Chicago: Rand-McNally.

Forsyth, D. R., & Strong, S. R. (1986). The scientific study of counseling and psychotherapy: A unificationist view. *American Psychologist, 41,* 113–119.

Fretz, B. R. (1981). Evaluating the effectiveness of career interventions [Monograph]. *Journal of Counseling Psychology, 28,* 77–90.

Gelso, C. J. (1979a). Research in counseling: Methodological and professional issues. *The Counseling Psychologist, 8*(3), 7–35.

Gelso, C. J. (1979b). Research in counseling: Clarifications, elaborations, defenses, and admissions. *The Counseling Psychologist, 8*(3), 61–67.

Gelso, C. J. (1982). Editorial. *Journal of Counseling Psychology, 29,* 3–7.

Gelso, C. J. (1985). Rigor, relevance and counseling research: On the need to maintain our course between Scylla and Charybdis. *Journal of Counseling and Development, 63,* 551–553.

Gelso, C. J., Betz, N. E., Friedlander, M. L., Helms, J. E., Hill, C. E., Patton, M. A., Super, D. E., & Wampold, B. E. (1988). Research in counseling: Prospects and recommendations. *The Counseling Psychologist, 16,* 385–406.

Gelso, C. J., Spiegel, S. B., & Mills, D. M. (1983). Clients' and counselors' reactions to time-limited and time-unlimited counseling. In C. J. Gelso & D. H. Johnson, *Explorations in time-limited counseling and psychotherapy* (pp. 14–62). New York: Columbia University, Teachers College Press.

Goldman, L. (1976). A revolution in counseling research. *Journal of Counseling Psychology, 23,* 543–552.

Goldman, L. (Ed.) (1978). *Research methods for counselors.* New York: Wiley.

Goldman, L. (1979). Research is more than technology. *The Counseling Psychologist, 8*(3), 41–43.

Gronsky, B. R. (1982). Research and the counseling psychologist: A comparison of researchers and practitioners. Unpublished doctoral dissertation, University of Maryland, College Park.

Gurman, A. S., Kniskern, D. P., & Pinsoff, W. M. (1986). Research on marital and family therapies. In S. Garfield & A. Bergin (Eds.), *Handbook of psychotherapy and behavior change* (3rd ed., pp. 565–626). New York: Wiley.

Heppner, P. P., & Anderson, W. P. On the perceived non-utility of research in counseling. *Journal of Counseling and Development, 63,* 545–547.

Hill, C. E. (1982). Counseling process research: Philosophical and methodological dilemmas. *The Counseling Psychologist, 10*(4), 7–20.

Hill, C. E., Carter, J. A., & O'Farrell, M. K. (1983). A case study of the process and outcome of time-limited counseling. *Journal of Counseling Psychology, 30,* 3–18.

Hill, C. E., & Gronsky, B. R. (1984). Research: Why and how? In J. Whiteley, N. Kagan, L. Harmon, B. Fretz, & M. Tanney (Eds.), *The coming decade in counseling psychology* (pp. 149–159). Schenectady, NY: Character Research Press.

Hoshmand, L. (1989). Alternate research paradigms: A review and teaching proposal. *The Counseling Psychologist, 17,* 3–80.

Howard, G. S. (1984). A modest proposal for a revision of strategies for counseling research. *Journal of Counseling Psychology, 31*(4), 430–442.

Howard, G. S. (1985). Can research in the human sciences become more relevant to practice? *Journal of Counseling and Development, 63,* 539–544.

Howard, G. S. (1986). The scientist-practitioner model in counseling psychology: Toward a deeper integration of theory, research, and practice. *The Counseling Psychologist, 14,* 61–105.

Hubble, M. A., & Gelso, C. J. (1978). Effects of counselor attire in an initial interview. *Journal of Counseling Psychology, 25,* 581–584.

Jones, A. S., & Gelso, C. J. (1988). Differential effects of style of interpretation: Another look. *Journal of Counseling Psychology, 35,* 363–369.

Kaul, T. J., & Bednar, R. (1986). Experiential group research: Results, questions, and suggestions. In S. Garfield & A. Bergin (Eds.), *Handbook of psychotherapy and behavior change* (3rd ed., pp. 671–714). New York: Wiley.

Kiesler, D. J. (1971). Experimental designs in psychotherapy research. In A. Bergin & S. Garfield (Eds.), *Handbook of psychotherapy and behavior change* (pp. 36–74). New York: Wiley.

Krumboltz, J. D. (Ed.) (1966). *Revolution in counseling: Implications of behavioral science.* Boston: Houghton Mifflin.

Krumboltz, J. D. (1968). Future directions for counseling research. In J. Whiteley (Ed.), *Research in counseling.* Columbus, OH: Merrill.

Krumboltz, J., & Mitchell, L. K. (1979). Relevant rigorous research. *The Counseling Psychologist, 8*(3), 50–52.

Lambert, M. J., Shapiro, D. A., & Bergin, A. E. (1986). The effectiveness of psychotherapy. In S. Garfield & A. Bergin (Eds.), *Handbook of psychotherapy and behavior change* (3rd ed., pp. 157–212). New York: Wiley.

Magoon, T. M., & Holland, J. L. (1984). Research training and supervision. In S. Brown & R. Lent (Eds.), *Handbook of counseling psychology* (pp. 682–715). New York: Wiley.

Myers, R. A. (1986). Research on educational and vocational counseling. In S. Garfield & A. Bergin (Eds.), *Handbook of psychotherapy and behavior change* (3rd ed., pp. 715–738). New York: Wiley.

Neimeyer, G., & Resnikoff, A. (1982). Qualitative strategies in counseling research. *The Counseling Psychologist, 10*(4), 75–86.

Oppenheimer, B. T. (1984). Short-term small group intervention for college students. *Journal of Counseling Psychology, 31,* 45–53.

Patton, M. J. (1984). Managing social interaction in counseling: A contribution from the philosophy of science. *Journal of Counseling Psychology, 31*(4), 442–456.

Polkinghorne, D. E. (1984). Further extensions of methodological diversity for counseling research. *Journal of Counseling Psychology, 31,*(4), 416–429.

Pepinsky, H. B., & Pepinsky, P. N. (1954). *Counseling theory and practice.* New York: Ronald Press.

Phillips, S. D., & Bruch, M. A. (1988). Shyness and dysfunction in career development. *Journal of Counseling Psychology, 35,* 159–165.

Rychlak, J. F. (1968). *A Philosophy of science for personality theory.* Boston: Houghton Mifflin.

Scherman, A., & Doan, R. E. (1985). Subjects, designs, and generalizations in Volumes 25–29 of the *Journal of Counseling Psychology. Journal of Counseling Psychology, 32,* 272–276.

Stone, G. L. (1984). In defense of the artificial. *Journal of Counseling Psychology, 31,* 108–110.

Tracey, T. J., Hays, K. A., Malone, J., & Herman, B. (1988). Changes in counselor response as a function of experience. *Journal of Counseling Psychology, 35,* 119–126.

Tunnell, G. B. (1977). Three dimensions of naturalness: An expanded definition of field research. *Psychological Bulletin, 84,* 426–437.

Watkins, C. E., & Terrell, F. (1988). Mistrust level and its effects on counseling expectations in black client–white counselor relationships: An analogue study. *Journal of Counseling Psychology, 35,* 194–197.

Whiteley, J. M. (1984). A historical perspective on the development of counseling psychology as a profession. In S. Brown & R. Lent (Eds.), *Handbook of counseling psychology* (pp. 3–55). New York: Wiley.

Part II

Fundamentals of Counseling and Psychotherapy

Chapter 5

The Therapeutic Relationship

When the beginning student first thinks about what personal counseling or psychotherapy is all about, he or she probably focuses on what psychologists view as technical factors. That is, the student thinks of therapy in terms of the application of psychological techniques and procedures, and he or she also focuses on the idea that these techniques and procedures are applied by an expert. This expert is quite knowing, and has at least a lot of the answers to the client's problems.

The *application of techniques by an expert,* in reality, is only part of what counseling or therapy is. The "other part" of therapy, often the most important part, is what we shall be concerned about in this chapter: *the relationship that develops between the client and counselor.* We shall examine the place of the counselor-client relationship in counseling; just what is meant by a relationship; the components of the therapeutic relationship; the factors that allow for a good relationship; and what are called "facilitative conditions" that, when present to a high degree, appear to promote constructive change in clients.

THE IMPORTANCE OF THE THERAPEUTIC RELATIONSHIP

Human beings are social animals. They live through a series of interrelationships, forming and being formed by interactions with other people. Much of what people come to feel and be is directly and indirectly related to the quality of the associations they have had with others. Much has been

> written about the quality of these formative relationships. If relationships help to form troubled lives (in the natural environment), then new relationships are needed to help change troubled lives. . . . the relationship that develops between patient and psychotherapist can be especially powerful in stimulating personality change. Despite the long history of successful and unsuccessful relationships the patient has had, the relationship that develops with the therapist, *quite apart from the techniques the therapist uses* [italics added], can facilitate the patient's growth. (Lambert, 1983, p. 1)

The above quote is the beginning paragraph of a recent book devoted entirely to the counselor-client relationship, its causes and effects, in a variety of approaches to counseling and therapy. Based on years of both empirical research and counseling experience, nearly all professionals who practice counseling, as well as those who study it, would agree with Lambert's above statement that the counselor-client relationship is very important. Furthermore, many if not most therapists believe that the relationship is the bottom line—the key factor in successful counseling. As Highlen and Hill (1984) have stated in their extensive review of the factors affecting client change in personal counseling: "Certainly everything else that transpires is inextricably embedded in the matrix of this relationship. . . . In order for the counselor to become a potent source of influence in client change, a bond between the participants must be developed. If this solid base is not established, clients will not risk themselves to engage in the 'pain of change'" (pp. 360–361).

Although virtually all practicing counselors would view the relationship as important, there are wide differences of opinion as to just how important it is to successful counseling. Some, such as Highlen and Hill (1984), see the counselor-client relationship as the *sine qua non* of effective intervention. Others go even further. They suggest that not only is the relationship the most important factor in change, but that certain relationship conditions are all that is needed for successful therapy. These conditions are both *necessary and sufficient* for constructive behavior and personality change in a wide range of interventions (see Patterson, 1984).

On the other side of the ledger, there is probably only a handful of therapists, mostly those who align themselves with a radical behaviorism (see Chapter 8), who see the relationship as unimportant. Still, on this same end of the continuum, but a step closer to the middle, some view the counselor-client relationship as important, but running a rather weak second to technical factors, for example, counselor techniques, in terms of what promotes client change. At about the midpoint on this continuum of importance is probably the therapist who views the relationship as very important and who sees a good relationship between therapist and client as a necessary factor for positive change, but not a sufficient factor. Other factors, such as counselor techniques, client characteristics, and so forth, are also important.

As will be discussed later in greater detail, conceptions of the role and importance of the therapeutic relationship seem to follow closely one's theoretical orientation. In terms of *the way in which* the relationship affects clients and client change, Prochaska (1979) suggests that the counselor-client relationship can be seen as (a) one of the *preconditions* for therapy to proceed (as in rational-emotive or perhaps behavior therapy); (b) an *essential process* that itself produces change (as in certain humanistic approaches); or (c) a primary *source of content* to be talked about and processed in therapy (as in most of the psychodynamically oriented approaches). In terms of *importance,* in the humanistically oriented approaches such as person-centered therapy, existential therapy, and gestalt therapy, the relationship is highly central to client change. This is also the case in most of the psychodynamically oriented therapies (e.g., Freudian analysis, neoanalytic approaches, Adlerian therapy). Thus, although the humanistic and psychodynamic therapies work with the counselor-client relationship in different ways, they both view it as deeply important.

In the learning-based approaches (behavior therapy, cognitive therapy, rational-emotive therapy, etc.), on the other hand, views of importance appear to range from those few who contend the relationship to be unimportant to those who see it as moderately important. Some learning-oriented therapists do indeed see the relationship as more central to change than we have implied, but the general tendency is for learning-oriented therapists to view relationship factors as second in importance to counselor techniques. There have, however, been recent changes among learning-oriented counselors regarding conceptions of the therapeutic relationship, and these changes will be examined in Chapter 8.

THE THERAPEUTIC RELATIONSHIP DEFINED

Despite the fact that the relationship has been a key construct in theory, practice, and research for many years, little effort has gone into defining what a therapeutic relationship is, and how relationship factors may be differentiated from nonrelationship factors. The inattention to definition is most surprising on the part of theories placing the relationship at the center of change. For example, in relationship-oriented therapies such as client-centered therapy (now called person-centered therapy; see Chapter 9), no more effort seems to have been put into matters of definition than in other approaches in which the relationship is not so crucial. These relationship approaches most often discuss so-called relationship conditions that are necessary and/or sufficient for positive change to take place. The conditions represent qualities and/or behaviors in the therapist, and the client's role essentially is to perceive or take in the conditions. For example, from the time of Rogers' (1957) famous statement about the necessary and sufficient conditions for positive change in therapy, virtually all client-centered therapists have viewed empathic understanding on the part of the counselor as one of these conditions. Thus, if constructive change is to take place, the counselor must empathically understand the client (as defined later in the chapter), and the client is to perceive the counselor's empathy.

Although therapist-offered conditions may be quite important, perhaps even necessary, they do not help us much in attempting to define what a relationship is and is not. Along with being conditions that contribute to a relationship rather than necessary elements of a relationship, they are one-sided. Therapist-offered conditions minimize the role of the client in the relationship and do not incorporate the reciprocal interaction and influence that must be part of a dyadic relationship.

A definition that does capture the reciprocal nature of relationships has recently been offered by Gelso and Carter (1985). This definition is simple and general: "The relationship *is the feelings and attitudes that counseling participants have toward one another, and the manner in which these are expressed*" (p. 159). In this definition, the techniques used by the counselor that come from his or her theory may be influenced by and influence the relationship, but these techniques do not define the relationship. For example, the interpretations offered by the psychoanalytic therapist are techniques, and they are prescribed by that therapist's theory of counseling (i.e., psychoanalytic theory of therapy). Likewise, when the behavior therapist uses conditioning techniques, we could not say that is the relationship. This therapist is following the dictates of his or her theory of counseling.

Thus, the counseling interaction consists of two elements. The first is the relationship, as defined above. The second is the technical side, consisting of the techniques used by the counselor and the theoretically dictated roles that the counselor and client engage in; for example, in client-centered therapy, the client expresses his or her feelings in the moment, as she or he experiences them, and the counselor seeks to empathically understand the client.

The differentiation between relationship and technical factors in therapy can be useful in helping us understand this highly complex enterprise. Yet, following Gelso and Carter (1985), more often than is probably recognized, relationship factors color and give shape to how technical factors are actualized in counseling. Thus, often subtle feelings and attitudes the counseling participants hold toward one another will strongly influence just how they enact their theoretically prescribed roles.

On the counselor's side, for example, if the counselor is psychoanalytically oriented and thus places a premium on the technique called *interpretation,* how and what that counselor feels toward the client will influence the nature, depth, frequency, length, and content of the interpretations that are offered. Even when the counselor is astute in his or her ability to understand his or her own feelings and not let them interfere with the work, even then these feelings must color the interpretations.

Not only does the relationship influence how the counseling participants enact their theoretically prescribed roles, but these roles also affect the relationship. For example, whether the counselor primarily reflects feelings, interprets, gives advice, or engages in conditioning exercises will each affect the relationship differently. Also, it goes without saying that the *manner* in which these roles are enacted both is affected by the emerging relationship and influences and alters that relationship.

In sum, then, although relationship and technical factors can be thought of as two elements of any therapeutic encounter, the two are highly interdependent. Each affects the other to a marked degree. In terms of the relationship, it often emerges silently, as the participants' feelings and attitudes toward one another develop. The therapist and client each do what they are supposed to do, according to the counselor's theory and the client's needs and compatibility with that theory. Ordinarily, the relationship comes to the fore either when something goes awry (e.g., when negative feelings arise) or when something special happens (e.g., the client feels especially moved by a feeling expressed by the counselor).

In attempting to capture the complexity of the relationship, we conclude this section with a quote from a psychologist who has devoted his career to studying the meanings of therapeutic relationships. In commenting on Gelso and Carter's definition, Barrett-Lennard (1985) provides a discussion that highlights the richness, fluidness, and indeed the elusiveness of the therapist-client relationship:

> One may think of a (dyadic) relationship as being centered on the qualities and contents of experiencing of the two participant individuals with, and toward, one another. This covers a lot of territory but it does not fully encompass the ways in which the participants communicate with each other, the messages that are passed back and forth, the moment-by-moment or generalized image that A has of B's awareness of A, or of B's feeling toward A, and likewise in respect to B's image of A's interperceptions. Neither of these levels fully encompasses "a relationship" as an emergent entity that develops a life and character of its own, existing in intimate *inter*dependence with the single-person components, a "we" in the consciousness of member persons and a distinctive "you" or "they," or the like, as seen from the outside. Any of these levels of relationship can be viewed in terms of what is present or typical at a given time in the life of the relationship, or from a developmental standpoint; and interest may center on the interior process of the relationship,

> or on the ways the relationship system maintains itself or is altered under the influence of external forces. (p. 282)

COMPONENTS OF THERAPEUTIC RELATIONSHIPS

As was the case with defining the relationship, ironically few psychologists have devoted attention to the parts or components into which the relationship might be divided. Perhaps that was so because those who were most concerned with the relationship were, for many years, devoting themselves to the study of the counselor-offered relationship conditions (e.g., empathy, unconditional positive regard, and congruence, as discussed in the latter part of this chapter). Although research on these conditions has been quite fruitful, uncovering many interesting findings, it may have interfered with further theorizing about the relationship.

In any event, from the time of some of Sigmund Freud's early writing (Freud, 1912/1959), at least some psychoanalysts have occupied themselves with theorizing about different dimensions of therapeutic relationships. Although in psychoanalysis the transference element of the relationship has always garnered the greatest interest, from Freud on, a number of analysts have proposed that there is more of interest to analysis than the transference relationship. Freud himself believed that there were two significant components to analytic relationships. The first was the transference proper, or the neurotic transference. This component needed to be analyzed and worked through. Juxtaposed with this neurotic transference, however, were what Freud called the "friendly" and "affectionate" feelings of the analysand toward the analyst. Although these feelings were also part of the transference (i.e., were distortions of the analyst), Freud felt them to be essential to successful analysis. They should not be interpreted to the analysand as transference.

Other psychoanalysts over the years developed formulations about components of the relationship that went beyond or at least were different from the neurotic transference; but it remained for Ralph Greenson (1967) to theorize that analytic relationships could be divided into three parts: the working alliance, the transference proper, and the real relationship. Greenson's writing has had an important impact within psychoanalysis. Recently, Gelso and Carter (1985) extended Greenson's propositions to essentially all theoretical approaches (not only psychoanalysis). In a pantheoretical statement, they proposed that *"all therapeutic relationships consist of these three components [working alliance, transference, real relationship], although the salience and importance of each part during counseling or therapy will vary according to the theoretical perspective of the therapist and the particulars of a given therapy"* (p. 161).

In the remainder of this section we shall examine these three components of therapeutic relationships, drawing heavily on Gelso and Carter's extended discussion and incorporating research findings that have appeared subsequent to that treatise. Before beginning our discussion, it should be underscored that, although we discuss the three components as separate constructs, they are in fact quite interrelated in counseling practice. The way in which they operate together will be explored at the end of this discussion. It should be kept in mind that the three components are seen by Gelso and Carter, and by the present authors, as being applicable to all relationships. They are in no way restricted to psychoanalysis.

The Working Alliance

Perhaps of all the constructs studied in the last few years in counseling and psychotherapy, the working alliance (also labeled *the helping alliance, the working relationship,* and *the therapeutic alliance*) has received the greatest attention. As of this writing, a number of systems and inventories have been developed to measure the alliance (see Alexander & Luborsky, 1986; Horvath & Greenberg, 1986; Marmar, Horowitz, Weiss, & Marziali, 1986), and the emerging research results are quite positive regarding the effects of the working alliance on the process and outcome of different therapies. Many theoreticians and researchers view the working alliance as one of the most promising general constructs in counseling.

What is the working alliance? What are its ingredients? What counselor and client characteristics and behaviors facilitate or inhibit its development? Following Gelso and Carter's thinking, we may consider the working alliance as *the alignment or joining together of the client's reasonable and observing side (the reasonable/observing ego in psychoanalytic terms) with the counselor's working or "therapizing" side (the counselor's observing ego applied to the counseling) for the purpose of facilitating the work of counseling.* This definition is based on the notion that two rather disparate qualities exist in human personality. The first is that which permits us to "stand back" and reasonably observe phenomena, including ourselves, and our own functioning, motives, and feelings. This is the side that could be seen as the reasonable/observing ego. The second quality allows us to experience and feel unreflectively and may be viewed as the experiencing side of the ego or the experiencing ego.

In therapies that may be considered expressive or insight-oriented treatments (e.g., psychodynamic and humanistic therapies), and perhaps in the behavioral and cognitive therapies as well, the client needs to be able to oscillate between the experiencing and observing sides of his or her personality. Thus, the client needs to be able to feel and experience, and then look and reflect upon those feelings and experiences.

Once again, in the working alliance the counselor and client's reasonable sides join together so that each can successfully carry out their roles in the work. Both counselor and client share a reasonable belief that this experience will be worthwhile for the client, and because of this, both are committed to their collaboration in the work.

What makes the working alliance so important? Not only does it reflect the participants' commitment to the work, and an intent to collaborate, but it also is what allows the client to continue in the work during difficult times. For example, if and when the client's defenses and negative transference reactions push him or her in the direction of discontinuing counseling, it is the working alliance that most potently aids the client to stand back from these feelings and recognize them as defensively based. Thus, although the alliance is always important during the counseling experience, it is especially important during difficult times between the counselor and client.

Probably the most seminal theoretical statement about the working alliance as it operates across diverse forms of psychotherapy has been offered by Edward Bordin (1979). Bordin proposes that the alliance consists of three parts: agreement between counselor and client on the goals of counseling, agreement about the tasks of the work, and the emotional bond that forms between the participants. Agreement on goals implies that the participants share the goals of the work, regardless of whether this agreement is explicitly stated or indeed whether the goals themselves are explicitly stated. Agreement on tasks implies that therapist and client also share a common view of how those goals may best be attained. Here it is important to understand that Bordin is not talking about tasks as structured work tasks. Rather, he is referring to any of the in-therapy or extra-therapy role behaviors expected of the participants. For example, in most forms of therapy an expected client task is for that client to talk about himself or herself and to express feelings. In analysis, the in-therapy task is for the analysand to free-associate, whereas in more structural treatments, a frequent task is for the client to carry out homework assignments. In any event, if the alliance is to be strong, client and counselor need to have sound agreements on the value of the main tasks of a given therapy. Last but not least, there needs to be an attachment between counselor and client if the alliance is to be strong.

In our way of thinking about working alliance, agreement on tasks and goals, and bonding, contribute to the strength of the alliance. In turn, the strength of the alliance facilitates agreement on tasks and goals as well as emotional attachment. Thus, there is a reciprocal causal relationship between alliance and the three dimensions discussed by Bordin. Implicit in this reciprocal relationship is the fact that the working alliance exists on a continuum, ranging from weak or nonexistent to very strong. Relatedly, bonding and agreement on tasks and goals also exist on continua, varying in the same way as does the working alliance.

As should be clear by now, the working alliance is interactive in that both the counselor and the client contribute to it. Regarding the counselor's contribution, we would expect a number of qualities and behaviors to be important. The counselor's professional concern, compassion, and willingness to persist in the work seem highly pertinent. Also, the well-known "facilitative conditions" of empathic understanding, unconditional positive regard, and congruence (to be discussed in detail later in this chapter) would appear to be vital to a strong alliance. Just as is the case with the client, if the alliance is to be strong, the counselor must make use of his or her reasonable or observing side so that the feelings he or she experiences toward the client may be appropriately used. Counselors experience a range of emotional reactions to clients, and it is imperative that we use our reasonable/observing capacities to understand these reactions. Then, as a bottom line, we must try to use our emotional reactions in the service of the client, to the client's benefit, and not in antitherapeutic ways.

In terms of the client's contribution to the working alliance, probably the most essential feature is a capacity to trust. Without this, there can be no healthy bonding, no positive attachment. As uncovered in a recent study by Gaston, Marmar, Thompson, and Gallagher (1988), client defensiveness or resistance tends to negatively affect the alliance, at least in brief therapy (analytic, behavioral, and cognitive) with depressed elderly patients. Perhaps most basically, though, the client must have a strong enough, reasonable, observing side, or ego, to allow him or her to stand back and observe what is transpiring in him or her and in the work.

Gelso and Carter present a number of theoretical propositions aimed at furthering research on the working alliance. Their long article, along with the five reaction papers following it, should be consulted by the reader who is interested in studying this construct further. In terms of research support, probably the clearest finding at this early stage of empirical investigation is that *the strength of alliance, as measured within the first few sessions of counseling or therapy, is related to a wide variety of measures of outcome. The stronger the alliance in the first few sessions the more positive are the results of counseling.* This finding appears quite robust, as it holds up for both brief and longer-term therapy, for counseling from a range of theoretical perspectives (analytic, behavioral, cognitive, humanistic, gestalt, etc.), and with several different types of alliance measures (Adler, 1988; Horvath & Greenberg, 1986; Luborsky, Crits-Cristoph, Alexander, Margolis, & Cohen, 1983; Marmar, Gaston, Gallagher, & Thompson, 1987).

In sum, the findings do appear to support the proposition that it is quite important to establish a sound working alliance very early in counseling. This formation of an early alliance is especially important in briefer counseling, in which the counselor does not have the luxury of time to devote to the gradual cultivation of an alliance. Based on the authors' counseling experience, we would go even further and suggest that the greatest attention needs to be given to promoting this aspect of the total relationship, for, without an alliance, it is hard to imagine the work of therapy being done with much ultimate effectiveness.

Just what constitutes a sound or sufficiently strong working alliance may depend on a host of factors. For example, interventions that are more emotionally demanding upon the client may require a stronger alliance than less demanding treatments. Also, the alliance may need to be especially strong during certain critical points in the therapy, for example, when negative transference or certain resistances threaten the work or when the client feels particularly vulnerable. Finally, certain aspects of the alliance may need to be stronger at certain times in the work. An example of the latter may be that early in the work the agreement on tasks may be essential, whereas later in the counseling the bonding aspect may be more important.

In summary, although the concept of an alliance has been in the counseling literature for many years, it is not until relatively recent times (the late 1970s and especially the 1980s) that hypotheses about its operation in a variety of forms of therapy have been offered and empirically tested. Much remains to be done, however. The topic of the working alliance is, at this time, one of the most fertile ones in counseling psychology for empirical investigation and sound theory development. It is also a construct that is highly relevant to counseling psychology practice.

The Transference Configuration

The second component of the therapeutic relationship that will be discussed has historically been embedded in psychoanalytic theory. Indeed, many consider the discovery of transference to be Freud's most significant achievement, and modern psychoanalysis is defined by many as the systematic analysis of the transferences (see Chapter 9).

Despite its centrality in psychoanalytic theory, one may consider transference (and countertransference) to be a part of all therapeutic encounters, and to be a component of all therapeutic relationships. In fact, as Freud (1912/1959) clearly formulated, transference can be seen as occurring in all human relationships. It is a natural human tendency that becomes magnified and intensified in therapeutic relationships because of the nature of such relationships. That is, because therapeutic interactions focus on help giving, with one person seeking to provide conditions for psychological growth in another, the tendency to experience and manifest transference reactions becomes heightened.

Just what is transference? Despite the great complexity of this construct, two basic conceptions may be educed from the literature. The first is the classical Freudian view. In that view, transference is seen as the reliving of Oedipal issues in the therapy relationship. The therapist is reacted to as if he or she were any or all of the participants in the client's early Oedipal situation, most often the client's mother and/or father. Because of the exclusive focus on the Oedipal context, this definition is quite narrow and restrictive, and of course requires that the therapist share the psychoanalytic view of the critical importance of the Oedipus complex in human development.

In viewing transference as a component of all therapeutic relationships, a broader conception of this construct is in order. In this broader conception, transference may be defined as *a repetition of past conflicts with significant others such that feelings, behaviors, and attitudes belonging rightfully in those earlier relationships are displaced onto the counselor or therapist.* To the extent that the client's reactions to the counselor are transference-based, the client is responding to the counselor *as if* the counselor represented aspects of the transference source, for example, mother, father, sibling. It is important to understand that the client does not really think or believe that the therapist *is* mother, father, or sibling when transference reactions are occurring. Rather, the client transfers significant aspects of the parents' reactions toward him or her from earlier times onto the therapist, such that the therapist is erroneously assumed to be exhibiting those reactions (motives, attitudes, feelings, etc.).

In transference situations such as those discussed above, the client may react to the therapist as if the therapist does not like him or her, is being critical, will abandon him or her, is not trustworthy, is perfect, is wonderful, and so on. In other words, an almost infinite array of affects, characteristics, motives, and behaviors may be attributed to the counselor erroneously. Inspection of these client perceptions, sometimes over long periods of time, usually reveals them to be displacements from earlier significant relationships. Examples of transference reactions from cases actually worked with by one of the authors are given below.

■ *Case 1:* Over many sessions, this client felt sure that the therapist could give her solutions to her life problems, which in fact were profound. She felt that the therapist really knew the solutions but was withholding them. He was not giving her her fair share—what she deserved to have. Because of this she experienced a chronic sense of deep anger toward the therapist. During one session in which she angrily criticized and pleaded with the therapist to "tell her," he pointed out the bitterness in her request and how her feelings must echo feelings from long ago. She responded by tearfully expressing how she never got her share from her parents, how she was never taken care of. This interaction was a critical step in the work toward her coming to understand her transference and work through the conflicts underlying them. ■

■ *Case 2:* Despite the fact that the client experienced the therapist's empathy and concern in an ongoing way, during periods of the work he responded to the therapist as a critical, demanding, and deeply attacking figure. The sound working alliance and the client's strong observing ego helped him stand back from these feelings and come to grips with where they were coming from. A good bit of the work centered on the client's conflicts with a highly critical, demanding father, and the effects of this relationship on his self-concept and relationships with others. ■

■ *Case 3:* During the early weeks of a long counseling experience, this client, among other things, could never break silences by offering new material. Her mind would go blank. She feared and fully expected that the therapist would feel critical of her initiating new topics and of any material she might initiate, despite the reality of the treatment situation; that is, her initiation was welcomed. A significant portion of the counseling focused on this client's injurious relationship with her mother, a deeply narcissistic woman who had few boundaries, and whose needs this client had to constantly attend to. In close relationships, this client consistently carried with her a sense that the only way she could be cared about was if she, in effect, denied any of her needs and attended to the other's. She became a stranger to her own needs, and much of the counseling aimed at helping her learn about what she wanted and needed, and psychically disengage from the often unconscious entanglement with mother. ■

Just as in all counseling relationships, in these three cases there were many transference elements. We have presented what may be seen as single "strands" of these transferences so as to clarify how transference reactions may occur in counseling. As a way of further clarifying this complex concept, the following rules of thumb about transference may be useful.

1. *Transference is always an error.* By definition, the perceptions the client has of the counselor, when transference-based, are erroneous. They represent displacements that were appropriate (not an error) to other relationships, from another time and place. It needs to be stated here that by no means are all perceptions the client has of the counselor erroneous, nor are all emotional reactions clients have toward their counselors based on misperceptions. It is important for the counselor to understand which reactions are realistic and which are based on transference.
2. *Transference may be positive or negative.* The misperceptions that are part of transference reactions are just as likely to be positive as

negative. Thus the client may project positive attitudes into the counselor, based on needs tied to past conflictual relationships, for example, because of the client's deprivations with a parent, she or he may need to see the counselor as more loving or powerful than is realistically the case. Because counselors' feelings are most often positive, and because the counseling role is a positive one, positive transferences are often more difficult to appreciate *as transferences* than are negative transferences.

3. *The emergence of transference in the counseling is facilitated by the therapist's neutrality and ambiguity.* The concept of neutrality is one of the most misunderstood in all of the psychotherapy and counseling literature. By neutrality we do not mean bland indifference or lack of caring. Instead we refer to the therapist's not taking sides and not imposing his or her values and beliefs on the client. Ambiguity is a similar but not identical concept. It refers to the tendency not to present a clear picture of one's feelings, life, and attitudes; and counselors as well as theoretical approaches to counseling vary widely in the extent to which they endorse the concept of ambiguity.

   In any event, it is generally agreed that counselor ambiguity and neutrality create an environment in which transference is more likely to develop and emerge fully. This is not to say that transference does not occur in active therapies, where the therapist is very open about his or her values and may take sides. It occurs there, too; but ambiguity and neutrality allow it to develop and come into the open more fully and in a way that many counselors believe to be less "contaminated" (by the reality of the counselor). It must be added that the extent to which transference *should* be encouraged to develop and emerge is not nearly agreed upon by counselors. As shall be seen in Chapters 7, 8, and 9, theories vary widely on this point.

4. *Transference is not conscious.* Although the client's feelings toward the counselor may be fully conscious, the fact that they are displacements from other, earlier relationships is not. Some approaches to counseling (especially the psychodynamically based ones) seek to make them conscious, with the aim of resolving or correcting transference distortions.

5. *Transferences are most likely to occur in areas of greatest unresolved conflict with significant others earlier in one's life.* The final rule of thumb implies that humans are more likely to misperceive the present based on the past (i.e., erroneously project the past into the present) in areas in which there were significant unresolved

> conflicts in past important relationships. Thus, for example, if a central area of unresolved conflict in one's childhood had to do with dependency, issues around dependency are likely to be evidenced in the transference relationship with the therapist.

It should be reiterated that what we have presented above are rules of thumb about the operation of transference in counseling and therapy. Some of these are a basic part of the definition of transference (e.g., it is always an error, it is not conscious); others have never been tested in a rigorous scientific manner. The concept of transference (and countertransference, as will be discussed next) is one of the most complex in psychology today, and it has been extremely difficult to develop methods of studying it scientifically. That is because theoretical propositions that incorporate unconscious processes are not easily tested with traditional scientific methods. Only in recent years have some sound procedures been developed and used (see examples in Luborsky, 1984; Weiss & Sampson, 1986). Unfortunately, however, because the concept of transference historically has been embedded in psychoanalysis, nearly all the research has focused on its operation in psychoanalysis or analytic therapy. Given our proposition that the transference configuration is a component of all therapies, more research should be conducted on hypotheses about transference as it operates across diverse forms of therapy. Such work is now in its infancy. (See, for example, Gelso, Hill, & Kivlighan, 1991.)

How does transference operate in different forms of therapy? How is it handled and how should it be dealt with by the counselor? We refer the reader to subsequent chapters of this book (Chapters 7, 8, and 9) and to Gelso and Carter (1985) for detailed discussion of these complex questions. For now, suffice it to say that, although we propose that transference is a component of the therapy relationship in all forms of counseling, some approaches more than others provide conditions allowing the transference to develop more fully, and then work with these reactions with the aim of helping the client gain insight into them. Generally, the psychoanalytically based approaches do this. Other approaches pay less attention to transference.

In general, transference will develop and become manifest to a greater extent in therapies that view it as central and aim to work with transference reactions. At the same time, there is evidence that it does occur even in therapies in which it is viewed as unimportant (see studies by Rhoads & Feather, 1972, and Ryan & Gizynski, 1971, regarding the operation of transference in behavior therapy). Counselors of all theoretical persuasions should be trained at least to recognize signs of transference and to deal with transference issues when they are interfering with progress. As Gelso and Carter (1985) discuss, therapists can do this and still remain faithful to the theoretical approaches they are practicing. For example, the behavior therapist can help the client understand transference difficulties that are negatively affecting the counseling, without violating any principles of behavior therapy.

Countertransference: The Counselor's Transference. Given that the client-counselor relationship is a two-way street, involving contributions from both participants, it is important to look at the counselor's contributions to the transference configuration. As implied earlier, the counselor can behave in ways that evoke certain transference reactions, and in this way the counselor will contribute to the client's transference. But it is important to note that the counselor also contributes his or her own transference reactions, and these are called countertransference.

Just as we propose that client transference occurs in all therapy, so too is countertransference seen as universal. No matter how emotionally mature the counselor, and how effectively he or she has overcome inevitable conflicts, the counselor is a human being, and as such will have areas of unresolved conflict. These sore spots contain the issues that are likely to develop into countertransference reactions. This occurs when material presented by the client touches areas of unresolved conflict in the counselor.

The above discussion may seem to imply that there is some agreed-upon definition of countertransference. Actually, this construct has been one of the most confused and confusing ones in the history of psychology (and of psychoanalysis). A wide array of definitions can be found in the literature. These range from the broadest one, called the *totalistic* definition, to the narrowest one, called the *classical* definition. The totalistic definition of countertransference views this phenomenon as including virtually all of the counselor's emotional reactions to the client. Thus, realistic reactions, not based on particular conflicts within the counselor, will be seen as countertransference, just as will conflict-based reactions.

The classical definition of countertransference is the "counselor's transference to the client's transference." This is very narrow in that only client transference reactions, and not reactions that are nontransferential, can be the trigger for countertransference. An intermediate definition may be the most useful one. Countertransference can thus be defined as *the counselor's transference to the client's material—to the transference and nontransference communications presented by the client.* As Langs (1974) suggests, countertransference may be seen as "one aspect of those responses to the patient which, while prompted by some event within the therapy or the therapist's real life, are primarily based on his past significant relationships; basically they gratify his needs rather than the patient's therapeutic endeavors" (p. 298).

Is countertransference therapeutic or antitherapeutic? Does it hinder or help progress in counseling? The answers to these questions depend upon whether countertransference is considered an overt behavior or an internal experience in the counselor. Earlier writing, usually in psychoanalysis, appeared to focus on external behavior, what the analyst *did* with the client based on internal conflicts in the work. When viewed as an external behavior, countertransference is something to be controlled and ideally to be worked through, because it is important that therapists not act out their own conflicts with and on their clients.

In recent times, countertransference has more often been viewed as an internal experience in the counselor (Giovachinni, 1975; Epstein & Feiner, 1979). When seen in this way, if properly handled, countertransference can be extremely helpful to counseling. (See empirical studies by Peabody & Gelso, 1982, and Robbins & Jolkovski, 1987.) For example, if the counselor uses his or her internal countertransference-based experiences to better understand the impact of the client on him or her and on others, this can greatly benefit the work. This requires that the counselor, in fact, be willing to focus on his or her feelings toward the client when these are experienced as conflictual. It also requires that the counselor is willing and able to try to understand where these feelings come from in his or her own life, a task that can be anxiety-provoking but extremely important.

In summary, like transference, countertransference is seen as a component of all therapy relationships. The countertransference experience can be for better or worse, depending on the counselor's willingness to inspect his or her own experience, and the roots of his or her conflict-based reactions to clients. Unfortunately, also just as with transference, empirical research on countertransference has been sparse. There is, however, at least one systematic review of the clinical and empirical research literature on countertransference (Singer & Luborsky, 1977), and some recent empirical efforts in counseling psychology (Hayes & Gelso, 1991; Peabody & Gelso, 1982; Robbins & Jolkovski, 1987). This is only a beginning; a great deal more research is needed on this construct.

The Real Relationship

Coexisting in an interrelated way with the working alliance and transference components of the counseling relationship is a third component. Gelso and Carter (1985) label this the "real relationship," following the lead of psychoanalyst Ralph Greenson (1967). Although we will use the term *real relationship,* this term can be confusing, implying as it does that relationships vary in how "real" they are. All relationships are of course real ones in the sense that they actually exist; and it is probably safe to say that none exists any more than others.

The construct of "real relationship" is conceptualized as having two main defining features: genuineness and realistic perceptions. Counseling relationships would rate high on the real-relationship component if both participants were highly genuine and perceived each other in a realistic (undistorted) way. Conversely, lack of genuineness and realistic perceptions would make for a low rating on this component.

The concept of genuineness has been a central one in counseling and therapy for many years, especially in the humanistic therapies (e.g., person-centered, gestalt). When genuineness is discussed in the counseling literature, what is usually being referred to is the *therapist's* genuineness; and, especially in the humanistic approaches, therapist genuineness is seen as an important facilitative factor.

What is meant by *genuineness?* We define it as the ability and willingness to be what one truly is in the relationship, to be honest, open, and authentic. As noted above, the counseling literature has tended to focus on therapist genuineness, and in this sense has neglected the fact that the relationship goes two ways. In order for the relationship to be high in genuineness, both parties must be open, honest, and authentic, or at least they must work to express these qualities with each other. As Greenberg (1985) puts it, in a genuine relationship, the two participants in the counseling situation are "stubbornly attempting to dispense with appearances and reveal themselves as they truly are in the moment" (p. 254). Along a similar vein, a relationship that is highly genuine would tend to be what is often described as an *I-thou relationship.* To follow Greenberg's thinking further, the genuine involvement in an I-thou relationship is seen as "the attempt for people to break down barriers between inside and outside, between image and experience, and to communicate intimately their moment-to-moment inner experience" (p. 254).

Because the counselor and client's roles are different ones in the relationship, however, their expression of genuineness is quite different. From the client's side, he or she is expected to try to express feelings, thoughts, and inner experience essentially at all times, although it is of course not expected that the client will always be successful at accurately expressing these inner qualities. In this sense, though, the client is expected to be genuine, or struggle to be so, throughout the work.

The counselor's contribution to a genuine relationship is more complicated than is the client's role. No approach to counseling and therapy would advise the counselor to say whatever is on his mind, and express or act out his or her feelings unreflectively. Relatedly, Greenberg (1985) points out that: "The relationship is therefore not a strictly mutual I-thou relationship in which the counselor is equally acknowledged and confirmed by the client in an ongoing fashion" (p. 255). Greenberg refers to philosopher Martin Buber's (1958) famous book on the I-thou relationship, and cites Buber's term, "one-sided inclusion," as fitting counseling relationships because of the different roles. Thus, one can have an I-thou relationship in counseling, but it is different from the ordinary I-thou relationship. The counselor puts many of his or her needs aside and is in the service of the client's needs and growth for the time of the work. Returning to the issue of genuineness, the extent to which and ways in which the counselor should be open, honest, and authentic must depend upon what is best for a given client at a given point in the work. In this sense, the counselor must practice a kind of "controlled spontaneity"—expressing what he or she feels, what is on his or her mind, after reflecting on what is best for the client and deciding that expression of this feeling would be appropriate.

In summary, the counselor spends much of the time in counseling paying attention to the client and his or her expressions and commenting on these. The counselor thinks about what is going on in the work, in the client, in himself or herself, and in the relationship. At certain points the counselor may express his or her emotions and feelings toward and about the client. It must be emphasized, however, that our comments do not imply that the counselor ought to be *disingenuous* or dishonest at any point. Although whether and how particular feelings ought to be directly expressed is open to debate, we would contend that there is no place in counseling for counselor dishonesty or disingenuousness.

The second aspect of the real relationship is *realistic perceptions.* Here the participants perceive each other in a realistic and accurate way, undistorted by transference experiences or other defenses. From the first moment of contact, at least some of the therapeutic relationship contains such realistic perceptions on the part of *both* client and counselor. We emphasize the term *both* here because some theoretical approaches (particularly the psychoanalytically based ones) appear to imply that, whereas the therapist's perceptions may be mostly realistic from the beginning of the work, all or nearly all of the client's perceptions are transference-based. On the contrary, not only does the client perceive or "subceive" aspects of the counselor realistically, but this realistic or accurate picture builds and increases throughout the work. Relatedly, as transference distortions are worked through (whether or not they are interpreted to the client as such), realistic perceptions take their place, at least in part.

Even counselors who practice the "blank screen" notion of counseling (discussed in Chapter 7), in the sense of being highly ambiguous about themselves and their personal opinions, communicate their personhood in numerous ways—from their office decor to their attire and general appearance to their sense of humor to the questions they ask, and so forth. And even clients with very strong transference proclivities and tendencies to distort will be able to perceive the counselor realistically to an extent.

How important is it for the relationship to be on the positive side (characterized by highly genuine and realistic perceptions on the part of both participants) of a real-relationship continuum? All forms of therapy would probably advocate that the therapist perceive the client realistically (e.g., undistorted by countertransference reactions and other personal needs). Virtually all would want the client to perceive the counselor accurately or, more importantly, to be moving in the direction of accurate perception. Similarly, client genuineness would be seen as a plus in virtually all approaches. The most controversial element, though, is counselor genuineness. The when, how, and to-what-extent of counselor genuineness varies significantly across therapies, as shall be discussed in greater detail later in the book. At the same time, no theory suggests that the counselor wear a professional facade that misrepresents who he or she is as a person.

What does research tell us about the real relationship in counseling? The answer to that is simple: no research exists on this construct as such. Thinking about components of a therapeutic relationship is very recent, and it has been only a few years since Gelso and Carter discussed the real relationship as it operates across different forms of counseling. At the same time, there is a great deal of research on one of the elements of the real relationship: therapist genuineness. This shall be discussed in the next section on therapist facilitative conditions. For in-depth reviews of the empirical research on therapist genuineness, among other therapist factors in counseling, the reader is referred to papers by Beutler, Crago, and Arizmendi (1986) and Orlinsky and Howard (1986).

A Perspective on Relationship Components

We noted in the beginning of this section that the three components of the therapeutic relationship are interrelated in practice. We shall now conclude this section by discussing how they are interrelated and how they might be expected to operate together in counseling.

Early in counseling, the working alliance is especially important. The reasonable sides of the counselor and client will need to join together, to bond, so that the value of working together can be appreciated, and emotional threats to the emerging relationship can be looked at without destroying what has begun to build. The counselor and client must also come to agree, implicitly or explicitly, on the goals and tasks of counseling, as discussed earlier. Utmost attention needs to be given to the cultivation of this alliance early in counseling. Initial positive transference and a positive real relationship aid considerably in alliance development. Even though transference reactions are displacements from earlier relationships (i.e., errors, as described earlier), if they are positive, they can help create warm, friendly feelings that serve to solidify the working bond between counseling participants. In a like manner, if each participant feels positively toward the other, who is seen realistically and who has genuinely expressed himself or herself, the working alliance will be strengthened. In this way, genuine and realistic caring, which itself creates and is part of a personal, emotional bond, also furthers the working bond of the alliance.

In turn, when the working alliance is sound, the client is able to experience negative feelings toward the counselor in the transference relationship, without these feelings injuring the work. In fact, the strength of the alliance allows one to work through the negative transferences and thus further strengthen the total relationship. On the other hand, when negative transference develops early in the work and before a strong working alliance has had a chance to develop, it is important, perhaps essential, that these feelings be explored and their transference roots uncovered. Without this, the alliance may be irreparably damaged by the negative transference, and the relationship may end or stagnate. (See Horwitz's 1974 examination of such phenomena based on a 20-year process outcome study done at the Menninger Clinic.)

As counselor and client continue to work together and their alliance strengthens, we would expect the real relationship to strengthen. The client is able to be increasingly genuine and to perceive the counselor more realistically. The working alliance facilitates this and thus is a factor in the strengthening of the real relationship, just as the real relationship affects the working alliance.

What is the developmental course of the three components during counseling? As indicated earlier, the working alliance is most salient early in the relationship. After the early phase, when it becomes established to a satisfactory degree, the alliance tends to fade into the background (see Hartley & Strupp, 1982), only coming to the fore when needed, for example, when the relationship is threatened by negative feelings that may result from transference. The real relationship, on the other hand, may well build throughout the relationship, becoming most salient in the later phases of the work, when the participants come to know each other most deeply, have become increasingly genuine, and perceive each other most realistically. Transference continues throughout counseling, but is increasingly understood by the client (Graff & Luborsky, 1977; Luborsky, 1985), at least in therapies that focus on these transference reactions. In therapies that do not, we would expect the transferences to become less salient as other phenomena are attended to—unless these transferences are injurious to the work. In such cases, they need to be dealt with and resolved, or the effects can be irreparably damaging.

In summary, each component of the counseling relationship develops in its own way, although each is also interdependent on the others. Additional theory and some beginning research are needed to further our understanding of the course of development of the various components in both successful and unsuccessful counseling.

FACILITATIVE CONDITIONS AND THE COUNSELING RELATIONSHIP

At several points in this chapter reference has been made to therapist-offered conditions, necessary and sufficient conditions, and relationship conditions. All of these references pertain to a set of conditions initially formulated over thirty years ago by Carl R. Rogers (1957), the founder of client-centered therapy, which is now known as *person-centered therapy* (see Chapter 7). Rogers' original theoretical statement was one of the most influential in the history of counseling psychology. It has generated a great deal of research and had a profound effect on counseling practice. In this section of Chapter 5 we shall explore the major conditions proposed by Rogers in some detail, as these conditions are crucial to the counselor-client relationship as defined earlier.

As a preface to his famous statement, Rogers asked, "Is it possible to state, in terms which are clearly definable and measurable, the psychological conditions that are *both necessary and sufficient* [italics added] to bring about constructive personality change?" (1957, p. 95) Rogers answered his question by stating the following six conditions:

> 1. Two persons are in psychological contact.
> 2. The first, whom we shall term the client, is in a state of incongruence, being vulnerable or anxious.
> 3. The second person, whom we shall term the therapist, is congruent or integrated in the relationship.
> 4. The therapist experiences unconditional positive regard for the client.
> 5. The therapist experiences an empathic understanding of the client's internal frame of reference and endeavors to communicate this experience to the client.
> 6. The communication to the client of the therapist's empathic understanding and unconditional positive regard is to a minimal degree achieved.
>
> *No other conditions are necessary. If these six conditions exist, and continue over a period of time, this is sufficient. The process of constructive personality change will follow.* (p. 96; italics added)

According to these conditions, the client needs to be in contact with the counselor and needs to be in a state (i.e., incongruence, anxiety, vulnerability) that makes him receptive to help. The client also must perceive or take in what the counselor has to offer. Despite the importance of these client contributions, though, the features of Rogers' statement that have been given the greatest attention over the years are 3, 4, and 5 above, the three therapist-offered conditions. As implied in Rogers' own work, as well as the research of many others, the three therapist-offered conditions, or the relationship conditions, constitute the bulk of his theoretical statement.

Before discussing each of the three conditions, we should clarify our use of the term *facilitative conditions.* Much of the research evidence suggests that the therapist-offered conditions are not sufficient (see reviews by Beutler et al., 1986; Gurman, 1977) for positive counseling outcomes in many or most cases. In other words, more is needed than just these three conditions (or even the six conditions originally specified by Rogers). Also, evidence suggests that these conditions are best not viewed as necessary, as it is conceivable that at least some clients in some kinds of counseling treatment change positively when these therapist-offered conditions are only present to a minimal degree. Yet, as will be elaborated later in the chapter, it appears that these conditions do in most cases facilitate positive change and are important for change. Thus, the conditions discussed below are labeled facilitative conditions, although they are viewed as unnecessary in some cases and certainly not sufficient in most.

Empathic Understanding

Of the three facilitative conditions, that which has the greatest appeal theoretically and clinically, and which probably has received the greatest amount of empirical support in terms of being associated with positive counseling outcomes (Orlinsky & Howard, 1986), is empathic understanding. Indeed, it is hard to envision effective counseling if the counselor is not able to empathize with the client and his or her issues. Therapists from virtually every theoretical orientation have noted the importance of empathy. (See, for example, Kohut's 1984 in-depth discussion of the importance of empathy in psychoanalysis, and Deffenbacher's 1985 discussion of its role in cognitive-behavior therapy.)

In describing his view of empathy, Rogers (1957) tells us:

> To sense the client's private world as if it were your own, but without ever losing the "as if" quality—this is empathy, and this seems essential to therapy. To sense the client's anger, fear, or confusion as if it were your own, yet without your own anger, fear, or confusion getting bound up in it, is the condition we are attempting to describe. When the client's world is this clear to the therapist, and he moves about in it freely, then he can communicate his understanding of what is clearly known to the client and can also voice meanings in the client's experience of which the client is scarcely aware. (p. 98)

Shortly after Rogers' seminal statement, G. T. Barrett-Lennard (1962), who had studied with Rogers, published an inventory that sought to measure empathic understanding and the other therapist-offered conditions from the vantage point of the client receiving counseling. Over the years, Barrett-Lennard has done careful and important research on the *Relationship Inventory* (RI) and revised it several times (see Barrett-Lennard, 1986). Because of that, the RI continues to be the most effective method of measuring the facilitative conditions in a manner that is true to Rogers' theory. Some items from the RI will help clarify the meaning of empathy. Pluses indicate high, and minuses low, empathy.

(+) He appreciates exactly how the things I experience feel to me
(−) He may understand my words but doesn't see the way I feel
(+) He usually understands the whole of what I mean
(−) Sometimes he thinks *I* feel a certain way, because that's the way he feels
(+) He realizes what I mean even when I have difficulty saying it

In his initial definition and many of his subsequent writings (e.g., Rogers, 1975), Rogers stressed that empathy and the other conditions were *attitudes and subjective experiences with the therapist.* Yet, as Hackney (1978) notes, over the years a shift occurred in how empathy was viewed. More and more it came to be seen as a communication *skill* and less and less as a subjective experience that could be expressed by the therapist in a variety of ways. Increasing stress was placed upon the idea that empathy was observable, measurable, and readily trainable—that is, often requiring only a few hours of training (see Carkhuff, 1969; Truax & Carkhuff, 1967). What Rogers and many others (see Bozarth, 1984) had seen as "a way of being" was reduced and narrowed to a trainable skill.

As part of this development, it appeared that empathy became almost equated with the counseling *technique* called *reflection of feeling,* the technique in which the counselor paraphrases or reflects back to the client the feelings involved in what the client has just communicated (see Chapter 6). Bozarth (1984) points out that many in the counseling field came to believe that reflection of feeling *is* empathy and empathy *is* reflection of feeling.

Although the technique of reflection may aid the counselor in expressing his or her empathy, equating the two oversimplifies and excessively narrows the concept of empathy. In his thoughtful clarification of why empathy and reflection must be differentiated, Bozarth (1984) presents the following multiple-choice item, asking his reader to indicate which statement is the most empathic: (1) I'm having strong sexual feelings toward you; (2) When I took my Volkswagen engine out, the car rolled down the hill, hit the rabbit pen, etc., etc.; (3) You feel as though you have lost contact with the physical world. The third response is a standard reflection of feeling, but Bozarth presents compelling case data to show how alternatives 1 and 2 were highly empathic. For example, in alternative 2, the client experienced an intense and painful communication block in one session. She began the next session by asking the therapist, "What have you been doing?" He responded by telling her a nearly session-long story about his car. She later expressed appreciation that the therapist did not try to force her to reconfront her struggle; she needed a respite from it. She also described how the session helped her identify the core of her difficulties.

The above shows how nonreflective responses can be empathic. On the other side of the ledger, reflections, even accurate ones, may signify a lack of empathy. One of the authors vividly recalls an instance when a colleague accurately reflected another colleague's underlying feelings during a meeting, resulting in the recipient tearfully and, to her, shamefully breaking down. This colleague, at that time, neither needed nor wanted someone to illuminate her underlying feelings, and doing so was a deeply unempathic act, although it entailed an accurate reflection of feeling.

There are many ways in which one can become empathic. As Hackney (1978) recommends, the counselor needs to "experience the feeling, first, comprehend it as best you can, then react to it" (p. 37). Modes of being empathic can and should be based on who the therapist is as a person, who the client is as a person, the therapist-client interactions, and probably some other factors. In essence, according to Bozarth (1984), what is needed is *idiosyncratic empathy* in which the empathy that is subjectively experienced is expressed in a way that fits the counseling participants and their relationship. Numerous responses (silence, reflection of feeling, interpretation, storytelling, etc.) may express empathy.

Before leaving our discussion of empathic understanding, we should note two recent and important developments in research and theory on this construct. The first development is that empathy is increasingly being viewed as a multistage process (Barrett-Lennard, 1981, 1986; Gladstein, 1983). Gladstein points out that several conceptualizations of empathy seem to include some common stages. First, empathy is experienced emotionally, through a process of identification with the client. This is not complete identification. Rather, it is a process in which the counselor to some extent experiences what the client feels and yet maintains the necessary separateness. Second, there is cognitive activity, in which the counselor consciously sifts through the client's expressions and considers their meanings to the client. Third, in Rogers' (1975) and Barrett-Lennard's (1986) conceptualizations, there is a communication of that empathy to the client; and, as discussed above, this communication may take many forms. Finally, there exists the client's "sense and perception of the degree to which the therapist is attuned and actually 'with' him, or her, in immediate personal understanding" (Barrett-Lennard, 1986, p. 446). As further noted by Barrett-Lennard, it is useful to conceptualize the stages of empathy as recycling throughout the counseling encounter.

The second recent development in research and theory on empathic understanding has been the growing awareness that there are different kinds of empathy. In an important contribution, Gladstein (1983) has reviewed empathy literature from social, developmental, and counseling psychology and has concluded that in each of these fields basically two kinds of empathy are discussed, each with significantly different implications for counseling. The first is *affective* empathy, in which the counselor identifies with the client and, essentially, *feels* what the client feels. The second type is *cognitive* empathy, in which the counselor "takes in" the client's perspective and *comprehends* what the client feels.

Gladstein (1983) presents a thoughtful discussion of how each of these types of empathy may or may not be helpful, depending upon what the goals of counseling are, what stage the counseling is in, and what the client's preferences are in the relationship. The key point is that certain kinds of empathy may be helpful or not helpful, and that simple statements about how empathy helps are not sufficient.

Finally, awareness that empathy is a multistage process and that there may be different types of empathy may help resolve one of the most confusing and disturbing findings in the empathy literature. A number of studies have noted that different measures of empathy are modestly related to one another, at best. Although puzzling at first glance, this finding makes sense because the various measures are tapping different aspects and stages of empathy. Thus, one would not expect them to be highly interrelated (see Barrett-Lennard, 1981; Gladstein, 1983).

Unconditional Positive Regard

Of the three facilitative conditions, unconditional positive regard is the most controversial, and perhaps also the most complex. At various points in the history of this construct, it has been viewed as synonymous with any and all of the following terms: warmth, nonpossessive warmth, acceptance, unconditional acceptance, respect, regard, and caring.

In Rogers' (1957) original theoretical statement, he discussed unconditional positive regard in this way:

> To the extent that the therapist finds himself experiencing a warm acceptance of each aspect of the client's experience as being a part of that client, he is experiencing unconditional positive regard. . . . It means that there are no *conditions* of acceptance, no feeling of "I like you only *if* you are thus and so." It means a prizing of the person. . . . It is at the opposite pole from a selective evaluating attitude—"You are bad in these ways, good in those." It involves as much feeling of acceptance for the client's expression of negative, "bad," painful, fearful, defensive, abnormal feelings as for his expression of "good," positive, mature, confident, social feelings, as much acceptance of ways in which he is inconsistent as of ways in which he is consistent. It means a caring for the client, but not in a possessive way or in such a way as simply to satisfy the therapist's own needs. It means a caring for the client as a *separate* person, with permission to have his own feelings, his own experiences. (p. 98)

As can be seen from Rogers' original definition, virtually all of the terms that have been used interchangeably with unconditional positive regard are included in his formulation. As Lietaer (1984) points out, some of the controversy and ambivalence surrounding the concept of unconditional positive regard is due to the fact that Rogers did not elaborate much further or at least did not examine some of the problems with the concept.

The controversy surrounding the concept of unconditional positive regard most basically relates to the notion that the therapist can be unconditional in his or her reactions to clients. Critics maintain that it is unrealistic to expect a therapist to experience any feelings toward a client without conditions. In this way, the concept of unconditionality runs into conflicts with the third facilitative condition, genuineness, or congruence. Except in extremely rare circumstances, critics argue, one cannot be unconditionally positive in one's regard for the client and genuine or congruent—simply because unconditionality is not possible.

Responses to these criticisms have been twofold. First, the extent to which a therapist experiences unconditional positive regard can be viewed as a matter of degree. Rogers himself made this point in his "necessary and sufficient conditions" paper (Rogers, 1957). As Berenson and Carkhuff (1967) noted a number of years ago, completely unconditional positive regard exists only in theory, and from a clinical and experiential viewpoint the most accurate statement is that the effective counselor experiences unconditional positive regard during many moments of his or her contact with the client. At times, the therapist experiences only a conditional regard, and perhaps at times the regard is negative.

The second response to the criticisms of the concept of unconditional positive regard entails an important distinction. Lietaer (1984) argues persuasively that in considering the concept of unconditionality, one must distinguish the client's inner experience from his or her external behavior. Unconditionality refers to acceptance of the client's experience (feelings, fantasies, thoughts, desires). Lietaer states: "My client ought to experience the freedom to feel *anything* with me; he should sense that I am open to his experience and will not judge it" (p. 46). Lietaer, however, goes on to note that this receptiveness to the inner experiential world of the client does not mean that all behavior is equally welcome: "Both within and without the therapeutic relationship there can be specific behaviors of which I disapprove, would like to change, or simply cannot accept" (Lietaer, p. 48). At the same time, it is important that the counselor attempt to look beyond the behavior of which he or she disapproves. The counselor should try to understand the behavior from the perspective of everything the client has experienced in his or her life. Lietaer adds: "Without approving of it, I accept his behavior as something that is there 'for the time being' and go with him into the personal problems that lie behind it" (p. 47). In being unconditional, though, Lietaer underscores that, whatever the counselor's reactions to the client's behavior, the counselor must *"keep on valuing the deeper core of the person, what she basically is and can become"* (p. 47).

Given the complexity of the concept of unconditional positive regard, it is not surprising that studies have shown it to be multidimensional. That is, the concept appears to be composed of several relatively independent dimensions (see Barrett-Lennard, 1986; Gurman, 1977; Lietaer, 1984). In terms of the dimensions that are important across different forms of therapy, the two that Barrett-Lennard (1986) formulates seem most pertinent: *level of regard* and *unconditionality of regard.* He defines level of regard as "the overall level or tendency of one person's affective response to another" (p. 440). Positive regard entails warmth, liking, caring, "being drawn toward," and valuing the client in a non-possessive way. Examples of positive items (the first three below) and negative items (the last three) from Barrett-Lennard's aforementioned Relationship Inventory are:

She respects me as a person.
I feel appreciated by her.
She cares for me.
I feel that she disapproves of me.
She feels that I am dull and uninteresting.
At times she feels contempt for me.

Whereas level of regard pertains to the degree of positive or negative feelings toward the client, unconditionality of regard refers to the degree of constancy in accepting the client, or, as Lietaer states, the extent to which the client is accepted without *if*s. Unconditionality of acceptance implies that the therapist's basic attitude toward the client does not fluctuate according to the client's emotions or behavior. Positively (first two) and negatively (last two) worded conditionality items from Barrett-Lennard's Relationship Inventory suggest how this construct may be operationalized:

How much he likes or dislikes me is not altered by anything that I tell him about myself.
Whether the ideas and feelings I express are "good" or "bad" seems to make no difference to his feelings toward me.
Sometimes I am more worthwhile in his eyes than I am at other times.
Depending on my behavior, he has a better opinion of me sometimes than he has at others.

Congruence

Congruence, or genuineness, as it is often termed, has been considered a foundation variable since Rogers' initial statement. This means that, as Barrett-Lennard (1986) notes, empathy, positive regard, and unconditionality cannot have their desired effects if the therapist is not congruent, or genuine. In fact, theoreticians such as Barrett-Lennard question whether one can really be empathic or unconditionally positively regarding in the absence of congruence. In this sense, congruence sets an upper limit on the degree to which the other conditions can exist and have their expected effects. (Stating these terms in an either/or fashion helps to clarify how the concepts operate interactively. In fact, each is better seen as existing on a continuum, with the *extent* of congruence influencing the *extent* to which one can be empathic and regarding.)

What do we mean by the term *congruence,* or *genuineness?* The concept of genuineness was discussed earlier in this chapter as part of the "real relationship" in counseling. We shall now examine this condition further. Rogers (1957) believed that congruence meant the following:

> within the relationship he [the counselor] is freely and deeply himself, with his actual experience accurately represented by his awareness of himself. It is the opposite of presenting a facade, either knowingly or unknowingly. . . . It should be clear that this [being congruent] includes being himself even in ways which are not regarded as ideal for psychotherapy. (p. 98)

Then, regarding whether the counselor must be congruent at all times, Rogers tells us that:

> It is not necessary (nor is it possible) that the therapist be a paragon who exhibits this degree of integration, of wholeness, in every aspect of his life. It is sufficient that he is accurately himself in this hour of this relationship, that in this basic sense he is what he actually is, in this moment of time. (p. 98)

When one studies Rogers' observations, a number of questions about congruence arise. Why does Rogers refer in the above paragraph to congruence as implying integration or wholeness? Is the congruence between one's underlying experience and awareness of that experience, between that underlying experience and one's overt communication with the client, between awareness and communication, or among all of these levels? How does congruence relate to therapist spontaneity and to acting out of one's impulses in counseling? In an effort to be congruent, to what extent should the therapist focus on expressing his or her own feelings to the client?

These complex questions have been addressed over the years by Rogers and a number of other theoreticians who have studied the facilitative conditions. As we shall see, the answers must be interrelated. For example, in response to why Rogers seems to equate congruence with integration and wholeness, from its inception, the concept of congruence has implied a consistency among the different levels of experience. One's underlying experience, awareness, and communication are all consistent. In this sense, the person is integrated. Clearly, when theorists who write about the facilitative conditions discuss wholeness and integration, they do not mean that the therapist has all positive feelings, or has no problems of his or her own. In Rogers' first statement above he makes that clear. The counselor may have negative feelings in the relationship, and be whole, integrated, and congruent if he or she is able to be nondefensively aware of these feelings and share them when appropriate. But, again, integration and wholeness refer to a consistency among the various levels of experiencing and communication.

The concept of *experience* or *experiencing* as it relates to counselor congruence is complicated and requires further clarification. Barrett-Lennard (1986) notes that experience

> includes all of the ways in which the person is aroused and active at a given moment which *could,* in the nature of the human organism, register and be integrated in conscious awareness. Implied is the notion that persons may be more or less "open to experience" at a given time, as a function both of situational and personality determinants. (p. 444)

If the counselor is not "open to his or her experience," then what is experienced at an underlying level will not be in awareness. In effect, the counselor is not conscious or aware of this experience, and to that extent there is incongruence between experience and awareness. This state also will create incongruence between experience and overt communication with the client, because experience tends to be expressed indirectly to the client, verbally and nonverbally, and this may contradict what the therapist overtly communicates.

We noted in our earlier discussion of the real relationship in counseling that the concept of counselor genuineness is controversial. Although no theoretical approach advocates therapist phoniness or disingenuousness, approaches differ in the extent to which they advocate the counselor's sharing his or her feelings about the client, the counseling, and the relationship directly with the client. In general, the psychoanalytic approaches promote *less* direct sharing of counselor feelings, and the humanistic approaches promote *greater* sharing. Virtually no legitimate approach, though, would advocate the counselor's acting out his or her impulses with the client, discussing his or her personal problems with the client except in some unusual circumstances, or telling the client whatever is on the counselor's mind. In terms of direct communication of negative feelings about the client or the relationship, the humanistic perspective would generally support such expressions and, in fact, view them as extremely important, especially if the counselor's experienced feelings were interfering with his or her counseling effectively and experiencing empathy and regard.

Finally, as for the other facilitative conditions, items from Barrett-Lennard's Relationship Inventory provide operational examples of the concept of congruence. The first two items are positively stated for congruence and the last two are negatively stated:

I feel that she is real and genuine with me.
I feel that what she says nearly always expresses exactly what she is feeling and thinking as she says it.
At times I sense that she is not aware of what she is really feeling with me.
I believe that she has feelings she does not tell me about that are causing difficulty in our relationship.

A Perspective on Facilitative Conditions

As was noted at the beginning of this discussion of the facilitative conditions, research over the years strongly supports the contention that these conditions are generally not sufficient and probably not even necessary in some cases. Yet the research also just as clearly suggests that the conditions are indeed facilitative. They are facilitative of a constructive, positive counseling process and of a range of desirable outcomes.

Actually, the history of research on these conditions is not as stable, and the results not as consistent, as the statement above might lead one to believe. Shortly after Rogers' statement about the "necessary and sufficient conditions," research studies rather quickly accumulated attesting to the positive effects of the conditions. It appeared that some bottom-line conditions had been discovered and that these conditions seemed among the most powerful ever studied in counseling and psychotherapy (see Truax & Carkhuff, 1967; Truax & Mitchell, 1971). Beginning around the early 1970s, though, more negative results began to emerge. This occurred when investigators who were perhaps more skeptical of Rogers' theory sought to test it rigorously and in a context different from Rogers' client-centered therapy (the theoretical position from which the conditions originated). Because of these negative results and the many concerns voiced about the methodology of the earlier research, disappointment set in about the facilitative conditions (see, for example, the review by Parloff, Waskow, & Wolfe, 1978).

The most recent reviews, incorporating research in the 1980s, present a more balanced picture. First, the conditions do have a positive effect on a range of indicators of the outcomes of counseling, although that effect does not seem as powerful and far-reaching as the research of the 1960s and early 1970s suggested. Second, the extensive recent reviews (i.e., Beutler et al., 1986; Orlinsky & Howard, 1986) as well as a notable earlier one (Gurman, 1977) clearly indicate that the facilitative conditions are much more strongly related to a range of counseling outcomes when these conditions are *based on the client's perception rather than on the ratings made by outside judges (who, for example, base ratings on taped segments of sessions).* In other words, when the client rates his or her therapist in terms of the facilitative conditions (on, for example, Barrett-Lennard's Relationship Inventory), these ratings will be much more related to how the counseling turns out (e.g., effective, ineffective) than will ratings of the facilitative conditions as viewed by outside raters. Although some observers believe this indicates that the facilitative conditions are not that important, in our view this finding is entirely consistent with Rogers' initial theory. Rogers' focus was on the client's perception of the relationship as the most important indicator of the effects of the conditions, not on "objective" ratings made by nonparticipants in the relationship.

A third noteworthy feature of recent reviews is that the effects do not seem equivalent for the different conditions. In Orlinsky and Howard's (1986) thorough review, for example, empathic understanding seems to have a more consistent positive effect across studies than does congruence, although congruence does seem important also, especially (again) from the client's perspective. In terms of important directions for future research on the facilitative conditions, we refer the reader to these excellent reviews as well as discussions by Rice (1983) and Watson (1984).

RELATIONSHIP COMPONENTS, FACILITATIVE CONDITIONS, AND THE THERAPEUTIC PROCESS

Do the facilitative conditions, as discussed above, and the relationship components, as explored earlier in this chapter, interrelate during counseling? If so, how would this occur? All that can be offered is theoretical speculation. Research is needed to help inform this speculation.

Gelso and Carter (1985) have suggested that the facilitative conditions are probably central in the development of the working alliance. Thus, the working alliance will be more positive and stronger to the extent that the therapist is empathic, unconditionally and positively regarding, and congruent.

Gelso and Carter also speculate that the facilitative conditions may have their effect *through* the alliance they foster. We would go a step beyond this and suggest that the therapist-offered facilitative conditions have their effect on the client through their effects on the transference and real relationship, as well as on the working alliance. For example, the therapist who is high on empathy, unconditionality, positive regard, and congruence will probably foster positive transference. At least as important, though, the counselor who is facilitative, and experienced as such by the client, will create the kind of safe climate that allows the client to explore negative transference reactions when they occur. If one feels deeply understood, cared about, and accepted personally with few if any conditions by a therapist who is experienced as genuine, the exploration and expression of negative feelings when they boil up are more possible. Of course, given a sound alliance (which, too, is affected by therapist facilitativeness), the client is better able to stand back, observe, and ultimately understand these feelings for what they are, that is, transference.

The counselor's facilitativeness both affects and *is a part of* the real relationship. It will be recalled that genuineness is one of the defining features of the real relationship, and of course counselor genuineness is one of the facilitative conditions. In this sense, facilitativeness is part of the real relationship. Also, though, the facilitative therapist will promote realistic and genuinely positive feelings on the part of the client toward that therapist. We would then expect a reciprocal effect. To the extent that the client experiences and expresses positive feelings toward the therapist, in the context of the real relationship, the therapist will do likewise.

The above discussion would appear to imply that therapist facilitativeness is a basic causal factor, having desirable effects on the counseling outcomes and a favorable impact on the relationship components. Yet clinically we know that some clients are easier to be facilitative with than others. Thus, the client affects how facilitative the therapist can and will be. An important research direction is the study of both the client factors, and relationship factors that promote or retard therapist facilitativeness.

SUMMARY

The relationship in counseling and therapy is defined as the feelings and attitudes that counseling participants have toward one another and the manner in which these are expressed. A distinction was made between relationship factors and technical factors in counseling, although it was suggested that the relationship that develops between counselor and client will influence how technical factors are enacted in the work.

The way in which the relationship affects the counseling process is seen differently in the various theoretical approaches to counseling. Most counselors and therapists, however, view the relationship as a very important part of counseling, and research supports this view.

The therapeutic relationship consists of three components: the working alliance, the transference configuration, and the real relationship. The *working alliance* is defined as the alignment of the client's reasonable and observing side with the counselor's working, or therapizing, side for the purpose of facilitating the work of counseling. The construct of the working alliance is one of the most promising in all of counseling psychology in terms of its effect on the counseling process and its outcome.

Client transference is defined as a repetition of past conflicts with significant others such that feelings, behaviors, and attitudes belonging rightfully to those earlier relationships are displaced onto the counselor. Five rules of thumb were offered to clarify the concept of transference: (1) Transference is always an error; (2) Transference may be positive or negative; (3) The emergence of transference is eased by therapist neutrality and ambiguity; (4) Transference is not conscious; and (5) Transferences are most likely to occur in areas of greatest unresolved conflict from earlier in life. Client transference occurs in all therapies. Counselor transference, too, is a given. The latter, *countertransference,* is a potential aid to the therapist in understanding the client and the counseling process, *if* the therapist is willing to focus his or her attention on conflictual feelings that may be experienced toward the client.

The real relationship consists of the realistic and genuine perceptions the participants have of one another. The real relationship, expectations of the counselor and the client regarding it, and the differing roles of the participants all interact during the course of counseling.

One of the most influential theoretical statements in the history of counseling psychology was Carl Rogers' formulation of the necessary and sufficient conditions for effective therapy. These conditions were presumed to be part of the counselor-client relationship, which, in turn, was seen as the most important ingredient of effective counseling. Of the conditions Rogers theorized about, the three that have been most focused on in theory, research, and practice are the therapist-offered conditions of *empathic understanding, unconditional positive regard* (including both unconditionality and positive regard), and *congruence.* The research evidence strongly suggests that these conditions are indeed facilitative, although they are generally not sufficient, and at times probably not necessary. The conditions are especially important in their relationship to counseling outcomes when measured from the vantage point of the client.

More research is needed on the manner in which the facilitative conditions and the relationship components interact in counseling.

References

Adler, J. V. (1988). *A study of the working alliance in psychotherapy.* Unpublished doctoral dissertation, University of British Columbia.

Alexander, L. B., & Luborsky, L. (1986). The Penn Helping Alliance Scales. In L. Greenberg & W. Pinsoff (Eds.), *The psychotherapeutic process.* New York: Guilford.

Barrett-Lennard, G. T. (1962). Dimensions of therapist response as causal factors in therapeutic personality change. *Psychological Monographs, 76* (43, Whole No. 562).

Barrett-Lennard, G. T. (1981). The empathy cycle: The refinement of a nuclear concept. *Journal of Counseling Psychology, 28,* 91–100.

Barrett-Lennard, G. T. (1986). The Relationship Inventory now: Issues and advances in theory, method, and uses. In L. Greenberg & W. Pinsoff (Eds.), *The psychotherapeutic process.* New York: Guilford.

Berenson, B. G. & Carkhuff, R. R. (Eds.) (1967). *Sources of gain in counseling and psychotherapy.* New York: Holt, Rinehart and Winston.

Beutler, L. E., Crago, M., & Arizmendi, T. G. (1986). Research on therapist variables in psychotherapy. In S. Garfield & A. Bergin (Eds.), *Handbook of psychotherapy and behavior change* (3rd ed.). New York: Wiley.

Bordin, E. S. (1979). The generalizability of the psychoanalytic concept of the working alliance. *Psychotherapy: Theory, Research and Practice, 16,* 252–260.

Bozarth, J. D. (1984). Beyond reflection: Emergent modes of empathy. In R. Levant & J. Shlien (Eds.), *Client-centered therapy and the person-centered approach.* New York: Praeger.

Buber, M. (1958). *Between I and thou.* New York: Scribner.

Carkhuff, R. R. (1969). *Helping and human relations* (Vols. 1 and 2). New York: Holt, Rinehart and Winston.

Deffenbacher, J. L. (1985). A cognitive-behavioral response and a modest proposal. *The Counseling Psychologist, 13,* 261–269.

Epstein, L., & Feiner, A. H. (Eds.) (1979). *Countertransference: Therapist contributions to the therapeutic situation.* New York: Jason Aronson.

Freud, S. (1959). The dynamics of transference. In E. Jones (Ed.) & J. Riviere (Trans.), *Collected papers* (Vol. 2). New York: Basic Books. (Original work published in 1912.)

Gaston, L., Marmar, C. R., Thompson, L. W., & Gallagher, D. (1988). Relation of patient pretreatment characteristics to the therapeutic alliance in diverse psychotherapies. *Journal of Consulting and Clinical Psychology, 56,* 483–489.

Gelso, C. J., & Carter, J. A. (1985). The relationship in counseling and psychotherapy: Components, consequences, and theoretical antecedents. *The Counseling Psychologist, 13,* 155–243.

Gelso, C. J., Hill, C. E., & Kivlighan, D. M. (1991). Transference, insight, and the counselor's intentions during a counseling hour. *Journal of Counseling and Development, 69,* 428–433.

Giovachinni, P. L. (Ed.) (1975). *Tactics and techniques in psychoanalytic therapy: Vol. 2, Countertransference.* New York: Jason Aronson.

Gladstein, G. A. (1983). Understanding empathy: Integrating counseling, developmental, and social psychology perspectives. *Journal of Counseling Psychology, 30,* 467–482.

Graff, H., & Luborsky, L. (1977). Long-term trends in transference and resistance: A report on quantitative-analytic methods applied to four psychoanalyses. *Journal of the American Psychoanalytic Association, 25,* 471–490.

Greenberg, L. (1985). An integrative approach to the relationship in counseling and psychotherapy. *The Counseling Psychologist, 13,* 251–260.

Greenson, R. R. (1967). *The technique and practice of psychoanalysis* (Vol. 1). New York: International Universities Press.

Gurman, A. S. (1977). The patient's perception of the therapeutic relationship. In A. Gurman and A. Razin (Eds.), *Effective psychotherapy: A handbook of research.* New York: Pergamon.

Hackney, H. (1978). The evolution of empathy. *Personnel and Guidance Journal, 57,* 35–38.

Hartley, D. E., & Strupp, H. H. (1982). The therapeutic alliance: Its relationship to outcome in brief psychotherapy. In J. Masling (Ed.), *Empirical studies of psychoanalytic theories* (Vol. 1). Hillsdale, NJ: Erlbaum.

Hayes, J., & Gelso, C. J. (1991). Effects of therapist-trainees' anxiety and empathy on countertransference behavior. *Journal of Clinical Psychology, 47,* 284–290.

Highlen, P. S., & Hill, C. E. (1984). Factors affecting client change in individual counseling: Current status and theoretical speculations. In S. Brown & R. Lent (Eds.), *The handbook of counseling psychology.* New York: Wiley.

Horvath, A. O., & Greenberg, L. S. (1986). The development of the working Alliance Inventory. In L. Greenberg & W. Pinsoff (Eds.), *The psychotherapeutic process.* New York: Guilford.

Horwitz, L. (1974). *Clinical prediction in psychotherapy.* New York: Jason Aronson.

Kohut, H. (1984). *How does analysis cure?* Chicago, IL: University of Chicago Press.

Lambert, M. J. (Ed.) (1983). *A guide to psychotherapy and patient relationships.* Homewood, IL: Dow Jones-Irwin.

Langs, R. J. (1974). *The technique of psychoanalytic psychotherapy* (Vol. 2). New York: Jason Aronson.

Lietaer, G. (1984). Unconditional positive regard: A controversial basic attitude in client-centered therapy. In R. Levant & J. Shlien (Eds.), *Client-centered therapy and the person-centered approach.* New York: Praeger.

Luborsky, L. (1984). *Principles of psychoanalytic psychotherapy.* New York: Basic Books.

Luborsky, L. (1985). Psychotherapy integration is on its way. *The Counseling Psychologist, 13,* 245–249.

Luborsky, L., Crits-Cristoph, P., Alexander, L., Margolis, M., & Cohen, M. (1983). Two helping alliance methods for predicting outcome in psychotherapy. *Journal of Nervous and Mental Disorders, 171,* 480–491.

Marmar, C. R., Horowitz, M. J., Weiss, D. S., & Marziali, E. (1986). Development of the therapeutic rating system. In L. Greenberg & W. Pinsoff (Eds.), *The psychotherapeutic process.* New York: Guilford.

Marmar, C. R., Gaston, L., Gallagher, D., & Thompson, L. W. (1987). *Therapeutic alliance and outcome in behavioral, cognitive, and brief dynamic psychotherapy in late-life depression.* Paper presented at the annual conference of the Society for Psychotherapy Research, Ulm, West Germany.

Orlinsky, D. E., & Howard, K. I. (1986). Process and outcome in psychotherapy. In S. Garfield & A. Bergin (Eds.), *Handbook of psychotherapy and behavior change* (3rd ed.). New York: Wiley.

Parloff, M., Waskow, I., & Wolfe, B. (1978). Research on therapist variables in relation to process and outcome. In S. Garfield & A. Bergin (Eds.), *Handbook of psychotherapy and behavior change* (2nd ed.). New York: Wiley.

Patterson, C. H. (1984). Empathy, warmth, and genuineness in psychotherapy: A review of reviews. *Psychotherapy: Theory, Research and Practice, 21,* 431–439.

Peabody, S. A., & Gelso, C. J. (1982). Countertransference and empathy: The complex relationship between two divergent concepts in counseling. *Journal of Counseling Psychology, 29,* 240–245.

Prochaska, J. O. (1979). *Systems of psychotherapy: A transtheoretical analysis.* Homewood, IL: Dorsey Press.

Rhoads, J. M., & Feather, B. F. (1972). Transference and resistance observed in behavior therapy. *British Journal of Medical Psychology, 45,* 99–103.

Rice, L. N. (1983). The relationship in client-centered therapy. In M. Lambert (Ed.), *A guide to psychotherapy and patient relationships.* Homewood, IL: Dow Jones-Irwin.

Robbins, S. B., & Jolkovski, M. P. (1987). Managing countertransference feelings: An interactional model using awareness of feeling and theoretical framework. *Journal of Counseling Psychology, 34,* 276–282.

Rogers, C. R. (1957). The necessary and sufficient conditions of therapeutic personality change. *Journal of Consulting Psychology, 21,* 95–103.

Rogers, C. R. (1975). Empathy: An unappreciated way of being. *The Counseling Psychologist, 5,* 2–10.

Ryan, V. L. & Gizynski, M. N. (1971). Behavior therapy in retrospect: Patients; feelings about their behavior therapies. *Journal of Consulting and Clinical Psychology, 37,* 1–9.

Singer, B., & Luborsky, L. (1977). Countertransference: A comparison of what is known from the clinical vs. quantitative research. In A. Gurman & A. Razin (Eds.), *Effective psychotherapy: An empirical assessment.* New York: Pergamon.

Truax, C. B., & Carkhuff, R. R. (1967). *Toward effective counseling and psychotherapy.* Chicago, IL: Aldine.

Truax, C. B., & Mitchell, K. M. (1971). Research on certain therapist interpersonal skills in relation to process and outcome. In A. Bergin & S. Garfield (Eds.), *Handbook of psychotherapy and behavior change.* New York: Wiley.

Watson, N. (1984). The empirical status of Rogers' hypotheses of the necessary and sufficient conditions for effective psychotherapy. In R. Levant & J. Shlien (Eds.), *Client-centered therapy and the person-centered approach.* New York: Praeger.

Weiss, J., & Sampson, H. (1986). *The psychoanalytic process.* New York: Guilford.

Chapter 6

The Counselor's Response to the Client: Tactics and Techniques of Counseling

In Chapter 5 we examined the counselor-client relationship as one of the two vital elements of counseling. Within the context of this ever developing relationship exists the second key element—the techniques used by the counselor in his or her work with the client. Such techniques consist of the actual verbal and nonverbal responses made by the counselor to the client. The term *tactics* is often used interchangeably with *techniques,* and in this chapter we use the latter as a shorthand term for both.

In this chapter, we describe the range of techniques used in counseling. In doing so, we are not seeking to provide the student with a cookbook on how to counsel. Rather, the aim is to give an overall picture of the kinds of responses counselors make to clients in an effort to promote positive change. We first present an overall classification of the levels of counseling technique and then discuss the differing types of techniques or responses within each level.

Just what is meant by the term *technique* in counseling? In fact, there are a range of definitions in the literature, and these vary from the most general to the very specific. An example of the most general definition is provided by Highlen and Hill (1984), who conceptualize technique as "anything the counselor performs within the session" (p. 366). A more specific and probably typical definition is that offered by Harper and Bruce-Sanford (1989). These authors define technique as: "A defined tool or method that is employed by the counselor in order to facilitate effective counseling or positive behavior change in the client" (p. 42).

Implied in the more specific definitions such as Harper and Bruce-Sanford's is the idea that techniques are deliberate. That is, they are verbal and nonverbal responses made by the counselor with the conscious intent of fostering certain behavioral or internal reactions in the client. Also, techniques are ordinarily connected to theory. For example, client-centered counselors (Chapter 9) use different techniques than do behavioral counselors (Chapter 8). And psychoanalytic theory supports techniques that are still different from those advocated by client-centered and behavioral approaches. Thus, each theory has both its own vision of the counselor-client relationship, as discussed in the previous chapter, and the techniques to be used in counseling, as will be explored in this one.

It is useful to think of technique in both the more general and more specific senses, as the following discussion will make apparent. Before proceeding, however, a caution is in order about the idea and use of techniques in counseling (i.e., especially with reference to the more specific usage of the term *technique*). Over the years, many counselors and theoreticians have worried that the field could become too "technique-oriented" and focus on the simplistic use of a set of techniques without deeper understanding. There also has been much concern that basic counselor attitudes (e.g., empathy, regard, congruence) could easily be neglected if the counselor focuses too much on techniques.

The view advocated in this book is that techniques (again, using the more specific definition) are extremely important in counseling, but that they must be used in a context. As Brammer and Shostrom (1982) remind us, the value of techniques is very limited unless the counselor has a good understanding of the therapeutic goals for which he or she is striving, of the basic attitudes that are central to counseling (such as those discussed in Chapter 5), and of the theoretical assumptions to which the techniques are tied. In essence, the use of techniques without a broader understanding of counseling will be ineffective in the long run. Brammer and Shostrom (1982) bring this point home when they note that: "One characteristic of a charlatan is blind adherence to pat techniques applied indiscriminately to all clients" (p. 172).

LEVELS OF COUNSELING TECHNIQUE

As a way of systematizing the numerous variables that may be considered under the heading "counselor techniques," two leading counseling researchers, Highlen and Hill (1984), suggest a classification scheme of techniques affecting client change. These researchers use the most general definition of technique, that is: "anything the counselor performs within the session." Their classification scheme was organized so that the first categories contained the most specific and clearly observable levels of counselor response. Counselor responses in these more specific categories typically are not theoretically derived (connected to any theory of counseling). The latter categories tend to contain more abstract and general variables that must be inferred from behavior (are not directly observable) and are often derived from a theory of counseling.

Below is presented a modification of Highlen and Hill's (1984) classification scheme. Some of the categories used by Highlen and Hill have been deleted, and changes in the ordering of techniques have provided a clearer continuum, from specific and observable to general and abstract. In the remainder of this chapter, counseling techniques under four of the five levels will be discussed. Level 4, encompassing general strategies, will be examined in the next three chapters.

Level 1. Nonverbal Behavior. Behavior that is not expressed through formal language, for example, facial expression, eye movements, body language, nonlanguage sounds, silence, the way in which things are said, counselor touch.

Level 2. Verbal Behavior. The classes of verbal responses counselors make with clients, for example, minimal encouragers, approval, information, direct guidance, open and closed questions, paraphrase, interpretation, confrontation, self-disclosure.

Level 3. Covert Behavior. The intentions behind the counselor's overt responses to the client; the counselor's internal plans and strategies for the counseling.

Level 4. General Strategies. Broader procedures that are ordinarily tied to theory, for example, the empty chair technique, systematic desensitization.

Level 5. Interpersonal Manner. The general ways in which the counselor "comes across" to the client, for example, expertness, attractiveness, trustworthiness.

Nonverbal Behavior

Imagine yourself in counseling with a psychologist whose actual words to you seem to convey caring, interest, and respect as you relate some emotionally painful experiences. At the same time, this counselor looks out the window rather than at you most of the time, speaks in a flat and emotionless tone of voice, sits with arms folded while leaning back in an easy chair, and when sitting up frequently taps his or her foot. Despite the counselor's positive words, you would not have to be a psychologist yourself to feel that something was wrong here, and to feel hurt by the psychologist's nonverbal responses. You probably would not stay around for counseling very long unless this changed. (We *hope* not!)

As far-fetched as this example may seem to you, both authors have observed counselors whose nonverbal behavior was vastly inconsistent with their verbal behavior. (Our observations have been largely of students just learning to be counselors, but unfortunately such inconsistencies also occur occasionally among experienced counselors.) Effective counselors, on the other hand, are aware that they are *always* communicating with clients through a wide range of nonverbal mechanisms, realizing that they, and their clients as well, cannot *not* communicate messages and cues nonverbally. These counselors pay attention to their own and their clients' nonverbal behavior and are able to "read" such behavior effectively. At the same time, effective counselors are not overly preoccupied with their bodies as a source of nonverbal communication. It does appear, however, that the most effective counselors are able to use their bodies as instruments of communication with clients without this interfering with the naturalness of their counseling.

Categories of Nonverbal Behavior. As discussed by Highlen and Hill (1984), nonverbal behavior comprises a number of areas, the most frequently studied of which are: paralinguistics, facial expression, kinesics, visual behavior, proxemics, and touch. Over the past two decades, a great deal of research has been done on each of these topics in the areas of interpersonal communication in general and counseling in particular.

Paralanguage pertains to *how* things are said rather than *what* is said. Paralinguistic cues qualify how a word or verbal message is sent or received. For example, the flat and emotionless voice tone used by the counselor described at the beginning of this section was a paralinguistic cue, qualifying as it did the counselor's verbal expression of interest, caring, and respect, making that expression, in effect, less believable to the client. In addition to voice tone, paralanguage includes spacing of words, emphasis, inflection (loudness, and pitch), pauses, various nonlanguage sounds (e.g., moans, yells), and nonwords ("uh," "ah"). Examples of paralinguistic cues often seen in counseling are laughter, yawning, speaking in a low voice, pausing between words, silence, raising of voice, stuttering or constant restatement, using a high-pitched voice, deep sighing, deliberate coughing, swallowing unnaturally, heavy breathing, and responding with "uh-huh," "uh," and "um." (See Harper & Bruce-Sanford, 1989, for examples of what each of these cues might mean in counseling in our culture.)

The face and facial expression are a second area of nonverbal behavior. Based on their extensive review of the research literature, Harper, Wiens, and Matarazzo (1978) conclude that facial expression may be the most important of all nonverbal cues in counseling. The importance of the human face as a communicator is summarized by Knapp (1972):

> The face is rich in communicative potential. It is the primary site for communicating emotional states; it reflects interpersonal attitudes, it provides

> nonverbal feedback on the comments of others; and some say that, next to human speech, it is the primary source of giving information. For these reasons and because of its visibility, we pay a great deal of attention to what we see in the faces of others. (pp. 68–69)

The importance of facial expressions to clients is demonstrated effectively in a study by Lee, Uhlemann, and Haase (1985). Counseling interviews of 20 minutes' duration were conducted by graduate students training to be counselors. The clients were undergraduate students who volunteered to discuss personal concerns in a study of counseling techniques. Among other things, the researchers were interested in whether these clients' judgments of their counselors' nonverbal behavior correlated with the clients' perceptions of how expert, attractive, and trustworthy the counselors were. In fact, of the eight nonverbal categories studied, counselor facial expression (indicative of warmth and concern) and timely smiling were the best predictors of clients' perceptions that their counselors were expert, attractive, and trustworthy.

Kinesics pertains to body movements other than facial expression and eye movements. In the example used to begin our discussion of nonverbal behavior, the counselor's leaning back, folding of the arms, and tapping of the foot were body movements that fit this category. Ekman and Friesen (1969) have categorized body movements into four types. *Emblems* are movements that can clearly substitute for words, for example, waving goodbye. *Illustrators* are movements that occur at the same time as speech and serve to clarify visually what is being said, for example, dropping one's head in cupped hands to indicate sadness. *Regulators* monitor the flow of verbal interaction, for example, head nods, shifts in posture. Finally, *adaptors* are body movements without conscious communicative purpose, although they are often indicators of inner thoughts and feelings, for example, head scratching, foot tapping, biting one's lips.

The study of kinesics in counseling has a fairly long history. For example, approximately twenty-five years ago Fretz (1966) found that counselors' forward body lean and direct body orientation were related to positive evaluations of counseling by clients. In a more recent study by Maurer and Tindall (1983), it was found that when experienced counselors deliberately used the same arm and leg positions during career counseling as did their high school student clients, these clients gave higher empathy ratings to the counselors than when counselors used different arm and leg positions (despite the fact that counselors in the two conditions were matched on empathy!). Thus, how the counselor uses his or her body in counseling communicates something to the client, whether or not the client is aware that she or he is so affected. Also, the counselor's, as well as client's, feelings are often evidenced through body movements, even when they are not conscious or evidenced in the words used (as in the use of adaptors described above).

Looking and gaze aversion is a fourth category of nonverbal behavior. The extent to which interactants look at each other and how they look at each other during their interaction are clearly important communicators in relationships in general and counseling in particular. Most counseling studies of nonverbal behavior use counselor-to-client eye contact as one of the key nonverbal counselor behaviors. For example, Tyson and Wall (1983), in arranging an experiment on what they viewed as responsive and nonresponsive nonverbal behavior, considered counselor eye contact 80 percent of the time as responsive and 20 percent of the time as nonresponsive. Regarding the importance of this nonverbal category, Lee et al. (1985) found counselor eye contact to be related to clients' ratings of counselors' expertness, attractiveness, and trustworthiness as counselors.

One element of eye contact often ignored is its relationship to cultural and racial factors. Highlen and Hill (1984), for example, point to research suggesting that whites and blacks have different norms for eye contact. Whites more often look while listening, whereas blacks are more likely to not look while listening. Furthermore, as Sue and Sue (1977) discuss, some cultural groups may avoid eye contact as a sign of respect and deference. As always, racial and cultural factors need to be incorporated by the counselor to be maximally effective.

Proxemics refers to the area of nonverbal behavior dealing with the structure and use of space in human interaction. Perhaps the most important scientific work on this topic has been done by Hall (1963, 1968), who notes four distance zones among middle-class Americans: intimate (0–18 inches), personal (1.5–4 feet), social (4–12 feet), and public (12 feet or more). If cultural factors affect eye contact, they seem even more influential in personal space. Hall (1963), for example, discusses the major differences between Americans and Arabs in how much space they prefer between interactants. In counseling, at least where the participants are white, middle-class Americans, Lecomte, Bernstein, and Dumont (1981) found that intermediate distances between counselor and client (approximately 50 inches) resulted in the most effective communication from both parties.

The final and probably most controversial area of nonverbal behavior is that of *touch* in counseling. Some therapists (e.g., Wolberg, 1967; Langs, 1973) maintain that touch should never occur in counseling or therapy, with the possible exceptions of handshakes, for example, upon meeting, after initial sessions, before or after vacations, at termination. Similarly, most counselors have a conservative bias about touching clients, believing that this nonverbal behavior should be engaged in with great caution. The concern about physical contact is that it may overstimulate clients' dependency, arouse sexual impulses or fears of the counselor's sexual motivations, and move the counseling away from being a "talking cure" and toward physical acting-out. Within this conservative bias, some counselors do believe that certain kinds of physical contact with clients are appropriate and even helpful in certain, specific situations. For example, in moments of crisis or great emotional pain, touching the client's hand can helpfully communicate concern and provide comfort.

Just as opinion about touch is controversial, the research findings have been mixed. As Suiter and Goodyear (1985) summarize, some studies have shown certain kinds of touch (e.g., of the client's hand, arm, shoulder) to have positive short-term effects, whereas other studies have demonstrated no effect. On the other hand, when counselors and clients watched videotapes of therapy, Suiter and Goodyear found that the counselor's semi-embrace of the client on tape resulted in lower evaluations of that counselor's trustworthiness. Apparently, this degree of physical contact symbolized greater intimacy than both counselors and clients felt appropriate.

The Deliberate Use of Nonverbals in Counseling. As noted earlier, the effective counselor knows that nonverbal communication is always occurring between him or her and the client. Also, this counselor is able to use his or her body as an instrument of communication, that is, as an intentional means of communication. Are there any suggestions that may be offered to the beginning counselor regarding how specific nonverbals may be used? Authors who discuss beginning counseling skills, often called microskills because of their specific nature, usually outline certain nonverbals. For example, in what may be the most prominent skills-oriented text in counseling, Egan (1986) uses the acronym SOLER as a device for teaching various nonverbal behaviors as a starting point for beginning counselors. It should be emphasized that Egan is appropriately tentative and flexible about them. Not only does he stress the need for flexibility in application but he emphasizes that his guidelines relate most to North American culture. The five prescriptions in Egan's SOLER are the following.

S: Face the client Squarely: that is, adopt a posture that indicates involvement. Egan notes that facing someone "squarely" is considered a posture of involvement, and communicates the message, "I'm available to you; I choose to be with you." Egan also notes that the word *squarely* need not be taken literally. What is important, he underscores, is that the bodily orientation you adopt conveys a message of involvement.

O: Adopt an Open posture. Crossed arms and legs may communicate defensiveness and lessened involvement, whereas an open posture can be a sign that you are open to what the client is able to share. Again, the term *open* need not be taken literally, as Egan notes that if your legs are crossed, that does not necessarily mean that you are uninvolved. The important thing is that the counselor ask himself, "To what degree does my posture communicate openness and availability to the client?"

L: Remember that it is possible at times to Lean toward the client. Leaning toward the other person often communicates that "I'm with you and interested in what you have to say right now," whereas leaning back or slouching may communicate "I'm not that interested" or even boredom. Egan also notes, though, that leaning too far forward or doing so too soon may be anxiety-provoking to the client. It may be experienced as a demand for too much closeness, too soon. Perhaps the most effective helpers are not rigid but are able to move backward and forward naturally and flexibly, according to what is happening in the counseling.

E: Maintain good Eye contact. Fairly steady eye contact is natural in personal discussions and tends to communicate attention and interest, although the racial and cultural modifiers of this rule of thumb, as noted above, must be kept in mind. At the same time, one can maintain such steady and intense eye contact, that the client feels he or she is being "analyzed." Generally, though, a high degree of eye contact (that is not staring or too intense for the client) communicates the appropriate interest. Egan notes that although there is no problem with occasionally looking away, if you catch yourself doing so frequently, this may be a clue about your reluctance to get involved.

R: Try to be relatively Relaxed while engaging in these behaviors. To Egan, this means two things—not fidgeting nervously or engaging in distracting facial expressions and, second, becoming comfortable with using your body as a vehicle of involvement and expression. When you feel comfortable engaging in the behaviors, Egan suggests that they will then help you focus attention on the client and punctuate your verbal dialogue through the use of nonverbals.

Although microskills such as the above were offered as clear prescriptions by counseling authorities in the past, more recent thinking, aided by research, has helped us become aware that suggestions such as SOLER may only be used as rough and very tentative guidelines. Egan makes this clear, as we have noted; authors such as Highlen and Hill (1984) emphasize this point even more strongly. They believe that each counselor-client dyad may establish its own set of rules for nonverbal behavior and that each dyad needs to be studied individually rather than trying to establish a universal set of nonverbal qualities applicable to all. Our view is somewhere in between that of the microskills group and the individualized view suggested by Highlen and Hill. We can establish some general principles or guidelines, but there will be great variability from case to case. And, to further complicate matters (which matches the great complexity of the real world of counseling), certain verbal or nonverbal behaviors may be used unconsciously by the counselor to compensate for other nonverbals. Highlen and Hill use the example of good eye contact compensating for a backward lean. As another example, Hermansson, Webster, and McFarland (1988) found that when the counselors they studied were instructed to lean backward or forward, their verbal behavior compensated for their nonverbals; for example, they were the most empathic when experimentally required to lean backward!

Verbal Behavior: The Response Modes Approach

Much of what goes on between counselor and client is at a verbal level. Over the years, there has been a great deal of research attention given to counselor verbal behavior, and a number of approaches to understanding and classifying the counselor's verbal behavior have been developed (see Patton & Meara, 1983; Tracey & Ray, 1984; Hill, 1985, for examples of three major approaches).

A most useful approach to understanding counselor verbal behavior is called the *response modes* approach. Here, the focus is on the grammatical structure of the counselor's verbal response, rather than on the content. Thus, for example, we classify counselor responses into categories or types, such as reflection, advice, question, and interpretation; and we look at how these types relate to a wide range of other variables in counseling. Of the different approaches, the response modes approach has been the most extensively studied over the years. For the most part, when one observes a counseling session, the observer can readily and reliably (with a little training) classify virtually all of the counselor's responses by using a response modes approach. Because of this, and because counselors must typically learn the different response modes as part of their training, we shall focus the remainder of this section on these responses. Note that such response modes are what we ordinarily mean when we talk about techniques, that is, when using the more specific definition of technique, as discussed earlier.

Hill (1990) has noted that there are over thirty different measures of, or systems for, classifying counselor response modes. Although naturally there are variations among the systems, there are probably more similarities than differences. They all appear to include the following six techniques or counselor response modes in their classifications: question, information, advice, reflection, interpretation, self-disclosure (Elliott et al., 1987). Using a slight modification of the classification system developed by Hill (1985, 1986), let us now look at each counselor response. Note that there are 11 different response modes in this system, and they are divided into four general categories: minimal responses, directives, information seeking, and complex counselor responses.

Minimal Responses. In Hill's system of categorization the first two response modes are called *minimal encouragers* and *silence.* These response modes are really not "verbal" in the strict sense; they fit the paralinguistic category discussed in the last section. We shall briefly discuss them, though, because of their frequency in the typical counseling interview.

The minimal encourager is a very short phrase that may show simple acknowledgement, agreement, or understanding. It usually reflects acceptance of the client, and encourages the client to continue talking. The minimal encourager tends to be neutral in that it does not imply approval or disapproval (see below), even though it usually seeks to show acceptance.

Examples of minimal encouragers are "Go on," "I see," and "Okay." The most commonly used minimal encourager is the response "Mm-hm." In the development of client-centered therapy (see Chapter 9), "Mm-hm" was seen as an indication of simple acceptance of the client, and this usage has continued today. Benjamin (1987) tells us that this response generally indicates permissiveness on the therapist's part, suggesting to the client, "Go on, I'm with you; I'm listening and following you." Despite the intended acceptance, phrases like "Mm-hm" can at times be used too frequently, so that the flow of the session is impeded by the seemingly constant use of "encouragers."

It is probably safe to say that beginning counselors undervalue silence. It makes them anxious, as they feel they must be *doing* something. In fact, silence may be filled with meaning. Silence may facilitate counselor and client getting closer, emotionally touching; or it may indicate that something is awry in the working alliance. Generally we like to differentiate "pregnant silences" from "empty silences." In a pregnant silence, the client is doing his or her "work," for example, thinking or feeling about what is transpiring. In an empty silence, little positive is going on and the client typically shows signs of anxiety, such as fidgeting. Our general rule of thumb is that pregnant silences should not be interrupted by the counselor, whereas empty silences should. Also, Benjamin (1987) notes that unless the counselor is very sure of what he or she is doing, extensive silences should be avoided. A minute of meaningful silence is a long time!

Directives. The category of *directives* involves directing the client to do something. In using directives, the counselor may try to get the client to continue what he or she is already doing (the response mode of approval) or provide information or guidance regarding what the client should do.

When the therapist uses the response mode of *approval,* he or she may be offering support, explicit approval of some aspect of the client or the client's behavior, reassurance, and/or reinforcement. Sympathy also fits this category, although counseling educators and theorists generally agree that offering sympathy is not a desirable counseling response, except under unusual circumstances. Responses within the response mode of approval may be very short, for example, "Very good," or they may be much longer. Examples of specific responses that fit this category are: "It'll get better," "Don't worry about it," "I think you did the right thing," "Everyone feels that way from time to time," "Right, you're right," "That's really tough to handle," "It'll be hard," "I'm concerned about you."

As Benjamin (1987) notes, when we offer reassurance, we are saying, in effect, that the client needs an external influence to keep him or her going or to get started, and this we shall provide. Benjamin uses the following examples that range from mild to heavy reassurance:

CL. (client) I can't face him.
CO. (counselor) You haven't tried; it may not be as hard as you think.
CO. I'm not so sure; I rather suspect you can.
CO. Can't you; that's one man's opinion and this man thinks otherwise.
CO. Of course you can. I really can't be there but I'll be there in spirit.
CO. It's hard, I know; but you can and you must.

There is evidence in the therapy literature that it is helpful to show approval of and support for the client as a person and in a general way (see Hill, 1989, 1990), but counseling can also be too supportive. One can be so supportive that the client's own strengths are not marshalled. Also, as with all techniques, it is crucial that we differentiate effective from ineffective use. Well-timed support or reassurance can indeed move the client forward, whereas certain kinds of reassurance offered in certain ways may be experienced as hollow and impede client growth. For example, implying that "everything will be okay" is often experienced as a lack of empathy, and such reassurances may interfere with the client's working through affects that need to be lived and experienced.

The second response mode under directives is called *providing information.* Counselor responses that fall into this category supply information to the client in the form of facts, data, opinion, or resources. The information that is given may be related to the counseling process, the counselor's behavior, or counseling arrangements such as meeting time and place, fee, and so forth. Examples of providing information are:

CL. So what do you make of these interest test results. What do you think are my best interests?
CO. It looks like your strongest interests are in wildlife management, although there is also a second group of interests that seem to involve sales.

CL. The time went by so fast. Now that I've talked to you, I'm really glad I came. How often do we meet?
CO. We meet weekly, for up to 12 sessions, which is the session limit at the center. (In addition to providing this information, an effective response here would acknowledge the client's positive feelings and perhaps express enthusiasm, also.)

The provision of information in counseling can be quite important. Certainly we do not support the caricature of the "nondirective" counselor who takes his or her nondirectiveness so seriously that he or she never provides information:

CL. (passing a counselor in the hallway) Could you tell me where the men's room is?
CO. You are wondering and unsure of where the men's room is.

At the same time, the counselor can become too involved in being an expert information giver, forgetting the fact that simple information rarely has an impact on underlying feelings and attitudes. The counselor also needs to be sensitive to the possibility that the client seeks information as a way of avoiding self-exploration and possibly painful feelings.

The third response mode under directives is *direct guidance.* This involves directions, suggestions, or advice offered by the counselor. Whereas the mode of providing information involves giving facts and data, direct guidance requests or suggests that the client *do* something. One can think of direct guidance as being of two kinds: that which offers advice or directions within the session, and that which does so outside the session.

Examples of direct guidance within the session are:

CO. Relax right now and take a deep breath.
CO. I would like you to tell me whatever crosses your mind when you think about your mother. Try not to edit and don't worry about how irrational or silly you may feel it sounds.

Examples of direct guidance regarding behavior outside the office are:

CO. I really think it would be a good idea to talk this over with Jim.
CO. I think you should talk with your math professor about why you had problems with the exam last week.
CO. As homework, I would like you to keep a record of how many times you feel anxious during each day, and of what was occurring at those moments.

The use of direct guidance, especially in the form of advice to the client regarding behavior outside the counselor's office, has always been a controversial issue. Many counselors do not believe advice should be given, except in extraordinary circumstances, whereas in the therapies that are more "directive," advice is seen as a desirable element of the process. In our view, all therapists need to sort out for themselves whether they have the right, as Benjamin (1987) puts it, "on moral, professional, or simply human grounds to give advice. If I conclude that I do not, I should say so openly and clearly" (pp. 234–235). We also agree with Benjamin that the first step in responding to a request for advice should be to explore what the client thinks about the situation being discussed and what alternatives have been considered—and what the client's hopes and fears are regarding the conflict situation:

> **CO.** I realize that you are terribly concerned about this. Perhaps if you can tell me the various alternatives you have considered and how you feel about them, we may be able to arrive at something that makes sense to you. (from Benjamin, 1987, p. 234)

Often such an exploration eliminates the need for advice from the counselor. The client is able to follow his or her own dictates.

Information Seeking. Counselor responses used to elicit information of some sort from the client are classed as *information seeking.* Generally, there are two counselor response modes here: *closed questions* and *open questions.* Closed questions are used by the counselor to gather data, and they typically request a one- or two-word answer, a "yes" or "no" or a confirmation. Examples are:

> **CL.** I just don't think I am studying enough in geometry. The problem is more the time I'm putting in than my study skills.
> **CO.** How many hours a night do you study for geometry on the average?

> **CL.** Jane and I finally got away for a weekend without the kids.
> **CO.** Did you have a good time?

> **CL.** My boyfriend thinks I ought to lose 10 pounds.
> **CO.** What do you weigh?

Open questions, rather than delimiting the client's response, seek client exploration or clarification. One usually is not looking for a specific and short answer when asking an open question. Using the same client statements as given above, examples of open questions might be:

> **CL.** I just don't think I am studying enough in geometry. The problem is more the time I'm putting in than my study skills.
> **CO.** What do you think gets in the way of your studying more?

> **CL.** Jane and I finally got away for a weekend without the kids.
> **CO.** What was the experience like for you?

CL. My boyfriend thinks I ought to lose 10 pounds.
CO. What are your feelings about losing the weight?

As you can see from these responses, the counselor, when using open questions, is seeking to facilitate exploration by the client. This exploration may pertain to the client's feelings, thoughts, behavior, and/or personality dynamics.

Although both open and closed questions have their place among counseling techniques, and may be helpful at times, many of those who write about technique believe questions are much overused in counseling. Benjamin (1987) presents this view emphatically when he states that:

> Yes, I have many reservations about the use of questions in the interview. I feel certain that we ask too many questions, often meaningless ones. We ask questions that confuse the client, that interrupt him. We ask questions that the client cannot possibly answer. We even ask questions that we don't want the answers to, and consequently, we do not hear the answers when they are forthcoming. (p. 134)

At the same time, Benjamin goes on to discuss how open questions are superior to closed questions, a view shared by many researchers and trainers (e.g., Egan, 1986; Hill, 1989). Benjamin (1987), in expressing this general viewpoint, tells us: "The open question may widen and deepen the contact; the closed question may circumscribe it. In short, the former may open wide the door to good rapport; the latter usually keeps it shut" (p. 136).

The research on therapist techniques tends to support this perspective on questions. In Hill's (1989) intensive study of eight psychotherapy cases in which highly experienced therapists conducted the therapy, clients typically gave low helpfulness ratings to closed questions. This technique created a feeling in the clients of being interviewed rather than being invited to become emotionally involved in a therapeutic relationship. The findings of Elliott, Barker, Caskey, and Pistrang (1982) are in line with those of Hill.

Open questions, on the other hand, were found to be helpful in some of Hill's cases but not in others. Some clients apparently like the challenge involved in the open question, whereas others experience them as too threatening. It seems clear that the effectiveness of open questions in counseling depends on many factors—for example, how well-timed the questions are, whether the client is ready for them, the issues with which the client is dealing, and of course the specific nature of the question being asked.

Complex Counselor Responses. In Hill's (1985) classification system, called the *Counselor Verbal Response Modes Category System,* the four *complex* counselor response modes or techniques include: paraphrase, interpretation, confrontation, and self-disclosure. These four response modes are complex in that they are more abstract than the other modes, and each of them may be divided into two or more subtypes. Also, their effectiveness depends greatly on complex and often subtle issues of timing, precise phrasing, and sensitivity to the client's dynamics and feeling states at the moment as well as more generally. Because of these considerations, the four complex techniques are more difficult to learn, and certainly more difficult to master, by counselors. Let us examine each of these techniques.

Paraphrase: The technique of paraphrase may be divided into four kinds of responses that have much in common with each other: restatements, reflections, nonverbal referents, and summaries. All four basically paraphrase, mirror, or summarize what the client has communicated to the counselor, either at the verbal or the nonverbal level. The counselor does not add his or her perspective to the communication but, rather, gives back to the client what the counselor hears the client expressing.

When the counselor verbalizes a *restatement,* she or he essentially restates or rephrases what the client has said, usually using similar but fewer words. In a good restatement, the counselor's expression is clearer and more concrete than the client's, and this fosters the client's examination of what he or she is expressing.

> **CL.** I just don't know if I have produced enough to be promoted to the next level at the university, and if I'm not I'll have to begin looking around for what I can find, for another job.
> **CO.** You're not sure if you'll make the cut and may need to find a new job.

> **CL.** It has just seemed like one thing after another this year. There was my wife's illness, and then Heather's accident was almost more than I could take. Now my eight-year-old son has to have this operation. I just wonder if it will ever end.
> **CO.** It just seems like the problems never stop and you're wondering if they ever will.

In contrast to a restatement, a *reflection* rephrases the client's expression with explicit attention to the feelings involved in that statement. These feelings may have been stated by the client or they may be implicit. In the latter case, the feelings are inferred by the counselor from the client's nonverbal behavior or from his or her total communication. To reflect feelings that are unstated, the counselor must listen empathically, and often a deeply empathic kind of listening is required. Unlike in interpretation, the therapist does not in reflection add his or her viewpoint, but rather brings to the surface those feelings underneath the client's words. The counselor in this sense is a mirror to the deeper feelings the client may be struggling to explore. The vignette below exemplifies this sort of reflection.

CL. It's hard to talk about this stuff or even to think about it. I mean, I've been complaining about not having a relationship for a long time, and now that there's a possibility, what do I do.
CO. It's upsetting to see how fearful and avoiding you are of just what you thought you wanted.
CL. That's for sure. I just don't know if John is the person for me. He seems too nice, and yet he has everything I *should* want. I just don't know.
CO. You're feeling just so confused about whether you want John or should want John.
CL. Yes, but as I think about it, that's the way I've always been. When someone cares about me and is good to me, I move away; when someone doesn't want me, I want them. What a mess this is. Will I ever improve?
CO. You feel discouraged, wondering if you will ever connect when the other person cares.

The *nonverbal referent* is similar to reflection and restatement but points to the client's nonverbal behavior as an indication of his or her feelings. Nonverbals here may refer to body posture, facial expression, tone of voice, gestures, and so forth.

CL. I don't know what's wrong. I should be happy with Sally's attention but I'm not.
CO. Your face has a sad expression as you talk about this.

CL. But, darn it, I do care about John, despite his craziness and social discomfort.
CO. Your voice was very soft as you said that.

CL. I feel happy in this relationship for the first time ever.
CO. Your voice sounds alive when you say that.

The final kind of paraphrase is called a *summary,* which verbalizes the major themes in what the client has expressed. The summary may cover a part of a session, the entire session, or the treatment as a whole. Examples are:

CO. It looks like the basic issue you've been struggling with today is your fear of relationships and how you avoid involvements that are good for you.
CO. In sum, you've spent several weeks sorting through what you want and have come to realize engineering isn't it. You are now focusing on management and feel really good about that.

As a general technique, the four types of paraphrase have a long history in counseling and therapy. Beginning in the 1940s, paraphrase became a prominent verbal technique as what was called nondirective therapy (later client-centered, then person-centered therapy) became popular. But even therapists who are not client-centered, or nondirective, with their clients use paraphrases. Hill (1989), for example, found paraphrase to be one of the most frequently used techniques among the eight experienced therapists in her study, none of whom were client-centered in their theoretical orientation.

Each of the four types of paraphrases may be of significant help to clients. They show the client the therapist is listening and enable the client to continue exploration. Paraphrases also let therapists check out their understanding of what clients are saying. On the other hand, as with all techniques, paraphrase can be misused. Continual use of restatement can be an irritant to the client, especially if the counselor approaches exact restatement of the client's verbalizations. Egan (1986) drives this point home when he states that: "Accurate empathy is not mere parroting. The mechanical helper corrupts basic empathy by simply restating what the client has said" (p. 109).

We agree with Egan that the effective counselor is always looking for the core of what is being expressed—that he or she becomes highly expert at finding that core and communicating it to the client. This kind of response is more likely to be reflection than restatement. And, in fact, in Hill's (1989) intensive analysis, reflection was experienced by clients as the most helpful of the paraphrase techniques. It made clients feel accepted and facilitated their getting in touch with their feelings.

Interpretation: Of the complex counselor responses, interpretation is probably the most complex. It requires greater skillfulness, in our view, and may have the greatest potential for both moving the client forward and interfering with progress. Whereas paraphrase techniques stay with the client, and give back to him or her what the therapist hears in that client's expression, interpretations *go beyond* what the client has stated or recognized. An interpretation usually offers new meaning and points to the causes underlying the client's actions and feelings. Here the therapist's frame of reference emerges as he or she reframes the client's material in terms the therapist's view of what is happening. This seeks to help the client see things from a new perspective and in a new way.

The complex nature of interpretation is underscored by the fact that this response encompasses several different types. In Hill's category system, for example, five types are described.

A common type of interpretation *establishes connections between seemingly isolated statements, problems, or events.* For example, to a client who has been discussing his fear of giving speeches, his low self-esteem, and his problems with relationships, the counselor may eventually point out how all three problems are interconnected, and, furthermore, how this client's excessive standards and expectations of himself appear to underlie each problem.

A second type of interpretation *points out themes or patterns in the client's behavior or feelings.* An example of this type might occur in response to the client who continues to become disenchanted with jobs after having high hopes initially. The counselor might note, "Each time it seems that you feel very excited about the possibilities of a job, and then when you see the inevitable problems, you turn away." The counselor might follow this interpretation with an open question about what the meaning of this pattern might be, or the counselor can provide a further interpretation, assuming of course that the client has provided enough material, for example, "Based on what we have been talking about, I suspect that your turning away is a way of dealing with your fear of failing." This follow-up statement demonstrates how the skilled therapist can connect two or more different types of interpretations within the same response.

The last interpretation above pointed to the client's underlying defense ("turning away") against anxiety (fear of failure). This type of interpretation falls within the third type discussed by Hill (1985), that is, *interpretation of defenses, resistance, or transference.* Interpretation of transference is probably the central technique in psychoanalytic treatment. Here the therapist points out how the client's perceptions of the therapist's feelings, behavior, or attitudes are distortions based on past relationships, usually with father or mother. (See the discussions of transference in Chapters 5 and 7.) In an effort to help the client gain insight, the counselor shows the client how she or he is reacting to and perceiving this counselor as if she or he were a significant person in the client's childhood. For example:

> **CL.** I just can't seem to talk to you comfortably about my gayness. It's as if you are sitting there and quietly judging me, thinking I'm an unmasculine shit. Even though you seem accepting of me, I can't trust that, and have this fear that you are critical of me as a person. I half expect you to start yelling at me, to really explode.
>
> **CO.** As I listen to you I'm struck with how you are seeing me as so similar to the way your father was. It's as if you're putting father into me.

The fourth type of interpretation *relates present events, experiences, or feelings to the past.* When making this type of interpretation, the therapist aims to help the client see how present problems and conflicts are tied to the past—are causally linked to that past. We say to the client, in effect, "You are misperceiving the present or behaving in ways that hurt you or others in the present because of these issues or experiences in your past." For example:

CL. I don't know—I just seem to avoid men who are good for me, and get hooked up with these bastards who abuse me. And I turn into such a nag. Nag, nag, nag—I nag so much that I'll turn them into bastards even if they aren't to begin with. I just don't know why I do these things.

CO. It seems like you consistently get into, and create, situations that are just like your mother and father's relationship when you were a child.

The fifth and final type of interpretation in Hill's system entails *giving a new framework to feelings, behaviors, or problems.* Counselors use this technique to provide clients with a fresh, new way of looking at some aspect of themselves and their lives. Hill exemplifies this process as follows:

CL. He just never does anything around the house, and he goes out drinking with the guys all the time. I get stuck taking care of the kids and doing everything around the house.

CO. He seems to be saving you from any decision about what you are going to do with your life and your career.

We began the discussion of interpretation by noting how complex this technique is and how, more than most techniques, it can be for better or worse—it can help or hurt the client. Probably more than any technique, the issues of *depth* and *timing* are absolutely crucial in determining whether an interpretation has its desired effect. Throughout psychoanalytic theory on technique, for example, one finds a great sensitivity to the use of interpretations that are only slightly ahead of the client's level of insight, enabling the client to take a short step forward in understanding. In this sense, the "good interpretation" is never a depth interpretation, or at least it is never so deep that it does not make contact with the client's awareness. In terms of timing, an effective interpretation must be made when the client can absorb it—can take it in, so to speak. No matter how accurate or well-stated an interpretation may be, if it is ill-timed, the client's response will not be what the therapist is hoping for—one of insight and awareness.

Another factor in whether interpretations are helpful relates to the characteristics of the client. In an important article on research on interpretation, for example, Spiegel and Hill (1989) suggest that clients with higher levels of self-esteem, psychological-mindedness, and cognitive complexity are the most receptive to interpretive approaches to counseling. Such people seem to like and profit from the therapist's explanations, even though they may not always agree with them (Hill, 1989). The other side of this coin is that counselors need to be aware of the kinds of people who do not profit from such approaches and to use interpretations guardedly if at all with such clients.

In fact, the research on the helpfulness of interpretation is more positive than for any other technique. In fact, interpretation, along with approval, are the only techniques consistently found to be helpful (Hill, 1989, 1990). It can be concluded from this that therapists, on the whole, are well aware of the complexity and potential power (for better or worse) of interpretation, and they tend to use it with appropriate caution and skill.

Confrontation: The next technique to be discussed is a controversial one because for many therapists and clients it conjures up the image of attacking and being attacked. In fact, this technique of *confrontation* may be gentle as well as aggressive, and, although some confrontations may be explicitly hostile, we believe the most effective ones are embedded in a caring relationship and are not hostile or attacking.

In her Counselor Verbal Response Category System, Hill (1985) indicates that confrontation points to some discrepancy or contradiction in the client's behavior, thoughts, or feelings. When defined in this way, a confrontation usually has two parts. In the first part, the therapist states or refers to some aspect of the client's behavior; and in the second part, which often begins with a *but,* the discrepancy is presented. Note that, unlike interpretations, confrontations do not state the cause of the discrepancy. Typically the confrontation seeks to help the client become aware of contradictions he or she was previously unaware of, unwilling to face, or unable to deal with.

A more general definition of confrontation, as provided by Egan (1986), views confrontation as any therapist response that challenges the client's behavior. The challenge may focus on discrepancies (as in Hill's definition), distortions, evasions, games, tricks, excuse making, and smoke screens in which clients involve themselves, but that keep them from solving their problems. The purpose of confrontation, according to Egan, is to invite clients to challenge the defenses that hinder growth.

An example of confronting a discrepancy between the client's words and behavior (or between verbal and nonverbal behavior) might be:

CL. I've been looking forward to coming to this session today because I get so much out of our work together.
CO. You say this but you were 15 minutes late and have been sitting silently with your arms folded. (The counselor might follow up this confrontation with an open question, e.g., "What do you make of this difference between what you've expressed and your behavior?")

A slight modification of a case noted by Egan (1986) provides a good example of confronting distortions. Eric, a young homosexual male, blames his problems on an older brother who seduced him during his early years of high school:

CO. Eric, every time we begin to talk about your sexual behavior, you bring up your brother.
CL. That's where it all began!
CO. Your brother's not around any more. . . . Tell me what Eric wants. But tell me as it is.
CL. I want people to leave me alone.
CO. I don't believe it because I don't think you believe it. . . . Be honest with yourself.
CL. I want some one person to care about me. But that's deep down inside me. . . . What I seem to want up front is to punish people and make them punish me.

As discussed with respect to interpretation, the technique of confrontation can be for better or worse. In Hill's (1989) intensive analysis, some clients responded well to confrontations, whereas others experienced them as too upsetting, even when the responses were presented very gently. Some clients found confrontations uncomfortable but profited from them nonetheless. Part of being sensitively empathic and skillful as a therapist is knowing when and how to confront clients. In general, confrontations work best within the context of a trusting relationship wherein the client feels understood and cared about. Egan (1986, pp. 227–228) presents the following guidelines for the use of confrontation in such a way that clients are likely to make use of the feedback that is involved:

1. *Avoid labeling.* Derogatory labels, in particular, make clients feel put down and increase resistance to feedback. Words such as *dumb, selfish, arrogant, manipulator, lazy,* and so forth, should be avoided, both because they are not effective and convey a lack of respect for the other person.

2. *Describe the situation and the relevant behaviors.* Rather than labeling, describe the context and self-limiting behaviors as specifically and accurately as possible. Even when you do this, don't dump everything on the client at once. You are not trying to build a case for a trial!

3. *Describe the impact or consequence of the behavior.* Point out how relevant parties (e.g., the counselor, client, significant others) are affected by the behavior in terms of both emotions and behavior. Note, though, that this should not be done with all confrontations; do this selectively.

4. *Help clients identify what they need to do to manage the problem.* Showing clients alternatives, or, even better, helping them explore

alternatives, can be valuable when you challenge some aspect of their behavior.

Self-disclosure: The final technique to be discussed is also a controversial one. The merits and liabilities of self-disclosure have been debated for many years in the counseling and therapy literature. Generally, humanistic counselors (see Chapter 9) believe therapist self-disclosure can be a very helpful way of facilitating a genuine I-thou relationship between counselor and client. When counselors self-disclose, they take themselves off the therapist pedestal and show themselves to be human beings, just like clients. To the humanist, this is a notably positive development. At the other end of the continuum are the traditional psychoanalytic therapists (see Chapter 7). To the analytic therapist, disclosure contaminates the emerging transference and, more importantly, may foster clients' consciously or unconsciously imitating the therapist, rather than seeking to understand themselves.

Generally, self-disclosure may be divided into *involving* statements and *disclosing* statements (McCarthy & Betz, 1978). In the involving disclosure, the counselor communicates to the client his or her feelings or perceptions, usually (but not always) in the moment, and about the client and/or relationship. Examples of such statements might be: "Sometimes, like right now, it's real hard to know how to respond to you in a way that would feel helpful," or "I feel sad as I listen to your continual attacks on yourself," or "I feel like we have had a good relationship, and although I know we must end now, it's a loss for me as well." Disclosing statements reveal something about the counselor or his or her life that does not directly relate to the client or the relationship. These disclosures may be of facts about the therapist; similarities between the therapist and client, including how they feel; or therapeutic strategies used by the therapist. Examples of disclosing statements in these different categories might be: "If someone responded to me that way, I, too, would have a lot of feelings—anger, helplessness, and so on" (disclosure of similarities in feelings); "I understand because I have two teenagers also" (disclosure of similarities); "One of the things that has worked well in my practice and my life has been to listen carefully and not interrupt" (disclosure of strategy); "I got my degree in counseling psychology from Ohio State in 1970 and have been practicing for 20 years" (disclosure of facts).

In addition to the division between involving and disclosing types of self-disclosure, we can make a further distinction. Self-disclosures may be either *positive* or *negative.* Positive disclosures are reassuring in that they support, reinforce, or legitimize the client's perspective, for example: "I, too, feel very good about our work and our relationship" (Hill, Mahalik, & Thompson, 1989). The negative disclosure, on the other hand, tends to be challenging in that it confronts the client's perspective, way of thinking, or behavior, for example: "You say it's okay, but if someone responded to me in that way, I'd feel pretty upset" (see Hill et al., 1989).

Although the research is mixed, the evidence generally seems to favor the merits of involving over disclosing statements, and positive over negative disclosures. At the same time, if offered skillfully, each of these kinds of disclosures may have a positive impact. It is notable, for example, that in her intensive analysis, Hill (1989) found that clients felt therapist self-disclosures were the most helpful of all responses. Also, self-disclosures led to the greatest amount of client self-exploration, as compared to other response modes. It is important to note here that Hill's therapists, who tended to be psychoanalytic, used self-disclosures very sparingly; that is, it was the *least* used of all techniques. Yet when used, it made an impact. Thus, judicious and cautious use of self-disclosure can be facilitative in counseling. Frequent self-disclosures, on the other hand, may serve the counselor's needs more than the client's.

The Frequency, Patterning, and Intent of Verbal Techniques. Because research has found a particular response mode or technique to be effective does not mean that the more it is used the better will be the counseling. Conversely, because some techniques have been shown to be minimally effective does not imply that they should not be used at all.

As an example of the effective techniques, much research has demonstrated the technique of interpretation to be a helpful mode. Yet, for an interpretation to be effective, it is important that the counselor patiently await the right moment to offer one. Many counselors do not make interpretations at all during about the first half of a therapy session. Rather, they wait for material to accumulate and then fit one or more interpretations into the latter part of the session. Often several sessions may go by before an interpretation is offered even by the analytic counselor, who values this technique above all others. This same point may be made for self-disclosure. Recall that this was the least frequently used technique, as well as a uniformly helpful one in clients' eyes. It must be reiterated that frequent use of self-disclosures tends to interfere with therapeutic movement.

On the other side of the ledger, a technique like the closed question is minimally effective, and clients most often evaluate it in a neutral fashion. Yet there are times in treatment when it is important to ask closed questions, for example, when the counselor needs to gather information about a client.

The *patterning* of techniques may well be as or more important than the particular techniques used. Thus, how the therapist combines techniques in a given treatment may be highly influential. For example, Hill (1989) has uncovered some fascinating evidence that interpretations are most often used in the context of approval, are preceded by questions, and are followed by suggestions. Could it be that the interpretations were helpful because of the context in which they were embedded? This seems to make sense especially given their emotionally challenging or disruptive nature. When using both confrontations and interpretations, it may be particularly important to do so within a context of supportive techniques.

The final point in this section is in fact prefatory to the next: that is, what the therapist is aiming for or intending with a given response may be more important than the technique or response itself in terms of the effect on a client. This brings us to the issue of *therapist intentions,* a topic that is just beginning to be studied in counseling psychology.

Covert Behavior

It will be recalled that the most general definition of techniques was "anything the counselor performs within the session" (Highlen & Hill, 1984, p. 366). When viewed in this general way, counselors' *internal* responses to clients and to the counseling situation may be seen as at least a part of their techniques. This internal, or *covert,* level is the third level of counseling technique (the first and second being nonverbal behavior and verbal behavior).

The internal responses of the counselor to the client and the counseling situation are extremely important because they significantly influence the counselor's treatment of the client, verbally and nonverbally. Thus, what the counselor thinks, feels, hypothesizes, and plans has a major impact on the counseling process. As surprising as it may seem, there has not been a great deal of empirical study of the covert behavior of the counselor. Within the last few years, though, an extremely promising line of research has emerged. This work, like the response modes approach just discussed, has been spearheaded by Hill and her colleagues. It focuses on a variable called counselor *intentions.* Let us look at these intentions as an example of the internal processes that influence counseling.

Intentions may be defined as "a therapist's rationale for selecting specific behavior, response mode, technique, or intervention with a client at any moment within the session" (Hill & O'Grady, 1985, p. 3). Thus, an intention is the *cognitive* component that mediates the specific responses counselors make to their clients. As such, intentions get us closer to what therapists think about what they are doing. They give us a glimpse of the *why* behind counselors' overt behavior, that is, behind the ostensible treatment.

To determine what therapists intend when they respond to clients, Hill and her colleagues conducted a series of studies. Generally, they had therapists listen to tapes of their sessions with clients and note what their intentions were behind each response. Based on studies using this method, Hill and O'Grady (1985) devised a list of 19 such intentions. Although some of these overlap with each other and may be clustered to shorten the list, it is useful to look at all 19 as a general guide. These are outlined in Table 6–1.

Although the study of counselor intentions is very recent, a number of valuable findings have already emerged. (See Fuller & Hill, 1985; Hill & O'Grady, 1985; Hill, Helms, Tichenor, Spiegel, O'Grady, & Perry, 1988.) It does seem clear that intentions are linked to the counselor's actual verbal responses. For example, when counselors intend to stimulate client insight, they are most likely to use the response mode of interpretation and least likely to use the mode of approval; when counselors seek to facilitate the exploration of feelings, they are most likely to use open questions and reflections, least likely to give information.

Table 6–1
LIST OF INTENTIONS

1. **Set limits:** To structure, make arrangements, establish goals and objectives of treatment, outline methods to attain goals, correct expectations about treatment, or establish rules or parameters of relationship (e.g., time, fees, cancellation policies, homework).
2. **Get information:** To find out specific facts about history, client functioning, future plans, and so on.
3. **Give information:** To educate, give facts, correct misperceptions or misinformation, give reasons for therapist's behavior or procedures.
4. **Support:** To provide a warm, supportive, empathic environment; increase trust and rapport and build relationship; help client feel accepted, understood, comfortable, reassured, and less anxious; help establish a person-to-person relationship.
5. **Focus:** To help client get back on the track, change subject, channel or structure the discussion if he or she is unable to begin or has been diffuse or rambling.
6. **Clarify:** To provide or solicit more elaboration, emphasis, or specification when client or therapist has been vague, incomplete, confusing, contradictory, or inaudible.
7. **Hope:** To convey the expectation that change is possible and likely to occur, convey that the therapist will be able to help the client, restore morale, build up the client's confidence to make changes.
8. **Cathart:** To promote relief from tension or unhappy feelings, allow the client a chance to let go or talk through feelings and problems.

Table 6-1 (*Continued*)

9. **Cognitions:** To identify maladaptive, illogical, or irrational thoughts or attitudes (e.g., "I must be perfect").
10. **Behaviors:** To identify and give feedback about the client's inappropriate or maladaptive behaviors and/or their consequences, do a behavioral analysis, point out games.
11. **Self-control:** To encourage client to own or gain a sense of mastery or control over his or her own thoughts, feelings, behaviors, or impulses; help client become more appropriately internal rather than inappropriately external in taking responsibility for his or her role.
12. **Feelings:** To identify, intensify, and/or enable acceptance of feelings; encourage or provoke the client to become aware of or deepen underlying or hidden feelings or affect or experience feelings at a deeper level.
13. **Insight:** To encourage understanding of the underlying reasons, dynamics, assumptions, or unconscious motivations for cognitions, behaviors, attitudes, or feelings. May include an understanding of client's reactions to others' behaviors.
14. **Change:** To build and develop new and more adaptive skills, behaviors, or cognitions in dealing with self and others. May be to instill new, more adaptive assumptive models, frameworks, explanations, or conceptualizations. May be to give an assessment or option about client functioning that will help client see self in new way.
15. **Reinforce change:** To give positive reinforcement or feedback about behavioral, cognitive, or affective attempts at change to enhance the probability that the change will be continued or maintained; encourage risk taking and new ways of behaving.
16. **Resistance:** To overcome obstacles to change or progress. May discuss failure to adhere to therapeutic procedures, either in past or to prevent possibility of such failure in future.
17. **Challenge:** To jolt the client out of a present state; shake up current beliefs or feelings; test validity, adequacy, reality, or appropriateness of beliefs, thoughts, feelings, or behaviors; help client question the necessity of maintaining old patterns.
18. **Relationship:** To resolve problems as they arise in the relationship in order to build or maintain a smooth working alliance; heal ruptures in the alliance; deal with dependency issues appropriate to stage in treatment; uncover and resolve distortions in client's thinking about the relationship that are based on past experiences rather than current reality.
19. **Therapist needs:** To protect, relieve, or defend the therapist; alleviate anxiety. May try unduly to persuade, argue, or feel good or superior at the expense of the client.

Source: Reprinted from Hill and O'Grady (1985).

Counselor intentions also seem clearly linked to theoretical orientation. For example, counselors who are psychoanalytic in their orientation more often have intentions to promote insight and feeling exploration. Behaviorally oriented counselors, on the other hand, are more likely, in their responses to clients, to intend to promote change, reinforce change, and set limits.

Another interesting finding about intentions is that different ones are used at various points within a given session. In the beginning of a counseling session, the most frequent counselor intentions are to clarify and get information; but as the session develops, the intentions of catharsis, insight, and change become more prominent. This progression during a session makes sense clinically. Counselors begin sessions intending to sort out information and clarify what the client is expressing. Then, as things get clearer with the unfolding of the session, the counselor moves closer, seeking to deepen the client's understanding and emotional experience and to promote change. This progression of intentions has been found to occur, with some variations, across an entire counseling experience as well as within a given hour (see Hill & O'Grady, 1985).

How Intentions Operate in Counseling. How are intentions played out in a counseling experience? Each client brings to counseling his or her own set of problems and issues, as well as a unique personality. Using the lenses that are inevitably colored by his or her personality and theoretical orientation, the counselor takes in and processes the material offered by the client. This is usually a tremendous amount of material, and the counselor processes it in an incredibly quick and sophisticated manner (Hill & O'Grady, 1985)—the parallel to a computer is inescapable. Based on their experience and theoretical orientations, counselors organize this client material or data according to goals they wish to accomplish at given points in a session. These goals (intentions) may be conscious in the therapist, or they may not be in awareness. Nevertheless, the intentions guide the counselor's choice of interventions.

A given intention can be implemented through a range of responses, both verbal and nonverbal. Hill and O'Grady (1985) use the example of a counselor intending to intensify client feelings. The counselor may do any of the following: lean forward, touch, reflect feelings, be silent, confront, self-disclose, respond with particular warmth, and so on. As noted above, however, therapists will refrain from making responses for a given intention as well; for example, if they want to intensify feelings, they typically will not give information. The counselor's choice of the intervention(s) used to implement a given intention depends on many factors—comfort with various techniques, theoretical orientation, and understanding of the client's dynamics and response patterns.

In any event, following the intervention, the client will then make a response based on his or her immediate integration of the intervention. In turn, the client's response helps shape the counselor's subsequent intention (and intervention). This process continues throughout the counseling encounter. Each participant, counselor as well as client, adjusts his or her responses to the immediate response of the other, combined with all that preceded. The counselor's intentions are thus continually shaped by the client, and these intentions, in turn, continually affect both the counselor's intervention and the client.

Interpersonal Manner: The Counselor and Interpersonal Influence

The final level of technique to be examined in this chapter is called "interpersonal manner" by Highlen and Hill (1984). This is the most abstract and global of the technical levels discussed so far and does not refer to specific behaviors and techniques. Rather, interpersonal manner refers to constellations of verbal and nonverbal behaviors that sum up the personal style of a counselor. At the most general level, manner entails how the counselor comes across to the client, and is defined by the impressions that the counselor creates in his or her clients.

Highlen and Hill point out that the variables of interpersonal manner (attitudes, involvement, communication patterns) compose the gestalt of overt behavior. These variables are numerous, including those of empathy, positive regard, and congruence. Thus, issues of technique (as examined in this chapter) come to overlap with the issues of counselor-client relationship (as discussed in Chapter 5).

In this final section we shall focus on a set of variables that have been studied extensively in counseling psychology for more than two decades and that are often referred to as the counselor's *social influence.* The major initial theoretical statement about social influence in counseling was offered by Stanley Strong (1968), and much of the development of this line of thought is a testimony to Strong's theoretical work and empirical research.

In drawing from research and theory in social psychology, Strong proposed that counseling was a process of social influence in which the counselor sought to influence the client toward attitude and behavior change. He theorized that counselors' attempts to induce change in clients created a state of cognitive dissonance. Clients, as do all humans, would then seek to reduce dissonance, and they could do this in any of several ways. In essence, they could either (a) change in the direction advanced by the counselor, or (b) not do so, for example, by discrediting the counselor or issue. Strong hypothesized that outcome (a) would be the most likely to the extent that clients perceive their counselors as being high in the qualities of *expertness, attractiveness,* and *trustworthiness* (EAT).

In line with the above propositions, Strong formulated counseling to be a two-stage process. In the first stage, the counselor does what is necessary to enhance the client's perceptions of the counselor's EAT. Then, in the second stage, the counselor influences client change. The specifics of this attempt to influence are not spelled out. Apparently any of a range of specific procedures may be used, as advocated by the different theoretical approaches to counseling (see the next three chapters).

The key constructs in social influence theory are E, A, and T. According to Strong (1968), expertness is the degree to which the counselor is seen as a source of valid assertions. Perceptions of E may be affected by "(a) objective evidence of specialized training such as diplomas, certificates, and titles, (b) behavioral evidence . . . such as rational and knowledgeable arguments and confidence in presentation, and (c) reputation as an expert" (p. 216). Counselor attractiveness is based on "perceived similarity to, compatibility with, and liking for" the counselor (Strong, 1968, p. 216). Strong feels that the facilitative conditions discussed in Chapter 5 critically influence clients' perceptions of counselor attractiveness. Counselor self-disclosure also is seen as central. Finally, counselor trustworthiness, according to Strong, is based on "(a) reputation for honesty, (b) social role, such as physician, (c) sincerity and openness, and (d) lack of motivation for personal gain" (p. 217).

Because of the cogency, clarity, and testability of Strong's theoretical statements (Strong, 1968; Strong & Matross, 1973), dozens of studies have been done over the past two decades on counselor social influence. Because client-perceived E, A, and T, often referred to as "source characteristics," are so central to the theory, much of the research has examined what factors may be included under these three variables and how to enhance clients' perceptions of them. Among other things, the research has generally supported Strong's original statements about what factors affect perceptions of this well-known triad. A major addition in recent years, though, has been the discovery of the great importance of the counselor's *nonverbal behavior* in the client's perceptions of E, A, and T. Generally, the nonverbals in the acronym SOLER appear to affect such client perceptions.

How important are E, A, and T for Strong's stage 2, the actual attempt to influence change? Surprisingly little research has been directed at this stage. The results generally support the importance of client-perceived E, A, and T in counseling outcome (Heppner & Claiborn, 1989), but this is still an open question. For an overview of this entire line of research—its findings, problems, and methods—the reader is referred to two major monographs. The earlier research has been summarized and analyzed by Corrigan, Dell, Lewis, and Schmidt (1980); research in the last decade has been critically examined by Heppner and Claiborn (1989).

Despite the great amount of research devoted to it over many years, counselors have always questioned the usefulness of social influence theory. It has never been clear, for example, just how the theory may be applied to practice. At first glance, it may appear that the theory dictates that the counselor do whatever is necessary to make himself or herself appear expert, attractive, and trustworthy—that nothing else is needed, as change will follow automatically from the client's perceptions of these source characteristics. If one follows this approach, what results is a caricature of counseling, with a focus on superficial appearances rather than the deeper, more central qualities that make for good counseling.

Social influence theory and its application is in effect a very general, pantheoretical set of principles about behavior change. This theory, in our view, should *not* be applied in any direct, straightforward fashion. Knowing about E, A, and T and integrating such knowledge into one's general theory of counseling may help the counselor understand the process and at times offer some hints about application. But the focus of counseling should be on understanding the client (and one's own reactions to the client and situation), developing the relationship, and applying one's substantive (e.g., psychoanalytic, behavioral) theory of counseling to the situation. The use of techniques, as discussed in this chapter, is best seen as occurring within this context. Furthermore, within this context, it is rare that the practitioner should seek to *appear* expert, trustworthy, and attractive. Rather, she or he should seek to *be* truly expert in his or her practice, genuinely trustworthy, and perhaps an attractive human being in the most general sense.

SUMMARY

There is a range of definitions of the term *techniques,* from the most general ("anything the counselor performs with the client") to the more specific ("a tool or method employed by the counselor to facilitate effective counseling"). Using the most general definition, four levels of technique exist: (1) nonverbal behavior, (2) verbal behavior, (3) covert behavior, and (4) interpersonal manner.

The general domain of nonverbal behavior comprises *paralinguistics, facial expression, kinesics, visual behavior, proxemics,* and *touch.* The effective counselor is aware that he or she is always communicating with clients nonverbally and that the client, too, is doing so. With experience the counselor learns to use nonverbals to enhance counseling. The acronym *SOLER* is a way of summarizing how the counselor might deliberately use nonverbal behavior to enhance counseling.

In the *response modes approach,* the focus is on the grammatical structure of the counselor's verbal response, rather than the content. Response modes are what is ordinarily meant by the term *technique,* when used in the more specific sense. Hill's (1985) Verbal Response Category System serves to classify response modes, eleven of which can be distinguished: *minimal encouragers, silence, approval, providing information, direct guidance, open and closed questions, paraphrase, interpretation, confrontation, and self-disclosure.* It is important that techniques such as response modes be used in the context of an understanding of counseling goals and a stable counselor-client relationship. The theoretical basis for applying techniques must also be understood.

Covert behavior can be discussed in terms of the *intentions* behind the counselor's response to the client. The study of counselor intentions is an exciting new area of inquiry that shows great promise in furthering our understanding of counseling processes and outcomes.

The fourth level of technique, *interpersonal manner,* involves a set of variables that have been given great attention in counseling psychology research: *counseling as a social influence process.* According to Strong's (1968) two-stage process in counseling, counselors first enhance the client's perceptions of the counselor's *expertness, attractiveness, and trustworthiness* (E, A, and T). In the second stage, the counselor influences behavior and attitude change, which is facilitated by the client's positive perceptions of E, A, and T. The direct applicability of social influence theory to counseling is, however, controversial and limited.

References

Benjamin, A. (1987). *The helping interview.* Boston: Houghton Mifflin.

Brammer, L. M., & Shostrom, E. L. (1982). *Therapeutic psychology: Fundamentals of counseling and psychotherapy* (4th ed.). Englewood Cliffs, NJ: Prentice-Hall.

Corrigan, J. D., Dell, D. M., Lewis, K. N., & Schmidt, L. D. (1980). Counseling as a social influence process: A review [Monograph]. *Journal of Counseling Psychology, 27,* 395–441.

Egan, G. (1986). *The skilled helper* (3rd ed.). Monterey, CA: Brooks/Cole.

Ekman, P., & Friesen, W. V. (1969). The repertoire of non-verbal behavior. *Semiotica, 1,* 49–98.

Elliott, R., Barker, C. B., Caskey, N., & Pistrang, N. (1982). Differential helpfulness of counselor verbal response modes. *Journal of Counseling Psychology, 29,* 354–361.

Elliott, R., Hill, C. E., Stiles, W. B., Friedlander, M. L., Mahrer, A. R., & Margison, F. R. (1987). Primary response modes: A comparison of six rating systems. *Journal of Consulting and Clinical Psychology, 55,* 218–223.

Fuller, F., & Hill, C. E. (1985). Counselor and helpee perceptions of counselor intentions in relation to outcome in a single counseling session. *Journal of Counseling Psychology, 32,* 329–338.

Fretz, B. R. (1966). Postural movements in a counseling dyad. *Journal of Counseling Psychology, 13,* 335–343.

Hall, E. T. (1963). A system for the notation of proxemic behavior. *American Anthropologist, 65,* 1003–1026.

Hall, E. T. (1968). Proxemics. *Current Anthropology, 9,* 83–108.

Harper, F. D., & Bruce-Sanford, G. C. (1989). *Counseling techniques: An outline and overview.* Alexandria, VA: Douglass Publishers.

Harper, R. G., Wiens, A. N., & Matarazzo, J. D. (1978). *Nonverbal communication: The state of the art.* New York: Wiley.

Heppner, P. P., & Claiborn, C. D. (1989). Social influence research in counseling: A review and critique. *Journal of Counseling Psychology* [Monograph}, *36,* 365–387.

Hermansson, G. L., Webster, A. C., & McFarland, K. (1988). Counselor deliberate postural lean and communication of facilitative conditions. *Journal of Counseling Psychology, 35,* 149–153.

Highlen, P. S., & Hill, C. E. (1984). Factors affecting client change in individual counseling: Current status and theoretical speculations. In S. Brown & R. Lent (Eds.), *Handbook of counseling psychology* (pp. 334–396). New York: Wiley.

Hill, C. E. (1985). *Manual for the Hill counselor verbal response modes category system* (rev. ed.). Unpublished manuscript, University of Maryland.

Hill, C. E. (1986). An overview of the Hill counselor and client verbal response modes category systems. In L. Greenberg & W. Pinsoff (Eds.), *The psychotherapeutic process: A research handbook* (pp. 131–160). New York: Guilford.

Hill, C. E. (1989). *Therapist techniques and client outcome: Eight cases of brief psychotherapy.* Newbury Park, CA: Sage.

Hill, C. E. (1990). Review of exploratory in-session process research. *Journal of Consulting and Clinical Psychology, 58,* 288–294.

Hill, C. E., Helms, J. E., Tichenor, V., Spiegel, S. B., O'Grady, K. E., & Perry, E. (1988). The effects of therapist response modes in brief psychotherapy. *Journal of Counseling Psychology, 35,* 222–233.

Hill, C. E., Mahalik, J., & Thompson, B. J. (1989). Self-disclosure. *Psychotherapy, 26,* 290–295.

Hill, C. E., & O'Grady, K. E. (1985). List of therapist intentions illustrated in a case study and with therapists of varying theoretical orientations. *Journal of Counseling Psychology, 32,* 3–22.

Knapp, M. L. (1972). The field of nonverbal communication: An overview. In C. Stewart & B. Kendall (Eds.), *On speech communication: An anthology of contemporary writings and messages.* New York: Holt, Rinehart and Winston.

Langs, R. J. (1973). *The technique of psychoanalytic psychotherapy* (Vol. 1). New York: Jason Aronson.

Lecomte, C., Bernstein, B. L., & Dumont, F. (1981). Counseling interaction as a function of spatial-environmental conditions. *Journal of Counseling Psychology, 28,* 536–539.

Lee, D. Y., Uhlemann, M. R., & Hasse, R. F. (1985). Counselor verbal and nonverbal responses and perceived expertness, trustworthiness, and attractiveness. *Journal of Counseling Psychology, 32,* 181–187.

Maurer, R. E., & Tindall, J. H. (1983). Effect of postural congruence on client's perception of counselor empathy. *Journal of Counseling Psychology, 30,* 158–163.

McCarthy, P. R., & Betz, N. E. (1978). Differential effects of self-disclosing versus self-involving counselor statements. *Journal of Counseling Psychology, 25,* 251–256.

Patton, M. J., & Meara, N. M. (1983). The analysis of natural language in psychological treatment. In R. Russell (Ed.), *Spoken interaction in psychotherapy.* New York: Irvington Publishers.

Spiegel, S. B., & Hill, C. E. (1989). Guidelines for research on therapist interpretation: Toward greater methodological rigor and relevance to practice. *Journal of Counseling Psychology, 36,* 121–129.

Strong, S. R. (1968). Counseling: An interpersonal influence process. *Journal of Counseling Psychology, 15,* 215–224.

Strong, S. R., & Matross, R. P. (1973). Change processes in counseling and psychotherapy. *Journal of Counseling Psychology, 20,* 25–37.

Sue, D. W., & Sue, D. (1977). Barriers to effective cross-cultural counseling. *Journal of Counseling Psychology, 24,* 420–429.

Suiter, R. L., & Goodyear, R. K. (1985). Male and female counselor and client perceptions of four levels of counselor touch. *Journal of Counseling Psychology, 32,* 645–648.

Tracey, T. J., & Ray, P. B. (1984). Stages of successful time-limited counseling: An interactional examination. *Journal of Counseling Psychology, 31,* 13–27.

Tyson, J. A., & Wall, S. M. (1983). Effect of inconsistency between counselor verbal and nonverbal behavior on perceptions of counselor attributes. *Journal of Counseling Psychology, 30,* 433–437.

Wolberg, L. R. (1967). *The technique of psychotherapy* (2nd ed.). New York: Grune & Stratton.

Chapter 7

The Psychoanalytic Approach

There are virtually dozens of theories of counseling and psychotherapy today, and indeed each practitioner may be seen as developing his or her own unique theory. At the same time, it is possible to combine the most prominent theories into three main clusters. In this chapter and the following two, we shall examine the three theory clusters that have been dominant in counseling psychology and in the counseling and therapy that is practiced by counseling psychologists. These clusters may be labeled *psychoanalytic,* (including Freudian approaches, their derivatives, and departures), *learning* (including the behavioral, cognitive, and cognitive-behavioral approaches), and *humanistic* (or existential-humanistic).

Many excellent presentations of theories of counseling are available. Our goal in the following three chapters is not to duplicate these. Rather, we aim to delineate the major ingredients of each of the three theory clusters, exemplify treatment approaches and procedures within each, and clarify the place of each perspective in counseling psychology. Key references will enable the student to pursue each individual theory in greater depth.

Will the real psychoanalytic practitioner please stand up? If this question were asked to a large group of therapists, those who stood would probably represent a dizzying array of viewpoints about personality development, health and psychopathology, and psychological interventions. It is not surprising that the beginning student often feels overwhelmed by the enormous diversity of views and approaches within the general psychoanalytic perspective. This diversity, along with the awesome complexity inherent in psychoanalytic theories, makes it hard for the beginner to decipher just what is and is not psychoanalytic. With experience, practice, and much reading, things do get clearer, although the seasoned practitioner and scholar does not have an easy time with this question either.

One of the principal goals of this chapter is to provide the reader with a framework for understanding common ingredients of the multifold approaches found under the psychoanalytic umbrella. We will also explain how psychoanalysis fits with counseling psychology.

We begin by taking a glimpse at the life and personality of the originator of psychoanalysis, Sigmund Freud. Subsequently we (1) examine some distinctions that too often remained unclarified and are frequent sources of confusion for the student attempting to comprehend the psychoanalytic perspective; (2) discuss eight common ingredients of psychoanalytic approaches; (3) present in detail James Mann's time-limited psychotherapy, as an example of an approach to psychoanalytic treatment that seems well suited to counseling psychology; and (4) conclude with a discussion of the relationship of psychoanalysis to counseling psychology—the ways in which these two endeavors have not meshed, and how their "fit" has become much better in recent years. Research issues and findings related to psychoanalytic interventions are also presented in the final section of the chapter.

It should be noted that the material in this chapter assumes the reader has a beginning understanding of basic psychoanalytic concepts such as Freud's psychosexual stages (e.g., oral, anal, phallic stages, and the Oedipus complex), structures of the psyche (id, ego, super ego), defense mechanisms, and levels of consciousness (unconscious, preconscious, conscious). Excellent discussions of these concepts are provided by Prochaska (1979) and Hansen, Stevic, and Warner (1986). The advanced student can consult Brenner's (1973) classic work.

THE FIRST FREUDIAN AND THE BEGINNINGS OF PSYCHOANALYSIS

All fields of psychology in which counseling interventions are involved must be indebted to psychoanalysis and especially to Sigmund Freud for the beginning development of therapeutic treatment. It was Freud, after all, who discovered and developed the "talking cure," the treatment upon which the entire field of verbal counseling has been built. Because of the profound impact of Freud and his early work on all approaches to psychological intervention, it is worth examining his life and the early psychoanalytic movement in some depth.

Sigmund Freud was born in 1856 in Freiberg, Moravia (formerly Austria, now Czechoslovakia). His father, Jakob, was a wool merchant in Vienna, where Freud lived from the age of four. Jakob was married twice; Sigmund was the first child of Jakob's second marriage, to Amalie, a 20-year-old woman who was also 20 years Jakob's junior. Jakob and Amalie bore seven other children, so Sigmund was the oldest child of a large family. Freud's childhood seems to have been a relatively happy one. Jakob was a liberal-minded Jew with progressive views. He was apparently a loving father with a good sense of humor, although he seemed to represent discipline and authority to Sigmund. Freud's relationship with his father seemed somewhat distant. Freud's mother is described as having a lively personality, and she gave Sigmund considerable affection and attention. She was proud of her first-born, and Sigmund remained fond of her until her death at 95 years of age.

A deep scholarly orientation pervaded Freud's life from very early on. His great intellectual capacity was recognized early by his family, and it was established that he would be a scholar. His destiny was incontestable: Freud's study-bedroom was the only one in his house equipped with an oil lamp—the other members' rooms had candles. Freud was a precocious reader, who studied a great deal. He began to enjoy Shakespeare at the age of eight, and as a teenager, ate his evening meals in his room so he would lose no time from his studies. Freud's passion for learning and understanding never faded. In fact, although Freud was steeped in psychoanalytic practice throughout most of his adult life, his most passionate interests revolved around understanding what makes people tick—the workings of the human psyche—rather than in providing psychological help.

Freud received his M.D. from the University of Vienna in 1881, after which he took a position at the city's well-known general hospital. There he engaged in general medical services, and also spent five months studying brain anatomy and neuropathology under Theodore Meynert at a nearby psychiatric clinic. His practice flourished, and he wrote books on aphasia and infantile cerebral paralysis. It looked as though the young Freud was destined for a smooth and lucrative career. Things were not to be easy, though, for Freud's restless and creative genius goaded him to new and deeper understandings of the human psyche—understandings that were to be the source of much professional ferment and emotional pain in his life. In his practice, he began to see patients with hysterical disorders and in 1886 presented his first paper on hysteria. It was badly received by his medical colleagues. This was probably the first in what became a long series of rejections for one of the great minds of our time.

While a medical student, Freud had met Joseph Breuer, a prominent general practitioner 14 years his senior. They became friends, and their friendship continued over the years. Breuer discussed with Freud a case he treated from 1880 to 1882, the now-famous case of Anna O, in which a variety of symptoms, including conversion reactions, were cured by means of hypnosis and the free discharge of emotions, called *catharsis.* Freud was fascinated by this case and by what he felt to be a remarkable discovery. Following his return in 1889 from the Nancy School, where he studied hypnotic suggestion with Bernheim and Liebault, Freud further tested the new method of catharsis, or abreaction, along with hypnosis.

He and Breuer eventually published the case of Anna O in *Studies in Hysteria* (1895), but the book did not receive the acceptance they had hoped for. The medical profession of that time explained all symptoms on the basis of some organic lesion; if a physical problem could not be found, it was assumed that something in the brain was the culprit. As Freud continued to develop his views about the sexual basis of the neuroses, things heated up further. When Freud theorized that hysterical and other symptoms were, at their core, the results of sexual repression, Breuer withdrew from the work. Freud essentially worked alone, and was the object of professional ridicule by fellow physicians. He was seen as a crackpot, and his private practice nearly dried up. For example, in early 1900 Freud reported that he had had no new cases for months, and his financial outlook was again bleak. Having a wife, six children, and a mother to support (Freud's father had died) surely added stress.

The final years of the 19th century were crucial for Freud and psychoanalysis. During this period, Freud worked essentially alone. He began his self-analysis as a way of understanding the psyche and resolving some personal neuroses, and further developed his theories about sex, producing one of his most important works, *The Interpretation of Dreams* (1900). He soon was to discontinue the use of hypnosis. Too many patients could not be hypnotized, and too many of the "cures" were short-lived. Instead, Freud began to use a procedure he called *free association* to get his patients to remember repressed material from their past, and thus began the revolutionary new method, psychoanalysis.

Freud's work began to receive positive recognition in the early 1900s. Although he continued to work largely alone, during this time Freud met a number of men who were to form the inner sanctum of psychoanalysis. For example, in 1902 he initiated weekly discussions in his home with a small group of budding analysts—the famed Vienna Psychoanalytic Society. Given the great struggles and isolation that Freud endured during his initial years of developing psychoanalysis, as well as some aspects of his character structure, it was perhaps inevitable that psychoanalysis would become a system revolving around the beliefs of one man.

As the first decade of the 20th century was drawing to a close, Freud's views were becoming increasingly influential. A major marker of the great recognition he and psychoanalysis were beginning to receive was the invitation from G. Stanley Hall for Freud to give a series of lectures in the United States, commemorating the 20th anniversary of Clark University. Freud's lectures had a great impact on that august body, including the famous William James, who became a supporter of psychoanalysis.

Interestingly, although Freud's genius is now almost universally recognized, he often complained of not having been given a better brain. He believed that his main virtue was his courage, an assertion that could hardly be denied. He also once stated that his next best attribute was his self-criticalness, and this seems equally inarguable. These qualities, courage and self-criticalness, constantly pushed Freud to further his and our understanding of the deepest aspects of the human psyche in the face of professional rejection and even humiliation. His self-criticalness also must have been part of his continual analysis, reanalysis, and modification of his own views.

Freud often changed his views, and did so even when giving up a cherished theory was painful to him. Yet he had difficulty with others deviating from his position, especially if they used the term *psychoanalysis* as a label for their theorizing. Psychoanalysis was Freud's creation, and he alone could decide what rightfully belonged in its province. Once Freud was convinced that a theory was valid, he maintained it with complete conviction. He could not admit contradiction. As Ellenberger (1970) noted, his opponents viewed this as intolerance, whereas Freud's followers saw this trait as a passion for truth.

Whatever the case may be, Freud inarguably was deeply passionate about his intellectual pursuits, and he had an enormous capacity for work. A look at his daily schedule gives a picture of how totally devoted he was to it. On a typical day, Freud saw his first patient at 8 A.M., and continued his clinical practice until 1 P.M., with a five-minute break between sessions. At 1 P.M. he had lunch and took a walk with his family. He then saw more patients from 3 until 9 or 10 P.M., followed by dinner and another walk with his wife. He then returned to his study and wrote from 11 until 1 or 2 A.M. This amounted to about an 18-hour workday. In commenting upon this, Prochaska (1979) notes the irony that a man whose professional life was so devoted to understanding sex appeared to have left so little time in his life for his own sexuality.

Freud was a man of compassion, who cared deeply about his patients and people in general. His courage and passion for knowledge, though, truly stand out. These qualities were evidenced clearly in how he dealt with his terribly painful cancer of the jaw and palate. In 1923 he was operated on for this cancer, the first of 33 such operations. For 16 years Freud suffered agonizing pain. His speech, hearing, and eating were seriously affected. Despite the worsening cancer, Freud worked on, usually without medication (which he felt clouded his thinking), until his death in 1939. Some of his most profound works were produced during these years, including *An Outline of Psychoanalysis* (1940), his final statement about revised psychoanalytic theory.

For in-depth reading on Freud's life and the background of the psychoanalytic movement, the reader is referred to the three-volume biography by one of Freud's most trusted colleagues, Ernest Jones (1953, 1955, 1957).

PSYCHOANALYTIC INTERVENTIONS: SOME KEY DISTINCTIONS

To understand modern psychoanalytic thought, it is helpful to make some key distinctions that are often ignored in the psychoanalytic literature. Three such distinctions are discussed below.

Theories of the Person vs. Theories of the Treatment Process

Psychoanalysis is a diverse and complex set of assumptions, theories, and laws about how human beings develop as they do. There are psychoanalytic personality and development theories, and psychoanalytic theories of health and psychopathology. Under the broad umbrella of psychoanalysis, such theories of personality and psychopathology often take divergent forms. For example, in addition to traditional or Freudian psychoanalytic theory, we have theories labeled "object relations" (both British and American schools), "ego analytic," "self-psychological," and "interpersonal." Although overlapping, each contains different formulations about why human beings develop as they do. We call these viewpoints about human personality development, health, and psychopathology *theories of the person.*

In addition to developing theories of the person, psychoanalysis formulates theories of the treatment process. Such theories examine, for example, what goes on during analysis or therapy between the therapist and client and how the client's issues are expected to unfold within the hour and during the course of treatment. Psychoanalytic theories of treatment examine the techniques that the analyst or therapist is to use with the client and, more generally, how the therapist is to behave during the sessions.

Most psychoanalytic practitioners would agree that the therapist should strive for a deep understanding of both psychoanalytic theories of the person and psychoanalytic theories of intervention. At the same time, it is important to keep in mind that these two theories are by no means the same. One can conceptualize the individual client in psychoanalytic terms (using any psychoanalytic theory) but provide treatment that is decidedly nonanalytic. On the other hand, if the therapist conceptualizes the treatment process in analytic terms (e.g., focus on interpretation and insight, transference and countertransference), she or he has probably also relied upon psychoanalytic formulations of the person.

The central point here is that when we talk about psychoanalysis, we need to be clear on whether we refer to formulations about the person (his or her personality, development, degree of health, and degree or kind of psychopathology) or about the treatment being offered.

Psychoanalytic Theory vs. Psychodynamic Theory

Although the terms *psychoanalytic* and *psychodynamic* are often used interchangeably, it is useful to differentiate them. The term *psychodynamic* is the broader of the two. This term has different meanings to different people, but even differing definitions share the assumption that underlying processes (feelings, ideas, impulses, drives, etc.) influence much of overt behavior; that these underlying processes are often not at the conscious level; and that humans frequently use defense mechanisms to keep anxiety-provoking feelings, ideas, and impulses out of conscious awareness. Theories that are psychodynamic in nature may or may not be psychoanalytic (Robbins, 1989). For example, gestalt therapy is an explicitly psychodynamic theory, but just as clearly it is not psychoanalytic.

What then makes a theory *psychoanalytic?* In addition to incorporating unconscious processes and defense mechanisms (as do psychodynamic theories), virtually all modern psychoanalytic theories also believe in (a) stages of development, whether they be psychosocial stages as in Erikson's (1950) theories, or psychosexual stages as in Freud (1923/1961); (b) the interplay of instinctual, biological, and social determinants (although theories of course vary in their emphases on these three levels); and (c) the centrality of mental functions or structures as the basic causes of our thoughts, feelings, and behavior (see Robbins, 1989). These ingredients are discussed further in the section, "Common Elements Among Psychoanalytic Approaches."

The distinction between psychodynamic and psychoanalytic theories largely pertains to theories of the person. When referring to theories of the treatment process, the distinction is much less clear and not especially useful. This is particularly so when we go beyond classical approaches to psychoanalytic intervention, as discussed below.

Levels of Psychoanalytic Intervention

When examining psychoanalytic interventions (the term *psychodynamic* also fits here), it is useful to differentiate among four levels of treatment: psychoanalysis proper, analytically oriented therapy, supportive-analytic therapy, and analytically informed therapy.

Psychoanalysis Proper. Psychoanalysis is the most intensive and depth-oriented form of therapeutic intervention. Sessions occur usually between three and five times a week, and analysis is virtually always long-term. Length of treatment is typically from three to seven years. Analysis is carried out by a certified psychoanalyst, who, until recently, was trained in this country as a medical doctor. After receiving the M.D. degree with a specialization in psychiatry, the psychoanalyst receives several years of additional training in psychoanalysis from one of the many psychoanalytic training institutes. In very recent years, training in psychoanalysis has opened up to psychologists (Slavin, 1989). Such training follows completion of the doctoral degree in psychology.

Psychoanalysis proper is ordinarily carried out with the analyst sitting behind the analysand, while the analysand in turn reclines on a couch. The analysand's main task is to *free-associate,* that is, to say whatever comes to mind without editing or trying to formulate intellectually the meaning of his or her associations. Another task of the analysand is to report dreams to the analyst. From the time of Freud's seminal work on the meaning of dreams (Freud, 1900/1938), dreams and their interpretation have held a special place in psychoanalysis. Analysts believe that dreams provide a powerful way of accessing the analysand's unconscious. On reporting dreams during the analysis, the analysand is asked to free-associate to parts of the dream. The analyst subsequently offers interpretations as to the meanings of these dreams in terms of the analysand's dynamic issues.

The analyst's task throughout the analysis is to be noninterfering, to offer what Freud called "even-hovering attention," and to make interpretations as the emerging material from the analysand makes sense to him or her. These interpretations should be close to the analysand's level of awareness and experience; for if they become too removed from what the analysand is feeling, the treatment can become a sterile, intellectual exercise.

Three interrelated features of the analyst's interactions with the analysand deserve special note, for they are fundamental to psychoanalysis. First, throughout the work the analyst seeks to maintain what is called the *analytic attitude.* This attitude is one in which the analyst's most basic mission is to engage the analysand in an exploration, an investigation, of the analysand's internal world. Virtually all of the work is aimed at fostering this in-depth exploration and the resulting insights.

The second feature of the analyst's interaction with the analysand is the analyst's stance toward gratifying the analysand's wishes or demands to be loved and taken care of in the analysis. Given that all therapeutic interactions involve a strong press toward giving and receiving help, it is inevitable that the analysand experiences these wishes or demands. Yet the analyst follows Freud's *rule of abstinence* and in doing so avoids direct expressions of affection and advice. There are two good reasons for this.

First, directly gratifying affectional and dependency needs runs the risk of fueling these needs and thus increases the likelihood that the analysand will become too attached to the treatment rather than to the goal of resolving his or her problems. Second, when such needs are gratified in the analysis itself, it is less likely that the issues underlying them will become conscious. Thus, gratification works against the analyst's mission of fostering insight.

The third element of the analyst's interaction that deserves special note is very much related to the first two. This element involves the analyst's stance of *neutrality and ambiguity.* This stance is often misunderstood by the beginning student, who interprets it as a kind of coldness, aloofness, or impersonality. This is far from the case in good analytic work. The analyst is deeply involved in the analysand's inner experience, and the analyst certainly cares about the analysand (see Greenson, 1967; Langs, 1976). Neutrality, however, implies that the analyst does not take sides in the analysand's struggles. Although the analyst is on the side of the analysand's healthy ego, he or she does not, for example, agree or disagree with the analysand's feelings toward significant others in his or her life and generally does not take a position on what the analysand should do in his life. Again, the analyst's job is to help the analysand understand himself or herself as deeply as possible; taking a position on what the analysand should do or who is right or wrong in the analysand's struggles interferes with the analyst's main job.

The concept of ambiguity, similarly, implies that analysts should refrain from displaying too much of their own issues, lives, viewpoints, and so forth. Such restraint provides an atmosphere in which the analysand's issues may unfold without their being confounded by the analyst's. The analyst's ambiguity also permits the analysand to project feelings and thoughts onto him, and in this way the all-important transferences are allowed to develop more purely than would be the case if the analyst's person intruded on the work.

During the course of analysis, as the analysand continues to free-associate and the analyst carries out the tasks discussed above, the analysand naturally regresses in his or her associations. That is, the analysand's associations and memories continually move backward in time (although not in a straight line). As this happens, the analysand gets more and more into the childhood conflicts and issues that form the fabric from which the present problems derive. Also, as this occurs, transference reactions, as discussed in Chapter 5, continue to develop and build.

If there is a pivotal point around which psychoanalysis revolves, it is this unfolding transference. Indeed, many analysts (e.g., Kernberg, 1975) define psychoanalysis itself as *the systematic analysis of the transferences.* As these transferences develop, they become increasingly intense, until what is called a transference neurosis emerges. During this transference neurosis, it is as if great amounts of energy are invested in the analyst, and the core of the analysand's neurosis gets funneled into and fuels the analysis. At this stage the analyst becomes very central to the analysand.

It must be remembered that transferences are by definition distortions of the analyst. As defined in Chapter 5, transference is a repetition of past conflicts with significant others, displacing feelings, behaviors, and attitudes belonging rightfully in those earlier relationships onto the analyst or therapist. In psychoanalysis, the key to helping the analysand resolve neurotic conflicts resides in providing insight into the distortions involved in the transferences. As the transference intensifies, the analyst maintains his or her ambiguity and neutrality, and this permits the continuing unfolding of these projections. The cure in analysis occurs as the transferences are repeatedly interpreted, worked through, and resolved. The analyst's timing in offering interpretations is crucial.

As the transferences are worked through, the analysand develops deep insight into how his or her early conflicts cause him or her to distort and misperceive the self and others. The analysand's defenses become reduced so that he or she can lead a better life. Again, the aim of analysis is this depth insight, most centrally of the analysand's hidden needs and issues, as manifested in the transferences. There is an assumption that the amount and type of transference that develops in analysis reflect in a deep and significant way the analysand's interpersonal and intrapersonal conflicts outside of the analytic setting. Thus, working through the transferences in analysis deeply and positively affects the analysand's relations with others as well as with the self. It results in deep-seated changes in personality structure.

Psychoanalytically Oriented Therapy. Much of what is called psychoanalysis in beginning texts is really psychotherapy with an analytic orientation, rather than analysis proper, as described above. In psychoanalytic therapy the client and therapist usually sit face-to-face. Sessions are usually once or twice a week, and the duration of the work may be anywhere from a few months to a few or even several years. Although practitioners of psychoanalytic therapy may be certified psychoanalysts, they may also be psychologists, psychiatrists, and psychiatric social workers who are not analysts but who have training in psychoanalytic treatment.

Differences between analysis proper and analytic therapy are generally differences of degree rather than kind. Because of the less frequent meetings, analytic therapy is not considered as intensive a treatment as analysis. Although transference reactions are central in this therapy, the therapist does not seek to cultivate the transference neurosis. Relatedly, free association may be used at times during analytic therapy, but it is not the *modus operandi* as in analysis. The focus tends to be on the problems the client is having in his or her life and what is going on inside, the intrapsychic factors, that have made the client come to grief. Just as there is somewhat less focus on transference in this therapy, there is greater emphasis on helping the client cope with and solve real-life problems (as opposed to purely intrapsychic issues).

The therapist's stance in analytic therapy is very similar to the analyst's stance, and again the differences are matters of degree. Interpretation is still the major technique, but deviations from this interpretive stance are more frequent in therapy. The analytic therapist still subscribes to the analytic attitude, follows Freud's rule of abstinence, and maintains neutrality and ambiguity. But the therapist is more willing to depart from these positions, to be involved in a give-and-take interaction with the client, and to guide the session more actively. The goals of psychoanalytic therapy are similar to those of analysis, although psychoanalysts make the arguable point that the changes occurring in this treatment are not as pervasive and deep as in analysis.

Supportive-Analytic Counseling. Supportive-analytic counseling typically occurs in once-a-week sessions and takes place in a face-to-face context. This form of analytic intervention may last anywhere from a few sessions to several years. Long-term supportive-analytic therapy is most often indicated for clients who have severe emotional problems but for whom the more insight-oriented therapies are either not clinically dictated or are not possible because of situational constraints—for example, the client cannot afford more than once-a-week therapy, or the client needs supportive work. Briefer supportive-analytic counseling occurs when the client seeks help through a crisis and/or when the client or the situation does not allow for long-term, insight-oriented work. The supportive-analytic therapist may be a psychoanalyst, psychologist, psychiatrist, or social worker.

Supportive-analytic therapy is different from analysis proper and analytic therapy in that the therapist is clearly more supportive in this approach and strives less for depth insight. In treating the client, the therapist has made the decision that he or she needs support and will not respond well to an insight-oriented approach. As part of the supportive stance, the therapist may provide appropriate suggestions, reassurance, and reinforcement to facilitate the client's positive steps in resolving life problems and to boost self-esteem. The therapist may at times take an educational posture, providing information and even teaching when necessary.

Analytically Informed Therapy or Counseling. Analytically informed counseling is actually not on the same continuum as the three interventions discussed above, but is included here because in our opinion, it is the psychoanalytically related intervention that is most often used by counseling psychologists and other nonpsychoanalyst psychologists. In this treatment, psychoanalytic theories of the person are used to inform the work—to gain an understanding of the client and his or her dynamics as well as of how these dynamics are expected to play out in counseling or therapy. But the techniques and procedures used by the counselor are many and varied. In essence, the therapist uses an analytic theory of the person but does not necessarily use an analytic approach to the treatment. Rather, the therapist is technically eclectic, in the sense that she or he uses whatever techniques and procedures seem to best fit the client.

An example of analytically informed therapy might be that of a therapist working in a university counseling center who conceptualizes student-clients in terms of dynamics and defenses and even formulates these defenses as id-ego conflicts, just as a classical psychoanalytic theorist would. This therapist, however, uses a range of techniques that take into account the fact that treatment at his or her center is brief and time-limited, having, for example, a 12-session duration limit. With a given student-client, for example, the therapist might use primarily gestalt therapy techniques (see Chapter 9) along with verbal reinforcement of behavior changes in the desired direction (see Chapter 8). Reflective techniques (Chapter 9) are also used to help the client explore feelings. All these techniques together might help shorten the treatment time from that if strictly analytic techniques, procedures, and attitudes were used, for example, analysis of transference, interpretation, analytic attitude, abstinence. The therapist also has greater latitude in terms of technique than is the case with supportive-analytic therapy, and, unlike that treatment, this analytically informed counseling may or may not be supportive.

As the reader would suspect, analytically informed therapy may be practiced by counselors from several disciplines. It may occur once, twice, or even three times a week, and the duration of treatment depends more on the treatment setting than anything inherent in the treatment itself. In fact, techniques of treatment are often selected to fit the setting. For example, different techniques might be used in a university mental health clinic specializing in brief therapy than in a private clinic specializing in longer-term treatment.

A Perspective on Levels of Psychoanalytic Intervention. The main factor that differentiates psychoanalytically oriented practitioners is their theory of the person. Thus, for example, a psychoanalytic-self psychologist following the theories of Heinz Kohut (1971, 1977, 1984) would attend to somewhat different aspects of the personality than would an analytic practitioner using orthodox Freudian theory. These practitioners would attend to different issues because the theories they espouse make different, often divergent, statements about how personality develops, how intrapsychic problems occur, and the forces or factors that serve to foster health and psychopathology. At the same time, however, and with some notable exceptions, the levels of analytic intervention discussed above cut across the differing psychoanalytic theories of the person. Thus, our discussion of psychoanalysis proper applies largely without regard to the analyst's perspective: object-relations, ego-analytic, self-psychological, or orthodox Freudian. The different perspectives guide the practitioner's understanding of the person, and suggest the content for the practitioner to focus on; but these theories generally say little about the process of treatment inherent in our above discussion of levels of analytic intervention.

COMMON ELEMENTS AMONG PSYCHOANALYTIC APPROACHES

There are many different psychoanalytic theories of the person, each in some way an extension or modification of Freudian theory. What do these different theories have in common? We briefly referred to such common elements when differentiating the terms *psychoanalysis* and *psychodynamics.* It is time now to elaborate the eight common elements, in terms of psychoanalysis as both a theory of the person and as an approach to treatment.

Psychic Determinism

Generally speaking, scientific theories in psychology are deterministic. This term implies that behavior is caused or determined and may thus be explained in terms of those causes or determinants. Psychoanalytic theories are no different from other scientific theories in this sense. Where psychoanalytic theories do tend to differ, however, is in their emphasis on *intrapsychic* factors as determinants. Such an approach may be most readily contrasted to behavioristic theories (Chapter 9), which are also deterministic but which do not look inside the person's mind or psyche for causes. For the behaviorist, causes are to be found outside the person, in terms of the outside reinforcers and punishers of behavior. In psychoanalytic theories, in contrast, a variety of factors (biological, social, familial) are seen as shaping the person's intrapsychic world early in life. Once this intrapsychic world or psyche is formed, it becomes a crucial determinant of behavior. The psyche contains the basic structures in the form of id, ego, super ego; basic drives, wishes, beliefs, conflicts, and needs; and differing levels of consciousness.

One derivative of the principle of psychic determinism that has great implications for psychoanalytic treatments is that because virtually all of the client's behaviors are caused by the interplay of these intrapsychic forces, all behavior in treatment is seen as meaningful. Everything the client does and says has purpose, meaning, and relevance to the therapist's understanding of and working with that client, and psychoanalytic practitioners place a premium on understanding their clients in terms of these intrapsychic determinants.

The Genetic-Developmental Hypothesis

A fundamental assumption of all psychoanalytic theories is that the past crucially determines the present and that in order to understand the present inter- and intra-personal functioning of the client as fully as possible, we need to examine the person's past. By the past is usually meant the person's childhood years, and the more classical analytic theories tend to focus on the earliest years as the key in personality development. For example, in analytic theories such as orthodox Freudian, object-relations, and self-psychological theories, the first six or seven years of life are seen as crucial to the development of one's basic personality.

The genetic-developmental hypothesis not only implies that the client's childhood is crucial in personality formation and in health/psychopathology, but this model also incorporates the idea of developmental stages. Thus, Robbins (1989) notes that all contemporary psychoanalytic theories believe in stages of development. Just what defines these stages, however, may differ across the various analytic theories. Freudian theory, for example, posits what are called *psychosexual* stages—oral, anal, phallic, latency, and so forth. For a clear discussion of these stages, with implications for counseling interventions, the reader is referred to Patton and Meara's (1991) work. Erikson's theory, on the other hand, conceptualizes personality development in terms of a series of *psychosocial* stages (see Erikson, 1950, 1968).

The psychoanalytic implications of stage theory become clearer when we consider two additional concepts, *fixation* and *regression*. Using the earlier years as an example, as children pass through the various stages of development, whether psychosexual or psychosocial stages, their healthy development is facilitated by the parents gratifying their psychological needs to an optimum extent. Too much gratification or, as is more often the case, too much deprivation of needs that become most pressing during given stages will result in fixation or regression, or both. Part of the child's psyche becomes stuck (fixated) at the stage in which he or she experienced too much frustration, or the psyche regresses back to an earlier stage at which there was neither too much nor too little frustration. Once fixation or regression occurs during development, the remnants of this tend to show themselves in one's personality throughout development. The seeds of the neuroses and other psychological difficulties are to be found in the person's childhood experiences of frustration or overgratification of needs and in the resulting tendency to become fixated or to regress. (See Fenichel's 1945 psychoanalytic classic for a full discussion of fixation and regression.)

What are the implications of the genetic-developmental hypothesis for intervention? Just as the past determines the present, and just as the seeds of human emotional problems are contained in childhood, so the most powerful and far-reaching treatments facilitate the in-depth exploration of childhood issues. Even more, the most powerful treatments, from the analytic perspective, aid the client in emotional reliving and working through of the early experiences that form the core of his or her neurosis. (Note that we are not talking about a sterile, intellectual inspection of the past, but, rather, an emotional reliving of it in the present.) It is not that all psychoanalytically based treatments do, in fact, require this exploration and reliving. Many do not, especially for practical reasons, for example, time constraints. And analytic practitioners generally would agree that effective treatment can be carried out in the absence of an in-depth examination of the past. Yet psychoanalytic theories believe that such examination makes for the most effective intervention.

The Centrality of the Unconscious

In essentially all psychoanalytic theories of the person, primacy is placed on forces outside of the person's conscious awareness that motivate behavior. In Freud's earlier theorizing, the conscious mind had only a relatively minor role in determining behavior. Of the three structures of the mind or psyche (id, ego, and super ego), early Freudian psychology was largely an id psychology. It was the id, the part of us that is most primitive and unconscious, that provided all psychic energy. The ego, much more of which was conscious, depended entirely on the id for its energy.

During Freud's later years, he placed much more importance on the ego and on conscious processes and choices. This trend was greatly furthered by the ego-analytic tradition, especially as pioneered by the work of Hartmann (1950). We shall have more to say about this development in a later section. For now, suffice it to say that in contemporary psychoanalytic theory, consciousness plays a much more significant role in personality development, and in the development of health and pathology, than in the earlier Freudian theory.

Be that as it may, unconscious factors are still seen as extremely important in personality development within all analytic theories, and the most effective interventions work, at least to an extent, to make the unconscious conscious. Underlying and unconscious beliefs, wishes, and needs are seen as being implicated in most or all pathological symptoms and behaviors. And from an analytic perspective, the most effective treatments must go beyond work on those symptoms or overt and maladaptive behavior. Rather, interventions need to work with and through the unconscious, core conflicts underlying the symptoms. This value on making the unconscious conscious can be seen in Freud's famous dictum regarding the goals of analytic treatment: "where there was id there shall be ego."

Most analytic practitioners, it should be stressed, would agree that treatment may still be effective without making the unconscious conscious or resolving core unconscious conflicts. Results of a major process-outcome study of analytic interventions conducted at the Menninger Clinic do, in fact, support the view that durable changes can occur in the absence of such resolutions (see Horwitz, 1974). The general view, though, is that (a) unconscious processes are tremendously important in personality development, and (b) the most effective treatments help clients, at least to some extent, become conscious of previously unconscious conflicts, beliefs, and so forth.

The Role of Defenses

The concept of defense is a key one in contemporary psychoanalytic theories. As discussed by Brenner (1973) and further clarified in Patton and Meara (1991), a defense is any operation of the mind that aims to ward off anxiety or depression. Defenses are usually thought about in terms of the now well-known defense mechanisms, for example, repression, denial, rationalization, intellectualization, isolation, projection, displacement, and reaction formation. In essence, one may experience wishes, impulses, thoughts, beliefs, or affects that are seen as bad or potentially harmful to oneself. For example, they threaten loss of love from parental figures; abandonment; or punishment, either from one's conscience or external figures. These wishes (for example) are prevented from becoming conscious, and thus from causing anxiety or depression, by the use of defenses. The wishes are usually seen as coming from the id, and it is the ego that erects defenses against them to protect the individual from internal punishment (from the super ego) or external harm.

Although defense mechanisms are often seen as operations of the ego, one can view them more broadly as any intrapsychic operations that reduce anxiety or other painful states. Thus, personality traits, attitudes, and perceptions could serve as defenses. For example, the character trait of extreme orderliness may serve as a defense against anxiety caused by the individual's impulses or wishes to be messy and out of control. Why such wishes would cause anxiety in the first place may be explained in terms of the specifics of the individual's interactions with parents, often during the anal stage, the psychosexual stages during which issues of control are primary.

Regarding treatment, psychoanalytic interventions seek to affect defenses. The aim may be to reduce or eliminate defenses or to help the client institute healthier defenses. Through working with and on the client's defenses, the treatment helps previously unconscious or subconscious reactions to become conscious and thus to be under the client's rational control. Working through defenses also frees up the energy that had been expended unconsciously in maintaining these defenses so that it may be used for healthier purposes. In effective therapy, the therapist is highly sensitive to the issue of the client's need for his or her defenses. Therapeutic interventions are paced such that defenses are worked on and through as the client is emotionally ready to give them up.

Repetition and Transference

From the time of Freud's early theorizing, psychoanalytic theorists have noted how the individual's past unresolved problems get repeated and lived out in present life, and, in turn, how the individual's emotional problems in the present are tied to unresolved conflicts in the past. Freud's in-depth analysis of the compulsion to repeat, the *repetition compulsion,* was his attempt to struggle with and understand why the conflictual past is so often repeated in the present and why in fact people distort the present so that it becomes consistent with the past (see Gelso & Carter's, 1985, discussion, pp. 169–173). This concept of repetition has become a deep and inherent part of contemporary as well as earlier psychoanalytic theory, and the repetition of unresolved conflicts tends to be viewed as a universal aspect of the human experience.

Examples of the kind of repetition we are referring to abound in clinical practice and in everyday life. The client who has experienced too much or too early loss (emotional or physical) in her early years with parents tends to carry with her a fear of being abandoned by others. She responds to friends and lovers as if they were similar to her parents, clings to them for fear of being again abandoned and thus pushes others away. The client who constantly oscillates between defiance and excessive obedience with authority figures (bosses) at work is repeating in the present the early and unresolved issues with a dominant father, toward whom the person felt fearful when defiant and angry when obedient. The client who needs to attract and conquer women but loses interest after doing so is acting out the unresolved conflict originating in his relationship with mother and father much earlier in his life.

Psychoanalytically based interventions seek to help the client understand repetitions such as those above, and through this understanding the client is able to perceive the present more accurately or at least to better control the repetitions. It should be noted that analytic treatment would not seek to help the client understand and work through all such repetitions. Rather, the therapist or analyst will tend to focus on certain core issues and the repetitions stemming from them. Usually, the focus would be on the issue or issues that were causing the greatest suffering in the client's life.

A key point regarding analytic treatment and repetition is that the unresolved issues going back to earlier times in the client's life tend to get played out in the treatment hour itself, especially through the transferences that are developed toward the therapist/analyst. This fact gives the therapist a powerful tool for dealing with neurotic repetitions. That is, as sufficient material unfolds to allow for convincing interpretations, the therapist is able to point out to the client how he or she is distorting in the present, real-life situation of the therapy, and how these distortions (i.e., transferences) represent repetitions. Therapist and client can thus work together to seek understanding of the client's issues underlying the distortions.

The Role of the Client-Therapist Relationship

In one large-scale investigation of psychotherapy (Sloane, Staples, Cristol, Yorkston, & Whipple, 1975), the researchers noted that for the psychoanalytic therapists they studied, the client-therapist relationship and psychoanalytic treatment were almost synonymous. The client-therapist relationship is extremely central to the process and outcome of treatment in virtually all contemporary psychoanalytic interventions.

In trying to understand the particular ways in which the relationship is central, it is useful to think back to Chapter 5, where components of the therapeutic relationship were discussed: the working alliance, the transference configuration, and the real relationship. Although all contemporary psychoanalytic approaches to treatment would agree that a sound working alliance is essential if analytic work is to be effective, the real hallmark of psychoanalytic interventions is attention to the transference relationship, including therapist countertransference. For what we have labeled "psychoanalysis proper," cultivation, interpretation, and working through of the transferences are the heart of treatment. For analytic interventions other than analysis proper, transference is still central, in terms of its unfolding and interpretation in the work and/or its use as a vehicle to aid the therapist in understanding the client's dynamics. The real relationship, on the other hand, has not been an important part of psychoanalytic thinking, although because of conceptualizations such as Greenson's (1967), greater emphasis on the real relationship has appeared in recent years.

Interpretation and Other Techniques

In the sense of verbal response modes as discussed in Chapter 6, the single technique that distinguishes psychoanalytic treatments from other therapies is *interpretation.* In psychoanalysis proper, as Greenson (1967) notes, interpretation is the ultimate and decisive instrument. Other techniques are seen as deviations from this baseline and are to be used only in exceptional circumstances. For example, when conducting psychoanalysis the analyst may on rare occasions offer direct guidance, but for him or her to do so, there would need to be a clear and pressing need, for example, an indication that the analysand will do something that would have long-term and very negative consequences. When such deviations in technique occur, the general rule of thumb in analysis is to analyze, at some point in the future, the client's issues that made these deviations necessary, so that depth insight can be fostered.

The aim of interpretations is to provide insight, that is, to help make conscious what was heretofore unconscious. The analyst allows the analysand's material to unfold during the hour or a series of hours and, when the time is right, offers an interpretation. Such interpretations seek to illuminate the hidden connections between aspects of the analysand's communications and/or uncover hidden causes. In fact, as Greenson (1967) clarifies, rather than making a single interpretation, the analyst usually offers a series of partial interpretations over a period of sessions, each aimed at shedding light on particular dynamics. Great emphasis is placed on offering interpretations that are well-timed, constitute an effective dosage, and are tactfully presented. Timing is perhaps the most complex of these issues. Interpretations are well-timed if the client is ready to hear and work with them, and for this to be the case, sufficient material pertinent to that interpretation needs to have already come to light. Only then will there be enough emotional evidence to make the interpretation convincing to the analysand or client.

In psychoanalytic treatments other than psychoanalysis proper, interpretation is still a key technique, although greater latitude is permitted to the therapist. As we move from analysis proper to analytically oriented therapy to supportive-analytic therapy, there is an increasing flexibility in technique. More active techniques, even those in the category of directives (see Chapter 6), may be used, of course very carefully and with a well-thought-out rationale. Still, interpretation is seen as the most powerful change-oriented technique. (These comments would not apply so clearly to what we have termed "analytically informed" therapy, because this form of therapy is eclectic regarding techniques.) An especially helpful discussion of the interpretive process within the context of psychological counseling is presented in Patton and Meara's recent book (1991, Chapter 4).

The Ideal of Insight

Baker (1985) states that, broadly speaking, all forms of psychoanalytic treatment tend to share five basic psychotherapeutic goals: (1) a reduction in the intensity of irrational impulses and a corresponding increase in the mature management of instinctual striving; (2) an enhancement of the repertoire, maturity, effectiveness, and flexibility of defenses used by the individual; (3) the development and support of values, attitudes, and expectations based on an accurate assessment of reality and that facilitate effective adaption; (4) the development of capacity for mature intimacy and productive self-expression; and (5) lessening of punitiveness of super ego and perfectionism rooted in the demands and prohibitions of the conscience.

What is the mechanism or vehicle for the attainment of these goals? The central, internal mechanism in psychoanalysis is called *insight*. Thus, it is through insight, attained during the treatment hour and beyond, that the client is enabled to move forward and attain the healthy goals noted by Baker. Such insight fosters healthy goal attainment through essentially two means. First and foremost, through the self-awareness that comes with insight, the client experiences increased conscious control (Baker, 1985). When needs, impulses, and strivings are brought under conscious control, the client is better able to make logical choices and is less driven by self-destructive and nonproductive patterns of behavior. The second means through which insight facilitates attainment of healthy goals is called "objectification of the self." In essence, through insight, the client is better able to stand back and observe himself or herself and thus gain a clearer and more accurate perspective.

What precisely do we mean by *insight?* Patton and Meara (1991) define insight as client and therapist production and understanding of factors within the client that contribute to his or her emotional difficulties. Within the treatment itself, client insight may pertain to any of a number of arenas: how present conflicts are related to past issues; the defenses being employed; the feelings and needs being covered; how one's conflicts are being played out in current life; how these conflicts are being acted out in the transference relationship with the therapist, and so forth.

In psychoanalytic writing, two kinds of insight are often differentiated. *Intellectual* insight reflects an understanding of cause-effect relationships in one's life but lacks depth because it does not connect this understanding to one's feelings. It is more like observing the self from a distance, without the feelings that go along with what is being observed. *Emotional* insight, on the other hand, connects affect to intellect—the client is emotionally connected to his or her understanding. As the client comes to understand his or her issues, strong feelings are likely to surface. The simultaneous experience of self-understanding with these feelings is insight in the most powerful and curative sense, emotional insight.

We must note that not all treatments of a psychoanalytic nature strive for depth insight. The shorter-term, more focused treatments (e.g., less than six months), while often insight-oriented, tend to promote more limited insight into one or a few central problem areas. In addition, even longer-term work of an analytic nature may not strive for depth insight when the therapist believes that support is the client's crucial need. This may be especially the case with the more troubled client whose fragile ego and/or degree of dysfunction dictates supportive strategies. Nonetheless, in contemporary psychoanalytic approaches of all types, insight tends to be seen as the most powerful vehicle for deep and durable change in the client, and it is to be sought whenever the clinical situation allows.

TIME-LIMITED PSYCHOTHERAPY: AN APPROACH FOR COUNSELING PSYCHOLOGISTS

Of the many different psychoanalytic approaches to treatment, the ones that seem most relevant to the counseling psychologist are those that shorten the usually very long-term nature of psychoanalytic treatment. Such approaches have become popular in recent times for many reasons (see Johnson & Gelso, 1980; Strupp & Binder, 1984). Examples of these treatments include Sifneos' (1979) short-term anxiety-provoking psychotherapy; Mann's (1973) time-limited psychotherapy; the time-abbreviated treatments originated by the Tavistock Group (Malan, 1979); the work of the Montreal Group (Davanloo, 1980); and Strupp and Binder's (1984) time-limited dynamic psychotherapy. All of these approaches share some common assumptions about brief analytic interventions: (a) clients who have long-standing psychological problems could be treated with dynamically based therapy in a much shorter time than had been previously thought; (b) basic principles of psychoanalytic/psychodynamic treatment could be applied to time-limited treatments; and (c) time-abbreviated therapies could effect lasting changes in the client's basic personality.

In this section, we shall discuss one approach that seems well suited to the work of counseling psychologists: James Mann's (1973) Time-Limited Psychotherapy, or TLP. This psychoanalytic approach is compatible with counseling psychology's emphasis on clients' strengths, is suited to work with intact personalities, and places a premium on brevity. TLP uses a 12-session limit, which is established at the beginning or in the early phase of the work. This limitation fits well with the growing emphasis in professional psychology in general on abbreviating treatments (Gelso & Johnson, 1983).

In focusing on TLP, we do not mean to imply that it is the only brief, dynamic approach suited to the work of the analytically oriented counseling psychologist. Our aim in presenting Mann's approach in some detail is to provide an example of how psychoanalytic principles are applied systematically to a brief therapy. Each of the other brief analytic/dynamic therapies noted above, however, also has relevance to counseling psychology. Strupp and Binder's (1984) time-limited dynamic therapy, for example, has some features very similar to Mann's, and may be the treatment of choice when more extended time-limited work (25–30 sessions) is preferred. The counseling psychology student (or agency) interested in time-limited analytic treatment may well study both approaches in tandem in developing his or her own time-limited strategies.

James Mann's Time-Limited Psychotherapy

James Mann (Mann, 1973; Mann & Goldman, 1982), a Boston psychoanalyst, has developed an approach to time-limited therapy that, more than any others, seeks to capitalize on universal human conflicts about time on the one hand and separation and loss on the other. His time-limited psychotherapy (TLP) has an explicit 12-session duration limit, and a beginning, middle, and ending phase.

Personality, Dynamics and Dysfunction. According to Mann, the recurring life crisis of separation-individuation is the basis upon which his TLP rests. This crisis is rooted in the separation-individuation phase of life, which occurs from around the third month through the third year of life. During this phase, individuals must psychologically separate from their primary caretakers, usually the mother, if they are to develop their own selves and individuality. Yet there always is a conflict about such separation, for it entails giving up the wonderful gratification and omnipotence tied to the mother-infant bond. Giving up such things is always a loss, and this is perhaps the original loss in a long series of losses which the individual inevitably faces throughout life. A key loss that stems from separation and individuation is that of a sense of infinite time. As the person grows, she or he must face the fact that time is finite, that life itself must end.

If the issues around separation from mother during the separation-individuation phase are not handled effectively by the parents, the individual is left with a special vulnerability to issues of separation and loss. Since parenting around this issue, as with all issues, is imperfect, however, all of us have some conflicts about separation. These conflicts are fueled throughout life by the losses most people typically experience, even as they gain new things, for example, the losses incurred at weaning, the Oedipal stage, puberty, college or work, marriage, birth of children, menopause, and old age. In addition to the typical losses involved in such life events and stages, Mann points out, there are countless experiences throughout life that revive repeatedly the sense of loss and anxiety related to the separation-individuation phase. Loss of money, of power, of a relationship, of self-esteem, and of a job—these are obvious examples, but there are many other subtle losses that form a constant accompaniment to life.

The failure to master the basic separation anxiety tied to loss undergirds what Mann sees as four fundamental and universal conflict situations. Every client who participates in TLP will experience one or more of these conflicts: (a) independence vs. dependence, (b) activity vs. passivity, (c) adequate vs. diminished self-esteem, and (d) unresolved or delayed grief. While dealing with the specific dynamics and central problem of each individual, TLP also focuses on one or more of these four conflicts. Furthermore, because the four conflicts are all rooted in the basic issue of separation-individuation, TLP also addresses directly the client's deep-seated experience of separation and loss. Let us now examine how all of this comes about.

Treatment Agreement and Guidelines. TLP begins with between one and three consultation interviews, during which the therapist seeks to understand the client's *central issue,* and the guidelines for treatment are clearly established. Once the therapist has decided that 12-session TLP is suitable, this limit is presented very explicitly during the initial phase. The 12 sessions, typically held weekly, begin at this point.

When Mann presents this time-duration guideline to his clients, he goes so far as to mark the ending date of his calendar in the presence of the client, driving home the point that the treatment relationship is limited in time. This limitation sets into motion a series of dynamic events (described in the next section) that is the key feature of TLP. Clients will at times ask the therapist if he or she believes that 12 sessions will be enough, given that the issues may be long-standing. The response is always a clear and unequivocal "yes," as the therapist's confidence in the treatment is essential.

A crucial event is the therapist's delineation of the client's central issue. Here the therapist makes use of his or her psychoanalytic understanding to detect an underlying, dynamic theme or pattern in the client's life that has roots in the past and that represents the client's ongoing emotional problems. Mann refers to the central issue as reflecting the client's *present and chronically endured pain.* This central issue may not be the same as the client's expressed reason for seeking help. For example, a male client may be anxious, depressed, and in marital conflict. He may believe that his conflicts with his spouse are what are causing his problems. The therapist, on the other hand, while agreeing that marital conflicts are a precipitant, may conclude on the basis of the material the client presents that an unresolved grief reaction with an earlier figure is the root of the client's difficulties.

The manner in which the central issue is presented to the client is of great importance. Although the therapist's understanding may be in terms of complex psychoanalytic theory, the central issue should never be expressed in technical jargon. Rather, it must be couched in terms of feelings or maladaptive function. When the therapist detects this area of present and chronically endured pain, and expresses it to the client in feeling or behavioral terms, the client is likely to experience the therapist's empathy and to feel a sense of closeness. An example of Mann's statement of the central issue occurs in his work with a 31-year-old married man who sought help because of his consuming fear of failing, and difficulty in studying for, his college courses. The client's past and present background included an alcoholic father who had committed suicide, a one-month-old son who had been found dead in his crib five years ago, a boss (to whom he had been close) who had died suddenly a year ago, a chronically ill mother, and a constant fear of being fired from his job. Mann expressed the central issue for treatment thus: "Because there have been a number of very painful events in your life, things have always seemed uncertain, and you are excessively nervous because you do not expect things to go along well. Things are always uncertain for you" (1973, p. 20).

Once the central issue is established, the therapist maintains his or her focus on it, making sure not to deviate into other issues or problems. To be effective, TLP must be a focused therapy. To be sure, the client's past is explored and connected to the present, but this exploration is limited to experiences directly relevant to the central focus. Note, however, that the therapist's initial statement of the central issue, as in the above examples, is often global and becomes increasingly sharpened as TLP proceeds.

Sequence of Dynamic Events. The strict time limit and the clear statement of a central issue set into motion a series of dynamic events. Proscription of time runs counter to and stirs up the unconscious and infantile fantasy of timelessness and unending union with an all-giving parental figure. The time limit and statement of a central issue also give the client a sense that his or her problems are understandable and can be resolved. The client experiences *at once* a sense of optimistic urgency, pessimism, and disappointment.

TLP consists of three stages, each lasting roughly three or four sessions. In the first, negative feelings about termination and endings are repressed, as is indeed the termination date itself. The limitation of time, the selection of a central focus that is both consciously meaningful and connected to significant unconscious issues, and the therapist's confidence that something can be done in a short time all come together to mobilize the client's optimism. An intensely positive transference develops in this initial stage. As a result of these positive affects, Mann asserts that one regularly sees rapid symptomatic improvement during the first stage. The client feels better and seems to be getting better. Important aspects of the current problem, how the client has coped with it, and its roots in the past are all explored. The client bares his or her soul. There is a great temptation on the part of the therapist to explore peripheral issues, but he or she must refrain from doing so. Instead, the therapist maintains the focus and actively seeks to understand and support the client in his or her exploration.

As the work continues into the second stage, the client's enthusiasm begins to wane. The client says, in effect, "There is so much to be done, and so little time." This is a clear signal to the therapist that the honeymoon is over. Negative transference takes the place of the previous positive transference. Mann notes that the characteristic feature of any middle point is that "one more step, however small, signifies the point of no return . . . the client must go on to a conclusion that he does not wish to confront. The confrontation that he needs to avoid and that he will actively seek to avoid is the same one he suffered earlier in his life; namely, *separation without resolution from the meaningful, ambivalently experienced person*" (1973, p. 34). As these feelings and defenses emerge, the therapist's stance, while still supportive of the client's simultaneous growth strivings, becomes more interpretive. The therapist begins to interpret how feelings about the therapist and about ending are tied to earlier feelings about separation and about transference sources, usually parents. All of this is done within the context of the central issue.

Emerging feelings about separation and endings signal entrance into the third and final stage. According to Mann, the last three or four sessions must deal insistently with the client's reaction to termination. This does not mean that the total focus of the sessions is on ending, but, rather, that issues about ending are a central theme during the last stage. The therapist is tempted here to evade such termination work, since she or he, too, has conflicts around separation. Yet such work must not be avoided. Attention to termination and helping the client see how feelings about separation relate to the central problem and stem from unresolved issues in the past, are deeply growth-enhancing. They not only help the client grow in terms of the central focus but also help him or her work through separation issues as manifested in one or more of the four conflict situations (independence-dependence, activity-passivity, self-esteem, unresolved grief).

The Therapist and the Client in TLP. The therapist is more active in TLP than in most analytic interventions, especially psychoanalysis per se. The therapist is questioning, encouraging, supportive, and educative. Regarding this last role, although the therapist should never lecture, she or he may provide information to the client when that seems useful. As the second stage is entered, the therapist becomes more interpretive. She or he seeks to clarify and interpret the client's resistances and, especially in the latter part of the treatment, works with client transferences. Unconscious feelings from the past, their invasion into the present, and their intrusion into the therapy relationship are interpreted and worked through. Of special interest are conflicts around the client's "feeling or behavioral style" as this relates to unresolved issues in the past and the present. It must be kept in mind, though, that this interpretive work occurs in a setting of warmth, empathy, encouragement, support, and optimism.

In keeping with counseling psychology's emphasis on clients' strengths, Mann notes this precondition for the successful practice of his TLP: "the conviction that, given a modicum of help, all human beings have emotional, intellectual, and adaptive assets that they are ready to channel into reasonably gratifying directions. It is imperative that we appreciate . . . what a patient can do for himself" (Mann, 1973, p. 51).

For what kinds of clients might TLP be contraindicated? Are there clients who are especially well suited to this treatment? Generally, TLP is suitable for a broad range of clients. It is not so much the severity or type of client disorder that determines suitability as degree of client motivation for treatment and the ability of client and therapist to establish a central issue. However, Mann affirms that some clients are clearly unsuitable: those who are so severely depressed that they cannot negotiate or even tolerate a treatment agreement; those who are acutely psychotic; and those whose desperation in life centers around the need for, and incapacity to tolerate, close relationships. This last group may fit into the broad category labeled as borderline personality disorders. Although some borderline clients may respond well to TLP, individuals within this category are generally doubtful candidates.

The applicability of TLP to counseling psychology is indicated in Mann's statements about the clients who are ideally suited to TLP. College students who are suffering from what Mann calls "maturational crises" and who, relatedly, have problems revolving around separation-individuation fit neatly into the issues TLP aims to address. These separation-individuation issues, along with the degree of flexibility of this client group, make the termination phase of TLP a genuine growth-consolidating experience, according to Mann. The time limit in TLP addresses the client's desire and need for independence; the treatment helps such a client mature, separate from childhood in a healthy way, and grow.

Comments on Time-Limited Psychotherapy. Although TLP is a creative approach to abbreviating lengthy treatment, some questions may be raised about its emphasis on separation-individuation. Issues of separation and loss are absolutely crucial in this approach, and yet both the beginning student and the seasoned counselor alike may well disagree as to whether such a focus is a necessity. Perhaps not all clients who are suitable for brief therapy or counseling have basic issues of separation, and it is not clear that great emphasis on such issues during the termination phase is as essential as Mann suggests. Empirical research does suggest, however, that from the client's perspective issues of termination should be dealt with in counseling, and in fact such issues are dealt with by most counselors (Marx & Gelso, 1987; Miller et al., 1983). The question is whether Mann overemphasizes separation and loss.

Be that as it may, the delineation of a central issue and the maintenance of a focus on that issue are worthwhile aspects of this brief analytic intervention. The selection of an underlying issue that clarifies how the client's present pain is connected to the past and to the client's attempts to cope is clearly true to the analytic roots of TLP. It aims to go well beyond simply treating overt symptoms. The focus on the client-therapist relationship, with a particular emphasis on transference, is also true to the analytic focus, although like many brief analytic treatments and in contrast to longer-term analytic therapies, Mann also emphasizes the importance of the therapist's being active, supportive, and guiding.

Perhaps the major deficiency of TLP is the lack of research to support (or refute) its effectiveness. To be sure, several studies are presented by Gelso and Johnson (1983) that support the value of 12-session counseling with college students in which Mann's ideas were emphasized. And one study (Miller et al., 1983) suggests that the stages proposed by Mann did occur in time-limited counseling performed by a general group of therapists familiar with Mann's theory. All of this research was done at one university counseling center, however, and much more research is needed.

THE PSYCHOANALYTIC APPROACH IN PERSPECTIVE

An important and lively strand of psychoanalytic thinking in counseling psychology throughout the years is seen in the writing of Bordin (e.g., 1968, 1980) and King (e.g., 1965). Both these theoreticians have made thoughtful and valuable efforts to apply psychoanalytic concepts to the needs of counselors who, for example, work with relatively normal clients in educational settings. Yet over time the influence of psychoanalysis on counseling psychology has tended to be marginal because, for a variety of reasons discussed below, there were some deep incompatibilities between the two fields. As we shall see, however, recently things have changed substantially.

From Strange Bedfellows to Compatible Partners

Historically psychoanalysis and counseling psychology could be seen as strange bedfellows for several reasons. For one, the focus in psychoanalysis on lengthy treatment, often lasting many years, ran counter to counseling psychology's emphasis on brevity. Whereas counselors were interested in abbreviating interventions often to a few sessions, within psychoanalysis there appeared to be an ethos suggesting that only very extended treatments were valuable. A second source of incompatibility historically pertains to the tendency within psychoanalysis to focus on psychopathology, or underlying lack of health, in contrast to counseling psychology's focus on people's assets and strengths. In this area, the two fields actually seemed to move in opposite directions: psychoanalysis paid attention to the deficits or pathology of even relatively healthy people, whereas counseling psychology focused its energies on the strengths of even very disturbed clients. Third, over the years psychoanalysis has singled out internal, or intrapsychic, factors to explain human behavior, whereas counseling psychology has placed its focus at once on the person (intrapsychic), the environment (external), and the person-environment interaction as the root causes of behavior.

Things have been changing in recent times, however, so that the two fields have become more compatible. The differences noted above are still present, but are much less extreme than in the past. In the early chapters of this book we discussed changes in counseling psychology. Let us now look at some of the changes in psychoanalysis that have made it more compatible with the work of the counseling psychologist. These changes are most evident in two lines of thinking that have been highly influential in recent years in psychoanalysis: the neo-Freudian perspective, exemplified by such writers as Adler, Jung, Rank, Fromm, Fromm-Reichman, and Sullivan, and the ego-analytic/object-relations perspective, exemplified in the writings of Hartman, Erikson, A. Freud, Winnicott, Guntrip, Klein, Kernberg, and Kohut. The formulations of this last group extend the writings that Freud began during the latter part of his career. To delve into the writing of each of these famous psychoanalysts would require a volume in itself. Let us simply note some of the relevant key features of their work.

First, in contrast to classical psychoanalytic theory of the person as detailed by Baker (1985), the neo-Freudian and ego-analytic/object-relations approaches place greater stress on the environmental, cultural, and interpersonal factors that contribute to psychological health and maladaptive behavior. In addition, Freud's psychosexual stages (e.g., oral, anal, phallic) are often translated into psychosocial stages during which the maturing human's experiences with significant others (often referred to as object relations) are the key determinants of development. Furthermore, such factors are seen as influencing behavior throughout life. Rather than being determined by what occurred during the first six or so years of life, psychological development is seen as a lifelong process: Significant tasks and maturational changes occur throughout adult life.

Both the neo-Freudian and ego-analytic/object-relations approaches pay significant attention to psychological health and the processes of normal development. In addition, they pay much attention to positive human strivings for creativity, mastery, and the capacity for love. The ego analysts, for example, view the ego as independent from the id (in contrast to classical theory, which sees the ego as deriving all of its energy from the id); the ego's function goes well beyond creating defenses against anxiety. The ego also serves to help people *adapt*—to stress, to life situations, to interpersonal relations, and so forth. The emphasis is on coping and even mastery, rather than simply defense.

One of the difficulties with classical psychoanalytic theory that has limited its relationship with counseling psychology is its inattention to female sexual development and portrayal of women as psychologically inferior. Classical analytic concepts such as penis envy seem archaic and sexist and have been scientifically unsupportable. Neo-Freudians, however, have been much less likely to conceptualize female development in such a manner and have demonstrated willingness to seriously study female sexual development. At the roots of this change has been the neo-Freudians' reformulation of the dynamics of the Oedipus complex, which they are more likely to see in psychosocial, rather than sexual, terms.

Finally, the movement during the past two decades toward abbreviating the length of analytic interventions has taken a huge step in making analytically based treatments more suited to counseling psychology, at least as practiced in places like university counseling centers and other community mental health agencies. The brief or time-limited therapy concepts of Mann, Davanloo, Strupp and Binder, Sifneos, and Malan, as noted in the last section, are particularly significant in this respect.

Science, Research, and Psychoanalysis

One major area of incompatibility historically between psychoanalysis and counseling psychology has been their divergent viewpoints about scientific research. Psychology (including counseling psychology) has deeply invested in its self-definition as a science (as well as a field of practice), seeing controlled empirical research as a major way in which science is to be practiced.

Psychoanalysis has also seen itself as a science (as well as a field of practice), but from Freud on has taken a pessimistic stance toward the value of controlled empirical research. Stated in the extreme (which was all too frequently also the norm), the view has been that controlled research could not possibly help understand the great complexities of human personality and of the psychoanalytic treatment situation. In fact, the only kind of research that could be revealing is that done by a psychoanalyst *during* psychoanalysis. In this view, the psychoanalyst's observations and inferences during the psychoanalytic treatment process constitute science and, furthermore, are the only kind of research that can help us understand the human psyche and the psychoanalytic treatment situation.

Unfortunately, there are enormous scientific problems with such research: the psychoanalyst's biases, which are free to invade the process; the nearly total lack of controls and control groups; extremely global observations; and so forth. Such problems, however, seemed either to be unrecognized within psychoanalysis or were seen as problems that simply had to be lived with. Moreover, undergirding this viewpoint of science was belief that truth could be revealed through the expert psychoanalyst's observations of the analysand—these serve as both a sufficient vehicle for theory construction and an adequate method for testing theory.

Historically, psychology was not without its contribution to the problem. Stated in the extreme (which was all too frequently the norm), the only road to truth and only viable form of good science in psychology, was the controlled experiment, preferably done under laboratory conditions, whereby very specific forms of overt behavior could be studies with great precision. Anything else was seen as subjective and thus unscientific.

Fortunately, things have changed in recent years to bring psychoanalysis and psychology closer together in their views of science and research. Psychoanalysts and psychoanalytic psychologists have clearly become more accepting of controlled empirical research. Such research is evident in publication outlets such as *Psychoanalytic Psychology,* published by the Division of Psychoanalysis (Division 39) of the American Psychological Association. This journal, first published in 1984, has as a primary goal the fostering of basic research and the integration of clinical and research findings (Lewis, 1984). Although it appears that psychoanalysis as research is still the most prominent approach, there is growing recognition of the need for scientific controls, and, in fact, the quantity of controlled research has been growing, especially in psychoanalysis within psychology (in contrast to psychoanalysis within medicine). At the same time as these changes in psychoanalysis have occurred, views of acceptable scientific methods in psychology in general have broadened. This is most clearly seen within counseling psychology in the "alternative methodology movement" (see Chapter 4). Counseling psychologists in particular are becoming much more accepting of research that focuses on the individual, is done in a field setting, does not seek great experimental control, and seeks to examine broad patterns of behavior and subjective meaning.

What has controlled research revealed about psychoanalytic interventions? In regard to psychoanalysis proper, it is extremely difficult to do controlled outcome research on this treatment, given its long-term nature. Thus, little research exists; the findings that do exist, however, are favorable. Psychoanalysis, from a variety of perspectives (e.g., Freudian, object-relations), does appear to have positive effects on analysands on a variety of dimensions, effecting, for example, deeper personality change (Horwitz, 1974; Lambert, Shapiro, & Bergin, 1986).

The picture is equally positive for psychoanalytic-oriented counseling or therapy. Controlled outcome studies indicate that clients who receive such treatments improve, on the whole, in a range of ways, including when the interventions are relatively brief and/or time-limited (Lambert et al., 1986; Sloane et al., 1975). Undemonstrated is psychoanalytic-oriented interventions' superiority to any other theoretical approach. All major approaches appear to be effective. Yet to be clarified is which approach is most effective for which clients under what conditions.

In addition to research on the outcome of psychoanalytic interventions, during the past decade significant research has been done on the *process* of such treatments. Although this research is too extensive to summarize here, it is worth noting that the most significant work has been done on the client-therapist (-analyst) relationship. Such research focuses on the role of the working alliance and on the development and effects of transference (see, for example, Luborsky, et al., 1979; Weiss & Sampson, 1986).

To supplement what has been but a brief sample of psychoanalytic theory, we recommend Baker (1985) and Prochaska (1979). Both give excellent overviews of the fundamentals of psychoanalysis that examine differences among various analytic theories as well (object-relations, ego-analytic, self-psychology). Garske and Molteni (1985) provide an excellent review of the briefer psychodynamic therapies, as do Strupp and Binder (1984) as part of their presentation of their own short-term therapy. Within counseling psychology, Bordin's (1968) classic work on psychological counseling is well-grounded in psychoanalytic theory, and King (1965) provides a valuable discussion of the use of analytic principles in counseling. For the student who is interested in delving into psychoanalytic counseling, we strongly recommend *Psychoanalytic Counseling* by Patton and Meara (1991), which presents a cohesive framework for understanding and conducting counseling from the perspective of both classical psychoanalytic theory and Heinz Kohut's psychoanalytic self psychology.

SUMMARY

The originator of psychoanalysis and all talking cures was Sigmund Freud. His great genius, courage, and thoughtfulness were evident throughout his career and are part of his legacy to psychoanalysis as a science and as an approach to psychological treatment.

In getting a grasp on psychoanalysis, it is useful to make a number of distinctions. First, psychoanalysis is both a *theory of the person and of the treatment situation.* Second, the terms *psychodynamic* and *psychoanalytic* must be distinguished: The former is broader than the latter and includes approaches that are nonanalytic. Third, there are different levels of psychoanalytic treatment, namely, psychoanalysis proper, psychoanalytic psychotherapy, supportive-analytic counseling or therapy, and psychoanalytically informed therapy. Psychoanalysis proper is the most long-term and intensive of these. Psychoanalytically informed therapy makes use of psychoanalytic theories of the person to understand the client but uses whatever treatment techniques best fit the client and his or her situation.

Eight common ingredients of psychoanalysis as theory of the person and of the treatment situation are: (1) psychic determinism, (2) the genetic-dynamic hypothesis, (3) the centrality of the unconscious, (4) the role of defenses, (5) repetition and transference, (6) the therapeutic relationship, (7) techniques in psychoanalysis, and (8) insight as the ideal outcome of psychoanalysis.

Of the many psychoanalytic treatment approaches, those most relevant to the counseling psychologist seek to abbreviate the typically long-term nature of analytic treatment. A number of short-term approaches have become popular in recent years. One example of how psychoanalytic principles have been applied to brief therapy is the time-limited psychotherapy (TLP) of James Mann. This 12-session therapy revolves around the universal issues of separation and loss. In the first session or so, the therapist delineates a central focus for the work, which is maintained throughout. This focus represents the client's present and chronically endured pain. The therapist's stance in TLP is active and supportive, although persistent emphasis is laid on interpretation and insight. Transference, especially around loss and separation, is actively interpreted, mainly during the last stage.

Stressing clients' strengths, TLP is particularly well-suited to younger clients (e.g., college students) with developmental problems. In this way, it is highly compatible with counseling psychology.

Over the years psychoanalysis and counseling psychology, once strange bedfellows, have become potentially compatible partners. Research on psychoanalytic interventions strongly supports the efficacy of such treatments, although there is no evidence that psychoanalytic treatments are more or less effective than others. Research on the process of analytic treatments recently has focused on the therapeutic relationship, especially on transference and the working alliance.

References

Baker, E. (1985). Psychoanalysis and psychoanalytic psychotherapy. In S. Lynn & J. Garske (Eds.), *Contemporary psychotherapy: Methods and models.* Columbus, OH: Merrill.

Bordin, E. S. (1968). *Psychological counseling.* New York: Meredith Corporation.

Bordin, E. S. (1980). A psychodynamic view of counseling psychology. *The Counseling Psychologist, 9(1),* 62–70.

Brenner, C. (1973). *An elementary textbook of psychoanalysis.* New York: International Universities Press.

Breuer, J., & Freud. S. (1955). Studies on hysteria. *The standard edition of the complete works of Sigmund Freud* (Original work published in 1895.) (Vol. 2, pp. 1–305). London: Hogarth Press.

Davanloo, H. (Ed.) (1980). *Short-term dynamic psychotherapy.* New York: Aronson.

Ellenberger, H. (1970). *The discovery of the unconscious.* New York: Basic Books.

Erikson, E. (1950). *Childhood and society.* New York: Norton.

Erikson, E. (1968). *Identity, youth, and crisis.* New York: Norton.

Freud, S. (1938). *The interpretation of dreams.* In A. A. Brill, *The basic writings of Sigmund Freud.* New York: Random House. (Original work published in 1900.)

Freud, S. (1949). *An outline of psychoanalysis.* New York: Norton. (Originally published in 1938.)

Freud, S. (1961). The ego and the id. In J. Strachey (Ed. and Trans.), *The standard edition of the complete psychological works of Sigmund Freud* (Vol. 19, pp. 3–66). London: Hogarth Press. (Original work published in 1923.)

Garske, J. P., & Molteni, A. L. (1985). Brief psychodynamic psychotherapy. In S. Lynn & J. Garske (Eds.), *Contemporary psychotherapy: Models and methods.* Columbus, OH: Merrill.

Gelso, C. J., & Carter, J. A. (1985). The relationship in counseling and psychotherapy: Components, consequences, and theoretical antecedents. *The Counseling Psychologist, 13,* 155–243.

Gelso, C. J., & Johnson, D. H. (1983). *Explorations in time-limited counseling and psychotherapy.* New York: Columbia University, Teachers College Press.

Greenson, R. R. (1967). *The technique and practice of psychoanalysis* (Vol. 1). New York: International Universities Press.

Hartmann, H. (1950). Comment on the psychoanalytic theory of the ego. *The Psychoanalytic Study of the Child, 5,* 74–96.

Horwitz, L. (1974). *Clinical prediction in psychotherapy.* New York: Jason Aronson.

Johnson, D. H., & Gelso, C. J. (1980). The effectiveness of time limits in counseling and psychotherapy: A critical review. *The Counseling Psychologist, 9(1),* 70–82.

Jones, E. (1953). *The life and works of Sigmund Freud* (Vol. 1). New York: Basic Books.

Jones, E. (1955). *The life and works of Sigmund Freud* (Vol. 2). New York: Basic Books.

Jones, E. (1957). *The life and works of Sigmund Freud* (Vol. 3). New York: Basic Books.

Kernberg, O. (1975). *Borderline conditions and pathological narcissism.* New York: Jason Aronson.

King, P. T. (1965). Psychoanalytic adaptations. In B. Stefflre (Ed.), *Theories of counseling.* New York: McGraw-Hill.

Kohut, H. (1971). *The analysis of the self.* New York: International Universities Press.

Kohut, H. (1977). *The restoration of the self.* New York: International Universities Press.

Kohut, H. (1984). *How does analysis cure?* Chicago, IL: University of Chicago Press.

Lambert, M. J., Shapiro, D. A., & Bergin, A. E. (1986). The effectiveness of psychotherapy. In S. Garfield & A. Bergin (Eds.), *Handbook of psychotherapy and behavior change* (3rd ed.). New York: Wiley.

Langs, R. J. (1976). *The bipersonal field.* New York: Jason Aronson.

Lewis, H. B. (1984). *Psychoanalytic Psychology,* (Editorial). *1,* 1–5.

Luborsky, L., Bachrach, H., Graff, H., Pulver, S., & Christoph, P. (1979). Preconditions and consequences of transference interpretations: A clinical-quantitative investigation. *Journal of Nervous and Mental Disorders, 169,* 391–401.

Malan, D. H. (1979). *Individual psychotherapy and the science of psychodynamics,* London: Butterworth.

Mann, J. (1973). *Time-limited psychotherapy.* Cambridge, MA: Harvard University Press.

Mann, J., & Goldman, R. (1982). *A casebook in time-limited psychotherapy.* New York: McGraw-Hill.

Marx, J. A., & Gelso, C. J. (1987). Termination of individual counseling in a university counseling center. *Journal of Counseling Psychology, 34,* 3–9.

Miller, J., Courtois, C., Pelham, J., Riddle, E., Spiegel, S., Johnson, D., & Gelso, C. (1983). The process of time-limited therapy. In C. Gelso & D. Johnson, *Explorations in time-limited counseling and psychotherapy.* New York: Columbia University, Teachers College Press.

Patton, M. J., & Meara, N. M. (1991). *Psychoanalytic Counseling.* New York: Wiley.

Prochaska, J. O. (1979). *Systems of psychotherapy: A transtheoretical analysis.* Homewood, IL: Dorsey.

Robbins, S. B. (1989). Role of contemporary psychoanalysis in counseling psychology. *Journal of Counseling Psychology, 36,* 267–278.

Sifneos, P. (1979). *Short-term dynamic psychotherapy: Evaluation and technique.* New York: Plenum.

Slavin, J. H. (1989). Post-doctoral training for psychologists in psychoanalysis. *Psychologist Psychoanalyst, 9,* 8–11.

Sloane, R., Staples, F., Cristol, A., Yorkston, N., & Whipple, K. (1975). *Psychotherapy versus behavior therapy.* Cambridge, MA: Harvard University Press.

Strupp, H. H., & Binder, J. L. (1984). *Psychotherapy in a new key.* New York: Basic Books.

Weiss, J., & Sampson, H. (1986). *The psychoanalytic process: Theory, clinical observation & empirical research.* New York: Guilford.

Chapter 8

The Behavioral and Cognitive Approaches

The theory cluster discussed in this chapter is actually a combination of two overlapping approaches to counseling, behavioral and cognitive. As will be seen, each approach relies heavily on the other in the modern practice of counseling, and the two perspectives are theoretically compatible. The cognitive and behavioral approaches, along with the currently popular combination of the two, called *cognitive-behavioral therapy,* have become a major force in the practice of counseling psychology. For example, in Watkins, Lopez, Campbell, and Himmell's (1986) national survey of counseling psychologists, nearly half of the respondents who claimed a single theoretical orientation (as opposed to the eclectics, who combined orientations) aligned themselves with either behavioral or cognitive approaches. Furthermore, almost a fourth of the eclectic counselors favored behavioral or cognitive theories.

We begin this chapter by giving a brief historical review of the development of behavioral and cognitive approaches. This is followed by an examination of nine basic assumptions common to both. In reviewing these assumptions, it will become clear that, just as with the other major theory clusters, there is no single behavioral or cognitive approach that dominates the current counseling scene. Rather, the present-day practice of behavior therapy and its cognitive cousin is marked by diversity and heterogeneity, which many believe to be a sign of health and growth.

The third section of the chapter delves into specific methods and techniques of the two approaches, exploring their common ground as well as their distinctiveness. After reviewing behavioral procedures, two primarily cognitive therapies are singled out and summarized. Finally, the chapter concludes with a perspective on behavioral and cognitive therapy in today's practice of counseling psychology.

AN HISTORICAL SKETCH

Of the two approaches reviewed in this chapter, the behavioral developed much earlier. Wilson (1989) notes that two historical events overshadow all others in the development of behavior therapy. The first is the rise of behaviorism—the theoretical and philosophical foundation of at least early behavioral treatments—at the beginning of this century. In the United States, the leading figure in this movement was John B. Watson. Watson's viewpoints were a reaction to the then prevalent "introspectionist" theories, which proposed that to understand human behavior one must look inside. In contrast, Watson posited that such "mentalistic" approaches were unscientific and not very fruitful. Psychology ought to be the study of *overt* behavior. Watson saw human behavior as fully caused by environmental factors (those outside the person), and he believed that behavior could be fully understood as a result of learning. This extremist position implied that humans could learn to be anything, could learn and unlearn any and all behaviors—virtually any human could be conditioned to become a doctor, a lawyer, a criminal, and so forth.

Watson's position, popular in the earlier part of this century, has been widely rejected in recent years. The call of behaviorism has been taken up by more sophisticated versions, the primary example being B. F. Skinner's radical behaviorism. Although Skinner saw internal events, as well as one's biological makeup, as important, he promoted the view that human behavior is best understood and modified through the study of overt stimuli and behavior. Operant conditioning principles (i.e., principles of reinforcement and punishment), in the Skinnerian view, are the most powerful ones in determining behavior. Skinner's views have had a deep impact on both behavior therapy and psychology in general.

The second historical event crucial to the development of behavior therapy was experimental research on the psychology of learning and the consequent discovery of principles of classical and instrumental conditioning. The most seminal event took place near the turn of the century: Russian physiologist Ivan Pavlov's experiments demonstrating classical conditioning principles, as revealed in the salivation responses of dogs. Around the same time in this country, E. L. Thorndike was developing his famous law of effect, in which he detailed how behavior was learned according to principles of reward and punishment.

Similarly, in the late 1930s, Skinner elaborated the principles of instrumental learning with his work on operant conditioning.

These two interrelated events, the rise of behaviorism and the development of the experimental study of learning, however, did not quickly pave the way toward behavioral therapy. Applications of conditioning principles to clinical problems had in fact occurred early in the century. For example, in the 1920s, Mary Cover Jones had demonstrated the use of conditioning in overcoming certain fears in children. Likewise, in the 1930s, O. Hobart Mowrer and E. Mowrer had used conditioning procedures (which remain effective today) to treat bed-wetting problems in children. Yet such behavioral treatments did not take hold in applied psychology, for, as Wilson notes, they were seen as simplistic by practicing psychologists. In the schism that developed, behavioral treatments were seen as part of academic-experimental psychology, whereas practitioners were most often psychodynamically oriented, and concerned themselves with clients' unconscious issues and motivations.

Enter Behavior Therapy

It remained for Joseph Wolpe (1958) to present what may have been the single most important book in the development of behavior therapy, *Psychotherapy by Reciprocal Inhibition.* Until that time, counselors and therapists lacked a set of techniques that would allow them to apply conditioning principles to their work with clients. For several years Wolpe, working in his clinic in South Africa, devised and applied behavioral techniques to his work with clients. Like the psychoanalysts, Wolpe theorized that all neurotic problems were caused by anxiety. But here the similarity to psychoanalysis ended. Wolpe used a combination of classical conditioning theory and Clark Hull's then-popular learning theory as the basis for his work. Anxiety was learned through conditioned autonomic reactions, and Wolpe devised several techniques to extinguish this anxiety. The most widely cited and used of these was Wolpe's systematic desensitization, which continues to be a powerful behavioral treatment today (Deffenbacher & Suinn, 1988). Moreover, Wolpe maintained that fully 90 percent of the adult neurotic patients he treated with his behavioral approaches improved markedly.

By the time Wolpe presented his ground-breaking work, another behavioral therapist, Hans J. Eysenck (1952), had already published one of the most controversial papers in the history of counseling and therapy. Eysenck reviewed existing studies on the outcomes of psychoanalytic and eclectic psychotherapy with neurotic clients and found that their improvement rates were no better than for neurotics receiving no formal therapy. About two-thirds of both groups improved significantly. Although the validity of these findings was debated for years and have been decisively refuted only in recent years (Lambert, Shapiro, & Bergin, 1986), they had a profound effect on the professionals training to be counselors and therapists in the 1950s and 1960s. When Eysenck's findings were seen in light of Wolpe's claim of very high cure rates in behavioral therapies (and that of other behavior therapists, including Eysenck himself in the early 1960s), the popularity of these approaches increased dramatically.

After its healthy birth in the late 1950s, and christening in 1959 by a parent figure (Hans Eysenck), behavior therapy grew quickly in the 1960s. As Rimm and Cunningham (1985) note, psychologists seeking an alternative to psychodynamic approaches found a convincing one in an amalgamation of Skinner's operant conditioning and Wolpe's classical conditioning. The 1960s began with the appearance of the first textbook in behavior therapy, Eysenck's (1960) *Behavior Therapy and the Neurosis.* Within counseling psychology, the behavioral banner was carried most effectively by John D. Krumboltz and Carl E. Thoresen, and behavioral treatments developed so quickly that Krumboltz wrote about the *Revolution in Counseling* (Krumboltz, 1966).

The 1960s ended as significantly as they had begun. Albert Bandura (1969) published the tremendously influential *Principles of Behavior Modification.* Among the many important aspects of this book was the concept of *modeling,* or *imitation learning.* Bandura reasoned that classical and operant conditioning were insufficient to explain how people learn. (In trying to learn to fish or hunt, using the principles of operant conditioning, you would receive reinforcement only after appropriate responses—a highly inefficient way to learn.) People also learn by observing others, models so to speak, and *then* by being reinforced for performing whatever was modeled.

The Cognitive Revolution

As the behavior therapies mushroomed in the 1960s, another therapeutic approach was just beginning to take shape. The seeds of the cognitive approach were planted with the 1962 publication of Albert Ellis' famous *Reason and Emotion in Psychotherapy.* In it, he argued that our feelings and behavior are caused by our cognitions, that is, what we think and say to ourselves. Ellis' rational-emotive therapy gained in popularity during the 1960s, but it was not until the 1970s, when it was joined by the cognitive revolution in psychology in general, that it flourished.

Behaviorism was the ruling force within psychology in general from the time of Watson through the 1960s. In the 1970s, however, theories about how cognitive processes determined behavior not only caught on, but appeared to become the ruling force among theories of behavior.

Within applied psychology, including cognitive psychology, this movement was evidenced in the increased popularity of Ellis' approach, and perhaps even more significantly, in the incorporation of cognitive concepts *within* behavioral counseling approaches. Bandura (1969) was one of the original forces promoting such an integration of cognitive and behavioral theories. Behavior therapists continued to be concerned with overt behavior, but also began to pay close attention to the interaction of thoughts, beliefs, values, and other internal and cognitive mechanisms, and how these affect behavior. For example, one of the most important investigated concepts in recent years is Bandura's (1977) concept of self-efficacy (people's beliefs about what they are able to do). Self-efficacy has been found to influence a wide range of behaviors, for example, sports performance, social skills development, educational achievement, and career development (see the review by Maddux & Stanley, 1986).

As part of this cognitive revolution, a number of treatment theories were developed. Although some of these cognitively oriented theories were developed within the behavioral tradition and some outside of it, all are compatible with behavior therapy in that they make use of behavior therapy techniques and can be conceptualized in learning terms. Beck (1976), for example, developed a cognitive therapy best known for its treatment of depression but which has much wider applications. His approach is basically cognitive, but employs many behavioral methods. Meichenbaum (1977), on the other hand, developed a form of counseling that from the beginning sought to integrate cognitive and behavioral notions.

Whereas behavior therapy discovered "mind" (cognition) in the 1970s, according to Wilson (1989), the 1980s witnessed growth in the interest in feelings and emotions and how these states interact with cognitions and overt behavior. Also, within behavior therapy much greater attention was given to the biological bases of behavior, including "biobehavioral" interactions (O'Leary & Wilson, 1987). The student who is interested in an in-depth analysis of the history of behavior therapy might consult Kazdin's 1978 book-length treatment of this subject.

BASIC APPROACHES AND ASSUMPTIONS OF BEHAVIORAL AND COGNITIVE TREATMENTS

Although counseling encompasses a wide range of cognitive and behavioral treatments, Wilson (1989) provides a useful framework in identifying four basic approaches. These four differ in the extent to which each focuses on overt behavior or cognitive processes. Before discussing the nine common assumptions of the behavioral and cognitive perspectives, we shall briefly summarize these four approaches.

The Four Basic Approaches

First, *applied behavior analysis,* or radical behaviorism, focuses exclusively on overt behavior, with cognition seen as excess baggage—unnecessary to the understanding and modification of behavior. Its leading spokesperson has been B. F. Skinner, and operant conditioning (see below) has been its main procedure.

Second, the *neobehavioristic mediational stimulus-response model* makes use of the learning theories of such eminent psychologists as Clark Hull, Neil Miller, and Kenneth Spence. Mediational models pay attention to what goes on inside the organism. Wolpe's systematic desensitization (SD, described later) is a prime example of such a model. SD seeks to extinguish anxiety (an internal response). As part of this process, the client uses imagery (another internal event) to visualize scenes that arouse anxiety. Internal processes are considered to follow the same laws of learning as do overt behaviors.

The third approach within the behavioral and cognitive perspectives is the *social learning theory* approach. The premise of this approach is that behavior is a function of three interactive systems: behavior itself, environmental influences, and cognitive processes. Albert Bandura (1977), a leading spokesperson for social learning theory, maintains that people's actions themselves produce the environmental conditions that, in turn, influence subsequent behavior. At the center of all this, though, are the internal cognitive processes (beliefs, values, expectancies). These processes determine how environmental events are perceived and interpreted. Although learning principles are central in how behavior (including cognitive behavior) is shaped, the human is a self-directing agent of his or her own behavior change.

The fourth approach, *cognitive behavior modification,* includes theories developed within the mainstream of behavior therapy (e.g., Meichenbaum, 1977; Goldfried, 1988), as well as those formulated from a more distinctly cognitive perspective (e.g., Ellis, 1989; Beck & Weishaar, 1989). The cognitive behavior modification approach is very similar to the social learning approach, but focuses to an even greater extent on cognitive processes in explaining and modifying behavior. Although they use a learning model and behavioral techniques, cognitive behavior modifiers believe that the most effective treatments work directly and intensively on people's self-defeating cognitions.

Nine Basic Assumptions

In discussing the nine basic assumptions of the behavioral and cognitive perspectives, we do not mean to imply that all these assumptions are uniformly held by all counselors. Indeed, there is so much diversity, even among the strictly behavioral approaches, that many critics have wondered if behavior therapy really exists. At the same time, much greater differences mark the behavioral and cognitive cluster versus the psychoanalytic and humanistic cluster of approaches than the cognitive and behavioral cluster. In discussing the nine assumptions, we shall try to make clear what differences exist *within* the behavioral and cognitive approaches as well as *between* them and the psychoanalytic and humanistic perspectives.

Attention to Overt Behavior and Processes Close to Overt Behavior. Virtually all behavioral and cognitive therapies pay close attention to overt behavior, although the radical behaviorists (applied behavior analysts) are the only ones who focus exclusively on such overt processes. As one moves more toward the cognitive side of the continuum (with cognitive modification at the end point), the counselor's attention will shift toward more internal processes, such as cognitions. At the same time, the amount of attention given to the modification of overt behavior is high in all of these approaches, even the explicitly cognitive ones, and is greater than that for the other theory clusters, for example, psychoanalysis.

Even when behavior therapists' attention shifts away from overt behavior, they will be inclined to address processes nearer the surface (nearer overt behavior) than will, for example, psychoanalytic therapists. Thus, in Wolpe's systematic desensitization, counselors seek to work directly on conditioned anxiety (an internal state), and cognitive therapists may go even further and work with the cognitions presumed to cause that anxiety. Psychoanalysts, on the other hand, tend to posit a number of forces even further removed from overt processes. A phobia may be seen by the analyst as a defensive maneuver stemming from the unconscious need to restrict anxiety to one situation rather than a range of them. This anxiety, in turn, may be conceptualized as stemming from unconscious childhood fears of punishment, tied to the wish to do away with father and the accompanying wish to win mother over. Here we have an unconscious defense (the phobia itself) caused by even more deeply unconscious fears, in turn, caused by equally deep unconscious wishes! Contrast this to Wolpe's view, in which the phobic avoidance and internal anxiety are seen as conditioned reactions to the feared object or situation.

The Belief that Behavior, Including Cognitive Behavior, Is Learned and Can Be Unlearned and Relearned. Although nearly all theories of personality and therapy now assume that human functioning is a result of the interaction of biological predispositions and environmental factors, the behavioral and cognitive approaches focus more on how humans go about learning behavioral, emotional, and cognition reactions and patterns. Despite biologically based predispositions, behavior still tends to be learned, the three basic models of learning being instrumental learning, classical conditioning, and modeling. Furthermore, it is *not* assumed that maladaptive behavior is acquired through processes different from those for adaptive (healthy) behavior. Both are acquired according to the same fundamental principles of learning. Just as behavior is learned according to certain principles, it can be unlearned and relearned. The same principles may be used to explain this unlearning and relearning process. Let us look briefly at each of the three forms or models of learning and the principles they include.

Instrumental learning. In this form of learning, often referred to as operant conditioning, behavior is seen as controlled by its consequences. The consequence, *positive reinforcement,* is anything that increases the probability of a response. If a counselor, for example, responds favorably ("Great idea!") when her career-counseling client says he plans to gather more information, and if such a favorable response is followed by increased information-seeking, we would term the counselor's response a positive reinforcer. Positive reinforcement is seen as the most powerful procedure through which behavior is learned.

In like fashion, *negative reinforcement* is anything that increases the probability of a response as a result of avoiding something negative that would have occurred had the escape behavior not been emitted. An example of this would be a client whose avoidance of public speaking is strengthened by the relief that comes from avoiding such activity. A similar concept, *punishment,* refers to the aversive consequences of a response and is often followed by a decrease in that response. For example, a student whose question is ridiculed by a professor would likely decrease his or her questioning. However, the use of an aversive stimulus often has undesirable side effects, so behavior therapists usually prefer a second kind of punishment—the removal of a positive reinforcement. An often used example of this form of punishment is called *time out* (see Rimm & Cunningham, 1985). Typically, the individual is taken to a place lacking the usual reinforcers (the misbehaving child is placed in a room holding no rewarding stimuli such as toys or TV).

The final concept to be mentioned under operant conditioning is *shaping,* or *approximation,* whereby a person is rewarded for successively closer approximations of the desired behavior or end-state. For example, a young child utters "mmmm" in the presence of his mother and is reinforced by her pleasurable response. Then the child is similarly reinforced for uttering "ma," and then only for the gold-star response: "Ma, ma!"

Classical conditioning. This form of learning was discovered by Pavlov in his experiments with dogs. When a stimulus that is neutral is paired with a stimulus that has an effect—the *unconditioned stimulus* (UCS); for example, food in the presence of hungry dogs—the associated *neutral stimulus* begins to elicit the same effects as the UCS. In other words, the bell becomes a *conditioned stimulus* (CS), in that, just like the food, it elicits salivation in the dog. The dog's response to the food, or UCS, is called an *unconditioned response* (UCR); its response to the bell, once the bell becomes a CS, is called a *conditioned response* (CR). Even after the dog is conditioned, its CR will *extinguish* if the CS is presented repeatedly without at least an occasional occurrence of the UCS. (This is similar to extinction of an operant response when reinforcement does not occur.)

In both classical and operant conditioning, two additional principles are crucial to the learning process. The first is *stimulus generalization,* the process through which a person generalizes from a specific conditioned or reinforced stimulus to others. For example, the male client who has learned to trust his mother may also tend to trust other women unless there is reason not to trust. The child who has learned to stay away from fast-moving cars also stays away from other fast-moving objects. However, both accurate and inaccurate generalizations are possible. Thus, a principle called *discrimination,* the learning of proper differentiations among stimuli, must work in tandem with stimulus generalization. The client who grew up with an emotionally destructive father needs to learn not to generalize her reactions to all males, but to discriminate among males regarding their capacity for kindness versus destructiveness.

There are innumerable examples of how classical conditioning may operate in the learning and unlearning of complex behaviors, and the student is invited to come up with such examples as they may apply to the counseling situation. One point we add here is that classical conditioning is no longer seen as the simple pairing of a single US with a single CS. Rather, as Wilson (1989) notes, the correlations between entire classes of stimulus events can be learned. The examples above of generalizing from mother or father to other women or men demonstrate such global conditioning.

Modeling. The third form of learning, modeling, is also referred to as *imitative learning* and *vicarious learning.* Much human behavior is learned by observing others (the *models*), doing what they do, and emotionally experiencing and imitating what they are seen experiencing. Much of what we learn could not be learned at all, or could be learned only very inefficiently, without modeling.

Of the three forms of learning, modeling is the newest to be theorized about, and some psychologists continue to believe that modeling is only a subset of classical and operant conditioning. It is true that aspects of operant and classical conditioning are part of the modeling process. For example, to an important extent, modeling occurs because the behaviors exhibited by the model are reinforced, in either the model or learner, or both. Yet modeling seems distinctive enough to warrant its separate discussion. Think about learning any complex skill (flying an airplane, driving a car, becoming an effective counselor) through only operant and classical conditioning (that is, without modeling). It is hard to imagine learning with any degree of efficiency or, in some cases, even safety. At the same time, one can readily see how the other two forms of learning may be added to modeling. In learning to be a counselor, you observe others both directly (on film, in practice sessions) and through reading. But you also receive reinforcement of appropriate counseling reactions and approximations of them. Further, you may observe others as they experience emotional responses to certain client behaviors; and, through vicarious classical conditioning, you may experience the same reactions to such behaviors when you begin counseling.

Before concluding this discussion of the three forms of learning (instrumental learning, classical conditioning, and modeling), it should be emphasized that the purely cognitive therapists, like the behavior therapists, tend to conceptualize their clients' problems, and how these problems are modified, in learning terms. Ellis (1989), for example, talks about how individuals are socially conditioned to perceive and cognize in certain ways. In like fashion, Beck (Beck & Weishaar, 1989) endorses social learning theory and the importance of reinforcement in his attempt to understand how cognitive processes develop, go awry, and can be changed.

The Melding of Behavioral and Cognitive Approaches in Practice. Although the primarily cognitive approaches to counseling (such as Ellis' rational-emotive therapy and Beck's cognitive therapy) were developed outside the mainstream of behavior therapy, behavioral and cognitive approaches tend to be melded in the present-day practice of counseling psychology, so that practitioners usually consider themselves cognitive-behavioral counselors rather than one or the other. This melding has occurred both because (a) the cognitive theories have explicitly stated their use of behavioral techniques and their conceptualization of human behavior in learning terms, and (b) the most popular behavior therapy theories consider internal constructs (e.g., cognition) crucial to development and change.

As implied in (b) above, the behavior therapy scene has encountered dramatic changes in recent years. Applied behavior analysis, a form of radical behaviorism focusing on only overt behavior, was a dominant force in American psychology (including applied psychology) in the not-so-distant past. In the 1990s, however, few radical behaviorists still practice. Social learning theory, as represented by the work of Albert Bandura, its leading spokesman, now prevails. Internal constructs, such as expectancies, values, thoughts, and self-efficacy, are key concepts in this approach. Overt behavior still receives much attention in social learning theory, but internal cognitive concepts are now studied in addition to external behavioral concepts. Thus, the modern behavioral counselor is usually a cognitive-behavioral counselor.

The Predominance of the Present. All cognitive and behavioral approaches place a premium on the here and now. Problems reside in the present and thus it is the present that requires attention in counseling. To be sure, virtually all agree that the past is important in shaping present cognitive and behavioral patterns. Thus, behavioral and cognitive therapists are interested in the client's learning history, and many gather careful assessment data about it. A counselor may, for example, solicit detailed information about the development of a client's social phobia because the sheer duration of this phobia over time is relevant to the methods of treatment. In the same way, the counselor examines past performance because this reveals important information about the client's assets.

Although the assessment of the client's learning or reinforcement history is seen as valuable, even crucial by some, treatment focuses on the present problem. Few, if any, behavioral-cognitive counselors seek in-depth insight into material buried in the client's past; such insight is not seen as especially helpful in resolving current problems. The past may be very interesting, but its revelations alone change nothing. Nevertheless, behavioral and cognitive counselors may indeed search for other kinds of insight—for example, insight into what clients are telling themselves, or insight into the conditions under which certain fears occur. But these are kinds of insight very different from that sought in psychoanalytic or even humanistic treatments.

The emphasis on the here and now clearly separates the cognitive-behavioral counselor from the more classical psychoanalytic therapist. On the other hand, centeredness on the present in cognitive and behavioral approaches is similar to the orientation of humanistic counselors.

Taking the Presenting Problem Seriously. A client seeks counseling because of anxiety about speaking in class. The problem has become more pressing because this client has just been admitted to a graduate program in counseling where the class sizes are very small and an emphasis is placed on class discussion. The behavioral counselor would make a careful assessment of this problem—its frequency, intensity, and duration—but would likely view the speaking problem as the key intervention issue. The cognitive therapist may go a step beyond and work on the cognitive beliefs that contribute to the speech anxiety, but this counselor will also stay very close to the presenting problem.

The psychoanalytic or humanistic counselor, on the other hand, may view the speaking problem as a symptom of other issues. These issues are generally seen as unconscious (by the analytic therapist) or outside awareness (by the humanist). What needs treatment is not the symptom but the "real" cause, which underlies it. The primarily behavioral counselor, however (differing somewhat from the cognitive), will treat the symptom itself. In fact, behavioral counselors have traditionally adhered to the expression: "The problem is the symptom, and the symptom is the problem."

The Importance of Specific, Clearly Defined Goals. Behavioral and cognitive counselors have a particular aversion to counseling goals that are stated in global—or what they consider "fuzzy"—terms. Thus, goals such as "self-actualization," "personality reorganization," and "resolution of core unconscious conflicts" have always been eschewed by such counselors. Even when clients seek counseling for such reasons, and express their goals in these terms, the behavioral-cognitive counselor works hard to help them be clear and specific. In fact, the counselor usually tries to *operationalize* what constitutes client improvement, that is, tries to state goals so that they are readily measurable and subject to public scrutiny.

An example of this might be seen in a female university student who seeks counseling because she vaguely senses that she does not think highly enough of herself. Careful assessment reveals that this client holds unattainable standards, and harshly criticizes herself when she fails to meet these. The counselor also observes that she tends to denigrate herself verbally. The counselor and client enunciate three goals: The client is to make fewer self-deprecating remarks, reduce her self-critical cognitions, and develop more attainable standards. Such specific problems and goals can be worked on through a variety of behavioral and cognitive interventions. They can also be readily measured.

Similarly, with a client who seeks counseling for specific problems, goals are likewise stated in terms of specific behavioral and emotional changes as much as possible. For example, an agoraphobic client who fears both enclosed spaces and the outdoors may have counseling goals expressed in terms of increasing the frequency of his visits to a local food store, and lowering his anxiety level during such visits. The client suffering from depression might seek to smile more, make fewer self-blaming comments, engage in a greater number of positive activities, and achieve a more favorable score on an inventory of depression.

A Value on the Active, Directive, and Prescriptive Counselor Role. Behavioral and cognitive counselors work actively with their clients to develop the goals of counseling. As counseling proceeds, the counselor's stance (much more than for humanistic and psychoanalytic counselors) is active, directive, and prescriptive. Thus, the counselor will actively guide the client during the interview; make suggestions about what the problem is and how it can best be resolved; suggest activities to be engaged in *within* the interview (e.g., role-playing, imagery, and desensitization); and prescribe client behaviors *outside* the interview. Such outside activities, called *homework,* are a hallmark of the behavioral and cognitive approaches. Much in treatment is accomplished *between* sessions, through what the client finds out about himself, practices, and attempts as the result of homework assignments.

Cognitive and behavioral counselors are thus far from the stereotype of the silent analytic counselor. They do not hesitate to talk during the session. In return, the counselor expects parallel client activity. As Wilson (1989) makes clear: "Perhaps more than any other form of treatment, behavior therapy involves asking a patient to do something such as practice relaxation training, self monitor daily caloric intake, confront anxiety-eliciting situations, and refrain from carrying out compulsive rituals" (p. 256).

The Counselor-Client Relationship as Important But Not Sufficient. When behavior therapy first hit the applied-psychology scene in the late 1950s and early 1960s, it presented itself as the super-scientific alternative to treatment approaches such as client-centered therapy and, especially, psychoanalysis, both of which were portrayed as something less than scientific. In the behavior therapy literature, the apparent need for rigor was expressed in the use of impersonal language, such as "experimenter and subject" for "therapist and client." Given the premium placed on scientific objectivity, the role of the client-counselor relationship was downplayed as a "soft" factor. It was not a readily observable, overt behavior and did not lend itself to rigorous, scientific measurement.

As behavior therapy has matured and become more open to the study and treatment of internal processes, and as notions of science and what is scientific have expanded and liberalized (see Chapter 4), the role of the counselor-client relationship has received much greater attention. Virtually all cognitive and behavioral counselors now express the belief that effective treatment is much more than the application of a set of techniques, and that the counselor-client relationship is very important to the change process. At the same time, unlike Carl Rogers and devotees of the person-centered approach, cognitive and behavior therapists do not believe that a good relationship is in itself sufficient to bring about durable change. The relationship is important, rather, inasmuch as it sets the stage for the effective use of techniques. The role of the relationship as seen by current behavior therapists is portrayed by Brady (1980), as follows:

> In general, if the patient's relationship with the therapist is characterized by belief in the therapist's competence . . . and if the patient regards the therapist as an honest, trustworthy, and decent human being with good social and ethical values (in his own scheme of things), the patient is more apt to invest himself in the therapy. Equally important is the quality and tone

> of the relationship he has with the therapist. That is, if he feels trusting and warm toward the therapist, this generally will facilitate following the treatment regimen, will be associated with higher expectations of improvement, and other generally favorable outcomes. The feelings of the therapist toward the patient are also important. If the therapist feels that the patient is not a desirable person or a decent human being or simply does not like the patient for whatever reasons, he may not succeed in concealing these attitudes toward the patient, and in general they will have a deleterious effect. (pp. 285–286)

The relationship in behavioral therapies is important but is not an end in itself. It provides leverage for the counselor to have the client follow the treatment regimen. Thus, the role of the relationship is very different than in either psychoanalytic or humanistic interventions. (See Chapter 5 on the therapeutic relationship and Chapters 7 and 9 on psychoanalytic and humanistic counseling, respectively.)

The Value of Empirical Data and Scientific Methods. There have been so many changes in behavior therapy over the years that its very definition is not very clear. This confusion has become especially salient as behavior therapy has incorporated cognitive theory and as cognitive therapy has adopted both behavioral techniques and learning theory as basic explanatory tools. At the same time, it is possible that the only assumption or element common to all so-called behavioral and cognitive approaches is the great value placed on careful empirical study of treatment techniques. Probably more than counselors of any other theoretical persuasion, the behavioral counselor sees himself or herself as an applied behavioral scientist who gathers scientific data and uses research findings about specific treatments in his or her counseling.

Given the great emphasis on specificity in behavioral counseling, it is not surprising that practitioners value careful and precise investigations of specific treatment techniques for use with particular client populations. The aim is to build an armamentarium of specific techniques of scientifically demonstrated effectiveness for use with certain client problems in particular situations.

METHODS AND PROCEDURES OF BEHAVIORAL AND COGNITIVE APPROACHES

In this section we summarize a variety of selected assessment and treatment procedures and methods often used by behavioral and cognitive therapists. We follow with a presentation of two primarily cognitive theories of counseling, Ellis' rational-emotive therapy and Beck's cognitive therapy. This section constitutes, however, only a skeletal summary of some frequently used methods and procedures. For a fuller presentation, the reader is referred to book-length discussions by O'Leary and Wilson (1987) and Rimm and Masters (1979), and to chapter-length treatments by Prochaska (1979), Rimm and Cunningham (1985), and Wilson (1989). The discussion below relies heavily on the presentations of Rimm and Cunningham (1985) and Wilson (1989).

Assessment Procedures

The first task of the cognitive-behavioral counselor is to develop a sense of rapport and trust with the client. The counselor listens sensitively and empathically as the client discusses the presenting problem. The emerging relationship allows the counselor to seek information from the client that might be too upsetting to divulge in the absence of such a bond. In the initial meeting or meetings, the therapist seeks full understanding of the client's presenting problem. Using his or her theory of behavior and counseling as a guide, the counselor elicits detailed information about the client's problem—how and when it developed, its duration, frequency, intensity, and severity, and the situations in which it occurs. The client's thoughts and feelings about the problem and how the client has tried to cope with it (including past attempts at counseling) are explored. The counselor looks carefully for the environmental and cognitive influences that may be maintaining the problem and that may be expressed through the client's thoughts, feelings, or behavior.

As Wilson (1989) indicates, cognitive and behavioral counselors rarely ask "why" questions, for example, "Why do you get anxious before exams?" or "Why do you feel stressed out at work?" Such questions may be central to the assessment work of the psychoanalytic therapist, but cognitive and behavioral therapists strongly prefer *how, when, where,* and *what* questions as they seek to understand the factors maintaining the problem behavior and situation. The counselor relies heavily on the client's self-reports but does not necessarily take them at face value. Instead, the therapist looks for ways in which the client's reports seem inconsistent or otherwise inaccurate. Such inconsistencies are gently probed or silently noted for later use. As an effort to develop a picture of the problem and its context, the counselor helps the client be as specific as possible, particularly in terms of how, when, and where the problem is manifested.

As aids in assessment, the counselor uses a variety of techniques in addition to verbal interaction. Among the most prominent are role-playing, guided imagery, self-monitoring, behavioral observation, and psychological testing. In using *role-playing,* the counselor may ask the client to role-play a particular interpersonal situation that seems to be troubling. The counselor can take the role of the person with whom the client is having difficulty or can engage in role reversal, whereby the client plays the other person while the therapist plays the client, or both these activities. Such role-playing provides the counselor with some preliminary behavioral observations of the client, and it also helps the client see more clearly what motivates the interaction with the person with whom he or she has a problem.

In *guided imagery* the counselor asks the client to create a visual image of the problem situation and then verbalize this image to the counselor. This enables both counselor and client to get a step closer (than does simple verbal explanation) to what actually goes on in the problem situation and to what the client thinks and feels in that situation. *Self-monitoring* entails the client's keeping a careful daily record of events or reactions that indicate the main problem. For example, the client with anxiety problems may keep a record of situations in which she or he feels anxious, the amount of anxiety experienced, and what triggered the anxiety. As a result, both client and counselor should develop a clearer, more detailed picture of the problem and what is maintaining it.

Unlike the other techniques, *behavioral observations* are ordinarily used by people other than the client (e.g., parents, teachers, hospital personnel) and are made in the client's natural environment (school, home, hospital), where the problem is occurring. The behavioral counselor shows these people how to observe and record the client's behavior objectively. Most often, this procedure is used from an operant-conditioning perspective. The observer learns to observe the client's behavior, for example, in the classroom or at home and note the reinforcers and punishers that may influence the behavior. The observers can then be taught how to modify their own behavior so as to help change the client's behavior. For example, parents often learn about reinforcement procedures and how their own behavior may reinforce the problematic behaviors of their child. The parents can then be taught how to use reinforcements to produce the desired behaviors.

Psychological tests, questionnaires, and checklists are used by behavioral and cognitive counselors, but only when these measure specific qualities directly relevant to the client's problem situation or behavior. General psychodiagnostic tests, such as the Minnesota Multiphasic Personality Inventory, or the varieties of projective devices, are clearly *not* favored. Instead, checklists and questionnaires that assess, for example, fears, anxiety, depression, or assertiveness may be quite useful to get a preliminary picture of the level of severity of the client's problem and determine how the degree of this severity changes across the course of treatment.

As a final note, it must be added that assessment does not stop after the presenting problem has been fully studied. The behavioral-cognitive counselor continues assessment throughout treatment. In such counseling, in fact, assessment is an integral part of the ongoing treatment.

Behavioral and Cognitive Treatment Procedures

More than counselors of any other theoretical orientation, the behavioral-cognitive counselor attempts to match specific treatment techniques to particular client problems. Techniques are selected on the basis of all aspects of the client's problem, the research literature on the effectiveness of the techniques, and the counselor's own clinical judgments about what will work best with the client. Below is a sample of behavior therapy techniques. As we present these, it is important to keep in mind that in actual treatment, various methods are usually combined and that both cognitive and behavioral procedures are frequently used with the same case.

Operant Conditioning. Operant conditioning is both a set of principles that explain how behavior is learned and a technique for modifying behavior. The use of operant-conditioning techniques may occur in the counselor's office as well as in the environment in which the client's problems occur. Let us look at within-session operant conditioning first.

If the client feels a sense of positive connection to the counselor or at least values the counselor's expertise, he or she will be receptive to the counselor's views and reactions. The counselor in this instance can be a potent reinforcer of behavior change. The behavioral counselor decides which behaviors are to be changed and, if within-office reinforcement techniques seem to fit the situation, the counselor will apply them, usually verbally. For example, in working with a client trying to resolve some career problems and move in a more suitable career direction, the counselor may believe that it is very important for the client to seek occupational information. If the counselor senses that the client will tend to resist such activity, he or she will verbally reinforce (e.g., "Great idea!" or "That sounds like a real step in the right direction") any hints on the client's part that such information would be helpful. Then, as the work proceeds, the counselor positively reinforces the client's expressed willingness to seek information. Positive reinforcement is thus combined with a shaping procedure. Such methods have been found to be highly effective in promoting occupational information-seeking.

In the above example, positive reinforcement is used to increase a response. What about operant-conditioning procedures to extinguish a behavior? Using an out-of-session example, suppose a mother, Ms. Weary, seeks counseling because her three-year-old child, Jimmy, has recently been having frightful, disruptive temper tantrums in which he holds his breath and throws his toys. The counselor carefully interviews Ms. Weary about the conditions under which the problem occurs and finds that they only occur in the presence of the mother, who has just begun a new job that allows her less time at home with Jimmy. The counselor decides to visit the Weary house to directly observe the situation. It becomes apparent that Ms. Weary picks up her son warmly, and verbally expresses affection, whenever he grows angry. Jimmy is thus getting reinforced for angry behavior. Further discussion reveals that Ms. Weary feels guilt about being away from home, although her new job is stimulating and a clear step forward for her vocationally. The counselor works with Ms. Weary to help her to stop reinforcing Jimmy's angry behavior and ignore it instead. Ms. Weary is to leave the room whenever the tantrums begin. The counselor also suggests that she provide Jimmy with lots of physical and verbal affection when he behaves well. The father, too, who often would get preoccupied with work issues while spending time with the child, is shown how to be more reinforcing when the child is well-behaved. In a short time, Ms. Weary, who has been keeping careful records as part of the counseling, reports that Jimmy has essentially stopped his tantrums, is getting lots of loving from both parents, and seems happier generally.

Desensitization. Systematic desensitization (SD) is one of the most thoroughly studied behavioral interventions for extinguishing anxiety and other fear-based responses; it has been found effective for a wide range of anxiety-related problems (Deffenbacher & Suinn, 1988). Growing out of studies that sought to remove conditioned fears in animals, it was adapted for use with humans by Joseph Wolpe (1958). The idea is that when anxiety is systematically paired with an incompatible state, the anxiety will disappear as a result of counterconditioning or will be inhibited, according to the principle of *reciprocal inhibition.* The response used most frequently to inhibit anxiety is relaxation, specifically deep-muscle relaxation.

SD comprises four steps (Deffenbacher & Suinn, 1988). The first is to give the client a rationale for the procedure. This should be stated in a nontechnical manner, and impart the concept that fears are learned and thus can be unlearned through desensitization. The second step is relaxation training. The client is usually taught progressive deep-muscle relaxation, a technique Wolpe adapted from Jacobson (1938). The client is also asked to remember a specific experience in which she or he felt deeply relaxed, and the counselor helps the client construct a scene around this. Third, the counselor and client work together to construct a visual hierarchy of anxiety-arousing scenes, ranging from non-anxiety-arousing to extremely upsetting, all related to the specific problem. For example, if the client is seeking counseling because of exam anxiety, the most upsetting scene may picture that student sitting in a classroom about to receive the final exam from the teacher. Visual hierarchies typically include 8–15 scenes, none of which should elicit much more anxiety than those next to it. Usually the counselor tries to space scenes evenly according to their anxiety-arousing potential.

The final step in SD is desensitization proper, in which the scenes in the hierarchy are, step-by-step, paired with relaxation. Typically, after the client is deeply relaxed, the counselor asks him or her to visualize the least anxiety-arousing scene in the hierarchy. If the client feels any significant anxiety when visualizing this scene, he or she is to raise a finger. If this happens, the client is instructed to visualize the highly relaxing experience they initially worked on. If no anxiety is felt after two or more trials of the first scene, the counselor asks the client to visualize the next one on the hierarchy. If anxiety is experienced, the counselor drops back to the previous scene and repeats the visualization of that scene two more times. This process continues until the client is able to visualize all scenes on the hierarchy without anxiety. Termination of counseling occurs when the client is able to experience success in dealing with the actual feared situation—for example, the test-anxious client is able to take exams with relative ease; the person with a phobia is able to perform activities that he or she was phobic about earlier.

One variant of SD is *in vivo desensitization.* The procedure is the same as in SD, except that the hierarchy is presented in real life. The housebound agoraphobic client may have a hierarchy that begins with stepping outside the house and ends with shopping at the local grocery store. The counselor usually accompanies the client in moving through the hierarchy. If the client becomes anxious, she or he is assisted in relaxation behavior. In vivo desensitization can be a powerful procedure and is recommended whenever it is viable. To be effective, however, the counselor must have full control over the implementation of the hierarchy. This is not always feasible, for example, when anxiety is tied to public speaking, social interaction, or sexual situations.

It should be noted that the progressive relaxation component of SD is often used as a treatment in itself and can be an effective procedure for coping with anxiety and stress. Another variant of SD, called *covert sensitization,* is used to extinguish undesirable behaviors such as alcoholism and certain sexual disorders, for example, exhibitionism. Here, the client is asked to imagine aversive consequences in response to the undesired acts. An alcoholic might be asked to imagine nausea at the thought of a drink, an exhibitionist to imagine being handcuffed in public by the police. A hierarchy of scenes that depict the unwanted behaviors is developed, and each scene is presented in a step-by-step fashion until the client is able to control the problem behavior.

Flooding. In certain ways, flooding is the opposite of SD. SD seeks to minimize anxiety by pairing small doses of it with a contradictory state (e.g., deep relaxation). Flooding maximizes anxiety. The agoraphobic client might be asked to imagine being away from home, in a crowded supermarket, without having first gone through a hierarchy of scenes.

The anxiety here will be quite high, but it usually dissipates if the client stays with the scene long enough. Thus, through repeated exposure to high-anxiety scenes, in the absence of any actual harm, anxiety becomes extinguished.

A form of flooding that is frequently used is *in vivo flooding,* which has been found effective with agoraphobias. Again using a trip to the supermarket as our example, the client might first approach the task in a graduated fashion (as in vivo desensitization). Then, once the client is able to approach the supermarket, the counselor may go with the client to the market, urging him or her to stay there regardless of the anxiety, until the anxiety subsides. The principle, again, is that anxiety will disappear if not reinforced. The client sees that he or she is not endangered, that nothing bad happens, so the anxiety eventually dissipates.

Flooding is a potentially useful method, but it is also clearly a high-stress method that inexperienced counselors should not try without supervision. Rimm and Cunningham (1985) point to evidence that flooding may be especially effective, for example, with agoraphobics, when combined with drug therapy. Medication, such as tricyclics or MAO (monoamine oxidase) inhibitors, is administered first, and then followed by the application of in vivo flooding.

Assertiveness and Social Skills Training. Counselors often work with clients who are inhibited in expressing their emotions and who do not stand up for themselves. Such people lack assertiveness, a skill that behavioral and cognitive counselors have worked with considerably over the years. The major strategy used within assertiveness training is called *behavior rehearsal.* Here the counselor helps the client specify situations in which he or she is unassertive. The counselor then plays the role of the person toward whom the client wants to be more assertive while the client role-plays assertiveness. The client pays attention to his or her feelings during and after the role-playing; the counselor observes specific strengths and weaknesses, positively reinforcing positive behavior and non-judgmentally noting the negative. In addition, the therapist often models effective assertive behaviors for the client. Therapist modeling is especially effective if the client lacks knowledge about effective assertiveness; it also gets the client in touch with what it feels like to be the target of the modeled response.

Following counselor modeling, the client imitates the modeled responses, and the counselor verbally reinforces improvements (*shaping*), attending to both verbal and nonverbal client behavior. If the client is working on expressing negative emotion, it is best to have the client begin with a mild response. Doing so aims at reducing the chances that the target person will be "backed into a corner" and forced to respond defensively (Rimm & Cunningham, 1985). In case the minimal responses are not effective, assertiveness training helps the client learn how to escalate assertions. Also, it may be best for the counselor to "fade out" both modeling and reinforcement during treatment, since modeling does not occur in the real world and the client must learn to be *self-reinforcing.* This fading out is thought to lead the client to greater self-directed mastery and persistence in his or her natural environment (Rimm & Masters, 1979).

Participant Modeling. In discussing assertiveness training, and at other points, we have commented on the use of modeling in counseling. The term *participant modeling* (or equivalents such as *contact desensitization, demonstration plus participation*) is often used to describe a specific set of procedures that involve the counselor's modeling through demonstration, followed by the client's imitation of the modeled responses. These procedures are carried out in a graduated fashion. Participant modeling has been found effective for a wide range of specific fears and anxieties and is currently being used a great deal to treat social phobias (e.g., agoraphobia).

Consider the steps that might be taken with participant modeling in treating the client suffering from agoraphobia. The goal of treatment might be for the client to be able to walk comfortably to the local food market. The first step would be to teach the person relaxation techniques, with a focus on deep breathing. The next step would be for the counselor to walk out onto the client's sidewalk, in the client's full view, and then do some deep breathing. Then, the counselor and client together would walk out onto the sidewalk, with the counselor offering instruction and support. Finally, the client would perform this task alone, using the skills she or he has just learned. This same procedure (counselor first, the client and counselor together, and finally client alone), is used for each step, the final step being the goal—the client's comfortably walking to the local market. At each step, the counselor should positively reinforce the client's behavior with verbal praise.

Self-Control Procedures. Self-control methods grew out of behavior therapists' desire to help clients control their own destiny rather than be passive recipients of conditioning procedures. Self-control methods emphasize the client as an active agent who can cope and exert effective control in problem situations. These methods are most appropriate in situations where natural reinforcements are long-term and no short-term reinforcements are available for the desired behavior. An example is academic performance, wherein effective study behavior is usually not reinforced soon after it occurs. Rather, the student must wait until the next exam or even the end of a semester for reinforcement. Such delays make it extremely difficult to learn new desired behaviors or extinguish old, undesirable ones. Self-control methods provide short-term reinforcements until the longer-term reinforcers become available.

Clients who use self-control methods serve as their own therapists in administering their own rewards and punishments. Because of this, therapists often give such clients instruction in behavior modification, with particular emphasis on operant-conditioning principles. Thus, clients are taught basic learning principles, the importance of reinforcement being contingent on given behaviors, and the idea of stimulus control (Rimm & Masters, 1979).

Behavior therapists now use a range of self-control procedures (Bandura, 1977; Kanfer, 1977). Kanfer and his colleagues have devised a multistage procedure for helping clients enhance their self-control, a procedure that has been particularly effective in the treatment of obesity (Rimm & Cunningham, 1985). The first stage entails the client's carefully monitoring his or her behavior, for example, the frequency of eating (how much, how fast, how often) and the surrounding situations (when watching TV, late at night). This gives the counselor and client a baseline for the problem behavior. The second stage entails establishing goals. It is essential that these be specific, reinforceable, and short-term. Thus, the counselor might work with the client to specify daily caloric intake. When goals are short-term, the client is able to experience more reinforcements, and when goals are specific, the client has a clearer sense of what is needed.

The third step is the actual treatment, in which the self-control methods are applied. Rimm and Masters (1979) detail the following procedures for the treatment of obesity: (1) removing undesirable foods from the house, particularly high-calorie foods that do not require preparation; (2) changing eating behavior, for example, returning eating utensils to the table between bites, taking short breaks during the meal; (3) stimulus-narrowing—restricting eating to certain places; (4) having the client eat in situations where he or she does not typically overeat; (5) reinforcing improvements in eating behavior; and (6) encouraging competing responses, for example, taking a walk while delaying eating.

Contingency Contracting. Contingency contracting, which relies on operant-conditioning principles, is a form of behavioral management in which the rewards and punishments for desired and undesired behaviors are established in advance, frequently by a *written contract* with the client (Rimm & Masters, 1979). The first step is assessment. The counselor and client work together to specify the behaviors that need to be modified. They may work toward increasing the frequency of desired behaviors that occur too seldom or decreasing undesirable behaviors undertaken too often. During assessment, counselor and client decide on who will dispense the rewards and punishments (e.g., client, parent, or teacher), and what these will be. Rewards might be money, praise, being allowed to attend movies—anything that the client enjoys. Punishments usually entail withholding the preferred rewards. During the assessment, it is helpful to get a baseline for the target behaviors. Note that such monitoring and recording of the behaviors is also useful during treatment, to get a clear picture of change. Also, seeing change is in itself reinforcing.

Treatment involves simply enforcing the contingencies. Again, this can be done by the client (a self-control method) or someone else. The reinforcers should be applied each time the target behavior is manifested. If this is not possible, "points" can be given for each performance of the target behavior. After reaching a specified amount, the points would convert into a reward or punishment. A good example of contingency contracting as a self-control procedure might be a college student who seeks help because of poor study behaviors. The counselor and client would work together to specify the desired study behaviors to be rewarded and the undesirable ones to be punished. Care would be taken to allow for rewards for effective short-term steps (shaping); for example, if the student typically studies only a half-hour per day, points or rewards could be given for studying one hour per day at first, with study time gradually increasing. With the counselor's guidance, the student would decide on the reinforcers. These could include self-praise, often an effective reinforcer. Note that the treatment occurs *between* sessions. During the sessions themselves, the counselor and client review progress and adjust the contract if needed. The counselor could also provide verbal reinforcement for desired behavior.

Cognitive Restructuring. On a cognitive-behavioral spectrum, the methods and procedures discussed so far would be found on the behavioral end. Cognitive restructuring, on the other hand, is the one overarching method that would be found on the cognitive end. The assumption underlying this method is that, in one way or another, what clients say to themselves and how they say it (their self-talk, or cognitions) determine or shape their problems. Thus, cognitive restructuring entails helping clients change their cognitions.

Cognitive restructuring is a broad term that includes identifying and changing anxiety-causing cognitions. As detailed by Meichenbaum and Deffenbacher (1988), these cognitions may be in the form of cognitive *events,* cognitive *processes,* cognitive *structures,* or all these. Cognitive events are what people say to themselves, and the images they have, that they are aware of and can report. Cognitive processes operate at an automatic and "unconscious" level and include the *way* people process information—how they appraise events, selectively attend to and remember events, and incorporate information consistent with their beliefs. Cognitive structures are even broader, constituting the individual's assumptions and beliefs about the self and the world in relation to the self. There is clearly much overlap in these three concepts, and it may be useful to think of them as existing on a continuum ranging from specific thoughts to global assumptions. The latter have a pervasive and general effect on how people behave and feel.

A wide variety of cognitive approaches now exists, but as Meichenbaum and Deffenbacher (1988) note, all cognitive restructuring procedures include the following: (1) evaluating how valid and viable are the client's thoughts and beliefs; (2) assessing what clients expect, what they tend to predict about their behavior and others' responses to them; (3) exploring what might be a range of causes for clients' behavior and others' reactions; (4) training clients to make more effective attributions about these causes; and (5) altering absolutistic, catastrophic thinking styles (discussed below under rational-emotive therapy).

TWO PRIMARILY COGNITIVE APPROACHES TO COUNSELING

Below we summarize the two most prominent cognitive approaches to therapy, Ellis' rational-emotive therapy and Beck's cognitive therapy. We single out these because each is a theory of therapy in and of itself, is well-known, and has substantial research support. Both are cognitive-behavior therapies, relying on principles of learning and using behavioral methods in addition to focusing on cognitive change. But, at the core, the two approaches are more cognitive than behavioral, because they posit that cognitions are the primary motivators of behavior and emotions, and that changing cognitions provides the most effective treatment.

In addition to the two approaches discussed below, the interested student may consult Goldfried's (1988) rational restructuring, a method that provides more structure to Ellis' rational-emotive therapy and a greater focus on personal coping skills. Also, Meichenbaum's stress inoculation training (see Meichenbaum & Deffenbacher, 1988) is substantially cognitive and has proven effective for many anxiety-related problems.

The Rational-Emotive Therapy of Albert Ellis

Albert Ellis began his clinical practice by conducting psychoanalytic psychotherapy but found that such treatment did not yield the degree of change that he sought, particularly given the long duration of analysis. As a consequence, he developed his own system of therapy, labeled *rational-emotive therapy* (RET). The work that provided the basis for this treatment and for all Ellis' subsequent and prolific writing was his *Reason and Emotion in Psychotherapy* (Ellis, 1962). A recent overview of rational-emotive therapy (RET) is presented in Ellis (1989).

The most fundamental aspect of RET is what Ellis calls his *ABC theory.* A client's emotional reactions and behavior (C) follow some activating event (A). This event may be any stimulus in the environment—a rejection, a reaction from another person, a low grade on an exam, and so forth. This significant activating event (A) may seem to be the cause of C, but is not. Rather, the client's emotional reactions or consequences are caused by B—the individual's cognitions. These cognitions include what the client tells him or herself about A and about the self in relation to A; they are internalized sentences the person utters, so to speak. The cognitions of B may also be broader, representing the client's belief system. Emotional difficulties are caused when the person's cognitions are irrational and self-defeating. The job of RET is to correct these irrational beliefs and replace them with rational and emotionally healthy beliefs.

Ellis (1989) uses as an example of irrational beliefs at point B a woman with severe emotional problems who is rejected by her lover. This troubled woman does not simply feel that it is undesirable to be rejected. Rather, she is inclined to also believe that "(a) it is *awful;* (b) she *cannot stand* it; (c) she *should not,* must not be rejected; (d) she will *never* be accepted by any desirable partner; (e) she is a *worthless* person because one lover has rejected her; and (f) she *deserves to be damned* for being so worthless" (p. 199).

In his earliest work, Ellis listed 11 basic irrational, "senseless" ideas that are common in our culture and lead to neurosis. Perhaps the two most common ones (Goldfried, 1988) involve approval from others and perfection. An example of the former is: "If I am not liked and approved of by others, that is terrible and I am no good." An example of the latter: "If I don't do a perfect job at everything I try, then I am no good." The common element of such beliefs is "catastrophizing" (if this or that happens or does not happen, it would be terrible and a catastrophe), "musturbating" (such and such must happen or must not happen), and "absolutistic" thinking (this or that is always so).

Where do such irrational beliefs and schemas come from, and how are they to be treated? Although human beings have vast resources for growth, they also have powerful inborn tendencies to think irrationally and harm themselves. They are born with "an exceptionally strong tendency to want, to 'need,' and to roundly condemn (1) themselves, (2) others, and (3) the world when they do not immediately get what they supposedly 'need'" (Ellis, 1989, p. 205). These tendencies are then deeply influenced by one's family upbringing and by social conditioning; early conditioning is the most durable. The irrational beliefs, once conditioned, are maintained by the person's continual reindoctrination of himself or herself. By the time a client seeks counseling, his or her cognitive beliefs and assumptions are deeply ingrained.

Counseling is most effective if the counselor actively exposes and corrects the client's irrational, self-defeating thinking. Because irrational thinking is deeply ingrained, it requires active and powerful treatment methods to change. The more passive approaches, for example, psychoanalysis, are less effective than active and directive therapy. On the other hand, Ellis (1989), who does not mince words, tells us that irrational beliefs, such as those of the woman rejected by her lover, "can be elicited and demolished by any scientist worth his or her salt, and the rational-emotive therapist is exactly that: an exposing and nonsense-annihilating scientist" (p. 199). The rational-emotive therapist uses a wide range of techniques: role-playing, assertion training, operant conditioning, desensitization, humor, suggestion, support, and so forth. But above all, RET entails active, vigorous, logical *persuasion* to help the client see and change irrational thinking and behavior.

RET does not place value upon insight into the unconscious or childhood causes. Rather, RET therapists help their clients develop insights into how their own beliefs and assumptions, once learned, are the root causes of their problems, because clients keep reindoctrinating themselves. Once the client understands this, RET strives to give the client insight that only through *hard work and practice* will these irrational, self-defeating beliefs be corrected—and stay corrected. Only repeated rethinking and actions will extinguish the irrational beliefs. Ellis' view of RET is nicely capsulized in the following quote:

> Rational-emotive practitioners often employ a fairly rapid-fire active-directive-persuasive-philosophic methodology. In most cases, they quickly pin the client down to a few basic irrational ideas. They challenge the client to validate these ideas, show how they contain extralogical premises and cannot be validated; logically analyze these ideas and make mincemeat of them; vigorously show how they cannot work and why they will almost inevitably lead to renewed disturbed symptomatology; reduce these ideas to absurdity, sometimes in a highly humorous manner; explain how they can be replaced with more rational theses; and teach clients how to think scientifically, so they can observe, logically parse, and minimize any subsequent irrational ideas and illogical deductions that lead to self-defeating feelings and behavior. (Ellis, 1989, pp. 215–216)

The Cognitive Therapy of Aaron T. Beck

Aaron Beck, like Albert Ellis, was originally trained in psychoanalysis. In the early 1960s he investigated Freud's theory of depression as "anger turned on the self," but found that the data he gathered did not support the theory. Instead, Beck found that the basic problem in depression was in how patients processed information—their cognitive processing. Based on this research, Beck (1967) developed a cognitive theory of depression and subsequently a cognitive therapy for depression as well as other disorders (Beck, 1976). A recent overview of this cognitive therapy is provided by Beck and Weishaar (1989).

Cognitive therapy is a brief (typically 12–16 sessions), present-centered, active, directive, and problem-oriented approach to counseling. In these ways it resembles RET. Beck notes these similarities as well as Ellis' influence on the development of cognitive and behavioral therapies in general (Beck & Weishaar, 1989). Cognitive therapy differs from RET, however, in aspects of its theory of personality and maladaptive behavior, and in the manner in which the therapist works with the client. Unlike RET, cognitive therapy does not assume that the troubled person has "irrational beliefs" and that the disorder will be corrected by modifying these beliefs through persuasion. Rather, the therapist and client work collaboratively to find and understand the "dysfunctional" cognitive thoughts and underlying assumptions that are contributing to the client's problems. Also in contrast to RET, Beck theorized that each psychological disorder has its own, unique cognitive content. For example, people suffering from panic disorders show different cognitive content from those experiencing depression, obsessive-compulsive disorders, and paranoid problems. Each disorder requires a different approach to treatment.

Cognitive therapy uses a learning model to conceptualize how personality develops and how dysfunctional cognitive thoughts and assumptions form. Beck has delineated several kinds of systematic errors in reasoning (cognitive distortions) that appear when people are in distress. *Arbitrary inference* entails drawing conclusions in the absence of supporting evidence. An example of this might be the counselor who concludes after an especially difficult day with her clients, "I am an ineffective counselor." *Selective abstraction* involves conceptualizing a situation on the basis of a detail taken out of context; for example, a man becomes jealous on seeing his fiancee lean toward another man to hear him at a noisy gathering. *Overgeneralization* means abstracting a general rule from a few instances and applying it too broadly. For example, based on the indifferent response of students in one undergraduate class to a few of his lectures, a college professor concludes, "All students are alike; my lectures will never be well received." *Magnification and minimization* involve perceiving something as far more or less significant than it is, for example: "If I don't do well on this date, that will be a disaster"; "This course will be a piece of cake for me" (think of the situations in which this form of minimization occurs). *Personalization* entails attributing blame for some event to oneself without any evidence, for example, when an acquaintance does not return a woman's hello from across a crowded room, the woman concludes that "I must have offended him." Finally, *dichotomous thinking* is rigid, either/or thinking; for example, a man makes the cognitive assumption that "either women will reject and hate you or they will love you and give you everything you want."

Cognitive therapists, according to Beck and Weishaar (1989), are warm, empathic, and genuine as they try to understand how their clients experience the world and cognize their experiences. Unlike in Ellis' RET, cognitive therapists do not persuasively confront their clients' irrational beliefs. Rather, they work together with their clients in what Beck calls *collaborative empiricism.* Therapists often help their clients frame their thoughts and assumptions into hypotheses. When these hypotheses represent cognitive distortions, therapists will seek to help clients see the faulty logic. At other times, counselors devise "behavioral experiments" that require clients to test their hypotheses outside of the counseling session. A major therapeutic technique used by cognitive therapists is *Socratic dialogue.* Thus, therapists carefully develop a series of questions that they ask clients to promote learning. The purpose of this questioning is to help the client arrive at logical conclusions. Cognitive therapists do more than raise questions, though. They actively point out cognitive themes and underlying assumptions that appear to be working against their clients; they devise homework assignments aimed at helping clients see and correct dysfunctional thoughts, assumptions, and behavior; they use a wide range of both cognitive and behavioral procedures to correct faulty cognitions and behavior.

Four common specific cognitive techniques are decatastrophizing, reattribution, redefining and decentering. *Decatastrophizing,* or "what if" hypothesizing, helps clients think through the outcomes they most fear and to make plans to cope with them. *Reattribution* moves clients toward considering alternative causes for events and reactions. This technique is especially helpful to clients who erroneously take responsibility for events and others' reactions. *Redefining* the problem seeks to make it more concrete and specific, and to state it in terms of the client's behavior. For example, the client who feels "nobody cares about me" may be led to redefine the problem to: "I need to reach out to people and show that I care about them." *Decentering* is a technique for treating anxious people who believe they are the constant focus of others' attention. After exploring in detail the logic of this belief, the cognitive therapist designs behavioral experiments that test it. Beck and Weishaar (1989) use the example of an anxious student who believed everyone was focusing on him. This student was instructed to observe others carefully, and he became aware that some were taking notes, some daydreaming, some watching the professor, and so forth. He concluded that his classmates had other concerns.

THE BEHAVIORAL AND COGNITIVE APPROACHES IN PERSPECTIVE

The Efficacy of Behavioral and Cognitive Therapies

Abundant research has been carried out on the effects of behavior therapy, cognitive therapy, and cognitive-behavioral therapy, on these therapies in general as well as on specific behavioral techniques and procedures. From their beginnings in the 1950s, the behavior therapies have been shown to have positive effects on clients, as have the cognitive therapies and cognitive-behavioral amalgamations in more recent times. In the overwhelming majority of studies, behavioral and cognitive procedures have demonstrated effectiveness well beyond what would be expected using a control group of nontreated clients or subjects. Also, in comparison to the psychoanalytic and humanistic therapies (see Chapters 7 and 9), behavioral and cognitive approaches appear to fare *at least* as well. The typical finding is that all of the major approaches to counseling perform equally well. When differences have been found, however, between behavioral or cognitive therapies on the one hand, and psychoanalytic or humanistic therapies, on the other, outcomes have usually favored the cognitive and behavioral therapies (see reviews of research by Emmelkamp, 1986; Garfield & Bergin, 1986; Hollon & Beck, 1986; Lambert, Shapiro, & Bergin, 1986). It is not now clear, however, whether the small differences in favor of the behavioral and cognitive approaches are valid or are due to methodological problems in the research to date (Lambert et al., 1986).

The main, overarching question to which behavior therapy has addressed itself from its beginnings goes something like, "What techniques offered by which therapists work best when used with which clients possessing what kinds of problems?" (see Krumboltz, 1966; Paul, 1967). Referred to as the *"who, what, when,* and *where"* question of counseling research, this formulation contains the numerous specific questions that counseling psychology researchers need to address (Gelso & Fassinger, 1990). Behavioral and cognitive counselors have probably done more to address these multifold issues than anyone else in the applied psychology fields. Answers are elusive, however, and the overwhelming majority of studies comparing, for example, one cognitive or behavioral technique with another, tend to show no differences. Although some answers are now emerging, just how to match clients to treatments remains one of the most challenging research questions in behavioral and cognitive therapy (Deffenbacher, 1988).

In concluding this section, one further issue in behavior therapy presents itself. One early and potentially devastating criticism of behavior therapy by, for example, psychoanalysts was that when one treats a symptom, even if the treatment is successful, the underlying problem will just appear in another form. Unless the underlying problem is treated, the resolution of one symptom will be followed by the emergence of yet another symptom. Because this *symptom substitution* could be so damning to behavior therapy, the early behavior therapy researchers were sure to examine carefully whether empirical evidence existed to suggest such a phenomenon. In fact, of the numerous studies on this topic, none supports symptom substitution in behavior therapy. If anything, the hard data seem to suggest that successful treatment of a specific symptom or behavior in behavior therapy is likely to positively affect the person in other ways. For example, if a client with speech anxiety is successfully treated with systematic desensitization (see Paul's classic study and follow-up in Paul, 1966, 1967), the client is also likely to experience overall reduced anxiety and improved self-concept.

Counseling Psychology and the Behavioral and Cognitive Approaches

Most likely, behavioral and cognitive approaches are a major force in counseling psychology today because of their basic compatibility. In terms of counseling psychology's defining features, it can be seen that the cognitive and behavioral approaches also focus very clearly on clients' strengths or assets. In contrast to classical psychoanalysis, where it seems as if everything is a defense against something and pathology is latent in every behavior (we exaggerate to make the point), behavior therapy, since its inception, has been adroit in uncovering the client's strengths and building on those.

A second defining feature of counseling psychology that has made for an excellent fit with the cognitive and behavioral approaches is its emphasis on brevity in treatments. Although both counseling psychology and these learning-based approaches can admit, and are not opposed to, long-term treatments, the norm is brief treatment. Translated into duration of individual counseling or therapy, the behavioral and cognitive approaches are typically completed well within six months; probably the usual number of sessions is 10–12 (two to three months of counseling).

Finally, one of the principal defining features of counseling psychology has been attention to both the person and the environment (the person-environment interaction) in determining behavior. Yet it has seemed that in counseling psychology research and practice, the environmental part of the equation has often been left out. Of all the approaches to counseling, though, the learning-based ones do pay very close attention to the environment, in terms of what originally caused behavior, what currently serves to control it, and how to modify it.

Emphasis on environment or external factors has been especially strong in the behavior therapies.

Despite these ways in which counseling psychology and the learning-based approaches are highly compatible, the behavior therapies did not become a major force in counseling psychology until cognitive processes began to be addressed. In the earlier days of behavior therapy, when only external events and limited aspects of the person's internal life (e.g., autonomically based conditioned anxiety) were considered and treated, it seemed as though the center of the person was being left out of the equation. To many counseling psychologists, behavior therapy, true to its behaviorist roots, placed too little value on the worth and dignity of humans, viewing them instead as nothing but conditioned reactions, albeit complex ones. With the advent of social learning theory and the cognitive-behavioral approaches, however, this has changed. The human's interior is amply attended to in the dominant forms of learning-based approaches, and the individual is seen as an active agent in the learning process of living, rather than as a passive recipient of stimuli.

SUMMARY

In present-day counseling psychology, the behavioral and the cognitive perspectives rely heavily on each other, and most practitioners who lean toward cognitive and behavioral theories mix the two. Such theoretical orientation is called *cognitive-behavioral counseling.*

Of the two approaches to counseling, the behavioral developed first, growing out of the *behaviorism movement* that began in the early part of this century as well as out of the experimental research on the *psychology of learning* that had begun around the turn of the century. Principles of classical conditioning (as in Pavlov's experiments) and operant conditioning (as in the work of B. F. Skinner) were formulated. Behavior therapy itself was born in the 1950s, its most important early book, Joseph Wolpe's *Psychotherapy by Reciprocal Inhibition,* appearing in 1958. In the 1960s, behavior therapy began to pay attention to internal, cognitive processes such as expectancies, values, and beliefs. Albert Ellis, Albert Bandura, and Aaron Beck, each of whom stressed cognition in one way or another, contributed significantly to the cognitive revolution that deeply affected behavioral and cognitive counseling.

Nine basic assumptions of the cognitive and behavioral perspectives were discussed: (1) attention to overt processes; (2) the belief that behavior is learned, with a focus on classical, operant, and imitative learning; (3) the melding of cognitive and behavioral approaches in today's practice of counseling psychology; (4) the prepotency of the present in the conduct of counseling; (5) the fact that the client's presenting problem is taken very seriously by these approaches; (6) the great importance of specific and clearly defined goals in treatment; (7) the value placed on an active, directive, and prescriptive approach during counseling; (8) the view of the counselor-client relationship as important but not sufficient; and (9) the central value of controlled, scientific research in the practice of counseling.

A wide range of behavioral and cognitive procedures was described, from *operant conditioning* as it may be used in counseling, to *desensitization*, to the more cognitive procedure of *cognitive restructuring*. The two most prominent, primarily cognitive therapies are Ellis' *rational-emotive therapy* and Beck's *cognitive therapy*. The research on the effectiveness of behavioral and cognitive therapies shows them to be at least as effective as other therapies, and there is no support for the idea of *symptom substitution*.

The cognitive and behavioral approaches are a major force in counseling psychology today because they are highly compatible with counseling psychology's emphasis on human beings' assets, on treatment brevity, and on the person-environment interaction. The behavioral and cognitive approaches have become even more attractive to counseling psychologists in recent times because of the attention given to the internal life of the person.

References

Bandura, A. (1969). *Principles of behavior modification.* New York: Holt, Rinehart and Winston.

Bandura, A. (1977). *Social learning theory.* Englewood Cliffs, NJ: Prentice-Hall.

Beck, A. T. (1976). *Depression: Clinical, experimental, and theoretical aspects.* New York: Hoeber.

Beck, A. T. (1976). *Cognitive therapy and the emotional disorders.* New York: International Universities Press.

Beck, A. T., & Weishaar, M. E. (1989). Cognitive therapy. In R. Corsini & D. Wedding (Eds.), *Current psychotherapies* (4th ed., pp. 285–322). Itasca, IL: Peacock.

Brady, J. P. (1980). In M. Goldfried (Ed.), Some views on effective principles of psychotherapy. *Cognitive Therapy and Research, 4,* 271–306.

Deffenbacher, J. L. (1988). Some recommendations and directions. *The Counseling Psychologist, 16,* 91–95.

Deffenbacher, J. L., & Suinn, R. M. (1988). Systematic desensitization and the reduction of anxiety. *The Counseling Psychologist, 16,* 9–30.

Ellis, A. (1962). *Reason and emotion in psychotherapy.* New York: Lyle Stuart.

Ellis, A. (1989). Rational-emotive therapy. In R. Corsini & D. Wedding (Eds.), *Current psychotherapies* (4th ed., pp. 197–240). Itasca, IL: Peacock.

Emmelkamp, P. M. G. (1986). Behavior therapy with adults. In S. Garfield & A. Bergin (Eds.), *Handbook of psychotherapy and behavior change* (3rd ed., pp. 385–442). New York: Wiley.

Eysenck, H. J. (1952). The effects of psychotherapy: An evaluation. *Journal of Consulting Psychology, 16,* 319–324.

Eysenck, H. J. (Ed.) (1960). *Behavior therapy and the neurosis.* Oxford: Pergamon.

Garfield, S. L., & Bergin, A. E. (Eds.) (1986). *Handbook of psychotherapy and behavior change.* New York: Wiley.

Gelso, C. J., & Fassinger, R. E. (1990). Counseling Psychology: Theory and research on interventions. *Annual Review of Psychology, 41,* 355–386.

Goldfried, M. R. (1988). Application of rational restructuring to anxiety disorders. *The Counseling Psychologist, 16,* 50–68.

Hollon, S., & Beck, A. T. (1986). Research on cognitive therapies. In S. Garfield & A. Bergin (Eds.), *Handbook of psychotherapy behavior change* (3rd ed., pp. 443–482). New York: Wiley.

Jacobson, E. (1938). *Progressive relaxation.* New York: Brunner/Mazel.

Kanfer, F. H. (1977). The many faces of self-control, or Behavior modification changes its focus. In R. Stuart (Ed.), *Behavioral self-management.* New York: Brunner/Mazel.

Kazdin, A. E. (1978). *History of behavior modification.* Baltimore, MD: University Park Press.

Krumboltz, J. D. (Ed.) (1966). *Revolution in counseling: Implications of behavioral science.* Boston, MA: Houghton Mifflin.

Lambert, M. J., Shapiro, D. A., & Bergin, A. E. (1986). The effectiveness of psychotherapy. In S. Garfield & A. Bergin (Eds.), *Handbook of psychotherapy and behavior change* (3rd ed., pp. 157–212). New York: Wiley.

Maddux, J. E., & Stanley, M. A. (Eds.) (1986). Self-efficacy theory in social, clinical, and counseling psychology [Special Issue]. *Journal of Social and Clinical Psychology, 4*(3).

Meichenbaum, D. (1977). *Cognitive behavior modification.* New York: Plenum.

Meichenbaum, D., & Deffenbacher, J. L. (1988). Stress inoculation training. *The Counseling Psychologist, 16,* 69–90.

O'Leary, K. D., & Wilson, G. T. (1987). *Behavior therapy: Application and outcome* (2nd ed.). Englewood Cliffs, NJ: Prentice-Hall.

Paul, G. L. (1966). *Insight versus desensitization in psychotherapy.* Stanford, CA: Stanford University Press.

Paul, G. L. (1967). Strategy of outcome research in psychotherapy. *Journal of Consulting Psychology, 31,* 104–118.

Prochaska, J. O. (1979). *Systems of psychotherapy: A transtheoretical analysis.* Homewood, IL: Dorsey.

Rimm, D. C., & Cunningham, H. M. (1985). Behavior therapies. In S. Lynn & J. Garske (Eds.), *Contemporary psychotherapies: Models and methods* (pp. 221–259). Columbus, OH: Merrill.

Rimm, D. C., & Masters, J. C. (1979). *Behavior therapy: Techniques and empirical findings.* New York: Academic Press.

Watkins, C. E., Lopez, F. G., Campbell, V. L., & Himmell, C. D. (1986). Contemporary counseling psychology: The results of a national survey. *Journal of Counseling Psychology, 33,* 301–309.

Wilson, G. T. (1989). Behavior therapy. In R. Corsini & D. Wedding (Eds.), *Current psychotherapies* (4th ed., pp. 241–284). Itasca, IL: Peacock.

Wolpe, J. (1958). *Psychotherapy by reciprocal inhibition.* Stanford, CA: Stanford University Press.

Chapter 9

The Third Force: The Humanistic Approach

The humanistic approach includes an array of therapies such as client-centered, or person-centered; existential; gestalt; and experiential. These approaches are often combined under the rubric *third force* because they reached prominence later than the two dominant forces in American psychology during the first half of the 20th century, psychoanalysis and behaviorism.

The humanistic approach not only followed psychoanalysis and behaviorism chronologically; as Belkin (1980) points out, in both the United States and Europe, humanistic psychotherapy evolved as a reaction to the determinism of Freudian psychoanalysis and to the mechanism of the behavioristic approaches to studying and treating disordered behavior. To many humanistic thinkers, the Freudian approach, which views all behavior as determined by intrapsychic forces outside the control and consciousness of the individual, does worse than miss the mark in terms of the creative, intangible, and often unpredictable aspects of the human personality and spirit. Rollo May (1967, as quoted in Belkin, 1980), one of the leading theoreticians within the third-force approach, offers this trenchant critique of Freudian determinism:

> The danger of the Freudian system of analysis arises when it is carried over into a deterministic interpretation of personality as a whole. The system can become simply a scheme of cause and effect: blocked instinctual urge equals repression equals psychic complex equals neurosis. . . . the danger lies in the influence of Freudian theory in setting up a mechanistic, deterministic view of personality in the minds of the partially informed

> public. . . . *to imagine that the whole of the creative, oftentimes unpredictable, certainly intangible aspects of the human mind can be reduced to cause-and-effect mechanistic principles is sheer folly.* . . . *If such a determinism is accepted, human responsibility is destroyed*. (pp. 48–49, italics added)

Indeed, the attacks on behaviorism by humanistic theorists and therapists are at least as strong as May's critique of psychoanalysis. What is found objectionable is not only the strict determinism of the behavioristic approach but the exclusive focus on observable behavior (and nothing more) that has been so typical of American behaviorism until recent years (see Chapter 8).

Because of these concerns about psychoanalysis and behaviorism, humanism flourished as a social movement within counseling and psychotherapy in the 1960s, synchronizing with the expansiveness and hopefulness of that decade and the early 1970s. Names often associated with the humanistic movement in this country include Gordon Allport, Sidney Jourard, Abraham Maslow, Rollo May, and Carl Rogers. American humanism was closely linked to the existential psychotherapy movement in Europe, and in fact the two are often seen now as being highly similar if not the same, at least in terms of the practice of counseling and therapy. In Europe, the existential therapy movement aimed to integrate the insights of existentialism as a philosophy of human existence with the practice of psychiatry and psychotherapy. The major contributors to the European movement were Medford Boss, Ludwig Binswanger, Viktor Frankl, R. D. Laing, and Frederick Perls. Belkin (1980) notes that Rollo May has for years been the leading American spokesperson for existential psychotherapy.

Although the humanistic movement reached full bloom in the 1960s and 1970s in the United States, its seeds had been planted much earlier. Probably its most prominent proponent in counseling and psychotherapy was Carl Rogers, who completed his first major book on counseling in the early 1940s (Rogers, 1942) and whose seminal *Client-Centered Therapy* was published a decade later (Rogers, 1951). Also in the early 1950s Fritz Perls produced his fundamental theoretical statement about gestalt therapy (Perls, Hefferline, & Goodman, 1951), an approach that fits clearly within the humanistic realm.

The humanistic perspective grew up with, or at least alongside, counseling psychology. The formal beginnings of counseling psychology can be traced to the Northwestern Conference of 1951, the same year as the publication of Rogers' and Perls' seminal books. More important than chronology, though, is the deep influence that the humanistic approach has always had on counseling psychology. As will be seen, the humanistic approach to studying and working with human beings is extremely compatible with some of the central defining features of counseling psychology as delineated in Chapter 1.

Today, in fact, nearly half the counseling psychologists who are members of Division 17 of the APA follow one of the humanistic approaches to counseling (e.g., client-centered, existential, gestalt) as either their primary or secondary theoretical orientation (Watkins et al., 1986). Also, a high percentage of counseling psychologists (e.g., 40% in the Watkins et al. survey) view themselves as eclectic, and many of these eclectics report being strongly influenced by the humanistic perspective (Watkins et al., 1986).

HUMANISTIC ASSUMPTIONS ABOUT HUMAN BEINGS, COUNSELING, AND SCIENCE

Wide differences in technique separate practitioners adhering to theories within the humanistic perspective. For example, in the two approaches examined later in this chapter, person-centered and gestalt therapy, major differences exist in what might be called therapist activity, or directiveness. The gestalt therapist is, in a word, much more *active-directive* than the traditional person-centered therapist. At the same time, common assumptions about human beings, treatment, and science cut across all of the differing approaches under the humanistic umbrella. Six of these are especially applicable.

The Democratic Ideal

In Grummon's (1965) interesting and thoughtful description of client-centered counseling, "belief in the democratic ideal" is noted as a major assumption underlying Carl Rogers' theories. In fact, this belief is inherent in virtually all humanistic approaches. Although the democratic ideal is difficult to define, it can be summed up in terms of one of its most central tenets: *belief in the worth and dignity of each individual.* Another basic tenet is belief in the individual's right to his or her own opinions, thoughts, and interests. Further, each individual has the right, and the responsibility, to control his or her own destiny. The democratic ideal is best served by a society and social institutions that encourage the individual to be independent and self-directing (Grummon, 1965).

The value placed on the individual and individual choice has been a key element of the philosophy of humanism from its beginnings. Although this value does not negate concern for others or for broader social institutions, it does bespeak a kind of individualism peculiar to the humanistic tradition (Lowe, 1969). This individualism can be clearly seen in Fritz Perls' (1969a) Gestalt Prayer.

I do my thing, and you do your thing.
I am not in this world to live up to your expectations

And you are not in this world to live up to mine.
You are you, and I am I.
And if by chance, we find each other, it's beautiful.
If not, it can't be helped.

The Fundamental Predominance of the Subjective

Since the Renaissance, humanistic philosophers have placed a premium on humans' ability to reason. Within the counseling and psychotherapy community of humanists, however, equal value is placed on the subjective side of life. In fact, the humanistic therapist tends to see the subjective side of life as dominant in healthy functioning. Rogers elucidates this position thus: "Man lives essentially in his own personal and subjective world, and even his most objective functioning, in science, mathematics, and the like, is the result of subjective purpose and subjective choice" (Rogers, 1959, p. 191). Gestalt therapists' investment in subjective experiencing and the awareness and living of one's inner, subjective experiencing is unmistakable. On the other side of the ledger, equally clear is their view that to deny one's subjective experience by living in one's intellect is an indication of dysfunctioning.

The humanist's belief in the predominance of the subjective side is most powerfully stated by Rogers in the following passage:

> No matter how completely man comes to understand himself as a determined phenomenon, the products of past elements and forces, and the determined cause of future events and behaviors, he can never *live* as an object. He can only *live* subjectively. . . .
>
> The person who is developing his full potential is able to accept the subjective aspect of himself, and to *live* subjectively. When he is angry he is *angry,* not merely an exhibition of the effects of adrenalin. When he loves he is loving, not merely "cathected towards a love object." He moves in self-selected directions, he chooses responsibly, he is a person who thinks and feels and experiences; he is not merely an object in whom these events occur. He plays a part in a universe which may be determined, but he lives himself subjectively, thus fulfilling his own need to be a person. (pp. 20–21)

Grummon (1965) notes that one of Rogers' major conceptions of humans is that they are "wiser than their intellects." Effective functioning is brought about by living one's full experiencing, of which our conscious thinking is only a fraction.

The Tendency Toward Growth and Actualization

"A musician must make music, an artist must paint, a poet must write if he is to be ultimately at peace with himself." Thus wrote Abraham Maslow (1954, p. 91) in his first major theoretical statement about the human tendency toward actualizing of one's basic nature. For Maslow and essentially all humanists, human motivation is guided by much more than the need for drive-reduction, freedom from tension, and, the elimination of undesirable states. Humans are active, initiating organisms possessing an inherent tendency toward and capacity for growth and self-actualization. The capacity may be latent because of negative upbringing or any of the myriad factors that suppress an individual's potential, but it exists nonetheless, and can be released under the right conditions—for example, through effective education or therapy. Rogers defines this actualizing tendency as the "inherent tendency of the organism to develop all its capacities in ways which serve to maintain or enhance the organism" (1959, p. 196). He views the actualizing tendency as the fundamental characteristic of all life, applying to not only human beings but one-celled protozoans, flowers, wild animals, and everything that lives.

What constitutes this process of self-actualization? The answer to this question is best seen in the work of Abraham Maslow. Over a period of several years, Maslow studied self-actualized people and developed theories about human motivation and self-actualization. His writings continue to be a touchstone for humanistic counselors in this area.

Maslow defines the process as the "ongoing actualization of potentials, capacities and talents, as fulfillment of mission (or call, fate, destiny, or vocation), as a fuller knowledge of and acceptance of, the person's own intrinsic nature, as an unceasing trend toward unity, integration, or synergy with the person" (1968, p. 25). Maslow theorized the existence of a "hierarchy of basic needs" common to all humans. One's more basic needs are at the bottom of the hierarchy—the physiological requirements for air, water, food, shelter, sleep, and sex. These are followed in ascending order by the needs for safety and security, for belongingness and love, and for self-esteem and respect. At the top of the hierarchy are the growth needs, such as those for self-actualization. As needs at one level of the hierarchy are taken care of, people then strive to satisfy those at a higher level. Thus, one continually strives to move up the hierarchy toward self-actualization. Maslow believes all needs must be met if good mental health is to ensue. If they are not, a "deficiency condition" results, referred to as neurosis, personality disturbance, psychosis, and the like.

Because of his or her focus on growth and actualization, the humanistic counselor is often termed a *growth psychologist.* Psychologists within this perspective view mental health in terms of growth, personal maturity, and actualization, rather than the absence of psychopathological symptoms. Formulations of the mature, actualizing individual (Maslow, 1970) or the fully functioning person (Rogers, 1962) are used by the humanistic counselor as a gauge of mental health.

The Essential Trustworthiness of Persons

If we were to baldly categorize the humanistic, psychodynamic, and learning perspectives on the basic goodness or trustworthiness of human beings, the psychodynamic perspective would lean toward the bad or untrustworthy view. To exaggerate to make the point, humans in the psychodynamic model are at the core a bundle of instincts (the id) that must be tamed by later development (ego, super ego) if society is to survive. We are essentially irrational and driven by irrational impulses. From the learning (e.g., behavioristic) perspective, humans are at the core *tabulae rasae*—clean slates. We have no basic nature but rather learn to be what we are through conditioning and imitating.

In contrast to the psychodynamic and learning perspectives, the humanistic perspective has always taken a positive stance, believing human beings' basic rationality is an aspect of their trustworthiness. As Lowe (1969) has stated: "The first humanistic value is that man is a rational being. If man is valued as a creature who above all else is good, then the rationality which sets him apart from the animal is his crowning glory" (p. 99).

Terms such as *trustworthy, good, reliable,* and *constructive* are seen over and over in the writings of Rogers and other humanists. These humanists are by no means naive about the evil and untrustworthiness of many human acts, but tend to see them as a function of defensiveness that people have learned as an unhappy consequence of their environmental backgrounds. The essentially positive view of human nature is stated eloquently by Rogers (1961) as follows:

> I have little sympathy with the rather prevalent concept that man is basically irrational, and that his impulses, if not controlled, will lead to destruction of others and self. Man's behavior is exquisitely rational, moving with subtle and ordered complexity toward the goals his organism is endeavoring to achieve. The tragedy for most of us is that our defenses keep us from being aware of this rationality, so that consciously we are moving in one direction, while organismically we are moving in another. But in the person who is living the process of the good life, there would be a decreasing number of such barriers, and he would be increasingly a participant in the rationality of his organism. The only control of impulses which would exist, or which would prove necessary, is the natural and internal balancing of one need against another, and the discovery of behaviors which follow the vector most closely approximating the satisfaction of all needs. (pp. 299–300)

We should add that not all third-force counselors advocate this positive view of human nature. To the gestalt therapist, human nature is more a mixture of the good with the bad, and humans have equivalent potentialities for both. Even some recent person-centered theorists (e.g., Levant & Shlien, 1984) promote this mixed view. Yet there is no doubt that the legacy left to us by the humanist perspective over the years is one of optimism about human nature and its possibilities.

The Value of an Authentic Human Encounter in the Present

Each and every humanistic approach promotes the counselor's being "real," being involved in a person-to-person encounter, and focusing on the here and now in that encounter. Although early client-centered therapy tended to inhibit the role of the counselor and limit his or her responses to paraphrasing, significant changes have occurred over the years. A major aspect of these changes has been the increased permission given to counselors to be genuine in the therapeutic encounter.

Whereas this focus on authenticity developed in the later person-centered approach, it has always been a basic feature of other humanistic approaches. For example, in gestalt therapy, therapist authenticity occurs through an "I-thou" relationship between counselor and client (Greenberg, 1985). In the I-thou (as opposed to "I-it") relationship the therapist is fully present in the moment, and both participants are open to each other. The therapist cannot force the client to be open, but can be open him- or herself while maintaining the belief that the client will eventually enter the I-thou relationship.

Humanistic therapists do not suggest that the counseling relationship be fully reciprocal. After all, the client is the one seeking help and exploring his or her feelings, thoughts, and experiences. However active, the therapist attempts to put his or her self aside and enter the world of the client, albeit in a partial and temporary fashion. The I-thou relationship advocated by gestalt therapists and virtually all others within the humanistic perspective is not a strictly mutual one wherein the therapist is equally acknowledged and confirmed by the client (Greenberg, 1985). The therapist participates in the relationship with an I-thou attitude but does not seek confirmation from the client. Thus, the therapist's full presence in the moment, unreserved communication, and abiding involvement with another human being are what define his or her contribution to the "I-thouness" of the relationship.

Greenberg (1983) gives some good examples, from the gestalt perspective, of the kinds of responses the therapist makes that reflect this authentic, open, I-thou encounter. These examples are broadly applicable to all humanistic approaches:

> To engage at the level of I-thou, without the demand that the other confirm one, is the essence of the therapist's attitude when he or she enters into an I-thou dialogue. The therapist might share with the client what he or she feels in the first moment of their contact, "I feel eager to meet you and find out what it is you want," or later in the encounter might say, "When I hear you say that, I feel sad and I wonder how you feel." As the encounter

> intensifies, the therapist might give the client some feedback by saying, "My heart is pounding as I say this to you but I want to tell you that I find myself pulling away from you when you are like that" or "I am aware that I am not listening to you and I'm wondering if you're feeling involved in what you're saying." The therapist must also accept and share his or her own sense of self in the encounter: "I felt defensive when you didn't want to do what I asked and I found myself trying to force you to do it" or "I feel frustrated with your deadness and I realize I'm expecting you to be lively so I'll feel good about myself." Another important moment for the therapist to share is when he or she is feeling lost and doesn't know where to go with the client. An essential feature of all encountering is that the therapist must express his or her feelings in an undemanding way and be willing to explore with the client what these feelings are about. In addition, the therapist must express all his or her feelings by saying not only "I am angry" but also "I am afraid that I may alienate you when I say this." In this way, the therapist shares his or her total humanness. (p. 141)

Obviously, the above responses and the vision they reveal of the therapeutic encounter are very different from those promoted by the psychoanalytic and learning perspectives.

The Necessity of Scientific Methods Accommodating the Human Experience

The humanistic movement in psychology has not focused on counseling and therapy alone. Of almost equal concern have been the scientific study of human behavior and the methods used for such study. Humanistic theoreticians and researchers over the years have been critical, though, of a scientific orthodoxy that equated science with a specific method and restricted its subject matter. Thus, the humanistic psychologist strongly advocated methods beyond the traditional psychological experiment, usually done in an antiseptic laboratory environment. Relatedly, the humanist has been critical of the belief that behavior could be dissected into miniscule parts and then studied in terms of those parts. Likewise, the humanist has always deeply opposed the behaviorist notion that only overt behavior is the proper subject matter of psychological science.

In contrast, humanistic psychologists have promoted scientific heterodoxy (Maslow, 1970). They believe that scientific methods should fit the subject matter being studied, ranging from rigorous experiments to less controlled qualitative methods. The *wholeness* of human behavior needs to be addressed scientifically, rather than the study of human nature being reduced to a narrow obsession with microscopic parts. In this same vein, the proper subject matter of psychology must be the complex human experience, including all of those internal processes and experiences so hard to study neatly and simply. In research, humans are seen as active agents, capable of choice and of shaping their own destiny.

It will be recalled that in Chapter 4 we discussed alternative methodologies in scientific research in counseling psychology. Much of the attack on the "received view" and what is being called for by way of alternative methods has a clear connection to the humanistic tradition in psychology. Unfortunately this connection all too frequently goes unrecognized by advocates of alternative methodologies. Yet the roots of scientific heterodoxy are deeply embedded in counseling psychology because of humanistic influence.

We shall now look at the two humanistic approaches to counseling that have been the most prominent in counseling psychology: Carl Rogers' person-centered approach, and the gestalt therapy of Fritz Perls. Throughout the discussion we shall be mindful of the relationship of the two theories to counseling psychology and its practice.

THE PERSON-CENTERED THERAPY OF CARL ROGERS

As discussed in an interesting paper by Dolliver (1981a), theories of counseling and therapy are to an important extent a reflection of the lives, needs, and personalities of their creators. Nowhere is this clearer than in the two humanistic approaches that we shall discuss. In this section, we show a glimpse of the life and professional accomplishments of Carl Rogers, the founder and intellectual leader of person-centered therapy. We shall look at Rogers' background in some detail because, in our view, he is probably the most influential scientist-practitioner in the history of counseling. Rogers' effect on counseling psychology has been so pervasive that many of his ideas now seem like self-evident truths. They have become so ingrained in counseling that many counselors forget they ever came from Rogers!

Carl R. Rogers (1902–1987) was one of six children raised in a fundamentalist religious atmosphere. He attended grade school in a wealthy Chicago suburb before the family moved to a Wisconsin farm, where his engineer father applied scientific techniques to farming. Rogers (1973) had this to say about his family and early years:

> I knew my parents loved me, but it would never have occurred to me to share with them any of my personal or private thoughts or feelings because I knew these would have been judged and found wanting. . . . I could sum up these boyhood years by saying that anything I would today regard as a close and communicative interpersonal relationship with another was completely lacking during that period. My attitude toward others outside the home was characterized by the distance and the aloofness which I had taken over from my parents. I attended the same elementary school for seven years. From this point on, until I finished graduate work, I never attended any school for longer than two years, a fact which undoubtedly had its

> effects on me. Beginning with high school, I believe my hunger for companionship came a little more into my awareness. But any satisfaction of that hunger was blocked first by the already mentioned attitudes on my parents, and second by circumstances. (pp. 3–4)

It is easy to see how the counseling theory Rogers developed—focusing on a close, accepting nonjudgmental relationship between counselor and client—reflect the unmet needs of Rogers' childhood. The flexibility in Rogers' theory, as well as its ability to embrace new concepts, is also a reflection of his style and personality. Note, for example, these observations about Rogers, presented as a preface to Prochaska's (1979) extensive discussion of client-centered therapy:

> The air and aura about him were warm and gentle though his words were strong and poignant. He was willing to field any question and respond to even the most critical comments. When asked how he as a therapist could be both genuine and nondisclosing, he surprised us with his candor. He said that over the past several years of working first with psychiatric clients and then with growth-oriented groups, he had come to see that his model of a therapist as reflective and nondirective had been very comfortable for a person like him. For most of his life he had been basically rather shy and nondisclosing. In the sunny climate of California with its emphasis on openness in groups, he had come to recognize that too much of his former style was a convenient role that had protected him from having to reveal much of himself. It was clear that in therapy, as in his life, he was realizing more fully the genuineness he had always valued but never really actualized. In the 70th year of his life, when lesser individuals might be expected to cling to their cherished ways as therapists and theorists, Rogers continued to reflect an openness to new experiences even when it meant having to reject a way of being that had previously seemed so genuine. (p. 110)

After his years on the farm, Rogers majored in agriculture and then history at the University of Wisconsin. (Rogers is one on a long list of prominent psychologists whose undergraduate major was not psychology.) Breaking with his fundamentalist background, he then entered the very liberal Union Seminary in Manhattan to prepare for the ministry. After two years, Rogers again changed, this time to his lasting vocation, psychology.

Rogers completed his Ph.D. in clinical and educational psychology at Columbia University in 1931. Significantly, the theoretical emphasis during his graduate training was Freudian; Rogers' subsequent theory was in many ways a reaction to the orthodox psychoanalytic perspective.

Rogers' Path to the Person-Centered Approach

After receiving his doctorate, Rogers spent 12 years as an intern and then psychologist at a child guidance clinic in Rochester. There he developed theories of intervention based on his own personal experience. During this time, Rogers was influenced by the work of Otto Rank, a prominent psychoanalyst who had developed views about personality and therapy markedly different from those of orthodox psychoanalysis. Rogers was especially affected by Rank's views on human will and the prime importance of the relationship in therapy (as opposed to techniques).

In 1939 Rogers published his first book, *The Clinical Treatment of the Problem Child.* In it one can see the seeds of what eventually became his person-centered approach. In 1940, Rogers moved to Ohio State University so that he could be more involved in training psychologists to do counseling. In this stimulating environment, with a coterie of graduate students to help further his thinking, Rogers published the controversial *Counseling and Psychotherapy* (Rogers, 1942). In this book, Rogers stressed the importance of the counselor's being warmly receptive to the client and establishing a permissive atmosphere. Counseling was seen as essentially nondirective, with the client taking the lead in its progress. Thus, the basic nondirectiveness of therapy was established. Rogers also emphasized his antidiagnostic views, which were almost heretical for that time. Diagnosing the client, Rogers argued, was nontherapeutic at best, taking the counselor away from his or her primary focus, that of understanding the client's internal frame of reference and helping the client move in the direction that was best for that individual.

At Ohio State, Rogers also began what became a lifelong pursuit—scientific study of the counseling process. He and his students conducted a series of studies of nondirective counseling. Rogers and Francis P. Robinson organized separate but related research programs that made use of newly developed tape recorders to study counseling sessions. Audiotapes allowed researchers to witness for the first time what went on in counseling. The use of such tapes brought about major scientific breakthroughs in the study of counseling.

In 1945 Rogers moved to the University of Chicago to head that university's counseling center. He continued his vigorous research program, and in 1951 published what many consider his most significant book, *Client-Centered Therapy* (Rogers, 1951). The change in the name of his theory, from *nondirective* to *client-centered* therapy, reflected key modifications in Rogers' approach. Whereas the use of techniques had still been emphasized in *Counseling and Psychotherapy,* in the new book the therapist's attitudes toward the client became the focus—one that has remained and even been strengthened over the years. Also new in *Client-Centered Therapy* was the stress on counselor attention to the client's unstated and underlying feelings, rather than his or her words and explicit feelings.

The 1950s was a period of great productivity for Rogers and his colleagues and students. In fact, nearly all of the fundamental ideas about therapy formulated by this group were published or written during that decade. The book *Psychotherapy and Personality Change,* based on research on client-centered therapy, was published in 1954 (Rogers & Dymond, 1954). In 1957 Rogers presented his famous paper on "necessary and sufficient conditions" (Rogers, 1957) discussed in Chapter 5. Few, if any, articles in the history of counseling and psychotherapy have promoted so much research. At the end of the 1950s, Rogers presented his full view of the process of client-centered therapy, along with his theory of personality and interpersonal relationships (Rogers, 1959). His next book, *On Becoming a Person* (Rogers, 1961), presented a wonderful array of articles on therapy, science, life, education, and so on. It is lucidly and interestingly written for the lay audience as well as the professional, and remains as relevant today as when it was first published in 1961.

In 1957 Rogers had moved back to his home state. There, at the University of Wisconsin, he continued research on the "necessary and sufficient conditions," and sought to test his theories with one of the most difficult populations possible—hospitalized schizophrenics. The five-year study he organized may be the largest therapy study ever done, even to this day. The results provided only partial support for the effectiveness of client-centered therapy and the necessary and sufficient conditions, when applied to hospitalized schizophrenics (Rogers, 1967). Rogers and his collaborators had set themselves an extremely difficult task: They compared subjects of client-centered therapy *not* with an equivalent group of nontreated patients but with patients receiving the hospital's regular treatment program (including, for example, group therapy).

In any event, this work with schizophrenic patients brought about more changes in client-centered theory. The movement toward greater therapist openness and authenticity, already under way for several years, was further energized by the individual therapy experience with these difficult patients. Eugene Gendlin, one of the principal researchers in this project, was moved to comment that: "It is already certain that the patients did a great deal to us. I might say that our improvement has been remarkable. . . . Thus, for example, genuineness has changed for us from the mere absence of a false front, to a very active, self-expressive mode of making an interaction" (Gendlin, 1970, p. 284).

In 1964 Rogers left the university environment, moving to the Western Behavioral Sciences Institute in La Jolla, California to work with normal individuals and groups. In 1968, he helped to found the Center for the Study of the Person in La Jolla. There he worked to apply his theories to a wide range of situations, especially in relation to education, groups, and couples. The move away from therapy techniques and toward relationship attitudes reached fulfillment in 1974, with the change from *client*-centered to *person*-centered therapy. This second change was again not simply in name, but reflected what, over the years, had become an attitude toward life and being. Rogers noted in 1980 that:

> The old concept of "client-centered therapy" has been transformed into the "person-centered approach." In other words, I am no longer talking simply about psychotherapy, but about a point of view, a philosophy, an approach to life, a way of being, which fits any situation in which *growth*—of a person, a group, or a community—is part of the goal. (Rogers, 1980, p. ix)

Theory of Personality: Growth and Maladjustment

Rogers was always more concerned with the conditions for change and growth than with the roots of personality development. Because of this interest, his ideas about intervention came *before* his statements on personality. Yet he did offer formal conceptions of personality, its development and unfolding. Rogers' key formulations on this topic were published in his *Client-Centered Therapy* (1951, pp. 481–533) and later in a major chapter (Rogers, 1959). In his 1951 work he presented 19 propositions about personality development. Seven of these propositions seem to capture a major part of the theory:

1. Each individual exists in a continually changing world of experience of which he is the center.
2. The organism reacts to the field as it is experienced and perceived. This perceptual field is, for the individual, "reality."
3. Behavior is basically the goal-directed attempt of the organism to satisfy its need as experienced, in the field as perceived.
4. The organism reacts as an organized whole to this phenomenal field.
5. The best vantage point for understanding behavior is from the internal frame of reference of the individual himself.
6. A portion of the total perceptual field gradually becomes differentiated as the self.
7. Most of the ways of behaving which are adopted by the organism are those which are consistent with the concept of self.

Inspection of this list reveals the key elements of Rogers' personality theory. First, the theory is based on *phenomenology.* That is, it is the person's subjective perceptions of self and environment, his or her subjective experience and reality, that guide behavior. Second, and relatedly, each individual has his or her own private world, and to understand this individual we must enter this private world and seek to comprehend the individual from his or her internal frame of reference. "External" understanding—the kind that involves, for example, diagnosis by an expert—often leads us away from the internal frame of reference. Third, all persons develop a self-concept or self-structure. For Rogers, this self-concept contains the person's perceptions of him- or herself alone and interactively with his or her environment as well as the values attached to those perceptions. This self-structure is fluid and changing, but, once formed, serves to guide one's behavior and perceptions. Finally, persons' reactions are based on the whole of their self-structures and perceptions of themselves and their world, rather than on specific portions of their perceptions, as other theories might maintain.

Incongruence, Congruence, and the Fully Functioning Person

If all individuals are basically trustworthy and have a tendency toward self-actualization, why is there so much unhappiness in the world? What goes wrong so as to interfere with and often cripple people's actualizing tendencies? In several of his early papers, Rogers developed the client-centered (now person-centered) theory of maladjustment, in which *incongruence* is the key concept.

Maladjustment occurs when an incongruence, or rift, exists between one's self-concept and his or her organismic experiencing, that is, between the person's image of self and his or her inner experiencing. Why and how does this happen? As children develop, so does their inherent need for *positive regard* and *positive self-regard.* As experiences with the world (mostly family and primary caretakers) unfold, children also develop a self-concept. If children experience enough love, especially love *without* conditions, they develop a positive self-concept, and, just as important, do not develop *conditions of worth* (conditions under which they feel worthwhile). If, on the other hand, parents are too restrictive or conditional (telling the child, e.g., "We love you if you're a good boy or girl in the ways we define it"), the child develops these conditions of worth.

If our self-concept includes too many conditions of worth, it becomes rigid or "frozen," so that we lack a sense of positive self-regard. Thus, too many of our inwardly felt experiences (called "organismic experiencing") must be distorted or blocked from awareness, and we experience a sense of incongruence. Humans in this situation are at odds with themselves, for their self-concept and organismic experiencing are not unified, but in conflict.

When such incongruence occurs—and Rogers would add that it occurs ever so frequently in modern Western civilization—individuals are at cross-purposes and are vulnerable to psychological maladjustment. They can no longer live as integrated, whole persons. If such individuals were to perceive accurately what was being experienced at the feeling level, their self-concept would be threatened. This threat causes anxiety, which the individual defends against by either denying inner experience or misperceiving experience.

If, however, the child develops in an environment in which there are no or minimal conditions of worth, the self-concept is more flexible, and the person may thus acknowledge his or her organismic experiencing without feeling a threat to the self-concept. This congruence permits the actualizing tendency to do its work and helps the individual to become what Rogers calls a *fully functioning person.* The qualities of the fully functioning person reflect the humanistic assumptions discussed earlier as well as those of the person-centered theory of development as examined above. According to Burke (1989), fully functioning persons are increasingly (a) open to their experience; (b) accepting of their feelings; (c) capable of living in the present without preoccupation with past or future; (d) free to make choices that are best for them and to act on those choices spontaneously; (e) trusting of self and of human nature; (f) capable of balanced and realistic expressions of both aggression and affection; and (g) creative and nonconforming.

Counseling and Therapy Using a Person-Centered Approach

The person-centered view of counseling flows directly and logically from the humanistic assumptions discussed earlier and from the abovementioned formulations about personality development, incongruence, and full functioning. The counselor seeks gently to enter the client's subjective world, to understand this client from his or her internal frame of reference, and to provide an experience in which the person is accepted and cared about *without* conditions of worth. As Prochaska (1979) notes, whether the client seeks counseling because of inadequate functioning tied to perceptual distortion, because defensive symptoms are causing too much emotional pain, or because of a wish for greater self-actualization, the goals of therapy are the same: to increase the congruence between self-concept and organismic experience. The therapeutic relationship, especially its personal and emotional components, is the primary vehicle for this reintegration of self and experience. In fact, it is this relationship, in and of itself, that produces growth in the client. Rogers (1951, p. 172) makes this point decisively: "The process of therapy is seen as being synonymous with the experiential relationship between client and therapist."

Lest the reader get the impression that any kind of positive relationship will promote change, we hasten to add that, according to person-centered theory, it is only when certain relationship conditions predominate that constructive change occurs. To begin with, Rogers says, "I launch myself into the therapeutic relationship having a hypothesis, or a faith, that my liking, my confidence, and my understanding of the other person's inner world, will lead to a significant process of becoming" (1951, p. 267). This statement effectively summarizes relationship conditions that Rogers believes "necessary and sufficient" for constructive change to occur. Briefly, they are as follows:

1. Two persons, the client and counselor, are in psychological contact.
2. The client is in a state of incongruence, being vulnerable or anxious.

3. The counselor is congruent or integrated in the relationship.
4. The counselor experiences unconditional positive regard for the client.
5. The counselor experiences empathic understanding of the client's internal frame of reference.
6. The counselor succeeds in communicating conditions 4 and 5 to the client; the client perceives these conditions.

As discussed in Chapter 5, the conditions that have been given the greatest attention in person-centered therapy are 3, 4, and 5, which are the counselor's contributions to the relationship: congruence, unconditional positive regard, and empathy. It is crucial that the counselor enter the therapeutic relationship with these attitudes, and counseling techniques are simply the way of *implementing* these attitudes. Without these attitudes, all the polished techniques in the world will not produce effective therapy.

In Rogers' most recent discussion of the three facilitative conditions (Rogers, 1980), empathy is described as a way of being that is powerfully curative because: (a) the nonevaluative and accepting quality of the empathic climate facilitates clients taking a prizing, caring attitude toward themselves; (b) being listened to by an understanding other allows clients to listen more accurately to themselves, with greater empathy for their own organismic experiencing, their own vaguely felt experiences; and (c) clients' greater understanding and prizing of themselves opens them up to inner experiences that, in turn, become part of a more accurately based self-concept.

In discussing the profound impact of the therapists' empathic way of being with clients, Rogers also notes the paradox that these client changes, in effect, move clients toward the very attitudes that, in therapists, represented the necessary and sufficient conditions for helping others change—empathy, unconditional positive regard, and congruence! Thus, as one experiences the empathic way of being from another (e.g., a counselor), one develops attitudes toward oneself that enable one to become an effective therapist—for one's self. Although Rogers (1980) focused mostly on the empathic way of being, he also reiterated the person-centered view of the primacy of all three facilitative conditions. In comparing the influence of the three conditions, he noted that in ordinary life interactions (between members of a couple, teacher and student, colleagues, friends) congruence is probably the most important element. Since congruence or genuineness involves your letting the other person know your emotional state, Rogers believed it was the basis for living together in a climate of realness. In other situations, though, caring or prizing (i.e., unconditional positive regard) may be most important, for example, in nonverbal relationships such as those between therapist and profoundly disturbed client, between parent and infant, and between physician and very ill patient. Finally, Rogers believes that empathy may be the most important of the three conditions when "the other person is hurting, confused, troubled, anxious, alienated, terrified, or when he or she is doubtful of self-worth, uncertain as to identity" (1980, p. 160). For Rogers, the gentle and sensitive companionship provided by an empathic person helps to clarify and heal. As Rogers talks about this sensitively empathic person, it appears that empathy merges with the other conditions, and we are back to the trio operating in a creatively interactive way.

We have focused mostly on what the person-centered therapist is and does with clients. As a final comment, we add that there are as many "do not's" as "do's" in this approach. Thus, as Meador and Rogers (1984) note, person-centered therapists avoid with the client any expression that has an evaluative connotation. Nonevaluativeness is essential to their approach. Person-centered counselors also do not interpret meanings to clients, do not question them in a probing manner, and do not diagnose, reassure, criticize, judge, praise, or describe them. These "do not's" are crucial. A common misunderstanding is that the person-centered therapist provides a great deal of praise and reassurance. Not so. The therapist prizes the client as a person, but his or her unconditional regard and empathy do not translate into continual positive evaluation or reassurance.

The Person-Centered Approach in Perspective

Just what does the person-centered therapist do in a session? Despite the emphasis on attitudes and relationship rather than techniques, are there techniques that are favored by the person-centered approach? What differentiates the person-centered therapist from therapists of other persuasions?

In fact, everything we have seen (case presentations, examples of client-counselor interactions) indicates that the person-centered counselor responds to clients in a distinctive manner. His or her responses are, for example, "following" rather than "leading" responses. That is, the client's expressions are followed by the therapist, and paraphrasing responses are the most commonly used ones. Reflection of feeling is a predominant technique, as can be seen in virtually all of the cases Rogers himself has presented in the literature. At the same time, it would be inaccurate to equate the person-centered approach and the empathic way of being with one or a few techniques (e.g., reflection of feeling). Reflection is used because it fits nicely with person-centered theory and philosophy. Over the years an increasingly broad range of techniques has been permitted. The bottom line theoretically is that the techniques be in synch with person-centered theory and philosophy.

Person-centered therapy, from its beginnings, has always been a nondirective approach, even though the term *nondirective therapy* has now fallen into disfavor. Advocates of the person-centered approach believe that the term has come to connote a much narrower range of responses to clients than is desirable and seems to put the emphasis in the wrong place—on techniques. The nondirectiveness that has always been central to the person-centered approach might best be viewed as *noninterference.* The counselor trusts that if he or she creates the right relationship conditions, the client will move in ways that are most advantageous. In this respect, Meador and Rogers (1984) cite Martin Buber's quotation of Lao-tse as a good example of what the person-centered therapist would like to become:

> To interfere with the life of things means to harm both them and one's self. He who imposes himself has the small, manifest might; he who does not impose himself has the great secret might. . . . The perfected man does not interfere in the life of beings, he does not impose himself on them, but he helps all beings to their freedom. (Buber, 1957, pp. 54–55)

We have noted that from early in his career Rogers was deeply invested in the empirical study of his theories. What can in fact be said about the empirically demonstrated efficacy of the person-centered approach? Put simply, does it work? As with all approaches to counseling and therapy, the response to this simple question must be an unsatisfying "It depends." We always need to look beyond the simple "Does it work?" question, and focus on the more probing question, "How effective is this treatment, with what clients, under what conditions, as applied by which counselors?" Be that as it may, the person-centered approach has been studied extensively over the years, and the results of controlled studies have been largely positive, especially when the facilitative conditions are present to a high degree. In fact, in a recent and very extensive analysis of a huge amount of empirical literature, Orlinsky and Howard (1986) have found that the three facilitative conditions, especially empathic understanding, relate positively to counseling and therapy outcome in a wide range of situations and treatments, particularly when these facilitative conditions are assessed from the client's perspective (in keeping with Rogers' views).

The person-centered approach and the field of counseling psychology have always been highly compatible (Prochaska, 1979). The person-centered therapist's belief in human beings' inherent potential for growth and self-actualization is deeply ingrained within counseling psychology and is in keeping with the unifying themes of the specialty as discussed in Chapter 1, specifically, that of the focus on intact personalities and on assets or strengths. Also, because of belief in the inherent human tendency toward actualization, the person-centered approach has favored briefer treatments (the third unifying theme of counseling psychology discussed in Chapter 1) over extended treatment. Overall, throughout its development from nondirective counseling to client-centered therapy to person-centered therapy, this approach to life and intervention has had a profound impact on counseling psychology and its practitioners.

For more extensive and highly readable treatments, including case materials, the reader is referred to chapters by Meador and Rogers (1984), Prochaska (1979) Burke (1989), and Lynn and Garske (1985). Of Rogers' more recent writings, his *A Way of Being* (Rogers, 1980) is a wonderfully clear and interesting statement of current issues and directions. Levant and Shlien (1984) have also edited an entire book on new directions in the person-centered approach.

THE GESTALT THERAPY OF FRITZ PERLS

Just as the development of person-centered therapy is inextricably tied to the personhood and writings of Carl Rogers, the beginnings and advancement of gestalt therapy are a consequence of the personality and work of Fritz Perls. Although Rogers and Perls belong to the same camp—the humanistic, third-force, growth-oriented therapies—and share several basic assumptions about personality and therapy, it would be hard to find two people whose outward personalities differed more. If Carl Rogers, for example, was the prototypical warm, kindly, gentle minister (or grandfather in his advanced years), Fritz Perls can be seen as a sort of flamboyant, creative, and somewhat eccentric movie director.

Prochaska (1979) notes that as a person Fritz was much like his writings—both vital and perplexing. In his writings, and especially in his gestalt therapy workshops, he was keenly perceptive, provocative, manipulative, evocative, hostile, and inspiring. His great charisma, as well as his effectiveness, created an almost cultlike following, particularly among professionals who participated in his workshops and who went out and spread the gestalt therapy gospel. Consider how Carl Rogers' gentle and modest presentation of himself contrasts with Fritz's statement that "I believe that I am the best therapist for any type of neurosis in the States, maybe in the world. How is that for megalomania. At the same time I have to admit that I cannot work successfully with everybody" (Perls, 1969b, page unnumbered). If it was a gentle, soft-spoken grandfatherliness that people were looking for from Perls, they came away from encounters with him disappointed and frustrated; if it was a stimulating, lively, spontaneous, and genuine encounter his workshop participants wanted, they came away feeling enriched and enlightened (see Prochaska, 1979).

Frederich S. Perls (1893–1970) began his therapy career as a psychoanalyst. After obtaining his M.D. degree in 1920 from Frederich Wilhelm University, he studied at the Berlin and Vienna Institutes of Psychoanalysis. Within the psychoanalytic framework, he was strongly influenced by Karen Horney, Otto Rank, and especially Wilhelm Reich, who was Perls' psychoanalyst in the early 1930s. Although Perls practiced analysis throughout much of the first half of his career, it is hard to see him using an analytic approach or attitude. His irrepressible, spontaneous, outgoing, and aggressive character seems to us to run counter to the restraint and control required in effective analysis.

Along with his training in analysis, Perls knew and was heavily influenced by the leading gestalt psychologists of the time, for example, Kohler, Wertheimer, Lewin; and in 1926 he became an assistant to the eminent gestalt psychologist Kurt Goldstein at Goldstein's Institute for Brain-Damaged Soldiers. While at Goldstein's laboratory, Perls met his wife to be, Laura Posner. Many (e.g., Simkin & Yontef, 1984) view Laura Perls as the cofounder of the gestalt movement. She received her D.Sc. in 1932 from the University of Frankfurt. She was well-versed in general and gestalt psychology. Although Laura wrote little, within the gestalt movement she is considered a leader.

By the time of Perls' first book (*Ego, Hunger and Aggression,* 1947), he had moved away from Freudian theory, but it was not until 1951 that he took his dramatic departure from psychoanalysis. At that time, he published (with Ralph Hefferline and Paul Goodman) *Gestalt Therapy: Excitement and Growth in Personality.*

Fritz and Laura had fled Hitler's Germany for South Africa in 1934; soon afterward Fritz organized the South African Institute for Psychoanalysis. Then, with apartheid on the rise, the Perlses moved to New York in 1946. In 1952 they, along with the American psychologist Paul Goodman, formed the New York Institute for Gestalt Therapy. Run in the Perlses' apartment, the institute became the prototype for many gestalt therapy centers that sprang up around the country in the 1950s and 1960s. In 1960 Perls moved to California and in 1964 accepted an appointment at the Esalen Institute, where he held many of his training workshops and seminars along with gestalt leaders James Simkin, Walter Kempler, Irma Shepherd, and John Enright. It was during this time that he wrote two of his most interesting books. *Gestalt Therapy Verbatim* (1969a) is an engaging first-hand account of gestalt therapy and is generally considered Perls' best presentation of his approach. *In and Out of the Garbage Pail* (1969b) is a fascinating autobiography of one of the most creative and unusual personalities psychology has known. Perls spent the final year of his life, 1970, on Vancouver Island, where he was in the process of building a gestalt commune at the time of his death.

The gestalt therapy movement grew slowly at first and did not reach full force until the 1960s. The emotional climate of the 1960s, with its emphasis on self-expression in the here and now, seemed the ideal setting for gestalt therapy to take hold. And take hold it did. Belkin (1980) notes that no approach to therapy received more rapid popularity in a short time period than did gestalt therapy in the late 1960s and 1970s. It is hard to convey in writing the climate and the excitement of the gestalt therapy movement. Burke (1989) gets close with the following characterization:

> It is the late 1960s, and you are one of the lucky ones to attend a "human potential" seminar at the Esalen Institute, a center for workshops and training programs nestled between the mountains and the Pacific Ocean at Big Sur, California. You walk into a large room jammed with people, some seated on chairs, some sitting cross-legged on the floor, some standing along the sides. Every type of person imaginable appears to be here. There are young people, denim-clad, some a bit seedy. There are professional types, casually dressed, engaging in lively debate. There is even a psychoanalyst in the group, bearded, smoking a pipe, and looking more than a trifle uncomfortable in these environs. As a grandfatherly man walks into the room, the hum of conversations becomes a hush punctuated by cries of "Fritz, Fritz." Fritz is wearing a dashiki, and his round, smiling face peers out from an abundant white beard. What follows is a miracle to behold. One by one, like children before a Santa, members of the group volunteer to join Fritz at one end of the room on a "stage" set with three chairs, one for Fritz, one for the volunteer, and one empty. Fritz seems to know each person's soul, if not their names. One by one, he cajoles them, picks on them, intimidates them, surprises them. In response, they cry, laugh, scream, hug, and, from most reports, heal. (p. 252)

Burke (1989) points out that although the setting he has tried to capture seems, 20 years later, to be an unlikely one for training in therapy, it indeed was one in which many bright, young practitioners learned to become gestalt therapists. Scenes like the above were repeated over and over in the 1960s, and to many at the time (professional therapists as well as lay persons) Fritz Perls was a sort of guru, a one-man liberator of human potential (Burke, 1989).

Theory of Personality: Growth and Maladjustment

Neither Fritz Perls nor other gestalt therapists have developed a systematic theory of personality or psychopathology. Also, although many principles and procedures of counseling have been enunciated over the years, no comprehensive or definitive work is available. Perhaps this deficiency is related to Perls' view (a view widely endorsed in the gestalt arena) that gestalt therapy needs to be lived—writing about it misses its essence. The creation of comprehensive theories and definitive positions ignores the reality that the gestalt approach to therapy, like any living organism, is in a continual process of change and evolution.

The theory of personality that does exist is more a cluster of loosely connected ideas that have evolved from the clinical experience of gestalt practitioners, rather than an overall theory of personality. Careful examination of the gestalt literature, though, does suggest several themes related to personality development and to healthy versus unhealthy functioning. It must be underscored that gestalt therapy is not synonymous with gestalt psychology. Although Perls and other gestalt therapists drew some ideas from gestalt psychology, the personality theory of gestalt therapy is really a loose and unique mixture of psychoanalysis, phenomenology, existentialism, gestalt psychology, eastern religions, humanistic philosophy, and even behavioral psychology. Below we list and briefly discuss what appear to be central themes.

1. Humans are unified organisms and always function as *wholes.* Behavior is guided by the whole person; the whole determines the part.
2. The individual is continually faced with factors that disturb his or her balance and is continually seeking to restore balance or achieve equilibrium by satisfying his or her physical and organismic needs. The unmet need is the *incomplete gestalt* that demands completion.
3. Personality consists of many *polarities,* or opposites (e.g., strength and weakness, activity and passivity); in healthy functioning these polarities are integrated such that they work in harmony: the person is *centered.* In unhealthy functioning the polarities develop into splits, or dichotomies, throwing the person into a state of conflict.
4. The principle of *ecological interdependence* suggests that persons exist by differentiating self and other as well as by connecting self and other. The boundary between self and environment or other must be kept permeable to allow exchanges (*contact*); at the same time, the boundary must be firm enough for organismic autonomy.
5. Human regulation is, to varying degrees, based on acknowledgment of *what is* (organismic) or on arbitrary imposition of what the person believes *should be* ("shouldistic"). The former reflects and leads to healthy functioning, the latter to neurosis.
6. *Awareness*—of what one is feeling, sensing, experiencing in the present, the *here and now*—is the key to healthy development and change, and is the immediate goal of gestalt therapy.

What ties these diverse propositions together? Perls and other leading gestalt therapists are more concerned about healthy and unhealthy development than personality development per se. The healthy individual is responsible for himself or herself and seeks to be that self. As Perls (1969a, p. 70) asserts: "responsibility means simply to be willing to say 'I am I' and 'I am what I am'." If the individual seeks to be aware of his or her organismic needs, rather than living by "shoulds" or by some image of what is good, emotional health results. When this self-acceptance occurs, the polarities referred to above are accepted—for example, we accept our aggressive side as well as our gentle side; thus the sides are integrated rather than being at war with each other.

As implied, the mature person lives in the present, in the so-called here and now. This does not mean that the individual is a hedonist who is concerned only with his or her own ego needs. It does mean that preoccupations with the past and the future are largely given up, so that one lives one's experience in the now. Values and standards are part of the immediate experience. The gestalt therapist understands the need for values; what is unhealthy is the all-too-frequent tendency to be driven by internalized "shoulds" at the expense of who one basically is and what one needs. When taking the responsibility to be oneself and to live in the present, one follows Perls' suggestion to live and review every second afresh. In doing this the joy, excitement, and creative potential in our lives may be actualized.

Growth Gone Awry: The Layers of Neurosis

What happens to interfere with the process of growth and with the actualizing tendency in all of us? Why is it that so many people become stuck in the deadness of living out social roles, in childish dependency, and in functioning more like computers than humans? Although Perls did not develop a formal theory of the causes of what he called growth disorders, he did point to some childhood factors (Perls 1969a, 1970). To address the question of what goes wrong, we first have to look at Perls' concept of maturation. For Perls, "maturing is the transcendence from environmental support to self-support" (1969a, p. 30). Parents can impede this process by undersupporting the child, so that needed support is pulled away before the developing child is ready for independence. More common is the critical, imposing parent who knows what is best for the child. The child either follows these unempathic parents' dictates or runs the risk of losing love and approval. The child thus becomes fearful of independent behavior and becomes what he is "supposed" to become. The third and most common impediment to maturity is the parent's spoiling of the child. Parents, out of their own unmet needs, all too often give the developing child everything they did not have. The parents are afraid to frustrate the child's wishes, and yet such frustration is needed if the child is to move forward and develop his or her own self-support. If the home environment is so secure and gratifying that the child's every need is met, that child will not move forward but become stuck.

Whichever of these impediments occurs, the result is the same. Instead of learning to stand on his or her own two feet, "the child—or the childish neurotic—will use his potential not for self-support but to act out phony roles. These phony roles are meant to mobilize the environment for support instead of mobilizing one's own potential. We manipulate the environment by being helpless, by playing stupid, asking questions, wheedling, flattering" (Perls, 1970, pp. 17–18).

Perls and other gestalt therapists never developed a systematic or formal theory of neurosis (or *growth disorders,* as Perls liked to call them); but Perls did formulate an interesting concept of what he called the "layers of neurosis." These layers can be seen as the defensive shields that the person must work through to grow from neurosis to health. Because Perls placed no premium on consistency, the actual layers are somewhat different in two works published only a year apart (Perls 1969a, 1970).

There are five layers of neurosis that form what Perls viewed as the structure of neurosis. In combining Perls' publications on these layers, the first layer can be seen as the *phony,* or *synthetic,* level. The neurotic spends most of his or her time at this level, a level in which one plays roles and games, and tries to act out an ideal self-concept rather than being authentic. Perls describes this layer colorfully as follows: "We behave *as if* we are big shots, *as if* we are nincompoops, *as if* we are pupils, *as if* we are ladies, *as if* we are bitches, etc." Thus the neurotic has "given up living for his self in a way that would actualize himself. He wants to live instead for a concept . . . like an elephant who had rather be a rose bush, and a rose bush that tries to be a kangaroo. We don't want to be ourselves; we don't want to be what we are. We want to be something else, and the existential basis for being something else is the experience of dissatisfaction. We are dissatisfied with what we do, or parents are dissatisfied with what their child is doing. He should be different, he shouldn't be what he is; he should be something else" (1970, p. 20).

Once the person gets through the phony layer, she or he then must pass through the *phobic, impasse,* and *implosive* layers. Although the distinctions between these layers are very murky in Perls' writing, the key issue is that as persons become more real, they encounter the internal objections to being authentic—all of the "should nots" in their psyche. Beyond this is a sense of being stuck and of deadness. At this implosive layer persons contract and compress themselves. To move beyond this they must get into contact with the deadness involved in their imploding. When they do that, the next layer is entered. Implosion becomes explosion, as the *explosive* layer is experienced. The person comes to life, as this explosion is "the link-up with the authentic person who is capable of experiencing and expressing his emotions" (Perls, 1969a, p. 60).

The emerging healthy individual may explode into *grief* if he or she needs to work through loss experiences that had not been assimilated; *orgasm* if he or she is sexually blocked; *anger* if this feeling has been denied; and/or *joy* when there previously had been none. In fact, to be truly well-functioning, the individual must be capable of all four of these explosions or experiences. In response to questions about the dangers involved in the explosion layer, Perls noted that the one way the danger is diminished is through the process of "melting." When in therapy the client becomes moved, he or she begins to melt, to feel soft, or to cry, which is a kind of melting that buffers against a dangerous explosion. Yet, at the same time, "basically one has to be willing to take risks" (Perls, 1970, p. 23).

The Practices and Procedures of Gestalt Therapy: Exercises and "Games"

What do gestalt therapists actually do? No other major theory of counseling presents as wide an array of interesting and evocative techniques and procedures as does gestalt therapy. To begin with, in the response-modes sense (see Chapter 6), the main verbal technique is *confrontation.* The gestalt therapist vigorously confronts discrepancies in the client's presentation of himself or herself and challenges the client to express what he or she truly is and feels in the moment.

> "You are telling me you're sad, but you are smiling."
> "You say you're relaxed, but I see your feet are fidgeting."
> "You say you'd like to be strong but that's hard to believe right now because my fantasy is that you're a little baby."

These are the kinds of confrontations gestalt therapists often make. Discrepancies in the moment are noted, highlighting contradictions in what the client says, in what the client says and does, and between what the client says or does and what the counselor fantasizes about him or her.

Another response mode that typifies the gestalt therapist is *direct guidance.* The gestalt therapist often instructs the client about exercises (see below) and other behaviors that are desired in the moment. In addition, the gestalt therapist is probably more self-disclosing than any other kind of therapist, and *self-involving disclosures* about what is being experienced in the here and now with the client are the preferred kinds. On the negative side, the one response type that is clearly taboo in gestalt therapy is *interpretation.* This response mode seeks to get at the "whys" of behavior, whereas the gestaltists are more interested in "hows" and "whats." Interpretations more often than not lead to intellectualized responses that do not reflect immediate experiencing. To Perls, the search for underlying causes is useless at best. It takes the client away from where she or he needs to be.

Before discussing gestalt exercises, a word is in order about how material from the client's past is to be dealt with in the gestalt approach. The focus on here-and-now experiencing, with the aim of developing awareness, does not preclude the exploration of past experiences. The critical thing is that those past experiences be explored in a way that is alive in the present. Thus, the client isn't to simply talk about the past; she or he is to experience the past in the now. Gestalt therapists will often encourage this process by asking clients to be themselves during the past time being examined: for example, "Be the seven-year-old of your memories right now, and tell me what is going on for you."

Although Perls and other gestalt therapists have repeatedly cautioned against overreliance on techniques in the form of exercises, gestaltists do use a range of these strategies. We discuss some of these games and exercises here, both because they are valuable procedures in gestalt work and as a way of clarifying some of the major elements of gestalt counseling. It should be noted that the therapist is not to preplan the use of techniques. Following the rule of working with the present experience (the therapist's as well as the client's), the gestalt counselor uses exercises as they are felt to fit the moment.

The most concise and clear discussion of gestalt exercises or games is presented by Levitsky and Perls (1970). Use of the term *games* is deliberate; it highlights Perls' views that social interaction is filled with games. Indeed it is not particularly desirable to eliminate games. Rather, consistent with the gestaltists' focus on awareness, the goal is to become aware of one's games and to use them in a way that satisfies one's needs.

Games of Dialogue. As discussed earlier, gestalt therapy views personality as consisting of many polarities or opposites, for example, passive and aggressive, weak and strong, masculine and feminine, controlled and impulsive. In healthy functioning, these opposites are integrated—they coexist in an harmonious way and in fact support each other—for example, the dominant and submissive poles in us can each be given expression, and each helps the other become less extreme. The individual is *centered* when these polarities have been integrated. Often, however, there exists a split between the polarities, causing a state of conflict.

Games of dialogue are especially suited to situations in which such splits occur, and the aim of these games is to create full awareness in the client of the split. Awareness leads to resolution so that the person may become centered. In games of dialogue, the client is asked to stage a dialogue between the two parts of himself. With the counselor's guidance, each part is acted out and the dialogue goes on until it feels appropriate to stop. Often this dialogue is carried out with a "two-chair technique," whereby the client sits in one chair representing one side of the split and talks to the other side. Then, when he or she feels it is time to respond as the other side, the client switches chairs, and the dialogue continues.

Although, as we have noted, there exists a wide range of polarities in all of us, the one that has been given the greatest attention from gestaltists is called the *top-dog and under-dog split.* The top-dog is that side of personality that moralizes and lives in a world of "shoulds." Top-dog tends to be bossy and condemning. On the other side, under-dog tends to be childlike, impulsive, and irresponsible—this side makes excuses and passively resists responsibility. You can see how easy it would be for a split to exist between these two sides (note their similarity to the superego and id in psychoanalytic theory), and in fact it may help clarify the concept to consider how this polarity might exist in yourself. In any event, given the prevalence of the top-dog vs. under-dog split, many gestalt games of dialogue focus on it.

Unfinished Business. "Unfinished business" is a form of "incomplete gestalt" in gestalt psychology. Whenever unfinished business is detected in gestalt therapy (usually in the form of unresolved feelings), the client is asked to finish it. Clearly, any person will have a wide array of unfinished business in the interpersonal arena, for example, with parents, siblings, and spouses. In Perls' opinion, resentments are the most common and significant type of unfinished business.

"I Take Responsibility." In gestalt therapy a premium is placed on the person's taking responsibility for his or her feelings and actions. The client is asked to say "I won't" rather than "I can't," and is also asked to say "and I take responsibility for it" as an addendum to his or her perceptions, feelings, and actions. Thus, "I am aware that I am smiling when I talk about this painful feeling—and I take responsibility for it." Or, "I don't know what to say—and I take responsibility for it." Although this may seem like a foolish and mechanical game, it does eventually drive home the point that responsibility resides in the person for all behaviors and that we constantly make choices about what we do and feel.

Playing the Projection. Probably the major defense mechanism according to gestalt therapists is projection, and whenever the gestalt therapist sees signs of projections, the client is asked to play the projection, as a way of becoming aware of the parts of himself or herself that are being projected onto others. Thus, for example, if the client feels the therapist is being critical, the client is asked to play the critical therapist. Often a two-chair dialogue may be used to highlight the split occurring along with this projection.

Nowhere is playing the projection seen more vividly in gestalt therapy than in work on dreams. Such dream analysis is vastly different than in psychoanalysis. Whereas in psychoanalysis, the client is to free-associate to segments of the dream, in gestalt therapy the client is asked to actually be each and every object in the dream. Imagine, for example, a dream as follows (one actually reported by a client of one of the authors): "I was in the attic and a monster was looking at me hatefully. A little baby was sitting near the monster and was very frightened. The attic door slammed shut; I ran out and tripped over a cinder block." In a gestalt analysis, the client was asked to play the role of the monster, the baby, the cinder block, and the door that slammed shut. Each was eventually experienced as a warring part of herself, and the awareness that resulted took this client a step toward resolving these splits.

Reversals. As an example of a particular kind of split, the client's behavior is often seen as a reversal of underlying impulses. To bring about awareness of the hidden side, the gestaltist asks the client to play the opposite of what is being expressed. For example, the client who is expressing excessive timidity is asked to play an exhibitionist; the client who is hostile and critical is asked to be receptive and nonjudgmental; the client who is overly sweet is asked to play one who is unreceptive and attacking.

Exaggeration and Repetition. Exaggeration is aimed at helping clients understand body language. When unwitting gestures or movements seem to be significant communications (e.g., a wave of the arm, tapping of the foot), clients are asked to exaggerate the movement repeatedly so as to become more aware of its meaning. This attention to nonverbal behavior forms a significant part of gestalt treatment. In fact, probably no other theoretical persuasion is as attentive to nonverbal behavior. Gestaltists believe that the body is a crucial vehicle for communicating messages of which the client is unaware. Thus, attention to nonverbals helps greatly in the effort to enhance awareness. Earlier we noted confrontation as the major response mode used in gestalt therapy. Many such confrontations attend to discrepancies between verbal and nonverbal expressions.

The verbal counterpart of the exaggeration game is called "repetition." Here the gestalt therapist asks the client to repeat a statement over and over, and often in a louder and louder voice. This is done when the therapist suspects that the client is not hearing himself or herself or is emotionally glossing over verbalizations that are significant. The repetition and the increased loudness help the client really hear rather than just form words.

"May I Feed You a Sentence?" A game related to the repetition exercise is used when the therapist senses the client is unaware of or disowning an aspect of himself or herself. The therapist asks the client if he or she may feed the client a sentence, suggesting that the client say it and try it on for size. The therapist may ask the client to utter the sentence several times. The client in this way can test his or her reaction to the statement in terms of how well it "fits."

Marriage Counseling Games. Gestaltists use several exercises when working with couples. For example, the therapist may have partners face each other and take turns beginning sentences with "I resent you for." This work may be followed by beginning sentences with "I appreciate you for." Other games reflective of important relationship themes are "I spite you by," "I am compliant by," and "I see." This last preface, "I see," aims at helping discover what members of a couple see in each other. Perls felt that a major problem in marriages is that partners are in love with a concept rather than an individual. The "I see" game seeks to help the partners see each other as they really are.

When involved in the exercises we have just described, the gestalt therapist seeks to have the client follow some "rules." The most common rules are to (a) stay in the here and now; (b) communicate with the other person, the "thou," rather than an "it"; (c) use "I" language rather than "it" language (e.g., "I feel bad" rather than "*It* is a bad feeling").

Throughout all of the exercises and in fact throughout all of gestalt therapy there is one overriding goal, rule, and exercise: to make use of the *awareness continuum.* That is, the therapist seeks to facilitate the client's awareness—of bodily sensations, perceptions, and emotions. The therapist often asks the client to "stay with this feeling" as a way of heightening awareness. As noted earlier, if there is a key to health in gestalt therapy, it resides in being aware. As Fritz Perls urged: "Lose your mind and come to your senses."

The Gestalt Approach in Perspective

Just as there is a lack of clarity in person-centered therapy as to the role of therapist techniques, in gestalt therapy the role of the counselor-client relationship has been inconsistently and unclearly articulated. Although Fritz Perls was fond of the expression, "here and now, I and thou," in his own counseling it never seemed that Perls developed "I-thou" relationships. Dolliver (1981b), for example, has cogently pointed out how the interpersonal quality that is necessary for an I-thou encounter was missing in Perls' work with clients and workshop participants. His exclusive focus seemed to be on the client and on exercises to promote awareness, and the "I" was missing from his interactions.

Other gestalt therapists have noted this deficiency and have sought to strengthen the relationship component of gestalt therapy (e.g., Polster & Polster, 1973; Shepherd, 1970; Simkin & Yontef, 1984). For example, whereas Perls seemed never to examine or reveal his own feelings and biases in his work, Shepherd (1970) asserts that, "The therapist needs to listen carefully and admit, 'what you say is true of me' if it fits, rather than dealing with this as the patient's fantasy, and implying inaccuracy or distortion of perception [as Perls so often did]" (p. 237).

In fact, the apparent inconsistency and lack of clarity that mark the role of relationship in gestalt therapy appear to stem from its two distinct lines of thought on the role and importance of the relationship. Greenberg (1983) highlights this split when he notes that some gestalt therapists, in the Perls tradition, focus on the role of "therapist as teacher of the method," whereas others key in on the relationship. Those who take the role of teacher use techniques and exercises to help clients learn to focus attention on experiencing in the moment. For these counselors, I-thou relating is engaged in only as a means of teaching clients the significance of I-thou relationships. For the relationship-oriented gestalt therapists, however, the role of the authentic human encounter in the present is the key to change. These therapists seek to share themselves as part of the work and deemphasize the role of techniques and exercises.

Gestalt Therapy Now

What is the current status of gestalt therapy in counseling psychology? As a system of intervention, its creativity and confrontiveness (often aggressiveness when practiced by some gestaltists) fit beautifully with the turbulence of the late 1960s and early 1970s. The focus on the self, on "doing your own thing," seemed to capture the *Zeitgeist.* With the death of Fritz Perls and the arrival of a new era, however, the immense popularity of gestalt therapy has clearly waned (see Burke, 1989, for a sound critique). In a recent survey of a large sample of counseling psychologists (Watkins, Lopez, Campbell, & Himmell, 1986), for example, less than 5 percent of the participants claimed gestalt therapy as either their primary or secondary theoretical orientation.

In part, the decline in popularity of gestalt therapy is due to its lack of a research base. Few outcome studies have been conducted to support its effectiveness, partly because of the indifference among gestaltists to scientific study. Perhaps the deemphasis of intellect in gestalt therapy was inappropriately applied to research. If we should "lose our minds and come to our senses," perhaps scientific study is unnecessary. Relatedly, there has been a lack of intellectual criticalness among gestalt therapists regarding the theoretical inconsistencies, for example, between the gospel as preached by Perls and the way in which he conducted his practice (see Dolliver's [1981b] thoughtful analysis of the limitations of gestalt therapy).

Although few counseling psychologists are now gestalt therapists, the gestalt approach has had enormous influence on the field of counseling psychology. According to Burke (1989), many of the techniques and exercises created by Perls and others are used often by therapists in their day-to-day practice (e.g., requesting first-person pronouns, staying in the here and now, bringing out internal dialogues). As Burke also notes, a technique such as the two-chair technique and its variations is immensely versatile in its applications. In fact, this technique is exceptional in the gestalt literature in that a solid line of research does exist supporting its effectiveness (see Clarke & Greenberg, 1986; Greenberg & Webster, 1982).

Not only have the techniques been influential, the concept of an authentic I-thou relationship has become a central part of the work of many counseling psychologists. In no other theory is this so powerfully articulated, although (as noted above) there has been a split among gestaltists on the role of the relationship. For those who emphasize "I and thou," their message is clear, vivid, and convincing.

As with person-centered therapy, we have offered only a glimpse of some of the main ingredients of gestalt therapy. For more detailed discussion of gestalt counseling, we suggest chapters by Simkin and Yontef (1984), Prochaska (1979), Burke (1989), and Belkin (1980). Perls' (1969a) *Gestalt Therapy Verbatim* remains the classic work, although Polster and Polster's (1973) lucid and interesting book is more appealing conceptually than Perls' often literary approach. *Gestalt Therapy Now* (Fagan & Shepherd, 1970), remains more than twenty years after its publication, a definitive book of readings on gestalt therapy.

SUMMARY

Although the philosophy of humanism is rooted in much earlier times, humanistic approaches to counseling are a product of the mid-20th century. These approaches developed as a reaction to both psychoanalysis and behaviorism. As a group, they are aptly labeled the "third force" in psychology and counseling.

Although the different humanistic approaches vary in their specifics, they share several assumptions about human beings, counseling, and science, regarding: the democratic ideal as an essential value; the fundamental predominance of subjective experience; the inherent tendency of humans toward growth and self-actualization; the essential trustworthiness of people; the value of authentic human encounters in the present as a powerful way of helping clients grow and develop; and the necessity for scientific methods to fit the human experience if they are to enlighten us.

The two humanistic approaches that have had the greatest impact on counseling psychologists are Carl Rogers' person-centered therapy and Fritz Perls' gestalt therapy. Although Rogers' approach to counseling came before any theory of personality, he did develop a set of clear and consistent theoretical statements about personality development. His emphasis was phenomenological, emphasizing the need to understand the private world of the individual and the whole person, rather than isolated parts. The self and self-concept are key components in Rogers' personality theory. In his effort to delineate healthy and unhealthy development, he focused on the actualizing tendency, how it goes awry, and how it may be facilitated. Difficulties caused by the formation of *conditions of worth* are pivotal in humans' estrangement from themselves, whereas in healthy functioning congruence exists between inner experiencing and behavior.

To Rogers, the key to successful counseling lies not in techniques or in accurate diagnosis, but in the therapeutic relationship. In fact, the kind of relationship that is both necessary and sufficient for client change is marked, on the person-centered counselor's side, by empathic understanding, unconditional positive regard, and congruence.

Although techniques are deemphasized in person-centered therapy, counselors of this persuasion use mainly paraphrasing techniques, especially reflection of feeling. Clearly the person-centered approach to life and therapy is one of noninterference (the earlier term *non-directiveness* having fallen into disfavor).

Largely because of Rogers' own self-actualization as a scientist as well as a practitioner, his ideas have been subjected to careful and thorough scientific scrutiny. Many of them have been supported, and some not; but, in the main, client-centered therapy and now person-centered therapy have received empirical support for their effectiveness, at least with clients who are not severely disturbed. Rogers and his approach to treatment have had a profound effect on counseling psychology.

The gestalt approach of Fritz Perls also emphasized intervention more than personality development. Perls' theoretical statements about personality were unsystematic, although they were related to gestalt therapy formulations about treatment. Regarding neurosis, or growth disorders, Perls speculated that there are five layers to the neurosis—the synthetic, phobic, impasse, implosive, and explosive layers—each of which must be worked through if a person is to become mature.

In terms of verbal techniques or response modes, the gestalt therapist uses primarily confrontation, direct guidance, and self-involving disclosures. A hallmark of the gestalt approach is the use of exercises or games during counseling. Revealing key issues, these games/exercises include: dialogues; "unfinished business";

"I take responsibility"; "playing the projection"; role-playing reversals; exaggeration and repetition; "May I feed you a sentence?"; and marriage counseling games. The overriding goal in gestalt therapy, whether approached through exercises or the counselor-client relationship, is the creation of awareness in the here and now of one's subjective experiencing.

Regarding the counselor-client relationship, there has long been a division in gestalt therapy between those who emphasize their roles as teacher of the method and those who focus on the I-thou relationship. Perls created some confusion because he verbally emphasized the I-thou encounter, but in his counseling and workshops he was more the teacher of the method.

Although the popularity of gestalt therapy has clearly declined since its heyday in the late 1960s and early 1970s, many of its techniques and ideas continue to appeal, and have been incorporated by practitioners.

References

Belkin, G. S. (1980). *Contemporary psychotherapies.* Chicago, IL: Rand McNally.

Buber, M. (1958). *I and thou.* New York: Scribner's.

Burke, J. F. (1989). *Contemporary approaches to psychotherapy and counseling: The self regulation and maturity model.* Pacific Grove, CA: Brooks/Cole.

Clarke, K. M., & Greenberg, L. S. (1986). Differential effects of the gestalt two-chair intervention and problem solving in resolving a decisional split. *Journal of Counseling Psychology, 33,* 11–15.

Dolliver, R. (1981a). Personal sources for theories of psychotherapy. *Journal of Contemporary Psychotherapy, 12,* 53–59.

Dolliver, R. H. (1981b). Some limitations of Perls' gestalt therapy. *Psychotherapy: Theory, Research, and Practice, 18,* 38–45.

Fagan, J., & Shepherd, I. L. (Eds.) (1970). *Gestalt therapy now.* New York: Harper & Row.

Gendlin, E. T. (1970). Research in psychotherapy with schizophrenic patients and the nature of that "illness." In J. T. Hart & T. M. Tomlinson (Eds.), *New directions in client-centered therapy* (pp. 280–291). Boston: Houghton Mifflin.

Greenberg, L. S. (1983). The relationship in gestalt therapy. In M. Lambert (Ed.), *Psychotherapy and patient relationships* (pp. 126–153). Homewood, IL: Dow Jones-Irwin.

Greenberg, L. S. (1985). An integrative approach to the relationship in counseling and psychotherapy. *The Counseling Psychologist, 13,* 251–260.

Greenberg, L. S., & Webster, M. (1982). Resolving decisional conflict by gestalt two-chair dialogue: Relating process to outcome. *Journal of Counseling Psychology, 29,* 468–477.

Grummon, D. L. (1965). Client-centered theory. In B. Stefflre (Ed.), *Theories of counseling* (pp. 30–90). New York: McGraw-Hill.

Levant, R., & Shlien, J. (Eds.) (1984). *Client-centered therapy and the person-centered approach.* New York: Praeger.

Levitsky, A., & Perls, F. S. (1970). The rules and games of gestalt therapy. In J. Fagan & I. L. Shepherd (Eds.), *Gestalt therapy now* (pp. 140–149). New York: Harper & Row.

Lowe, C. M. (1969). *Value orientations in counseling and psychotherapy: The meanings of mental health.* San Francisco: Chandler Publishing.

Lynn, S. J., & Garske, J. P. (Eds.) (1985). *Contemporary psychotherapies: Models and methods.* Columbus, OH: Merrill.

Maslow, A. H. (1954). *Motivation and personality.* New York: Harper & Row.

Maslow, A. H. (1968). *Toward a psychology of being* (2nd ed.). New York: Van Nostrand Reinhold.

Maslow, A. H. (1970). *Motivation and personality* (rev. ed.). New York: Harper & Row.

May, R. (1967). *Psychology and the human dilemma.* New York: Van Nostrand Reinhold.

Meador, B. D., & Rogers, C. R. (1984). Person-centered therapy. In R. Corsini (Ed.), *Current psychotherapies* (3rd ed., pp. 142–195). Itasca, IL: Peacock.

Orlinsky, D., & Howard, K. (1986). Process and outcome in psychotherapy. In S. Garfield & A. Bergin (Eds.), *Handbook of psychotherapy and behavior change* (3rd ed., pp. 311–381). New York: Wiley.

Perls, F. S. (1947). *Ego, hunger, and aggression.* New York: Random House.

Perls, F. S. (1969a). *Gestalt therapy verbatim.* New York: Bantam.

Perls, F. S. (1969b). *In and out of the garbage pail.* Lafayette, CA: Real People Press.

Perls, F. S. (1970). *Four lectures.* In J. Fagan & I. L. Shepherd (Eds.), *Gestalt therapy now* (pp. 14–38). New York: Harper & Row.

Perls, F. S., Hefferline, R., & Goodman, P. (1951). *Gestalt therapy.* New York: Dell.

Prochaska, J. O. (1979). *Systems of psychotherapy: A transtheoretical analysis.* Homewood, IL: Dorsey.

Polster, E., & Polster, M. (1973). *Gestalt therapy integrated: Contours of theory and practice.* New York: Vintage Books.

Rogers, C. R. (1939). *The clinical treatment of the problem child.* Boston: Houghton Mifflin.

Rogers, C. R. (1942). *Counseling and psychotherapy.* Boston: Houghton Mifflin.

Rogers, C. R. (1951). *Client-centered therapy.* Boston: Houghton Mifflin.

Rogers, C. R. (1957). The necessary and sufficient conditions for therapeutic personality change. *Journal of Consulting Psychology, 21,* 95–103.

Rogers, C. R. (1959). A theory of therapy, personality, and interpersonal relationships, as developed in the client-centered framework. In S. Koch (Ed.), *Psychology: A study of science* (Vol. III). New York: McGraw-Hill.

Rogers, C. R. (1961). *On becoming a person.* Boston: Houghton Mifflin.

Rogers, C. R. (1962). Toward becoming a fully functioning person. In A. Combs (Ed.), *Perceiving, behaving, becoming, 1962 Yearbook* (pp. 21–33). Washington, DC: Association for Supervision and Curriculum Development.

Rogers, C. R. (Ed.) (1967). *The therapeutic relationship and its impact: A study of psychotherapy with schizophrenics.* Madison, WI: University of Wisconsin Press.

Rogers, C. R. (1973). My philosophy of interpersonal relationships and how it grew. *Journal of Humanistic Psychology, 13,* 3–15.

Rogers, C. R. (1980). *A way of being*. Boston: Houghton Mifflin.
Rogers, C. R., & Dymond, R. (1954). *Psychotherapy and personality change*. Chicago: University of Chicago Press.
Shepherd, I. L. (1970). Limitations and cautions in the gestalt approach. In J. Fagan & I. L. Shepherd (Eds.), *Gestalt therapy now* (pp. 234–238). New York: Harper & Row.
Simkin, J. S., & Yontef, G. M. (1984). Gestalt therapy. In R. Corsini (Ed.), *Current psychotherapies* (3rd ed., pp. 279–319). Itasca, IL: Peacock.
Watkins, C. E., Lopez, F. G., Campbell, V. L., & Himmell, C. D. (1986). Contemporary counseling psychology: The results of a national survey. *Journal of Counseling Psychology, 33*, 301–309.

Chapter 10

Diagnosis and Assessment

> Assessment, Evaluation, and Diagnosis. Procedures may include, but are not limited to, behavioral observation, interviewing, and administering and interpreting instruments for the assessment of educational achievement, academic skills, aptitudes, interests, cognitive abilities, attitudes, emotions, motivations, psychoneurological status, personality characteristics, or any other aspect of human experience and behavior that may contribute to understanding and helping the user.
>
> —American Psychological Association, *Specialty Guidelines for the Delivery of Services by Counseling Psychologists* (1981, p. 654)

Assessment is a highly controversial topic in counseling psychology. On the one hand, it is clearly linked to at least two of the themes of counseling psychology identified in Chapter 1: (1) educational and career development and (2) person-environment interaction. On the other hand, the emergence of client-centered and other humanistic approaches to counseling has led to serious questions about the role of assessment; other questions about the value of assessment emerged with the increased awareness of cultural diversity during the 1960s and 1970s. We argue that counseling psychologists cannot function properly without assessment procedures. Only with a better understanding of assessment and diagnostic procedures will counseling psychologists be able to advance the scientific understanding of human problems and select treatment strategies most appropriate for those seeking help.

How do we define assessment? Why is it necessary? To paraphrase Kleinmuntz (1982), assessment is systematic or standardized procedures for observing behavior. At a fundamental level, it is the psychologist's way of communicating. Although all persons are unique, there are many ways in which they are alike. Without ways to identify and communicate similarities and differences in behaviors, within and among individuals, psychologists could make no valid generalizations about people nor any predictions about them that would exceed a chance level of accuracy. For lawful relationships to develop, means must exist to determine, for example, what kinds of persons will be most satisfied in people-oriented as compared to data-oriented occupations. As another example, knowing that counseling strategies should differ for persons whose problem is depression as compared to dependency is useless information unless there is some way of assessing whether clients are depressed or dependent (or possibly both, if that is the case). Thus, assessment is central to both the science and practice of counseling psychology.

Though various aspects of assessment are common to all fields of applied psychology, there is one assessment tradition unique to counseling psychology: using assessment to help clients gain new information and perspectives about themselves. Counseling psychologists, more than any other mental health professionals, give tests and test results to clients as a way of stimulating exploration of current concerns. Assessments provide clients with a psychological snapshot which they can use to reflect on and understand themselves.

Why are "systematic or standardized procedures" needed for self-understanding? Too often this question is not addressed, and it is often glibly said, "No one can know us better than ourselves." But how well do people know themselves? Many persons make major decisions without an awareness of the values of personality styles that underlie those decisions. Most persons also do not know themselves very well with regard to the "normative" aspects of behavior. A woman may know that she is more adept with numbers than with spatial relationships, but does that mean that her spatial relationship skills are relatively poor compared to all other skills? Certainly in making career decisions, it is just as important to have an understanding of one's abilities and interests compared to others as it is to realize their place within one's own range of strengths and weaknesses.

In this chapter we shall look at a variety of topics that will help clarify both the promise and problems of assessment. The first section includes the intriguing history of diagnosis—one of the earliest and most controversial uses of assessment data—in counseling psychology. We look at the arguments for and against diagnostic procedures and, more importantly, how *appropriate* diagnostic strategies exemplify the scientist-practitioner in action. From this perspective, assessment must be carried out in a multitude of ways at various levels. The greatest hope for significant improvements in assessment is improved systematic integration of diverse approaches.

The second section presents descriptions of several types of assessment other than tests. Because assessment is too often thought of only as using psychological tests, we first present some of the values of interviews, behavioral ratings, and environmental assessment procedures.

The third and largest section focuses on psychological tests. First, we briefly review major concepts in evaluating and constructing psychological tests, so that readers can become educated users of tests and know when to consider developing alternative measures. Many current assessment measures are poorly suited to some of the most pressing contemporary research and practice problems. Often, well-trained counseling psychologists can develop or modify existing measures in ways that add significantly to the range of information needed to gain a fuller understanding of those the profession seeks to help. We then review the role of tests in both diagnostic assessment and counseling psychology research. We identify the tests most often employed by counseling psychologists, and briefly describe typical practice and research uses of major intelligence, interest, and personality measures.

We complete the chapter by reviewing some major strategic and ethical issues in test selection, test interpretation, and report writing. We also explore issues of the use of computers in testing. Realizing we cannot cover all tests and test issues in this chapter—there are many books devoted to each major topic reviewed here—we aim simply to acquaint the reader with the major concerns of assessment in counseling research and practice.

DIAGNOSIS: A DIRTY WORD?

Has diagnosis become a dirty word in counseling psychology? In many contemporary counseling books, diagnosis is barely mentioned, even though many pages and studies were devoted to it during the formative phases of the profession (Williamson, 1939; Robinson, 1950; Pepinsky & Pepinsky, 1954). For those early psychologists attempting to differentiate types of psychological problems in order to decide what kind of treatment to offer, it probably seemed quite logical to follow the medical model of examining symptoms, postulating different causes for these symptoms, and then surveying treatments to find the right one for a given set of symptoms.

A diagnosis of measles, pneumonia, or cancer tells something about how the illness came about, how long it is likely to last, the prognosis for recovery, and, most important, what treatment to provide. Unfortunately, psychologists' experience clearly indicates that psychological problems differ from physical diseases and illnesses in several ways that make medical-style diagnosis far less useful to them. The symptoms of psychological disorders are not as homogeneous as those of physical problems. Cases of pneumonia share far more symptoms in common with one another than do cases of schizophrenia. Moreover, psychological symptoms are displayed less consistently than are symptoms of physical illnesses. The person with measles or pneumonia has symptoms that are detectable at almost any given moment, but a depressed or anxious person may manifest his or her symptoms only occasionally in any given time period.

Compounding these problems is the fact that psychologists vary tremendously among themselves as to the variables to which they attend. Analytically oriented psychologists emphasize dynamics (Bordin, 1968), while behaviorists attend more to overt behaviors (Adams, Doster, & Calhoun, 1977; Krumboltz, 1966). Because various psychologists single out different aspects of the same client, it is not surprising that the reliability and consistency of psychological diagnostic systems leave much to be desired (Crites, 1969; Matarazzo, 1983).

Another issue is the lack of uniform linkage between diagnosis and treatment. In medicine, a given diagnosis almost invariably implies specific treatment options. In psychology, on the other hand, *one can better predict what kind of treatment a person will get by knowing the theoretical inclinations of the therapist than by knowing the problems of the client!* A cognitive-behavioral counselor's treatment of depression more closely resembles his or her treatment of anxiety than it resembles a psychoanalyst's treatment of depression. In short, traditional medically oriented diagnostic systems have not been very helpful to either counselors or their clients.

Even the problems of low reliability and limited usefulness are not necessarily the greatest limitations of diagnosis. During the early years of the profession, when more attention was being given to diagnostic systems, Rogers (1951) was simultaneously developing his theory of client-centered counseling. He clearly indicated that traditional diagnoses were in many ways *inimical* to the facilitating of client growth and development. We would like to identify three concerns that help explain the incongruence that counseling psychologists often experience when dealing with diagnosis.

The first of these concerns is the focus of medically oriented diagnostic systems on deficits and pathology. One of the unifying themes of counseling psychology is an emphasis on assets and strengths. Using strengths to actualize one's potential for growth is a major concept in Rogers' client-centered therapy, and is also the focus of many other humanistic developments of the mid-20th century. Experience has shown, in both medical and psychological settings, that any system that focuses on deficits often reduces the attention paid to the possibilities for growth and development.

A second concern is the disregard for individual complexity implicit in making diagnoses. Rogers found that many of the classical diagnoses he had been trained to use resulted in oversimplifications; he also felt that these diagnostic categories made people focus on *similarities* among individuals rather than their *unique differences.* Diagnosis, in such a perspective, promotes stereotyping and the attendant risks of overlooking each individual's potential. Finally, and of lasting concern to much of society at large as well as to psychologists, is the "labeling" aspect—the judgmental connotations attached to diagnostic categories. Labeling persons *schizophrenic* can have a tremendous impact on how other people treat them (see Stewart's 1970 study of how normally functioning people are treated when suddenly diagnosed and placed in a hospital, even though they make no changes in their typical ways of interacting with people). Relatedly, Szasz (1960) postulates that making a diagnosis has in many cases done more to aggravate a problem than to alleviate it. In his view, many "psychological problems" are in fact problems of adjustment in living, for which persons must take some responsibility. By providing a diagnosis, the psychologist implies a "disease," thus relieving the patient of responsibility for his or her actions.

All of these criticisms help to explain why diagnosis is a quite controversial topic in psychology, and why theorists such as Rogers vehemently object to "doing diagnoses." Yet the need for differentiation of clients remains, unless one takes the position that all clients should get the same treatment—an obviously untenable position. Krumboltz (1966) very early on specified that both researchers and practitioners in psychotherapy need to ask what works with whom under what conditions. The "with whom" part of this dictum requires a diagnostic system. Further, the desire for practitioner accountability that emerged in the 1980s reemphasized the need for some sort of diagnostic system. During that time, administrators of mental health agencies and insurance companies began to ask, in an attempt to control costs, what kinds of clients were receiving treatment for how long, and what constituted a reasonable amount to pay for treatment for a particular diagnosis.

The continued study of diagnosis has yielded some progress, albeit controversial, in the last decade and has pointed the way to even further progress. A product of that study is the third edition of the Diagnostic Statistical Manual, originally published in 1980 and revised seven years later (American Psychiatric Association, 1987), which is better known as DSM-III-R. (A more extensive revision, DSM-IV, is scheduled for publication in the mid-1990s.)

DSM-III-R

Nathan and Harris (1983) have provided a concise history, comparative analysis, and appraisal of diagnostic systems for mental disorders. From the late 19th-century pioneering efforts of Emil Kraepelin through World War II, several very different diagnostic systems emerged. The American Psychiatric Association took the leadership in developing a standardized system; their first manual was published in 1952, a second in 1968, and the third in 1980. Nelson (1987) has reviewed the criticisms of earlier systems which led to the third revision. Clearly, one of the major factors in the development of the new manual is the unreliability of earlier diagnostic systems. DSM-III, and DSM-III-R even more so, specifies more operational criteria than earlier systems, noting both inclusionary and exclusionary criteria. For any particular diagnosis, the manual lists characteristics that a client's problem must have as well as those which, if present, indicate it is something else. For example, in the diagnostic criteria for a panic disorder the following inclusionary and exclusionary statements appear: "At least three panic attacks within a three-week period in circumstances other than during marked physical exertion or in a life-threatening situation. The attacks are *not* [italics added] precipitated only by exposure to a circumscribed phobic stimulus" (American Psychiatric Association, 1987, p. 231). In contrast to earlier manuals, there is more emphasis on observable behaviors than causes.

For most psychologists, the DSM-III-R's most impressive feature is the multiaxial nature of this system. The large panel of mental health experts who developed the third edition clearly recognized that previous systems focused almost exclusively on symptoms clients displayed and did not take into consideration many other features of the client that were important in developing a treatment plan or making a prognosis. Table 10-1 presents example number one from the DSM-III-R manual. As can be seen in that table, there are five axes. The first axis focuses on clinical syndromes, the second on developmental and personality

Table 10–1
EXAMPLE OF HOW TO RECORD THE RESULTS OF A DSM-III-R MULTIAXIAL EVALUATION

Axis I:	296.23	Major depression, single episode, severe without psychotic features
	303.90	Alcohol dependence
Axis II:	301.60	Dependent personality disorder (Provisional, rule out borderline personality disorder)
Axis III:		Alcoholic cirrhosis of liver
Axis IV:		Psychosocial stressors: anticipated retirement and change in residence, with loss of contact with friends
		Severity: 3—moderate (predominantly enduring circumstances)
Axis V:		Current GAF: 44
		Highest GAF past year: 55

Source: From *Diagnostic and Statistic Manual of Mental Disorders* (3rd. ed., rev.) by American Psychiatric Association, Washington, DC. Copyright 1987 by the American Psychiatric Association. Reprinted by permission.

disorders, the third on physical disorders and conditions, the fourth on severity of psychosexual stressors, and the fifth on a global assessment of functioning. In the example in the table, the presenting problem was a single episode of severe depression. Additionally, the person has a history of dependence on alcohol. Also in evidence is the personality disposition of dependent personality, further described as one in "which the individual passively allows others to assume responsibility for major areas of his or her life because of the lack of self-confidence and an inability to function independently" (American Psychiatric Association, 1987, p. 325). As noted on Axis III, there is cirrhosis of the liver, most likely a result of alcohol dependency. The fourth axis identifies current stressors as anticipated retirement and changed residence, with loss of contact with friends. The fifth axis indicates that, during the past year, the person had shown adequate adaptive functioning, now somewhat lower since the episode of depression.

Notice how much richer a description these five axes provide than does the simple label "depression." The DMS-III-R focuses more on identifying all relevant aspects of the disorders, not just labeling persons. While this diagnostic system has been, and continues to be, criticized on several bases (Schacht & Nathan, 1977; Schacht, 1985), it is such a major improvement over previous systems that it has been widely adopted in most medically oriented settings and also in many community mental health clinics.

Diagnosis as a Process

All counselors engage in some form of diagnosis, whether implicit or explicit. Properly viewed, the diagnostic process can avoid, or at least minimize, many of the pitfalls reviewed above and result in more effective intervention and research strategies. All counselors need to keep in mind two major factors about diagnosis: (1) there are multiple sources of diagnostic information about each individual, and (2) diagnosis is a continuous dynamic process that lasts as long as the counseling relationship.

In addressing the concept that diagnosis must encompass multiple sources of information, two sets of constructs present themselves. The first set is an extension of the multiaxial concepts of DMS-III. From a psychologist's point of view, as compared to a physician's, much more attention needs to be given to (1) behaviors, (2) the environment, and (3) interpersonal relationships.

Since the 1960s, there have been many significant developments in behavioral assessment strategies (e.g., Ciminero, Calhoun, & Adams, 1977). Emphasis is on overt behaviors that can be reliably observed *and,* in so far as possible, on the variables that "control," that is, increase or decrease those behaviors. During the same past two decades, community and environmental psychologists have given increasing attention to the role of environment in determining a person's behavior. Building on Mischel's (1968) earlier concepts about the role of the environmental situation in determining a person's behavior, Moos and his colleagues have developed scales to show how school, the workplace, and the family environment all significantly impact individuals' behavior (e.g., Moos, 1974). Somewhat ahead of his time, Leary (1957) provided a seminal work on an interpersonal diagnostic system built on the premise that the only really useful diagnosis, especially for therapy, if not for all personality, was one that focused on how persons typically related to others *and* how others typically related to them, describing, for example, what reactions a person typically evokes from others. In Leary's view, only by knowing this information, as compared to symptoms or etiology, could one hope to predict, with reasonable accuracy, the person's future behavior *and* know how and where to intervene to change patterns that clients want to change. These developments have helped psychologists attend to behavioral, environmental, and interpersonal interactions as part of the diagnostic process.

A second set of constructs about sources of information for diagnoses also derives from the work of Leary (1957) in which he describes the need for multiple levels of information about an individual. In his view, assessments of an individual need to be made through (1) his or her public communications, such as ratings of public behavior, (2) conscious descriptions such as provided in self-report tests, (3) private symbolization as available in projective tests and dreams, and (4) unexpressed unconscious, material, that is, "interpersonal themes which are systematically and compulsively avoided by the subject at all the other levels of personality and which are conspicuous by their inflexible absence" (p. 80). (Leary was never able to solve the problem of how to assess this area except by its absence.) His last recommended level was that of (5) values reflected in "the subject's system of moral, superego judgments, his ego ideal. We refer here to the interpersonal traits and actions that the subject holds to be 'good,' 'proper,' and 'right'—his picture of how he should be and would like to be" (p. 80).

We do not suggest that Leary's five levels are the levels to which all *must* attend; other writers such as Kaplan, Colarelli, Gross, Leventhal, and Siegel (1970) have presented another model in terms of the ambiguity vs. clarity of structures of both the testing stimulus and the behavior expected of the client. The major point we wish to make is that obtaining information from these different types of assessments, even of the same behavior, gives psychologists the greatest latitude for developing more comprehensive and useful diagnostic views. Lanyon and Goodstein (1982) have nicely summarized the data showing that when clinicians are given several pieces of information of the *same* type, for example, scores from several interest inventories or several kinds of ratings, the diagnosis does *not* become any more accurate than when simply using one test score. *Only* when using test or interview information from different levels and/or kinds of assessment, (e.g., interview data and objective tests or behavioral ratings and projective tests), do we get noticeable improvements in accuracy of diagnosis. The greater the diversity of levels of information, the greater the likelihood that the diagnostic prediction will show some increase in validity. To summarize: the most useful diagnostic information must include four areas: symptoms (or expressed problems), interpersonal relationships, behaviors, and environmental factors. Each of these areas should be assessed, insofar as possible, at different levels by different types of assessments.

Turning now to the dynamic aspects of diagnosis, one can see immediate connections to the points made previously about the process of collecting diagnostic information. In the first place, all of the information called for above cannot possibly be gathered in one moment, nor is anyone intellectually capable of scanning and integrating all of that information simultaneously. It must be recognized that one is always in the process of constructing a fuller and fuller picture of the client. One often starts with clients' self-reported statements about their problems, then notes their observable behaviors, then moves on to information obtained through interviews and other measures about environmental factors, fantasies, and so forth. As long ago as 1954, Pepinsky and Pepinsky aptly described diagnosis thus: "hypothesis formulation and testing, a process of approximation and correction" (p. 198). We cannot emphasize too much the tentativeness with which one needs to hold one's formulations. As Lanyon and Goodstein (1982) found in their review, all too often the *first* information one obtains plays the most significant role in the diagnosis, just as in the primacy effect found by social psychologists—first impressions typically have a dominant and long-lasting effect. Moreover, according to Lanyon and Goodstein, those who hold an orthodox theoretical position make little change in their diagnostic views about a client even with additional information; they therefore achieve less accuracy in their diagnoses.

Until recently, there have been all too few studies on the processes that counselors and clinicians actually go through in making their diagnoses. For almost three decades, little progress was made beyond the earliest such studies by McArthur (1954), Koester (1954), and Meehl (1960), all of which found diagnosis more accurate when not approached with the rigidity of a single theoretical perspective. Lanyon and Goodstein (1982) reviewed somewhat more recent studies showing what factors can improve the accuracy of diagnoses; they found that expert feedback to counselors regarding the accuracy of their diagnoses (using prepared case materials) is, not surprisingly, one of the most important factors. Currently, much important research focuses on clinical hypothesis formation, that is, how one goes about building the kind of picture needed to make diagnosis a more reliable and useful process. Strohmer and his colleagues (e.g., Strohmer & Newman, 1983, Strohmer & Chiodo, 1984) have been examining how a variety of cognitive processes in social judgment relate to clinical hypothesis formation. From such studies and the application of computer-facilitated sequential analyses, psychologists may well identify in the coming decade more of the components and processes that can help them improve their diagnoses of clients. Remembering the Pepinskys' sage advice, the process needs to be one of "approximation and correction," a kind of hypothesis that is continually tested by new and incoming information.

There is yet another dynamic aspect to diagnosis in counseling and psychotherapy. By definition, effective therapy means the client is changing. To the extent that a counselor is helping the client change, this week's diagnosis will be less accurate than next week's. Again, all diagnostic thinking must be tentative. This perspective is one that even client-centered therapists acknowledge is useful.

TYPES OF ASSESSMENT OTHER THAN TESTS

The main purpose of this section is to clarify that assessment is *not* synonymous with psychological testing, despite this prevailing impression among many students and even counselors. We shall furnish brief descriptions of three other kinds of instruments—interviews, behavioral ratings, and environmental assessments—before our discussion of widely used types of psychological tests. For each of these kinds of assessments, we shall note some of the assets and limitations of each that apply not only to the kinds of diagnostic processes described above but also to other uses in counseling, for example, providing clients with information for making self-comparisons and stimulating explorations of alternative ways of functioning, researching topics such as normal development and coping, and evaluating the effectiveness of counseling interventions.

Note that none of these types of assessments is inherently better than the others. Each one has distinct contributions to make. In an ideal world, a truly comprehensive assessment might be possible. However, if one considers that the five levels of assessment Leary (1957) talked about can each be measured by multiple types of assessment, it can be seen that it would take many more hours and resources than are almost ever available to do a comprehensive assessment of even one individual. Consequently, choices need to be made, based on an understanding of what needs to be known about a person or group of persons at a given time.

Another important principle is that using only one type of assessment data is *always* a high-risk proposition. Drawing conclusions uniquely from a test or from behavioral observations or from client self-report entails significant risks of error. It is only when one can see common themes emerging from different types of assessment, preferably across different levels as well, that one can truly gain significant confidence in assessments. We feel so strongly about this point that our advice to students and professionals is that no important decision about a person should ever be made on the basis of one type of assessment data: try at least to compare behavioral observations and interview data with self-report data or test data. When such data do not point in the same direction, as is often the case, then further assessments must be made.

Interviews

Interviews, as a type of assessment, have a history as long as psychological tests. Over the years, numerous articles have analyzed their comparative strengths and weaknesses. Pope (1983) provides more than eight pages of references on the role of the interview as part of the assessment phase in psychotherapy and counseling. There are two specific kinds of information that are more readily available in interviews than in most other kinds of assessment. The first is a person's life history. No two individuals are exactly the same. The details of how a person developed, especially how he or she has progressed through life up to the present time, can be obtained in reasonable detail only through the interview. Counselors who work with abusive persons quickly learn that clients with the same personality test profiles are not necessarily equally likely to be repeat abusers; an individual's behavior in interviews is a critical component in assessing risk of repeat abuse.

Second interviews are also a rich source of behavioral observations, especially nonverbal behavioral information, for example, tone of voice, posture, gestures, habits such as nail biting, scratching, and so forth. Many of these behavioral observations lead to significant inferences that complement the data obtained from what the client says and from other sources of assessment. Counselors frequently find clients saying they are not concerned about a particular problem, yet showing many signs of anxiety, such as hand-wringing, hair-pulling, and fidgeting, whenever that problem is discussed.

The individuality of assessment that the interview allows is both its strength and its weakness. Interviews have often been labeled unreliable sources of information; that is, two or more different interviewers do not come up with the same conclusions based on interview data. There are at least four explanations for this unreliability. First, interviewers may well ask different questions and therefore receive different information. Secondly, different interviewers, because of the different impressions they make on clients, may elicit entirely different responses even when asking the same questions. Thirdly, interviewers make different observations during a session (no one is able to observe *all* of the behaviors that a client manifests during an interview). Finally, even if all interviewers have the same information or observations, they may interpret it differently. In an effort to address some of these problems, a structured interview questionnaire may be developed, so that the same questions are asked. There may even be "rules" specified for how to combine some of the information. To the extent that all of these more structured steps are taken, the interview becomes more and more like a test and, of course, becomes less responsive to an individual's uniqueness. Whether or not to interview as an assessment technique depends on the purpose of the assessment. If the information needed can be secured by existing psychological inventories or tests, then the more reliable test is preferable to the interview. However, in many cases, no standardized tests are available to answer the questions one wishes to ask; in such cases the interview should indeed be considered.

Behavioral Observation Ratings

Prior to the significant understanding gained in the last couple of decades about the value of specificity in behavioral observations, there were many kinds of more global ratings made in both employment and therapy settings. Many of the problems with ratings that are discussed in various textbooks on psychological measurement and I/O psychology can be addressed by developing more specific behavioral checklists related to the areas under study. Cauteda (1977) and Nelson and Hayes (1979) have provided examples of behavior ratings pertinent to the assessment of clients. Related to earlier points about the need for assessing different areas, Lazarus (1976) uses the acronym *Basic-ID* to support his position that it is important to make observations in at least seven different areas: behavior, affect, sensation, imagery, cognition, interpersonal relationships, and drug/health behaviors. Almost all areas can be observed either in an interview situation, in more naturalistic settings (such as work settings and waiting rooms), or in role-played settings (for example, having the client respond to a hard-sell telephone call as a way of observing assertiveness skills). Again, these different areas can be rated in a variety of situations for greater breadth of perspective.

There are a few limitations to note about behavioral ratings. First, any single behavior at any given time is never more than one sample of a person's behavioral repertoire. Although psychologists may be fond of saying that the best predictor of future behavior is past behavior, this predictive accuracy is modest at best. Consequently, like interview data and test data, behavioral ratings must be considered in a context of multiple samples of a person's behavior, which include both repeated behavioral ratings and other assessments.

In addition, those behaviors most easily observed are *not* always the most useful sources of information. For example, it is much easier to get reliable, widespread agreement on the significance of crossing of legs versus speech hesitancy, yet the former has rarely proven significant in any important assessment of an individual, whereas the latter has been a useful indication of stress (Kasl & Mahl, 1965).

Finally, even though behavioral ratings sound as though they should be easy to use—one simply "observes behaviors"—agreement is rarely unanimous among observers, at least initially. To gain the maximum reliability that behavioral ratings can offer, some training is needed for the observers or raters.

Environmental Assessment

In keeping with counseling psychology's emphasis on person-environment interactions, comprehensive assessments of an individual need to include a consideration of those environmental factors that can facilitate or restrict one's personal adjustment and development. While the term *environmental assessment* may call to mind factors like temperature, light, and space, we are referring here to psychological assessment of the interpersonal environment, including such factors as competition, cohesion, support, and coerciveness. Moreover, such assessment focuses on how the persons themselves describe the environment from their perspective. This technique, of course, is congruent with the phenomenological position that persons' perceptions may be more important in affecting behavior than "real world" effects. For example, whether or not one perceives one's parents as accepting may be more critical in later adjustment than whether or not the parents actually engaged in accepting behaviors as measured through behavioral rating scales.

Anastasi (1982) provides a brief history of the development of environmental assessment measures, especially in university and college environments in the 1960s. Holland's (1985) measures of work environment (see Chapter 12) have become a major component of diagnosis and treatment of career choice and adjustment problems. Environmental measures for other areas have been developed by Moos (1974) and his colleagues in the social ecology laboratory of Stanford University. They have developed separate assessment scales for environments such as psychological treatment programs, high school classrooms, college residences, and work settings. Although the questions on the scales vary according to a particular setting, their analyses indicate three major dimensions for assessing psychological environments: (1) relationships (e.g., involvement, peer cohesion), (2) personal growth (e.g., autonomy, task orientation), and (3) system maintenance and change (e.g., control, clarity). These scales have proved as useful for diagnosing group issues as personal issues—what the "implicit norms/rules" in a setting are that restrict a person's options, make one want to stay or get out, make one uncaring, and so forth. Such measures have been used all too seldom in individual diagnosis. However, as counseling psychologists work increasingly with culturally diverse clients, assessment of environmental factors becomes even more critical for understanding factors that interfere with opportunities for personal growth and development.

EVALUATING AND CONSTRUCTING PSYCHOLOGICAL TESTS

For readers who have not had prior coursework in the basics of psychological testing, we recommend a reading of "A Primer of Testing" (Green, 1981), before proceeding. His 11-page article describes the constructs and considerations that underlie the recommendations in this section on psychological assessment.

The terms in the heading of this section may seem reversed—evaluating before constructing? Our choice of order is deliberate. In this section we wish to identify a few major concepts every counseling psychologist needs to consider when planning to use any existing assessment instruments. Moreover, for certain problems one wishes to assess, especially as a researcher, there may be few if any measures that have adequate psychometric support or evidence of usefulness in past research. In these situations, and *only* in these situations where adequate measures cannot be found, we encourage counseling psychologists to develop appropriate assessment instruments. Before computers became readily available to almost every graduate student and professional counseling psychologist, development of assessment measures of any sophistication was beyond most persons' capabilities. That situation has changed radically. Now what were once considered complex analyses, such as measures of internal consistency of multiple-response items or factor and cluster analyses, can be executed on personal computers. Thus, the scientist-practitioner counseling psychologist is now able to routinely provide basic psychometric data on any newly developed measure or, for existing tests, psychometric data for unique samples (e.g., a culturally diverse population).

As Green (1981) makes clear, reliability and validity are the linchpins of test evaluation. Reliability refers to the consistency with which one measures something. Without consistency, one cannot develop validity, that is, predictable and useful relationships with other variables that are important to us, such as clients' mental health, employees' career adjustment, or adolescents' self-esteem. Our recommendation regarding reliability is that measures need to be evaluated for both *temporal* consistency and *internal* consistency. The former is most easily illustrated by test-retest reliability. One asks, "If a test is given this week and the same test is given two weeks later, how well do the scores correlate with each other?" The higher the correlation, the more reliable, or consistent, the results are said to be. Correlations of 0.80 or higher are seen as a minimal standard for practical use of tests, that is, making decisions about what course of action or treatment a client should follow. Such reliability is often seen as most critical for practitioners' use of psychological tests—if a client's scores differ radically on the same test two weeks apart, then clearly the test is of little use for understanding present, or predicting future, behavior.

Internal consistency refers to the homogeneity of a test. As both Green (1981) and Nunnally (1978) have argued persuasively: "A test gains its reliability and its power by adding up a large number of homogeneous items" (Green, 1981, p. 1005). Homogeneous items are found by inspecting the intercorrelations of all items in a test or subtest with each other. To do this, one uses a coefficient called "alpha," now a part of many computer software statistical packages. Researchers using current tests or developing their own will want to determine each instrument's internal consistency. Nunnally suggests that measures with internal consistency of below 0.70 may have greatly limited value in both practical and research applications. Efforts to demonstrate validity of such poorly defined measures may prove almost fruitless. He describes several ways in which efforts might be better expended for improving internal consistency, thereby allowing for greater potential development of valid relationships with the variables that are most important to counseling psychologists.

Two major recommendations can be made regarding counseling psychologists' appraisal of the validity of assessment instruments. Among the many kinds of validity (see Green, 1981) the validity question that should take precedence is "What evidence is there that the use of this test in the past has resulted in answering questions like the one I'm asking now?" For example, if one is asking a question about ego strength of a deaf client, is there any evidence that the test being applied has been used with deaf clients and has been shown to be significantly related to other accepted appraisals of ego strength? If one wishes to use a symptom checklist to assess whether a new treatment program is more helpful than another, can evidence be located that other researchers have found client changes in the symptom checklist as a function of psychological treatment? Much misuse of tests in practice as well as wasted efforts in research are the result of not having asked this particular question about validity.

A second recommendation regarding validity is related to Campbell and Fiske's (1959) now classic article on convergent and discriminant validity. Fully implementing their recommendations exceeds the capacity of all but the major test developers; however, their concept of discriminant validity has special importance for both researchers and practitioners in counseling psychology. Because so many of the concepts with which counseling psychologists work are abstract (e.g., self-concept, empathy, anxiety), there are likely to be many different meanings for each concept and, most importantly for the present discussion, numerous measures with considerable overlap despite different names (e.g., a values inventory and an interest inventory). Just as the accuracy of diagnosis improves if a psychologist uses distinctively different levels or types of assessment, so too does research benefit from using assessment instruments that are discriminantly different. Many research projects include multiple measures, but if those measures are highly intercorrelated, then little new information is gained. Quite simply, multiple tests with clients or in research should be selected according to their discriminant validity, that is, the statistical evidence of differences in what they measure, not only the differences in their titles. In the next section, we review four major kinds of tests.

PSYCHOLOGICAL TESTS: MAJOR TYPES

In this section we discuss what most people think of when they encounter the term *assessment*—that is, a psychological test. What is a test? "A psychological test is essentially an objective and standardized measure of a sample of behavior. . . . the psychologist proceeds in much the same way as a biochemist who tests a patient's blood or a community's water supply by analyzing one or more samples of it" (Anastasi, 1982, p. 22). Many shelves of books in college libraries are devoted to the thousands of psychological tests in existence. No one can keep count any longer of the millions of tests given each year in employment and educational settings.

Counseling psychologists are typically involved with only a few of these tests. According to both Fitzgerald and Osipow (1986) and Watkins, Campbell, and McGregor (1988), about two-thirds of all counseling psychologists regularly use some sort of psychological measures, mostly objective tests (see our later section on objective and projective tests). Note, however, that one-third use *no* tests. In fact, some counseling psychologists have used no psychological tests for the last 20 years, while others routinely assign more than 20 tests each week. Moreover, the particular tests given vary significantly among settings (Watkins, Campbell, & McGregor, 1988). In counseling centers, the tests most frequently used are the Strong Interest Inventory (SII) and the Minnesota Multiphasic Personality Inventory (MMPI). In hospital and clinic settings, the MMPI and the Revised Wechsler Adult Intelligence Scale (WAIS-R) are most frequently used. Even more variations appear in the other interest, personality, and ability measures that are used in these settings. In short, the various theoretical orientations of individual counseling psychologists, plus the demands of their work settings, create highly variable patterns of test usage, so it is vital that all counseling psychologists become acquainted with the major kinds of tests and what they can contribute to both practice and research problems. Only the informed counseling psychologist make an informed decision on whether to use psychological testing in any given situation. The purpose of the remainder of this section is to acquaint readers with those tests used most frequently by counseling psychologists, describing some of the typical client problems and research questions addressed by such tests.

Interest Measures

Considering all the types of psychological tests, counseling psychologists have been most visibly involved with the development of interest measures. Because counseling psychology has been the specialty most centrally involved in career development and career counseling, almost every key person in the history of interest measurement has also been a key figure in the leadership and scholarship of counseling psychology. By the 1920s psychologists began to see limits to the usefulness of focusing only on occupational abilities as predictors of occupational success. Increasing attention was given to the role of interests in understanding occupational success and adjustment. The work of E. K. Strong (1943), started in the late 1920s, laid the foundation for what has become the most widely used interest measure, the SII (Hansen & Campbell, 1985), given to well over a million people each year (Hansen, 1984).

The reasonable skeptic may ask, why does one need a measure of interests? Why not ask the person simply to express his or her interests? Hansen (1984) concisely reviews the decades of data showing how expressed interests and measured interests often disagree and examines the various hypotheses that have been put forward to explain why. These data, along with the literature on the significant contributions of measured interests in predicting who will stay in a position and find success in it, have led to not only several revisions of the interest inventory developed by Strong but to numerous other measures of interest, especially the Kuder Occupational Interest Survey (Kuder & Diamond, 1979) and the Holland Vocational Preference Inventory (VPI) (Holland, 1977). Although each of these measures has a somewhat different conceptual and empirical history, all have entered the counseling psychology mainstream as useful and adequately valid instruments in assisting clients to explore and choose satisfying and successful careers. Hansen (1984) and Walsh and Osipow (1986) provide concise descriptions of these measures.

Of the three measures, the SII clearly provides the widest range of information, which accounts for its extensive use. As of 1974, the SII began to include the six occupational themes of Holland's VPI and now includes scores on 23 basic interest areas (e.g., sales, teaching, medical sciences) and 207 occupational scales (e.g., optician, minister, travel agent) all grouped within the six occupational themes. Norms for both males and females in each of these areas are provided except in those few occupations where there are either too few females or too few males to develop a separate norm.

Probably every university and college counseling center includes the SII among its most commonly used tests. The wealth of information available in the various sections of the SII allows for extensive exploration of career options for those who have no idea what career to enter as well as for those who seek to confirm their interests. For students below the college level who are not planning to earn a college degree, a companion measure focused on nonprofessional occupations may be more appropriate. The Career Assessment Inventory (Johansson, 1976) is constructed in much the same way as the SII, furnishing a useful array of occupations for the non-college-bound client to consider.

The research uses of the interest inventories are as equally varied as the counseling uses. Almost every issue of the *Journal of Vocational Behavior* and the *Journal of Counseling Psychology* includes one or more research articles in which an interest inventory has been one of the major assessment techniques utilized. These investigations range from testing theoretically based models—for example, comparing the role of interests, self-efficacy, and thinking style as predictors of career and academic behavior (Lent, Brown, & Larkin, 1987)—to more basic descriptive research such as the validity and usefulness of the SII with various demographic groups (e.g., women and blacks).

Personality Measures

Although the history of the development of psychometrically based personality tests coincides chronologically with the development of interest measures, the diversity of personality measures far exceeds that of interest measures. The multiplicity of personality theories in the first half of the 20th century resulted in very different kinds of tests for almost every theory. This diversity is still reflected in the fact that Watson, Campbell, and McGregor (1988) found only two or three *interest and ability* measures recommended for inclusion in the training of counseling psychologists; however, no less than 12 *personality* tests were so included: the MMPI, the Sixteen Personality Factors, the California Psychological Inventory, the Myers-Briggs Type Indicator, the Edwards Personal Preference Schedule, the Millon Clinical Multiaxial Inventory, the Thematic Apperception Test, the Rorschach, the Draw-a-Person, the House-Tree-Person, the Bender-Gestalt, and sentence completion blanks. Brief descriptions of almost all these tests may be found in testing references, but the best overview for counseling psychologists is a book by Lanyon and Goodstein (1982) on personality assessment. It discusses the conceptual development of these tests and provides a brief synopsis of the critical literature on most of them.

It is important at this point to describe the distinction between objective and projective personality tests and the special issues this distinction raises for counseling psychologists. These two types of tests differ on several dimensions and can lead to quite different conceptualizations of a client. The clearest distinction is in the kind of response called for. Objective tests require that the client answer *true/false, agree/disagree, like/dislike,* or a similar set response to each statement on the test. In projective tests, the response called for is most always a "free" or open-ended response; for example, the client is shown a picture and asked to describe what he or she sees. The tests also differ in the structure of the *stimulus material,* that is, what is presented to the client. In an objective test, the stimulus is almost always a specific statement, whereas in a projective test it is much more likely a picture, an ink blot, or other deliberately ambiguous stimulus. When responding to such ambiguity, theoretically, the client projects himself or herself into the response. Projective testing was developed by adherents of the psychoanalytic approach as a way of assessing the unconscious experience. It is this private symbolized level of experience that Leary, as noted earlier, believes should be part of the full assessment of a client. By definition, one cannot get direct access to unconscious experience through client self-report because the client is not aware of what is in the unconscious. One needs, then, a situation where clients can project themselves so that the examiner can observe manifestations of their unconscious experience. Given the very different kind of responses obtained in objective and projective tests, the scoring also needs to be quite different. Objective tests are usually scored for specific scales, yielding numerical scores that can easily be compared to the scores of others. By comparing one person's scores to a measure's "norm" groups, judgments may be made about the strength of a particular characteristic in a person. Although recent developments with some of the projective techniques have moved in this direction (Exner, 1974, 1978), most projective techniques are scored much more subjectively. In such cases, examiners follow guidelines for assessing themes or ratios of types of responses that have been shown to have some diagnostic value and that appear to have at least logical connections with theoretical propositions about how unconscious experience might be manifested.

From a traditional research viewpoint, objective tests clearly have much more reliability and validity than any of the projective techniques. Moreover, projective techniques have historically focused largely on psychopathology. (It is important to note, however, that a focus on pathology is not an inherent part of projectives. Counseling psychologists who were so inclined could develop scoring techniques designed to describe the more normal developmental processes reflected in the projected unconscious.) Because of their questionable validity and their focus on psychopathology, projective techniques are infrequently used by counseling psychologists. In fact, controversy has arisen (Watkins et al., 1989) about whether counseling psychologists should be trained in projective techniques. With an increasing number of counseling psychologists entering hospital practice and independent practice instead of counseling centers, interest in projective techniques seems to be growing, but many counseling programs do not offer such training as a regular part of their curriculum.

Beyond the objective and projective distinction, there are other questions about whether counseling psychologists should use any personality tests developed primarily for pathological populations, particularly when the scales are of a pathological nature, such as *schizophrenic, paranoid,* and so forth. Such labels make it extremely difficult to provide an interpretation to a client without causing a great deal of anxiety, requiring much effort on the part of the counselor to find less pathologically oriented ways to describe the tendencies (Kunce & Anderson, 1984). Tests that measure less pathological aspects of personality are much more congruent with the themes of counseling psychology. Personality inventories like the Edwards Personal Preference Schedule (EPPS) (Edwards, 1959), with its need scales (e.g., dominance, nurturance) and the Myers-Briggs Type Indicator (Myers, 1975), which measures personality types such as introversion and extroversion, often have more appeal to counselors who want to use personality tests as part of personal and career counseling with the client. See discussions by Helms (1983) and Pinkney (1983) about applying the results of the tests just mentioned.

For the most part, personality inventories have been used in individual diagnosis, mostly to assess a client's degree of psychopathology. As discussed earlier, symptoms are not always regularly displayed. For example, it may be critical to assess judgments of depression, schizophrenic thinking, and inadequate control of impulsive behavior in determining what type of intervention and/or protection is needed when suicidal or homicidal issues are presented by a client. As only a sample of behaviors is seen in any one interview with an individual, a psychometrically well-developed test may provide a broad-based sample of behavior, thereby increasing, in a relatively efficient way, knowledge about the client.

By far, the most exhaustively researched personality assessment instrument is the MMPI, which is specifically designed to identify different types of psychopathology. Literally thousands of studies (Dahlstrom & Dahlstrom, 1979) have been made on its clinical and validity scales. Each person who takes this test receives a score on each of the scales, a score that is compared to that of a norm group to determine if the individual is, for example, scoring significantly high on "hypochondria" or "paranoia." Graham (1990) provides an excellent practical introductory guide on the MMPI and the recently published MMPI-2.

Although the MMPI first became prominent in the 1950s, it had become clear by the 1960s that the psychopathology of most individuals was much more complex than reflected by one high score on one scale. Thus, a diagnosis could not be given simply by looking at the highest score. The complexities of human behavior were better reflected by the relationships among the scales. The MMPI has proved most useful when considered in terms of examinees' profiles. Various "codebooks" describe the typical patterns on behavior, probable etiology, and prognosis for the most common combinations of high scores. Duckworth (1979) provides a codebook specifically useful for counseling psychologists in their work with college students. For counseling psychologists who wish to use the MMPI as part of the personality test results they give to clients, Kunce and Anderson (1984) have authored a chapter with a descriptive table listing the underlying dimension and the positive and negative counterpart behaviors for each scale. For example, the underlying dimension for the scale on hysteria is expression. The traditional pathological interpretation of high scores on this scale emphasizes such attributes as denial, psychosomatic reactions, and suggestibility. A more positive interpretation of high scores on this same scale emphasizes attributes such as empathy, responsiveness, sensitivity, and optimism.

Counseling psychology research makes far less use of the MMPI than of many other personality measures because of that instrument's pathological orientation. In research, it has been used mostly as a screening/diagnostic measure for selecting subjects for research on various kinds of treatment programs (e.g., Hill et al., 1983) or in correlating scores pertaining to psychopathology with other variables such as interests and job adjustment. For other research purposes, counseling psychologists have often used the California Psychological Inventory (Megargee, 1972), a measure structured much like the MMPI but focused on nonpathological populations and yielding scores on such attributes as sense of well-being, self-control, and achievement-via-conformance. The newer MMPI-2 may see more use in counseling research since it is now being used more frequently in psychological treatment research (Butcher, 1990).

Ability Tests

Contemporary counseling psychologists' low-level application of ability tests stands in direct contrast to the profession's history. Recall the immense role of ability tests in occupational selection at the beginning of the century and their formative influence on the profession. Much of the psychologist's work was devoted to the development of both general intelligence and special aptitude tests to help people choose between occupations requiring, for example, mechanical or numerical skills and those requiring spatial-relations or verbal skills. However, in the past century the world of work has changed radically. The majority of the workforce now occupies white-collar or service positions in which special mechanical or spatial-relations skills are rarely as important as general intelligence. Moreover, within the professions, the amount of general intelligence necessary to be successful does not differ much from that needed to succeed in college. For example, there are successful nuclear engineers whose general intelligence is no greater than that of average college students. Interests, persistence, and other motivational factors may bring success to those with slightly above average intelligence while their more brilliant colleagues stumble. College counselors rarely need any other ability information than that available from college entrance tests such as the Scholastic Aptitude Test (SAT) or the American College Test (ACT). (In a few instances, even at the college level, it is important to distinguish between and assess both general intelligence and special aptitudes; Anastasi (1982) and Goldman (1961) provide relevant differentiations and examples.)

A few counseling psychologists, however, may find themselves significantly involved with some of the more traditional aptitude tests and precollege-level group intelligence tests. Job Corps programs, the military, and similar organizations work with tens of thousands of men and women who do not enroll in higher education. For counseling psychologists working with such populations, a knowledge of the different kinds of general intelligence and specialized abilities tests, as well as an understanding of the norms of such tests, is absolutely essential. Anastasi (1982) is an excellent source of information in this area.

In Watkins et al.'s 1988 survey of counseling psychologists, the WAIS-R was the most widely used intelligence test (though his respondents recommended that counseling psychologists become familiar also with the Stanford-Binet, an individualized intelligence test that evolved from the very first intelligence test developed at the turn of the century). For what purposes do counseling psychologists use an intelligence test, especially one like the WAIS-R, which must be individually administered, requiring one or two hours of testing time? Why is the WAIS-R one of the tests most frequently used in hospitals and clinics by psychologists (clinical as well as counseling) but rarely used in counseling centers? The answer lies in the kinds of clients seen in those settings. In many cases, clients seen in hospitals or clinics have suffered injury or illness or psychological problems that have impaired their intellectual functioning.

The WAIS-R consists of five verbal and six performance subtests that must be individually administered in a one- to two-hour period, depending on the speed with which the examinee completes the measures. Several of the tests are timed; many of the five verbal tests allow for open-ended responses (e.g., Why should people pay taxes? How are work and play alike?). The performance tests require the manipulation of blocks, arranging pictures to tell a story, learning a code, and so forth. It takes many hours of supervised training to learn to administer this test effectively, but once it is mastered, the examiner can gain from the testing session a rich amount of information on how a person goes about solving different problems as well as how well they are solved. Norms are provided for ages 16 through 64, for performance and verbal IQs, and for a full-scale IQ. Separate but similar tests exist for younger persons: the Wechsler Intelligence Scale for Children and the Wechsler Preschool and Primary Scale of Intelligence.

An examiner is able to make critical observations, answering questions such as: Do some kinds of subtests stimulate more anxiety or more impulsivity than others? Does the client realize he or she is making mistakes? If so, how does this affect motivation to continue? The test allows also for an assessment of what kinds of cognitive tasks the client can do well and, conversely, has trouble with. Such assessment may be used (1) to understand lifelong difficulties the client may have had in responding to certain kinds of intellectual challenges or, (2) if the client has previously had no difficulties, to support the need for further neuropsychological testing (described in the next section). With the availability today of various brain scan techniques, far less use is made of psychological tests than previously in determining organicity, that is, brain pathology. However, the WAIS-R can be a most valuable source of information in terms of what deficits should be considered for rehabilitation. Brain scans can show only where there has been damage, not how it has affected the person's remaining ability. Are an attorney's reasoning processes as competent as they were before her brain tumor operation? Has the recovering alcoholic, believed to have suffered brain damage from heavy drinking bouts, retained enough eye-hand coordination skills to continue his job as a telephone assembly worker? Does the stroke victim retain sufficient planning ability to continue to take care of herself, shop, cook, manage her finances, and so forth? With information obtained from the WAIS-R, appropriate rehabilitation plans can be made regarding both daily living and occupational tasks for those recovering from various injuries and illness. For beginning students of individualized intelligence tests, two very concise and informative descriptions of the WAIS-R and its appraisal values are House and Lewis (1985) and Matarazzo and Matarazzo (1984). More specialized issues in using the WAIS-R for clinical and neuropsychological assessment are covered in Kaufman (1990).

The use of the WAIS-R, or any other intellectual measure, as a research instrument in counseling psychology is far less prevalent than the use of other kinds of psychological assessment. Clinical and developmental psychologists are more likely to conduct research utilizing intellectual measures. Where such tests appear in counseling psychology studies, they mostly function as descriptive measures of characteristics of a sample used in a given study.

Neuropsychological Tests

Counseling psychologists in hospitals, rehabilitation centers, and service centers working with the elderly increasingly find themselves needing some knowledge of neuropsychological testing. The complexity of brain-behavior relationships has required the development of highly technical and sophisticated batteries for comprehensive neuropsychological assessment, as well as some brief screening instruments used to identify the need for larger batteries or various radiological brain scans, for example, CAT and PET scans. Smith's (1983) article offers a brief introduction and Filschov and Boll's (1981) *Handbook of Clinical Neuropsychology* provides essential information on the development of neuropsychological assessment techniques. An increasing number of training programs and internships furnish some training in neuropsychological tests; those wishing to specialize in neuropsychological assessment may well choose to enter postdoctoral training programs.

USE OF TESTS

In this section we examine some core issues about the use of tests, especially with reference to the unique ways many counseling psychologists apply psychological tests. Unlike clinical, school, and I/O psychologists, who use psychological tests most often for reports presented to other professionals, counseling psychologists frequently communicate test results directly to the client. The client is the direct consumer. Duckworth (1990) elaborates the use of tests with clients as a method of (1) enhancing short-term therapy, (2) focusing on developmental issues, (3) aiding problem solving and (4) improving decision-making. As the typical primary goal is to have clients learn things about themselves that will help them to make changes in their personal or occupational lifestyle, it is critical for counselors to understand the factors in selection and interpretation that will affect what clients get out of test results.

Early counseling psychologists relied on their accumulated wisdom to choose those tests that would provide the most valuable information, and then they presented the results to the client, much as a physician does when confronting a medical problem for which he or she orders a blood test. One serendipitous effect of the previously discussed theoretical clashes over the role of diagnosis was investigations into how much clients benefited from the results of psychological tests. There have now been several decades of studies checking on clients' understanding of test results and their satisfaction with and use of the results in making changes in their lives (Goodyear, 1990). Many of the earlier investigations indicated that clients had shockingly poor understanding of the test results and often made little use of them in subsequent decisions (Goldman, 1972). These disappointing results, however, did stimulate the quest for more effective testing.

One major area of investigation has been that of involving the client in deciding what kinds of tests he or she would like to take, that is, making test selection part of the counseling process (Bordin & Bixler, 1946). (Such a procedure is, of course, very unlike what typically happens in a medical situation where the physician decides the test to be made.) The results of several studies of such client involvement suggest that the clients' subsequent use of test results is improved by having them take a more active part in the selection process (Brammer & Shostrom, 1977). We particularly like Brammer and Shostrom's description of general strategies for involving clients in deciding on what tests can help solve their presenting problem: "(1) The client and counselor decide from their discussion what types of data are needed to help solve his problem; (2) the counselor describes the various categories into which tests are classified; (3) the counselor recommends those specific tests which will give the kinds of data sought by the client and recommends against testing in areas where there are already sufficient data or where tests would not help much; (4) the counselor allows the client to react to the selections so that any doubts or negative feelings about tests can be worked through; (5) arrangements are made for the tests to be administered" (p. 288).

In practice, it is often found that tests cannot be selected until the second or third counseling session, perhaps even later. It is important to allow sufficient time for the client to explore what he or she already knows well about himself or herself and to frame the present problem in sufficiently concrete terms so that with the counselor he or she can explore choices from a variety of tests. In many cases, clients enter counseling wanting to take tests immediately and have to be helped to understand that the most beneficial use of tests will come about only after there has been a clear determination of what they need to know about themselves as well as which tests can best address those issues. These procedures prepare the client to participate in a discussion of the results. By being involved in the selection, the client has already learned something about what each test can and cannot do and has at least implicitly decided, "I want to learn what this test can tell me."

Just as there have been numerous studies of how clients' selection of tests can enhance what they get out of them, so too there have been many studies of test result interpretation. The results of these studies have, to say the least, not been conclusive as to how to maximize client understanding and satisfaction. Comparisons of (1) individual and group interpretation techniques, (2) computer-provided versus counselor-provided interpretation sessions, or (3) using or not using test profiles as part of the interpretation seem to result in *no* significant differences in client accuracy and attitude just as often as they result in significant differences (Herr & Cramer, 1988; Goodyear, 1990). All too often these studies have focused on a kind of test interpretation that is too brief and insufficiently integrated with the counseling process to permit an adequate evaluation of interpretation strategies.

Both Healy (1990) and Tinsley and Bradley (1986) have presented some strategies allowing for greater integration of test interpretation and the process of counseling. Healy's recommendations focus on what he labels a "Reformed Career Appraisal" in which the counselor acts more as a collaborator than an expert with the client. The basic concepts underlying his assessment model are similar to those of Tinsley and Bradley's (1986) two fundamental principles: "First, test interpretation must not be viewed as a discreet activity but conceptualized as part of the ongoing counseling process. . . . counselors who take 'time out' from being sensitive, warm, empathic and caring individuals while conducting test interpretations engage in a practice detrimental to the overall counseling process. . . . Second, it seems useful to think of tests as structured interviews designed to provide information about clients in an efficient manner. They should not be deified or thought of as magically providing answers" (p. 462). Several of Tinsley and Bradley's other recommendations are often overlooked by beginning counselors. We strongly urge any counselors who provide test interpretations to be thoroughly familiar with *all* their recommendations.

Their recommendations for counselors' preparation *before* meeting with the client for test interpretation include answering the question "What do these scores mean?" by generating ideas or hypotheses that integrate the test results with other information about the client. In this effort, specific care should be taken in evaluating the consistency of the different types of data. If test scores are in conflict with one another or with other information about the client, test scores must be verified; the counselor must be ready to explore any discrepancies as part of the test interpretation process with the client.

Tinsley and Bradley also recommend preparing clients for test interpretation by asking them what they remember about taking the test and what they thought of the test while completing it. Equally important is reviewing information discussed in previous counseling sessions which is relevant to the kinds of questions the test is designed to address. This review sets the context for the interpretation.

Concerning defensive reactions on the part of the client to either low or unflattering scores, these authors emphasize the importance of the client's goals in testing. Unflattering scores that are relevant to client goals become an important part of the information that needs to be considered for further counseling. Persons who want to change how they appear to others and yet are "out of touch" with what personality measures indicate about their styles can gain important perspectives on what areas need to be addressed. Clients whose interest or ability scores are incongruent with their occupational plans also need to explore what hurdles these scores may predict for them and weigh the costs and benefits of staying with that choice.

Some major debates have appeared in the counseling literature concerning whether the test interpretation session should include examining the actual profiles of scores. At one extreme, Bradley (1978) suggests that "truth in testing" requires that the test booklet, answer sheet, and profile all be available for the client to review. At the other extreme, Crites (1976) argues that this presentation of massive amounts of information often prevents the client from comprehending the results in a personally meaningful way. He cites some evidence for the value of client understanding when the counselor introduces only test results that are relevant to the topic under discussion. In this model, the client may never see a profile and in fact may never learn about the scores obtained on the scales not relevant to the specific questions he or she had. In practice, few clients are satisfied with this "partial feedback," because they took the "whole" test.

Recommendations based on strategies used by Gustad and Tuma (1957) address the issue of clients being overwhelmed by information. Before the actual test interpretation begins, the client is asked to make some self-estimates on a blank profile on the test. Since the profile sometimes includes a multitude of scales, clients are not asked to make predictions on every one, but, for example, on the Edwards Personal Preference Schedule, to rate what they believe will be their three highest needs scores as compared to their three lowest, or, on the Strong Interest Inventory, to mark the five occupations to which they think their interests will be most similar and the five to which their interest will be least similar. By making these predictions, two things have been accomplished. First, to get clients to make those predictions, the counselor explains the various categories of test results and how they were developed. Consequently, clients know before they get their own results what the profile looks like and what each section represents. Secondly, by having made their predictions, clients have been prepared for a discussion of how the results compare to their predictions. Disconfirmations, of course, provide much data for discussion in counseling. Although this procedure is time-consuming, it serves as a highly satisfactory method of enabling clients to fully understand their test results and to begin to make use of them in problem solving.

Test Report Preparation

Because counseling psychologists infrequently do testing for other professionals, counseling texts typically give less attention to preparing test reports than do clinical and school psychology texts. However, given the increasing number of counseling psychologists in hospital internships and in community mental health clinics (Cameron, Galassi, Birk, & Moss, 1989) it is important to be aware of a few major controversies about the preparation of test reports. The first issue to be noted has major implications for the format of the test report. Is the psychological testing to be considered an objective measurement of the person? Or is a test seen simply as one sample of behavior to be integrated with other information that will provide a better understanding of a client? From the former perspective, test results are most typically reported on a test-by-test basis, with observations and conclusions made about the functioning of the person on each individual test. First, there may be a paragraph on intelligence, then one on personality style, then one on possible indications of organicity. The psychologist may have been asked to give a person some tests with no more understanding of what the problem is than a lab technician who is asked to do a blood test has no idea of the reason for which the test was requested. In this model, any information that a test can give about a person's functioning, with comparison to any available norms, is listed as part of the report.

By the late 1950s, there were many criticisms of this particular style of test reporting, and questions were raised as to whether such reports were truly useful to professionals (Klopfer, 1983; Fischer, 1985). In the decades since, much more attention has been given to developing test reports that address specific client problems and that integrate the results of various tests with other information about the client. Tallent (1976) provides highly detailed recommendations for preparing such person-centered, as compared to test-centered, test reports. Klopfer (1983) has also furnished useful illustrations of how such reports may be varied in form and style for a variety of professionals such as attorneys, city managers, and social workers.

Fischer (1985) goes one step further. In a fascinating book, *Individualized Psychological Assessment,* she outlines procedures for including the client in the development of the understandings to be communicated to the professional person. She has her clients prepare their own reactive statements regarding their perceptions of the accuracy, adequacy, and usefulness of the results as reported by the psychologist. While such an approach might seem shocking in a traditional medical setting, Fischer details how the humanistic psychology movement can be "translated" into the assessment area through the involvement of the client in the preparation of such reports. She provides examples where she has involved clients such as schoolchildren, mental competency referrals, and employee evaluation referrals in commenting on her test reports on them.

The reader who consults both Tallent (1976) and Fischer (1985) will gain a wealth of perspectives, as well as very specific guidelines, on how to write test reports. Choice of style is, in many cases, greatly influenced by the agency requesting the test. Hospitals and clinics, and to some extent, schools and industries, specify particular formats. Psychologists who are knowledgeable about a variety of test-reporting techniques can help agencies examine alternative formats.

Computerized Testing

Rapid advances in computer technology have resulted in the increased use of computers in the administration, scoring, and interpretation of psychological tests. In all three areas, the computer has significant potential for enhancing the assessment process. For example: The use of a computer keyboard for administering tests reduces some of the test-taking errors inherent in using multipaged booklets and machine-scored answer sheets; for a variety of handicapped persons, a keyboard and video terminal may be much more effective for presenting test information than the usual paper-and-pencil formats; computers reduce scoring errors; computers can generate, as soon as the examinee is finished, a complex set of scores and profiles that would take many hours to prepare manually. However, computerization of testing also holds numerous risks, especially in the ready availability of test interpretations to untrained test users.

Sampson (1990a, 1990b) has reviewed the major assets and liabilities of computer-assisted testing. He argues specifically for the term *computer-assisted* (vs. computerized) because of concern over the risks he perceives for counselors. For instance, counselors may utilize tests they really do not know well because interpretations are presented by the computer; therefore, the counselor does not have to "study" the tests to interpret the results to the client. Without an adequate understanding of how and why a test has been developed and what it can and cannot do, there is danger of using a test inappropriately.

A related concern is the validity of the test interpretations provided through the software packages. Both Burke and Normand (1987) and Sampson (1990b) review the results of studies comparing different software packages whose interpretations of the same test for the same individual have produced, in some cases, quite different interpretations. This variety of interpretations serves as a reminder that there is not just one "truth" that comes from a given set of test results (even when provided by a computer!). It is essential that a computer-based test interpretation be evaluated carefully in the context of other information about the client. The results are still just one sample of behavior. Although systematic efforts have been made to ensure examination of the validity of various test interpretation packages (APA, 1986), it is absolutely essential that no one test interpretation be treated as the truth.

Special Ethical Issues

The last point brings us directly to consideration of three ethical issues particularly significant in psychological assessment: (1) appropriateness of choice of measures, (2) control of use of assessment measures, and (3) confidentiality of results and reports. Though, in one sense, the ethical standards reviewed in Chapter 3 subsume all of these issues, there are some especially sensitive questions all counseling psychologists should keep uppermost in their thinking when dealing with psychological tests. The subsection on use of tests in counseling in the APA's *Standards for Educational and Psychological Testing* (1985) specifically identifies the need for examining whether or not a test has the appropriate technical reliability and validity data to support its use with a particular client. For example, norms for the test should include persons with demographic backgrounds similar to that of the client. Careful consideration must be given to the appropriateness of tests for use with anyone who does not fit within typical middle-class norms.

The second ethical issue in testing is one that has received insufficient attention in relevant studies. Perhaps because counseling psychologists compose the specialty that typically presents the results of tests to clients, they are asked more than most other psychologists to share the use of the tests. Some clients are so pleased with their results they want to have other family members or friends take the test too. Sometimes clients ask to borrow a copy of the test booklet. Counselors sometimes have difficulty dealing with such requests. If the counselor will not give out a test, the client may feel as though the counselor is trying to hide something. Counselors must get clients to see that a test has value only in the context of other information and can only be understood through a careful review with the counselor, who is familiar with both the strengths and the weaknesses of the test. Unfortunately, the proliferation of computer-assisted testing has heightened the perception that tests are readily available for "friends" and others, increasing the pressure on counseling psychologists. As a safety measure, most psychological tests are restricted as to what kinds of professionals may ethically order and use them.

The final ethical issue is that of confidentiality of test results and reports. In setting standards to protect the rights of test takers, the APA (1985) states concisely the needs of counselors: "Test results identified by the names of individual test takers should not be released to any person or institution without the informed consent of the test taker or authorized representative unless otherwise required by law. Scores of individuals identified by name should be made available only to those with a legitimate, professional interest in particular cases. Test data maintained in data files should be adequately protected from improper disclosure. Use of time sharing networks, data banks, and other electronic data processing systems should be restricted to situations in which confidentially can be reasonably assured" (pp. 85–86). Regrettably, these standards are not as easy to comply with as they are to read. In many professional situations, one is requested to release information to employers, deans, principals, and so forth, but has not been given permission to release it. No matter how legitimate a request may seem, it is illegitimately answered without the client's informed consent. Moreover, even when consent is given, only those with legitimate *professional* interests are to receive results. Needless to say, if it is one's boss making the request (e.g., a principal or dean), it is not easy to abide by the ethical code, yet one must always examine both the qualifications and purposes of the person intending to use the test results.

SUMMARY

Though psychological assessment is a major force in the history of psychology, it is a topic that has received relatively little attention in contemporary counseling psychology. Criticisms of diagnostic procedures and psychological tests during the 1950s and 1960s, respectively, led to this undervaluation. Diagnosis, which seems to be a "dirty word" to some counseling psychologists, is an implicit part of the counseling process. By conceptualizing diagnosis as a hypothesis-building and testing process, one can take explicit steps to evaluate clients and to ensure that they benefit from ongoing diagnostic procedures.

The second major section of this chapter explored the advantages and limitations of three major types of assessment instruments used by psychologists: interviews, behavioral ratings, and environmental assessment procedures. In regard to the evaluation and construction of psychological measures, counseling psychologists need to attend to both temporal and internal consistency as part of their evaluation of the reliability of assessment strategies. Further, beyond traditional validity considerations, counseling psychologists are well advised to assess (1) prior usefulness of measures for the kinds of questions being asked and (2) the *measured* discriminant validity of tests

—that is, Do tests with different names actually measure different variables? Following such recommendations will greatly enhance the contributions of assessments in both research and practice.

From among the hundreds of psychological tests and inventories used by counseling psychologists, three were illustrated in some detail to demonstrate counseling psychologists' use of interest, personality and, ability measures (the Strong Interest Inventory, the Minnesota Multiphasic Personality Inventory, and the Wechsler Adult Intelligence Scale, respectively).

The chapter's final section, on strategy and ethical issues in the use of tests, included a discussion of clients' roles in the selection of tests, interpretive strategies for improving clients' understandings of test results, contrasting styles of test report preparation, and issues in computer-assisted testing. Three special ethical concerns were described: appropriateness of choice of tests, control of use of assessment measures, and confidentiality of results and reports. Throughout the chapter, it became readily apparent that the scientist-practitioner model is a key part of counseling psychologists' use of and potential contributions to effective diagnostic and assessment procedures.

References

Adams, H. E., Doster, J. A., & Calhoun, K. S. (1977). A psychologically based system of response classification. In A. R. Ciminero, K. S. Calhoun, & H. E. Adams (Eds.), *Handbook of Behavioral Assessment.* New York: Wiley.

American Psychiatric Association (1987). *Diagnostic and statistical manual of mental disorders* (3rd ed., rev.). Washington, DC.

American Psychological Association (1981). Specialty guidelines for the delivery of services by counseling psychologists. *American Psychologist, 36,* 652–663.

American Psychological Association (1985). *Standards for educational and psychological testing.* Washington, DC.

American Psychological Association (1986). Guidelines for computer-based tests and interpretations. Washington, DC.

Anastasi, A. (1982). *Psychological testing.* New York: Macmillan.

Bordin, E. S., & Bixler, R. S. (1946). Tests selection: A process of counseling. *Educational and Psychological Measurement, 6,* 361–373.

Bordin, E. S. (1968). *Psychological counseling* (2nd ed.). New York: Appleton-Century-Crofts.

Bradley, R. W. (1978). Person-reference test interpretation: A learning process. *Measurement and Evaluation in Guidance, 10* (4), 201–210.

Brammer, L. M., & Shostrom, E. L. (1977). *Therapeutic psychology* (3rd ed.). Englewood Cliffs, NJ: Prentice-Hall.

Burisch, N. (1984). Approaches to personality inventory construction: A comparison of merits. *American Psychologist, 39,* 214–227.

Burke, M. J., & Normand, J. (1987). Computerized psychological testing: Overview and critique. *Professional Psychology, 18,* 42–51.

Butcher, J. N. (1990). *The MMPI-2 in psychological treatment.* New York: Oxford University Press.

Cameron, A. S., Galassi, J. B., Birk, J. M., & Moss, N. W. (1989). Trends in counseling psychology training programs. *The Counseling Psychologist, 17,* 301–313.

Campbell, D. T., & Fiske, D. W. (1959). Convergent and discriminant validation by the multitrait-multimethod matrix. *Psychological Bulletin, 56,* 81–105.

Cauteda, J. R. (1977). *Behavior-analysis forms for clinical intervention.* Champaign, IL: Research Press.

Ciminero, A. R., Calhoun, K. S., & Adams, H. E. (1977). *Handbook of behavioral assessment.* New York: Wiley.

Crites, J. O. (1969). *Vocational psychology.* New York: McGraw-Hill.

Crites, J. (1976). Career counseling: A comprehensive approach. *The Counseling Psychologist, 6*(3), 2–12.

Dahlstrom, W. G., & Dahlstrom, L. E. (1979). *Basic readings on the MMPI: A new selection on personality measurement.* Minneapolis: University of Minnesota Press.

Duckworth, J. C., (1979). *MMPI interpretation manual for counselors and clinicians* (2nd ed.). Muncie, IN: Accelerated Development.

Duckworth, J. (1990). The counseling approach to the use of testing. *The Counseling Psychologist, 18,* 198–204.

Edwards, A. L. (1959). *Manual for the Edwards Personal Preference Schedule.* New York: Psychological Corporation.

Exner, J. E. (1974). *The Rorschach: A comprehensive system* (Vol. 1). New York: Wiley.

Exner, J. E. (1978). *The Rorschach: A comprehensive system* (Vol. 2). New York: Wiley.

Filskov, S. V., & Boll, T. J. (Eds.). (1981). *Handbook of Clinical Neuropsychology.* New York: Wiley.

Fischer, C. G. (1985). *Individualizing psychological assessment.* Monterey, CA: Brooks/Cole.

Fitzgerald, L. M., & Osipow, S. H. (1986). An occupational analysis of counseling psychology: How special is the specialty? *American Psychologist, 41,* 535–544.

Goldman, G. (1961). *Using tests in counseling.* New York: Appleton-Century-Crofts.

Goldman, L. (1972). Tests and counseling: The marriage that failed. *Measurement and Evaluation in Guidance, 4,* 213–220.

Goodyear, R. K. (1990). Research on the effects of test interpretation. *The Counseling Psychologist, 18,* 240–257.

Graham, J. R. (1990). *MMPI-2: Assessing personality and psychopathology.* New York: Oxford Press.

Green, B. F. (1981). A primer of testing. *American Psychologist, 36,* 1001–1011.

Gustad, J. W., & Tuma, A. H. (1957). The effects of different methods of test introduction and interpretation on client learning and counseling. *Journal of Counseling Psychology, 4,* 313–317.

Hansen, J. C. (1984). The measurement of vocational interests: Issues and future directions. In S. D. Brown & R. W. Lent (Eds), *Handbook of Counseling Psychology* (pp. 99–136). New York: Wiley.

Hansen, J. C., & Campbell, D. P. (1985). *Manual for the SVIB-SCII.* Palo Alto, CA: Consulting Psychologist Press.

Helms, J. E. (1983). *A practitioner's guide to the Edwards Personal Preference Schedule.* Springfield, IL: Charles C. Thomas.

Healy, C. C. (1990). Reforming career appraisals to meet the need of clients in the 1990s. *The Counseling Psychologist, 18,* 214–226.

Herr, E. L., & Cramer, S. H. (1988). *Career guidance and counseling through the life span.* Glenview, IL: Scott, Foresman.

Hill, C. E., Carter, J. A., & O'Farrell, M. K. (1983). A case study of the process and outcome of time-limited counseling. *Journal of Counseling Psychology, 30,* 3–18.

Holland, J. L. (1977). *Manual for the Vocational Preference Inventory.* Palo Alto, CA: Consulting Psychologist Press.

Holland, J. L. (1985). *Making vocational choices* (2nd ed.). Englewood Cliffs, NJ: Prentice-Hall.

House, A. E., & Lewis, N. L. (1985). Wechsler Adult Intelligence Scale—Revised. In C. S. Newmark (Ed.), *Major psychological assessment instruments* (pp. 323–380). Boston: Allyn & Bacon.

Johansson, C. B. (1976). *Manual for the Career Assessment Inventory.* Minneapolis: NCS Interpretive Scoring Systems.

Kaplan, M. L., Colarelli, M. J., Gross, R. B., Leventhal, D., & Siegel, S. N. (1970). *The structural approach in psychological testing.* New York: Pergamon.

Kasl, W. V., & Mahl, G. F. (1965). Disturbance and hesitation in speech. *Journal of Personality and Social Psychology, 1,* 425–433.

Kaufman, A. S. (1990). *Assessing adolescent and adult intelligence.* Boston: Allyn & Bacon.

Kleinmuntz, B. (1982). *Personality and psychological assessment.* New York: St. Martins Press.

Klopfer, W. G. (1983). Writing psychological reports. In C. P. Walker (Ed.), *The Handbook of Clinical Psychology* (pp. 501–527). Homewood, IL: Dorsey.

Koester, G. A. (1954). A study of the diagnostic process. *Educational Psychological Measurement, 14,* 473–486.

Krumboltz, J. D. (Ed.) (1966). *Revolution in counseling.* Boston: Houghton Mifflin.

Kuder, F., & Diamond, E. E. (1979). General manual for the Kuder DD Occupational Interest Survey. Chicago: Science Research Associates.

Kunce, J. T., & Anderson, W. P. (1984). Perspectives on uses of the MMPI in nonpsychiatric settings. In P. McReynolds & G. J. Chelune (Eds.), *Advances in Psychological Assessment* (pp. 41–76). San Francisco: Jossey-Bass.

Lanyon, R. I., & Goodstein, L. G. (1982). *Personality assessment* (2nd ed.). New York: Wiley.

Lazarus, A. E. (1976). *Multimodal behavior therapy.* New York: Springer.

Leary, T. (1957). *Interpersonal diagnosis and personality.* New York: Ronald Press.

Lent, R. W., Brown, S. D., & Larkin, K. C. (1987). Comparison of three theoretically derived variables in predicting career and academic behavior: Self-efficacy, interest congruence, and consequence thinking. *Journal of Counseling Psychology, 34,* 293–298.

Matarazzo, J. G. (1983). The reliability of psychiatric and psychological diagnosis. *Clinical Psychology Review, 3,* 103–145.

Matarazzo, R. G., & Matarazzo, J. D. (1984). Assessment of adult intelligence in clinical practice. In P. McReynolds & G. J. Chelune (Eds.), *Advances in Psychological Assessment* (Vol. 6, pp. 77–108). San Francisco: Jossey-Bass.

McArthur, C. (1954). Analyzing the clinical process. *Journal of Counseling Psychology, 1,* 203–208.

Meehl, P. E. (1954). *Clinical versus statistical prediction.* Minneapolis: University of Minnesota Press, 1954.

Meehl, P. E. (1960). The cognitive activity of the clinician. *American Psychologist, 15,* 19–27.

Megargee, E. I. (1972). *The California Psychological Inventory Handbook.* San Francisco: Jossey-Bass.

Mischel, W. (1968). *Personality and assessment.* New York: Wiley.

Moos, R. (1974). *The social climate scales.* Palo Alto, CA: Consulting Psychologist Press.

Myers, I. B. (1975). *Manual: The Myers-Briggs Type Indicator.* Palo Alto, CA: Consulting Psychologist Press.

Nathan, P. E., & Harris, S. C. (1983). The diagnostic and statistical manual of mental disorders. In C. E. Walker (Ed.), *The handbook of clinical psychology* (pp. 302–343). Homewood, IL: Dow Jones-Irwin.

Nelson, R. O. (1987). DSM-III and behavioral assessment. In C. G. Last & N. Hersen (Eds.), *Issues in Diagnostic Research* (pp. 303–327). New York: Plenum.

Nelson, R. O., & Hayes, S. C. (1979). Some current dimensions of behavioral assessment. *Behavioral Assessment, 1,* 1–16.

Nunnally, J. (1978). *Psychometric theory* (2nd ed.). New York: McGraw-Hill.

Pepinsky, H. B., & Pepinsky, P. N. (1954). *Counseling: Theory and practice.* New York: Ronald.

Pinkney, J. W. (1983). The Myers-Briggs Type Indicator as an alternative in career counseling. *Personnel Guidance Journal, 62,* 173–177.

Pope, B. (1983). The initial interview. In C. E. Walker (Ed.), *The handbook of clinical psychology* (pp. 344–390). Homewood, IL: Dorsey.

Robinson, F. P. (1950). *Principles and procedures in student counseling.* New York: Harper.

Rogers, C. R. (1951). *Client-centered therapy.* Boston: Houghton Mifflin.

Sampson, J. P. (1990a). Computer-assisted testing and the goals of counseling psychology. *The Counseling Psychologist, 18,* 227–239.

Sampson, J. P. (1990b). Computer applications and issues in using tests in counseling. In C. E. Watkins, Jr., & V. L. Campbell (Eds.), *Testing in counseling practice.* Hillsdale, NJ: Erlbaum.

Schacht, T. E. (1985). DMS-III and the politics of truth. *American Psychologist, 40,* 513–521.

Schacht, T., & Nathan, P. E. (1977). But is it good for psychologists? Appraisal and status of DSM-III. *American Psychologist, 32,* 1017–1025.

Smith, A. (1983). Clinical psychological practice and principles of neuropsychological assessment. In C. E. Walker (Ed.), *The handbook of clinical psychology* (pp. 445–500). Homewood, IL: Dorsey.

Stewart, R. B. (1970). *Trick or treatment.* Champaign, IL: Research Press.

Strohmer, D. C., & Chiodo, A. L. (1984). Counselor hypothesis testing strategies: The role of initial impressions and self-schema. *Journal of Counseling Psychology, 21,* 510–519.

Strohmer, D. C., & Newman, L. A. (1983). Counselor hypothesis testing strategies. *Journal of Counseling Psychology, 30,* 557–565.

Strong, E. K. (1943). *Vocational interests of men and women.* Palo Alto: Stanford University Press.

Szasz, P. S. (1960). The myth of mental illness. *American Psychologist, 15,* 113–118.

Tallent, N. (1983). *Psychological report writing* (2nd ed.). Englewood Cliffs, NJ: Prentice-Hall.

Tinsley, H. E. A., & Bradley, R. W. (1986). Test interpretation. *Journal of Counseling and Development, 64,* 462–466.

Walsh, W. B., & Osipow, S. H. (Eds.) (1986). *Advances in vocational psychology* (Vol. 1). Hillsdale, NJ: Erlbaum.

Watkins, C. E., Jr., Campbell, B. L., Hollifield, J., & Duckworth, J. (1989). Projective techniques: Do they have a place in counseling psychology training? *The Counseling Psychologist, 17,* 511–513.

Watkins, C. E., Jr., Campbell, V. G., & McGregor, P. (1988). Counseling psychologists' uses of and opinions about psychological tests. *The Counseling Psychologist, 16,* 476–486.

Watkins, C. E., Jr., & Campbell, V. L. (Eds) (1990). *Testing in counseling practice.* Hillsdale, NJ: Erlbaum.

Williamson, E. G. (1939). How to counsel students. New York: McGraw-Hill.

Chapter 11

Cultural Diversity and Cross-Cultural Counseling

There is ever-accumulating evidence of inadequacies in psychologists' training for, and responsiveness to, cultural diversity. In this chapter we first define the terms *cultural diversity* and *cross-cultural counseling*—we believe the latter should be used far more broadly than it is by most psychologists. Second, we briefly explore some of the literature illustrating the practice and research problems that have occurred for numerous clients and counselors because of reliance on the values and beliefs of "white culture" (Katz, 1985). The third section of this chapter is devoted to approaches that can help *all* counseling psychologists be sensitive to the multiple ways that cultural diversity can have an impact on their clients and, most importantly, provide a framework for considering what it takes to become competent as a cross-cultural counselor.

It is the intent of this chapter to provide an enriched understanding of the many sources of diversity in contemporary society. There is much to be learned about similarities and differences both within and among various diverse groups—for example, Asian-Americans, the hearing impaired, homosexuals, and religious fundamentalists. New knowledge is critical; Alexander Pope's adage that "a little learning is a dangerous thing," when applied to counseling and cultural diversity, translates as: "Enlightened stereotypes can be as dangerous as bigoted stereotypes." Counseling psychologists must develop awareness and competencies that will enable them to contribute to the development of all individuals, regardless of their backgrounds or lifestyles.

SOME PRELIMINARY DEFINITIONS

> Cultural and individual differences. . . . Programs must develop knowledge and skills in their students relevant to human diversity such as people with handicapping conditions; of differing ages, genders, ethnic and racial backgrounds, religions, and lifestyles; and from differing social and individual backgrounds. (APA, 1979, p. 4)

This statement from the accreditation standards of the American Psychological Association intentionally casts a wide net over what is to be included in attending to human diversity. All too often, for "majority" persons, the term *diversity* brings to mind visible, racial, ethnic groups, or VREGs (Cook & Helms, 1988). Culture, however, takes many forms. Empirical literature demonstrates the comparative inadequacies of research and counseling strategies for each of the categories named in the above APA statement. Before examining that literature, we need to define five terms. Though the definitions we give are all drawn from current literature, there is considerable controversy about how broadly each of those terms should be used. Many psychologists feel that broad usage results in inadequate attention to the concerns of any one group.

Culture is a term frequently associated with international, often distinctively different groups (e.g., South Pacific Island societies) but has increasingly been linked with race and ethnicity (Casas, 1984). Smith and Vasquez (1985) define culture as "shared values, shared perceptions of reality, and shared symbols that people have by which their thinking and interpersonal relationships are conducted" (1985, p. 532). Sundberg (1981) notes that culture so shapes everyone's lives that most people are not aware that there are alternative ways of viewing human nature, time, and existence. Thus, a lack of understanding of others is often not malevolent but rather a result of lack of awareness of the "filters" through which daily experiences are interpreted. Especially for those not part of any identified minority group, the culture may be largely invisible, not part of any conscious awareness.

In contrast to the term *culture,* the term *race,* as noted by Casas (1984), is often thought of as a biological classification based on physical characteristics and genetic origins; however, race in social contexts has much more to do with what people believe about it than its biological components. Because race is a highly visible "marker," it becomes a major component of interpersonal interactions when people hold sets of beliefs about a particular race.

Ethnicity is a far more limiting term than *race* and is environmentally rather than genetically based in that it describes a group of persons who share a unique social and cultural heritage. Most of us have some identifiable ethnic heritage. Not only are there many ethnicities within a single race, but also, much less recognized is the fact that ethnicity often crosses racial lines. Ethnic Puerto Ricans, for example, include persons from at least three major racial groups.

Minority is a term that clearly needs to be understood, not in terms of statistical relationships (women outnumber men in our society but are often considered a minority group), but rather as defined by Wirth: "a group of people who, because of physical or cultural characteristics, are singled out from the others in society in which they live for differential and unequal treatment, and who therefore *regard themselves* [italics added] as objects of collective discrimination" (1945, p. 347). Under this definition, then, minorities include such persons as those with various handicaps, alternative lifestyles, and values and beliefs not widely shared by the majority or at least the most powerful members of society. As less powerful members of society, this definition suggests, all these types of minorities experience various forms of "oppression" and limits to their opportunities as a result of their "group membership." On this basis, some writers now prefer the term *oppressed groups* to *minorities.*

Relatedly, Smith and Vasquez (1985) critically note that it is important to distinguish influences and behaviors that originate from cultural differences as compared to those that come from deprivation and discrimination inherent in a minority status. Of course, in countless cases, clients may be experiencing stresses that result both from cultural as well as from minority status.

Racism, as compared to *race,* is the term most pertinent to the topic of this chapter. Ridley defines the term thus: "Racism is defined as any behavior or pattern of behavior that systematically tends to deny access to opportunities or privileges to one social group while perpetuating privileges to members of another group" (1989, p. 60). Ridley also differentiates prejudice from racism, clarifying that racist acts can occur completely apart from either positive or negative prejudices, that is, preconceived judgments or opinions without sufficient knowledge. "Well-intentioned people can still behave to the detriment of others, especially when they are misinformed. . . . Anyone is capable of behaving in a racist manner, *including ethnic minorities themselves* [italics added]. . . . Many acts of racism occur because people lack valid information or are misinformed about other cultural groups" (Ridley, 1989, p. 58). Dealing with these inadequacies in people's knowledge will be one of the major foci of our discussion on multicultural competence.

Cross-cultural counseling is the last term to be defined in this section. In past decades, this term often referred to counseling with international students. We share the emerging current view that cross-cultural counseling should refer to *all* counseling that deals with clients whose values and perceptions of reality (see definition of *culture*) are different from the counselor's. From this perspective, men counseling women or women counseling men are engaging in cross-cultural counseling. An Asian-American counseling a Hispanic, an atheist counseling a fundamentalist, and a black 25-year-old counseling a black 85-year-old are all engaged in cross-cultural counseling. Defined in this way, cross-cultural counseling is not a single approach or technique but rather an orientation that, as we shall see later, encompasses special knowledge, attitudes, and skills. Have we made the term so inclusive that *all* counseling is cross-cultural? We answer: Yes, to the extent that every counseling relationship needs to be examined for the potential contribution of cultural diversity to the origins of the client's problem, to the client's understanding of the problem, and to the development of relevant options for coping with the problem. Given this definition, it is essential to identify first the barriers that make cross-cultural counseling so vital to a wide range of clients, then to discuss the attitudes, knowledges, and skills that are needed to turn the frequent oppressive consequences of cultural diversity into "positive, life-enhancing qualities" (Thomas, 1985, p. 661).

BARRIERS AND BIASES

There are now over two decades of literature that document biases among mental health professionals (e.g., psychologists, psychiatrists, counselors), regarding both their expectations of and treatment of female and/or ethnic minority clients. Atkinson and Hackett (1988) have also reviewed the evidence of bias and discrimination regarding many nonethnic minorities such as the elderly, handicapped, homosexuals, and so forth.

Why are such biases so pervasive? Are psychologists and other mental health specialists particularly bigoted, mean-spirited people? In the last decade, the work of several writers enabled the helping professions to gain an understanding of how such biases are developed and maintained. As noted in the definition above, culture creates ways of perceiving and thinking, a "worldview" that each person holds but that lies beyond immediate awareness and that leads to pervasive assumptions about how all other persons perceive the world and the factors which cause them to act the way they do. Those who are most like the dominant group of a culture, for example, the white middle-class in America, are typically least aware of their culture. They are, according to Wrenn (1962), culturally encapsulated; their culture is largely invisible. Middle-class white males have just as much culture as any other group that can be identified (Helms, 1990); however, because that group has been the most powerful as a group in Western society, many whites may have little awareness of what constitutes "white culture" (Katz, 1985). It is only when one has sustained experience with another culture that one begins to see very different ways of looking at the world. Therefore, understandably, though ironically, nonwhites in the USA are often in the best position to inform whites about what constitutes "white culture."

The white middle-class worldview, as developed in the United States, emphasizes "rugged individualism" (Sue et al., 1982; Katz, 1985) whereby independence and autonomy are highly rewarded and it is assumed that the individual can control the environment. In fact, there is almost the sense that to become a winner (notice the implicit competition), it is one's duty to master and control nature. When these concepts are translated into counseling, the "logical" conclusion for treatment is that problems are rooted in the client's intrapsychic processes and that the locus for responsibility for change lies primarily within the client. This view also stresses the goal of individuation, that is, "standing on your own two feet," being the "captain of your own fate," and not having to rely on anyone. As Richardson and Johnson (1984), Sue (1978), Katz (1985), Dahlquist and Fay (1983), and LaFromboise, Trimble, and Mohatt (1990) have all documented, these particular values pose numerous conflicts with the "cultures" of being female, Asian-American, black, Hispanic, and American Indian, respectively. For example, consider first the emphasis on competitiveness and being female in American culture. Any regular reader of a city newspaper can recall cases in which women who had won many law cases or important sales contracts complained they were not offered partnerships or promotions while men of lesser accomplishments were offered such positions. The reasons given for denying women the positions included that they were too cold, too independent, or too aggressive—the very attributes looked for in males. However, because such characteristics are "unfeminine," they penalize women.

Dahlquist and Fay (1983) cite evidence of such conflicts that is more pertinent to ethnic minorities. We noted above the importance of independence in traditional white middle-class culture. Yet for all the major racial ethnic minorities in American society, there is considerable evidence that dependence on family and group relationships is an extremely strong value. Thus, one is forced to make the choice of being autonomous and rejecting the expected interdependence with family or clan or of being part of the family and being seen as weak and dependent by the dominant group in our society.

Compounding these dilemmas is the fact that the "rugged individualism" perspective emphasizes inadequacies of individuals in the creation and maintenance of their problems—what has come to be known as a "person blame," or "victim blame," orientation. Richardson and Johnson (1984) provide an excellent illustration of the conundrum in which we place clients when person-blame orientations are taken with minorities. They note the popularity of the concept of fear of success in the 1970s, a concept that suggested women achieved less than men because of their fears of the penalties of being seen as successful; that is, they would no longer be valued as women. The initial response of psychologists was that it was the *woman* who needed to change, that is, overcome her fear of success. Intervention strategies were designed to reduce these fears. Yet as noted in the example above, in many situations in society, when a woman does succeed, she may be "punished" in highly visible and painful ways. Thus by getting the person to change *without* changing the environmental context, one is really preparing clients to enter punishing situations rather than ones of mastery.

Psychologists' views about what causes psychological problems and how they should be treated have been derived largely from theories of human behavior developed by middle-class males and tested largely on the same population—the most educated segment of American society during the first three hundred years of its history. Whether most counselors and therapists realize it or not, their interventions may be considered sociopolitical acts (Katz, 1985). As Katz notes, "White culture serves as a foundation for counselor training, research and practice" (1985, p. 615). Therefore, since the goal of counseling has typically been seen as helping persons adjust and adapt, the strategies of counseling have been typically oriented, regardless of the counselor's background, to helping persons choose behaviors that adapt to "white cultural values" and role definitions rather than develop individual identities that may or may not fit those values.

"There has been a growing alarm among many psychologists that our psychological theories and service delivery systems have helped perpetuate rather than ameliorate the second-class citizenship of women. A particular concern has been the too frequent tendency to consider female clients maladjusted if they did not fit into restrictive sex roles and to encourage them to adjust to these roles rather than develop their own identities" (Hill et al., 1979, p. 2). Sue et al. (1982) also describe, in their position paper on cross-cultural counseling, how traditional counselor training promotes the status quo, even when it may be promulgating limited opportunities for groups of clients.

A real danger to clients, then, lies in unexamined and unrealistic expectations counseling psychologists may have as a result of their own worldviews and their cultural stereotypes about people (e.g., gender, race/ethnicity, lifestyle preference). This danger can exist at both the "etic" and "emic" level of analysis. *Etic* is a term that cross-cultural researchers use to describe an approach external to a particular culture and that some define as "universal norms" (Lopez et al., 1989). (The reader must keep in mind that universal norms are not truly agreed-upon universals, but rather the perceptions one has about fundamental reasons why people interact and behave as they do.) Lonner (1985) explains *etic* and *emic* as follows: "thus to 'impose an etic' is cross-cultural jargon for employing a construct *as if* it has the same meaning in the target or non-originating culture. . . . An emic approach, on the other hand, rather than imposing constructs, would endeavor to discover from *within* a culture that which is important to the culture; the use of standardized tests or other exported methods are usually considered inappropriate, ethnocentric, or both" (pp. 601–602).

To oversimplify for a moment, the task of the counseling psychologist is to be able to maintain a balance in obtaining and utilizing etic and emic information, especially when any discrepancy exists between the cultures of the counselor and client—whether it is a function of age, gender, race/ethnicity, lifestyle, religion, or whatever. Since the basic knowledge of human development and interventions, as typically taught in all psychology, is predicated on being universal (i.e., etic), it is only natural that there is heavy reliance on the etic in working with any client. In fact, it can be argued that to ignore all the etic would be just as disastrous as over-relying on it as the totality of all one needs to know. The emic also needs to be more consistently attended to, than it typically is, in working with any client different from the counselor, whether the counselor be black, white, handicapped or fully able, secular or religious, and so forth. Ibrahim (1985) argued that counseling psychologists need to keep a three-dimensional model in mind in which one is constantly trying to understand the (a) client's personal worldview as it overlaps with the (b) client's subculture (emic analysis) and (c) the majority culture (etic analysis). Looking at these overlaps or lack of overlap is, from her viewpoint, the primary source of diagnostic information. Obviously, one can use such information only if the counselor or therapist is well versed in the knowledge and skills of specific cultural groups as well as the majority culture. The next section reviews deficiencies in the cultural awareness of counselors and therapists.

ILLUSTRATIVE STEREOTYPES IN THE TREATMENT OF CLIENTS

Empirical literature continues to accumulate that demonstrates how counselors often limit the opportunities for culturally diverse persons in achieving their full potential. Looking first at some of the literature on biases about women, most often cited is the work by Broverman et al. (1970) on sex role stereotypes and clinical judgments of mental health. After asking a variety of mental health specialists to describe healthy adults, healthy adult males and healthy adult females, they found that the healthy adult female was described significantly differently than the healthy adult. Healthy females were described as less objective, less competitive, and less independent but more emotional and more submissive than males.

As Nickerson reports, there is other "damning evidence . . . from the . . . APA Report on Sex Bias and Sex Role Stereotyping in Psychotherapeutic Practice (1975). The Task Force, in arriving at its findings and conclusions, reviewed the research literature on this topic and surveyed women psychologists, obtaining documentation of sex stereotypic practices that female psychologists themselves had encountered. This report documents psychotherapeutic sex bias in the areas of (a) fostering of traditional sex roles; (b) expectations and devaluations of women; (c) sexist use of psychoanalytic concepts; and (d) responding to women as sex objects, including the seduction of women in therapy" (1979, p. 5).

More recently Barak and Fisher (1989), after careful reviews of over two decades of research on counselor and therapist gender bias, have raised questions as to the universality of such bias. That such biases always have and still do exist among some professionals is not questioned. Barak and Fisher point out that some of the "bias" problems that remain have their roots in long-standing psychological tests, intervention methods, and clients' own stereotypes as well as counselor or therapist biases. Although one might argue that much progress has been made in terms of increased awareness of gender issues since the 1960s, with a recent survey showing the majority of clients found to be treated in a gender-fair manner (Sesan, 1988), careful attention to issues of gender bias needs to be a continued priority of researchers and practitioners. Denmark, Russo, Frieze, and Sechzer (1988) have provided a succinct and illustrative list of 22 areas where sexism still occurs, not only in research on counseling and therapy but also in basic psychological research.

Many negative stereotypes about racial and ethnic minorities also appear in the psychological literature. Specifically related to counselors' biases, Bloombaum, Yamamoto, and James (1968) found practicing therapists holding attitudes toward Mexican-Americans, blacks, Asian-Americans, and Jews that clearly reflected cultural stereotypes. More recently, Casas (1984) notes that studies looking at counselors' expectations of minorities included the following: "Blacks were believed to have high rates of drug addiction and personality disorders, American Indians were prone to alcoholism and suicide, Hispanics were described as exhibiting tendencies toward drunkenness, criminal behavior, and undependability" (p. 802). Yet, when social class is controlled, few if any actual differences are found in degrees of pathology between various ethnic minority groups and the majority culture. In other words, when either middle-class blacks or Hispanics are compared with middle-class whites, major differences are not found in patterns of psychopathology. Thus, the stereotypes attributed to racial classes often have their basis not in race or ethnicity but in the socioeconomic structure. As noted by Smith and Vasquez (1985), since being a minority often means encountering discrimination and deprivation, there is often confusion as to whether differences are a function of ethnicity or race or a function of the discrimination and deprivation.

Stereotypes about racial and ethnic minorities also continue to proliferate on the basis of what may be accurate but easily misleading data about usage of psychological services. For example, recently Snowden and Chung (1990) have studied the ethnic discrimination marking psychiatric hospitalization. As recently as 1990, it was found that: "Blacks and Native Americans are considerably more likely than Whites to be hospitalized; Blacks are more likely than Whites to be admitted as schizophrenic and less likely to be diagnosed as having an affective disorder; Asian-Americans/ Pacific Islanders are less likely than whites to be admitted, but remain for a lengthier stay, at least in state and county mental hospitals" (p. 347). These differences in hospital rates, if not considered in conjunction with other data such as socioeconomic status, the capacity of the family or the culture to tolerate or support a dysfunctional person, and access to and use of other services, can lead to biases among psychologists, who may diagnose considerably more psychopathology in various minority groups than actually exists. Many more careful epidemiological and longitudinal analyses are needed before conclusions can be made about levels of pathology based on hospitalization patterns.

Kite and Deaux (1987) document at length the negative stereotypes held regarding homosexuals. Moreover, they note that for this minority, not only are there many stereotypic behaviors associated with that lifestyle, but also that those very behaviors, when observed in persons whose sexual preferences are unknown, lead to erroneous conclusions regarding sexual preferences. Women described as masculine are more likely to be assumed to be homosexual, as are men whose behaviors are described as effeminate. Morin (1977) reviews much of the research evidence that shows the invalidity of the stereotypes held about the behaviors and psychological adjustment of homosexuals. Most of the stereotypic behaviors of homosexuals appear widely in male and female gender roles and do not reflect sexual preferences. Although unflattering stereotypes exist for many groups, including white males (e.g., engineers have repressed psychological lives and therefore make bad clients), the primary concern for counseling psychologists needs to be whether these stereotypes influence how their clients are treated. Perceptions based on class membership rather than on individualized assessment of the client are more likely to lead to a limited perspective as to how much the client can improve or what the client can do. These effects are the danger of stereotypes whether or not there is validity to any of them. This is verified by the evidence of what happens to minority clients in counseling sessions.

Concerning visible racial ethnic minorities, there has been a long series of studies, ever since the 1970s, showing that VREGs come to mental health centers in lower per capita proportions than do whites. Perhaps even most troubling, the drop-out rates for blacks, Asian-Americans, Hispanics, and American Indians run as high as 50 percent versus 30 percent for whites (Sue & Sue, 1977). The assumption that is reasonably and typically made on the basis of these studies is that such clients are not finding counseling services adequate. A recent review by Worthington (1989) shows that similar kinds of data can be found when dealing with religious clients. Atkinson and Hackett (1988) provide a historical review of the problematic results of counseling and therapy with other nonethnic minorities including the disabled and the elderly. Their review clearly suggests there is much to attend to in providing effective counseling to minorities. The remainder of this chapter explains what has been learned about potentially helpful strategies.

MATCHING COUNSELOR AND CLIENT

One of the earliest reponses to data on the underutilization of mental health services by a minority and to evidence questioning the effectiveness of traditional counseling with both women and ethnic minorities, was to suggest that such clients should be counseled by persons with similar demographic backgrounds. One of the primary recommendations of the Vail Training Conference for Psychologists (Korman, 1974) was to make significant increases in the number of female counselors (who then held less than a third of the professional counseling and psychotherapy positions, as compared to more than half as of this writing) and minority counselors in order to provide a greater number of culturally similar counselors.

Concomitantly, many studies were undertaken regarding client preferences for culturally similar counselors and, more importantly, regarding counseling's perceived effectiveness when provided by a counselor who was culturally similar to the client. By the end of the 1970s, numerous studies had been completed looking at the conditions under which female clients preferred female counselors and at the effects of female/female counselor-client pairs as opposed to male-counselor/female-client pairs. Fitzgerald and Nutt (1986) provide a succinct review of the results of such studies. Young single women are likely to benefit more from having a female therapist. For all other female clients, there is much less clear evidence that female are more effective than male counselors. Fitzgerald and Nutt (1986) do note that there is sufficient evidence to suggest that there are certain circumstances in which it may be more desirable for a female client to be seen by a female counselor:

> For instance, the victims of rape, incest, and domestic violence may respond in a more trusting and open manner to women therapists than to males. Similarly, women with sexual concerns, as those seeking abortion

> counseling, may feel more comfortable working with female counselors. Highly vulnerable in the one-down power relationship that is exemplified by the traditional male-therapist/female-client dyad, submissive female clients may benefit greatly from working with a woman therapist who effectively models assertiveness and appropriately shares responsibility for the counseling process of the client. . . . Finally, it is likely that issues of job discrimination and sexual harassment would warrant working with a female therapist. (p. 199)

It must be emphasized that the authors do not think that males cannot possibly be effective counselors in these situations, rather that, in these circumstances, "open discussion with the client regarding her preference, combined with professional judgment, appears to be the most appropriate course at present" (p. 200).

Both Casas (1984) and Dahlquist and Fay (1983) provide reviews of the now almost countless studies that have been conducted with VREGs' preferences for culturally similar counselors. Both document relatively strong evidence for the preferences of black clients for counselors of the same race; the data for other ethnic groups are considerably more mixed, with many studies showing no differences while others do obtain significant differences. Casas notes the difficulties in drawing conclusions because of the widely varying research paradigms and methodologies that are used in these studies.

Reviewing numerous studies of the actual effectiveness of counseling in ethnically similar vs. ethnically dissimilar counselor-client dyads, Atkinson (1983) concluded that such research offers little support for the superiority of ethnic matching. Most authors of such studies conclude that competence and empathic understanding are much more important ingredients in the effectiveness of counseling than racial/ethnic similarity of the dyads.

Far less literature exists for groups that are culturally diverse in ways other than race and ethnicity, but what is available seems consistent—more religious clients express preferences for clearly identified religious counselors (Worthington, 1989). The elderly often prefer to see counselors who are at least middle-aged (Donnan & Mitchell, 1979). However, preferences notwithstanding, there are little data to support that counselor-client matching on these characteristics provides more effective counseling. On the other hand, preference data may be important, in and of itself, especially in terms of making a mental health service attractive to potential clients. Given, for example, the relatively strong preferences of blacks for black counselors, an agency that has no black counselors may have far fewer black clients than one that does, even if the black clients who come to the agency receive competent services from white counselors.

The research on matching of counselors and clients led to a focus on how to increase the number of culturally diverse counselors rather than how counselors from any background, "majority" or "minority" themselves, could become more effective in providing services to culturally different clients. Thoughtful reviewers of the many areas of research (e.g., biases, matching of counselors and clients, underutilization of mental health services) have, however, now opened new horizons in exploring cultural diversity. Understanding recent developments in the concepts of biculturalism and racial identity may be fundamental in achieving competence as a cross-cultural counselor—the focus of the final section of this chapter.

BICULTURALITY AND RACIAL IDENTITY

As the mental health professions began to pay more attention to systematic differences in culturally diverse groups, researchers and practitioners could clearly identify that overgeneralizations were frequently being made. Research findings of significant correlations between women's sense of self-efficacy and their choice of nontraditional careers did not mean that *all* women with a high sense of self-efficacy chose a nontraditional career or vice-versa. Evidence that VREGs drop out of counseling in the first six sessions more often than other clients did not mean that all VREG clients drop out of counseling. Investigators, primarily in the areas of racial and ethnic diversity, have been developing conceptual models to explain how clients may vary significantly *within* the identified culturally diverse group.

Studies of several Hispanic and Asian-American ethnic groups have incorporated the concept "level of acculturation" in understanding how client preferences for, expectations of, and needs from counseling will differ. Level of acculturation may be defined as the degree to which a client has adopted the values and lifestyles of the predominant culture as compared to maintaining the values and lifestyles of his or her culture of origin. Various scholars such as Sue and Sue (1985), Padilla and Lindholm (1984), Ponterotto (1987), Sanchez and Atkinson (1983), and Atkinson, Morton, and Sue (1989) have identified how the level of one's acculturation can affect, for example, preferences for a certain type of counselor.

One of the side effects of the concept of level of acculturation is the expectation that "well-adjusted" persons will be those who adopt the value system of the majority culture. In fact, some might see part of the role of counseling as helping the person make such an adaptation. The reactions of society, at large, to ethnic persons is often that their problems are due to their social maladaptation. All too often, such conclusions are reached without realizing that adaptation could put the culturally-at-odds person in the painful dilemma of having to reject the values and ideals of the persons who love and support them most, namely their family and friends. Moreover, persons who value their subculture are often seen as deficient. Yet many persons establish highly competent lifestyles that incorporate values of both the majority culture and their subculture.

Two concepts receiving increasing attention help explain how some persons seem to manage "the best of both worlds." The concept of biculturality applies most clearly to persons from ethnic subcultures who manage to live so competently, even if not always comfortably, both within the majority society as well as their own ethnic community. Szapocznik, Scopetta, de los Angeles Arnalde, and Kurtines (1978) found that the best psychological adjustment among Cuban immigrants occurred among those who could negotiate both cultural worlds, each with its own set of values and patterns of interpersonal relationships. These authors, for their part, suggest that more attention should be given to the promise and processes of biculturalism instead of emphasizing assimilation into the majority culture.

One might also view the concept of androgyny as a kind of biculturality for male and female. As Cook (1987) explicates so clearly, androgyny incorporates the assertive, achieving aspects traditionally associated with masculinity and the sensitive, interpersonal relationship orientation associated with femininity: "It is assumed that masculinity and femininity are independent, positive trait dimensions existing in everyone, to some extent" (p. 473). This concept of androgyny suggests that a person who is high on both kinds of behaviors has the greatest potential for adaptation. Note that a person can be high on both masculinity and femininity, low on both, or high on one and low on the other. Cook's review of the empirical studies found androgynous persons to be more adjusted, more satisfied with life, receiving more positive evaluations from friends, and scoring higher on self-esteem.

Obviously, to make such a combination means that the person has found values that are not necessarily antithetical at all times. For example, the more one's subculture devalues competition, the more difficult it may be to participate in much of the majority culture of the United States. On the other hand, since all persons have multiple roles, it may be possible, for example, to be competitive in the work situation but retain communal/cooperative-style functioning for all family, social group, and avocational roles. Lastly, it must be emphasized that biculturality need *not* be viewed as the new standard for all to meet. Honoring cultural diversity means seeing how one might work out effective adaptation either within one's culture of origin *or* within the "majority" culture *or* in a bicultural combination.

The other major new horizon in understanding counselors' adjustment to diverse cultures is that of racial identity. Helms (1984, 1990) and

Parham (1989) have extensively investigated models of racial identity to help explain variability in the psychological development of American blacks and whites as well as to account for the diverse results that have been obtained in pairings of white and black counselors and clients. Several critical components of the construct of racial identity go beyond the concept of biculturalism, addressing questions, for example, about why some clients will not even acknowledge cultural differences that are affecting their interactions while others will angrily focus on little else. Managing basic identity issues can help counselors understand resistance and reactance during counseling, as they deal with such conflicts. Holding promise for other cross-cultural areas such as dealing with handicaps and alternative lifestyles, the racial identity model has been used so far to describe how whites and blacks develop racial identities and to analyze issues in interracial counseling dyads.

The origin of the black racial identity model is to be found in the 1960s, when large numbers of American blacks began to change their self-images and interactions with the majority culture. While some became heavily involved in the "Black Power" movement, others retained virtually unchanged their previous lifestyles. Cross (1971) developed a four-stage model to explain the "Negro-to-Black conversion" experience. His four stages, described below, have served as the basis for an extensive number of studies on how racial identity influences value orientation, self-esteem, self-actualization, and counselor preference (see Parham, 1989; Helms, 1990). (Subsequent study of white racial identity led Helms and her colleagues [1990] to formulate a very different set of stages, to be described later.)

> *Pre-encounter.* In the first stage the person is prone to view the world from a White frame of reference. . . . the person has accepted a deracinated frame of reference, and because his or her reference is usually a White normative standard, he or she develops attitudes that are very pro-White and anti-Black. *Encounter.* This second stage is characterized by an individual experiencing one of many significant (shocking) personal or social events that are inconsistent with his or her frame of reference. For example, a Black person who views his or her race as not important and wishes to be viewed and accepted simply as a "human being" is denied access to living in an exclusive neighborhood because of skin color. . . . *Immersion–Emersion.* This stage represents a turning point in the conversion from the old to a new frame of reference. . . . The person begins to immerse him[self] or herself into total Blackness, clinging to various elements of Black culture and simultaneously withdrawing from interactions with other ethnic groups. . . . This stage is also characterized by a tendency to denigrate White people while simultaneously glorifying Black people. . . . *Internalization.* This stage is characterized by the individual achieving a sense of inner security and self-confidence through his or her Blackness . . . by psychological openness, ideological flexibility and a general decline in anti-White feelings. Although still using

> Black as a primary reference group, this person moves to a more pluralistic, nonracist perspective. (Parham, 1989, pp. 189–190)

As Helms has so clearly illustrated (1984), racial identity has significant implications for whether or not a black client can form a therapeutic alliance with a white counselor. A preencounter client may largely ignore the racial implications of any of his or her experiences; the immersion/emersion client may focus on little else. Somewhat to the surprise of many counselors, black clients who have reached the state of internalization may seem quite like preencounter clients in their tendency to avoid talking about racial issues. Yet, if the topic is initiated by the counselor, preencounter clients will largely deny the relevance of such issues while internalized clients will be able to talk quite comfortably about their understanding of the relevance of the issue and how they cope with it.

It became very clear to Helms and her colleagues, in their work on black racial identity that, just as blacks vary significantly in their affect and cognitions regarding race, so do whites. In her recent book (Helms, 1990), she outlines both the conceptual and empirical foundations underlying the development of a white racial identity. From her research she has suggested six stages that fall within two major phases. The first three stages deal with the abandonment of racism, the second three with the development of a nonracist white identity. Although the model is still in its early stages of development, the results of research with whites in both counseling and social interactions support the hypotheses generated from the model. Given the increasing number of cross-racial interactions in counseling and therapy, a description of the six stages may be particularly thought-provoking for whites who have not thought much about their racial identity. The suggested six stages are as follows:

> *Contact.* As soon as one encounters the idea or the actuality of Black people, one has entered the contact stage of identity. . . . Behaviors thought to characterize Contact people are limited social or occupational interaction with Blacks. . . . in such interactions, the White person uses the Black person to teach him or her about what Black people in general are like and often uses social stereotypes of Blacks as the standard against which the Black person is evaluated. Comments such as "You don't act like a Black person" or "I don't notice what race a person is" are likely to be made by Contact persons. . . .
>
> *Disintegration.* . . . It is probably during this stage . . . that the person first comes to realize that in spite of mouthings to the contrary, Blacks and Whites are not considered equal and negative social consequences can besiege the White person who does not respect the inequalities. Moreover, the Disintegration stage may be the time in which the person comes to realize that the social skills or mores he or she has been taught to use in interacting with Blacks rarely work. Thus the person in disintegration may not only

perceive for the first time that he or she is caught between two racial groups, but may also come to realize that his or her position amongst Whites depends on his or her abilities to successfully "split" her or his personality. . . . Which alternative [from Festinger's three ways of reducing dissonance] the White person chooses probably depends on the extent to which his or her cross-racial interactions are voluntary. It seems likely that the person who can remove himself or herself from interracial environments or can remove Blacks from White environments will do so. . . . Attempts to change others' attitudes probably occur initially among Whites who were raised and/or socialized in an environment in which "White" liberal attitudes . . . were expressed. However, due to the racial naivete with which this approach may be undertaken and the person's ambivalent racial identification, this dissonance-reducing strategy is likely to be met with rejection by Whites as well as Blacks. . . .

Reintegration. In the reintegration stage, the person consciously acknowledges a White identity. In the absence of contradictory experiences, to be White in America is to believe that one is superior to people of color. . . . He or she comes to believe that institutional or cultural racism [is] the White person's due because he or she has earned such privileges or preferences. Race related negative conditions are assumed to result from Black people's inferior social, moral, and intellectual qualities, and thus, it is not unusual to find persons in the reintegration stage selectively attending to and/or reinterpreting information to conform to societal stereotypes of Black people. Honest discussion of racial matters is most likely to occur among same-race peers who share or are believed to share a similar view of the world. Active expression may include treating Blacks as inferior and involve acts of violence or exclusion designed to protect White privilege. . . .

Pseudo-Independent. . . . In this stage, the person begins to acknowledge the responsibility of White racism and to see how he or she wittingly or unwittingly perpetuates racism. . . . The . . . stage is primarily a stage of intellectualization. . . . To the extent that feelings concerning racial identity issues are allowed to emerge, there are apt to be feelings of commiseration with Blacks and perhaps disquietude concerning racial issues in White peer groups . . . Though the person may seek greater interaction with Blacks, much of the interaction involves helping Blacks to change themselves so that they function more like Whites on White criteria for success and acceptability rather than recognizing that such criteria might be inappropriate and/or too narrowly defined . . .

Emersion/Immersion. . . . The person in this stage is searching for the answers to the questions: "Who am I racially?" and "Who do I want to be?" and "Who are you really?" . . . He or she may participate in White consciousness raising groups whose purpose is to help the person discover her or his individual self-interest in abandoning racism and acknowledging a White racial identity. Changing Black people is no longer the focus of her or his activities, but rather the goal of changing White people becomes salient. . . .

Autonomy. . . . In this stage, the person no longer feels a need to oppress, idealize or denigrate people on the basis of group membership characteristics such as race because race no longer symbolizes a threat to him or her.

> Since he or she no longer reacts out of rigid world views, it is possible for him or her to abandon cultural and institutional racism as well as personal racism. Thus, one finds the Autonomous person actively seeking opportunities to learn from other cultural groups. One also finds him or her actively becoming increasingly aware of how other forms of oppression (e.g., sexism, ageism) are related to racism and acting to eliminate them as well. (Helms, 1990, pp. 55–66)

In the fullest explication of her model of black-white counselor dyads, Helms (1984) describes what behaviors may be expected both from a black client and a black counselor at each of the five stages of black racial identity and from a white client and a white counselor at each of the six stages of white racial identity as well as four different kinds of probable interactions depending on the stages of the counselor and client. In such interracial dyads, one can have parallel, crossed, progressive, or regressive relationships, each with quite different effects for the processes and outcomes of counseling:

> When counselors and clients are the same race, a parallel relationship is one in which the counselor and client belong to the same stage of racial consciousness and necessarily share the same attitudes about Blacks *and* Whites; . . . a crossed relationship is one in which the counselor and client belong to opposite stages of racial consciousness, defined as having opposing attitudes about both Blacks and Whites; . . . a progressive relationship is one in which the *counselor's* [italics added] stage of racial consciousness is at least one stage more advanced than the client's; . . . a regressive relationship is one in which the *client's* [italics added] stage of development is at least one stage more advanced than the counselor's. (Helms, 1990, pp. 140–141)

From the descriptions of these interactions, it should be fairly obvious that the client in a cross-racial dyad, whether the counselor is black or white, has the chance to move toward healthier stages in a progressive relationship, that is, where the counselor is at least one stage ahead of the client. In the crossed, regressive, or parallel relationships one can expect that different kinds of impasses and frustrations will be experienced by the counselor and/or the client: "The specific implications of parallel and crossed relationships will probably differ depending upon whether the counselor and/or client is Black or White and whether the counseling is intra- or cross-racial; but by identifying the counselor and client's racial consciousness stages, it should be possible to make predictions about the quality of their counseling relationship as well as possible counseling outcomes" (Helms, 1990, p. 141). In fact, Carter (1990) was able to demonstrate that in black-white counseling relationships, racial identity attitudes were a more significant predictor of the quality of the relationships than race alone. Some of Helms' students have begun extending the concept of models of identity to show that individual differences within various groups of cultural diversity (e.g., handicapped, religious) can be systematically categorized in ways that will help explicate the processes and outcomes of counseling. Most importantly, counseling psychologists need to become accustomed to looking *beyond* the demographic labels that so often mark the beginning and end of considerations of cultural diversity.

ACHIEVING COMPETENCE IN CROSS-CULTURAL COUNSELING

As stated earlier in this chapter, the question of cultural diversity needs to be considered in *every* counseling relationship, addressing the differences in counselor and client beliefs, attitudes, values, and perceptions that affect the usefulness of certain counseling techniques and strategies. It must be emphasized that cultural diversity needs to be *considered*—it may or may not be a major aspect of the counseling in any given relationship.

More so than any other topic discussed in this book, competence in cross-cultural counseling is still in its infancy. As Ponterotto and Casas found as late as 1987, very few counseling programs had much formal coursework or training available in the area of cultural diversity. However, they did note that by the 1980s programs showed more interest in developing such materials.

In 1990, the APA published ten detailed "Guidelines for providers of psychological services to ethnic and culturally diverse populations" (APA, 1990). These guidelines were built on the research that has focused on (1) the impact of ethnic-racial similarity in the counseling process, (2) minority utilization of mental health services, (3) relative effectiveness of styles of therapy, (4) cultural values in treatment, (5) appropriate therapy and counseling models, and (6) skills for working with specific ethnic populations.

In this next section we identify some of the key references and strategies that can be used to address the most critical areas identified by two major task forces in counseling psychology (Principles concerning the counseling and therapy of women, 1979; Sue et al., 1982) that specifically addressed the counseling needs of women and ethnic minorities. Their recommendations have broad applicability to working with other culturally diverse groups as well. Tables 11–1 and 11–2 present both groups' recommendations organized according to (1) attitudes/beliefs, (2) knowledge, and (3) skills as the essential components in achieving competence in multicultural counseling. The final section of this chapter deals with emerging concepts on how counselors can most effectively acquire these attitudes, knowledge and skills.

Table 11–1
PRINCIPLES CONCERNING THE COUNSELING AND THERAPY OF WOMEN

The principles presented here are considered essential for the competent counseling/therapy of women.

1. Counselors/therapists are knowledgeable about women, particularly with regard to biological, psychological and social issues which have impact on women in general or on particular groups of women in our society.
2. Counselors/therapists are aware that the assumptions and precepts of theories relevant to their practice may apply differently to men and women. Counselors/therapists are aware of those theories and models that proscribe or limit the potential of women clients, as well as those that may have particular usefulness for women clients.
3. After formal training, counselors/therapists continue to explore and learn of issues related to women, including the special problems of female subgroups, throughout their professional careers.
4. Counselors/therapists recognize and are aware of all forms of oppression and how these interact with sexism.
5. Counselors/therapists are knowledgeable and aware of verbal and non-verbal process variables (particularly with regard to power in the relationship) as these affect women in counseling/therapy so that the counselor/therapist-client interactions are not adversely affected. The need for shared responsibility between clients and counselors/therapists is acknowledged and implemented.
6. Counselors/therapists have the capability of utilizing skills that are particularly facilitative to women in general and to particular subgroups of women.
7. Counselors/therapists ascribe no pre-conceived limitations on the direction or nature of potential changes or goals in counseling/therapy for women.
8. Counselors/therapists are sensitive to circumstances where it is more desirable for a woman client to be seen by a female or male counselor/therapist.
9. Counselors/therapists use non-sexist language in counseling/therapy, supervision, teaching and journal publications.
10. Counselors/therapists do not engage in sexual activity with their women clients under any circumstances.
11. Counselors/therapists are aware of and continually review their own values and biases and the effects of these on their women clients. Counselors/therapists understand the effects of sex-role socialization upon their own development and functioning and the consequent values and attitudes they hold for themselves and others. They recognize that behaviors and roles need not be sex based.
12. Counselors/therapists are aware of how their personal functioning may influence their effectiveness in counseling/therapy with women clients. They monitor their functioning through consultation, supervision or therapy so that it does not adversely affect their work with women clients.
13. Counselors/therapists support the elimination of sex bias with institutions and individuals.

Table 11–2
CHARACTERISTICS OF THE CULTURALLY SKILLED COUNSELING PSYCHOLOGIST

Beliefs/Attitudes	
1. The culturally skilled counseling psychologist is one who has moved from being culturally unaware to being aware and sensitive to his/her own cultural heritage and to valuing and respecting differences. 2. A culturally skilled counseling psychologist is aware of his/her own values and biases and how they may affect minority clients.	3. A culturally skilled counseling psychologist is one who is comfortable with differences that exist between the counselor and client in terms of race and beliefs. 4. The culturally skilled counseling psychologist is sensitive to circumstances (personal biases, stage of ethnic identity, sociopolitical influences, etc.) which may dictate referral of the minority client to a member of his/her own race/culture.
Knowledge	
1. The culturally skilled counseling psychologist will have a good understanding of the sociopolitical system's operation in the United States with respect to its treatment of minorities. 2. The culturally skilled counseling psychologist must possess specific knowledge and information about the particular group he/she is working with.	3. The culturally skilled counseling psychologist must have a clear and explicit knowledge and understanding of the generic characteristics of counseling and therapy. 4. The culturally skilled counseling psychologist is aware of institutional barriers which prevent minorities from using mental health services.
Skills	
1. At the skills level, the culturally skilled counseling psychologist must be able to generate a wide variety of verbal and nonverbal responses. 2. The culturally skilled counseling psychologist must be able to send and receive both verbal and nonverbal messages accurately and "appropriately."	3. The culturally skilled counseling psychologist is able to exercise institutional intervention skills on behalf of his/her client when appropriate.

Attitudes and Beliefs

Looking first at how to achieve the needed developments regarding attitudes and beliefs, if we have been at all successful thus far in this chapter we hope that readers have a heightened sense of some of the awareness called for by principle 2 regarding women (Table 11–1) and characteristic 1 under "Beliefs/Attitudes" for culturally skilled counselors (Table 11–2). In an ideal world, presentation of valid knowledge would be sufficient to change attitudes, but as social psychologists learned many decades ago, changing attitudes, especially ones widely shared in the dominant culture, can be an extremely difficult task. Reading, in most cases, will not be enough. Katz (1978) has developed perhaps the most illustrative and compelling kinds of exercises needed to sensitize persons to the racial attitudes that most persons hold but are unaware of. The exercises she recommends can bring into sudden awareness behaviors that are routinely engaged in without any idea how they affect others. Consciousness-raising groups have been another strategy often effective for dealing with the attitudes therapists hold about women's "nature" and "place" (Brodsky, 1973); similarly, such groups have been used to confront fears about homosexuality and inappropriately assumed limitations of various groups of handicapped persons.

Changing attitudes mostly requires participation in some experience that will challenge previously unexamined beliefs. The experience may be an especially discomforting one, as few, if any, counselors consciously intend to hurt or limit someone's opportunity. Yet they learn everyday behaviors in many cases have had precisely that effect.

One of the best-known procedures for raising counselors' consciousness about both their unacknowledged attitudes and lack of awareness about a cultural group is the triadic training model of Pedersen (1979). In this model, the counselor and client from different cultural backgrounds are "assisted" by an "anticounselor." The anticounselor is someone from the same cultural group as the client who acts as an alter ego, personifying the client's problem. The anticounselor has been trained to say deliberately out loud thoughts that the client is expected to have in reaction to the counselor's questions and suggestions. The counselor can then see the meanings and consequences questions and statements have for someone who is not part of the counselor's culture. A skillful anticounselor can accomplish in minutes what might take group consciousness-raising experiences many hours (and which might never be accomplished through extensive reading or professional experience!). Moreover, as Pedersen (1979) points out, in the simulated "laboratory" counseling exercises he describes, the counselor can learn "(l) how to become less defensive when under attack or when receiving strong negative feedback from a client, and (2) how to recover from a mistake once it has been made" (pp. 413–414).

Knowledge Base

Psychology, as a discipline, has been perhaps more responsive in identifying and developing the knowledge base than in promoting attitude change. Part of this responsiveness is related to the fact that knowledge is often best communicated through the written word. Unlike attitude change or skills acquisition, where individual interpersonal experiences are essential, a knowledge base can be gained by reading. The pertinent literature for counseling research and practice with women has been described by Johnson and Scarato (1979) and by Fitzgerald and Nutt (1986). Moreover, three entire issues of *The Counseling Psychologist* (Fitzgerald & Harmon, 1973; Birk & Tanney, 1976; Hill et al., 1979) as well as the handbook chapter by Richardson and Johnson (1984) all provide extensive discussion of issues critical to counselors' knowledge for enhancing women's development.

For other culturally diverse groups, the literature is less distinctly focused; however, pertinent articles regarding VREGs are readily available in references such as Jones' (1980) *Black Psychology,* Helms' (1990) *Black and White Racial Identity,* Sue and Morishima's (1982) *The Mental Health of Asian Americans,* Sue and Moore's (1984) *The Pluralistic Society,* Snowden's (1982) *Reaching the Underserved: Mental Health Needs of Neglected Populations,* Jones and Korshin's (1982) *Minority Mental Health,* and Pedersen's (1985) *Handbook of Cross-cultural Counseling and Psychotherapy.* For counseling American Indians, the most focused work is that of LaFromboise, Trimble, and Mohatt (1990). For working with the elderly, Santos and VandenBos (1981) provide a number of edifying articles. For most of the nonethnic minorities, Atkinson and Hackett (1988) is the most concise reference. For religious persons, Worthington's (1989) review furnishes numerous pertinent references.

The rationale for acquiring a knowledge base is that there are, for each culturally diverse group, beliefs, attitudes, and ways of perceiving the world that may differ from the counselor's. By becoming acquainted with these differences in perceiving and thinking, the counselor is more able to "connect" with his or her clients and form the kinds of therapeutic alliances described in earlier chapters. Furthermore, when dealing with clients from any culturally diverse background, an understanding is also needed of how history and sociopolitical forces have shaped both clients' views of themselves and their opportunities as well as counselors' views of clients and their opportunities. Without such knowledge, counselors may find themselves working in a cultural straitjacket that severely limits what clients can gain from counseling.

The base of knowledge needed is far more extensive than simply some specifics about counseling identifiably culturally diverse groups. It must also include: (1) explanation of the physical and developmental factors that influence psychological development, for example, in women and the aged, (2) and descriptions of the sociocultural factors influencing client perspectives, about what constitutes, for example, family, being "a man" or "a woman," or illness. Such knowledge is critical; impasses in counseling are often a result of a counselor's assuming that a client feels and thinks the same way she or he does.

Sue and Zane (1987) have noted that the credibility of the counselor is impaired if the counselor's (a) conceptualization of the problem, (b) suggested means for problem resolution, or (c) goals for treatment are incongruent with the way the client perceives the world. Such impairment severely diminishes the potential for an effective therapy alliance. Sue and Zane (1987) add that they do not intend

> to imply that therapists should simply strive to match clients. At times, the client's belief systems may be inappropriate; he or she may need to learn new and (previously considered) incompatible responses. The client may hold inappropriate goals or the therapist may have to define other goals in order to address the client's primary problem. Nevertheless, therapists should realize that incongruities in conceptualization, problem resolution, or goals often reduce credibility. This diminished credibility needs to be restored or increased by demonstrating the validity of the therapist's perspective. Moreover, the incongruencies should alert the therapist to the need to reexamine treatment strategies. For example, are the treatment decisions guided by the therapist's limitations in understanding the culture and context of the client or by well-thought-out outcome considerations for this client? (p. 41)

Skills

Recently more attention has been given than previously to the adequacy of counseling skills needed to be a competent cross-cultural counselor. No matter how well aware counselors might be of their own attitudes, as well as sensitive to perceptual and value differences of clients and knowledgeable about any given culturally diverse group, unless they can communicate this awareness and knowledge through "ability to devise innovative strategies, vis à vis the unique client's needs" (Ponterotto & Casas, 1987, p. 433), then the primary goal of delivering effective cross-cultural counseling services cannot be accomplished. Just as there is no substitute for practicum experience for learning basic counseling skills, there is no substitute for learning cross-cultural counseling by seeing clients who are significantly different from oneself and receiving supervision that focuses on the awareness needed to make assessments and plan appropriate strategies. Regretfully, it must be acknowledged that most of the clients seen in graduate student practica are not from backgrounds dissimilar to the counselor's and only rarely will a practicum student have a supervisor who emphasizes cultural emic factors in the dyads instead of etic elements.

Johnson (1987) notes that there are so few opportunities in normal social interactions and counseling to practice intercultural communication that he proposes greater use of a laboratory approach, that is, arranging for experiential demonstrations as part of counselors' training. He examines several models that have been developed to enhance learning from simulated intercultural interactions (Birnbaum, 1975; Pedersen, 1979; Kasse, 1980). A laboratory exercise approach also "legitimizes" directly dealing with the intercultural issues:

> In many respects it is a violation of social protocol to engage in conversation about race, gender, ethnicity, religion, social class, or age group differences. Likewise in counseling, many beginning counselors and trainees are disinclined to raise such issues in the context of training practice or field setting out of fear they will disrupt the relationships they have tried so hard to achieve. All too frequently, this posture of blindness to differences undermines their credibility with ethnic minority clients. The laboratory experience seems to help participants achieve greater sense of balance with cultural material. This notion of balance, not overemphasizing culture at the expense of sensitivity or vice versa, is potentially a true index of the kind of expertise required of a multicultural counselor. (Johnson, 1987, p. 327)

Pertinent exercises can be found in or adapted from techniques in all of the references noted in the two preceding paragraphs.

Less structured means for acquiring skills in cross-cultural counseling derive from the concept of *cognitive empathy* as an effective way to engage in cultural role taking. Scott and Borodovsky (1990) argue that traditional concepts of empathy cannot be achieved in most cross-cultural counseling dyads. A white person cannot affectively know what it is like to grow up black in America; a 25-year-old cannot affectively know what it is like to be a frail 80-year-old. They point out that in such dyads one must rely on cognitive empathy, that is, learning about the client's culture "by simply asking the client about her or his culture. . . . Thus the counselor can meet the client at different levels on the basis of her or his cognitive understanding [even though the counselor] cannot penetrate the client's intrapsychic structure on the effective level" (Scott & Borodovsky, 1990, pp. 169–170). A counselor who is sensitive to cultural considerations will readily ask about aspects of the client's background that may have an impact on the progress of counseling.

Carney and Kahn (1984) have suggested effective cross-cultural counseling skills should be gained through a series of developmental training of stages. Their model aims to stimulate changes in attitudes and knowledge as well as in skills. Their work is clearly related to earlier work by Knefelkamp, Widick, and Strode (1976), based on cognitive developmental theory, in the latter's suggestions for how to prepare both male and female counselors for counseling women. Carney and Kahn (1984) note the importance of both challenge and support:

> Challenges prod trainees to expand their knowledge and attitudes by presenting new ways of viewing other cultural groups, or by presenting alternative methods of counseling those who are culturally different. Supports include a training atmosphere that promotes personal sharing and trust. . . . the appropriate learning environment for trainees at early stages of development provides a high degree of structure, offers a limited set of personal challenges and has clear direction provided by the trainer. Learning at later stages is promoted by a fading of structure, increasingly diverse challenges, and a greater personal responsibility taken by the trainees. (p. 112)

According to this view, the value of training experiences that focus on attitudes, knowledge, or skills will vary according to the identity development of the trainee. Consequently, training models need to be planned to incorporate a diversity of levels of counselor functioning. This position is empirically supported by the work of Neimeyer, Fukuyama, Bingham, Hall, and Mussenden (1986) who, when comparing pro-counselor and anticounselor triad models of cross-cultural training concluded that "the more confrontive anticounselor model may be better suited to the advanced student who has already developed some level of confidence and skill in cross-cultural interactions. . . . In contrast, the pro-counselor model might be more appropriate for beginning counselors by providing them with an experience of success to alleviate their anxiety in cross-cultural interactions" (p. 439).

Moreover, because of the sensitivity of many of the issues in any cross-cultural training model, there needs to be high levels of support as well as challenge, though the two may need to be inversely related as trainees progress. For example, at the beginning levels, a great deal of support and modest challenges may be more effective, whereas in later stages of development, trainees can handle greater levels of challenge with more limited amounts of supervisory support. Such patterns have been well discussed in the literature on supervisory models (e.g., Stoltenberg & Delworth, 1987).

The concept of stages of developmental training in cross-cultural counseling training has recently been enlarged to include readiness in dealing with racial issues (e.g., Ponterotto, 1988; Lopez et al., 1989; Helms, 1990). The work of these authors suggests that at each of the stages of Carney and Kahn's model, one experiences different conflicts. For example, for those who are at relatively early stages of racial awareness, the conflict will be between their ethnocentric worldview and the more egalitarian views of counseling. However, as they have not yet truly experienced racial awareness, they are "unlikely to entertain cultural hypotheses as explanations for the client's presenting problem" (Lopez et al., 1989, p. 379). Trying to immerse these counselors in the knowledge base would be ineffective. The material in the knowledge base is attended to only when attitudes start to shift about the importance of issues of cultural diversity.

Then, as counselors become more aware of racial or cultural differences, they are first likely to respond to them in stereotypic fashion; moreover, lacking knowledge about techniques, counselors choose to act in an outwardly detached scholarly manner, applying etic techniques with which they are familiar. It is in this stage that one can begin to combine new knowledge about cultural diversity with the awareness of the need to pay continual attention to cultural differences in making assessments and using alternative interventions.

As the counselor recognizes the importance of race, the conflict may shift to managing feelings of guilt and responsibility and to feeling overwhelmed by the alternative strategies available. The greatest need in moving from the third stage to the fourth stage is to be able to organize attitudes, knowledge, and skills in a meaningful way and to overcome one's worries about one's own ethnocentrism. At the highest levels, the counselor can begin to form both a comfortable self-identity as a nonracist individual and begin to make appropriate tests of hypotheses about which kinds of etic or emic explanations are most useful for a particular client. According to Lopez et al. (1989): "In the final stage of development, therapists are expected to more discriminately generate cultural explanations and then reject or accept such explanations after carefully considering multiple hypotheses. This careful evaluation of all plausible hypotheses is likely to represent a disconfirmation hypothesis-testing strategy in which clinicians seek evidence to disconfirm cultural or non-cultural hypotheses alike" (p. 376).

In this statement, the essence of the scientist-practitioner model becomes apparent yet again. Achieving competence as a cross-cultural counselor includes first the development of *attitudes* that will allow counseling psychologists to examine all counseling interactions for sources of cultural diversity that may affect assessments and interventions. It then includes the development of *knowledge* that leads to informed hypotheses to test in planning interventions. Finally, it includes the development of *skills* to carefully evaluate and choose interventions that will attend not only to the intrapsychic forces of clients but also to the environmental issues that affect a client's opportunities for growth and development.

SUMMARY

In today's world, counseling services are being provided to an increasingly diverse clientele. Researchers have learned much in the past two decades about how limited counseling theories and strategies have been for facilitating the development of individuals with diverse ethnic and cultural backgrounds. Among the terms *diversity, culture, race, ethnicity, minority, racism,* and *cross-cultural counseling,* both the first and the last have much broader applicability than is often understood. If appropriate consideration is to be given to the cultural factors present in counseling relationships, it must be understood that cross-cultural counseling refers to *all* counseling that deals with clients whose values and perceptions of reality are different from the counselor's. Every counseling relationship needs to be examined for the relevance of cultural diversity to the origin of the client's presenting problem, to the client's understanding of the problem, and to the development of relevant options for coping with the problem.

Biases of mental health professionals and white middle-class worldviews have added to the barriers to the opportunities of many of those identified as minorities in achieving their potential. Evidence on the effects of such biases is most extensive for women, ethnic minorities, and homosexuals.

The third major section of this chapter reviewed the limitations of early research that tried to address the problem of diversity by matching counselor and client. Newer research models on biculturality and black and white racial identity have helped us understand why such matching is not always effective. Even more importantly, they show what counselors must do, whatever their cultural background, to achieve competence in cross-cultural counseling.

Various kinds of attitudes, knowledge, and skills have been recommended to realize this competence. Empirical evidence suggests the need for stages of development in the training of counselors dealing with multicultural issues. It will be the task of future counseling psychologists to conduct the research necessary to determine the effectiveness of these recommendations.

References

Acosta, F.X., Yamamoto, J., & Evans, L.A. (1982). *Effective psychotherapy for low income and minority patients.* New York: Cleum Press.

American Psychological Association. (1979). *Criteria for accreditation of doctoral training programs and internships in professional psychology.* Washington, DC.

American Psychological Association (1990). *Guidelines for providers of psychological services to ethnic and culturally diverse populations.* Washington, DC.

American Psychological Association Task Force on Sex Bias and Sex Role Stereotyping in Psychotherapeutic Practice (1975). *American Psychologist, 30,* 1169–1175.

Arrendondo-Dowd, P., & Consalves, J. (1980). Preparing culturally effective counselors. *Personnel and Guidance Journal, 58,* 657–660.

Astin, H. S. (1984). The meaning of work in women's lives: A sociological model of career choice in work behavior. *The Counseling Psychologist, 12,* 117–126.

Atkinson, D. R. (1983). Ethnic similarity in counseling psychology: A review of the research. *The Counseling Psychologist, 11*(3), 73–92.

Atkinson, D. R., & Hackett, G. (Eds.) (1988). *Counseling non-ethnic American minorities.* Springfield, IL: Charles C. Thomas.

Atkinson, D. R., Morton, G., & Sue, D. W. (Eds.) (1989). *Counseling American minorities: A cross-cultural perspective* (3rd ed.). Dubuque, IA: William C. Brown.

Barak, A., & Fisher, W. A. (1989). Counselor and therapist gender bias? More questions than answers. *Professional Psychology: Research and Practice 20,* 377–383.

Birk, J. M., & Tanney, M. F. (Eds.) (1976). Counseling women II. *The Counseling Psychologist, 6*(2), 2–64.

Birnbaum, M. (1975). The clarification group. In K. Benne, L. Bradford, J. Gibb, & R. Lippet (Eds.), *The laboratory method of changing and learning.* Palo Alto, CA: Science and Behavior Books.

Bloombaum, N., Yamamoto, J., & James, Q. (1968). Cultural stereotyping among psychotherapists. *Journal of Consulting and Clinical Psychology, 32,* 99.

Brodsky, A. (1973). The consciousness-raising group as a model for therapy with women. *Psychotherapy: Theory, Research, and Practice, 10,* 24–29.

Broverman, I., Broverman, D., Clarkson, F., Rosenkrantz, P., & Vogel, S. (1970). Sex role stereotypes and clinical judgments of mental health. *Journal of Consulting and Clinical Psychology, 34,* 1–7.

Carney, C. G., & Kahn, K. B. (1984). Building competencies for effective cross-cultural counseling. *The Counseling Psychologist, 12*(1), 111–119.

Carter, R. T. (1990). Does race or racial identity attitudes influence the counseling process in black and white dyads? In J. E. Helms (Ed.), *Black and white racial identity* (pp. 145–164). New York: Greenwood Press.

Casas, J. M. (1984). Policy, training, and research in counseling psychology: The racial/ethnic minority perspective. In S. D. Brown & R. W. Lent (Eds.), *Handbook of counseling psychology* (pp. 785–831). New York: Wiley.

Cook, D. A., & Helms, J. E. (1988). Relationship dimensions as predictors of visible racial/ethnic group students' perceptions of cross-racial supervision. *Journal of Counseling Psychology, 35,* 268–274.

Cook, E. P. (1987). Psychological androgyny. *The Counseling Psychologist, 15,* 471–513.

Cross, W. E. (1971). The Negro to Black conversion experience: Towards a psychology of black liberation. *Black World, 20*(a), 13–27.

Dahlquist, L. M., & Fay, A. S. (1983). Cultural issues in psychotherapy. In C. E. Walker (Ed.), *The handbook of clinical psychology: Theory, research, and practice* (pp. 1219–1255). Homewood, IL: Dow Jones-Irwin.

Denmark, F., Russo, N. F., Frieze, I. H., & Sechzer, J. A. (1988). Guidelines for avoiding sexism in psychological research. *American Psychologist, 43,* 582–585.

Donnan, H. H., & Mitchell, H. D. (1979). Preferences for older versus younger counselors among a group of elderly persons. *Journal of Counseling Psychology, 26,* 514–518.

Fitzgerald, L. E., & Harmon, L. W. (Eds.) (1973). Counseling women. *The Counseling Psychologist, 4*(l), 2–101.

Fitzgerald, L. F., & Nutt, R. (1986). The Division 17 principles concerning the counseling/psychotherapy of women: Rationale and implementation. *The Counseling Psychologist, 14,* 180–216.

Helms, J. E. (1984). Toward a theoretical explanation of the effects of race on counseling: A black and white model. *The Counseling Psychologist, 12*(4), 153–165.

Helms, J. E. (Ed.) (1990). *Black and white racial identity: Theory, research and practice.* New York: Greenwood Press.

Helms, J. E., & Parham, T. A. (in press). The development of the Racial Identity Attitude Scale. In R. L. Jones (Ed.), *Handbook for Tests and Measurements for Black Populations* (Vols. 1-2). Berkeley, CA: Cobb and Henry.

Hill, C. E., Birk, J. M., Blimline, C. A., Leonard, N. M., Hoffman, M. A., & Tanney, M. F. (Eds.) (1979). Counseling women III. *The Counseling Psychologist, 8*(1), 2–64.

Ibraham, F. A. (1985). Effective cross-cultural therapy: A framework. *The Counseling Psychologist, 13,* 625–638.

Ivey, A., & Authier, J. (1978). *Microcounseling: Innovations in interview training.* Springfield, IL: Thomas.

Johnson, M., & Scaroto, A. M. (1979). A knowledge base for counselors of women. *The Counseling Psychologist, 8*(1), 14–16.

Johnson, S. D. (1987). Knowing that vs. knowing how: Toward achieving expertise through multicultural training for counseling. *The Counseling Psychologist, 15,* 320–331.

Jones, E. E., & Korchin, S. J. (Eds.) (1982). *Minority mental health.* New York: Praeger.

Jones, R. L. (Ed.) (1980). *Black psychology.* New York: Harper & Row.

Kasse, P. (1980). *Training for the cross-cultural mind.* Washington, DC: Society for Intercultural Training and Research.

Katz, J. H. (1978). *White awareness: Handbook for anti-racism training.* Norman, OK: University of Oklahoma Press.

Katz, J. H. (1985). The socio-political nature of counseling. *The Counseling Psychologist, 13,* 615–624.

Kite, M. E., & Deaux, K. (1987). Gender belief systems: Homosexuality and the implicit inversion theory. *Psychology of Women Quarterly, 11,* 83–96.

Knefelkamp, L. L., Widick, C. C., & Strode, B. (1976). Cognitive-developmental theory: A guide to counseling women. *The Counseling Psychologist, 6,* (2) 15–19.

Korman, M. (1974). National conference on levels and patterns of professional training in psychology. *American Psychologist, 29,* 441–449

LaFromboise, T. D., Trimble, J. E., & Mohatt, G. B. (1990). Counseling intervention and American Indian tradition: An integrative approach. *The Counseling Psychologist, 18,* 628–654.

Leong, F. T. L. (1986). Counseling and psychotherapy with Asian-Americans: Review of the literature. *Journal of Counseling Psychology, 33,* 196–206.

Lonner, W. J. (1979). Issues in cross-cultural psychology. In A. J. Marsella, R. G. Tharp, & T. I. Cibrowski (Eds.), *Perspectives on cross-cultural psychology.* New York: Academic Press.

Lonner, W. J. (1985). Issues in testing and assessment in cross-cultural counseling. *The Counseling Psychologist, 13,* 599–614.

Lopez, S. R., Grover, K. E., Holland, D., Johnson, M. J., Kain, C. D., Kanel, K., Mellins, C. A., & Rhyne, M. C. (1989). Development of culturally sensitive psychotherapists. *Professional Psychology: Research and Practice, 20,* 369–376.

Morin, S. F. (1977). Heterosexual bias in psychological research on lesbianism and male homosexuality. *American Psychologist, 32,* 629–637.

Nickerson, E. T. (1979). How helpful are the helpers? A selected review of sexist help practices. *The Counseling Psychologist, 8*(1), 5.

Neimeyer, G. J., Fukuyama, M. A., Bingham, R. P., Hall, L. E., & Mussenden, M. E. (1986). Training cross-cultural counselors: A comparison of the pro-counselor and anti-counselor triad models. *Journal of Counseling and Development, 64,* 437–439.

Padilla, A. M., & Lindholm, K. J. (1984). Hispanic behavioral science research: Recommendations for future research. *Hispanic Journal of Behavioral Sciences, 6,* 13–22.

Parham, T. A. (1989). Cycles of psychological nigrescence. *The Counseling Psychologist, 17,* 187–226.

Pedersen, P. (1978). Four dimensions of cross-cultural skill in counselor training. *Personnel and Guidance Journal, 56,* 480–484.

Pedersen, P. (Ed.) (1979). Counseling clients from other cultures: Two training designs. In M. F. Asante, E. Newmark, & C. A. Blake (Eds.), *Handbook of intercultural communication* (pp. 405–419). Newbury Park, CA: Sage.

Pedersen, P. (Ed.) (1985). *Handbook of cross-cultural counseling and therapy.* Westport, CT: Greenwood Press.

Pomales, J., & Williams, V. (1989). Effects of level of acculturation and counseling style on Hispanic students' perceptions of counselor. *Journal of Counseling Psychology, 36,* 79–83.

Ponterotto, J. G. (1987). Counseling Mexican-Americans: A multi-modal approach. *Journal of Counseling and Development, 65,* 308–312.

Ponterotto, J. G., & Casas, J. M. (1987). In search of multicultural competence within counselor education programs. *Journal of Counseling and Development, 65,* 430–434.

Ponterotto, J. G. (1988). Racial consciousness development among white counseling trainees: A stage model. *Journal of Multicultural Counseling and Development, 16,* 146–156.

Principles concerning the counseling and therapy of women (1979). *The Counseling Psychologist, 8*(l), 22.

Richardson, M. S., & Johnson, M. (1984). Counseling women. In S. D. Brown & R. W. Lent (Eds.), *Handbook of counseling psychology* (pp. 832–877). New York: Wiley.

Ridley, C. R. (1989). Racism in counseling as an aversive behavioral process. In P. Pedersen, J. G. Draguns, W. J. Lonner, & E. Trimble (Eds.), *Counseling across cultures* (3rd ed., pp. 55–77). Honolulu: University of Hawaii Press.

Sanchez, A. R., & Atkinson, D. R. (1983). Mexican-American cultural commitment, preference for counselor ethnicity, and willingness to use counseling. *Journal of Counseling Psychology, 30,* 215–220.

Santos, J. F., & VandenBos, G. R. (Eds.) (1981). *Psychology and the older adult.* Washington, DC: American Psychological Association.

Scott, N. S., & Borodovsky, L. G. (1990). Effective use of cultural role taking. *Professional Psychology: Research and Practice, 21,* 167–170.

Sesan, R. (1988). Sex bias and sex-role stereotyping in psychotherapy with women: Surveyed results. *Psychotherapy, 25,* 107–116.

Smith, E. M. J., & Vasquez, M. J. T. (Eds.). (1985). Cross-cultural counseling. *The Counseling Psychologist, 13,* 531–684.

Smith, E. M. J. (1989). Black racial identity development: Issues and concerns. *The Counseling Psychologist, 17,* 277–288.

Snowden, L. R. (Ed.) (1982). *Reaching the underserved: Mental health needs of neglected populations.* Beverly Hills, CA: Sage.

Snowden, L. R., & Chung, F. K. (1990). Use of inpatient mental health services by members of ethnic minority groups. *American Psychologist, 45,* 347–355.

Stoltenberg, C. D., & Delworth, U. (1987). *Supervising counselors and therapists: A developmental approach.* San Francisco: Jossey-Bass.

Sue, D. W. (1978). Eliminating cultural oppression in counseling: Toward a general theory. *Journal of Counseling Psychology, 25,* 419–428.

Sue, D. W. (1980). *Counseling the culturally different: Theory and practice.* New York: Wiley.

Sue, D. W., & Sue, D. (1977). Barriers to effective cross-cultural counseling. *Journal of Counseling Psychology, 24,* 420–429.

Sue, D. W., & Sue, D. (1985). Asian and Pacific Islanders. In P. Pedersen (Ed.), *Handbook of cross-cultural counseling and therapy* (pp. 141–146). Westport, CT: Greenwood.

Sue, D. W., Bernier, J. E., Durran, A., Feinberg, L., Pedersen, P., Smith, E. J., & Vasquez-Nuttall, E. (1982). Position paper: Cross-cultural counseling competencies. *The Counseling Psychologist, 10*(2), 45–52.

Sue, S., & Moore, T. (Eds.) (1984). *The pluralistic society: A community mental health perspective.* New York: Human Services Press.

Sue, S., & Morishima, J. K. (1982). *The mental health of Asian Americans.* San Francisco: Jossey-Bass.

Sue, S., & Zane, N. (1987). The role of culture and cultural techniques in psychotherapy: A critique and reformulation. *American Psychologist, 42,* 37–45.

Sundberg, N. D. Cross-cultural counseling and psychotherapy. A research overview. In A. Marsella & P. Pedersen (Eds.), *Cross-cultural counseling and therapy.* New York: Pergamon.

Szapocznik, J., Scopetta, M., de los Angeles Arnalde, M., & Kurtines, W. (1978). Cuban value structure: Treatment implications. *Journal of Consulting and Clinical Psychology, 46,* 961–970.

Thomas, C. W. (1985). Counseling in a cultural context. *The Counseling Psychologist, 13,* 657–664.

Wirth, L. (1945). The problem of minority groups. In R. Linton (Ed.), *The science of man in the world crisis.* New York: Columbia University Press.

Worthington, E. (1989). Religious faith across the life span: Implications for counseling and research. *The Counseling Psychologist, 17,* 555–612.

Wrenn, G. (1962). The culturally encapsulated counselor. *Harvard Educational Review, 32,* 444–479.

Part III

Key Intervention Areas

Chapter 12

Counseling Psychologists as Career Psychologists

The theoretical and empirical contributions to psychology that are most distinctively identified with counseling psychology lie primarily in the area of career psychology. In fact, among doctoral psychology training programs, training in career development and career counseling are rarely found outside of counseling psychology programs.

This uniqueness within psychology does not signify that counseling psychologists are the only professionals attending to career development. Whereas the topics presented in the chapters up to the present one have overlapped mostly with clinical psychology, career psychology shares common ground mostly with industrial/organizational (I/O) psychology. Moreover, career psychology brings counseling psychologists into interdisciplinary contact with sociologists and economists who work on some of the same "world-of-work" problems, using approaches and methodologies indigenous to their own specialties.

A major distinction of career psychology is its primary emphasis on "normal development." Since the work of Parsons (1909) and the vocational guidance movement at the beginning of the 20th century (see Chapter 2), a major focus in research has been to examine how persons typically go about making vocational decisions.

SOME DEFINITIONS

First of all, several terms must be clarified: *vocational choice, vocational guidance, vocational psychology, career development, career psychology, career counseling, educational development,* and *educational counseling. Vocational choice* is a behavioral term—all persons choose or do not choose to engage in a vocation. Studies of the antecedents, correlates, and consequences of this choice, or lack of choice, constitute a major portion of the literature in career psychology. (Vocational choice and occupational choice are essentially interchangeable terms. Sociologists and economists tend to prefer *occupational,* whereas psychologists tend to prefer *vocational.*) *Vocational guidance* consists of the processes developed to help individuals with the assessments and reasoning needed to make wise career choices. The even broader term, *vocational psychology,* has been defined by Crites (1969) as the study of vocational behavior and development, vocational behavior including all "responses the individual makes in choosing and adjusting to an occupation" (p. 16). Vocational development "is considered to be a construct which is inferred from the systematic changes that can be observed in vocational behavior over time." (p. 17)

The terms *career development, career counseling,* and *career psychology* grew out of theory and research in vocational psychology in the 1950s and 1960s. Much of the research in those decades turned to developmental psychology to understand the processes of vocational choice and development. Noting that most persons engage in several vocations during their lives, Super (1980) promoted use of the term *career* to cover the sequence of major positions held by a person throughout his or her preoccupational (student) years, working years, and retirement years. *Career* refers to all work-related roles, such as those of student, employee, and retiree, as well as to relevant avocational, familial, and community activities. *Career,* then, is the preferred adjective in the context of life-span implications of vocational behaviors and developmental processes.

The terms *educational development* and *educational counseling* may seem, at first reading, particularly out of place in this chapter. However, if one considers education as part of career development (and in contemporary technological society, education becomes more and more a critical factor in career possibilities), then it can be seen that choices of courses and institutions of higher education, and performance in those settings, are inextricably involved with career psychology. Even the earliest counseling psychologists working in college and university counseling centers quickly saw that problems in the educational plans and/or performance of many students affected their career development. Some leading counseling psychologists have focused on issues in selecting and predicting success in colleges (Astin, 1987). Other counseling psychologists have specialized in the development of remedial systems for students whose study skills and other motivational factors have kept them from achieving their potential. The most widely researched study skills method, the SQ3R (Survey, Question, Read, Recite, and Review), was developed by one of the "charter members" of the profession, F. P. Robinson (1961).

The remaining sections of this chapter examine first the relation of career psychology to both society at large and to individual adjustment. The next and largest section is devoted to an exploration of five diverse approaches to the study of career psychology. The final section deals with the growing bodies of literature on the role of gender and race in career psychology.

CAREER PSYCHOLOGY: A DIVERSITY OF APPROACHES

How can we account for the nearly 100 years of almost uninterrupted attention to career psychology? From one perspective, career choices are simply a few of the many choices made in everyone's life—whether to marry, to buy a house, to take a vacation, and so forth. On the other hand, Freud, according to Erikson (1950), wrote explicitly about the positive relationship to one's mental health of the ability to love *and to work.* The last half of this century has seen a continual accumulation of empirical evidence in support of this principle. Loftquist and Dawis (1984) cite some of the classic studies of the impact of work on life satisfaction and mental health. Perhaps most intriguing is the study of Palmore (1969), who found that work satisfaction was a better predictor of *longevity* than physicians' ratings, use of tobacco, or genetic factors. The annual reviews of vocational literature, published each October in the *Journal of Vocational Behavior,* include an increasing number of studies that show how work adjustment and job stress affect not only the individual worker's mental health but also spouse and family (Greenhaus & Parasuraman, 1986). Thus not only is the choice of a career central to one's lifestyle (Osipow, Walsh, & Tosi, 1980), it is also a vital aspect of the physical and emotional well-being of the individuals themselves and their families.

Socially and economically, there are yet other driving forces behind career psychology. Recall the role of both world wars in advancing the vocational guidance movement. Using human resources effectively was, and continues to be, the major impetus for governmental support of the development of occupational classification, selection, and promotion procedures. Some jobs demand specific talents; putting employees in positions without these talents is at best economically wasteful and, in a war effort, at worst, potentially catastrophic. On a less dramatic basis, everyday issues like absenteeism and job turnover are two of the highest, most preventable costs businesses incur. Each year, hundreds of thousands of dollars are invested in research to find out what steps can be taken to increase workers' satisfaction, a factor directly linked to absenteeism and job turnover (Loftquist & Dawis, 1984).

From the societal (as compared to the economic) viewpoint, a well-functioning society is one in which there are low levels of social alienation, that is, one in which few persons are found who are not contributing to, or possibly even interfering with, the processes of communal living. Worker dissatisfaction is a major component in social alienation. It is not difficult to recall how much social unrest has occurred in times of high unemployment and/or when groups of individuals are systematically denied the opportunity to enter and succeed in valued careers. The continued underemployment of vast numbers of women (Betz & Fitzgerald, 1987) and ethnic minorities (Smith, 1983) is today's manifestation of the continued relationship between social problems and career development.

Indeed, career psychology continues to be central to both the profession of counseling psychology and to society at large, as individuals cope with the technological revolutions of the 20th and now fast-approaching 21st century. As a consequence, the literature in career psychology is burgeoning. Slaney and Russell (1987) noted that the number of articles and books published on career psychology in 1986 increased 1100% over 1976!

Next we provide a brief introduction to five diverse approaches to the study of career psychology. Most of the research on career choice, and much of the research on career adjustment, can be conceptualized within one of these frameworks. Most importantly for our purposes, three of these approaches underlie the career counseling models to be explored in Chapter 13. Our purpose here is simply to provide an introduction to each of these very different approaches, both their varied assumptions and the diverse types of research they have generated. As with personality theory, no one approach has been shown to be distinctly better than all the others, each one serving to contribute to the development of the profession.

Holland's Theory of Vocational Personalities and Work Environments

The first theoretical approach to be explored is perhaps the best exemplar of counseling psychology's emphasis on the interaction of personality and environment. Incorporating this relatively recent emphasis, Holland's interactional theory is clearly linked to the earliest approach to career development, known as the "trait and factor approach." Growing out of some of the limitations of the trait and factor approach, Holland's work has resulted in the development of the most frequently investigated and widely used career assessment and intervention techniques.

The Trait and Factor Approach. The trait and factor approach implements Parsons' (1909) basic model of career guidance, which involves matching an understanding of oneself and the world of work by a process of "true reasoning." The simplest form of this model underlies the concept held by many people throughout the world that each job requires a certain set of skills and that success is simply a matter of matching "the right person with the right job." Many persons who seek career counseling say that all they want is an assessment of their abilities and a list of the jobs that those abilities fit. The limitations of such a simplistic interpretation are explored in later sections of this chapter.

On the other hand, much evidence has been accumulated over the years that assessments of an individual's abilities and interests can significantly predict occupational success far beyond chance levels. Brown, Brooks, & Associates (1990) cite the statistic that over a third of the variance in predicting occupational success can be accounted for simply by knowing measured abilities of workers. Thus, the trait and factor approach has provided a statistically valuable foundation for career psychology.

Career counselors, however, early on saw inadequacies in simple matching of clients' abilities and job requirements. Many persons have the requisite abilities but for personal reasons do not wish to enter a profession. Consider teaching as one example. Most college graduates have the intellectual ability necessary to enter the teaching profession, and many such graduates are interested in helping other persons. Yet, for reasons such as status, income, and peer and parental influences, the majority of college graduates do not become teachers. Thus, a variety of factors keep many graduates from entering a profession that is a good "match" for their measured abilities and interests.

On the job side of the coin, there are an equally large number of reasons for inadequacies in a simple matching approach. The issue is largely one of the immense variety of activities subsumed under any one job title—among the over 20,000 titles that exist in the United States. Consider what seems to be a relatively narrow occupation, that of oceanographer. Some oceanographers focus their work on alternative energy resources; others are involved in movements of the ocean that affect weather; still others are concerned largely with the biology of life in the oceans. Even within each of these categories, according to some further variation, these persons may be involved in research, applied design technology, or even promotion and sales of innovative processes.

John Holland, based on his experience as a career counselor in military and educational settings and on his work throughout the 1950s on the development of new interest measures, became astutely aware of the limitations of simple matching of persons' traits and job requirements. In perhaps one of the finest manifestations of the value of the scientist-practitioner model, he drew upon his experiences as a counselor and researcher to develop a theoretical model that addressed some of the limitations of the trait and factor approach.

The RIASEC Model. Holland (1985a) very succinctly states the principles that underlie the development of his approach to career psychology and, more specifically, that explain how persons make vocational choices:

> The choice of a vocation is an expression of personality. . . . Interest inventories are personality inventories. . . . Vocational stereotypes have reliable and important psychological and sociological meanings. . . . The members of a vocation have similar personalities and similar histories of personal development. . . . Because people in a vocational group have similar personalities, they will respond to many situations and problems in similar ways, and they will create characteristic interpersonal environments. *Vocational satisfaction, stability and achievement depend on the congruence between one's personality and the environment in which one works* [italics added]. (pp. 7–10)

Note that this is *not* a matching of job requirements with an individual's ability, but rather a matter of how much *congruence* there is between the personality type of the individual and the nature of the environment in which the work is done.

Holland's work on the development of the Vocational Preference Inventory (1977), an interest measure, made clear to him that interests could be categorized into far fewer types than there were occupations. Based on various analytic approaches, Holland was able to identify six different types of interests people have. Moreover, by assessing environments through descriptions of people *in* those environments, Holland also described six work environments corresponding to the six interest profiles. Drawing on Linton's (1945) *The Cultural Background of Personality* and the interaction theories we noted in Chapter 2 (Lewin, 1935), Holland finally proposed the person-environment interaction, or congruence, principle.

Central to understanding the application of this theory are the descriptions of the six different types of personalities and the environments to which they correspond (for the succinct descriptions of these see Holland, 1985a). Each type begins with one of the six letters R-I-A-S-E-C. (We present here only the types of interests, not the corresponding environments.)

> Realistic type. . . . a preference for activities that entail the explicit, ordered, or systematic manipulation of objects, tools, machines, and animals; and an aversion to educational or therapeutic activity. . . .
>
> Investigative type. . . . a preference for activities that entail the observational, symbolic, systematic, and creative investigation of physical, biological, and cultural phenomena in order to understand such phenomena; and an aversion to persuasive, social, and repetitive activities. . . .
>
> Artistic type. . . . a preference for ambiguous, free, unsystematized activities that entail the manipulation of physical, verbal, or human materials to create artforms or products; and an aversion to explicit, systematic, and ordered activities. . . .
>
> Social type. . . . preference for activities that entail the manipulation of others to inform, train, develop, cure, or enlighten; and an aversion to explicit, ordered, systematic activities involving materials, tools, or machines. . . .

> Enterprising type. . . . a preference for activity that entails the manipulation of others to attain organizational gains or economic gains; and an aversion to observational, symbolic, and systematic activities. . . .
>
> Conventional type. . . . the preference for activities that entail explicit, ordered, systematic manipulation of data, such as keeping records, filing materials, reproducing materials, organizing written and numerical data according to a prescribed plan, operating business machines and data processing machines to attain organizational or economic goals; and an aversion to ambiguous, free, exploratory, or unsystematized activities. (Holland, 1985a, pp. 19–22)

Typical occupations fitting the various types include: (1) realistic: landscape architect and air traffic controller, (2) investigative: economist and biologist, (3) artistic: editor and photographer, (4) social: athletic coach and minister, (5) enterprising: real estate sales agent and radio/TV announcer, and (6) conventional: receptionist and accountant.

Again, guided by a great deal of statistical analysis, Holland has been able to develop the hexagon provided in Figure 12-1. This model shows that realistic types are more closely related to, for example, investigative or conventional types than to social types. Essential to the definition of these six types of personalities and environments are the relationships between them, the most important of these being, according to Holland, congruence, consistency, and differentiation. *Congruence* is simply the relationship between the person type and the environment in which he or she is working. For a person whose primary type is artistic and who works in an artistic environment a fully congruent match has been made. The match of an artistic person to a conventional environment is totally incongruent ("conventional" is opposite "artistic" on the hexagon). *Consistency* refers to how closely a person's interests are related to each other. A person who has primarily realistic interests but also strong social interests is a less consistent person than one whose strongest interests are realistic and investigative. Again, refer to the hexagon proximities of types. The principle of consistency states that the more consistent persons are in their interests, the more predictable they are as to the occupation in which they will find success and satisfaction. Similarly, the concept of *differentiation,* that is, attaining clearly higher scores on some of these six scales than others, postulates that more differentiated people will be more predictable as to which kind of occupation they will choose and remain in. Conversely, the person who has a "flat profile," that is, undifferentiated, is one for whom no serious gambler would bet a lot of money in predicting that person's eventual career choice.

Holland's theoretical work led to the development of several unique assessment tools and interventions. He is perhaps best known for the Self-Directed Search (1985b), a career counseling intervention combining

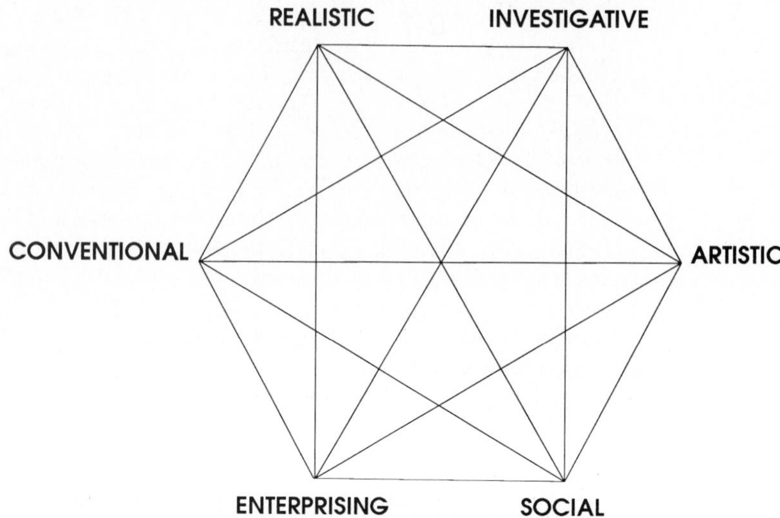

FIGURE 12–1 The RIASEC Model. A hexagonal model for defining the psychological resemblances among types and environments and their interactions. From John L. Holland, *Making Vocational Choices*, second edition (1985). Used by permission.

self-assessment and self-help. In fact, the Self-Directed Search (SDS) grew out of Holland's interest in providing a measure that would not only avoid the separate answer sheets and machine scoring of other vocational interest inventories but also would help students move *beyond* simply learning about themselves. His goal was to facilitate examinees' becoming involved in the "true reasoning" stage of decision making that Parsons (1909) had earlier identified as a critical step in effective vocational choice. In the past 20 years, Holland and his colleagues have refined this measure, which gauges occupational stereotypes and includes a variety of self-assessments such as competencies and occupational daydreams. By following the self-scoring directions, each person obtains a three-letter code representing his or her "personality type." The scores obtained are then used in conjunction with an occupational finder listing over 1000 occupations arranged according to various three-digit RIASEC codes. Notice that the matching concept is still present as in the trait and factor approach, but the match is now between the *environment* and the *personality* typology rather than between an identified skill needed in a job and the measured ability of a person. Equally important, each three-digit code represents numerous options.

The SDS is now one of the most widely administered inventories in career psychology, with hundreds of thousands of persons from age 15 to retirement taking the measure each year. The number of studies on the measure has increased almost geometrically over the past decade. Extensive studies of the hexagonal model have supported its validity (Brown, Brooks, & Associates 1990; Holland, 1985a); the SDS has been supported in hundreds of studies showing its effect on self-understanding, satisfaction with current choices, and the number of vocational possibilities being considered (Holland, 1985b).

Any theoretical viewpoint that attracts so much attention also attracts criticism. Readily acknowledged is the fact that although the hexagonal model contributes more to our understanding of vocational choices than the basic trait and factor approach, the theory does not readily explain how and why people develop the personality profiles reflected in their RIASEC codes. These topics are addressed by some of the other approaches explored later in this chapter.

In summary, we have provided a very brief introduction to the major concepts of Holland's productive approach. The concept that environments are best defined by looking at the people in them is one increasingly attended to by I/O psychologists in their work on "climate" (Schneider, 1987). The RIASEC model of person-environment fit is now being used to explain human behavior beyond the field of work, for example, in assessments of marital and family interactions (Bruch & Gilligan, 1980), and to explore the effectiveness of psychotherapy in treatment of problems such as depression and passivity (Mahalik, 1990). Also, Holland's emphasis on environment in understanding the dynamics of choice has helped others focus on the role of environmental constraints, especially their effect on the career choices and development of those who are not part of the mainstream of society (Gottfredson, 1986). (This issue is further elaborated below under sociological approaches.)

Super's Developmental Self-Concept Approach

> The process of career development is essentially that of developing and implementing self-concepts; it is a synthesizing and compromising process in which the self-concept is a product of the interaction of inherited aptitudes, physical make-up, opportunity to play various roles, and evaluations of the extent to which the results of roleplaying meet with the approval of superiors and fellows. (Super, 1984, p. 195)

Super, like Holland, became aware of the limitations of the trait and factor model, although he too recognized the validity of its matching aspects. Super's initial research and theorizing spans the beginning years of the profession of counseling psychology. During that time he was simultaneously immersing himself in the then emerging literature on developmental psychology and in Carl Rogers' phenomenological work on the self-concept. Drawing on his acquaintance with the developmental literature, he was able to address the very questions that Holland's theory and the trait and factor theory were poorly equipped to handle, that is, questions on how preferences develop. Super's application of developmental theory to career processes made clear the now somewhat obvious, but then less so, observation that vocational behavior varies according to our "developmental age." To capture the essence of such age changes, he first incorporated the work of occupational sociologists Miller and Form (1951). They outlined five stages of growth: childhood; exploration, or adolescence; establishment, or young adulthood; maintenance, or middle adulthood; and decline, or old age. Within each of these age periods, the critical question, according to Super, is, "What are the appropriate vocational behaviors for someone in this age-group?"

By the mid-1950s Super had developed longitudinal research projects to answer this question with empirical data. The concept that persons would engage in quite different vocational behaviors at different ages and that different behaviors would have more or less successful outcomes, developed into the concept of career maturity. If measures could be developed to assess how well an individual was filling appropriate age-related tasks, then one could come up with a vocational maturity quotient for individuals, determining how far below or beyond their chronological age they were in terms of vocational development. One of the most tangible results of Super's approach to career psychology has been the development of a variety of career maturity measures. Westbrook (1983) has reviewed the assets and liabilities of the measures of career maturity that have been developed in the past 20 years.

While there have been both philosophical and empirical debates about what constitutes career maturity, one critical finding did emerge from Super's investigation of what constituted career maturity among ninth-graders. From his massive study of biosocial, environmental, vocational, personality, and achievement factors, Super found that later adjustment in careers was predicted most clearly by what could be called planfulness during the ninth-grade years. Contrary to then prevailing concepts that ninth-graders who had decided what they wanted to do would have an advantage and be more successful later in life, it was found that the career decisions of ninth-graders were often poorly grounded and unstable: that is, they did not stay the same over time. The best predictor of later vocational adjustment was not having reached a decision, but rather being actively oriented toward gathering career-relevant information. The tremendous effects of these findings were summarized by Osipow (1983):

> Super suggested, based on such data, that the school curriculum should "foster planfulness" aimed at helping youngsters become aware of their level

> of occupational aspirations and the general amount of education required to achieve that level. This self-knowledge could be developed without specifically deciding on an occupational goal, which would be premature in the ninth grade. In fact, rather than restrict occupational choice possibilities at that age, the school should exert its efforts to broaden occupational perspectives and to teach the student to use available resources for exploration effectively. In this statement lie the roots of the Career Education movement. (p. 163)

We cannot emphasize enough what a radical concept this was in the 1960s. Our entire educational system had, for decades, been organized according to students choosing specific vocational and academic tracks by grade nine to get the best start on their future careers.

Super's work also addressed the process of vocational development through the incorporation of Rogers' views on how self-concept develops and changes. As a result, Super introduced the proposition that only when persons know themselves sufficiently well can they examine the opportunities available in their environments to find the roles that can implement their self-concepts. Note that, as in Holland's theory, "matching" occurs, but it is not between job requirements and abilities (trait and factor approach) or between personality and environment (Holland's approach). Rather the match is between how a person sees himself or herself and what kind of careers provide an opportunity for the individual to continue to be the way he or she is (or the way he or she wants to become if a change in self is desired.)

As one goes through life, self-concepts may change (most readers probably have a somewhat different concept of themselves than they had when 12 years old). As self-concepts change, career aspirations and choices may need to change to become more congruent. Changes in physical abilities, marital situation, or life values in the adult years serve as an impetus for looking at new kinds of vocational roles. Thus, Super's construct of self-concept implementation through career choice provides a major window through which to look at the process factors missing in the Holland and trait and factor approaches.

More recently, Super has begun looking at how vocational behaviors apply to other life roles, such as homemaker, citizen, and "leisurite," that is, a consumer of leisure-time activities. Studies of career patterns and development in other cultures, often initiated or led by Super, have helped him understand the applicability of the self-concept theory to these other life roles. These cross-cultural investigations have also led Super into an assessment of the different values that people in diverse societies and cultures have regarding various life roles. Part of his research now focuses on demonstrating the importance of *work salience,* that is, how much importance one gives to work as a role. Differences in how each person values work are beginning to be seen as a critical component in how and why people make different lifestyle and occupational decisions at various age levels.

The two approaches reviewed thus far have generated a great amount of research, much of which confirms their contribution to the understanding of both the content (Holland) and process (Super) of vocational development (Brown, Brooks, & Associates, 1990). We turn now to three other approaches that have had far less impact both conceptually and empirically but which help to explain the complexities of career-relevant behavior.

Krumboltz's Social Learning Approach

Krumboltz and his colleagues began a series of studies in the 1960s, the results of which have helped them to articulate a set of propositions describing career decision making (Krumboltz, Mitchell, & Jones, 1976) and the development of preferences. Drawing first on experimental analyses of behavior (Skinner, 1938), then upon Bandura's (1977) social learning theory, their theory extends beyond basic behavioral principles to explain how perceptions of interactions with the environment influence thinking and how that thinking influences subsequent behavior.

According to the propositions of Krumboltz and his colleagues, the interactions of four categories of factors influence career decisions: (1) genetic endowment and special abilities, including factors such as race, sex, physical appearance, intelligence, artistic ability, and so forth; (2) environmental conditions and events, such as number and nature of job opportunities; and social policies; (3) learning experiences; and (4) task-approach skills. We shall look first at how the social learning approach focuses on the last two categories and then at how those categories interact with the first two categories to shape career choices.

In the social learning approach, three major types of learning are identified. The first two are similar to the operant and classical conditioning models taught in introductory psychology. Here, *instrumental learning* experiences are identified as those that occur when one experiences a positive outcome for a behavior instead of being punished for its occurrence. According to the basic principles of behavior analysis, persons most often repeat those behaviors for which there are positive outcomes. For example, if one successfully completes a science project or a scouting merit badge, or receives praise for making one's own clothes, these behaviors are much more likely to be repeated. Conversely, if one is unable to complete a set of math problems or is ridiculed for how he or she dances, then these behaviors are much less likely to be repeated.

Associate learning is the term used to describe the associations developed between a neutral event or stimulus with an emotionally laden one, such as the classical conditioning of salivation to a bell in Pavlov's dogs. For example, if a youngster's only experience with plush furnishings comes from waiting in a dentist's office, he or she may decide that being a dentist is the way to achieve a comfortable life and, desiring such a life, choose dentistry as a career. This example may seem an oversimplification, but Krumboltz and his colleagues (1976) have documented numerous examples of pervasive generalizations that have resulted from the effect of a single stimulus or event. The latest television and film heroes, from lawyers to gymnasts to fighter pilots, often have a statistical impact on the number of applications to corresponding career-training programs. Conversely, and just as importantly, if school, for example, is an unpleasant experience, teaching is unlikely to be one's chosen profession.

The third kind of learning that needs to be considered in developing career preferences is *vicarious learning*. New behaviors and skills can be learned simply by observing the behaviors of others through media such as books, movies, and television. Think of how one dance after another has spread throughout the country because of its display on television. Or more specifically in regard to career developments, Krumboltz and his colleagues (1976) have shown that students can learn how to obtain occupational information simply by observing someone else go through the process. Relatedly, as part of counselor training, watching someone else conduct counseling interviews can provide some valuable vicarious learning.

Is it simply a few critical learning experiences that shape career decisions? One of the major contributions of *social learning* theory, as compared to orthodox experimental analysis of behavior, is its attention to the mental processes involved in how humans generalize their experience. It is these generalizations that have the greatest impact on choices. In other words, through generalization, the results of a few experiences can lead someone to expect the same results from a broad class of similar experiences.

Mitchell and Krumboltz (1984) describe three sets of generalizations specific to the social learning approach to career development. They speak of self-observation generalizations, worldview generalizations, and task-approach skills. By self-observation generalizations, they refer to the statements persons make to themselves based on their previous experiences. That is, the experiences each person has lead to generalizations about whether or not he or she can do something (task efficacy) and from those generalizations to generalizations about what one's interests and values are. Someone unskilled at fixing a bike, compared to a friend who is adept at it, might well conclude that he or she has neither mechanical skills nor interests. These generalized self-observations are very similar to the self-concept that Super talks about as a critical factor in career choice.

The worldview generalization in the social learning model is simply this same kind of generalization extended to the environment. Based on the three kinds of learning just described, certain assumptions are made about various careers; that is, stereotypes of careers are developed. (It is these stereotypes which form the basis of Holland's theory. Thus, the self-observation and worldview generalizations provide a direct connection between the social learning approach and Super's and Holland's theories.)

The task-approach skills outlined by Krumboltz and his colleagues (1976) are perhaps the most unusual feature of their theory. These concepts go beyond some of the specifications of social learning theory to help explain the choice and action phases central to vocational behavior and development. In task-approach skills one can see the interactions among learning environments, genetic components, and environmental influences. Most basically, the opportunity for certain kinds of learning experiences is shaped by both environmental influences and genetic endowment factors. Short persons do not have many opportunities for outstanding success as basketball players. On the other hand, the many very tall people in the Masai Mara territory in Kenya also do not have much opportunity for successful basketball playing experiences; in the former case it is a matter of genetic reasons and in the latter, environmental. To give an example more closely related to career development and choice, it is not extraordinary to find a previously successful dental student with such poor spatial relationship skills that he or she fails dentistry school laboratory courses and is forced to make a new career choice even though prior instrumental (academic courses) and associative learning experiences (remember the plush office) led the person for 23 years to expect to be a dentist!

Considerable literature from both experimental and survey studies support the significance of the three different kinds of learning. Recent studies show even more clearly how the results of self-observation generalizations, worldview generalizations, and task-approach skills affect career decisions (Betz & Hackett, 1981; Fassinger, 1985).

The social learning approach is also uniquely beneficial in explaining deficits in career development. Mitchell and Krumboltz (1984) list six reasons for the development of self- and worldview observations that lead to inappropriate choices, or even more often, to avoidance of making a decision or choice that could lead to more satisfying results: "(1) drawing faulty generalizations ('I'm the only person in my class who is afraid of public speaking'), (2) making self-comparisons with a single standard ('I'm not as warm as Carl Rogers, so I could never be a counselor'), (3) exaggerating the estimates of the emotional impact of an outcome ('If I don't succeed in business school I just couldn't stand it'), (4) drawing false causal relationships ('To get ahead, you just have to be in the right place at the right time'), (5) being ignorant of relevant facts ('High school English teachers spend their day helping eager students to appreciate the finer points of literature') and (6) giving undue weight to low probability events ('I wouldn't accept a job in California because it's going to fall into the ocean during the next earthquake')" (p. 266).

Krumboltz and his colleagues identify at least three therapeutic strategies particularly well suited to changing these various kinds of inappropriate beliefs. In his development of rational emotive therapy, Ellis (1970) refers to irrational beliefs; Beck (1976), in his development of cognitive therapy, refers to inaccurate or dysfunctional beliefs; Meichenbaum (1977) applies cognitive behavior modification strategies to what he calls stress- and anxiety-producing beliefs. Keller, Biggs, and Gysbers (1982) succinctly explain how each of these therapeutic approaches can be used for helping clients with inappropriate career-related beliefs.

In summary, the social learning approach has helped specify a number of behavioral processes. The approach is particularly strong in describing how an individual arrives at a particular choice. The next approach reviewed also has this focus but from a very different theoretical perspective.

Psychodynamic Approaches

Each of the three approaches reviewed thus far has drawn on a major theoretical framework in psychology: Holland on the personality-environment interaction, Super on developmental models, Krumboltz on social learning. The fourth approach to career psychology we shall explore is derived from yet another psychological theory—Freudian analytic or, more broadly, psychodynamic theory. While career-related theory and research is less extensive for this approach than for the other three, it does, in many ways, complement them and may, like social learning theory, be uniquely helpful in explaining some of the problems in career development.

There are two major theorists who should be included within the scope of psychodynamic approaches to career psychology. Both Bordin (1968) and Roe (1956) have written books describing their dynamic views of counseling and including studies specifically related to vocational behavior. Both of these writers use the psychodynamic concept that all persons have basic innate needs to be satisfied and that what people choose to do in work, in play, and in interpersonal relationships is a result of how successful their early childhood experiences were in gratifying those needs. To the extent that one's needs are unsatisfied or were satisfied in inappropriate ways, one will become fixated on those unmet needs and make inappropriate choices in adult life while seeking satisfaction.

Bordin and Roe have each focused on different kinds of needs in their extension of dynamic theory to vocational development. Bordin has stayed close to the Freudian developmental scheme with its oral, anal, and phallic stages. In researching representative occupations of the three stages, he and his colleagues distinguished, for example, social workers (oral—nurturing and telling are key activities), accountants (anal—retaining money is a key activity), and plumbers (phallic—fitting male and female pipe ends together). They were able to confirm a number of hypotheses about the kinds of early events and experiences and types of interactions with parents that each of the three groups would have in accordance with the concept that unsatisfied needs in these stages would determine career choice.

Roe found more congenial Maslow's (1954) hierarchy of needs, ranging from the most basic physiological and safety needs through the higher-order needs for beauty and self-actualization. Lower-order needs are seen as more potent, if not satisfied, and so strongest in driving adult behavior. Focusing on the child-parent interaction, Roe also deviated from more traditional analytic theory, seeking to examine whether parents' concentration on, acceptance of, or rejection of their children would have predictable results on how children chose occupations, that is, deciding to work with people as compared to things.

Osipow (1983) has provided one of the best reviews of the research supporting the propositions of each of these writers. Conducting any research in the psychodynamic approaches is extremely difficult. The concepts are not easily defined in concrete terms; much of the data collected must be retrospective, that is, culled from what investigators ask adults to remember about their early childhood experiences and their relationships with their parents. Added to these problems is the fact that the results obtained from such studies have typically been inconclusive. For every study yielding significant results, another yields contradictory or nonconfirming data or no significant group differences.

Following the work of Bordin and Roe, other researchers have focused on the psychodynamic concept of identification and its relation to career development. Identification used in this way refers to the desire to be like the person identified with. Identification of a person with one's mother or father has been examined as a component of career preferences and choices. Osipow has also reviewed the more extensive literature in this area, literature that yields modest evidence to support the concept that stronger identification with the father can result in choices for more traditionally masculine professions and stronger identification with the mother for more traditionally feminine professions. Although there is considerable concern in current times about labeling any profession as masculine or feminine, these results may simply indicate the complex factors entailed in persons' entering non-traditional professions (e.g., women choosing engineering, men choosing nursing).

Despite problems of design and inconclusive results, which have limited the role psychodynamic research has had in advancing the field of career psychology, the approach does illuminate problems of misorientation in vocational development. For clients completely unable to make career decisions or who find themselves persisting in careers, or related coursework, that provide no satisfaction (and possibly much frustration), the counselor might successfully explore the possibility of fixations on certain need gratifications and/or problems such as guilt and disappointment related to identification with family, for example, parents or siblings.

Interestingly, to conclude our brief discussion of four psychological approaches to the study of career development, we signal the role that the "self" plays in each. In the dynamic approach just reviewed, the "unaware" self is what is driving the choice of behaviors; in the social learning approach the generalized self-view is a major factor in choices; in Super's developmental approach, choices represent an implementation of the self-concept; in Holland's person-environment perspective, the person's view of himself or herself in one of the six profiles is the determinant. In the final approach to be reviewed, emphasis shifts from the self to the environment.

Sociological Approaches to Career Development

In the last several decades it has become clear to psychologists, especially in studying vocational adjustment of workers, that a broader interdisciplinary perspective is necessary. In this brief section we identify the major sociological concepts that are needed to complement the psychological perspective in understanding career choice and adjustment.

"The sociological approach is fundamentally based on the notion that elements beyond the individual's control exert a major influence on the course of life, including educational and vocational decisions. Supporters of this view suggest that the degree of freedom of occupational choice a person has is far less than might at first be assumed and that one's self-expectations are not independent of the society's expectations" (Osipow, 1983, p. 225). Osipow includes, in his perspective the "chance" approach to career development, that is, being in the right place at the right time. What he notes, most interestingly, is that although both psychologists and sociologists will acknowledge that chance plays some part in a given decision, "the psychologists are likely to be annoyed with chance variables and ignore them if possible while sociologists are more likely to be interested in the phenomena of chance and study it" (p. 226).

The other approaches we have reviewed seem, at least implicitly, to assume an open occupational system, that is, one in which persons are able to choose any occupation for which they have the appropriate interests and abilities. Both sociologists and psychologists have often focused on the role of ability in career psychology and sought to determine whether or not our society is a true meritocracy in which all persons can advance according to their ability. Sociologists have and continue to gather evidence to the contrary about the openness and the meritocratic aspects of the workplace in American society. Osipow (1983) and Hotchkiss and Borow (1984) review considerable research showing that factors such as socioeconomic class, gender, and race have a significant impact on what choices will be made and what positions and earnings will be achieved *even when ability levels are the same.* More specifically, evidence continues to appear that women and minorities typically earn less when having the same training and ability as white males. These findings underpin, of course, many of the current cases regarding discrimination, affirmative action, and pay equity.

Even among white males, the research findings indicate the strong effect of a father's socioeconomic class on the occupational choices and attainments of sons (much more so than daughters). Some of this influence is direct, as in the case where a son inherits a family business. Another direct influence is seen in rural or isolated areas with a single predominant employer, such as mining or manufacturing of a particular sort. In such locations, there is a much greater probability that sons will enter their father's occupation. Of perhaps greatest importance are the indirect effects evident in parents' socioeconomic class on the educational opportunities and attainments of their children. There is, of course, considerable evidence in this country that education is *the* major factor in occupational mobility and advancement. Consequently, anything affecting the amount of education one obtains affects eventual occupational choice and attainment. Higher socioeconomic status not only provides the funds for more advanced education but also has at least indirect, if not direct, effects on the attitudes that children have toward education. Parents who themselves have not had higher education may be living in areas where neither they nor their peers see much value in education. For children who grow up in communities where 90 percent of the students go to college there is a high differential probability of their attending college even when their ability levels are essentially identical to those of children in another community where less than 50 percent of the students go to college. In short, socioeconomic class plays a large role in the opportunity structure, a role that may override ability, interest, and personality variables.

Furthermore, considering critical influences in vocational behavior in the adult working years, sociologists also present quite different sets of data than psychologists. Hotchkiss and Borow (1984) review the long series of studies by Kohn and his colleagues which look at whether psychological functioning affects job choices or whether job choices influence employees' psychological functioning. Remember, from Super's viewpoint, persons seek jobs that will implement their self-concepts. Theoretically, persons change jobs to find a better implementation of the self-concept. Kohn and his colleagues, however, have concluded that the direction of influence works in the opposite way, that is: "the job exerts a stronger contemporaneous affect on the psychological variable than the psychological variable exerted on the nature of the job" (Hotchkiss & Borow, p. 159). Because psychologists and sociologists usually work from their own disciplinary frames of reference, their approaches have seemed almost mutually exclusive—explanations for career choice had to be either sociological or psychological. With advances in computer programs for more complex statistical analyses and in what is called sequential modeling analyses, the time has clearly come for both psychologists and sociologists to conduct studies of career development that include both personal and environmental variables. From such studies investigators will be able to ascertain, first, whether they are really looking at different variables or simply the same phenomena with different names, and, second, how these variables, if different, each contribute to the variance in career behaviors.

We previously noted that race and gender were major sociological factors in career development. Much of these data have only recently received significant attention from counseling psychologists. Almost all of the first four theoretical approaches reviewed were developed largely through the study of white males, the primary population in career paths and in higher education. Because of rapid changes in contemporary culture in the number of ethnic minorities and women entering higher education and the workforce, it is essential that we provide a brief overview of some of the major trends in the emerging literature.

CAREER PSYCHOLOGY AND GENDER

Betz and Fitzgerald (1987) have reviewed 25 years of literature on the changing work roles of women in America. Since World War II, the percentage of working women in the United States has increased threefold; the percentage of working mothers has increased tenfold. The earliest research in the career psychology of women focused on (1) differences in men's and women's interests, and (2) the factors that went into a woman's decision to choose between homemaking and combining homemaking and a career (choosing "career only" was not even offered as an option in many of these early studies).

Differences in men's and women's interests that existed in the 1930s and 1950s, when the major interest inventories were developed, resulted in measures that did not include scores for women for occupations such as senior C.P.A., real estate sales person, or psychiatrist. By the mid-1970s a debate raged about whether interest measures were sex-biased (the preferred term now is *gender-biased*—see Zunker, 1986) and whether different forms and/or scoring techniques could eliminate that bias. The debate was most instructive as to what constitutes bias as well as to the limits of empirical approaches and statistical methods in solving emotionally charged issues. While many interest measures were changed to eliminate clear instances of bias, most of the measures could only update their database. Recall, for example, that the Strong Interest Inventory is constructed by comparing an individual's inventory responses to the interests of people already in the field. How does one compare a woman's responses to a profession such as funeral director if indeed there are no female funeral directors to compare them to? Is it adequate to compare her responses to her male counterparts? Until recently, similar problems applied for men as well, there being very few male flight attendants or male nurses, for example. The various interest inventories incorporate in diverse ways continuing gender differences in interest patterns. Only time can tell whether the changes seen in men's and women's work roles in the last few decades will finally reflect increasing similarity in men's and women's interests.

The rate of change in women's aspirations and expectations is discouraging to some. Betz and Fitzgerald (1987) cite the long and continuing list of studies that show that males and females, from preschool through the college years and on into adulthood, have highly differentiated views about what are "women's" occupations and what are "men's." These stereotypes, promulgated in media from school textbooks to television ads, are probably the major factor in the small number of women who enter what are called the nontraditional professions, for example, in engineering and the sciences. Much of the research of the past 15 years has been devoted to understanding what factors encourage women's interests in such careers, thereby overcoming the stereotypes that still emerge in the kindergarten years. Betz and Fitzgerald's (1987) book presents a succinct review of factors that have been found to facilitate women's career development. Many of the factors they list—for example, attending same-sex schools, androgynous upbringing—have not been found to influence men's choices. Farmer (1985) and others have been designing theories of career development that incorporate these kinds of factors. Farmer's model perhaps is the least complicated in specifying that one needs to look at three sets of interacting influences: background variables such as gender and ethnicity, psychological variables such as self-concept and attitudes, and environmental variables such as availability of role models and support from family. Betz (1989) provides some provocative perspectives on environmental variables in her presentation of the "null environment hypothesis," showing how the lack of a supportive educational environment results in fewer opportunities for women than for men. That is, given men and women of the same above-average ability level but who both receive no encouragement to go to college, a higher proportion of the men are likely to attend college.

A final issue that clearly differentiates women's career choice and adjustment relates to the choices women must make about whether and how to manage both a career and a family. From the 1950s to 1980s instead of analyzing what factors influence the choice of either homemaking or career, studies increasingly examined how women manage careers and family roles simultaneously. Gilbert's (1987) review of studies of dual-career families and Betz and Fitzgerald's (1987) work on the interface of work and home are particularly instructive:

> Women who work appear to be at a psychological advantage compared to their non-working counterparts, particularly when they work because they wish to do so. This advantage translates into increased power and influence in their marital relationships and into higher levels of self-esteem. Although the home-work interface appears to be quite difficult to negotiate, particularly when there are children involved, there is little evidence that husbands and children of working wives suffer any deleterious effects. . . . Working women do indeed work very hard, and they retain a great majority of the household and childcare tasks performed by their counterparts who do not engage in paid employment. Although the research on coping suggests that attempts to meet all expectations at home and work (i.e., the superwoman syndrome) is not healthy for women, many do engage in this pattern. (pp. 208–209)

The continuing issues of child care and part-time work and how they affect both men's and women's advancement in careers will probably be a major focus of research studies in the 1990s.

CAREER PSYCHOLOGY AND RACE

Some of the findings we have just discussed regarding women apply to racial and ethnic minorities as well. Just as preschool children have strong sex stereotypes about jobs, there is evidence that elementary school children from racial and ethnic minorities already differentiate among careers that are appropriate or inappropriate for them (Frost & Diamond, 1979). These stereotypes may be shared by teachers and counselors, who wittingly or not influence the students' choices at all levels.

An increase in the number of studies of women's career development in the past couple of decades has been accompanied by a slight, even if much slower increase, in the number of studies of the career development of racial/ethnic minorities. Despite the broad range of topics studied, such as vocational aspiration and realism, career maturity, attitudes toward work, and validity of interest measures, the results of such studies remain surprisingly inconclusive. It seems that for every study that finds racial and ethnic group differences on these variables, another study finds no significant differences. However, both Osipow (1983) and Smith (1983) note that most of these studies have confounded race and socioeconomic levels so that the inconclusiveness may be due to variations in samples. Until adequate controls are made for socioeconomic background and educational level, investigators will probably continue to find contradictory results when making racial and ethnic comparisons. What is most clear for racial/ethnic minorities, as for women, is that the attainment of higher levels of education does not reap the same reward in terms of salaries earned or opportunities for promotion (Updegrave, 1989). Indeed, those factors clearly suggest that career opportunities are not based on a pure meritocracy but rather that factors like gender and class have a significant impact.

It is these limits to opportunities that Smith notes reduce the validity of many of the career theories discussed in this chapter. All but the sociological approaches at least implicitly assume that one is free to choose a career that is congruent with one's personality, that implements self-concept, or that satisfies basic drives. To the extent that economic factors such as recession reduce the number of available jobs, all persons are affected, but minority groups especially. In times of recession, unemployment rates rise faster for minority than for nonminority persons. Equally limiting for those from disadvantaged backgrounds, primarily the racial and ethnic minorities in this country, is the reduction in opportunities to complete high school and to pay for a college education. As noted earlier, education, in today's technological society, is one of the major factors in establishing career mobility. Those from disadvantaged backgrounds are particularly handicapped in having "freedom of choice."

Smith (1983) also discusses the implications of the emerging underclass in today's society for the issues of career psychology: "The emergence of the underclass as a permanent fixture of our nation's social structure represents one of the most significant class developments in the past two decades. Its existence challenges the cherished American belief that one can pull oneself up by one's bootstraps, if only one has enough motivation, enough drive" (p. 164). As a specific illustration of this problem, she describes Raspberry's (1981) report of a project where employers were offered total reimbursement for wages paid to disadvantaged youths who had gone through a training program. Less than one in five of the employers wanted to consider taking these youths as employees. "It seems clear that employers tended to see the youngsters as not worthwhile, even when no money was involved. On the other hand, 80% of those who did participate found the youths' work habits, attitudes and willingness to work average or better; three fourths found their performance improving over time and two thirds said the young workers required no more supervision than they had originally anticipated" (p. 30). Past studies of workers who have been in traditional careers or who have graduated from institutions of higher education have not provided the theories or concepts needed to understand the difficulty of the long-term unemployed and the working poor, many of whom come from disadvantaged ethnic and racial backgrounds.

Further study is needed of the patterns of career choices of various racial/ethnic groups. Larger proportions of Asian-Americans choose science careers than any other racial group; blacks and Hispanics choose education and social sciences in larger numbers, and degrees in engineering and the sciences in lower numbers, than whites and Asian-Americans. Given that career choices of the blacks and Hispanic groups are among the lowest paid in today's society, their opportunities for economic gain and advancement are all the more limited. Do these patterns of choice reflect subjective preference or externally imposed expectations? As national efforts have been mounting to expand the nontraditional career choices of women, increasing interest is being shown in the career horizons of racial minorities. Perhaps the greatest challenge for career psychologists is to determine how both women and racial and ethnic minorities can gain access to the full range of careers commensurate with their abilities, with equitable opportunities for promotion and economic reward.

SUMMARY

Career psychology is perhaps one of the oldest and most central components of counseling psychology. The most distinctive theoretical and empirical contributions counseling psychology has made to psychology are in the area of career development. The robustness of career psychology as a field of research and practice for nearly one hundred years (Borgen, 1984) is no doubt related to the implications of career psychology for both individual and societal well-being. Career adjustment is important for both the mental and physical health of individuals as well as for the economic and social health of a society.

The major part of this chapter was devoted to the presentation of four approaches to the study of career psychology. The first was Holland's six-part RIASEC model, built upon the earliest matching approach in career psychology, known as the trait and factor approach. By shifting the focus from a match between persons' abilities and job requirements to the congruence of persons' assessment of themselves with the actual job environment, Holland has been able to show how incorporation of person-environment models significantly enhances the accuracy of predictions about people's career choices and whether they stay in those careers. Currently, investigations of the applicability of this model continue, for every age from junior high through the retirement years.

Super drew on mid-20th century concepts in both developmental psychology and Rogers' theory of personality in formulating his developmental approach to career psychology. Shifting the focus from what the choice will be to *how* the choice is made led him to theorize that persons seek careers that implement their self-concept and keep or change jobs depending on the extent to which they implement their self-concept. Moreover, by emphasizing developmental processes, Super made a unique contribution in identifying what kinds of career-relevant processes should be occurring at various ages. Instruments were developed to assess completion of developmental and corresponding career maturity at the different levels. Through longitudinal studies, Super was able to identify the processes in adolescence which lead to more effective career adjustments in the adult years. His findings radically altered the nature of career interventions for young adolescents.

Using the social learning approach, Krumboltz and his colleagues continued to focus on the processes of how choices are made. By incorporating basic principles of learning and generalization, the social learning approach explains how a career-relevant self-concept develops. This model has been especially useful in examining misorientation in career development, that is, how various mistaken beliefs lead to unsatisfactory vocational choices. The specificity of the model is particularly helpful in devising interventions to rectify inappropriate notions that affect career choice.

Psychodynamic approaches to career psychology are far less developed both empirically and conceptually than the other three psychological approaches described. The difficulty in conducting research in psychodynamic models and in linking early life experiences with adult career-related behavior makes the psychodynamic approach one of the most difficult with which to work. However, like the social learning approach, psychodynamic approaches are particularly useful in explaining why clients often seem "stuck" in maintaining poorly adjusted career behaviors. As will be seen in the next chapter on career interventions, psychodynamic approaches may be particularly useful for helping individuals understand those blocks that keep them from making appropriate and satisfying decisions.

The sociological approach stands in contrast to the psychological models of career psychology. The sociological approach stresses that factors other than psychological ones may be of immense importance in career-related decisions. Even more critically, in contrast to psychologists' view that jobs are chosen and kept to be congruent with or to satisfy psychological conditions, the sociological data suggest that staying in jobs is the result of people's changing psychological aspects of themselves. Or, stated more boldly, when there is job dissatisfaction, effective solutions are possibly found in helping clients change themselves to fit the job instead of in changing jobs to better fit the client's self.

The second major contribution of the sociological approach is that it calls attention to the various factors such as gender and race that moderate relationships between psychological variables and career behaviors. Recent data show the limitations of existing theories and studies when applied to women and ethnic/racial groups. Theories must be developed and studies conducted that will assist both women and racial and ethnic minorities in gaining access to the full range of career opportunities commensurate with their abilities.

References

Astin, A. W. (1987). *American freshmen: 20 year trends, 1966–1985.* Los Angeles: Higher Education Research Institute, University of California.

Bandura, A. (1977). *Social learning theory.* Englewood Cliffs, NJ: Prentice-Hall.

Beck, A. T. (1976). *Cognitive theory and the emotional disorders.* New York: International University Press.

Betz, N. E. (1989). Implications of the null environment for women's career development and for counseling psychology. *The Counseling Psychologist, 17,* 136–144.

Betz, N. E., & Fitzgerald, L. F. (1987). *The career psychology of women.* Orlando, FL: Academic Press.

Betz, N. E., & Hackett, G. (1981). The relationships of career-related self-efficacy expectations to perceived career options in college women and men. *Journal of Counseling Psychology, 28,* 399–410.

Bordin, E. S. (1946). Diagnosis in counseling and psychotherapy. *Educational and Psychological Measurement, 6,* 169–184.

Bordin, E. S. (1968). *Psychological counseling* (2nd ed.). New York: Appleton-Century-Crofts.

Borgen, F. H. (1984). Counseling psychology. *Annual Review of Psychology, 35,* 579–604.

Brammer, L. M., & Shostrom, E. L. (1982). *Therapeutic psychology* (4th ed.). Englewood Cliffs, NJ: Prentice-Hall.

Brown, D., Brooks, L., & Associates (1984). *Career choice and development.* San Francisco: Jossey-Bass.

Brown, D., Brooks, L., & Associates (1990). *Career choice and development* (2nd ed.). San Francisco: Jossey-Bass.

Bruch, M. A., & Gilligan, J. F. (1980). Extension of Holland's theory to assessment of marital and family interaction. *American Mental Health Counselors Association Journal, 2*(2), 71–82.

Crites, J. O. (1969). *Vocational psychology.* New York: McGraw-Hill.

Crites, J. O. (1978). Career maturity inventory. Monterey, CA: CTV/McGraw-Hill.

Crites, J. O. (1981). *Career counseling: Models, methods, and materials.* New York: McGraw-Hill.

Ellis, A. (1970). *The essence of rational psychotherapy: A comprehensive approach to treatment.* New York: Institute for Rational Living.

Erikson, E. (1950). *Childhood and society.* New York: Norton.

Erikson, E. (1959). Identity and the life cycle. *Psychology Issues, 1* (entire issue).

Farmer, H. S. (1985). Model of career and achievement motivation for women and men. *Journal of Counseling Psychology, 22,* 363–390.

Fassinger, R. E. (1985). A causal model of career choice in college women. *Journal of Vocational Behavior, 27,* 123–153.

Frost, F., & Diamond, E. E. (1979). Ethnic and sex differences in occupational stereotyping by elementary school children. *Journal of Vocational Behavior, 15,* 43–54.

Gilbert, L., & Rachlin, V. (1987). Mental health and psychological functioning of dual-career families. *The Counseling Psychologist, 15,* 7–49.

Gottfredson, L. S. (1986). Special groups and the beneficial use of vocational interest inventories. In W. B. Walsh & S. H. Osipow (Eds.), *Advances in vocational psychology.* Hillsdale, NJ: Erlbaum.

Greenhaus, J. H., & Parasuraman, S. (1986). Vocational and organizational behavior, 1985: A review. *Journal of Vocational Behavior, 29,* 115–176.

Holland, J. L. (1977). *Manual for the Vocational Preference Inventory.* Palo Alto, CA: Consulting Psychologists Press.

Holland, J. L. (1985a). *Making vocational choices: A theory of vocational personalities and work environments.* Englewood Cliffs, NJ: Prentice Hall.

Holland, J. L. (1985b). *The Self-Directed Search Professional Manual.* Odessa, FL: Psychological Assessment Resources.

Hotchkiss, L., & Borow, H. (1984). Sociological perspectives on career choice and attainment. In D. Brown & L. Brooks (Eds.), *Career choice and development* (pp. 192–234). San Francisco: Jossey-Bass.

Keller, K. E., Biggs, D. A., & Gysbers, N. C. (1982). Career counseling from a cognitive perspective. *Personnel and Guidance Journal, 60,* 367–370.

Krumboltz, J. D., Mitchell, A. M., & Jones, G. B. (1976). A social learning theory of career selection. *The Counseling Psychologist, 6*(1), 71–80.

Lewin, K. (1935). *A dynmamic theory of personality: Selected papers.* New York: McGraw-Hill.

Linton, R. (1945). *The cultural background of personality.* New York: Century.

Loftquist, L. H., & Dawis, R. V. (1984). Research on work adjustment and satisfaction: Implications for career counseling. In S. D. Brown & R. W. Lent (Eds.), *Handbook of Counseling Psychology* (pp. 216–237). New York: Wiley.

Mahalik, J. (1990). Holland's RIASEC model as a predictor of counseling process. Unpublished doctoral dissertation, University of Maryland, College Park.

Maslow, A. H. (1954). *Motivation and personality.* New York: Harper & Row.

Meichenbaum, D. (1977). *Cognitive behavior modification,* Morristown, NJ: General Learning Press.

Miller, D. C., & Form, W. H. (1951). *Industrial sociology.* New York: Harper & Row.

Mitchell, L. K., & Krumboltz, J. D. (1984). Social learning approaches to career decision making. In S. Brown & L. Brooks (Eds.), *Career choice and development* (pp. 235–280). San Francisco: Jossey-Bass.

Myers, R. A. (1986). Research on educational and vocational counseling. In S. L. Garfield & A. E. Bergin (Eds.), *Handbook of psychotherapy and behavior change* (pp. 715–738). New York: Wiley.

Osipow, S. H. (1983). *Theories of career development* (3rd ed.). Englewood Cliffs, NJ: Prentice-Hall.

Osipow, S. H., Walsh, W. B., & Tosi, D. J. (1980). *A survey of counseling methods.* Homewood, IL: Dorsey Press.

Palmore, E. (1969). Predicting longevity. *The Gerontologist, 9,* 247–250.

Parsons, F. (1909). *Choosing a vocation.* Boston: Houghton Mifflin.

Raspberry, W. (1981). Employers ignore young urban blacks. *Buffalo Evening News,* June 25, 1981. (Syndicated column, *Washington Post*).

Robinson, F. P. (1961). *Effective Study* (Rev. ed.). New York: Harper.

Roe, A. (1956). *The psychology of occupations.* New York: Wiley.

Schein, E. H. (1982). Increasing organizational effectiveness through better human resource planning and development. In R. Katz (Ed.), *Career issues in human resource management.* Englewood Cliffs, NJ: Prentice-Hall.

Schneider, B. (1987). The people make the place. *Personnel Psychology, 40,* 437–453.

Skinner, B. F. (1938). *The behavior of organisms: An experimental analysis.* New York: Appleton.

Slaney, R. B., & Russell, J. E. A. (1987). Perspectives on vocational behavior, 1986: A review. *Journal of Vocational Behavior, 31,* 111–123.

Smith, E. J. (1983). Issues in racial minorities' career behavior. In W. B. Walsh & S. H. Osipow (Eds.), *Handbook of vocational psychology* (Vol. 1, pp. 161–222). Hillsdale, NJ: Erlbaum.

Super, D. E. (1957). *The Psychology of Careers.* New York: Harper.

Super, D. E. (1980). A life-span, life-space, approach to career development. *Journal of Vocational Behavior, 16,* 282–298.

Super, D. E. (1984). Career and life development. In S. Brown & L. Brooks (Eds.), *Career Choice and Development* (pp. 192–234). San Francisco: Jossey-Bass.

Updegrace, W. L. (1989, December). Race and money. *Money,* pp. 152–172.

Walsh, W. B., & Osipow, S. H. (1983). *Handbook of vocational psychology* (Vols. 1–2). Hillsdale, NJ: Erlbaum.

Westbrook, B. W. (1983). Career maturity: The concept, the instrument, and the research. In W. B. Walsh & S. H. Osipow (Eds.), *Handbook of vocational psychology* (Vol. 1, pp. 263–303). Hillsdale, NJ: Erlbaum.

Zunker, B. G. (1986). *Career counseling: Applied concepts of life planning.* Monterey, CA: Brooks/Cole.

Chapter 13

Career Counseling and Career Interventions

When work is a pleasure, life is a joy;
when work is duty, life is slavery.

—Maxim Gorki

In this chapter we shall see how Parsons' (1909) vocational guidance for adolescent boys in the early 1900s has now been expanded to career counseling and career intervention procedures for almost everyone, ages 5 to 75. We use the two terms *career counseling* and *career intervention* primarily to avoid the implicit limitations of the more traditional term *career counseling.* Most people think of counseling as a one-to-one interaction or, at most, small-group counseling. Yet research and program developments of the last 30 years have shown that career development can be facilitated and enhanced by a broad range of interventions, ranging from a highly structured set of classroom activities to a computer program to an individualized relationship that is essentially indistinguishable from personal counseling. Thus we join Myers (1986) in using the term *career interventions* to cover this broad range; the term *interventions,* of course, subsumes traditional individual or small-group career counseling.

The theories of career development reviewed in the last chapter have all had a great impact on how career counseling and career interventions have developed. Despite theoretical variations, almost all interventions include components to enhance participants' knowledge of self, knowledge of the world of work, and decision-making processes for combining these two areas of knowledge. To understand better both the diversity and commonalities of career interventions, we will first examine three types, each based on a different theoretical model but each incorporating the three components noted above. First we will describe a computerized version of career exploration for college students based on Super's developmental model. Then we will present a structured group counseling program based on Holland's model as it applies to a group of middle-aged, high-school-educated employees who have recently lost their jobs. Finally, we will examine psychodynamically oriented individual career counseling with a 35-year-old administrative assistant seeking "to get out of a rut" she has "failed to escape" in the last ten years.

Following these illustrations, we review the research evidence showing the significant impact of diverse career interventions, which a research procedure called meta-analysis has determined sometimes exceeds that of personal counseling. The final section of this chapter highlights the ever-increasing range of career counseling and intervention activities engaged in by counseling psychologists in kindergarten and elementary schools, in high schools and colleges, in hospitals, in rehabilitation centers, in career development centers, and in employee assistance programs in business and industry.

CAREER INTERVENTIONS: THREE ILLUSTRATIONS

We have chosen examples not only for their diverse theoretical origins but also for the diversity of settings and modalities they illustrate, including a college counseling center, an employee assistance program, and independent practice (setting) and an interactive computerized career guidance system, structured group counseling, and individualized personal counseling (modalities). Though three theoretical models in three settings with three different modalities are described, it is important to note that almost all of the examples are interchangeable. There are counseling centers, employee assistance programs, and independent practices that offer computerized, structured group, and individual counseling. A client may take part in any one or possibly two or three of these services depending on the presenting problems.

Group and individual approaches to career counseling can easily be adapted to fit any of the theories reviewed in the previous chapter. Crites (1981) provides a useful schema for identifying the methods and tools used in these diverse theoretical approaches to career counseling. Computerized approaches have also been developed for a variety of theoretical models. Zunker (1986) provides an excellent brief review of nine different computerized approaches; we describe only one of them here. The fundamental components of most of these systems are essentially similar.

DISCOVER: A Computerized Career Guidance System

In the early 1960s, even while computers were in their infancy, at least in the public's eye, some career counselors foresaw their immense value in addressing all three components of career counseling: gaining information about oneself, gaining information about the world of work, and putting those two together in making some decision. Especially valuable was the computer's huge memory base for dealing with information on the world of work. Filled with books on the various occupations, counselors' libraries still do not provide much detailed information on the more than 20,000 careers available in today's society. Computers could also assist individuals in using information about themselves (e.g., abilities and interests) to identify which of these careers are suitable. Able to sort multiple parameters in just milliseconds, computers can handle the almost limitless number of permutations produced through combinations of interests, abilities, values, and experience. The computer career guidance systems such as DISCOVER incorporate both self-assessment and interactive sections that help students and clients increase and organize information about themselves and at the same time teach them strategies for using that information in identifying occupations to consider.

Like all the computerized career guidance systems, DISCOVER is a program that can be used almost totally on one's own or in conjunction with the help of a counselor. Career counselors can have the program available on a personal computer to be used on a "sign-up" basis just as one might use the PC-ROM unit in a college library for computerized bibliographic searches. Most counseling psychologists prefer to have some initial contact with career clients to ensure that they have concerns appropriate for the use of computer-assisted career guidance. For example, a person who comes in knowing that he very much wants to be an artist but whose parents want him to be a physician is not going to find much help in a computerized approach. On the other hand, the client who has no firm ideas about what careers might be attractive is an ideal candidate for using the DISCOVER program as a way to identify and explore alternatives. Once a set of alternatives has been identified, the counselor can help the client plan strategies for further exploration and decision making.

DISCOVER now includes nine modules for college students: (1) beginning the career journey, (2) learning about the world of work, (3) learning about yourself (knowledge of self), (4) finding occupations, (5) learning about occupations (knowledge of the world of work), (6) making educational choices, (7) planning next steps (decision making), (8) planning the career, and (9) making transitions. (Note that the three common components of career interventions are well covered.)

While the first two modules are primarily for orientation to and information about the world of work, the third is designed to help the client develop more information about himself or herself in terms of interests, abilities, values, and experiences. The program includes inventories for each of these areas, all of which can be completed at the computer. Alternatively, instead of using the briefer, less standardized measures, one can enter a client's results from major standardized inventories and tests such as Holland's Self-Directed Search, the Strong Interest Inventory, the Differential Aptitude Tests, or the Armed Services Vocational Aptitude Battery. For whatever scores one enters, a summary of results is provided. This summary can be printed for later review. (In fact, clients can print any page of the display in the entire program, including the units designed to teach about the work classification system and later modules providing comparisons of jobs related to clients' specific skills, interests, values, and so forth. In other words, each client can create his or her own personalized information packet.)

Based, then, on Super's concept that one makes the best career choices when one can implement one's self-concept in terms of interests, abilities, values, and experiences, the computer generates a list of options that fit the client's particular pattern. The program also allows more emphasis to be given to any one of these areas if the client feels, for example, that interests should be more important than experiences in deciding on career choices. An intriguing feature of this particular module is the "why not" section. If jobs the client thought might be interesting do not appear on the list, he or she can ask the computer, "Why not?" The computer will show what that job requires in the way of interests, abilities and values and how it does not fit with the client's. At that point, this feature invites the client, of course, to consider whether he or she wants to reexamine some of his or her values or interests in making a career choice. Thus, does one change one's career choice to fit current values, interests, and so forth, or does one reconsider the importance of these relative to career choice? This step is the clearest manifestation of the concept of career choice as implementation of the self-concept.

Module 5 provides the opportunity to examine detailed information on 15 different topics, such as work tasks, ways to get training, employee outlook, and so forth, for the occupations corresponding to a client's particular self-assessment. In addition to the occupations that come up on a client's list, according to self-assessment, one can inquire about any of 400 different occupations on which one would like the latest information.

The sixth module, on making educational choices, focuses on choosing different kinds of training in terms of education and majors. The seventh, or planning, module is for those who are ready to take specific steps toward further education such as graduate school or toward developing job-seeking skills. The eighth module, on planning a career, incorporates

Super's concept of the "career rainbow," that is, looking at how, over the lifespan, one's work role will interact with other roles, such as those of parent, citizen, homemaker, spouse/friend. The final module, on making transitions, is designed especially for those who have come back to school after being in other roles and/or who find themselves in a "career crisis," such as that caused by beginning graduate school and wondering if that is the right decision. Based on the work of Schlossberg (1981) regarding transition factors that create significant adjustment problems, the program helps determine "the temperature" of a transition and then, using cognitively oriented stress-management skills, explains how to reduce the temperature of the transition by coping with the various stresses and problems the transition is causing.

Obviously, some of these modules are more important for some persons than others; one always has the choice of not even starting a module or starting it and, seeing that it is not really helpful, simply "signing off." At the completion of the use of DISCOVER and after getting the printout of all parts of the program wanted for further reference, the client can leave the information in the computer so as to come back and use it again or, if completely finished, erase all responses. At completion, all clients or students are asked to provide an evaluation of the helpfulness of the various modules; in this way the developers continually receive information about how to make the program more useful and user-friendly.

As an example of how a counselor might typically use this program in a university counseling center, the following procedures might be followed. After completing a standard interview, a counselor could describe the various modules to the client, explaining what kinds of information they provide and then assist the client in choosing the modules that are most helpful. The client's "homework" would be to complete one or more selected modules before the next counseling session. The following counseling session would be devoted to exploring what the client had gained. This step helps the client more clearly articulate what has been learned and allows the counselor to determine if appropriate understandings have been acquired. Client and counselor then examine what further modules need to be completed and/or decision-making steps to complete.

Structured Outplacement Group Counseling

Our next illustration is of the use of Holland's Self-Directed Search (1985a), a self-assessment measure based on his person-environment interaction approach, as the cornerstone of an outplacement program provided by a major manufacturing company that has found it necessary to dismiss 130 assembly-line workers. Outplacement counseling is a concept rapidly gaining acceptance among employers. Economic downturns, mergers, and technical change are among the major reasons for which large companies sometimes find themselves having to make significant reductions in their employee workforce. Companies have learned that, for the relatively small cost of the kind of program described in this section, they can reduce the ill will that firings create in the community (and possibly avoid lawsuits) (Schlossberg & Leibowitz, 1980). Perhaps most importantly, such a program can help terminated workers find suitable new employment. When such goals can be accomplished, there may also be significantly reduced personal and societal costs in terms of unemployment benefits and welfare.

We provide here a brief overview of a 12-hour outplacement program offered in six two-hour sessions. The opening two hours are the least structured and most like a typical therapeutic group counseling session, providing opportunity for a catharsis of participants' feelings of frustration, rejection, and loss of control over their lives. Although the content of the session may seem strikingly depressing, under skillful group leaders the employees will show some of the benefits that Yalom (1985) has so often shown accompanies effective group work, for example, the realization that other people have the same concerns and a sense that somebody cares enough to listen. Many workers, for example, may not have talked about their problems with anyone else and so felt alone in their feelings of rejection, anger, or depression. If unattended, these feelings may well keep employees from engaging in an active search to find new kinds of employment. Failure to find new employment after three to six months can result in significant mental health and physical health problems for both employees and their families (Mallinckrodt & Fretz, 1988).

The second two hours are devoted to countering the passivity and negativity often shown in the first two hours. As further described in Chapter 16, a large number of structured counseling programs have been developed to address issues of low self-esteem, as well as other relevant job-search topics such as communication skills and assertiveness training. Choosing from a variety of structured exercises as described in, for example, Drum and Knott (1977) and Danish and D'Augelli (1983), the group leader can begin to help the employees find that they do have other strengths they can call upon, that they still have areas in their lives over which they have control, and that they have coping skills they have used in other situations to get them out of tough times. In short, the goal of the second two hours is to mobilize and activate the employees' coping resources.

The third and fourth two-hour components of the program are designed to increase employees' career options. It is here that the Self-Directed Search (SDS) is used. While those familiar with the SDS may be surprised to see it used with adults who have already been in the job market (since it is often seen as a preferred instrument for high school students and those who have not yet entered the job market), with blue-collar employees, as in the present example, it is precisely the kind of instrument needed to help employees look at a variety of options they have not previously considered. Many blue-collar employees, especially those in jobs not requiring high-level skills, entered a position, not because of any special training or interests but simply because it was a well-paying job that was available after they finished high school or left their last job. The most typical reaction of unskilled blue-collar employees is to look first for any other job in the area that pays about the same or to look for the same kind of job available in another company, preferably nearby. There may be few if any of the same kinds of jobs available in that community and, of course, all of the dismissed employees will probably be competing for whatever few slots might be available. Using the SDS helps overcome this narrowness of options.

After the workers have taken and scored the SDS, with a chance for individuals to get clarifications from the counselor, many of their basic questions about the instrument can be answered from a booklet called "You and Your Career" (Holland, 1985b). It explains a great deal about the Holland person-environment model that was described in the last chapter but in a way that is directly related to SDS results and helps persons see how to use their SDS scores for exploring alternative occupations. Repeatedly the SDS has been shown to yield increases in "self-understanding, (and) the number of vocational alternatives considered" (p. 1, Holland, 1985a).

Following the two-hour section in which the SDS is completed and associated materials reviewed, the next session of the program focuses on group exploration of these results. The group now examines the relevance of their occupational aspirations to their obtained codes and begins, with the assistance of both other group members and the counselor, to identify the kinds of skills they have obtained in their present position that might be utilized in the various jobs identified in their personal SDS codes. Other members of the group serve as immediate resources, oftentimes having some knowledge if not actual experience in some of the jobs that appear on other employees' lists. Thus, group members help each other see various possibilities.

The last two sessions of the outplacement program focus on job-getting skills. First is resume writing, helping participants see how best to present the various skills learned in their previous jobs. Next comes training in job-interviewing skills. (Because this session, especially, requires a lot of individual monitoring and because of the value of giving everybody a chance to take part in group discussions, each group should be limited to no more than 10 or 12 persons. A company with many layoffs may need to run several groups.)

To the extent that more time can be made available in this phase, workers would, after receiving basic instruction on preparing resumes, bring them back for review and critique by each other in order to learn how best to present themselves. More importantly, with additional available time, they will role-play job interviewing and begin to set specific goals in applying for jobs. Azrin & Basalel (1980) have developed highly effective job club programs that include these components, especially designed for those without high levels of education. For those who are sufficiently motivated and have at least a high-school reading level, the popular self-help book *What Color Is Your Parachute?* (Bolles, 1986) covers many of these same areas in a most humorous and effective manner.

In summary, the outplacement program added the component of "therapeutic" group counseling to the knowledge-of-self component of career counseling with specific attention to how past experiences/skills can be incorporated into self-knowledge. The use of the SDS expands the workers' knowledge of related areas in the world of work. The third component of career counseling, decision making, is achieved in this program by a focus on tailoring job-getting skills to workers' choices.

Individual Psychodynamic Career Counseling

The psychodynamic approach to career interventions is probably best illustrated by individual counseling. From a report of such counseling it is easy to see how intrapsychic processes are manifested in work-adjustment problems. Moreover, in the following illustration one can see how the frustration of the work experience spills over into other aspects of both physical and mental health. This example also illustrates how one can hardly distinguish between personal counseling and career counseling. Further, the fact that career counseling here addresses problems of personal adjustment as well as career adjustment calls attention to the too often neglected perspective of career counseling as a mental health intervention. Brown and Brooks (1985) noted, in their excellent article on this topic, that, since the 1960s evidence has increased substantiating the contribution of career counseling to improved personal adjustment. As the number of counseling psychologists in independent practice increases, more counseling psychologists are becoming aware of the need, by many clients, for greater integration of psychotherapy and career counseling.

Before beginning this illustration, it is worth noting that no psychological testing has been included in this case. Contrary to many stereotypes of career counseling, it is possible to work effectively without tests, especially when the client and the counselor are able to work together to generate the critical information. If this particular case had progressed in a quite different way, psychological testing might have been called for at some point. However, as the case developed, tests were unnecessary for the client to progress.

Given the individualized nature of this particular case, it is probably easiest to begin by looking first at the intake notes, that is, the notes made when the client first came to the counselor. Following these will be some of the weekly case notes of the counselor, revealing the topics of the various sessions and the progress being made. After each set of notes we have added some commentary of our own, showing how this case exemplifies some of Bordin's (1968) concepts of psychodynamic career counseling. (All case notes have been appropriately altered to protect confidentiality.)

Intake Note: Sheila is a 35-year-old administrative assistant who came for career counseling to get out of a rut she has been in for ten years. She began full-time work at age 20 as a legal secretary following two years of community college. In both high school and while attending a community college, she took mostly business courses. The attorney she worked for initially joined others in a large firm; she has had several promotions during her 15 years with them and has been the "office manager" (in her words), though she lists her title as administrative assistant, for four years. There is no opportunity for further promotion or new positions within the firm. Sheila feels that the money and benefits are good for someone with her education, however she is increasingly bored with her job and wants to change but has no idea what to consider. She has lived with her mother since her father died five years ago, just as Sheila was separating from the man she had married four years earlier. She said little about the marriage except that "I wasn't exciting enough for him." She dates only occasionally. Relatively low self-esteem is readily apparent, but she reports no other signs of depression. Says she has numerous minor physical ailments—"I'm a hypochondriac." Talks readily though not with any psychological sophistication. She has no prior experience in psychotherapy. Minimal probing of sensitive areas (e.g., her husband) yields much defensiveness. Trying to discuss relationships of her career and personal life during counseling may be quite threatening.

Diagnosis: Bordin and Kopplin (1973) developed a diagnostic system of five major categories for dynamic understanding of vocational development problems: synthetic difficulties (minimum psychopathology, problem is in overcoming realistic obstacles and/or integrating diverse interests), identity problems, gratification conflicts (approach-avoidance conflicts with a given choice), overt psychopathology, and change orientation (the client is dissatisfied and wants to change himself or herself by changing vocational choice). Since the counselor did not see overt psychopathology in this client but did find some lack of satisfaction with other roles in life as well as work, it seems quite likely that the change orientation diagnosis is particularly relevant in this case. The counselor, at this point, had too little information about identity formation to know if these kinds of problems were present. Gratification conflicts are also probably part of the problem given that she gets some important need satisfied by her present job, yet other needs, like challenge, are totally unmet. The next set of notes was made after Sheila's first regular counseling session.

Session One Notes: Sheila seemed more agitated in this session. She is feeling some urgency for doing something, anything, to get out of the present work situation. I tried to check out particular areas on the job that might have created a sense of urgency but got nothing. She reports feeling trapped in her routine. No stimulation from work, or home, or friends. No close friends, bowls once a week with friends from high school days. She is the only one without a husband or serious boyfriend. I have a strong sense that her routine, while frustrating to her as she "takes stock" at age 35, has been a major source of security. The possibility of change is probably at least as frightening as it is attractive.

A Psychodynamic Model for Vocational Counseling: Bordin (1968) sees the career counselor's task as "how to go about facilitating an optimal self-confrontation under conditions of minimal anxiety. . . . The major problem is to avoid either overly superficial, abortive self-examination or seduction into an equally abortive psychotherapy" (p. 429). The first important component is to explore how the client seeks gratification, that is, gains satisfaction from various aspects of life, including not only job but also home and social life. The counselor has obviously begun in this first session to explore these various areas, and will want to continue to do so during the next couple of sessions. The counselor will also expect Sheila to become somewhat impatient with these explorations of areas other than her job situation because she came for "career counseling." The counselor will need to help Sheila understand that the best career choices are made by gaining an understanding about how to find sources of gratification in one's life. Getting the client to make relevant self-confrontations yet keeping the focus of the counseling on the career problem is "a fine line" (p. 430) that Bordin recognizes career counselors must face.

In the later sessions the counselor will use a great many comparisons as a way of facilitating self-confrontation. For example, "On the one hand, you feel very competent in your job but, on the other hand, have no idea what those competencies are. Therefore, you can't think of any alternative career choices," and, "On the one hand, the responsibility of taking care of your mother has made you feel helpful and appreciated yet, on the other hand, greatly limits what job options you might consider."

Session Four Notes (Sessions two and three are not discussed here): Today's theme was security. Sheila has clearly grasped the security she gets from her routines and how that makes any change scary. She is also beginning to see that she has a very limited view about her competencies both on the job and socially. Her ex-husband seems to have stimulated that sense of inadequacy in ways she has not yet really described, in fact, I am not sure she has really been able to admit them to awareness. The combination of security in present routine and a limited sense of competence severely limits availability of options that could be considered. I plan to focus on understanding the dynamics of the need for so much security in hope of helping her take a risk or make some minor change in some part of her life. This seems more workable to me, in our time-limited relationship (Sheila was seen in an agency with a 12-session limit for individual counseling) than trying to significantly expand her limited sense of competence.

Comment: The counselor has followed one of Mann's (1973) suggestions here for working in time-limited therapy, that is where the client is seen for a limited number of sessions, say, 7 to 20. In dynamically oriented time-limited counseling, the counselor tries to focus on *one* of the major themes in the person's lifestyle that may be an impediment to having more gratification. While all of the different areas that the client has brought up could potentially be worked on in psychotherapeutic relationships, this could require months of counseling. The counselor chose the theme of security as the one where progress might be made most rapidly for helping the client understand its pervasiveness and implications and to make some small steps to change its hold on her life.

Session Seven Notes (Sessions five and six are not discussed here): Excitement! Sheila has decided to enroll in an evening program for older students who want to earn a bachelor's degree. She told me, in a very didactic way, that this was a good decision for her since it did not change any other routines that were satisfying to her yet it gave her a new challenge. She is not sure that she meets her own standard of "what it takes to get a college degree," but feels she is at least as bright, if not brighter, than any of the persons she supervises who have college degrees. She criticized me for not being more enthusiastic about what she called her "big step." She was right in one sense, but I was considering whether this was an action that would prematurely end our exploration of her security needs and other possible options that she might consider.

Comment: The counselor has quite legitimate concerns about a possible "abortive self-examination" (Bordin, 1968, p. 429) or what others might call "flight into health" (seizing on the very first option that makes one feel somewhat better). Notice, however, how Sheila is beginning to think about herself in a more purposeful, psychological way. While she initially came to counseling saying implicitly, "You get me out of this rut," she has now, on her own, taken a step that brings some change into her life and provides gratification where she had none before. She had reached what Bordin calls the stage of critical decision in the struggle for growth and change. Now look at what happens three sessions later after Sheila had the opportunity to work on changes.

Session Ten Notes: Sheila seems confident about her choice and has already completed enrollment for a composition course next semester. The security—or more precisely, play-it-safe style, originated in her earliest years—both her parents led their lives that way and she was always taught that "a bird in the hand is worth two in the bush." She sees the course she will be taking as not only a new challenge, but also a new way to get out of the house and meet new friends, other changes she has been wanting to take. She feels no need for further counseling at this time; feels it has been very helpful to look at herself. She asks if she could return after taking some courses to consider "what then." For now, "I can easily tolerate my job if there is something challenging somewhere in my life."

Comments: Although this outcome is hardly typical of career counseling—that is, Sheila made no change in her job—those who counsel "midlife" clients will not be at all surprised with the result. One can achieve life satisfaction in many ways, sometimes through changes in jobs, but just as often through changes in other aspects of one's life. When one weighs both the advantages and disadvantages of a current job situation, a current marital situation, or current social life, the conclusion might well be that the risk of change in one area, such as work, may outweigh the benefits of a change and that more gratification might be achieved by changes in another aspect of life, such as one's social life. (Conversely, marriage counselors know that many marriages suffer because of job problems and that changes in the job situation can be a critical component in improving a marital relationship.) Sheila made a small change and (recall the concepts explored in the last chapter regarding social learning theory) to the extent that she experiences the challenges of the college courses as successful ones, she will be more willing to risk other changes in life.

Two years after the end of counseling, Sheila saw her counselor in a shopping mall parking lot and said she was still taking courses and had recently moved away from her mother's home to share an apartment downtown with a friend she met at work. She had stayed in the same job, becoming more and more convinced that it paid better and was as tolerable as most of the jobs that people in her classes had. For now she was taking a variety of classes, not even worried about getting a degree and stated, "I might come back to see you if I ever have to decide what I want to do when I grow up."

Some Observations on Illustrations: There are innumerable possibilities for adapting the different theoretical approaches to yet other settings, for example, schools, rehabilitation centers, hospitals, and to diverse modalities such as classes, workshops, groups, computer-assisted programs, and individual counseling. Several textbooks, for example, Zunker (1986) and Herr and Cramer (1988), are devoted to these various kinds of interventions.

EVALUATING CAREER INTERVENTIONS

Although various forms of career guidance and counseling have been practiced for nearly a century, it was not until the late 1970s and 1980s that systematic reviews of the studies of effectiveness of such counseling began to appear. The good news from these reviews is that most of them consistently find positive effects from a wide variety of different types of career interventions, whether the review is the more traditional review of the literature (Fretz, 1981; Holland, Magoon, & Spokane, 1981) or meta-analyses (Baker & Popowicz, 1983; Oliver & Spokane, 1981; Spokane & Oliver, 1983). (Meta-analysis refers to a set of statistical procedures that can be applied to the results obtained in a collection of empirical studies, in this case, studies of the "treatment" effects of career interventions.) While Fretz (1981) concluded that the positive effects were small, even though consistently found for different kinds of interventions, Spokane and Oliver (1983) argued that the effects were substantial. It is perhaps interesting to note that in comparing the results obtained in meta-analyses of career interventions with the effects obtained in meta-analyses of psychotherapy, the average effect size (the major statistic used in meta-analyses) for career counseling is slightly larger than that obtained in meta-analyses of most psychotherapy. These results also indicate fewer cases of career counseling than psychotherapy resulting in deleterious effects. Baker and Popowicz (1983), focusing on career education studies, obtained a somewhat smaller effect size but still found consistently positive effects from these broader-based interventions.

Oliver and Spokane (1988) went on to determine whether there were particular kinds of career interventions that were more effective than others. Their analyses of the studies published between 1950 and 1982 were amazingly extensive and resulted in the conclusion that "individual counseling seemed to yield the biggest gain for amount of time spent with the client/student. Career classes did have a slightly larger effect size but typically included many, many hours of career related 'treatment'. When we calculated the ratio of effect size to number of sessions, individual career counseling emerged as the most effective intervention per unit of time involved. Obviously, though, a group or class intervention reaches far more people at one time than does individual intervention and consequently has a cost advantage" (pp. 457–458).

The less-than-good news about these reviews of results can be seen in questions raised by Myers (1986) and Rounds and Tinsley (1984). First, many of the evaluation studies have as their "outcome measures" (dependent variables) what are often called instrumental outcomes, that is, for example, gaining occupational information, gaining self-knowledge, and learning some decision-making skills. The assumption is that such skills are instrumental in subsequently obtaining and performing satisfactorily in new career choices. Unfortunately, very few studies on the effects of career counseling have focused on those variables which are ultimately much more important to individuals and to society, for example, job-getting skills, job performance, low levels of depression, or other psychological adjustment variables. Hanson (1981) conducted one of the most commendable of such studies, focusing on adults in the workforce rather than college students. He found that an extensive career development program offered in an industrial setting resulted, six months later, in employees being rated by their supervisors as improved in the quality and quantity of their work and in their morale and communications skills. The important message for counseling psychologist researchers is to focus more on these career-implementing and performance variables beyond the more easily and more immediately measured instrumental behaviors.

There are two other major limitations in career intervention evaluation data that need to be noted. Although the positive effects seem clear, the studies have provided little understanding about what counseling procedures account for those changes. Holland, et al. (1981) argued that the effects are due to four common features of treatment: (1) components that provide exposure to occupational information; (2) components that promote cognitive rehearsal of vocational aspirations; (3) components that provide a cognitive structure for organizing information about self, occupations, and their relations; and (4) components that facilitate social support or reinforcement from counselor or workshop members. The conclusions were largely inferential; there have been no studies which clearly demonstrate whether any or all of these components are necessary. Rounds and Tinsley argue persuasively for the development of "dismantling and constructive" strategies. For example, using Holland et al.'s (1981) propositions, two treatments could be compared in which one of the components would be deleted from the program to see whether or not it resulted in decreased effectiveness. The constructive effort would simply do the reverse: a program would be offered with perhaps only two of the components, then another one offered with three components, a method that would determine the incremental role of the third component in relation to the other two. There are, of course, many other factors that one could hypothesize are effective in treatment; if researchers are to gain knowledge about why career counseling works, they will need to conduct studies where they systematically add or delete components to assess the effectiveness of each.

Yet one other issue remains: Do clients with specific attributes or diagnoses benefit more from one kind of career counseling than another? Thus far, very few studies in career counseling have looked at whether the effects of treatment vary in any way related to client characteristics. While Fretz (1981) provided much of the rationale and suggested some categories for conducting what are known as client attribute–treatment interaction studies, relatively few of these complicated studies have been conducted. One clear illustration of the potential effectiveness of this kind of work is found in that of Kivlighan, Hageseth, Tipton, and McGovern (1981). Their study separated participants into person-oriented and task-oriented types. Their hypothesis was that the person-oriented participants would have better outcomes from group counseling which involved learning through interaction and that the task-oriented participants would have better outcomes from counseling which involved learning through individual problem solving. The results confirmed their hypothesis, with subjects in treatments that matched their personality types showing greater gains in vocational maturity and engaging in more information seeking. Thus they provide an affirmative answer to the question of whether or not some clients will benefit more from one kind of treatment than another. At this point, however, few such studies have been done. There is not only the difficulty of getting a sufficient number of subjects of any one type, at any one time, in order to run such studies, there are also too few theoretical propositions regarding which kinds of clients should benefit the most from a given treatment. Finally, as noted by Rounds and Tinsley (1984), there are no career problem diagnostic schemes that clearly indicate different kinds of interventions for different kinds of clients.

In summary, although much evidence continues to be amassed on the very positive effects of career interventions, investigators are only beginning to discover why career counseling works and to question whether more attention should be given to matching particular treatments to particular kinds of clients. While these remain important issues for scientific study of career interventions, the predominance of the positive effects has made itself felt in the marketplace. In the final section of the chapter we shall see how the range of career interventions has been steadily expanding into all sorts of age groups and settings during the past 20 years.

CAREER INTERVENTIONS: THE EXPANDING MARKET

In today's world, on any given day, career interventions are taking place in myriad settings with nearly every age and demographic group imaginable. We need to note here that counseling psychologists differ somewhat on how broadly they are willing to define career interventions. Spokane (1990) speaks of centrifugal and centripetal forces in defining career interventions. The *centripetal force* is "one that moves the field toward restrictive definitions of career counseling as a variant of psychotherapy. . . . Adherents of this centripetal position argue that . . . progress in career counseling will result, then, when we develop a psychotherapy-based model for understanding and predicting the change process underlying career treatments . . . The *centrifugal* definition uses the term career intervention to refer to any activity designed to enhance an individual's ability to make effective career decisions" (pp. 286–287). In this section, we shall use this broader, more inclusive centrifugal definition of career interventions.

We also must note that in many of the settings for today's career interventions, the involvement of counseling psychologists, trained at the doctoral level, is often in training and consultation roles, "indirect service" roles described more fully in the chapters on structured groups and consultation. Whether the setting be schools, colleges, workplaces, or hospitals, the counseling psychologist is likely to encounter significant demands for both direct *and* indirect career services and will need training and experience in both kinds of roles in order to be maximally prepared for this expanding market for career interventions. As a way to illustrate some of the indirect service roles, some examples will be given of both training and consulting roles of counseling psychologists in career intervention programs in three settings: schools and colleges, the workplace, and hospitals. These descriptions are by no means exhaustive; they are but a sampling of the diversity of roles that have been increasing steadily throughout the past decades as society struggles with both the societal and personal costs of career choice and adjustment problems.

Schools and Colleges

There are numerous "in service" or "continuing education" career-related workshops counseling psychologists conduct for other professionals. Looking first at schools and colleges and starting at the lower age ranges, counseling psychologists have been involved with providing in-service training to kindergarten teachers to help them understand how to broaden the occupational sex role concepts of preschool children beyond the stereotypes already learned by age five (see previous chapter). By teaching how occupational stereotypes develop, the counseling psychologist can help teachers develop a better understanding of how to choose materials and activities that will help the children realize that occupational choices are not necessarily linked to specific genders.

Also in schools and colleges, there are numerous consultation opportunities for career-relevant program development and program evaluation. One of the current hot topics for which many programs are being developed is how to increase the number of students entering scientific and technological careers. Both elementary and high school systems have sought the help of counseling psychologists in exploring ways in which occupational information can be incorporated into the science curriculum in such a way that a greater number of students might learn about and therefore, one hopes, consider the possibilities of careers in those areas. At a more advanced level, many colleges of engineering around the country are putting a great deal of effort into developing programs to recruit and retain more women and ethnic minorities in engineering programs. Quite often counseling psychologists are involved as consultants both to identify the factors that lead to groups avoiding these nontraditional choices as well as to develop programs that provide students with the kinds of learning experiences that Krumboltz and his colleagues (see Chapter 12) identified as being so critical in the development of preferences.

At the college level, the counseling psychologist may also be involved in developing and supervising courses on career decision making for undecided college students. Recall that Spokane and Oliver (1983) found career courses to have significant impact on the desired outcomes of career interventions.

Another career-related training and consulting role of counseling psychologists on college campuses relates to study skills. As noted in the previous chapter, from the very beginnings of counseling psychology in university settings, it was clear to many counselors that a major part of implementing one's career objectives was learning how to study effectively so that one's academic *performance* would be up to the level of one's academic *potential.* Until recently, study skills programs and courses were often part of counseling center services or counseling psychology training programs. When, during the 1960s and 1970s, college opportunities were extended to a much wider range of the population than previously attended college, expanded study skills programs became a specialized service in their own right, often directly part of academic affairs as compared to being part of counseling centers or student affairs offices. Myers has frequently reviewed studies conducted by counseling psychologists that have shown the contribution of efficient study skills to academic performance. In his latest review (1986) he notes the growing role of principles of behavior modification in increasing the effectiveness of study skills training. In perhaps the most comprehensive review of interventions to improve college students' academic "role functioning," Kirschenbaum and Perri (1982) conclude that these interventions lead to improvement in grades in about one third of the studies and to reduced anxiety and better study skills attitudes in one half of the studies. Interventions that included more than one component—for example, anxiety reduction, study skills, and self-control—yielded the most durable effects.

The Workplace

In the workplace, the counseling psychologist may also be involved in both direct and indirect teaching as well as considerable consultation on program development. In a variety of industrial settings, seminars on career transitions, preretirement planning, managing job stress, and so forth, are increasingly common offerings, part or all of which are developed and/or taught by a counseling psychologist. Indirect service, through in-service training in the workplace, also has its part. The counseling psychologist may frequently be called on to make presentations to or provide short seminars for managers and/or administrators on topics such as managing the alcoholic employee, coping with interpersonal friction among employees, and strategies for assisting employees who no longer show the same commitment and promise they did earlier in their careers. Moreover, counseling psychologists, especially with their understanding of the kinds of stresses and strains that transitions can bring (Schlossberg, 1981; Brammer & Abrego, 1981) are particularly well prepared to help companies develop both selection programs and supportive counseling programs for employees and their families when significant changes in job function and/or location are involved. The many other present and emerging roles for counseling psychologists in industry are well described in the special issue of *The Counseling Psychologist* (Vol. 10(3), 1982) on counseling psychologists in business and industry.

Hospitals

Psychologists from both clinical and counseling psychology backgrounds are finding an increased number of roles in general medical surgical hospitals. The rapid growth of behavioral medicine has expanded the number of roles for psychologists in hospital settings; an increasing number of counseling psychology programs furnish specialized training in behavioral medicine.

Although one does not ordinarily think of behavioral medicine as closely related to career interventions, counseling psychologists are finding in hospital settings that significant problems in career adjustment are posed in the recovery process of patients who have had, for example, cardiac surgery or closed-head injuries. Just 20 years ago, many of these patients would have died, but recent technological advances in surgery have enabled them to return, with some change in patterns of activities, to productive lives. Methods for managing required changes in personal and career adjustment are a major contribution that counseling psychologists bring to the hospital setting. While much of that service is delivered through traditional one-to-one counseling with the clients, helping the staff understand the need for those services often results in "continuing education" (the medical equivalent of "in-service education" for teachers) for psychiatrists, clinical psychologists, and other professionals, who are aware of the patient's concern about making a living after recovery yet do not understand how to address the problem. As one recent counseling psychology graduate, working in a closed-head injury program, put it: "This is *real* counseling psychology; helping both the patient and the staff, both of whom are so focused on identifying the deficits and limitations, realize that the patient still has many assets that can be utilized as part of the recovery program."

SUMMARY

Research and program developments in recent decades have resulted in a broad range of interventions that have produced significant effects on the career development of individuals. These interventions range from classroom activities to computer programs to individualized relationships that are essentially indistinguishable from personal counseling. The bulk of this chapter was devoted to three illustrations of career interventions. Each example was based on one of the theoretical models described in the previous chapter (developmental, person/environment interaction, psychodynamic). Moreover, each example illustrated a different modality (computer, group, and individual) in a different setting (university counseling center, employee assistance program, independent practice). As noted in the chapter, all three aspects of the examples are quite interchangeable, that is, for each of the theoretical approaches described in the previous chapter, interventions can be developed in all three modalities, that is, computer-assisted, group, or individual interventions. Moreover, comprehensive career services in any setting, from counseling centers to employee assistance programs to independent practices, would be able to provide services in all of these modalities.

Given the variety of interventions, an important question is whether some are more helpful than others. In the last decade, a wide variety of reviews and meta-analyses have documented the impact of career interventions on the career development and adjustment of diverse groups of students, workers, and clients. The average effects of career counseling are slightly greater than those typically obtained in meta-analysis of psychotherapy. However, measurements have been largely on more immediate outcomes such as gaining occupational information and self-knowledge. Ultimately, the profession needs to demonstrate that career counseling has an impact on persons obtaining and retaining jobs in which they are more productive and satisfied. Another limitation apparent in the reviews is that the studies that have been conducted have not identified what it is in career interventions that contributes to the gains that are made. Are some components of the interventions more essential or more effective than others? What are the necessary and sufficient conditions of effective career interventions? Can some types of clients benefit more from one kind of career intervention than from another kind? These are the important questions for current investigators of career interventions.

The last section of the chapter described the increasing number of training and consultation roles counseling psychologists play in making career interventions. In schools and colleges, as well as in hospitals and the workplace, these roles enable counseling psychologists to have an impact on the career development and career adjustment of a greater number of staff, students, and employees than could ever be obtained simply from individual counseling. Career counseling and career interventions provide some of the best opportunities for counseling psychologists to implement the preventive, developmental, and remedial roles so central to the profession.

References

Azrin, N. H., & Basalel, V. A. (1980). *Job club counselor's manual.* Baltimore: University Park Press.

Baker, S. B., & Popowicz, C. L. (1983). Meta-analysis as a strategy for conducting effects of career education interventions. *Vocational Guidance Quarterly, 31,* 178–186.

Bolles, R. N. (1986). *What color is your parachute?* Berkeley, CA: Ten-Speed Press.

Bordin, E. S. (1968). *Psychological Counseling* (2nd ed.). New York: Appleton-Century-Crofts.

Bordin, E. S., & Kopplin, D. A. (1973). Motivational conflict and vocational development. *Journal of Counseling Psychology, 20,* 154–161.

Brammer, L. M., & Abrego, P. J. (1981). Intervention strategy for coping with transitions. *The Counseling Psychologist, 9*(2), 19–35.

Brown, D., & Brooks, L. (1985). Career counseling as a mental health intervention. *Professional Psychology: Research and Practice, 16,* 860–867.

Crites, J. O. (1981). *Career counseling: Models, methods and materials.* New York: McGraw-Hill.

Danish, S. J., & D'Augelli, A. R. (1983). *Helping skills II. Life development interventions.* New York: Human Sciences Press.

DISCOVER: A computer-based career development counselor support system (1984). Iowa City, IA: American College Testing Foundation.

Drum, D. J., & Knott, E. F. (1977). *Structured groups for facilitating development.* New York: Human Sciences Press.

Fretz, B. R. (1981). Evaluating the effectiveness of career interventions (monograph). *Journal of Counseling Psychology, 28,* 77–89.

Gottfredson, L. S. (1986). Special groups and the beneficial use of vocational interest inventories. In W. B. Walsh & S. H. Osipow (Eds.), *Advances in Vocational Psychology.* Hillsdale, NJ: Erlbaum.

Hanson, M. C. (1981). Career counseling in organizational groups. In D. H. Montross & C. J. Shinkman (Eds.), *Career development in the 1980's: Theory and practice.* Springfield, IL: Thomas.

Herr, E. L., & Cramer, S. H. (1988). *Career guidance and counseling through the lifespan.* Glenview, IL: Scott Foresman.

Holland, J. L. (1985a). *The Self-Directed Search Professional Manual.* Odessa, FL: Psychological Assessment Resources.

Holland, J. L. (1985b). You and your career. Odessa, FL: Psychological Assessment Resources.

Holland, J. L., Magoon, T. M., & Spokane, A. R. (1981). Counseling psychology: Career interventions, research and theory. *Annual Review of Psychology, 32,* 279–305.

Kirschenbaum, D. S., & Perri, M. G. (1982). Improving academic competence in adults: A review of recent research. *Journal of Counseling Psychology, 29,* 76–94.

Kivlighan, D. M., Jr., Hageseth, J. A., Tipton, R. M., & McGovern, T. V. (1981). Effects of matching treatment approach and personality types in group vocational counseling. *Journal of Counseling Psychology, 28,* 315–320.

Mallinckrodt, B., & Fretz, B. R. (1988). Social support and the impact of job loss on older professionals. *Journal of Counseling Psychology, 35,* 281–286.

Mann, J. (1973). *Time limited psychotherapy.* Cambridge, MA: Harvard University Press.

Myers, R. A. (1986). Research on educational and vocational counseling. In S. L. Garfield & A. E. Bergin (Eds.), *Handbook of psychotherapy and behavioral change* (pp. 715–738). New York: Wiley.

Oliver, L. W., & Spokane, A. R. (1988). Career-intervention outcome: What contributes to client gain? *Journal of Counseling Psychology, 35,* 447–462.

Osipow, S. H. (1983). *Theories of career development* (3rd ed.). Englewood Cliffs, NJ: Prentice Hall.

Parsons, F. (1909). *Choosing a vocation.* Boston: Houghton Mifflin.

Rounds, J. B., & Tinsley, H. E. A. (1984). Diagnosis and treatment of vocational problems. In S. D. Brown & R. W. Lent (Eds.), *Handbook of Counseling Psychology* (pp. 137–177). New York: Wiley.

Schlossberg, N. K. (1981). A model for analyzing human adaptation to transition. *The Counseling Psychologist, 9*(2), 2–18.

Schlossberg, N. K., & Leibowitz, Z. (1980). Organizational support systems as buffer to job loss. *Journal of Vocational Behavior, 17,* 204–217.

Spokane, A. R. (1990). Self-guided interest inventories as career interventions. In C. E. Watkins, Jr., & V. L. Campbell (Eds.), *Testing in counseling practice.* Hillsdale, NJ: Erlbaum.

Spokane, A. R., & Oliver, L. W. (1983). The outcomes of vocational intervention. In S. H. Osipow & W. B. Walsh (Eds.), *Handbook of vocational psychology.* Hillsdale, NJ: Erlbaum.

Walsh, W. B., & Osipow, S. H. (1983). *Handbook of vocational psychology.* Hillsdale, NJ: Erlbaum.

Watkins, C. E., Jr., & Campbell, V. L. (Eds.) (1990). *Testing in counseling practice.* Hillsdale, NJ: Erlbaum.

Williamson, E. G. (1939). *How to counsel students: A manual of techniques for clinical counselors.* New York: McGraw-Hill.

Yalom, I. (1985). *Theory and practice of group psychotherapy* (3rd ed.). New York: Basic Books.

Zunker, B. G. (1986). *Career counseling: Applied concepts of life planning.* Monterey, CA: Brooks/Cole.

Chapter 14

Systems in Action: Family and Couples Interventions

Consider the following case example, and in doing so also think about these questions: Who is the client to be counseled? What treatment format would be used? How would the causes of the client's problems be conceptualized?

■ Parents seek psychological help for their 15-year-old son. In recent months he has been increasingly angry and belligerent at home and has been unwilling to help out around the house. His grades in school have dropped, and the parents are worried that he has been drinking and possibly involved in drugs. Because of his behavior, the boy has been upsetting his younger brother and sister. The parents say that they can no longer reach the boy, although they have tried everything. ■

Based on what you have read in the preceding chapters, your answers to the three questions we have posed would be relatively straightforward. Traditionally, the adolescent boy, who is seen as the "identified patient" in family therapy terms, would be the client. He would probably be seen in individual counseling, with the aim of facilitating greater responsibility, self-control, and adjustment, and of controlling and eliminating alcohol and drug involvement, respectively. The causes of the client's problems would be seen as residing in the client's psyche and related to underlying conflicts and complexes, by the psychoanalytically or humanistically oriented counselor. Alternatively, the behavioral counselor might conceptualize the client's problems as being tied to environmental contingencies that serve to control this adolescent's behavior.

In the present chapter, though, we present a different way of thinking about and treating human problems. The approach is called the *family therapy perspective.* From such a perspective, the answers to the three questions we have raised would be very different from those presented using the traditional, individual counseling perspective. For one, the troubled adolescent would probably not be seen as the client who is to receive treatment. The client to be treated would be the entire family and/or subunits within the family. Second, the treatment mode would probably not be individual counseling for the adolescent, but, rather, family counseling for the entire family or subunits, including for example, the parents. Finally, as to the causes of the adolescent's problems, they would be seen as residing in the family *system,* the system of interactions that have been established in the nuclear family, and possibly even the extended family.

To continue with our example, the family therapist might hypothesize that the boy's problems are a symptom of distress in the family (rather than simply a cause of such distress). A closer look at this family might reveal that the father behaves in a critical, dominating manner with the boy. The mother, who seems to passively submit to the father's authority, actually undermines his authority in numerous, often nonverbal ways. She might send the boy to the father for discipline but then passively disagree with the rules he establishes. The parents themselves may have many conflicts with each other, but these have gone underground, and attention to the teenager's rebelliousness helps the parents to avoid their own problems. The other children unconsciously seek to maintain their roles as the "good kids," and thus have some investment in their brother's being the "bad kid." In such a situation, individual treatment of the adolescent would probably not be very effective, because the family system itself is the problem. Much of this chapter will serve to elaborate and clarify the observations just made and in doing so will seek to give the reader the fundamentals of the family therapy perspective.

The treatment of families and couples (married or unmarried) and conceptualizing in terms of systems rather than individuals are among the most recent phenomena in professional psychology. This way of conceptualizing and helping originated in the 1950s, and it is only in recent years that the family therapy approach has become popular among professional psychologists. For example, it has been suggested that only in the 1980s did this approach really become prominent in counseling psychology (Gelso & Fassinger, 1990).

The remainder of the chapter begins with a brief description of the origins of the family therapy movement (including work with couples). The focus will be on the individuals and groups who originated working with families. We then present some of the key assumptions and concepts that appear to undergird most, if not all, approaches to family interventions. Following the presentation of key assumptions and concepts, we review the six major theoretical approaches to family interventions: psychoanalytic, experiential, behavioral, family systems, strategic, and structural. The chapter concludes with a discussion of the role of family and couples interventions in counseling psychology, and a presentation of established research findings about family therapy.

In presenting the key assumptions and concepts that underlie family interventions, we shall underscore the main features of what is called *general systems theory,* a theoretical stance that cuts across most of the different approaches to treatment. Finally, the six main approaches to working with family problems are reviewed in favor of a presentation of general principles of family interventions. This is so because general principles do not appear to exist in this young field. (Family therapy might be contrasted in this way to the more mature field of group counseling as discussed in Chapter 15.) Thus we believe that if family treatments are to be clearly presented, it must be through the review of major theoretical approaches.

THE BEGINNINGS OF FAMILY INTERVENTIONS

Throughout the history of professional psychology, the importance of the family in shaping the psyche and behavior of the individual has been recognized. Sigmund Freud, for example, was acutely aware of the role of the client's family background in this respect. Freud, and virtually all other therapists in the first half of this century, however, sought to isolate the family from the individual client's treatment. The aim was to free the client from the unhealthy influence of the family. In contrast, the aim of family therapists is to assist the family and the individual, through work on and with the family.

According to Foster and Gurman (1985), the earliest forerunners of family therapy interventions were the child-guidance and marriage counseling movements in the United States and England during the first half of the 20th century. Child-guidance and marital counselors developed treatment models that involved concurrent treatment of two or more family members, despite the prevailing view, which dictated that the individual be understood and treated.

The family therapy movement, which began in the 1950s, originated from two directions. One of these was the study of families in which one or more of the offspring became severely disturbed psychologically, that is, schizophrenic. As will be discussed below, a number of important family treatments stemmed from this original aim of understanding troubled families. The second source of family therapy was the independent work of several creative clinicians who began in the 1950s to experiment with family-based treatment. Let us look at some of the key figures in this movement.

The Palo Alto Group: Schizophrenia and Family Communications

According to Nichols (1984), one of the groups with the strongest claims to starting family therapy was Gregory Bateson's schizophrenia project in Palo Alto, California. Bateson was an anthropologist interested in studying communication in general. In the mid-1950s he formed the Palo Alto group, consisting of himself, Jay Haley, Don Jackson, John Weakland, and William Fry. Although the members of this group studied various topics related to communication, they joined together in studying communication within families as it might help explain the nature and causes of schizophrenia.

Among the many creative concepts about family communication developed by the Palo Alto group was that of the *double-bind.* Based on their observations of families in which one of the children suffered from schizophrenia, the Palo Alto group (Bateson, Jackson, Haley, & Weakland, 1956) hypothesized that schizophrenia resulted from the person's having to cope with confused and confusing communication within the family, usually from parent to child. Communications involving double-binds were a central part of such parent-child interactions. In such communication, the recipient (i.e., the child) repeatedly receives two related but contradictory messages of different levels (e.g., verbal vs. nonverbal) from the parent but finds it difficult or impossible to comment on the inconsistency. A classic example of this double-bind communication was given in Bateson et al.'s (1956) original article: A young man recovering from a schizophrenic reaction was visited in the hospital by his mother. When he embraced her, she stiffened. In response to this, he withdrew. She commented, "Don't you love me anymore?" His face reddened, and the mother responded, "Dear, you must not be so easily embarrassed and afraid of your feelings." The young man was caught in a double-bind. After the mother left the hospital, he assaulted an aide and had to be placed in seclusion.

Although the findings of the Palo Alto group had implications for family therapy, treatment or treatment research was not the group's mission. A second group in Palo Alto was concerned about treatment. The Mental Research Institute (MRI) was established by Don Jackson in 1958 and actually contained many of the same members as Bateson's Palo Alto group. (In fact, Bateson, himself, was a consultant to the MRI.) Within MRI, Jackson and Jay Haley developed and popularized a communications approach to the treatment of families (Nichols, 1984). Communications therapists are not concerned about *intra*psychic phenomena or about the childhood causes of clients' problems. Rather, the treatment of families (actually, usually married couples in the early days) was present-centered, directive, and sought to uncover the communication patterns and problems in the family.

Other Originators: Ackerman, Whitaker, and Bowen

Originally trained in psychoanalysis, Nathan Ackerman was a key figure in the early family therapy movement. As early as the 1930s he was writing about family dynamics, and in 1955 he organized and led the first session on family diagnosis at a meeting of the American Orthopsychiatric Association. In 1961 Ackerman, along with Don Jackson, founded the field's first professional journal, *Family Process*.

Whereas the communications therapists focused on overt communication, Ackerman was concerned about the intrapsychic effects of families on individuals (e.g., Ackerman, 1958). He conceptualized families as being emotionally separated into competing factions or dynamic coalitions, for example, mother and daughter or competing generations. Difficulties within families were seen in terms of "interlocking pathologies," since the problems of one person could not be understood separately from those of other family members. Although Ackerman focused a great deal on individuals' dynamics within the family, he was one of the first therapists to recommend that all members in the same household participate in all family therapy sessions. He also suggested that certain members be counseled individually as well as in the family group. As a therapist, he was far from the stereotype of the silent analyst. He believed the family therapist should be spontaneous and lively—at times she or he should provoke emotional reactions, at times siding with one member and at other times serving as a referee. The therapist should be deeply involved emotionally in the families she or he treats.

Carl Whitaker was among the first therapists to treat entire families, having worked with families even in the late 1940s. Whitaker is considered by many to be the dean of *experiential* family therapy (Nichols, 1984). This approach is closely related to gestalt therapy (see Chapter 9), and employs some of the same confrontational and experiential techniques. Like Fritz Perls, Whitaker is an extremely colorful man who is often irreverent, iconoclastic, and even outrageous.

The problem with families, says Whitaker, is that they are emotionally deadened. They have become rigidified into stereotyped routines, and what they need to free themselves is an emotionally alive therapist, who behaves spontaneously and presents them with an authentic human encounter. Whitaker was one of the first to promote the benefits of cotherapy (two therapists working together with couples and families).

When practicing such a spontaneous, no-holds-barred approach, a cotherapist can be invaluable in helping the therapist detect and modulate countertransference reactions.

The final "co-originator" of the field of family therapy has had perhaps the most profound influence of all, an influence that is just as powerful today as it was when the field began. Murray Bowen, who like so many of the early leaders came from a psychoanalytic background, began treating families while he directed a research project on schizophrenic families. He first treated family members individually, but by the mid-1950s came to see the family as the unit of disorder and shifted to working with the entire family. Although he began family work by being nondirective, he soon shifted to a structured and directive approach, believing that this was needed to stimulate movement in families entrenched in their problems. At the same time, from the beginning Bowen viewed it as essential that the family therapist remain objective and detached, lest he or she become embroiled in the family's pathology. His approach in this way is in stark contrast to that of Ackerman and Whitaker, whom we have just described. Murray Bowen's family systems therapy will be reviewed later in this chapter.

Bowen eventually became dissatisfied with his results when treating the entire family and in the early 1960s shifted to working with just the parents of troubled children. He believed it to be more helpful to all involved to have the parents work through their own relationship issues. Bowen and his followers have maintained this couples focus over the years.

We have given only a brief synopsis of the approaches taken by some of the main figures of the family therapy movement. There were many other early leaders. For a thoughtful and interesting review of the history and beginning years of the family therapy movement, the reader is referred to Nichols (1984).

KEY ASSUMPTIONS AND CONCEPTS OF FAMILY AND COUPLES THERAPY: SYSTEMS THEORY

The field of family therapy may be described as "a diverse set of perspectives having in common a *systems* perspective of behavior" (Foster & Gurman, 1985, p. 413, italics added). This systems perspective contains several concepts that most if not all family-oriented practitioners tend to share.

Before describing the concepts and assumptions, it should be noted that systems theory in family work draws heavily from what is called *general systems theory.* As a 20th-century phenomenon, systems theory has been applied widely to physical systems, and also extended to social and biological systems (P. Minuchin, 1985). Von Bertalanffy's (1968, 1974) writing on general systems theory is generally credited with having a profound effect on the family therapy movement, although family therapists have drawn at least as heavily from theoreticians in the field who have applied basic principles of systems theory to living systems such as families. Members of the Palo Alto group, as described earlier, have been leaders in the application of general systems principles (e.g., Bateson, 1972, 1979; Watzlawick, Beavin, & Jackson, 1967).

What are some of the basic assumptions and concepts of systems theory as applied to families? Following Patricia Minuchin's (1985) discussion, we describe the most basic concepts below.

Wholeness and Interdependence

Perhaps the most fundamental assumption of systems theory is that *systems are organized wholes, and elements within a system are necessarily interdependent* (P. Minuchin, 1985). When we talk about a system being an organized whole, we imply that this whole is greater than the sum of its parts. Thus, a family is more than the sum of the individuals in it. It also includes all of the interactions between and among those individuals and the unique ways in which these individuals interrelate. The concept of interdependence implies that the behavior of each part (e.g., each member of a family) is dependent to some extent on the behavior of every other part.

Family therapists are interested in the interactional patterns developed over time among family members and how these patterns regulate the behavior of members within this system. From the systems perspective, with the concepts of wholeness and interdependence in mind, it is most effective to study or treat a member of a family as part of an organized system, for that member can best be understood in context.

Circular Causality and Equifinality

Psychologists typically conceptualize behavior in terms of linear causality. Thus A (e.g., mother's rejection) is assumed to cause B (e.g., child's low self-esteem). According to systems theory, thinking in terms of linear causality does not yield a valid picture of reality. The problem goes beyond the simplistic nature of our example. Point A may be extended so that it includes many causes (e.g., the father's behavior, the mother and father's interaction, etc.), but this is still linear causality, with A and its subparts causing B.

A more valid way of thinking about causality, say the systems theorists, is what is called circular causality. Here A may cause B, which in turn causes A1, which in turn causes B1, and so forth. In other words, A and B mutually influence each other. Consider, for example, the domineering father, who stimulates dependency in his son, and when the son behaves dependently, the father increases his dominance. This, in turn, further robs the son of his self-confidence and he becomes more passive. The father reacts by taking over. In this example, father and son are involved in a causal pattern, with each affecting and reinforcing the behaviors of the other.

When working with a family system or subsystem, this circular causality shows itself consistently and powerfully to the counselor. It takes only a small amount of experience with couples, for example, to see that neither is the cause of the other's behavior, but rather that each influences the other in a circular way. As P. Minuchin notes, "the irreducible unit is the cycle of interaction" (p. 290).

A central concept that stems from the assumption of circular causality is that of *equifinality*. This concept implies that any family problem, regardless of its original causes, may be solved if modifications are made at any point in time in the system. Open systems are not governed by their initial conditions, and systems have no memories. Because of these features, the concept of equifinality suggests that the family therapist need not explore the past. The therapist may focus on the present and get the job done just as effectively and certainly more efficiently as when original causes are explored.

Most family therapists, even those who are psychoanalytically oriented, focus much of their energies on the present interactions within the family and believe that it is the current interaction within the system that perpetuates, if not causes, the problem. Foley (1989) uses the example of the man who began heavy drinking 20 years ago because of unresolved problems with his mother but drinks now because of unresolved problems in the present relationship with his wife. Following the principle of equifinality, the therapist may focus on the husband-wife interaction, and not the mother-son relationship, with just as positive an outcome.

Homeostasis and Change

Since Don Jackson (1957) of the Palo Alto group first theorized about *family homeostasis*, this concept has been a crucial one for family therapists. Just as a thermostat serves to maintain room temperature, family mechanisms serve to regulate the patterns of interaction within the family unit. Homeostasis maintains a constancy of functioning within the family. This does not mean that the family is rigid. As discussed by Nichols (1984), family homeostasis is seen as a nonstatic, dynamic state—a state of equilibrium in which the family may be at point A on one day and point B on another day. Although families seek to maintain the status quo, the result is not rigid invariance in behavior. Rather, the result may be stable variance; the family may vary from one day to the next, but the pattern of variability is stable.

Homeostatic processes in the family, on the whole, are adaptive. They allow the family to maintain a state of equilibrium. In disturbed families, however, the processes that serve to maintain homeostasis may also incorporate symptoms and maladaptive behavior as necessary parts of the system. Here, as P. Minuchin (1985) notes, the need to maintain established patterns makes the family rigid and inhibits needed changes. Resistance to change in therapy, for example, is seen as a homeostatic process.

An example of how psychological symptoms may serve a "positive" function, for example, to maintain the family balance, was offered many years ago by Jackson and Weakland (1959). They noted the case of a young woman who was diagnosed as schizophrenic, with one of her major symptoms being a deep and pervasive indecisiveness. Curiously, though, when she behaved decisively, her parents emotionally fell apart. The mother acted helpless, and the father became sexually impotent. Because of this, the parents had a hard time even being aware of instances when the daughter was decisive. Here we can see vividly how the daughter's seemingly pathological indecisiveness served to protect the parents from facing their own issues. As long as the parents focused on their daughter's deficits, their own could be avoided and homeostasis in the family maintained.

The literature of family therapy is virtually filled with examples of how symptoms serve a function in families and thus also serve to maintain balance. In fact, the concept of family homeostasis has been so powerful in family therapy that it took a long time to develop the companion concept of *morphogenesis,* or change (P. Minuchin, 1985). Just as systems seek to maintain homeostasis, they also strive to meet new challenges and circumstances in effective ways. As a family develops, it inevitably faces many challenges, and it must periodically reorganize (e.g., when an offspring leaves home for college).

Family theorists have described typical stages families go through as the family develops. For example, Carter and McGoldrick (1980) developed a six-stage model with the following order: (1) the unattached young adult, (2) joining of families through marriage, (3) family with young children, (4) family with adolescents, (5) launching children and moving on, and (6) the family in later life. Whatever the particulars of these stages, the point is that each stage contains its own crises and demands for change. The family must be able to meet these demands if it is to continue to function in a healthy way. When families cannot handle transitions, then family therapists may be needed to help the family see that its established patterns no longer suffice, to mobilize the family's resources for change, and finally to consolidate new, more adaptive patterns.

Systems, Subsystems, and Triangles

Another assumption of systems theory is that complex systems are made up of subsystems. Although the individual may be considered a subsystem, family therapists pay attention to larger subsystems within the family, for example, the parent subsystem (more complex than just the spouses in divorced or blended families), the sibling subsystem, the parent(s)-child(ren) subsystem, the grandparent subsystem, and so forth.

A kind of subsystem that has particular importance for family therapists is called the *triangle.* As theorized by Bowen (1976), triangles are viewed as the building blocks of all interpersonal systems, including families. Families may be seen as consisting of a series of interlocking triangles. Such triangles occur when tension arises in two-person subsystems. Thus, a third person or thing is triangulated into the relationship. For example, two lovers may have a stable relationship as long as the tension between them is low. When stress occurs, however, one of the lovers may feel the need to triangulate in a third person or thing, such as alcohol, a friend, or a psychotherapist. Unfortunately common examples of triangulation are husbands in a troubled marriage resorting to heavy drinking or affairs, and wives in such situations becoming overinvolved with the children, clubs, the family, and so forth. The classic example of triangulation in families exists when husband and wife are experiencing tension in their relationship, and as a means of avoiding it, focus on the children. Instead of fighting with each other, the parents concentrate on the kids. If the unresolved issues between parents are too great, one of the parents is likely to become overattached to one or more of the children, with the regrettable consequence that the child may develop emotional problems.

Family therapists typically pay close attention to the triangles that exist in the family system. One of the major tasks in most family interventions is to work with triangles so that unhealthy triangulations are modified. In the classic example above, the therapist would work with the couple, with the aim of helping them resolve their issues and reducing their triangulation with the children.

Boundaries, Rules, and Patterns

Most family therapists would subscribe to the systems theory concept that subsystems within the family are separated by psychological boundaries. Furthermore, a systems view suggests that family interactions across these boundaries are governed by unspoken rules and patterns (P. Minuchin, 1985).

The concept of emotional boundaries between subsystems of a family, one of the major theoretical advances in family interventions, was first proposed by Salvador Minuchin (Minuchin, 1974). More will be said about the concept of boundaries and rules when we discuss Minuchin's structural family therapy in the next section. For now, suffice it to say that boundaries are seen by S. Minuchin as invisible barriers surrounding individuals and subsystems. These boundaries regulate amount and kind of contact with others, and they serve to protect the separateness and independence of the family and its subsystems. When young children can interrupt their parents' conversation whenever the children wish, the boundary between the parent and child subsystems in the family is seen as too "soft," or *diffuse.* Likewise, if parents rush in to protect their children whenever the children experience some threat, the boundaries are diffuse. Diffuse boundaries tend to inhibit healthy development, especially in the area of autonomy. They lead to *enmeshment* between members of different subsystems.

On the other hand, boundaries may be *rigid,* which allows for little emotional contact between subsystems, resulting in *disengagement.* Using the example of parent and child subsystems, rigid boundaries and lack of emotional contact between these two subsystems allow for plenty of independence but also lead to emotional isolation.

MAJOR THEORETICAL APPROACHES TO FAMILY AND COUPLES TREATMENT

As noted at the beginning of this chapter, apart from the assumptions and concepts of general systems theory as just described, there are few general principles or techniques of family/couples treatment that cut across the different theoretical perspectives. There is no "family therapy approach" to assessment and intervention. Rather, there are clusters of theories that differ from one another in terms of the conceptual framework used to understand families; who is actually seen in treatment; the dimensions attended to in the assessment; and the treatment techniques used (Foster & Gurman, 1985).

The six approaches briefly reviewed below are: psychoanalytic, experiential, behavioral, family systems, strategic, and structural. Although space considerations permit us only to present the essential ingredients of each perspective, it must be kept in mind that there is often much variability in viewpoints *within* a given perspective as well as overlap between perspectives. For an extensive, thoughtful, and highly readable review of these systems and others, the reader is referred to Nichols (1984).

The Psychoanalytic Approach

Although psychoanalysis has traditionally been concerned with intrapsychic functioning of individuals, a number of theories have developed during the last half of the 20th century that focus more attention on relationships and human beings' inherent relatedness. Within the couples and family therapy domain, the major current theory of this nature is called *object relations theory.* Much of the present section will focus on this interesting brand of psychoanalytic theory.

In contrast to classic Freudian psychoanalysis, which focuses on biologically based drives revolving around sex and aggression, object relations theorists posit an innate human need for relationships (Fairbairn, 1952; Guntrip, 1969). In fact, object relations theory may be defined as, "the psychoanalytic study of the origin and nature of interpersonal relationships, and of the intrapsychic structures that grew out of past relationships and remain to influence present interpersonal relations" (Nichols, 1984, p. 183). The word *object,* as used by object relations theorists and indeed all psychoanalytic theorists, refers primarily to people and usually to people other than the self.

From birth on, the human being seeks sustaining relationships with significant others, especially of course with mother and father in early life. Like all psychoanalytic theories, object relations theory posits developmental stages, but these are quite different in many ways from the psychosexual stages posited by Freud (oral, anal, phallic, etc.). Rather, the stages generally revolve around the child's relationship with primary caretakers. The earliest stage, for example, involves profound dependency on the primary caretaker, usually mother. Subsequent stages focus on the differentiation of a self separate from caretakers and individuation of that self while maintaining connection to others. Parents need to respond to the growing child's needs during each of these stages. All parents will of course make mistakes, and most of us make many of them. What is needed is not perfection, but rather "good enough parenting"—for the parents who are able to respond appropriately, on the whole, to the child's needs. As supposed in all analytic theories, if the child's needs are too frustrated during the early stages, they will go underground but then show up later. What is of greatest interest to couples/family therapists is that these needs show themselves in the choice of and behavior toward love objects, and in terms of one's strengths and weaknesses as a parent.

In addition to a particular kind of theory about development as just summarized, the heart of object relations theory is how early relationships are "taken in" (internalized) by the person, and carried with him or her in subsequent relationships. In essence, the person forms internalized representations of early love objects such as parents, and these representations serve as a blueprint of sorts for subsequent relationships. The internal object representations profoundly affect the choice of subsequent love objects, behavior toward those persons, and perceptions of the objects. It must be understood that the internal representations only partly correspond to reality. They are always affected by the child's existing needs and drives.

Although object relations therapists do work with entire families and various family subsystems, it is safe to say that most analytic work involves the couple subsystem. Some of the most fascinating object relations theory has recently been developed on how marital partners choose each other and respond to each other in a way that matches the internal representations of early objects, such as mother and father (see Scarf, 1987).

The concept of *projective identification* is used by most object relations therapists as a key to the troubled interactions of members of a couple and of a family. When using this defense, the person unconsciously projects hidden feelings and ideas (which in turn reflect hidden object representations from childhood) onto the spouse or other significant objects. The person not only projects hidden parts of the self onto others but then identifies with those parts because these are, after all, parts of the self. In couples and family interactions, projective identification, ordinarily a complex concept, is even more complicated. The object (e.g., spouse) takes on these projections and then acts them out. For example, in his earliest years a husband has internalized the bad mother, represented as a hostile, rejecting object who will not provide him nurturance. He then sees rejection and hostility in his wife, even when it is not present in reality. Significantly, the wife "takes in" this projection, and acts out the role of the hostile, rejecting object. To carry this example further, the wife, too, has her internal object representations, for example, the cool, distancing father introject. She may project these into her husband, and he may in turn act them out. Thus, in the systems theory sense, we have a true system in operation, with definite circular causality. The cure, from an object relations perspective, is for each to learn to own and accept his and her own repressed parts (object representations) and, just as significantly, not to accept the projections of the other (Scarf, 1987).

Even when the "identified patient" is a child, in the object relations perspective the child is often seen as the carrier of the split-off (from consciousness) and unacceptable impulses of other family members. For example, in the case of the delinquent child, the parents are able to avoid facing certain of their own impulses, experience vicarious gratification of these impulses through the child, and still punish the child for expression of the impulses. The parents can act as the super ego while punishing the child for acting out the impulses of the parents' id. Nichols (1984, p. 194) uses the following telling example of this phenomenon:

> The J. family sought help controlling 15-year-old Paul's delinquent behavior. Arrested several times for vandalism, Paul seemed neither ashamed of nor able to understand his compulsion to strike out against authority. As therapy progressed, it became clear that Paul's father harbored a deep but unexpressed resentment of the social conditions which made him work long hours for low wages in a factory, while the "fat cats didn't do shit, but still drove around in Cadillacs." Once the therapists became aware of Mr. J.'s

strong but suppressed hatred of authority, they also began to notice that he smiled slightly when Mrs. J. described Paul's latest exploits.

The psychoanalytic family therapist assesses his or her cases in terms of both the dynamics of the individuals in the family and the dynamics of the family system and subsystems (Nichols, 1984). During the initial assessment, most analytic therapists would meet with the family as a whole (cf. Ackerman, 1961; Skynner, 1981). The aim of the initial work is to understand dynamics of the family as a whole as well as those of the individuals and subgroups within the family. Following this initial phase, a decision is made as to which members of the family should be worked with. Although modern psychoanalytic family therapists work with all imaginable combinations of family members, work with the couple dyad is the norm.

Although the psychoanalytic family therapist tends to be more active and directive than the psychoanalytic individual therapist (see Chapter 7), this treatment is clearly nondirective in comparison to other family/couples approaches. The therapist listens a great deal, and although this listening is very active, he or she is relatively quiet. Interpretation is the primary technique in most analytic approaches, and rarely would a therapist offer more than two or three interpretations in a session (Nichols, 1984). As in virtually all psychoanalytic approaches, great emphasis is placed on the client's transference, although in the case of couple and family therapies, this transference gets even more complicated than in individual treatment. Thus in evidence are transferences to the therapist from each of the family members as well as transferences between and among family members themselves. As Boszormenyi-Nagy (1972) points out, transference specifically to the therapist is less intense than in individual therapy. Both the real and transference reactions between and among other family members divert some of the energy ordinarily invested in the individual therapist.

The psychoanalytic family therapist usually prefers to work with families in a longer-term format than other approaches. The goal is personality change in individual members of the family. The object relations perspective clearly defines how that change is conceptualized. Terms such as *separation-individuation* (Katz, 1981) and *differentiation* (Skynner, 1981) are often used. In other words, the goal is for individuals to differentiate themselves (from other family members, e.g., parents), while at the same time maintaining and improving the quality of relationships with family.

The Experiential Approach

Experiential family therapy grew out of the humanistic psychology movement of the 1960s, and because of this it bears a close resemblance to the humanistic counseling perspective described in Chapter 9. The essential problem with families, just as with individuals, is that they are emotionally frozen and stuck; the job of therapists is to help the family and its members to become unstuck. This process entails learning to experience one's underlying feelings and to express what is experienced. Through such experiencing and expressing, members of the family both get in touch with themselves and are enabled to touch each other emotionally.

The leading exponents of the experiential approach to family work are Carl Whitaker (Whitaker, 1976; Whitaker & Keith, 1981), Virginia Satir (Satir, 1967), Walter Kempler (1973), and Ronald Levant (1983). As noted in the discussion of the beginnings of family therapy, Whitaker is considered by many to be the dean of experiential family therapy, for he was probably the first within this perspective to work with families and write about it. Experiential family therapy differs from most systems-oriented family work in its focus on expanding immediate personal experience, and in the early days of this approach, attention was directed much more to the individuals in a family than to the family system. To be sure, there was great stress on sharing among individuals in the family, but the individual emphasis was unmistakable. Also, unlike the systems therapists to be discussed later but similar to psychoanalytic family therapists, experiential therapists work to help members of the family get in touch with feelings that are hidden from awareness, the awareness of the individual as well as the awareness of other family members. In more recent years, experiential therapists have focused to a greater extent on the family as a system, on the interconnectedness of the family. As Nichols (1984) points out in his analysis of the experiential approach, experientialists now see the family as a team in which none of the players can perform effectively without the unity and wholeness of the group. Thus, individual problems are broadened to include the involvement of other family members, and members are invited to consider their own part in maintaining the behavior of other members with which they are unhappy.

As part of this movement toward the family and couples system, experiential family therapists are now more inclined to work with the entire family. Whitaker (1976), for example, believes the therapist should have at least a few meetings with the entire family, including three generations. He also believes that children should always be part of the work. Whitaker often invites extended-family members to early meetings as consultants rather than clients. Inviting grandparents as consultants, for example, helps reduce their resistance to attendance, facilitates their support of the treatment aims, and also gives a fuller picture of the family's dynamics.

Given the goals of emotionally unfreezing the family, the experiential therapists, like their cousins the gestalt therapists (Chapter 9) and encounter group therapists (Chapter 15), stress the importance of being open, not wearing a professional mask, and sharing immediate experience with family members. The spontaneous expression of the therapist is placed at a premium. An adherence to theory is often seen as a hindrance to the therapeutic process rather than an aid. Theory can provide a cover for the therapist, getting in the way of his or her spontaneous experience and expression. (Of course, this is a theoretical statement in itself!)

Just as theory is deemphasized by the experientalists, the use of cookbook techniques is eschewed. It is the person of the therapist, not a set of techniques, that is curative. Kempler underscores this point when he states that experiential therapy has no techniques, only people (Kempler, 1968). To further the experiential process, these therapists are quite active and directive. They involve themselves deeply and often provoke clients to do likewise. "Look at each other when you talk," "Say that again, only this time let your feelings be part of what you say," "You are whining—tell him to get off your back, but this time *mean it!*" These are the kinds of directives often used by experientalists.

The confrontational and provocative nature of experiential family therapy is made clear in a case example presented by Nichols (1984). After an information-gathering session, the L. Family was discussing Tommy's misbehavior. Mrs. L. and Tommy's sister were listing the "terrible things" Tommy did around the house. The therapist noticed how uninvolved Mr. L. seemed to be as he passively nodded in response to his wife's complaints. When asked about what he felt by the therapist, he responded minimally, and it seemed that in fact little was on his mind, at least consciously. The therapist did not know why this was, but she did know that she felt annoyed by the lack of involvement, and she decided to express this:

Therapist to Mr. L.: You know what, you piss me off.

Mr. L.: What? (He was shocked; people he knew didn't speak that way.)

Therapist: I said, you piss me off. Here your wife is concerned and upset about Tommy, and you just sit there like a lump on a log. You're about as much a part of this family as that lamp in the corner.

Mr. L.: You have no right to talk to me that way (getting angrier by the minute). I work very hard for this family. Who do you think puts bread on the table? I get up six days a week and drive a delivery truck all over town. All day long I have to listen to customers bitching about this, and that. Then I come home and what do I get? "Tommy did this. Tommy did that." I'm sick of it.

Therapist: Say that again, louder.

Mr. L.: I'm sick of it! I'm sick of it!

This interchange dramatically transformed the atmosphere in the session. Suddenly the reason for Mr. L.'s disinterest became clear. He was

> furious at his wife for nagging and complaining about Tommy. She, in turn, was displacing much of her feeling for her husband onto Tommy, as a result of Mr. L.'s emotional unavailability. In subsequent sessions, Mr. and Mrs. L. spent more time talking about their relationship, less and less was heard about Tommy's misbehavior. (Nichols, 1984, pp. 277–278)

The Family Systems Approach

A school of family therapy that strongly adheres to the main tenets of general systems theory is the family systems approach. Although a number of creative therapists have been involved in the refinement of this perspective, the prime mover has been Murray Bowen. He originated family systems therapy, has elaborated it over the years, and has been responsible for the training of many of its leading spokespersons.

Bowen has always been more interested in developing theories of how families operate than in creating techniques of treatment, because effective theories serve as guides to the treatment of family systems (Bowen, 1966, 1976). Bowen was originally trained as a psychoanalyst, and his family systems theory is decidedly psychodynamic, with many psychoanalytic elements. It is one of the most powerful and widely used theories of families and family interventions.

Bowen began theorizing about families in the 1950s, and although his theory has evolved, the most fundamental constructs have revolved around two sets of opposing forces. One set pulls the person into the family and makes for family togetherness, whereas the other set pushes the person toward individuality. The key assumption of the theory is that excessive and conflictual emotional attachments to one's family need to be resolved, rather than accepted passively or reacted against, if one is to differentiate into a mature personality and become a well-functioning parent (Bowen, 1976, 1978; Nichols, 1984).

Five interrelated concepts serve as the nucleus of Bowen's rich and far-reaching theory. We shall briefly summarize each of these.

Emotional Triangles. The notion of triangulation is a significant part of Bowen's theory. As discussed earlier, family systems therapists pay close attention to triangles in troubled families and work actively at helping their clients detriangulate. Couples, for example, are helped to work directly with their issues and to avoid triangulating a third person or object into their situation.

Differentiation of Self. Perhaps the most fundamental construct in family systems theory is differentiation, both as it occurs within a person and between persons. Undifferentiation, or fusion, occurs when people do not separate feelings from intellect but instead are flooded by their feelings. At an interpersonal level, the undifferentiated person tends to either absorb others' feelings or react against others. Such intra- and interpersonal undifferentiation is passed on from one generation to the next in families, and a central aim of all family systems therapy is to help clients learn to become differentiated within themselves and from other members of their nuclear and extended families. Helping an individual within the family or a couple become differentiated has a healthy effect on the entire family system.

Nuclear Family Emotional System. This concept refers to emotional entanglements that become transmitted from one generation to the next in families and that form unhealthy patterns. When lack of differentiation exists in the family of origin, the person is either emotionally fused with his or her parents or cut off emotionally from them. The consequence, though, is lack of differentiation within the person. Persons then unconsciously seek out mates with about an equal level of undifferentiation, and the two people form a new fused relationship. This will produce any of the following: (1) a defensive distancing between spouses, (2) overt conflict in the relationship, (3) psychological or even physical dysfunction in one of the spouses, or (4) projection of the problem onto one or more of the children.

Family Projection Process. Parents transmit their own lack of differentiation to their children through a kind of projection. As just noted, undifferentiation causes stress in the marital situation. Because of this, one or more of the children often get unconsciously triangulated into the process. A common scenario is for the husband to withdraw from his wife, and for the wife to project her needs into the children, such that she becomes fused with one of them. The husband unconsciously supports this entanglement because it relieves him of the stress of the relationship. The wife is also enabled to avoid the marital situation. The child, however, does not develop healthy differentiation and often becomes emotionally crippled. The parents then have to invest even more concern in the child, and the family pattern becomes deeply embedded.

Multigenerational Transmission Process. Not only do parents transmit their lack of differentiation to their children, but this transmission process goes on for several generations. Thus, in family systems theory the constructs of differentiation and fusion are applied to individuals, nuclear family systems, and the extended-family system. In each family, the children who are most affected by the family's fusion will go on to create families in which there is lack of differentiation, and the cycle continues. Along the way, some spouses and some children develop symptoms of emotional disorder, for which treatment is sought. These individuals become the "identified patient," but the problem of undifferentiation is an inherent part of the system.

Although problems inhere in the family system, Bowenians aim to help individuals differentiate, which in turn affects the system. Family systems therapists work with all combinations of family members, including individuals (Kerr, 1981). But it is the marital dyad they most often treat. In striking contrast to some of the family therapists described earlier (e.g., Whitaker, Ackerman), Bowenians believe it is crucial for the therapist to maintain an unemotional and rational stance with patients. If the therapist gets too emotionally involved, she or he will become triangulated, and be less effective.

In working with couples, family systems therapists do not encourage interaction between the members. These therapists invite each member to take turns interacting with the therapist, while the other member observes and tries to empathize. Clients are discouraged from becoming too emotional, since it is through the use of reason and intellect that one learns to be differentiated. This "deemotionalizing" is a distinctive feature of family systems therapy.

Bowen (1978) states that the therapist's functions are fourfold: (1) defining and clarifying the relationship between spouses, (2) keeping the self detriangulated from the family emotional system, (3) teaching the functioning of emotional systems, and (4) demonstrating differentiation by taking the "I position." Regarding this last function, the therapist must own his or her views and ideas and state them calmly. This serves as a model of differentiation to the couple.

Two other elements are vital in Bowenian therapy. First, if the treatment is long-term (e.g., beyond six months), family systems therapists will tend to include didactic methods, teaching clients about family systems and recommending that they attend relevant seminars. Second, as part of long-term treatment, family systems therapists encourage members of the couple to return home for visits so that they can further the process of differentiation in their extended families. During this phase, the treatment often resembles "coaching" (Bowen, 1976), and the time gap between sessions is widened, for example, to one meeting a month. Clients who are not differentiated often separate from their parents by emotionally cutting off the relationships. Family systems therapists want their clients to return to the system and form healthier relationships, where a sense of togetherness can exist within the context of differentiation.

The Strategic Family Therapy (SFT) Approach

Strategic family therapy (SFT) is actually a cluster of approaches with a common systems orientation to family problems and some shared conceptions of how treatment is best performed. Also called problem-solving therapy and systemic therapy, SFT is typically a short-term treatment in which the therapist is highly active and directive. The treatment is aimed at modifying overt behavior in the form of family members' communications with one another. SFT represents a controversial approach to treatment, as the therapist takes control of the interactions with his or her clients and actively manipulates clients into behaving more constructively. Virtually all strategic therapists agree on one point: insight is of no help and may in fact serve to deepen clients' resistance to change. What helps is behavior change, actively instigated by the therapist's directives.

There are many leading figures in the SFT movement, a movement that is currently one of the most powerful in the family therapy field (Goldenberg & Goldenberg, 1985). Creative and important contributions have been made by Jay Haley (1976) and Cloe Madanes (1981), a husband-and-wife team; the Milan (Italy) Group, led by Mara Selvini Palazzoli (Selvini Palazzoli, Boscolo, Cecchin, & Prata, 1978); Lynn Hoffman (1981) and her team at the Ackerman Institute; and the Brief Therapy Center of the Mental Research Institute in Palo Alto (Fisch, Weakland, & Segal, 1982).

On the whole, strategic therapists, like their behavioral cousins, focus treatment on the primary symptom presented by the family, usually in the form of maladaptive behaviors exhibited by the identified patient. These symptoms, however, are seen as originating in the family system and are treated within that system. Thus, the identified patient (often a misbehaving child in the family) is usually not isolated for treatment. He or she may be treated as part of family treatment, or the marital dyad may be worked with in an effort to resolve the child's symptom.

True to its systems theory roots, SFT conceptualizes the symptom in terms of circular sequences in the family. In addition, strategic therapists, borrowing Bowen's concept of triangles, view these circular sequences as usually involving three persons. A common sequence, noted by Haley (1976), is as follows: (a) Father becomes unhappy and withdraws; (b) child misbehaves; (c) mother deals with the misbehavior ineffectively; (d) father moves toward involvement with mother and child; (e) child behaves more appropriately; (f) mother becomes more effective, and expects more from the father and the child; (g) father becomes unhappy and withdraws.

Selvini Palazzoli and her colleagues (Selvini Palazzoli et al., 1978) think of troubled families as playing games that serve to maintain homeostasis in the family. Healthy systems balance homeostasis and change, and they do change when transitions in the family require it (e.g., when a first child enters the family, a child leaves the family, or a parent's vocational situation changes). Pathological families, however, seem to maintain the status quo at all costs.

A key distinction in SFT is that between first-order change and second-order change (Watzlawick, Beavin, & Jackson, 1967). First-order change involves "more of the same," as the family seeks change without changing the system. Such change is ineffective. Second-order change alters the system itself and is more likely to be effective. Troubled families only employ first-order change. Nichols (1984) notes, for example, that parents of a clinging, dependent child might change from telling the child to stay home to telling the child to go out and play as a way of facilitating independence. This does not work, however, because it does not alter the basic system pattern—dominant parents dictating to a dependent child.

In terms of interventions, strategic therapists work with any combinations of family members, and some even include the entire family and the extended family. Most common, however, is work with either the marital dyad or the parents along with one of the children, usually the identified patient. Unlike the experiential and family systems approaches, SFT usually does not entail the use of co-therapists, although strategic therapists do typically use consultation in the unique way. For example, consultants will often observe the therapy through a one-way mirror and even enter the therapy session to make active suggestions. As noted, SFT is symptom-oriented, and because of this it tends to be brief. Strategic therapists at Palo Alto's Mental Research Institute, for example, typically implement a treatment that continues for only ten sessions.

The most frequent technique used by strategic therapists is the directive. Clients are given directives for in-session behavior, but most often directives are given in the form of homework assignments. These directives may entail straightforward suggestions, or they may be in the form of paradoxical interventions, as described below.

Perhaps the most distinctive feature of SFT is the use of active therapist manipulations aimed at dramatically changing behavioral sequences in the family system. The most frequently used manipulations are those called *paradoxical interventions.* Dowd and Milne (1986) have offered an extensive discussion of such interventions in counseling psychology and family work. One of the most common forms of paradox is *symptom prescription.* Here the therapist instructs the client actually to engage in the behavior that the client seeks to eliminate. An example given by Watzlawick, Weakland, and Fisch (1974) took place in a family in which the mother rationalized her son's frequent misbehavior by stating, "It's all the result of psychological problems." Her strategic therapist directed the child to misbehave even more during the coming week, and the mother was to forgive him with even greater amounts of understanding. Here the mother can comply with the therapist's directive and come to see the problem as controllable. Alternatively, she could rebel against the directive, in which case a big step is taken toward solving the problem. The dynamics of such paradoxical interventions involve the client's being placed in a therapeutic double-bind, in which a positive outcome is accomplished, regardless of what the client does. Strategic therapists view this as a "no-lose" situation, in contrast to the pathological double-bind discussed early in this chapter, which involves a "no-win" situation.

Other paradoxical interventions involve symptom scheduling, restraining, and positioning. In *symptom scheduling,* the counselor directs the client to set aside a certain time to engage in the symptom. For example, a therapist might instruct the client who has problems with obsessive thinking to spend one hour a day, from 4:00 to 5:00 P.M., engaging completely in obsessive thinking. A *restraining strategy* involves cautioning the client against changing too rapidly and is often helpful with oppositional clients, who may oppose the counselor and undergo rapid change. *Positioning* occurs when the therapist agrees with the client's negative self-view, and may even exaggerate it.

Therapists are often uncomfortable with the confrontational quality of paradoxical interventions. Madanes (1981) uses *pretend techniques* as a way to insert a sense of playfulness into what might be an otherwise antagonistic process. She might, for example, invite a child to pretend to have the symptoms that everybody has been trying to get the child to abandon. Madanes here would also ask the parents to pretend to help the child have these symptoms. As a consequence of making it into something playful, the child often gives up the actual symptom.

Strategic therapists use paradox and straightforward directives very thoughtfully. They often meet with the entire family, and carefully observe the family's interactions with the therapist, with each other, with the identified patient in the family, across generational lines, and so forth. The therapist then decides on a treatment strategy, including the kinds of directives to use, to fit the problem or symptom. The therapist pays very close attention to the system factors that serve to maintain the presenting problem and that might also be the vehicle through which the problem is solved.

The Structural Approach

The structural approach entered the family therapy scene in full force in the 1970s and has remained one of the most popular and influential approaches to family intervention (Goldenberg & Goldenberg, 1985; Nichols, 1984). Structural theory is deeply embedded in systems theory, holding similar conceptions of how families operate and how to intervene with troubled families. It is an appealing theory in several ways. Structural theory offers ideas about the structure or underlying organization of families that make a great deal of sense to the practicing counselor. The theory of how families operate and how they go emotionally awry also has clear implications for assessment and treatment. Finally, a number of clear counseling techniques are suggested by the theory.

The founder and leader of the structural approach is Salvador Minuchin, whose ideas about family intervention took shape when he worked with multiproblem, economically impoverished families of delinquent children in the 1960s. Some of the most important and useful works on the structural approach have been presented by Minuchin (Minuchin, 1974—his definitive piece; Minuchin & Fishman, 1981), by Aponte and VanDeusen (1981), and by Umbarger (1983).

Three concepts form the nucleus of the structural theory of family functioning: structure, subsystems, and boundaries.

Family Structure. The concept of family structure may be defined as the organized pattern in which family members interact. All families have predictable patterns of interaction, and such patterns reveal the who, when, and how of family members' interactions. Patterns that are repeated develop into psychological structures. For example, a father may play the role of distant disciplinarian, whereas the mother may be affectionate but unable to set limits. This pattern may be manifested in numerous interactions between the spouses and their children when affection and discipline are at issue. These parental roles are a clear, even if implicit, part of the family's structure.

Part of the family's structure involves a number of unspoken rules about how members are to interact within and outside the family. Examples of such rules are that mother spends time with the children while father works; the children act up whenever the parents seem to have a conflict; father plans and orchestrates the family trips; family members do not share their feelings directly. Rules, patterns, and structure in families, once established, are highly resistant to change.

Subsystems. As noted in the earlier discussion of key assumptions in systems theory, all complex systems are divided into subsystems. Such subsystems may contain any number of people within the family, and subsystem groupings may be determined by age, generation, gender, interests, and so forth. Thus, there is usually a parent subsystem and a children subsystem, as well as less obvious ones—for example, the mother aligned with the male children, and the father forming another subsystem with the female child. Subsystems may be fluid in the sense that any individual within the family may belong to more than one subsystem. The mother in a particular family may be part of the spousal subsystem in certain ways, of the female subsystem in other ways, and the athletic subsystem in still other ways.

Boundaries. In all families there are invisible barriers that surround and to an extent insulate all individuals and subsystems, and Minuchin's notions about the characteristics of these boundaries are among the most interesting and significant concepts within structural theory.

Boundaries serve to control the amount of contact with those outside the boundary. As noted earlier, these boundaries range from being rigid to diffuse, with the boundary labeled "clear" being at the midpoint on the continuum. Neither of the extremes (rigid or diffuse) is healthy. Rigid boundaries permit little emotional contact with individuals or systems outside of the boundary, and this results in what Minuchin calls *disengagement.* Diffuse boundaries, on the other hand, are not solid enough, and foster too much emotional connection with outside individuals or systems. This results in *enmeshment.*

Disengaged individuals or subsystems tend to be isolated. Although this isolating permits independence and at times mastery, there is a cost. Disengagement also limits warmth, affection, and a sense of support. On the other side of the continuum, enmeshment allows for plenty of support and affection across subsystems. Enmeshed parents provide an abundance of love and affection. At the same time, the children are not given room to develop themselves as independent, effective individuals.

Structural therapists pay close attention to boundaries in families. If enmeshment exists (e.g., between any of the combinations of parent and child subsystems), structural therapists seek to solidify boundaries. If individuals or subsystems are disengaged, on the other hand, the therapist works to soften boundaries and open communication.

As regards interventions, structural therapists, like the strategic therapists described in the previous section, are very active, directive, and at times manipulative. Unlike the strategic group, however, structuralists do not work directly on presenting symptoms. Instead, they seek to modify structure, for the best and longest-lasting way to change problem behavior is to change the family patterns (structure) that maintain it. Structuralists typically work with families in which a child or adolescent is the identified patient, and they may work with any combination of family members, at times dealing with individuals and at times with different subsystems within the family. The therapist, for example, may meet with the entire family for a while. Then, feeling that the parent subsystem needs clearer boundaries from the child subsystem, the therapist may meet with the parents alone. In this same family, it may be clear that the father and son need their boundaries softened, and the therapist may also meet with this pair.

In his most comprehensive statement, Minuchin (1974) describes steps and techniques of structural therapy. During the first session or two the therapist seeks to "join" the family—to demonstrate respect for it and each of its members. At the same time, he or she is carefully observing structure, subsystems, and boundary issues. The therapist may have family members enact problem sequences. For example, if the husband complains that his wife is not communicating with him, the therapist may ask the husband and wife to talk this over in the session. As the therapist observes sequences and directs enactments, he or she is also making a diagnosis, not a DSM diagnosis but a structural one. The diagnosis includes *all* family members. It is not enough, for example, to know that a husband and daughter are enmeshed. The therapist must also learn the ways in which the wife is involved with both. She may also be enmeshed with the daughter, disengaged from the husband, or close to him. These patterns all call for different diagnoses and interventions.

After joining the family, observing interactions, and diagnosing the problem, structural therapists seek to change family patterns and boundaries. When Minuchin and other structural therapists intervene in these patterns, they do so in intense, forceful, and at times dramatic ways. Family patterns are usually entrenched, and it requires intensity and forcefulness to modify them. Structuralists pay particular attention to systems of circular causality in the family. The husband withdraws from the wife because she is emotionally demanding; the wife is emotionally demanding because the husband withdraws from her. The therapist intervenes in these circles, actively and forcefully points them out, and seeks to promote change.

Nichols (1984) gives a case example from his own work of how affective intensity is used to modify patterns and boundaries. A mother and daughter, a 29-year-old woman suffering from anorexia, were enmeshed in a rigidly structured family. The father, the only one who would express anger openly, was excluded from that subsystem. The mother had covertly taught the daughter to be fearful of the father's anger because of her own issues in dealing with it. During one session, the father expressed how isolated he felt from his daughter. He and the daughter both felt it was because of his anger, for which the daughter blamed him. Nichols asked the mother what she felt, and she expressed that it wasn't the father's fault, it was no one's fault. In an effort to get the mother's attention and begin to cut into the rigid system, Nichols exclaimed, "Like hell it isn't!" She asked what he meant, and Nichols replied, "It's *your* fault!" Nichols notes that the content—who was really afraid of anger—was not as important as the structural goal of reducing the destructive enmeshment between mother and daughter. Softening the father-daughter boundaries and strengthening the mother-father subsystem would also be important in this case.

Given the intensity of such interventions, structural therapists emphasize the importance of timing and having a sound diagnosis of the system and individuals prior to intervening.

Behavioral Approaches

Of all the approaches to family intervention discussed in this chapter, the behavioral approach most often incorporates the results of empirical research into the development of treatment guidelines. Although there is more evidence on the effectiveness of behavioral interventions than on other family therapies, this approach is often not even included in discussions of family therapy (e.g., Goldenberg & Goldenberg, 1985; Foley, 1989). This is so because the behavioral approach is generally not considered to be family therapy treatment in the sense that there is little attention to systems theory or the family as a system. The focus in behavioral treatment has tended, for example, to be on two-person situations. The marital couple and parent-child dyads have been given almost exclusive attention. The triad and the entire family system, so often the focus of family therapists, have tended to be ignored.

The behavioral approach is also unlike the other, more systems-oriented family therapies in that it most often conceptualizes family problems in terms of linear causality rather than circular causality. The behavioral family counselor seeks to isolate specific and concrete problem behaviors, identify what in the (usually) interpersonal environment is controlling them, and use behavioral techniques to reduce the problem behaviors while increasing positive behaviors.

Foster & Gurman (1985) note that this specificity of the behavioral approach is both a strength and a deficiency. It is a deficiency in that being highly specific about the enormously complex interactions that seem inherent in dysfunctional families is notoriously difficult. Without a framework for understanding the interactions in the family as a whole, identifying specific behaviors to be changed may be very limiting.

Behavioral family interventions rely on the same principles of learning discussed in Chapter 8 and on many of the same intervention techniques, as well. The learning model most often used in the family area is social learning theory, with particular attention to principles of operant conditioning in terms of what maintains undesirable behavior and what is needed to increase desirable behavior in couple and parent-child interactions. Just as in behavioral therapies in general, more attention has been given in recent years to the role of cognitive factors in behavioral marital and parent-child interventions.

Like most family therapists, behavioral counselors tend to be active and directive, and they emphasize their clients' active involvement in the treatment, as well. Behavioral counselors often serve as educators, teaching their family clients to apply learning principles and behavioral techniques and reinforcing desired behaviors in their clients. Behavioral family counselors have worked primarily in two general areas: marital counseling and parent training. In both these areas, treatment is preceded by a careful behavioral assessment to determine which behaviors are to be modified. A range of assessment techniques are used, as detailed in Chapter 8. The goal is to pinpoint target behaviors (those to be changed) and get a baseline of such behaviors. The frequency, intensity, duration, and situational context of target behaviors is analyzed. Great pains are taken to reduce presenting problems to specific, behavioral terms.

Numerous behavioral techniques and programs have been presented in the literature, in both the marital and parent training areas (Foster & Gurman, 1985). Only a general flavor of these procedures will be given here. In marital counseling, the therapist helps each spouse identify behaviors in the other that are desirable and to communicate what is wanted. The therapist also develops a behaviorally oriented treatment plan aimed at increasing the desired behaviors. Focus is more on increasing the positive than decreasing the negative. Various types of contingency contracting are frequently used. Here positive behavior of one member is made dependent on positive behavior of another. For example, Charlie agrees to spend a half hour with the children each night before bedtime if Jane does the dishes. Such a contingency is usually also balanced; for example, Jane goes on weekly hiking trips with Charlie if Charlie vacuums twice a week. In such contracting, it is important that none of the behaviors be objectionable to either member. Also, for problems that are too conflictual to be dealt with by simple contingency contracting methods, the behavioral counselor uses structured problem-solving techniques. The couple is taught to clearly define problems, discuss one problem at a time, listen to and paraphrase what the other has said, avoid verbal abuse, and state what they want in positive terms rather than deficiencies, for example: "I like the way you do . . . ," and "I would like it if you did . . ."

In behavioral parent training, behavioral principles are used to modify the behavior of the parent(s) and child, and the parent-child interactions. But if the child is brought for help as the identified patient, the behavioral counselor tends to accept that. At times, though, the problem the family seeks help with may not be the one the therapist judges to be appropriate for the first phase of treatment. For example, a family seeks help because the children seem to be fighting all the time. Upon observation, the therapist notices that the children fight with each other especially when the parents argue, which is often. The therapist is likely to judge that marital counseling is the best first step, that is, before working directly on modifying the children's behavior.

As a first step in parent training, the parent(s) is (are) taught to specify the problem behavior in the child or adolescent, record its frequency, and note the events that accompanied the problem behavior. The last step is aimed at determining what events might be the stimuli or reinforcers for the problem behavior. Then the parents are taught to intervene systematically, using behavioral techniques. The most common techniques involve operant conditioning, whereby desirable behaviors are positively reinforced and undesirable ones are either ignored or punished (see Chapter 8). Care is taken in selecting effective reinforcers, as children vary greatly in what is reinforcing to them. The Premack Principle (Premack, 1965) is a long-standing one followed in parent training. Thus, a high-frequency behavior is used as a reinforcer for a low-frequency but highly desired (by the parents) behavior. For example, let us say that the parents of Johnny, a five-year-old boy, are driven to distraction by his constant refusal to eat reasonably balanced meals (rather than just sweets). We find that Johnny's favorite activities are riding his tricycle and playing with his buddy, Stan, in the back yard. The Premack Principle would involve making Johnny's favored (high-frequency) behaviors contingent on his eating properly while reducing complaining behavior. This program might be implemented in steps, so that reinforcers would be given as desired behaviors approximate the end goals.

Time-out procedures (as noted in Chapter 8) are also often used in parent training in an effort to extinguish unwanted behavior. Here the child is usually taken to a place where the usual reinforcers are lacking (e.g., a room without TV, when she or he misbehaves). It is important, though, that appropriate behaviors be positively reinforced.

Despite their tendency to ignore systems, behavioral counselors have devised an arsenal of techniques that appear to modify behavior effectively in couple and parent-child interactions. From a systems perspective, what may be learned from these behavioral technologists is that changes in any part of the system have effects on other parts; recall the concept of equifinality discussed in the early part of this chapter. Even though a given behavior may be tied to numerous elements of the family structure, system, and subsystem, that behavior may be modified without directly altering the system; the resulting change may be long-lasting and, in itself, have a positive effect on the system.

FAMILY AND COUPLES THERAPY IN PERSPECTIVE

In this final section we discuss the current status of family therapy and its relationship to counseling psychology. We conclude by examining some of the major research findings in the family therapy field.

Current Status of Family and Couples Therapy

The growth of family therapy and its impact on the general field of counseling and psychotherapy during the past three decades have been astounding, by almost any criteria one cares to use (Gurman, Kniskern, & Pinsoff, 1986). For example, whereas in 1973 there existed only one professional journal in the family therapy field, there are now more than two dozen journals, this number including only those published in English. Gurman and his colleagues note that the frequency of new books is also remarkable.

Another sign of growth is membership in professional organizations pertinent to a field. In the family and couples area the major organization is the American Association for Marriage and Family Therapy. In 1970 that association had 973 members (Foster & Gurman, 1985). By 1975 the figure mushroomed to 7,000, and by 1985 had grown to almost 13,000 (Gurman et al., 1986). Our impression is that in the most recent years this growth has naturally leveled off, but the growth continues, and as Foley (1989) indicates, the future of the family therapy movement is bright indeed.

Another index of the current popularity of family and couples therapy deserves mention. In the United States alone, there are more than 350 training programs in family therapy, approximately half offering graduate degrees. Further, Gurman et al. (1986) estimate that as many as 15,000 people annually received family therapy training in the late 1980s.

Naturally, in a field growing at such a phenomenal rate, many issues will arise. One main issue pertains to the growth and integration of theoretical approaches to family intervention. Stated baldly, there has been tremendous growth but little integration. This is not surprising in a new field, for which theoretical approaches to practice must be developed. In any new field, one might first expect a pattern of development in roughly the following order: creation of many new approaches; the forming of "schools" revolving around the most prominent approaches; the fighting among schools as to which approach is best; the realization that there is no best way and that each approach will have its strengths and weaknesses; and, finally, the attempt to integrate different approaches, with still different methods and theories evolving from such integrations.

In the area of family therapy there are now a number of schools, and there has been plenty of battling about which is best. Efforts at integration of these multiple perspectives have begun only in the most recent years. As examples, the reader is referred to two thoughtful pieces: Lebow (1987) has discussed the strengths and limitations of integrating different approaches; Aradi and Kaslow (1987) provide a helpful discussion of how the practicing therapist may go about integrating diverse approaches into his or her treatment. Another general issue that seems to be an inherent part of the family therapy movement pertains to the balance between attention to the individual vs. attention to the family system. Perhaps in an effort to counter the overwhelming focus of the counseling and psychotherapy enterprise on the individual, family therapists have strongly emphasized the family system. In this movement toward a broader framework, often the individual seemed to be forgotten. Salvador Minuchin (Minuchin, Rosman, & Baker, 1978, p. 91), for example, worried about the danger in "denying the individual while enthroning the system." Within the family approaches, it is important that some problems be seen and treated as individual, that some be seen and treated as systems, but, most important, that the interrelationship of individuals and systems be examined. Foster and Gurman (1985) make this point nicely:

> There is a way in which systems thinking can obscure the fact that families, after all, are composed of feeling and thinking individuals. To embrace a strictly family systems framework may serve the purpose of understanding how a group of individuals in a family can be viewed as a system but it does not explain the interplay among the individuals so regarded. What is most compelling is the gritty task of explaining these interrelationships. (pp. 413–414)

Family Therapy and Counseling Psychology

Just as family therapy has grown dramatically in popularity in recent years, so too has it grown in popularity among counseling psychologists. For example, in a recent survey (Fitzgerald & Osipow, 1988), well over half of a large sample of counseling psychologists were involved in family and couples counseling, and, even more revealing, over 80 percent of a large sample of graduate students in counseling psychology desired to do family and couples work when they completed graduate school. Furthermore, surveys of counseling graduate students (Fitzgerald & Osipow, 1988), and training directors of counseling psychology doctoral students (Schneider, Watkins, & Gelso, 1988) clearly indicate that, not only is family and couples counseling of great interest to graduate students, but these counseling students view such work as an important part of their professional identity.

On the negative side, given the recency of the family and couples counseling movement, it appears that graduate training within counseling psychology has not yet caught up with the need for training. Thus, in the Schneider et al. (1988) study, the ratings made by training directors of counseling psychology doctoral programs suggest that such training is not as effective as it needs to be. What this probably means is that there are simply not enough graduate courses (practica and didactic courses) on family and couples therapy in these counseling programs. Given the growing interest in family and couples work among counseling psychology students and practitioners, we would expect the amount of training to increase substantially in counseling doctoral programs.

The studies we have just described, and in fact much of the material in this chapter, have combined couples counseling and family counseling. It appears, however, that couples counseling has been embraced to a greater extent than family treatment by counseling psychologists. For example, the national survey by Watkins, Lopez, Campbell, and Himmell (1986) revealed that nearly two-thirds of a large sample of counseling psychologists were involved in couples therapy, whereas less than half conducted family therapy. The reason for this difference pertains largely to job settings. Working so often at university counseling centers and treating college students, counseling psychologists have dealt with a client population whose main developmental tasks involve separation from the family, and families have been rarely incorporated into treatment. At the same time, given the importance for college-aged students of developmental tasks revolving around intimate relationships, couples therapy (whether or not the couple was married) has been a prime intervention. As counseling psychologists move into a wide range of settings and as the percentage of professionals who conduct independent practice increases, we expect greater involvement in family as well as couples treatments.

Research on Family Interventions

What does empirical research have to say about the effectiveness of family and couples interventions? Just as with virtually all types of recognized interventions, the evidence suggests that family and couples counseling *on the whole* are effective forms of treatment in resolving a range of problems. Beyond this global evaluation, family and couples researchers are just beginning to accumulate replicable findings about what we have referred to elsewhere as the "who, what, when, and where" question of counseling effectiveness (Gelso, 1979; Gelso & Fassinger, 1990). In other words, family and couples researchers are now tackling the many complex questions within the more general question—with what kinds of clients are what kinds of family and couples interventions effective in which ways when offered by which kinds of counselors using what techniques?

As with counseling research in general, we may divide research on family and couples counseling into two kinds: process research and outcome research. Research on the process of family and couples counseling (what leads to what within the session) has just begun in earnest during the past decade, and there are now a number of significant research programs in the United States. Summary of findings within this area is beyond the scope of this chapter. We refer the reader to the thoughtful and extensive analysis by Gurman et al. (1986).

Regarding treatment outcomes (the effects of counseling), the work history is longer, so more findings have accumulated. Based on their exhaustive reviews of dozens of studies, Gurman et al. (1986) and Foster and Gurman (1985) have been able to make a number of major conclusions. These are summarized as follows:

1. Family and couples therapy has been found to be beneficial in about two-thirds of the cases, and the effects have been clearly superior to no treatment (control groups).
2. The positive effects of both behavioral and nonbehavioral family and couples counseling typically occur in brief treatments, that is, 1–20 sessions.
3. Regarding the components of treatment, communication training appears to be a technique with sound empirical support.

4. When both members of a couple are in therapy conjointly in the face of marital problems, there is greater chance of positive outcomes than when only one member is treated.
5. The greater the number of family members included in family counseling the better the outcome; inclusion of the father is important.
6. Family therapy is as effective and possibly more effective than individual treatment for problems attributed to family conflict.
7. No support exists for the superiority of couples or family counseling in which two therapists work together simultaneously.
8. Therapist relationship skills (e.g., warmth, empathy) are important for successful family and couples therapy. They have effects above and beyond the effects due to the therapist's technical skill.
9. Family and couples therapy, just like individual therapy, at times results in clients' getting worse. In the family and couples area, such deterioration may be reliably related to therapists' providing little structure in early sessions combined with confrontation of highly affective material, rather than combining stimulating interaction with emotional support.
10. The developmental level of the identified patient (e.g., child, adolescent, adult) does not affect treatment outcomes. Neither do certain family variables such as the diagnosis of the identified patient, quality of family interaction, and family structure.

Throughout this chapter we have signaled key readings, in particular, major sources for each theoretical cluster. In terms of general readings on family therapy, Nichols' (1984) book, as noted, is a thoughtful and interesting treatment of all major approaches to family therapy. Foley's (1986) book is an excellent introduction for the beginning student. Gurman and Kniskern's (1981) handbook presents in-depth studies written by leaders of each major approach and is as useful today as it was when published over ten years ago. Foster and Gurman (1985) have written a useful review chapter on the major approaches, with many helpful case examples. Foley (1989) presents a review of family therapy whose perspective differs from that of the current chapter and thus provides a valuable supplement. Foley presents the family therapy approach and assumes that there is indeed an approach that cuts across the major perspectives.

SUMMARY

The family therapy movement, which began in the 1950s, originated from two sources: the Palo Alto studies of families in which one or more of the children was schizophrenic and the independent work of several creative clinicians who began to experiment with family therapy. Besides the Palo Alto group and the Mental Research Institute, the work of three clinicians had a profound effect on the new field of family therapy: Nathan Ackerman, Carl Whitaker, and Murray Bowen.

Family therapy was described as a *diverse set of perspectives having in common a systems perspective of behavior.* Several basic assumptions of systems theory as applied to families include: (a) systems are organized wholes with interdependent parts; (b) causality is circular rather than linear and one can effectively intervene at any point in a system; (c) systems seek to maintain homeostasis, but effective systems do change when needed; (d) systems contain subsystems, of which a major example is the triangle; (e) all systems have boundaries, rules, and patterns.

Six approaches to family and couples counseling were reviewed. The *psychoanalytic approach* most often uses object relations theory as a way to conceptualize couples and family dynamics. Attention is given to how objects are internalized and to their far-reaching effects on couples and families. *Projective identification* is a major defense in couples relationships. The *experiential approach* focuses on here-and-now feelings, therapist spontaneity, and confrontation to help expand couples' and families' immediate experience and to emotionally unfreeze the family. The *family systems* approach, originated by Murray Bowen, contains several major constructs about families: emotional triangles, differentiation of self, nuclear family emotional system, family projection process, and multigenerational transmission. The family systems therapist takes a rational approach in helping clients develop differentiation within the self and between the self and other family members. The *strategic approach* is brief, active, and symptom-oriented. Strategic therapists treat specific behaviors within a systems context. They are directive and at times manipulative, using straightforward suggestions as well *paradoxical interventions.* Minuchin's *structural approach* focuses on the constructs: (1) family structure, (2) subsystems, and (3) boundaries. Structuralists are active and directive, using affective intensity to unshake clients' embedded problems. They seek to influence the family's structure and to develop boundaries between subsystems that are neither rigid nor diffuse. The *behavioral approach* works most with couples or parent-child dyads in modifying specific behaviors through the use of behavioral techniques and principles. Of all the approaches it is *least* systems-oriented, but studies have shown behavioral couples counseling and parent training to be effective interventions.

The family and couples therapy movement has grown tremendously during the past two decades. Two key issues at this time are the need for integration among the diverse approaches and the need for balance between emphasis on the system and emphasis on the individual. The general area of family and couples intervention is growing in popularity in counseling psychology, although in the past greater interest has been shown in couples interventions than in family treatment. This may be due to the settings in which counseling psychologists have worked and may be changing in the future.

Research on family and couples therapy has confirmed the general effectiveness of this intervention. Researchers are now examining the *process* of family and couples counseling and the "who, what, when, and where" questions pertinent to the effects of these treatments.

References

Ackerman, N. (1958). *The psychodynamics of family life.* New York: Basic Books.

Ackerman, N. (1961). A dynamic frame for the clinical approach to family conflict. In N. Ackerman, F. Beatman, & S. Sherman (Eds.), *Exploring the base for family therapy.* New York: Family Services Association of America.

Aponte, H., & VanDeusen, J. (1981). Structural family therapy. In A. Gurman & D. Kniskern (Eds.), *Handbook of family therapy* (pp. 310–360). New York: Brunner/Mazel.

Aradi, N., & Kaslow, F. (1987). Theory integration in family therapy: Definition, rationale, content and process. *Psychotherapy, 24,* 595–608.

Bateson, G. (1972). *Steps in an ecology of mind.* New York: Ballantine.

Bateson, G. (1979). *Mind and nature.* New York: Dutton.

Bateson, G., Jackson, D., Haley, J., & Weakland, J. (1956). Toward a theory of schizophrenia. *Behavioral Science, 1,* 251–264.

Boszormenyi-Nagy, I. (1972). Loyalty implications of the transference model in psychotherapy. *Archives of General Psychiatry, 27,* 374–380.

Bowen, M. (1966). The use of family theory in clinical practice. *Comprehensive Psychiatry, 7,* 345–374.

Bowen, M. (1976). Theory in the practice of psychotherapy. In P. Guerin (Ed.), *Family therapy* (pp. 42–89). New York: Gardner Press.

Bowen, M. (1978). *Family therapy in clinical practice.* New York: Jason Aronson.

Carter, E., & McGoldrick, M. (Eds.). (1980). *The family life cycle: A framework for family therapy.* New York: Gardner Press.

Dowd, E., & Milne, C. (1986). Paradoxical interventions in counseling psychology. *The Counseling Psychologist, 14,* 237–282.

Fairbairn, W. (1952). *An object relations theory of personality.* New York: Basic Books.

Fisch, R., Weakland, J., & Segal, L. (1982). *The tactics of change: Doing therapy briefly.* San Francisco, CA: Jossey-Bass.

Fitzgerald, L., & Osipow, S. (1988). We have seen the future, but is it us? The vocational aspirations of graduate students in counseling psychology. *Professional Psychology: Research and Practice, 19,* 575–583.

Foley, V. (1986). *An introduction to family therapy* (2nd ed.). New York: Grune and Stratton.

Foley, V. (1989). Family therapy. In R. Corsini & D. Wedding (Eds.), *Current psychotherapies* (4th ed., pp. 455–500). Itasca, IL: Peacock.

Foster, S., & Gurman, A. (1985). Family therapies. In S. Lynn & J. Garske (Eds.), *Contemporary psychotherapies: models and methods* (pp. 377–418). Columbus, OH: Merrill.

Gelso, C. (1979). Research in counseling: Methodological and professional issues. *The Counseling Psychologist, 8*(3), 7–35.

Gelso, C., & Fassinger, R. (1990). Counseling psychology: Theory and research on interventions. *Annual Review of Psychology, 41,* 355–386.

Goldenberg, I., & Goldenberg, H. (1985). *Family therapy: An overview* (2nd ed.). Monterey, CA: Brooks/Cole.

Guntrip, H. (1969). Schizoid phenomena, object relations, and the self. New York: International Universities Press.

Gurman, A., & Kniskern, D. (Eds.) (1981). *Handbook of family therapy.* New York: Brunner/Mazel.

Gurman, A., Kniskern, D., & Pinsoff, W. (1986). Research on marital and family therapies. In S. Garfield & A. Bergin (Eds.), *Handbook of psychotherapy and behavior change* (3rd ed., pp. 565–623). New York: Wiley.

Haley, J. (1976). *Problem-solving therapy.* San Francisco, CA: Jossey-Bass.

Hoffman, L. (1981). *Foundations of family therapy.* New York: Basic Books.

Jackson, D. (1957). The question of family homeostasis. *Psychiatric Quarterly Supplement, 31,* 79–90.

Jackson, D., & Weakland, J. (1959). Conjoint family therapy: Some considerations on theory, technique, and results. *Psychiatry, 24,* 30–45.

Katz, B. (1981). Separation-individuation and marital therapy. *Psychotherapy: Theory, Research, and Practice, 18,* 195–203.

Kempler, W. (1973). *Principles of gestalt family therapy.* Oslo, Norway: Nordahls.

Kerr, M. (1981). Family systems theory and therapy. In A. Gurman & D. Kniskern (Eds.), *Handbook of family therapy* (pp. 226–264). New York: Brunner/Mazel.

Lebow, J. (1987). Integrative family therapy: An overview of major issues. *Psychotherapy, 24,* 584–594.

Levant, R. (1983). Client-centered skills training programs for the family. *The Counseling Psychologist, 11*(3), 29–46.

Madanes, C. (1981). *Strategic family therapy.* San Francisco, CA: Jossey-Bass.

Minuchin, P. (1985). Families and individual development: Provocations from the field of family therapy. *Child Development, 56,* 289–302.

Minuchin, S. (1974). *Families and family therapy.* Cambridge, MA: Harvard University Press.

Minuchin, S., & Fishman, H. (1981). *Family therapy techniques.* Cambridge, MA: Harvard University Press.

Minuchin, S., Rosman, B., & Baker, L. (1978). *Psychosomatic families.* Cambridge, MA: Harvard University Press.

Nichols, M. (1984). *Family therapy: Concepts and methods.* New York: Gardner Press.

Satir, V. (1967). *Conjoint family therapy.* Palo Alto, CA: Science and Behavior Books.

Scarf, M. (1987). *Intimate Partners: Patterns in love and marriage.* New York: Random House.

Schneider, L., Watkins, C. E., & Gelso, C. (1988). Counseling psychology from 1971 to 1986: Perspective on and appraisal of current emphases. *Professional Psychology: Research and Practice, 19,* 584–588.

Selvini Palazzoli, M., Boscolo, L., Cecchin, G., & Prata, G. (1978). *Paradox and counterparadox.* New York: Jason Aronson.

Skynner, R. (1981). An open-systems, group-analytic approach to family therapy. In A. Gurman & D. Kniskern (Eds.), *Handbook of family therapy* (pp. 39–84). New York: Brunner/Mazel.

Umbarger, C. (1983). *Structural family therapy.* New York: Grune and Stratton.

VonBertalanffy, L. (1968). General systems theory: Formulations, development, applications. New York: George Braziller.

VonBertalanffy, L. (1974). General systems theory and psychiatry. In S. Arieti (Ed.), *American handbook of psychiatry* (Vol. 1, pp. 1095–1117). New York: Basic Books.

Watkins, C. E., Jr., Lopez, F. G., Campbell, V. L., & Himmell, C. D. (1986). Contemporary counseling psychology: Results of a national survey. *Journal of Counseling Psychology, 33,* 301–309.

Watzlawick, P., Beavin, J., & Jackson, D. (1967). *The pragmatics of communication.* New York: Norton.

Watzlawick, P., Weakland, J., & Fisch, R. (1974). *Change: Principles of problem formation and problem resolution.* New York: Norton.

Whitaker, C. (1976). The hindrance of theory in clinical work. In P. Guerin (Ed.), *Family therapy: Theory and practice.* New York: Gardner Press.

Whitaker, C., & Keith, D. (1981). Symbolic-experiential family therapy. In A. Gurman & D. Kniskern (Eds.), *Handbook of family therapy* (pp. 187–225). New York: Brunner/Mazel.

Chapter 15

Therapeutic Groupwork: An Established Format

Both research and practice have now clearly demonstrated that individual counseling or therapy is effective for a variety of client concerns. Also, clients who seek counseling typically want individual help. Why then should counseling psychologists bother with group treatments such as group counseling and psychotherapy? Why not simply assign all clients to individual counseling? Doing so would certainly simplify the training of counseling psychologists, for then they could be trained only in individual interventions. Assigning all clients to individual treatments would also simplify agency practices, since counseling agencies would no longer need to worry about whom to assign to what interventions. Nor would agencies then need to grapple with logistical problems such as how to arrange for group meeting times.

In devising our answer to the above questions, we must first say that what is the simplest practice is often not the *most effective.* To begin with, group procedures allow for an efficient use of the counseling psychologist's time, as a number of individuals may be worked with simultaneously in a group format. More important than this efficiency, however, is the fact that group interventions such as group therapy, just like individual counseling, have been shown to be especially helpful for a range of concerns (Kaul & Bednar, 1986).

ADVANTAGES AND LIMITATIONS

Are there unique advantages to group interventions such as group counseling or therapy? Although the research evidence is as yet unclear about this, the major advantages of group treatment are generally seen as *interpersonal.* Thus, the client in group therapy learns by observing other group members, receiving feedback from others, giving feedback and being helpful to other group members, becoming part of a cohesive group, and, moreover, participating in the sharing and the give and take of this very personal form of interpersonal interaction.

It follows that clients who will profit most from group interventions are those whose difficulties are in the interpersonal arena. For example, clients who suffer from interpersonal anxiety, who are unsure of their relationship skills, who desire close relationships but for one reason or another shy away from them—all are prime candidates for group therapy. Group therapy also can be particularly effective in less obvious cases. For example, the client whose family dynamics breed secrecy and shame may experience enormous growth from a group experience in which his or her inner feelings are shared and accepted by other members. Likewise, the client whose major problem itself breeds secrecy and shame may find group therapy strikingly helpful. An example of this latter type might be the female incest survivor who participates in group therapy as a way of coming to grips with her sense of shame and self-blame about her incestuous experiences. Recent literature on women who have experienced the trauma of incest supports the idea that group treatments can be especially effective for these clients (Courtois, 1988). The unique efficacy of group therapy for the incest survivor has been stated in a particularly convincing way by one therapist who has worked with this client group in both individual and group formats:

> I can't tell you how many times I have worked with individual clients who were incest survivors on the "shame and blame" syndrome common to incest survivors, and no matter what I say or do as a therapist, I'm only one countervoice to years of self-blame and humiliation. Progress is often relatively slow. Put the same client into an incest survivor's group—she shares her horrible secret—and other people communicate their common experience, and she sees clearly that she is not to blame. The change in group therapy is so much more dramatic than in individual, it is a truly astounding experience for some. The relief often happens even after only one or two sessions. There is something about *universality* and *consensual validation* [see later discussion of these two factors] that occurs in group treatment that makes it extremely effective with incest survivors (Dr. Ruth E. Fassinger, Department of Counseling and Personnel Services, University of Maryland, personal communication, June 12, 1990).

The major advantages of therapeutic groups, as discussed by Corey and Corey (1987), are:

1. Participants can explore their style of relating to others and learn more effective social skills.

2. The group situation offers support for new behaviors and encourages experimentation. Members can try out new behaviors and decide whether they want to incorporate them into their repertoire outside the group.
3. More than in individual counseling, there is a re-creation of the everyday world in many groups, especially if the membership is diverse with respect to interest, age, background, culture, and problem type. When groups are heterogeneous in this way, members are able to contact a wide range of personalities, and receive rich and diverse feedback.
4. Members are able to learn about themselves through the experience of others; to experience emotional closeness and caring, which encourages meaningful self-disclosure; and to identify with the struggles of others.

Groups are not cure-alls, although some group leaders unfortunately see group treatments as the only means of effective behavior change. Also, as Corey and Corey (1987) tell us, some practitioners seem to believe that a very brief, intense group experience can remake people's lives. Unrealistic expectations of this sort can result in hurtful experiences for clients, especially those who also have such expectations. This is of course not a limitation of groupwork per se, since practitioners of individual counseling may also have the same sort of inappropriate expectancies. Some key limitations discussed by Corey and Corey (1987) are:

1. There is often a subtle pressure to conform to the group's expectations and norms. Some group members may take in these norms without questioning.
2. Some people get hooked on groups and turn the group experience into an end in itself, rather than a laboratory to learn new behaviors that can be used outside the group. The group experience becomes savored for its own sake, and no change occurs.
3. Not all persons are suited to groups. The authors underscore that the idea that groups are for everyone has done serious harm to the reputation of the group movement. Some individuals are too suspicious, too narcissistic, too hostile, or too fragile to benefit from treatments such as group therapy; and some can suffer emotional injury by participating in certain groups. This highlights the fact that counselors need to do thoughtful screening of potential group clients and that both the counselor and client need to weigh at the outset of therapy the possible benefits and drawbacks of the group experience.
4. Similar to the type described in number 2 above, some persons tend to make a group a place to ventilate their miseries and bare their souls. They seek total acceptance and understanding from

the group and make no attempt to do what is necessary to change their lives.

Obviously, considerable skill in client selection to begin with, and in group management subsequently, is needed to deal effectively with the potential problems listed above. With effective leadership (discussed later in the chapter), many of the limitations of groups can be worked with and transcended.

We would like now to take a step back and examine just what is meant by therapeutic groups and describe some of the major types of such groups as well as the backgrounds of these interventions. Then, in the remainder of the chapter, we explore leadership factors in groupwork, the stages of groups, the ingredients of effective groups, and some ethical issues in groupwork. We conclude the chapter with a discussion of the place of groupwork in counseling psychology, the research issues involved in group treatment, and findings in this area.

THERAPEUTIC GROUPWORK: DEFINITION, TYPES, AND BACKGROUND

To begin with, it is possible to define a *group* as "any aggregate of individuals among which some degree of interdependence exists." A *therapeutic group* may be defined as an "aggregate of interdependent individuals whose interaction is in pursuit of some shared goal or goals." The therapeutic group is always more than the sum of its individual parts because the group itself takes on its own life, its own psyche so to speak, and its own personality.

Therapeutic groups can include a wide range of interventions such as group psychotherapy, group counseling, encounter and growth groups, T groups, structured groups, and self-help groups. Below we describe each of these types of groups, in particular, group counseling/therapy, and briefly note the background of their development in counseling psychology.

Group Counseling and Group Psychotherapy

Group counseling tends to be more oriented toward prevention (vs. remediation) than does group psychotherapy. Also, group counseling is more likely to focus on the conscious concerns of the client, to include attention to educational and vocational issues as well as personal ones, to occur in educational settings (in contrast to medical or clinical settings), and to be used with clients within the normal range rather than with severely troubled persons. Group counseling is, on the whole, briefer than group therapy, with generally an upper limit of about 20 to 25 sessions. Group therapy, on the other hand, may continue for several years and is more likely than counseling to seek deep personality change in clients.

Although we have described the typical distinctions between group counseling and therapy, it should be emphasized that the differences are more of degree than kind. There is considerable overlap between the two, just as there is much overlap between the terms *counseling* and *therapy* (see definitions in Chapter 1). In fact, except at the extreme ends of the continuum, the differences become blurred or eliminated with most groups in counseling practice. Corey and Corey's (1987) description of group counseling really applies to both group counseling and therapy. According to these authors, participants in group counseling or therapy often have problems of an interpersonal nature, which are well suited to the group format. Clients are able to see a reenactment of their everyday struggles and problems unfold before them in the group. In the group, however, the client is able to work on and through these problems, with the feedback and help of group members. In this way the group provides a slice of reality to the client as well as a vehicle for change. Members are encouraged to get feedback from others about how they are seen, as well as to give such feedback. They also have the chance to re-experience early conflicts with significant others, and in the process of reliving, to work through old issues. The empathy and support of the group also allow members to identify what and how they want to change and to try out new behaviors. Clients can learn to respect individual and cultural differences and, at the same time, discover that on a deep level they are more alike than different. Life situations differ, but their pain and struggles are universal.

Despite the similarities and overlap between group counseling and therapy, the two have differing historical backgrounds. Group counseling, for example, has its roots in education and guidance; its beginnings may be traced to the vocational guidance movement in the early part of this century. Early guidance groups were mostly in the form of classes and the methods used in these classes were largely instructional (Gazda, 1984). The group psychotherapy movement can also be traced to the early part of the 20th century, but is usually seen as beginning with the work of Boston internist Joseph Hersey Pratt and his publication in 1906 of "The Home Sanitorium Treatment of Consumption." Like the early group guidance workers, Pratt's group procedures with his tuberculosis patients were largely inspirational and instructional. During this time period also, early psychoanalysts (Freud, Adler, Driekurs, and Furrow) were writing about group analytic work.

Although therapeutic groupwork was practiced throughout the early part of the century, it was not until the 1930s that it experienced a major growth spurt. The term *group counseling* may have been first used in 1931 by Dr. Richard D. Allen within a school setting, whereas in the same year J. L. Moreno first used the term *group therapy.* Moreno, an actor turned group therapist, is often seen as the father of group therapy and of the related fields of psychodrama and sociometry. He began experimenting with group therapy early in the century, and as a medical student in Vienna he organized and led group sessions for Viennese prostitutes. Before emigrating to the United States in 1925, Moreno established "The Theatre of Spontaneous Man," which attempted to represent the dramas of life for therapeutic staging. Moreno also developed the first group therapy journal, *Impromptu,* in 1931. Other individuals who had a major role in the mushrooming of group therapeutic procedures during this time period were Louis Wender, Paul Schilder, Lauretta Bender, Alexander Wolf, and Samuel Slavson. Slavson's work is of particular note. Ettin (1989) states that Slavson was a prominent proselytizer, prolific writer, and vigilant watchdog in the field of group therapy for more than half of his 91 years. Slavson founded the American Group Psychotherapy Association in 1943 and originated the *International Journal of Group Psychotherapy* in 1951. Many consider Slavson, rather than Moreno, to be the father of group therapy.

Training (T) Groups and Sensitivity Training Groups

The concept of T group (*T* for *training*) or what has come to be its synonym, sensitivity group, grew out of the work of Kurt Lewin. Lewin is considered by many to be the major researcher and theoretician of democracy in psychology (Schmuck & Schmuck, 1979), and the basic mission of the T group was to train democratic managers and administrators in business and industry. These training groups began with the birth of the National Training Laboratories (NTL) in 1947 at Bethel, Maine. NTL tried to create an environment where change could occur, especially interpersonal change, through laboratory training.

In the standard NTL-type T group, participants find themselves in an unstructured situation, in which it is their task to build out of their interaction a group that can help them meet their needs for support, feedback, and learning. The behaviors enacted by members as they participate in the group provide the material for analysis and learning. Thus, T group members have the chance to learn about how their behavior is seen by others, the roles they and others tend to play, ways of being more sensitive to others, and methods for understanding group dynamics. All of this is aimed at translating behavior into more effective democratic leadership. Time is usually provided for trainees to plan how they will apply their knowledge after the laboratory (Eddy & Lubin, 1971). T groups are oriented toward the here and now and are developmental and growth-oriented in nature, rather than remedial or even preventive. They may range from a one-day workshop to an ongoing group, although the typical T group may entail two or so weeks of intensive training.

Encounter and Growth Groups

Just as the 1930s witnessed a mushrooming of interest in group therapy, the 1960s saw heightened involvement in new kinds of therapeutic groups. Undergirding these new groups was a social-psychological movement, called the "human potential movement." In psychology, this movement was spearheaded by humanistic therapists such as Carl Rogers, Abraham Maslow, Herbert Otto, Jack Gibb, and William Schutz. The essential theme of this movement was that humans tend to actualize only a tiny fraction of their potential and that psychological interventions of a developmental nature can help them move toward self-actualization. Many of these interventions took the form of groups, the most prominent groups of the times called "encounter," or "growth," groups.

Thus, the encounter, or growth, group grew out of individuals' need to become more fully functioning. These groups aimed to help already well-functioning persons relate more effectively and intimately with others, reduce feelings of alienation, and become more aware of their feelings and direct experiencing rather than only their cognitive functioning. Encounter groups tend to promote such norms as openness, honesty, release of inhibitions, sharing, being on a feeling level, risking new behaviors, and being in the here and now (Peterson & Nisenholz, 1987). Such groups are usually emotionally intensive experiences, and the leader tends to take a more active and directive role than in most therapeutic groups. In the 1960s and early 1970s encounter groups often contained physical interaction among participants, and there was a good bit of experimenting with dance, art, massage, and nudity. In the more conservative climate of the 1980s and 1990s, there is much less of this sort of experimentation, and group leadership tends to be less active and aggressive. Although growth groups are not as popular as they once were, there is clearly still a place for them in counseling psychology, particularly given their focus on human potential and growth.

Finally, one additional type of growth group deserves note. The *marathon growth group* also grew out of the 1960s, and it, too, aimed at enhancing interpersonal openness, sensitivity, and intimacy. The distinguishing feature of the marathon group was its continuation over many hours or even days with only minimal breaks. The typical marathon group, for example, might occur over a weekend, with breaks only for eating and sleeping. The idea behind this procedure is that when interaction among participants occurs without the usual interruptions, people are more likely to take off their social masks and become genuine with one another. Although not now as popular as in the 1960s and 1970s, marathons are still conducted, usually as part of ongoing group therapy. Thus, the typical marathon group is held at some point during the ongoing life of a therapy group, with enough regular group therapy time after the marathon to work through issues that emerged during the intensity of the extended sessions. Marathons conducted in this way can be powerful adjuncts to group counseling or therapy.

Structured Groups

Just as the encounter group was a child of the 1960s, the structured group grew out of the social-psychological climate of the 1970s, with its emphasis on accountability of services and the need to provide efficient as well as effective treatments. The main features of the structured group are discussed in detail in Chapter 16. For now, suffice it to say that the structured group is oriented toward a single theme, and from this theme emerges the goals of treatment. For example, the theme might be assertiveness training, and the goals consequently would revolve around improving participants' assertiveness skills. Often based on behavioral principles such as reinforcement and shaping, structured groups tend to be brief, for example, 6–8 weekly sessions, lasting an hour and a half or two hours. Typically, the leader follows a predeveloped treatment manual in which the tasks for each session are spelled out. In terms of the developmental-preventive-remedial continuum, structured groups tend to be preventive. Over the years, the themes of such groups have emerged from issues that were reflected in the broader society. Examples of popular structured group themes are: stress management, adult children of alcoholics, assertion training, support for incest survivors, relationship skill training, women in transition, and eating disorders (e.g., bulimia).

Self-Help Groups

The final type of therapeutic group that we shall describe is often ignored in discussions of groupwork. Self-help groups, however, fulfill a critical need for many people that is not met by mental health workers. Self-help groups are composed of people with common interests and problems. They give participants a crucial support system, providing motivation to help them begin changing their lives. As Corey and Corey (1987) indicate, self-help groups stress a common identity based on a common life situation far more than any other type of group. Typically open (new members may enter the group at any time), these groups offer inspiration, hope, encouragement, and support, often to people who feel little hope to begin with. Examples of self-help groups are Alcoholics Anonymous, Weight Watchers, Mended Hearts, and Recovery. These groups are led by persons who struggle with the same problems as members (e.g., the recovering alcoholic in AA), rather than being professionally led.

GROUP LEADERSHIP: APPROACHES, TASKS, AND QUALITIES

The Leader's Focus

Over the years, there has been considerable controversy over whether the group leader ought to focus his or her observations on the group as a whole or the individuals within the group. A third possibility is to focus on the interactions between and among members.

Group-Centered Approach. The method of focusing on the group as a whole originated and received its strongest voice at the Tavistock Clinic in England (e.g., Bion, 1961). This approach is based on the idea that the group is an entity in itself and that individuals learn most by understanding this entity, how they fit into it, and how they contribute to it. In the extreme, the therapist's comments when following this method are rarely aimed at individuals but, rather, seek to clarify the underlying meanings and processes in the group as a whole.

Individual-Centered Approach. Examples of the individual-centered approach are psychoanalytic groups and certain gestalt therapy groups. In some gestalt groups, for example, the individual participant is placed into the "hot seat" and the counselor devotes his or her therapeutic energies for a period of time to that client and the issues he or she is experiencing at the moment. Other participants presumably learn through observing and identifying, although their comments are sought at times. Individual members take turns in the hot seat.

Interpersonally Centered Approach. In this third approach the main attention of the leader is given to the interactions between and among members. The focus tends to be how the members affect and experience one another.

As a way of clarifying the three approaches, imagine a group therapy client, Jane, entering her group for a given session, expressing that "I feel angry today—I've had this sense of irritation since yesterday, and today it has just gotten bigger and bigger. I feel so abusive toward this group, but don't know why." Consider the three therapist responses given below, and decide which of the three approaches they fit.

1. "I notice the group has responded with silence, like last week when Jim expressed irritation. Actually it feels more like silent irritation. I wonder what is happening in the group right now."
2. "Jane, could you share with us what these feelings are like [about] for you right now?"

3. "Jane, you looked at Jim when you said that, and now he's looking very responsive. Jim, what are you feeling right now about Jane's experience?"

Toward an Integrated Approach. Recent efforts have sought to integrate the group and individual approaches (the interpersonal approach fits well with both), as theory and research have suggested that neither extreme is very helpful (Horwitz, 1986). Basically two types of attempts at such integration have occurred. The first might be called the *alternation view.* There are certain points in the life of a group when the total membership is affected, for example, beginning phases, entry of new members, therapist's absence. At these points, group interpretations are most appropriate, since group behavior is best understood in terms of the dynamics of the entire group. When the group is functioning cohesively, however, work on individual (and interpersonal) issues is most effective.

The second integrative approach is the *common group tension* approach, exemplified by the work of Horwitz (1986). Within this approach it is theorized that a common group theme is always operative in the functioning of the group and that individual needs are always interacting with this underlying theme. Horwitz's approach is to offer interpretations and other comments to individuals, and after working with a few individuals, to detect the underlying group theme that begins to emerge. As this common group "tension" becomes clearer to the therapist, she or he then makes a group observation or interpretation. As an example of this approach, Horwitz describes a group in which, following a vacation by the therapist, virtually all members expressed often confused and confusing feelings of abandonment as well as guilt over such feelings. As these feelings were expressed in various ways by the individual members, the therapist focused on each individual's specific issues. As it became clear that the theme of abandonment was common to each member's concerns, the therapist made several interpretations about this and how it was affecting the life of the group.

The Leader's Tasks

In virtually all types of therapeutic groups, but especially in the less structured, more interactional ones such as group counseling/therapy and growth groups, there are common tasks in which the leader must engage. Although one could think of numerous leader tasks in therapeutic groupwork, Yalom (1985) has convincingly proposed that there are three fundamental tasks: (1) the creation and maintenance of the group, (2) group culture building, and (3) activation and illumination of the here and now.

Creation and Maintenance of the Group. The therapist's first crucial task is to create and convene the group. The importance of selecting and preparing members cannot be overemphasized. Research and clinical experience generally support the observation that certain types of individuals tend to do poorly in therapeutic groups. It is probably wise not to include persons who are paranoid, hypochondriacal, sociopathic, brain-damaged, acutely psychotic, or addicted to drugs or alcohol (unless the group is explicitly aimed at the drug-dependent person). Also, Yalom (1985) suggests that persons who have extreme difficulties with intimacy are not good group candidates (with the emphasis on the extreme), and those in an acute life crisis may need more individual attention than can be given in the group format. Finally, Yalom discusses at length the group "deviant," who should not be placed into an interactional group. What is meant by *deviant* is someone who cannot or will not examine himself or herself and his or her relationship with others in the group.

On the positive side, it is wise to select members who fit well with the group and to form groups with a reasonable balance of interpersonal styles. Try for a "reasonable diversity," while avoiding potential scapegoats and "misfits" (Dies, 1987). Considerable clinical skill is required to "screen in" suitable members and "screen out" those who will not do well in the group. Often more than one individual interview is required to perform this selection.

During the process of selection and during the early phase of the group's life, it is important that members be well informed about what groups are like, what can be expected of them, and what they can expect from others. Indeed, people have many misconceptions about what group therapy is like, and much of this misinformation is negative—for example, groups are unpredictable and will force individuals to reveal what they do not want to (Slocum, 1987). Correcting these misconceptions is a valuable beginning.

Once the group begins, the therapist's job is to deter anything that threatens the group's cohesiveness. Thus, the therapist works to prevent dropouts because these, more than perhaps anything else, will threaten the group's existence. Continued tardiness, absences, the formation of cliques within the group, certain kinds of socializing between members outside the group, and scapegoating all threaten the integrity of the group and require the therapist's intervention. The creation and maintenance of the group is so important in the early stages that, at times, the pressing needs of the individual must be put aside. Yalom uses the example of a group containing four core members who were male and who had trouble keeping female members. During two new female members' first group meeting, they were ignored. One of the male members entered the group late and immediately began discussing a problem he was having without acknowledging the new members' presence or existence. After a half hour, Yalom interrupted the client with the question, "Mike, I wonder what hunches you have about how our two new members are feeling in the group today?" This question turned the members' attention to how they had ignored the two new members and helped Mike begin to work on his tendency to ignore the needs of others.

Group Culture Building. Once the group becomes a physical reality, the counselor's main job is to develop it into a therapeutic social system. In seeking to do this, the counselor works to establish a code of behavioral rules (often unstated), or norms, that guide the interactions of the group members. This norm building is more complicated in group than in individual counseling. In individual counseling, the counselor is the only agent of change, but in group therapy other group members serve as perhaps the most potent agents of change. The therapist's task is to create a group culture that facilitates therapeutic interaction among members.

This therapeutic culture, as we have said, contains the norms that guide client behavior. Just what norms are we talking about? Active involvement, self-disclosure of immediate feelings, nonjudgmental acceptance of other members, spontaneity of expression, desire for self-understanding, dissatisfaction with at least some of one's present behavioral patterns, and the desire for change—these are the main norms (or values or "oughts") that the group leader works toward establishing.

Both group theory and research support the notion that the therapist facilitates the building of therapeutic norms through two roles: that of a *technical expert* and that of a *model-setting participant* (Dies, 1987; Yalom, 1985). The therapist functions as a technical expert when instructing the client about the rules of the group prior to the group's beginning and during the early stages. Such instruction is reinforced by the weight of the therapist's authority and experience and by the fact that the rationale presented by the therapist for these "rules" makes good, clear sense to the client.

During the early stages of the group, the counselor as technical expert can use a variety of means to help shape norms. Yalom (1985) provides examples of the methods available. If the therapist wants to create an interactional network in which the members freely interact rather than directing all comments to the therapist:

> you may implicitly instruct members in their pre-group interviews or in the first group sessions; you may, repeatedly during the meetings, ask for all members' reactions to another member or toward a group issue; you may wonder why conversation is invariably directed toward yourself; you may refuse to answer questions or may even close your eyes when you are addressed; you

> may ask the group to engage in exercises that teach patients to interact—for example, you may ask each member of the group, in turn, to give his or her first impressions of every other member; or you may, in a much less obtrusive manner, shape behavior by rewarding members who address one another—you may smile or nod at them, address them warmly, or shift your posture into a more receptive position. Exactly the same approaches may be applied to the myriad of other norms the therapist wishes to inculcate: self-disclosure, open expression of emotions, promptness, self-exploration, and so on. (pp. 119–120)

The therapist also shapes norms through serving as a model-setting participant. For example, by offering a model of nonjudgmental acceptance and appreciation of members' strengths along with their problem areas, the leader helps shape a group that is health-oriented. The therapist also models honesty, spontaneity, and human fallibility. This does not imply, however, that the counselor freely expresses all feelings. Clients' needs must take preeminence, as in any form of therapy; and the effective therapist models responsibility and restraint, as well as honesty and openness. Integrating such qualities as restraint and openness is no easy task, even for the seasoned counselor.

Activation and Illumination of the Here and Now. Some group counselors, depending on their theoretical orientation, will focus on material in the client's past, whereas others will attend only to the present. Whether the counselor's focus is primarily on past or present, however, group members live their group lives in the present, in the here and now. Thus, even when past material is being explored, it may be done so in a way that is fresh and alive in the present. To this extent, we agree with Yalom's suggestion that the activation and illumination of the here and now is one of the three primary tasks of group therapy.

According to Yalom, if the here-and-now focus is to be effective, it must consist of two interrelated tiers. The first tier is the "experiencing" one. The members must *live* with each other in the present. They develop strong feelings toward each other, toward the therapist, and toward the group. These here-and-now feelings need to be expressed, and indeed they form the main interactions in the group. As vital as this here-and-now experiencing (called "activation of the here and now") is, however, it is not enough. If all that group members do is express immediate feelings, they would have a powerful experience that would be soon forgotten, without behavior change taking place.

If clients are to change, the counselor must also *illuminate the here-and-now process.* Thus, the effective counselor helps members to observe and think about what is happening in their interactions and what the meanings are of those interactions. This is the cognitive component, the observing and thinking about one's experience; and, just as in individual therapy, it is critical to effective change in groups. Whereas the group members, with the aid of the counselor, are responsible for activation of the here and now, only the therapist is responsible for commenting on the process, for directing the client's attention to the meaning of what is happening in the group. We should also note that if only this second tier is actualized in the group, that would not be effective either. The interactions would be emotionally sterile.

The counselor has many techniques at his or her disposal in the effort to activate and illuminate the here and now. The bottom line, however, is noted nicely by Yalom (1985), when he suggests that counselors "think here-and-now." He further states that: "When you do so long enough, you automatically steer the group into the here-and-now. Sometimes I feel like a shepherd herding a flock into an ever-tightening circle; I head off errant, historical, or 'outside' statements like strays and guide them back into the circle. Whenever an issue is raised in the group, I think, 'How can I relate this to the group's primary task? How can I make it come to life in the here-and-now?' I am relentless in this effort, and I begin it in the very first meeting of the group" (p. 150).

The Leader's Personal Qualities

Just as in individual counseling, the personal qualities of the group leader or counselor are of utmost importance. Also as in individual counseling, the ability to offer a good relationship may be the most important of these. Thus, the group counselor's ability to experience and communicate (a) empathic understanding, (b) positive regard, warmth, and respect, and (c) genuineness or congruence, forms the groundwork of effective therapeutic groupwork. In group interventions, however, the relationship task is more complicated than in individual work. The leader not only must be effective in developing therapeutic relationships with his or her clients, the leader must also facilitate therapeutic relationships among the members of his or her groups.

In line with the above relationship qualities, Corey and Corey (1987) discuss 13 personal characteristics of effective group leaders: courage, willingness to model, presence, goodwill and caring, belief in group process, openness, nondefensiveness in coping with attacks, personal power, stamina, willingness to seek new experiences, self-awareness, sense of humor, and inventiveness. This list should be studied and integrated by the beginning group counselor. Let us elaborate on a few of these qualities below.

Courage. Courage is a personal quality that is all too infrequently addressed in both the individual and group intervention literature. It is probably an important trait for both counselors and clients. It may take courage as well as other ingredients for clients to take the risks involved in opening up in counseling and making the changes that need to be made. For group leaders, Corey and Corey (1987) believe that courage is reflected in their willingness to (1) be vulnerable, admitting to mistakes and taking the same risks that are expected of group members; (2) confront members even when they are not sure that they are right; (3) act on their beliefs and hunches; (4) be emotionally touched by their group members; (5) continually examine themselves and strive for a depth of awareness; (6) be direct and honest with members; and (7) express to the group their expectations (including fears) about the group process.

Willingness to Model. The group leader's functioning in a group serves as a model for all group members. Leader modeling was discussed above as one of the ways in which the leader facilitates the development of an effective group culture. Suffice it to say here that leaders can teach best by example, that is, by doing what they expect members to do. The leader role certainly differs from the member role. Yet the leader is not just an observer; she or he is a *participant-observer,* who engages in honest, timely, and appropriate self-disclosure and feedback. The leader need not and should not hide behind a professional façade.

Belief in Group Process. As a scientist-practitioner, the counseling psychologist who leads therapeutic groups must balance an appropriate scientific skepticism and thoughtful clinical judgment with a belief in the value of group treatment and the therapeutic forces in groups. The leader need not accept group efficacy on faith, for there is plenty of research evidence (as well as clinical evidence) that group treatment is effective (Kaul & Bednar, 1986; Dies, 1987). The belief in the efficacy of groups and of group process is especially important since what the counselor believes is bound to influence his or her behavior. In other words, the counselor who believes in the effectiveness of group process will behave in a way that actualizes that belief. On the other side of the ledger, Corey and Corey (1987) note that some therapists lead groups despite the belief that groupwork does not effect significant client change. Some lead groups mainly for money or power or because the agencies at which they work require them to lead groups. To do so is clinically unsound at best, for negative beliefs will tend to result in lessened effectiveness—a self-fulfilling prophecy of sorts. Indeed, leading groups while doubting their effectiveness is unethical.

Inventiveness. Inventiveness is another leader quality that is underemphasized. Corey and Corey (1987) assert that: "The capacity to be spontaneously creative—to approach each group with fresh ideas—is a most important characteristic for group leaders. Freshness may not be easy to maintain, particularly if a therapist leads groups frequently. Leaders must somehow avoid becoming trapped in ritualized techniques or a programmed presentation of self that has lost all life" (pp. 19–20). The ability to think up new techniques and new ways of approaching a group prevents group-leader burnout. As a way of staying fresh and reducing burnout, many group experts recommend co-leadership. Having a co-leader takes some of the strain off the leader; it also provides fresh interpersonal and technical input. One may also reduce the number of groups one leads when energy and enthusiasm are diminished.

Nondefensiveness. Criticism and other negative reactions toward the group leader occur in virtually all groups of any duration. The group counselor will be seen as structuring too much, structuring too little, not caring enough or caring too selectively, being too critical or demanding, and so forth. One reason for this is that the leader cannot be what everyone wants at all times. Second, many of the members will have issues related to authority, parenting, and helping; often when helping and authority are combined, as in the role of the group leader, reactions are inevitable. At the same time, the spirit of openness and sharing that must exist in groups encourages members to express and reflect upon whatever negative reactions they have. Some of the negative reactions will be earned, as the leader inevitably makes mistakes that produce them. Many of the negative reactions will be expressions of distorted perceptions (e.g., transferences) related to the leader-helper role. All of this is to say that when leading therapeutic groups, the counselor must not only expect some reactions but must be able to facilitate their expression and examination. Counselors who are easily threatened, who must have group approval, or who are hypersensitive to negative feedback are going to have a difficult time with leading groups.

THE LEADER'S THEORETICAL ORIENTATION TO GROUPWORK

There are as many theoretical orientations and approaches to therapeutic groupwork as there are to individual counseling and therapy. As a starter for the beginning group counselor, we provide a brief summary of the major group theoretical approaches that fit the individual approaches discussed in Chapters 7, 8, and 9. Thus, the summaries below relate to group approaches that are psychoanalytic, behavioral, rational-emotive, person-centered, and gestalt. Take note of how the approaches to groupwork connect to their individual counseling counterparts in the earlier chapters.

Psychoanalytic group counseling or therapy has very clear resemblances to psychoanalytic therapy as discussed in Chapter 7. Many view this form of treatment as individual therapy done in a group rather than as group therapy. The analytic group therapist usually focuses on individual members and on interpersonal interactions among them rather than on the group as a whole.

A key feature of psychoanalytic group therapy is viewing the group as a symbolic representation of each client's original family. Within the group setting, the member's interactions with other members and the leader reflect many of the unresolved issues that related to earlier times and places, with parents, siblings, and other significant persons. As clients' issues get relived in the present, the therapist seeks to help the client gain insight into these issues and work them through in the present. Transferences to the group leader and members are central phenomena that need to be understood and resolved. This working through of interpersonal issues from the past in the context of present relationships results in personality change, the goal of psychoanalytic groups.

Behavioral group interventions most often take the form of short-term structured groups as discussed in Chapter 16, for example, assertiveness, anxiety management, and stress reduction groups. Since such groups are considered to be a type of education, group leaders do a great deal of teaching. They take an active and directive (not dominating) stance in such work, the main goal being to apply behavioral principles to the group. The focus is on the individuals in the group rather than the group as a whole. The behavioral group tends to be structured, and a portion of most sessions may be taken up with leader instruction around some common theme (e.g., assertiveness). The group format has the advantage of allowing clients to practice new behaviors and receive reinforcement for appropriate changes. Homework assignments related to the behaviors being modified are usually key elements of behavioral group counseling. The leader applies a wide range of behavioral techniques, depending on the behaviors being modified. As in individual therapy, in the behavioral group focus is placed on overt and specific behaviors, the statement of precise goals, the formulation of a treatment plan, the application of behavioral, action-oriented methods, and the evaluation of outcomes.

Ellis' *rational-emotive* group therapy, like its behavioral cousin, is seen as a type of education, or more aptly reeducation. The therapist's main task is to help clients become aware of their irrational beliefs, see how these beliefs impede their happiness, and most importantly substitute rational, healthy beliefs for the irrational ones. The ultimate aim is to help clients internalize a rational philosophy of life. Ellis (1982) contends that rational-emotive therapy (RET) works well in very large groups (e.g., 50–100 "clients") or small groups (10–13 members). The therapist in this treatment uses a range of active-directive cognitive and behavioral techniques to accomplish the main tasks. Techniques include persuading, teaching, informing, disputing, role-playing, modeling, self-reinforcement, feedback, and skill training. Homework assignments are an almost inherent part of RET, and Ellis (1982) believes that they are even more effectively used in group than individual counseling.

As may be evident, the focus of RET in groups is the individual, and much of the interactions are between the therapist and individual clients. The dynamics of the group as a whole are seen as largely beside the point. Group intervention is often seen as the preferred mode by RET therapists, however, because it is efficient and because group members can be powerful allies of the therapist in changing others' irrational, self-defeating thinking. Thus, group members contribute comments, suggestions, and hypotheses; they also reinforce interventions offered by the therapist.

The *person-centered* approach to therapeutic groupwork grew out of Carl Rogers' work, initially his client-centered therapy with individuals, and subsequently (1960s and 1970s) his focus on encounter and growth groups. In the person-centered approach, the leader is more aptly called a "facilitator," as he or she seeks to enable the group and the individuals within it to develop itself and themselves (its and their own goals, directions, and procedures) rather than to lead the group in any traditional leader-oriented way. The facilitator in many ways participates as a member in this approach and in the process gives up the role and power of the expert. The leader's task is to create group conditions that will allow for self-actualization that is within the capacity of group members. The leader's attitudes, rather than techniques, are what matters most; the relationship attitudes of empathy, unconditional positive regard, and congruence are fundamental.

The person-centered facilitator has a deep trust in the ability of the group to develop its potential and to move in the direction of awareness and spontaneous expression of immediate experiencing, looking inward for answers, tolerance for ambiguity, openness to outside reality, and openness and expressiveness with others. These changes occur at the group level as well as at an individual level within the group. As you might guess, the person-centered approach is highly unstructured; it is the group's responsibility to create its own structure. Because of the lack of leader direction, such groups tend to flounder quite a bit in their early stages. But as the leader's attitudes of acceptance and understanding are internalized by the members, and as the members' actualizing tendencies emerge, person-centered groups develop into cohesive, self-directing organisms.

The *gestalt* therapy approach to therapeutic groupwork has as its goals enhancing the self-awareness of the individuals. Self-awareness is developed through consistent attention to immediate experiencing of rather than talking *about* feelings and thoughts. Actually there are two gestalt therapy approaches to groups. The first, developed by Fritz Perls in the 1960s, is in reality individual therapy done in a group. Individuals take turns in the "hot seat," a situation in which the therapist works with one member. As this is going on, other members are encouraged to observe and process and then to offer feedback and personal reactions to what has occurred. The second approach, which probably emanates from the work of Irving and Miriam Polster, is much more process- and interaction-oriented. The focus is still on awareness and experiencing, but the leader also seeks to foster spontaneous interaction among members as well as a group culture. Thus, the focus of the leader is on the group as a whole and the interactions of participants, as well as the individual.

Highly active, the gestalt leader facilitates awareness, experiencing, and spontaneous interaction through the use of a range of techniques, exercises, and experiments (see Chapter 9). At the same time, gestaltists are careful to emphasize the leader's person over techniques. Techniques should emerge spontaneously from the therapist as a person. The therapist must stay in close touch with his or her own experiencing in the group.

As summarized from the five theoretical perspectives given above, none of the approaches to therapeutic groupwork resembles very closely group counseling or psychotherapy as it is typically practiced. By "typical," we refer to relatively unstructured groups that have about six to ten members, are held once or twice a week for an hour and a half to two hours, continue for anywhere from six months to several years, and are closed in the sense that new members are added only on occasion. The focal points of the typical therapy group tend to be at all three levels: the individual, the group, and interaction among members. Immediate experiencing is of fundamental importance but so is the need to cognitively understand this experiencing of the group and its individuals. The leader is not highly directive, but neither is she or he nearly as nondirective as the person-centered therapist. This leader does assume the role of expert but uses this expertise to maintain the group, develop the group culture, and help the group focus on the present (see the previous section). She or he is not nearly as dominant or knowing as, for example, the rational-emotive group leader.

It is safe to say that the leader of group counseling/therapy as typically practiced is a combination of the above theoretical orientations and more. Yet some orientations have been more influential than others. The typical leader represents some amalgamation of psychodynamic (not strictly psychoanalytic—see the distinction in Chapter 7) and humanistic approaches to thinking about and leading groups. Within the humanistic approach, both gestalt and person-centered views have been a powerful influence on groupwork.

STAGES OF THERAPEUTIC GROUPS

Now that we have examined aspects of leader behavior in therapeutic groups, it is time to look at aspects of the group itself, namely how the group unfolds or develops. An extensive literature has been built up on group development, and there is general agreement within this research and clinical literature that therapeutic groups progress through different stages or phases of development (MacKenzie & Livesley, 1990). Tuckman (1965) appears to be the first to have summarized the literature on stages, labeling them as "forming," "storming," "norming," and "performing" (to which others later added "adjourning"). The number of stages that have been proposed varies from two to nine (Beck, 1974), but considerable similarities exist in the way these stages are described and their sequencing. Below we describe a sequence of four stages: exploratory, transition, working, and termination. This is probably the most commonly presented sequence in the literature.

First, it should be pointed out that all formulations of stages apply in a clear way only to groups in which membership is more or less closed. The closed group maintains the same or nearly the same membership throughout the life of the group, adding new members only on occasion. The open group on the other hand continually adds new members as members leave the group. Particularly in groups in which there is a frequent turnover of membership, the concept of stages becomes confounded. Stages may mark each member's development within the group, but no clear stagewise progression occurs for the group itself.

Exploratory Stage

During this beginning stage, members introduce themselves, tell why they are in the group and what they hope to get out of it. Some basic ground rules of the group are established early on. The interaction of group members tends to be on the superficial side. Issues of inclusion and influence are primary in this first stage. Members wonder if they will fit in and be liked and listened to and, as a result, try to present themselves in a way that is acceptable to others. There is also the question in each member's mind, however framed, of how much influence he or she will have in the group. In fact, as Bonney (1969) has noted, the group does consciously and unconsciously assign varying degrees of power and influence to each member.

There are often periods of silence and awkwardness in the early meetings, as members seek to find direction and wonder what the group really will be about, *really*. In the exploratory stage, members also wonder if the group is a safe place in which to share their inner feelings. Beginning efforts at self-disclosure are made, partly as a way of testing the waters. If members are able to express themselves, a beginning sense of group cohesion emerges. It is essential that a sense of trust be built up during this stage.

During this crucial and delicate stage, as discussed in the section on leadership, the group counselor helps to establish therapeutic norms through both a sensitive use of instruction and through his or her behavior. Thus, he or she functions both as the technical expert and as the participant-model. The primary mission of this stage is simply to maintain the group and to build a solid foundation.

Transition Stage

As the group moves beyond the exploratory stage, members will seek to disclose a bit more deeply. They go beyond talking about their background and presenting their beginning stories. This movement is not without ambivalence, however, as anxiety and defense also become heightened during the transition stage. Thus, there is the urge to move forward into deeper explorations and also the counterpoint, the flight away from more personal (and thus dangerous) ways of being.

As members move beyond superficial expressions, aggression seems to enter the scene. (Note that the term *storming* has been used for this stage.) Members will often alternate between "fight and flight," between aggressiveness and avoidance of emotions. Power and influence become even more central in the transition stage than they were during the exploratory stage. The leader is frequently the object of aggressive reactions, and at this stage such aggressiveness is often related to the leader's structuring and controlling too much or too little. Some members will seek to wrestle power from the leader, others will be sure to find the leader's shortcomings.

The major challenge to the leader in the transition stage is to intervene in a sensitive and timely way. The leader must offer both encouragement and challenge in helping clients face their resistances, which are tied to anxiety. These same leader ingredients must be used to help the group work with the conflict and negative feelings that are emerging in this stage. It is particularly important that the leader not be defensive or hostile in response to challenges or downright attacks from group members. The leader must at once be open about his or her feelings and maintain a therapeutic stance of helping the group explore itself. During this period, the leader also has to reinforce growth-enhancing behaviors such as acceptance and respect, constructively expressed feedback, nondestructive expression of disagreements, and deeper self-explorations and self-disclosures.

Working Stage

During the next stage, the group has already worked through many of its doubts and anxieties. Those who were not able to commit to the group or who should not have been there to begin with have already left. The group has a deeper sense of trust and cohesion, and members are able to express themselves deeply as well as give and receive feedback without great defensiveness. When confrontation occurs, it is done in a way that does not attack or judge the person being confronted. The leader is seen more realistically, and the individual is more ready to explore the transferences and other distortions that do occur. Leadership functions are more readily shared by members, without the power struggles characteristic of the transition stage. Members during the working stage feel accepted and supported in a deeper way than earlier and consequently are willing to risk new behavior. This support-risk sequence forms a spiral, such that support leads to greater risks and more openness, which leads to greater support and acceptance.

The working stage may be the most exciting one for the leader. The initial resistances and defensiveness have been worked through, therapeutic norms have been established, and members are able to live in the here and now. The leader can focus energies on facilitating continued and deepened exploration of the interpersonal and intrapersonal issues in the group. A crucial leader function during the working stage is to help members translate their understandings into constructive action, certainly within the group, but also outside the group. The leader of course continues to function as the participant-model, who confronts in a caring way and appropriately discloses ongoing reactions to the group.

Termination Stage

In the final stage of group development, ending, or termination, becomes the central issue. The duration of this stage will depend on the length of the group, with longer-term groups having longer termination stages. The major tasks of the group during this stage are looking back at what has been accomplished, looking forward in terms of members' plans and hopes for the future, and saying good-bye. It is fairly common for clients to initiate a "going around" procedure in which feedback is solicited from all other members. The group experience itself is usually evaluated as part of ending. Naturally, members tend to experience some sadness and anxiety about ending the group and the relationships that have been developed, although this is usually overshadowed by the sense of growth and accomplishment that has been evidenced during the life of the group. Self-disclosures tend to taper off in the final stage, as members are reluctant to open up new issues with the end of the group in close sight.

The group leader's main task during the ending phase is to help members face termination and deal directly with termination issues such as separation and loss, and with positive feelings as well. The leader provides a structure in which members can clarify the meaning of the group experience to them and think actively about how their learning may be generalized and continued after the experience ends. Positive development and behavior of clients are reinforced by the leader. In structured groups, the leader often helps members formulate specific contracts and homework assignments aimed at fortifying changes.

Now it is time to take a look at what makes for positive change in group interventions. This is discussed in the following section.

THERAPEUTIC FACTORS IN GROUPWORK

At the beginning of this chapter, we noted that research evidence clearly indicates that group interventions, on the whole, do foster change and growth in participants. What is it about these groups that helps people? What goes on in, for example, group therapy that facilitates the client's changing in a desirable way? Are there certain ingredients of group therapy and other therapeutic groups that allow for such change? In an extremely thoughtful formulation by one of the masters of group therapy and group therapy research, Irving Yalom (1985) has proposed that there are 11 therapeutic factors that are either mechanisms of change or conditions for change to take place in group therapy and other therapylike interventions. Yalom derived these factors both from his experience leading groups and from research findings, and his formulation has been a potent guide to theory and research on groupwork in recent years. As we define and discuss the 11 therapeutic factors, the reader should keep in mind that they are not independent of one another. Rather, they work together, interdependently, in a very complex way. Additionally, they operate in different ways for differing types of groups (discussed below). The 11 factors, along with brief definitions and discussion, are:

1. *Instillation of hope.* Clients often begin therapy feeling demoralized. If therapy is to be effective, clients need to begin feeling a sense of hopefulness—that they can change as a result of the treatment. Observing others in the group change is a major impetus to hope.
2. *Universality.* Many people enter counseling feeling isolated and alone in their problems, as if they are different from the rest of the human race in the conflicts that they experience. Universality, experienced early in the group, is the sense that we all have problems, that we are all alike in this way, and that others can understand and share our concerns.
3. *Imparting information.* Included here is instruction, given by therapists about mental health and illness and general psychodynamics, along with advice, suggestions, and direct guidance offered by the counselor and other group members. Instruction is especially pertinent in certain kinds of groups (e.g., structured

groups) and therapies (e.g., rational-emotive therapy). Although direct advice may not itself help, the interest and caring it implies may do so.

4. *Altruism.* The desire experienced by group members to help others is a key factor, since clients receive through giving. Not only does giving stimulate others to return the giving, but giving in itself often enhances one's sense of effectiveness and self-esteem. Clients can be enormously helpful to one another, for example, through support, suggestions, shared insights and experiences.

5. *The corrective recapitulation of the primary family group.* The ongoing group comes to resemble the client's original family, and the client tends to interact with the group in the way he or she did with the family. As early family experiences are relived, with the help of the therapist and other members, the client comes to resolve many central issues and change fixed patterns tied to unresolved issues.

6. *Development of socializing techniques.* Social learning or the development of social/interpersonal skills is fostered in all therapeutic groups, although the types of skills taught and how directly they are taught varies tremendously from group to group. Some groups train social interpersonal skills directly, others do so implicitly, mainly through feedback from members and leaders.

7. *Imitative behavior.* Clients learn in groups by identifying with leaders and other members. Although blind imitation may reflect unresolved problems, there is a healthy kind of learning through observing and identifying that occurs in therapeutic groups. Such learning may occur at a conscious level, but is more often than not unconscious.

8. *Interpersonal learning.* This is a particularly powerful factor. As a group unfolds (particularly a less structured one), it evolves into a social microcosm—a miniature representative of the individuals' social worlds. At the same time, the client becomes more open about the self and is able to display his or her interpersonal issues and problems. As this occurs, and with the help of feedback as well as self-observation, the client gains insight into his or her impact on others, maladaptive behavior with others, distortions in interpersonal relationships (e.g., transference), and his or her responsibility for relationships and the responses he or she gets from others.

9. *Group cohesiveness.* This is the parallel of the client-therapist relationship in individual counseling. In groups, it includes the client's relationship to the therapist, other group members, and the group as a whole. This has been an extremely elusive factor to define over the years, although it is seen as crucial by virtually all theoreticians of therapeutic groups, especially in less structured groups, and has been the subject of numerous studies. One may simply define it as the attractiveness of a group for its members, keeping in mind that there is a difference between group cohesiveness and individual member cohesiveness (the individual's attraction to the group). Groups with a greater sense of solidarity, bonding, or "we-ness" are high on cohesion. In cohesive groups, members are accepted, approved of, and have a sense of being "taken in." Group cohesiveness is not, in itself, a mechanism of change, but rather a precondition for group therapy to be effective in helping clients.

10. *Catharsis.* The release of emotions, the open expression of affect, is a necessary factor in groupwork, but it is not sufficient. For change to occur, the feelings that are released need to be understood, processed, and dealt with. Catharsis also helps through its interaction with other therapeutic factors. For example, members' catharsis enhances group cohesiveness, allows for interpersonal learning, and deepens members' sense of universality.

11. *Existential factors.* This factor is actually a constellation of factors revolving around one's basic and ultimate responsibility for his or her life and actions, one's basic aloneness, the recognition of one's mortality, and the inevitability of some human problems and pain. Although this factor was included by Yalom almost as an afterthought, some of the items within it have been rated by group therapy clients as extremely important in what they got out of their group experience.

We noted at the beginning of this section that the 11 therapeutic factors would be expected to operate differently for different types of groups. Research findings suggest that in personal growth groups and outpatient groups, for example, interpersonal learning (including self-understanding) and catharsis are seen as most important by clients, whereas clients in inpatient groups place more importance on instillation of hope and universality (Butler & Fuhriman, 1983; Yalom, 1985). In addition to type of group or setting, Yalom has proposed that the factors operate differently according to the stage of group development, as discussed in the preceding section. For instance, early in the group life, instillation of hope, universality, and imparting of information are seen as relatively more important. Factors such as altruism and cohesion are important throughout the life of the group, but their nature changes as the group matures. Early in therapy, altruism often takes the form of offering suggestions and asking help-oriented questions, whereas later on it may appear as a deeper caring and "being with." Cohesiveness first operates as a therapeutic factor through support, acceptance, and facilitation of attendance. It has its later effect, however, through the kind of deeper self-disclosure, confrontation, and conflict that are an inherent part of the interpersonal learning factor. Early-late differences such as these have been at least partially supported by research studies (Butler, 1981; Butler & Fuhriman, 1983; Kivlighan & Mullison, 1988). Research has tended to look at highly global group development in relation to the therapeutic factors (e.g., early vs. late). For a systematic theoretical discussion of how the factors operate across distinct stages of counseling, the reader is referred to MacDevitt (1987).

ETHICAL ISSUES IN THERAPEUTIC GROUPWORK

Professional ethics have been discussed already in depth in Chapter 3. Because there are some special ethical issues in therapeutic groupwork, however, we shall offer additional discussion below. Before doing so, we should note that ethical codes do exist that are focused specifically on groupwork, and these codes should be studied carefully by anyone who plans to work with groups. For counseling psychologists, the most relevant documents, in addition to those discussed in Chapter 3, are *Ethical Guidelines for Group Leaders* by the Association for Specialists in Group Work (ASGW, 1990); *Guidelines for Psychologists Conducting Growth Groups* (APA, 1973); and *Professional Standards for Training of Group Counselors* (ASGW, 1983). Also, Corey, Corey and Callanan (1982) have written a useful book entitled *A Casebook of Ethical Guidelines for Group Leaders.*

Four issues deserve special note: those of informed consent, confidentiality, involuntary participation, and training.

Informed Consent

Potential group members or clients have a right to know what they are getting into. Although this applies to individual as well as group treatments, it needs to be emphasized here because groupwork is often poorly understood or misunderstood by the public. People seem to have less accurate information about group treatments than individual ones.

Clearly informing potential members about the group should begin as soon as the leader or agency decides to recruit members. Announcements aimed at recruitment should include an explicit statement of the purpose, length, and size of the group; the leader's qualifications; and the financial cost of the intervention. Claims should not be made unless they can be supported by scientific evidence.

The matter of informed consent is related to leaders' making members aware of their rights and responsibilities as group participants. Those who join a group have a right to expect *at least:*

— a clear statement regarding the purpose of the group, procedures to be used, and the leader's policies and ground rules
— respect for member privacy
— freedom from undue group pressure or coercion from either members or leaders to participate in exercises or to disclose matters they are unwilling to discuss
— notice of any research involving the group, any observations of the group through one-way mirrors, or any audio- or videotaping of group sessions
— full discussion on the limitations of confidentiality (see below)

Confidentiality

The principles of confidentiality discussed in Chapter 3 apply to group interventions as well as other interventions. In groups, however, confidentiality becomes a more complicated matter than in individual treatment, because the leader must be concerned about other members in addition to the leader himself or herself maintaining confidentiality. This is no easy matter, because group members naturally want to talk about their group experiences with significant others in their lives.

The counselor needs to underscore the importance of confidentiality from the first contact with potential clients, for example, when members are being recruited and when groups are advertised. Confidentiality should also be discussed in the counselor's initial individual meeting with each member before the group, during the first group meeting, and at appropriate times during the group's evolution. It is the leader's job to note to members that confidences are usually broken by simple carelessness, and without any ill intent. Corey and Corey (1987) suggest that members will not violate confidentiality if they talk about *what* they learned in the group rather than *how* they gained insights or what they *did* in the group. For example, the male client who learns for the first time how he protects himself from fear of rejection by acting aggressively toward his intimates may share that he learned this in the group. However, he does not need to be specific about what went on in the group that sparked this insight. Cautions such as these are always important, but they are vital when members have contact with each other and with each other's friends and acquaintances outside the group, as in school settings.

The importance of confidentiality in group treatments cannot be overemphasized, for it is hard to imagine groups functioning as they must without a sense of trust that what members share will not be revealed outside the group. Because of this, some group leaders ask members to sign a contract agreeing not to discuss anything that goes on in sessions and not to reveal the identity of other members.

Involuntary Membership

Much of the theory and practice of therapeutic groupwork as discussed throughout this chapter hinges on voluntary membership. Participants seek out a group experience because of what they hope to learn. At times, though, groupwork is required. This may occur in psychiatric hospitals or prison settings, or in outpatient clinics as a court-mandated procedure (e.g., for someone charged with spouse abuse, delinquency, or substance abuse). Required groups for sex offenders is a fairly common practice in many inpatient settings. In other settings, potential clients are pressured into joining groups. One of the authors, for example, worked at a university agency in which, because of a very long waiting list, students seeking counseling had to wait for several weeks before being seen. To provide some service while students waited for individual counseling, the agency offered "transitional groups." This was a fine idea, except that students were often pushed to join these groups rather than remain on the waiting lists. A study of this procedure (Collins, Gelso, Kimball, & Sedlacek, 1972) revealed that the drop-out rates from such groups were exceedingly high, and significantly higher than when students simply waited for the treatment they preferred. Unless there are legal or moral issues that dictate requiring group experiences, it is at best unwise to make such requirements; at worst, it is unethical.

When it is appropriate to require a group experience, this still creates problems for the leader and the group. In such cases, the leader should at least facilitate the client's expression of feelings around this requirement. Also, it is appropriate for the leader to make clear that although participation is involuntary, members still have the right to discuss or hold back as they wish. On the other hand, it is the leader's job to facilitate members' opening up, so this represents a dilemma for both the leader and the involuntary member.

There are times when it is unclear whether or not group experiences ought to be required. An example of this gray area is whether groups ought to be required for graduate students who plan to lead therapeutic groups in the future. Certainly participation in some form of experiential groups is desirable, as unique learning occurs in this way, learning that is different from the more didactic, theoretical learning in formal courses. Also, one must wonder about the motivations and even competence of students who would choose not to participate while planning to lead groups. At the same time, many see mandatory therapy as a contradiction. In any event, Corey and Corey (1987) offer some sensible guidelines for when group experiences are required of students. First, if the program requires group therapy, for example, that program ought to make sure it is available, either free of charge or at rates that students can handle. Second, it is unethical for graduate faculty to require counseling for a fee and then to encourage students to become the faculty's own clients. Referral should be made to professionals who have no evaluative responsibility for the student.

Training in Therapeutic Groupwork

Therapeutic groupwork has had a shaky history in counseling psychology and other psychological specialties. On the one hand, there is much empirical evidence to suggest that group experiences tend to be effective in helping participants change in desirable directions, and this evidence has been around for a long time. On the other hand, unfortunate abuses have occurred in this area of psychological intervention. Some of these abuses are tied to the extreme practices in which some leaders engaged during the 1960s and early 1970s as part of the encounter group movement. Highly confrontive and aggressive leaders at times sought to push participants of encounter and marathon groups to do more and more emoting, seemingly for its own sake, and some clients were psychologically hurt by such aggressive pushing (Lieberman, Yalom, & Miles, 1973). Reports of nude marathons including a great deal of sexuality certainly did not help much, either in the eyes of the public or of well-trained professionals.

Fortunately, the excesses of that period are behind us. At the same time, therapeutic groups have become an established part of the psychological practice of counseling psychologists. Part of the problem of the 1960s and early 1970s, though, remains with us. In the group area perhaps more than any area, people with insufficient credentials and training seem to be willing to call themselves expert leaders.

The issue of training is further complicated by graduate training programs that expect students to lead groups after training only in individual counseling and therapy (Yalom, 1985). Fortunately, the attitude that training in individual counseling and therapy is sufficient for the practice of any form of intervention (e.g., group therapy) is changing; however, more than traces of that attitude can be found today.

What is the proper training for people who wish to lead therapeutic groups? Unfortunately, there is no clear-cut answer to this question, as different types of groups require different types of training. Yet some general guidelines are possible. In terms of academic training, in addition to basic course work in individual counseling and assessment received in a counseling psychology program, potential group leaders should take a minimum of one course in the theory and practice of therapeutic groups. In addition, the Association for Specialists in Group Work (1983) suggests the following types of experience in groupwork:

— critiquing of group tapes
— observing group counseling sessions
— participating as a member in a group
— co-leading groups with supervision
— practicum experience: leading groups alone with critical self-analysis of performance along with a supervisor's feedback
— internship: further work in leading groups under supervision

The ASGW also recommends specific knowledge competencies and skill competencies for group counselors. These guidelines should be consulted by students and training programs involved in therapeutic groupwork.

THERAPEUTIC GROUPWORK IN PERSPECTIVE

In this final section we address two key questions about therapeutic groups. First, what is the place of therapeutic groups in counseling psychology? Second, what are some of the major research findings and issues in this area?

An Established Format

As we noted in the section above, group interventions have not had a stable history in professional psychology. The excesses of the 1960s and 1970s were part of this problem. Additionally, the group field was slow to develop a solid research base. Without such a base, any area in psychology suffers diminished respectability and, more important, is at the mercy of passing fads and fancies. Finally, for many years groupwork was seen as desirable only if the personpower did not exist to treat all clients with individual counseling. Groups existed as fill-ins of sorts, to be used when demand for service clearly exceeded an agency's supply of providers. The group field was thus an undernourished stepchild of individual counseling and therapy.

Views have slowly but surely changed over the years, as it has become clearer and clearer that therapeutic groups are a viable and effective treatment for a big percentage of clients and as the excesses of past decades have given way to a more thoughtful approach to group treatment. Of course, we should add that some very positive things came out of the 1960s, and it would be extremely unfortunate if the group field became so cautious and conservative that the experimentation and spontaneity of groupwork were greatly diminished.

The change in attitude toward therapeutic groupwork has progressed to the point that counseling and therapy groups, growth groups, and structured theme-oriented groups have become established modes in the counseling psychologist's repertoire. In fact, Fuhriman and Burlingame (1990) now view the practice and investigation of group treatment as integral parts of the counseling psychologist's identity. Recent surveys of graduate students (Fitzgerald & Osipow, 1988) and training directors of counseling psychology doctoral programs (Schneider, Watkins, & Gelso, 1988) support this idea. Over 80 percent of the sample of graduate students reported wanting to do group counseling and structured groups as part of their subsequent careers, and such therapeutic groups were rated as an important part of these students' professional identity by the training directors and the students themselves.

Some Research Findings and Issues

In their extensive analysis of the existing research literature in group therapy and encounter-growth groups, Kaul and Bednar (1986) tell us that the evidence *unequivocally* suggests that group treatments are associated with client improvement in a wide range of settings. They further note that: "The data supporting this conclusion have come from a substantial number of independent investigations, with reasonably rigorous and varied experimental procedures" (p. 672). Also, although the findings comparing group treatments to other treatments are not quite so clear-cut, it does appear that group interventions are as effective, on the whole, as either individual intervention or drug treatments. Some of the concepts that have been studied most extensively in group research are (a) training members before the group on desired behaviors and functions, (b) self-disclosure and feedback, (c) group cohesion, and (d) leadership styles. Even summarizing the complex findings in each of these areas is beyond the scope of this chapter. The reader is referred to Kaul and Bednar's (1986) review on the first three topics and Dies' (1987) analysis in the area of group leadership. Yalom's (1985) theoretical discussion of the role of the 11 therapeutic factors as presented earlier in this chapter is an extremely useful guide to the variables that can be studied in relation to the processes and outcomes of group interventions.

On the negative side, Kaul and Bednar lament the slow progress of research in this area and the fact that really new findings are so slow to emerge. We badly need sophisticated research aimed at answering such basic questions as:

— how client improvement is mediated by group processes
— how the individual can affect group processes

— how varied group processes affect the individual
— what dimensions of psychological functioning are most amenable to change via group processes

It is not surprising that progress in group research is slow, for this is one of the most difficult (as well as interesting) areas to study in all of psychology (Dies, 1977). In making their point about the methodological difficulties one encounters in group research, Kaul and Bednar (1986) offer this clever analysis:

> For those of us who have not had the dubious distinction of trying to accommodate the staggering multitude of design problems involved in group research, let us briefly illustrate the problem. Suppose a researcher is interested in a question that involves two levels of a treatment condition and its effects on three levels of a personality variable. The most natural result of this basic form of a question is a randomized design with a 2 times 3 factorial arrangement of treatments. By the time our researcher accommodates the need for (1) multiple group design (8 to 10 groups per cell), (2) plausible placebo and control conditions, (3) replications involving different leadership styles and leader personality variables, (4) controls for test sensitization effects, (5) a large enough subject pool to allow for prescreening and selection with the personality inventory, and (6) one replication of the entire experimental process, we are talking about a research project that could involve 180 psychotherapy groups, 25 to 50 group leaders, and approximately 9,000 to 12,000 experimental subjects. Need we say more? One such experiment would exhaust the subject pool of several universities, the trained leaders of the same, as well as the funds from several granting agencies. (p. 674)

This example is of course a large exaggeration, as no study ever can accommodate all the methodological issues addressed here. (Recall the bubble hypothesis discussed in Chapter 4.) The difficulties in group research, though, suggest that progress will continue to be gradual. The more important fact is that research in therapeutic groups is a firmly embedded feature of the group movement, including its manifestation in counseling psychology.

In this chapter, we have tried to highlight some of the key elements of therapeutic groupwork. For more in-depth coverage of this topic, the reader is referred to Yalom's (1985) *Theory and Practice of Group Psychotherapy.* This is perhaps the most influential book today in the group therapy area, and it is relevant both to beginning students and seasoned practitioners. Corey and Corey's (1987) book is an excellent overall treatment of therapeutic groups for the beginning student, and Corey (1985) provides an equally excellent review of the different theoretical approaches to group counseling. Gazda (1984) will give a reader a clear picture of the similarities and differences in group counseling with different populations (e.g., the elderly, substance abusers, families). The

January 1990 (Vol. 18, No. 1) issue of *The Counseling Psychologist* presents valuable reviews on the topics of theme-oriented group therapy, career group counseling, time-limited group counseling, and comparison of group and individual therapy.

SUMMARY

The advantages of therapeutic groups are seen largely in the *interpersonal* area. Groups are particularly helpful to participants who have difficulties in this area, and groups help most with interpersonal issues. The disadvantages of therapeutic groups include the pressure to conform, the tendency of some clients to get hooked on groups and to try to use them as a place to ventilate their miseries rather than change, and the fact that groups are not suited to everyone. We defined the therapeutic group as "an aggregate of interdependent individuals whose interaction is in pursuit of some shared goal(s)." The background and characteristics of five kinds of therapeutic groups were given: (1) group counseling and group therapy; (2) growth, or encounter groups; (3) T groups; (4) structured theme-oriented groups; and (5) self-help groups. Of the differing kinds of groups, this chapter was particularly concerned with group counseling or therapy. These two terms were differentiated in the same way as the terms *counseling* and *therapy* were differentiated at the beginning of the book. In counseling practice the two terms and processes are usually melded.

There tend to be three different approaches to leading groups: (1) the group-centered approach in which the leader focuses on the group as a whole; (2) the individual-centered approach in which the leader focuses on the individuals in the group; and (3) the interpersonally centered approach in which the leader focuses on the interactions between and among individuals in the group. Integration of these three kinds of focus is seen as desirable.

The leader was seen as having three main tasks: (1) creating and maintaining the group, (2) facilitating the building of a group culture, and (3) activating and illuminating the here and now. Once the group becomes a physical reality, the leader's main job is to develop it into a therapeutic social system. To do this, the leader must actively shape the desired norms in the group. His or her role as a *technical expert* and a *model* were examined as potent vehicles for norm shaping. The personal qualities of the leader may be more important than the particular techniques that are used. Especially important among these personal qualities are courage, willingness to model, belief in group process, inventiveness, and nondefensiveness.

The leader's behavior is guided by his or her theoretical orientation. In the chapter, five orientations to groupwork were summarized, to coincide with the five theoretical orientations discussed in Chapters 7, 8, and 9: psychoanalytic, behavioral, cognitive, person-centered, and gestalt.

There is general agreement that stages exist in the development of closed groups, although the exact number of stages that are posited varies from theorist to theorist. We discussed and described four stages. In the *exploratory* stage, members get acquainted, and begin self-disclosing. Members wonder if they will be accepted and if the group will be safe. Cohesion begins to develop. In the *transition* stage, participants move toward deeper exploration and at the same time resist this deepening. Issues of power and influence are central, and aggression usually is evident, often toward the leader. In the *working* stage, cohesion is high, and members have moved toward deep self-exploration and feedback. Then, in the *termination* stage clients pull back somewhat as they face issues of separation. They look back, look ahead, and say good-bye.

Irving Yalom proposed 11 therapeutic factors that contribute significantly to group effectiveness. These factors operate differently according to type of group (e.g., college student growth group, in-patient therapy group, outpatient group) and stage of group development.

Four main ethical issues in groupwork were discussed: (1) informed consent, (2) confidentiality, (3) involuntary membership, and (4) training. We also noted that, although groupwork has had a shaky history in counseling psychology, it is currently an established format in the field and forms an integral part of the counseling psychologist's identity. Research has clearly supported the effectiveness of a wide range of group interventions; it appears that groups are as effective as individual treatment. The complexities of group research are numerous.

References

American Psychological Association (1973). Guidelines for psychologists conducting growth groups. *American Psychologist, 28,* 933.

Association for Specialists in Group Work (1983). Professional standards for training of group counselors. Alexandria, VA: American Personnel and Guidance Association.

Association for Specialists in Group Work (1990). *Ethical guidelines for group leaders.* Washington, DC: American Personnel and Guidance Association.

Beck, A. P. (1974). Phases in the development of structure in therapy and encounter groups. In D. Wexler & L. Rice (Eds.), *Innovations in client-centered therapy.* New York: Wiley.

Bion, W. R. (1961). *Experiences in groups.* New York: Basic Books.

Bonney, W. C. (1969). Group counseling and developmental processes. In G. Gazda (Ed.), *Theories and methods of group counseling in the schools.* Springfield, IL: Charles C. Thomas.

Butler, T. (1981). Level of functioning and time in treatment: Variables influencing patients' experience in group psychotherapy. *Dissertation Abstracts International, 41,* 2749B.

Butler, T., & Fuhriman, A. (1983). Curative factors in group therapy: A review of recent literature. *Small Group Behavior, 14,* 131–142.

Collins, A., Gelso, C., Kimball, R., & Sedlacek, W. (1972). Evaluation of a counseling center innovation. *Journal of College Student Personnel,* 141–145.

Corey, G. (1985). *Theory and practice of group counseling* (2nd ed.). Monterey, CA: Brooks/Cole.

Corey, G., Corey, M. S., & Callanan, P. (1982). *A casebook of ethical guidelines for group leaders.* Monterey, CA: Brooks/Cole.

Corey, M. S., & Corey, G. (1987). *Groups: Process and practice* (3rd ed.). Monterey, CA: Brooks/Cole.

Courtois, C. (1988). *Healing the incest wound.* New York: Norton.

Dies, R. R. (1977). Pragmatics of leadership in psychotherapy and encounter group research. *Small Group Behavior, 8,* 229–248.

Dies, R. R. (1987). Clinical implications of research on leadership in short-term group psychotherapy. *International Journal of Group Psychotherapy, 37,* 27–78.

Eddy, W. B., & Lubin, B. (1971). Laboratory training and encounter groups. *Personnel and Guidance Journal, 49,* 625–635.

Ellis, A. (1982). Rational-emotive group therapy. In G. Gazda (Ed.), *Basic approaches to group psychotherapy and group counseling* (3rd ed.). Springfield, IL: Charles C. Thomas.

Ettin, M. F. (1989). "Come on Jack, tell us about yourself": The growth spurt in group psychotherapy. *International Journal of Group Psychotherapy, 39,* 35–57.

Fitzgerald, L. F., & Osipow, S. H. (1988). We have seen the future, but is it us? The vocational aspirations of graduate students in counseling psychology. *Professional Psychology: Research and Practice, 19,* 575–583.

Fuhriman, A., & Burlingame, G. M. (1990). Group therapy: Introduction. *The Counseling Psychologist, 18,* 5.

Gazda, G. M. (1984). *Group counseling: A developmental approach* (3rd ed.). Boston, MA: Allyn & Bacon.

Horwitz, L. (1986). An integrated, group-centered approach. In *Psychotherapist's casebook.* San Francisco, CA: Jossey-Bass.

Kaul, T. J., & Bednar, R. L. (1986). Experiential groups research: Results, questions, and suggestions. In S. Garfield & A. Bergin (Eds.), *Handbook of Psychotherapy and Behavior Change* (3rd ed., pp. 671–714). New York: Wiley.

Kivlighan, D. M., & Mullison, D. (1988). Participants' perceptions of therapeutic factors in group counseling. *Small Group Behavior, 19,* 452–468.

Lieberman, M., Yalom, I., & Miles, M. (1973). *Encounter groups: First facts.* New York: Basic Books.

MacDevitt, J. W. (1987). Conceptualizing therapeutic components of group counseling. *Journal for Specialists in Group Work,* 76–84.

MacKenzie, K. R., & Livesley, W. J. (1990). A developmental model for brief group therapy. *International Journal of Group Psychotherapy, 37,* 101–115.

Peterson, J. V., & Nisenholz, B. (1987). *Orientation to Counseling.* Boston, MA: Allyn & Bacon.

Schmuck, R. A., & Schmuck, P. A. (1979). *Group processes in the classroom* (3rd ed.). Dubuque, IA: W. C. Brown.

Schneider, L. J., Watkins, C. E., & Gelso, C. J. (1988). Counseling psychology from 1971 to 1986: Perspective on and appraisal of current training emphases. *Professional Psychology: Research and Practice, 19,* 585–588.

Slocum, Y. S. (1987). A survey of expectations about group therapy among clinical and nonclinical populations. *International Journal of Group Psychotherapy, 37,* 39–54.

Tuckman, B. W. (1965). Developmental sequence in small groups. *Psychological Bulletin, 63,* 384–399.

Yalom, I. D. (1985). *The theory and practice of group psychotherapy* (3rd ed.). New York: Basic Books.

Chapter 16

Prevention and Outreach Interventions

Read the following titles of nine journal articles as if this were a test of your ability to find the common theme.

"Employee fitness and wellness programs in the workplace" (Gebhardt & Crump, 1990).

"Social support, social groups, and the cancer patient" (Taylor, Falke, Shapton, & Lichtman, 1986).

"Coping skills training: An evaluation of a psychoeducational program in a community mental health center" (Brown, 1980).

"A stress management training program for low-income women" (Marciniak, 1984).

"Bereavement groups: Techniques and themes" (Yalom & Vinogradov, 1988).

"A mobile unit as an adjunct to a community outreach program of education, screening, and counseling for sickle cell disease, nutritional anemia, and hypertension" (Duncan, Scott, & Castro, 1982).

"Cognitive relaxation and social skills interventions in the treatment of general anger" (Deffenbacher, Story, Stark, Hogg, & Brandon, 1987).

"Stress: Country-style: Illinois' response to farm stress" (Cecil, 1988).

"Alteration of Type A behavior and reduction of cardiac recurrence in post-myocardial infarction subjects" (Friedman et al., 1984).

Despite the immense diversity of topics and settings represented by these articles, their subject matter has involved counseling psychologists in what might variously be labeled prevention, outreach, and/or consultation. Chapters on these topics are often not included in texts related to counseling psychology. Yet many contemporary professional psychologists would argue that such topics are becoming most important for the 1990s; therefore, both this chapter and the next one review the conceptual and practical bases for these kinds of psychological interventions. The kinds of services listed above, in the titles of the journal articles, are the ones that will be increasingly needed as more stringent limits are placed on health insurance reimbursements for individual counseling and psychotherapy.

The first part of this chapter is devoted to (1) the meanings of the terms *prevention* and *outreach* for counseling psychology, (2) how these two different terms, and several associated terms and emerging psychological specialties, have developed historically, and (3) how these terms represent an intertwining of several of the themes of counseling psychology discussed in the first chapters of this book. The second section of this chapter first describes a now classic contribution of several counseling psychologists devoted to prevention and outreach—the cube model of dimensions of counselor functioning. One major outgrowth of this model has been the emergence of structured, theme-oriented groups as a way of addressing issues of prevention and outreach. In one sense, in today's professional psychology practices, structured groups are the generic model of outreach and prevention services, offered at work sites, schools, clinics, hospitals, prisons, and even in churches and community libraries. The common features of structured groups will be identified and then illustrated with examples that can be readily adapted to many of the settings just listed.

Because of some expressed concerns about the amount of training for and practice of prevention and outreach services by counseling psychologists, the final section of this chapter reviews a variety of impediments and criticisms that need to be addressed. Only by overcoming some understandable reluctance will present and future counseling psychologists be able to achieve their potential contributions regarding prevention and outreach.

DEFINITIONS: TWO SETS OF INTERTWINED TERMS

At the very beginning of this book, three basic roles of counseling psychologists were delineated: remedial, preventive, and educational/developmental. Most of the material in the preceding chapters on theory and practice has focused primarily on the remedial role of counseling psychologists. In the next two chapters, the focus shifts to the preventive and educational/developmental roles. Though these latter terms have been differentiated, the professional services counseling psychologists provide within these roles are very similar. In fact, the terms derive more from different historical contexts than from the particular goals or services they subsume. Thus, one could not reasonably be asked to label most of the programs described in this chapter as either prevention or educational/developmental or, alternatively, prevention or outreach. These terms, as used by psychologists, are typically used interchangeably, reflecting most often whether the practitioner is affiliated, in his or her thinking or work setting, with a medical perspective or with an educational perspective of human services.

The Medical Perspective

The term *prevention* has a long history in physical medicine. Most significant historical breakthroughs in medicine are typically identified as the discovery of something that would *prevent* the spread of a major disease, for example, protecting against rat bites as a way of preventing the spread of the plague, spraying for mosquitos as a way of preventing the spread of malaria, or practicing "safe sex" as a way of preventing the spread of AIDS. Specific attention to prevention in mental health has a much more recent history (Caplan, 1964). As recently as 1978, prevention in mental health was still labeled a new revolution: "The new revolution will involve major societal efforts of preventing mental illness and emotional disturbance. It will apply the best available knowledge, derived from research and clinical experience, to prevent needless distress and psychological dysfunction. It will, in the best public health tradition, seek to build strength and increase competence and coping skills in populations and thereby reduce the incidence of later disturbance" (Albee et al., 1978, p. 1827). (In light of our earlier note about the interchangeability of prevention and developmental services, notice even here the presence of developmental terms: "build strength," "increase coping skills".)

Prevention in the mental health area has been most fully explicated by Caplan (1964). His terms are often found in the literature on prevention, outreach, and consultation and are therefore worthy of brief review. In reviewing his terms one will quickly see that some kinds of prevention seem to overlap with remediation. It is perhaps best to consider a continuum rather than discreet categories between prevention and remediation or even between types of prevention. Caplan uses the terms *primary, secondary,* and *tertiary prevention.* He defines *primary prevention* as those steps taken to prevent the occurrence of a mental illness or psychosocial dysfunction, with the prevention activities directed toward a total population rather than individuals *before* they experience any of the problems they are at risk of encountering. Primary prevention programs include, for example, communication skills training for parents of young adolescents, support group interventions for new mothers who are at risk for experiencing postpartum depressions, and career education programs for undecided college students.

Secondary prevention involves the earliest possible identification and treatment of existing problems so as to reduce their intensity and duration. Crisis intervention counseling is a classic example of secondary prevention; providing frustrated employees with career counseling might also be seen as secondary prevention to the extent that it prevents the development of greater levels of general anxiety and depressive disorders.

Tertiary prevention is a manner of working with those who already have problems in ways that the highest levels of functioning can be restored and the recurrence of the problems is minimized. Clearly, secondary and tertiary prevention have significant overlap with remediation roles. In fact, some would argue that differences in use of the terms *counseling* and *psychotherapy* should reflect the differences between prevention and remediation. The emphasis of counseling psychology on brief interventions, designed to utilize a client's assets and strengths, is directly oriented toward both secondary (reduce intensity and duration of stress) and tertiary prevention (treat so as to minimize recurrence of the problem). If psychotherapy, then, is seen as purely remedial, the only goal is to restore the client to a previous level of functioning.

The most distinctive concept of the three is primary prevention. Nonetheless, even that term encompasses a potentially endless range of services. "Our reading for a year leads us to the conclusion that practically every effort aimed at improved child rearing, increasing effective communication, building inner control and self-esteem, reducing stress and pollution, etc.—in short everything aimed at improving the human condition, at making life more fulfilling and meaningful, may be considered to be part of primary prevention of mental health and emotional disturbances" (Kessler & Albee, 1977, p. 577).

It was in the 1960s that large numbers of psychologists first began to give attention to various kinds of prevention services, largely as a result of the report of the Joint Commission on Mental Illness and Health (1961) and the Community Mental Health Centers Act of 1963. Since that time at least two specialized fields of psychology have emerged that focus on these multiple levels of prevention. Largely in response to the call for more primary prevention activities, the specialty of community psychology emerged. As Zax (1980) has described in his history of this specialty, the legislative acts noted above resulted in much more attention to the development of new research programs and innovative treatment models. Almost all such programs gave increased attention to the environment in which the dysfunctional behaviors were occurring, a reaction against a medical perspective that problems are to be understood mostly in terms of individual, organismic pathology. Thus, within the profession of community psychology one finds many ardent social activists who are strongly critical of the limits of traditional personality theories as a way of explaining human behavioral problems. While it is well beyond the scope of this text to give further details of the history of community psychology, it is important to note that this newer specialty has been a major force in reminding psychology that many of the mental health problems in our society reside in "the less than optimal features of the society itself such as racism, sexism, poverty, unemployment, or restricted educational opportunity" (Blocher & Biggs, 1983, p. 10).

If the 1960s was the decade of the emergence of community psychology, then the 1970s can be seen as the decade of the emergence of health psychology, another specialty in which counseling psychologists are increasingly involved and with strong relationships to prevention. With the increasing attention, in recent decades, to the biological factors in psychological dysfunction, health psychology became one of the fastest growing new areas within psychology. Yet, like the definition for primary prevention noted above, the definition of health psychology is almost equally broad: "We can define professional health psychology as the conduct of interventions, derived from psychological science, aimed at altering health related experience or behaviors of individuals, either directly or through action upon the experience of behaviors of persons whose activities affect the health of others" (Rodin & Stone, 1987, p. 16). Many of the kinds of services listed in the article titles opening this chapter would easily be considered within the purview of prevention in health psychology. An edited volume on prevention in health psychology included topics such as adolescent smoking prevention, exercise programs for health promotion, coping with illness in childhood, and physician/patient communication (Rosen & Solomon, 1985).

Thus, counseling psychologists involved in prevention activities find themselves in significant interface with those in community psychology and health psychology. In fact, many counseling psychologists maintain professional memberships in one of those divisions within the APA as well as membership in the Division of Counseling Psychology.

The Educational Perspective

As noted in the first two chapters of this text, counseling psychology, especially in contrast to clinical psychology, developed as a profession in educational rather than medical settings. It is therefore not too surprising that many of the services that have been developed and promulgated under the term *prevention,* as developed in the medical perspective, have different labels when viewed from the educational/developmental perspective. During the 1960s, within the counseling profession, the term *outreach* was much more frequently used than *prevention* for very similar types of services. These differences in terminology are more than accidental. Passionate ideological feelings are involved as well. There is continuing concern with the medical perspective's focus on disease and pathology. To the extent that the term *prevention* is still linked to the medical model, prevention services may remain too narrow in scope: "It [community psychology] is still saddled . . . with a conceptual allegiance to the ill-conceived metaphor of mental health, with resulting ties to health service delivery systems and medical models of diagnosis and treatment that are limiting to its ultimate development and contributions" (Blocher & Biggs, 1983, p. 11). Similarly, Danish, D'Augelli, and Ginsberg (1984) affirm that "a new conceptual foundation is needed to direct prevention activities, one that is not based on a medical or a therapeutic-curative model. . . . We will propose a different conceptualization, that of life-span human *development*. . . . A model of prevention must be concerned with behavior over the life-span, with the continuity and discontinuity of development over time" (p. 523).

As cogently described by Drum and Figler (1973), professional activities labeled "outreach" grew out of counseling psychologists' efforts to aid the psychological development of students they served, that is, moving beyond remediation. As may be recalled from Chapter 2, from the beginnings of counseling psychology, through at least the 1960s, most counseling psychologists worked in schools and colleges. Outreach initially referred to innovative services provided by counseling psychologists within schools or colleges but provided outside of the offices in which they typically did one-to-one counseling or therapy.

Why were these "innovative" services developed and just what were they? There are at least three reasons for their development. The first was articulated by Warnath (1971), frequently cited as one of the most incisive critics of college counseling centers' failure to respond to student needs in the 1960s. "Every center is highly selective in the clientele who will seek its services, and unless the counselors reverse the process and seek out the problem areas which might use their attention, they will be unaware of many student needs they are neglecting. The pregnant girl, the potential draft resister, and the student hooked on drugs are unlikely to walk into a counseling center to ask for help from any counselor who may be available" (Warnath, 1971, pp. 58–59). To respond to such needs, Warnath believed, counselors must get out of their offices and develop innovative services, for example, setting up satellite locations for drop-in, "anonymous" one-session counseling in residence halls or student activities buildings. Additionally, there was a call for what were then very innovative services such as developing audiotapes for self-help programs. Self-help audiotapes on study skills, choosing careers and majors, and managing test anxiety were all new "outreach" services that were designed to reduce the frequency or at least intensity of typical college student developmental problems.

A second reason for the development of outreach services was the greatly increased attention to mental health services in the 1960s as a result of the previously mentioned Community Mental Health Centers Act. With a sudden increase in demand for mental health services, there were immense shortages of professional-level counseling psychologists to staff college and student counseling centers and community mental health centers. Much of the rationale for outreach activities evident in Drum and Figler (1973) is based on responding to such shortages by providing innovative group-based services.

The third reason is the most theoretically based: life-span development theory. Given this theoretical foundation, it is not surprising that it is the primary basis on which outreach activities have continued. The focus of developmental psychology has "aged" with the profession, with strongest emphasis on children, beginning in the 1920s, to a rapidly emerging emphasis on aging in the 1980s. Throughout the 1940s and 1950s there was an ever-increasing amount of literature on adolescent and college student development: intellectual development, moral development, and psychosocial development, especially identity development. By the late 1960s a variety of innovative psychological programs were being developed, based on the work of developmental psychologists such as Piaget, Kohlberg, Perry, and Erikson, that were designed to facilitate and enhance students' progress through various developmental stages and tasks.

The term *deliberate psychological education* (Mosher & Sprinthall, 1971) was used to describe a model curriculum that could be used to foster psychological development. The primary purpose was to reduce the occurrence of psychological stress and dysfunction. The course work in this curriculum was extremely varied. A "participant-observation" methodology was used for the study of the psychology of work whereby junior high students actually left the school to spend time at work settings. Another course taught the high school students to be "counselors" by studying "the generic processes of counseling and the general themes which adolescents bring to counseling. The course focuse[d] heavily on the processes of listening to another individual, listening for feeling and for ideas and learning to respond both to another person's feelings and his ideas" (Mosher & Sprinthall, 1971, p. 14). A study of the changes in psychological development of participants in these special programs found that, compared to control nonparticipants, they showed greater advances on both the Loevinger Ego Development Scale and Kohlberg Moral Judgment Scale.

Another area of developmental research, that of coping with life transitions, has also led to the emergence of new types of outreach services.

Many transitions are expected to occur at certain times of life (e.g., graduating from school, having children, retiring). Other transitions are less predictable but have an equal impact on new challenges they create for us (e.g., infertility, reaching a plateau at work, having a child who never leaves home). Schlossberg (1989) has noted that many transitions bring changes in our roles, relationships, routines, and in our assumptions about ourselves. The more changes there are, the more likely we are to experience psychological distress in undergoing them. If effective interventions are designed to help one prepare for such transitions (e.g., orientation courses for new college students, preretirement planning programs), then the probability of psychological dysfunction is reduced.

Thus far we have been describing outreach activities focused largely on (1) getting the counselor out of the office to reach persons that would otherwise not come for services and (2) interventions to facilitate normative development. Both of these kinds of activities are designed in part to fulfill the role of primary prevention, that is, avoid the development of significant problems that many persons experience as part of normal development and in coping with developmental transitions (Schlossberg, 1989). In brief, outreach has some of the same goals as primary prevention—keeping problems from happening. However, it needs to be emphasized that developmental interventions that are part of outreach are not just addressed to preventing problems but also have the goal of enhancing the eventual outcome of normal development. "Normal" development of identity in contemporary society may leave many persons with limited interpersonal relationship skills resulting in less than maximally effective marriages, co-worker relationships, and so forth. If one develops more effective skills in relating to adults, might one become more effective as a spouse and worker? The effectiveness and quality of life of individuals and society, then, can both benefit from developmental interventions. The development of such programs is now most often referred to as psychoeducational programming (e.g., Sprinthall & Scott, 1989).

Despite these differences in the ideology behind prevention and developmental interventions, the psychological services to accomplish both are typically quite similar. Moreover, such services most often are offered outside of the counselor's office. Therefore, throughout the rest of this chapter the terms *outreach, prevention,* and *developmental* are used almost interchangeably as they refer to psychological services. Simply remember that the terms developed in different historical contexts and that they have unique as well as shared meanings.

New Implications of the Definitions

Outreach and prevention services have special relationships to the definition of yet other newer terms now appearing in the rapidly changing market for psychological services. As the cost of all levels of health care escalates, increased attention is being given to both primary prevention programs (e.g., wellness programs at the worksite) and secondary prevention programs (e.g., group-based programs that address topical issues such as stress management). Just as shortages of mental health personnel in the 1960s led to increasing emphasis on outreach, so are the costs of one-to-one mental health treatment doing likewise in the 1990s.

One service setting that typically has a strong focus on outreach is employee assistance programs (EAPs). These programs are now being developed in many business settings and large governmental agencies. Toomer (1982) describes six roles for counseling psychologists in such business and industry settings, three of which are clearly in the areas of prevention and outreach: training/educator, human resources manager, and organizational specialist. (The other roles are counselor/therapist, researcher/program evaluator, selection/promotion expert.) In addition to providing outreach services like stress management programs for employees and basic relationship skills for managers and supervisors, counseling psychologists may also be involved in helping the organization identify what aspects of the work environment are detrimental to productivity and/or employee morale. As described in the chapter on career psychology, there is an abundance of literature showing the relationship of employee morale to such cost control factors in industry as turnover, absenteeism, and productivity: "Business or industrial organizations may be viewed as large human systems whose structure and culture have impact on many smaller systems, such as work groups, workers, and families of workers. Organizational systems also have an impact on larger human systems such as the community and society. Consequently, focusing remedial, preventive, and developmental interventions on aspects of the organizational system may be a powerful and parsimonious approach to enhancing human potential" (Minatoya, 1982, p. 27). Studies of an organization's effects on employees' psychological health also often lead to, for example, outplacement programs for employees who are being terminated, orientation programs for employees who are being transferred abroad, and retirement planning programs. All such programs address transition periods where individuals are at high risk for psychological problems.

Managed care is another setting in which outreach interventions are important. *Managed care* is a relatively recent term that applies to a group of health practitioners who contract with an employer to provide for most of the mental and/or physical health care needs of the employees. Since, in most such contracts, the group of practitioners is responsible for meeting many of the health service needs of the employees for a set price, many of these programs want to minimize the costs of expensive remedial treatments. Consequently, more attention is given to outreach programs as a way of reducing the frequency and severity of mental health disorders. Outreach programs on bereavement, dealing with broken relationships, and managing transitions such as midlife crises and retirement are all an extrapolation of programs originally developed for the college-age population and the transitions they face. Both EAPs and managed care programs are increasingly conducting periodic courses or seminars of two to six weeks duration just as many college counseling centers have, for nearly two decades, provided a variety of outreach theme-oriented groups throughout the academic year on topics such as stress, communications skills, self-esteem, and so forth.

In the next section, we describe a now-classic conceptualization of psychological services, developed by counseling psychologists, that increases the awareness of the multiple ways in which service deliverers can meet their prevention and developmental roles as well as their remedial role.

THIRTY-SIX FACES OF COUNSELING: THE CLASSIC MODEL

Despite the plethora of new roles for counseling psychologists that emerged in the 1960s and 1970s under the many labels just reviewed in the definition section, there was no systematic way to determine what balance was desirable and whether a psychological services center was being reasonably comprehensive in its offerings. Morrill, Oetting, and Hurst (1974) provided a three-dimensional cube (see Figure 16-1) to respond to this need for a systematic description of counselor functions. The cube has had seminal value not only in organizing what has been accomplished by the profession but also in pointing to what needs to be done in those "cells" of the cube where there are few if any existing services. Most counseling services continue to focus on just a few "faces" of the cube. Consequently, the well-prepared counseling psychologist uses the cube as a way to explore opportunities for prevention and outreach services in both current and emerging career settings.

The *purpose* dimension of the cube includes the roles of remediation, prevention, and development, emphasizing that "developmental interventions include those programs designed to enhance the functioning and developmental potential of healthy individuals and groups" (Morrill, Oetting, & Hurst, 1974, p. 357). The *target* dimension is one that is still too little attended to, given its generic applicability to psychological services in counseling centers, hospitals, industry, or managed care. Within this dimension, *primary group* refers to the group of persons who are most influential for an individual. These might include family members, roommates in a residence hall, or residents in a senior center or a life-care community. In this latter setting, other residents may be the closest the person

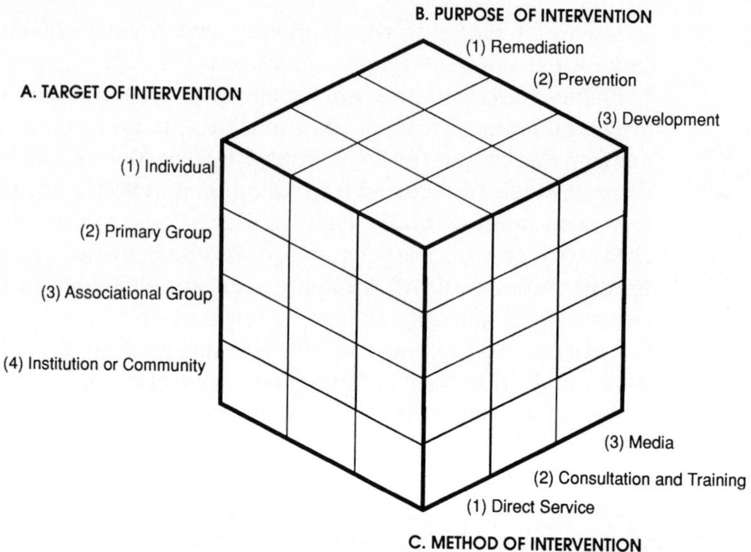

FIGURE 16–1 The Thirty-six Faces of Counseling. Courtesy of Weston H. Morrill, Ph.D.

has to "family," at least on an everyday basis. An *associational group* is one in which the individual is a member, such as a civic club, a church, or one's work setting. The faculty of any given department is an associational group; the nurses assigned to a particular hospital ward are an associational group; the employees assembling toasters in a small appliance plant are an associational group. Associational groups are, in turn, subunits of an institution, the final level in this dimension—for example, university, hospital, small appliance plant. For a civic or religious associational group, the larger context is the community, and one could argue that the model, when applied beyond the university setting, should use the label "institution/community." All too often, thought is given only to the dichotomy of individual vs. group without attention being paid to what different kinds of goals and programs one would have for individual vs. associational vs. institutional/community groupings.

The cube's third dimension of counselor functions, *method of intervention,* includes perhaps the least considered aspects of the model prior to the late 1980s. Although direct service has been the mainstream of professional psychology since its beginning and while new developments were made in consultation and training throughout the 1970s (see next chapter), only in the 1980s was much attention given the media, radio and TV as well as written self-help materials (see "Perspectives on self-help and bibliotherapy: You are what you read" [Craighead, McNamara, & Horan, 1984]).

One could argue that a truly comprehensive counseling service should have some available program for each of the 36 faces of counseling. It is probably easiest to conceptualize such a comprehensive set of services by choosing a method of intervention, such as media, and then asking what kind of media program is needed for each of the psychological *targets* of intervention with each of the different *purposes* (i.e., remediation, prevention, and development). To be fully comprehensive, one would need 12 media programs, whether written or audiovisual. Likewise, one could specify 12 sorts of consultation or training programs and 12 kinds of direct service.

It is certainly possible to see how some outreach might be done in every cell, whether it is simply moving direct service to a satellite center, for example, setting up an office in the student union to maximize initial interviews, or developing a preventive intervention for an international company in order to reduce the stresses of employee relocation. The frequent overlapping implications of a single outreach intervention for both development and prevention have already been described.

In the next section we describe the one type of outreach program that has seen the largest growth in counseling psychology in the past two decades. It is also a type of outreach which has both developmental and preventive implications. These interventions are what many counseling psychologists call "structured groups." The importance of structured groups is growing in the 1990s because they are just as applicable to emerging roles in employee assistance programs and managed care as they are in the college settings in which many of them were developed. We focus on three examples of structured groups because these most closely approximate a generic model of an effective outreach or prevention program.

STRUCTURED GROUPS AS GENERIC PREVENTION AND OUTREACH

Drum and Knott (1977) define a structured group as "a delimited learning situation with a predetermined goal, and a planned design to enable each group member to reach this identified goal with minimum frustration and maximum ability to transfer the new learning to a wide range of life events" (p. 14). They categorize the numerous kinds of structured groups that have been developed in the last 20 years within three broad groupings: *lifeskills* (e.g., assertion training, decision making, parenting skills), *life theme groups* (e.g., clarifying personal values, raising self-esteem, developing gender awareness), and *life transition groups* (e.g., for separated and divorced persons resolving personal loss). Each time a major new "diagnostic" concern becomes visible, relevant structured groups have typically emerged. Recent examples include groups for persons with eating disorders, adult children of alcoholics, and victims of date rape.

Most structured groups meet for a relatively small number of sessions, typically around six to eight. Some meet for even fewer sessions; a few go somewhat longer. Manuals are developed that provide a list of activities and objectives for each group session. Sessions typically last 90 minutes to two hours, but this amount of time can be shortened if essential, especially if the number of group sessions can be extended. The converse, however, is not recommended. That is, extending the length of each group session and reducing the total numbers of sessions is rarely recommended for the simple reason that it provides less time for group members to practice some of the skills or to explore some of the issues on their own time and in their own personal situations. Many structured groups include "homework" assignments for practicing certain skills in group members' own personal situations. As for any other skill, more practice time often provides the possibility for more efficient learning. In brief, the goals of most structured groups are not easily accomplished in a marathon all-day session.

Before describing some specific examples of structured groups it is worth examining the unique set of values they provide for consumers, be they clients, students, or employees, as well as for the staff or agency offering the program. As Drum and Knott (1977) cogently summarize, there are eight easily identifiable values inherent in the offering of structured groups. One, structured groups are "relatively non-threatening to participants and make the process of learning enjoyable. Through appropriately structured exercises they encourage people gently but firmly to increase their ability to try out new behaviors or examine issues they would normally avoid" (p. 24). Two, they take the mystery out of the process of self-discovery and self-enhancement, making it seem possible to change without undergoing intensive psychotherapy. Three, the implied contract in such groups is much more limited. "Each participant can enter into the group experience with a feeling of inner comfort that the group will stick to the stated goal and not attempt to restructure the whole personality" (p. 25). Four, structured groups, like all group treatment, have the advantage of helping the person realize that many others have the same kind of problem situation. The sense of being in it together provides a reassurance to the participant that he or she is not alone in this problem. Five, there is less stigma associated with taking part in groups that focus on common developmental or transitional needs using an educational-experiential format than there is in entering remedial counseling or therapy. Six, the interactions within such groups encourage change and growth while also providing the chance for group members to practice skills with other persons who are sharing their same problem. Seven, there is the opportunity for both peer and professional feedback related to the tryout of skills. Eight, structured groups, like all group interventions, provide an economical use of counselors' time. The needs and issues of many persons can be addressed in the same amount of hours that one-to-one counseling would provide for only one person.

We will briefly describe three structured groups as a way of helping the reader develop a closer acquaintance with such groups. It is important to note, however, that one of the best ways to learn about structured groups is to participate in such a group, just as it has often been suggested that one of the important ways to learn about counseling and therapy is to be a client.

The first structured group to be described is one on assertion training, a kind of structured group developed most extensively in the 1970s. It can now be considered as the classic model of structured groups. Assertion training groups are currently a standard part of the services of many counseling centers and women's centers, especially since problems of battered and unemployed women are often exacerbated by very low levels of assertiveness. In 1975 an entire issue of *The Counseling Psychologist* (Vol. 5, No. 4) was dedicated to an exploration of the structure and value of assertion training for a very wide range of populations (e.g., job interviewees, new professional consultants, the elderly). Ever since that time, evidence continues to accumulate on the positive effects of such training for participants from ages 14 to 65 (Richards, Burlingame, & Fuhriman, 1990).

Descriptions of specific goals and exercises for a diversity of structured groups are still most easily found in Drum and Knott (1973), for example, self-management, parenting skills, self-esteem, personal loss, and raising male consciousness. They also include a model of assertion training conducted in seven sessions. Much of the sense of what happens in such groups can be found in the following excerpts from their descriptions of the activities for each of the sessions.

Assertion Training

> Session 1: . . . trainers and group members introduce themselves. Trainers explain rationale for behavior therapy in general and assertive training in particular. Trainers explain that the skill of assertive behavior can be broken down into manageable behavioral components, such as eye contact and appropriate facial expression; body posture and appropriate hand movement; vocal tone, volume, and quality; and goal directedness. After each presentation of a behavioral component, the trainers model the contrast between ineffective and effective use of that component. Group members then pair up and alternately perform a related exercise. . . . trainers present assertive guideline: state the feeling that needs to be expressed as

clearly as possible, and state what you need from the other person. If appropriate, ask for respect from the other person for your feelings. . . . Trainers roleplay three pairs of scenes, one for each of the three types of assertion, i.e., objective, subjective and defensive. . . . Homework assignments: observe a good assertive role and study his/her behavioral components. In interactions with others be aware of your own behavioral components and actively bring them into play in order to make better contact. Describe the situations in your own life where you have been unable to be assertive and would like to be. Bring these written scenes to the [next] session. . . .

Session 2: Discussion of homework and sharing of past week's experiences. . . . Trainers explain some further behavioral goal guidelines in assertion. . . . trainer-client roleplays: half the group roleplays the less difficult of their two written scenes with one of the trainers as the "assertee". . . . immediately after the scene, the "asserter" views the videotape playback and critiques the behavioral component. If videotape is not available, then the group members can critique the "asserters" [on their] use of behavioral components. . . . the scene is played again as before with videotape. . . . the process can be repeated. . . . until the individual is comfortable with his/her performance and the group (and trainers) feels that progress has been made. Homework assignments: practice the quick relaxation techniques when feeling anxious. . . . members now make a behavioral contract with the group to be accomplished during the weeks; i.e., to express their feelings in a specific non-threatening situation.

Session 3: Discuss sharing of experiences in contracts. . . . three additional behavioral guidelines: good assertion is not aggression. . . . timing of an assertive response is critical. . . . before asserting, it is important that the individual internally reflect on the specific goal. . . . Roleplays with the second half of the group as described in session 2. Homework assignment: group members contract to act on a specific, real life objective approach assertion. . . .

Session 4: Discussion and sharing of contracts. . . . Trainers review principles covered in past sessions (briefly) and respond to issues raised. Role playing with group members second scene [from session 2]; homework assignment: group members contract to act on a specific real life defensive assertion. . . .

Session 5: Discussion and sharing of contracts. . . . Role playing with second half of group. Homework assignment: group members contract for real life subjective approach assertion.

Session 6: Discussion and sharing of contracts. . . . Group improvisational roleplays: Trainers and group members pick random assertive situations to roleplay; these should be situations which occur suddenly and for which an asserter must respond without prior rehearsal or planning (e.g., someone steps in front of you in line, someone takes your seat, people talk loudly at movies, etc.). . . . Announcement of time and date for session 7 (approximately one month later). Homework assignments: keep a continuous assertive diary for the coming month with entries for as many situations as can be charted; emphasis can be on both positive occurrences and the problematic skills areas. . . .

Session 7: Trainers facilitate free flowing discussion concerning clients' successes and problems with assertion. Role playing can be utilized to illustrate the issues being discussed. The issue of choice in assertion can be introduced by the trainers if not introduced by the group. Trainers elicit feedback on their personal and program performance. (Drum & Knott, 1977, pp. 62–81)

In these excerpts one can see the limited goals for each session. One can also see the opportunities there are for members to learn about specific interpersonal skills that they then get to try out in the relatively safe environment of a group of persons who share their concerns. Such group practice is then followed by the "homework" of trying to use the skill in personal situations, with the chance to come back the following week to discuss how those tryouts went, what changes might be made, and so forth. Whether the topic be communication skills in marriage, developing a plan to change careers, dealing with broken relationships, or coping with chronic pain, this same focused learning and practice format can be very effective for persons experiencing a similar type of problem.

Athletes Coaching Teens (ACT)

Another example of a structured group shares similarities in the specification of activities for each session but is much less narrowly focused in terms of *specific* goals. Moreover, this next example involves counseling psychologists training paraprofessional leaders, resulting in significant benefits for both leaders and participants. As described by Danish, Howard, and Farrell (1990) their Athletes Coaching Teens (ACT) program was developed primarily to serve the goal of drug prevention. However, in their careful study of the factors leading to drug use among their target population of middle school students, they found that, in addition to problems with drug use, there were strong relationships between alcohol and drug use and "unsafe sexual activity, aggressive behavior, school attendance, and school disciplinary problems . . . [and] a lack of optimism about the future" (p. 2). Given that perspective, the authors developed a prevention program focused on teaching life skills. "In other words, our approach has been to teach adolescents 'what to say yes to' as opposed to 'just say no'" (p. 3).

Applying concepts from Bandura's (1977) social learning theory, especially its emphasis on modeling (Thoresen, Hosford, & Krumboltz 1970), the authors decided to use professional, college, and high school athletes in various stages of the program. The professional athletes were used primarily to make presentations at school assemblies concerning goal setting and attainment and the problems associated with drug involvement, dropping out of school, and teen pregnancy. College-level athletes were then instructed by the authors in how to train selected high school students to be ACT leaders. These high school students were chosen by their schools for their athletic involvement, academic performance, and leadership qualities. "Because these high school students are regarded as positive role models who have grown up in the city and have attended the same middle school as the seventh graders, they are in a unique position to be effective teachers for middle school youth. Once high school athletes have completed the ACT training program, they implement a seven session program within middle school health classes" (Danish et al., 1990, p. 3).

There are seven 45-minute workshops with each one including a review of concepts taught in the previous workshops as well as a brief skit to introduce the lesson of the day. Opportunity for practice then follows. The content of each session is described as follows:

> *Dare to Dream:* in this workshop the ACT program and the high school leaders are introduced. Participants discuss the importance of dreams and learn to dream about their future.
>
> *Setting Goals:* in this workshop three characteristics of a reachable goal are presented (make the goal important to you, positive, and specific). Participants convert their dreams from Workshop 1 into reachable goals.
>
> *Making a Goal Ladder:* focuses on the importance of making a plan to reach a goal. Participants are taught the relationship between long and short term goals by selecting a current goal that directs them toward a future goal. Then they develop a goal ladder with a series of small rungs to help them reach their current goal. One of the rungs must be something they can accomplish during the ACT program.
>
> *Roadblocks to Reaching Goals:* participants learn how various roadblocks (drugs, teen pregnancy, dropping out of school, fighting, and so on) can prevent them from attaining their goals. Using timeliness and developing original stories they see the impact of roadblocks on the outcome of youths' lives.
>
> *Overcoming Roadblocks:* The acronym STAR is taught: *Stop* and chill out; *Think* of your choices; *Anticipate* the consequences of the choices; *Respond* with the best choice. Students practice using STAR in situations they could encounter at home or in school.
>
> *Rebounds and Rewards:* the participants' goal ladders are used to discuss rewards for accomplishing a rung on the ladder. Participants also discuss how to rebound from temporary setbacks such as when a goal becomes too difficult and seems unreachable.
>
> *Putting your ACT Together:* a series of "games" which provide an opportunity to integrate and apply the information covered in the previous workshops. This workshop is best conducted in a gym or outdoors. (Danish et al., pp. 3, 8)

By bringing such a program into the regular classroom, for an entire class of students, a very large number of students are reached; equally important, both the high school and college-level athletes receive training in communication and leadership skills regarding one of our country's most pressing contemporary social problems. Such training can enable them to become active volunteers themselves in developing and promoting similar programs in other settings as their own personal and professional lives develop.

Adult Children Of Alcoholics (ACOA)

Our final example of a structured group again shows the basic feature of high level of specification of activities even for a client group with significant adjustment problems. The structured group to be described was developed for *adult* children of alcoholics. During the 1980s, this client population emerged as one which could significantly benefit from treatment focusing on typical family problems that lead to difficulties in the psychological functioning of adults. The family problems may have occurred decades earlier but their consequences still affect the adults long after they have left home. The group described here is one that can be adapted for use with anyone from late teens to retirement age. (In fact, this kind of group serves to remind us that, no matter what our age, we shall always be, or shall always have been, someone's child.) The group to be described could be offered in any of a number of mental health service settings such as community mental health clinics or counseling centers, independent or group practices, or even in community service agencies, such as churches, libraries, and seniors' centers.

The program described below, a ten-session model developed by Perone (1989), is one of several that have been developed for this group of clients. It is based on findings regarding alcoholic families: "Alcoholic families are built on a basis of denial and avoidance. These families have secrets to hide which require a system of rigid rules and various roles for family members to play. Children from dysfunctional families, then, tend to become rigid and controlling themselves as a way of coping. . . . Adult children of alcoholics have difficulty trusting others, have difficulty identifying and/or expressing their feelings, and often cannot ask for what they need" (Perone, 1989, p. 1).

After an initial group session, utilizing any one of a number of different strategies typical in group work for members to become acquainted, the group members move, in the second session, to a focus on the family and how it has affected their current psychological functioning. Each member develops a "gene-o-gram" to describe his or her basic family membership and structure, an important foundation for subsequent sessions. The third session is built around the roles the participants play in their families. The session is based on the work of Black (1985) and introduces the role of the "responsible child," the "placating child," the "adjusting child," and the "acting out child." Group members discuss what role or roles they felt they and their siblings played in their families and help each other explore their own experiences.

In the fourth session, the focus is on the common characteristics of adult children of alcoholics, based on the work of Woititz (1983). After studying the 13 characteristics she lists, the group again spends time exploring which of those characteristics describe themselves. This group session helps lead to a realization of how much adult behavior is a result of the early family experience.

The fifth session is devoted to an experiential understanding of the concept of co-dependency. "Co-dependency results on focusing on the needs and behaviors of others. It has been described as the disease of 'lost self'" (Perone, 1989, p. 14). It is introduced as a learned pattern of behavior that can be unlearned by changing patterns under the control of the participant. Co-dependency results in twisted emotional equations—for example: being loved equals being desperately needed, being loving equals taking care of others, intimacy equals smothering, spontaneity equals rebellious behavior.

The sixth session builds on the previous one, to show how co-dependency affected communication patterns in the family. Group members use "family sculpting"; that is, other group members are used to represent other family members such as father, mother, sister, brother, or even a favorite animal. Once the family is "sculpted," the participant begins to break the co-dependent behavior by telling something to each of the family members that he or she has wanted to in the past but has not been able to. The purpose of the exercise is to be able to express previously suppressed feelings.

The seventh session focuses on the comparison of healthy vs. dysfunctional families, relying on the work of Whitfield (1987). The family system is studied in terms of ten differences between alcoholic families and healthy families; for example, the alcoholic family has rigid roles, or family secrets and conflict between members are denied and ignored.

The remaining three sessions are devoted to providing experiential exercises to break the "four rules" of the dysfunctional alcoholic family: the rule of rigidity (because of the unpredictable behavior of the alcoholic member, the family imposes more rules to gain some stability), the rule of silence (to keep the family secret), the rule of denial of what's happening (so that no one feels the responsibility for change), and the rule of isolation (not only to help keep the secret, but to keep family members' support focused on each other emotionally). Each of the exercises is designed to help participants experience somewhat more healthy interactions than they were able to experience in their families and to provide a safer environment for flexibility and spontaneity, expression of feeling, recognition and acceptance of problems, and intimate sharing with other persons.

Obviously, even more so than the other structured groups described, this is one in which group leaders would have to do a great deal of study about the kinds of psychological problems typically experienced by the adult children of alcoholics to design appropriate experiential exercises. As with all structured groups, one of the major benefits for members is the opportunity to share, with persons with the same kinds of problems, more positive interpersonal experiences.

This brief presentation of three programs, it is hoped, makes clear the potentially significant impact that structured groups can have for achieving the goals of prevention and outreach. Such programs are suitable for any number of different settings. Assertion training programs, when focused on career transition problems, can be a valued part of an employee assistance program. Substance abuse programs that involve professional athletes may be appropriate not only for school-aged youth but for many adults whose primary role models may also be accomplished athletes. Thus EAP or managed care programs, often serving large numbers of young adult males, may wish to offer some modification of the ACT program. Given the large number of persons living with substance abusers, structured programs similar to the one for adult children of alcoholics can be important offerings both in EAPs in work settings and in community settings such as neighborhood services centers, churches, and community mental health centers.

RHETORIC OR REALITY?

The question "Rhetoric or Reality?" is borrowed from Hansen (1981), who, while still a graduate student, wrote a most incisive critique of counseling psychology's commitment to primary prevention. Anxious to learn about and receive training in how to do primary prevention, she discovered that there were very few conceptualizations or empirical articles about prevention in counseling psychology journals and even fewer opportunities to take relevant courses and practica within counseling psychology programs: "It is startling to find, in recent issues of *The Counseling Psychologist,* a spate of papers urging counseling psychologists to redefine their role and become systems change agents, psychoeducators, and specialists in primary prevention. . . . this paper will seek to show that counseling psychology is, in fact, neither strongly committed nor systematically involved in primary prevention, that it is deeply ambivalent to preventive mental health" (p. 57).

We noted at the beginning of this chapter that prevention and outreach are topics that are often not covered in counseling psychology texts. At the same time, there have been references throughout previous chapters to the longstanding definition of counseling psychology, including the remedial, preventive, and developmental roles. This section is a bluntly honest presentation of several trenchant critiques of the ambivalence of counseling psychologists (and, others would add, almost *all* psychologists) regarding prevention and outreach. We conclude this section with our own prognosis for prevention and outreach and complete the chapter with a discussion of the more promising developments in the profession's work in these areas.

The data on research, training, and practice related to prevention and outreach all point to a limited role of these activities in counseling psychology. Krumboltz, Becker-Haven, and Burnett (1979), using the long-standing tripartite division of counseling psychologists' roles into the remedial, prevention and developmental, concluded in their annual review article that "prevention, unfortunately, continues to occupy last place in the hearts of counseling psychologists" (p. 588). Regarding training, Banikiotes (1977) found that outreach and consultation ranked 20th in curriculum offerings. A slightly later survey by McNeil and Ingram (1983) empirically confirmed Hansen's lament about training, showing that most counseling psychology programs either did not offer training in prevention and outreach or, at best, only a few students in the program took such a course. Training in development of outreach programs yielded even lower rates of participation than training in preventive principles and interventions.

The rhetoric and reality dichotomy is reflected as well in the occupational analysis of Fitzgerald and Osipow (1986), who show that, for the most part, fewer than half of all counseling psychologists do any work related to prevention services such as needs assessment and program evaluation, and spend relatively little time on those tasks when they are performing them. *Yet, they rate its importance to their identity as high as they rate most aspects of research.* Is it that employers do not want these kinds of services? One can hardly conclude that from surveys in both the late 1970s (Magoon & McDermott, 1979) and late 1980s (Kandell, 1988). In both these studies of what counseling center directors desired in employees (as compared to what was available among applicants for positions), prevention and outreach was typically seen as *being very desirable but not readily available.* On the other hand, for individual counseling and therapy skills, diagnostic skills, and crisis intervention skills, there was a much closer balance of availability and desirability. Kandell found one notable exception between the data from the late 1970s and 1980s. The availability of persons trained in structured groups radically increased such that the majority of candidates in the late 1980s had some preparation in this area.

How can one account for these apparent discrepancies in what has been identified as a vital role for counseling psychology since its beginning as a profession, yet recognize the failure of prevention, especially, and more recently, the failure of developmental interventions to capture the hearts of (or even receive much time from) most counseling psychologists? Osipow (1977), reviewing this dilemma over a decade ago, "formulated 'Osipow's Law' to epitomize [his] concerns. Remediation (in the form of psychotherapeutic interventions) drives out prevention in the form of counseling interventions where the two are present in the same agency" (p. 94). Osipow believed that the operating force behind this law was that more and more mental health services were being funded through third-party insurance payments, which according to most insurance companies' regulations are restricted to remedial interventions for diagnosed dysfunctions. Thus, what some professional leaders believe is most needed is not what is being paid for. Career counseling, communications skill groups, and stress management psychoeducational groups may all have higher benefits relative to costs yet often fail to qualify for mental health insurance payments. An increasing number of counseling psychologists are seeking to affect public policy so that more preventive services can be reimbursed by health insurance payments or included in managed care programs.

Sprinthall (1990) feels the same dilemma has increasingly affected developmental interventions. Despite extensive theorizing, program development, and research by counseling psychologists in the 1960s and 1970s, who proposed developmental interventions and deliberate psychological education, Sprinthall feels that, in the past decade, everything but remedial individual therapy has been receiving diminished attention. Commenting on Osipow's Law, he provides a valuable interdisciplinary perspective in noting that "the law is really a reminder of the power of the medical model. In that field [medicine] less than two percent of program resources and activities are devoted to prevention. . . . in other words it seems that the medical model is in. The educational, career, preventive development approach is being driven out [in training of counseling psychologists]" (p. 455). Especially distressing to Sprinthall is the fact that this change in priorities counters the research evidence on which psychology has always proudly said it bases its development of interventions: "From my view, one of the major ironies is that although we have apparently drifted away from our roots in prevention, education, and development, the bases for our original distinctiveness have increased. On one hand, there is problematic evidence to support the medical model for psychological diagnosis/treatment. On the other hand, there is increasing evidence in favor of the developmental and preventive. Ironically, we move toward the former and away from the latter" (p. 457). He then describes the few but expanding applications of psychoeducational developmental programs not only in schools but also in correctional centers and community settings.

Our prognosis for prevention and outreach research and services throughout the 1990s and on into the 21st century is that they will continue to receive at least slight but vital participation by counseling psychologists, just as they have for the past half-century. Prevention and outreach will remain small, in our view, not because they should, but because the entire health care system, as noted by Sprinthall (1990), is so dominated by the medical model that remedial efforts will continue to receive the bulk of funds and therefore provide the most employment. If public policy changes can be achieved for more adequate funding of prevention, much more rapid developments can be expected. Relatedly, there is significant growth in EAPs and managed care as a way of containing the runaway costs of treating all problems as needing long-term remediation. Outreach and prevention activities, properly designed, are some of the most cost-effective interventions that psychologists can provide. If, as expected, more job opportunities become linked to psychologists' ability to provide cost-effective interventions, then there is promise for increasing attention to prevention and outreach. Will counseling psychologists be trained to provide such services? Watkins (1985) has provided a useful outline of coursework and practicum experience that can be made an integral part of a counseling psychology program. His suggestions include a broad range of references that can be consulted to build on the concepts and principles outlined in this chapter.

EVALUATING PREVENTIVE AND OUTREACH INTERVENTIONS

As Sprinthall (1990) noted, the evidence for both primary prevention and developmental interventions has been remarkable. Baker, Swisher, Nadenichak, and Popowicz (1984) reviewed a large number of empirical evaluations of prevention strategies and, using meta-analytic techniques to combine the results of these studies, concluded that the treatment effect size was larger for such interventions than that found in meta-analytic analyses of the results of psychotherapy. In addition to such research on primary prevention strategies, there are now an ever increasing number of studies of all sorts of outreach endeavors which continue to yield significant results for their target populations. For two very different examples, consider the work of Taylor et al. (1986) showing that social support groups for persons suffering from cancer led to significantly decreased depression and the work of Burnette, Williams, and Law (1987) showing that, for Vietnam veterans who participated in discussion groups, self-management effectiveness increased and expression of anger scores decreased. Earlier we cited some of the significant findings for psychoeducational interventions with young adolescents and assertion training programs with a variety of populations.

The largest bodies of evaluative literature concerning outreach efforts are in the areas of stress management, wellness programs, and structured groups. In the area of stress management, several comprehensive evaluation review articles have appeared in recent years, all indicating positive effects for programs offered to many different ages in a variety of agencies such as schools, community mental health centers, work sites, prisons, and so forth (Ivancevich, Matteson, Freedman, & Phillips, 1990; Matheny, Ayerck, Pugh, Kurlete, & Silva-Cannella, 1986; Deffenbacher, 1988). In the area of wellness programs, while the empirical literature is more recent, an early summary has been provided by Gebhardt and Crump (1990), who concluded that: "Recent research using control groups has found relations between reduction in health care costs, absenteeism, and turnover and implementation of comprehensive health promotion programs" (p. 262).

In the area of structured groups, the largest group of evaluative studies has focused on the effects of communication skills. While the genesis of many such skills programs was primarily in counselor training programs during the 1960s, by the 1970s many of these skills programs had developed into significant outreach programs that have continued to be extended to many different populations. Comprehensive evaluations of the effectiveness of such programs in the family setting have been provided by Levant (1983) in his major treatise "Toward a counseling psychology of the family: Psychological-educational and skills-training programs for treatment, prevention and development." He summarizes the contributions of such skills programs for both marriage and parenting.

Binder and Binder (1983) concluded from their comparison of treatment modalities that communication skills training and behavioral approaches with populations of delinquents both have considerably more positive effects on recidivism rates than traditional psychotherapy and social casework. Kagan and Kagan (1990) continue to provide evidence of the usefulness of their Interpersonal Process Recall skills model of communication skills for a broad variety of situations such as improving the effectiveness of communication between physicians and their patients, aiding the rehabilitation of brain-injured patients, and enhancing the lives of lupus sufferers. A recent comprehensive review of the outcomes of structured groups has been provided by Richards, Burlingame, and Fuhriman (1990). They found 74 empirical articles reviewing what they call theme-oriented groups in 14 different categories (e.g., social skills, chemical dependency, sex crime victims, and parenting). While they found positive effects suggested in many of those articles, they found the studies, like much of the early research on psychotherapy and counseling, often characterized by inadequate specification of actual treatment and limited attention to control factors. Their review holds significant implications and cautions for those designing evaluations of structured-group outreach programs. For illustrative data on the effects of developmental interventions, the review by Danish, D'Augelli, and Ginsburg (1984) provides evidence of the significant contributions from programs such as community education about life-events for older adults, a peer contraceptive program, and retirement planning for professional athletes.

Many of these reviews and articles are quick to note a large number of limitations to the evaluative research on prevention and outreach. In addition to the all-too-frequent list of problems in research on almost any aspect of counseling (e.g., widely different measures used in the studies, lack of explicit descriptions of the interventions, limited sample sizes, and questionable control groups), prevention and outreach research has some unique problems related to the criteria against which they are assessed. For remedial treatment, it is logically clear that one is trying to alleviate the problem, and that some positive results should be visible by the end of treatment. However, for both prevention and developmental research, the criteria are conceptually quite different from remediation. There is no clear problem to "cure." Both prevention and developmental interventions share the goal of having a fewer number of problems for a given population at a specified future time, with the specified time usually being related to some sort of normative life event, for example, the transition from elementary to junior high school, marriage, or retirement. Beyond that, developmental interventions also have the goal of helping persons attain an enhanced outcome as they go through a developmental phase such as achieving independence as a young adult or managing a midlife career change. Defining what constitutes an enhanced outcome in a measurable way is a major challenge for researchers. It is easy to talk about "more productive" employees and "better" marriages, but much harder to get agreement on the criterion for "productive" or "better."

Few of these outreach programs have been compared to other kinds of treatments that might produce similar short-term or long-term effects. One of the major tasks for the 1990s will be to conduct such comparative research to determine the comparative costs and effectiveness of various approaches within or between the categories of remedial, preventive, and developmental interventions. This concern is significant when costs are at issue; for example, if a particular problem affects only a few persons, and preventive interventions would have to be offered to a large part of the population, then prevention could be more costly than remediation. On the other hand, for a topic such as stress, which seems to affect a very large part of the population, preventive interventions can be highly cost-effective, as has already been shown. Determining those areas in which preventive and/or developmental outreach programs can be the most cost-effective interventions would be one of the most valuable contributions counseling psychologists could make in the years ahead.

SUMMARY

The first part of this chapter was devoted to defining how the medical and educational perspectives have led to different terminology for prevention and outreach services. The term *prevention* is characteristic of the medical viewpoint and is most widely used now in the newer specialties of community psychology and health psychology. Distinctions are made between primary prevention, secondary prevention, and tertiary prevention. The goal of primary prevention is to prevent problems before they occur, secondary prevention is to alleviate the intensity and duration of problems, and tertiary prevention is to restore the client to the highest level of functioning possible and minimize the probability of the recurrence of the problem.

The terms *outreach* and *psychoeducational* derive from the educational perspective, more specifically, a life-span view of human development. Psychological tasks and transitions we all face become the primary focal point of interventions that can be designed to reduce psychological dysfunction as well as lead to *enhancement* of normal development. "Normal" development is not always ideal in terms of how satisfied people are on their jobs, in their marriages, in their relationships with their children, and so forth. The goal of enhancement is to help persons move through typical developmental stages in ways that will lead to an improved quality of life. New service settings such as employee assistance programs and managed care practices are providing an impetus for greater use of prevention and outreach interventions.

The second major section of this chapter described the classic cube model of counselor functions as a way of understanding the variety of services that fit within the remediation, prevention, and developmental roles of counseling psychologists. In addition, the cube's facets included the *target* dimension of individuals, associational groups, and institutions, and a *method of intervention* dimension including direct service, consultation/training, and media. The model is especially useful in helping counseling psychologists to think about the variety of services that could be provided in a truly comprehensive service setting, addressing especially the needs of those who might not voluntarily come to a clinic themselves but still need some sort of psychological services.

The major illustrations of services in this chapter were of structured groups, perhaps the most generic example of prevention and outreach services. Structured groups are limited learning situations designed to help participants reach an identified goal and to transfer their learning to a broader range of life events. These kinds of groups have grown widely during the past 20 years and can be broadly considered within three broad categories: (1) life skills (e.g., assertion training), (2) life theme groups (e.g., clarifying personal values), and (3) life transition groups (e.g., bereavement groups). Three examples of groups include: an assertiveness training group for college students, a drug prevention group for junior high school students, and a group for adult children of alcoholics. Each of these groups can be adapted to a wide variety of settings and age groups.

The final section of the chapter dealt with some of the controversies regarding how much counseling psychologists really use prevention and outreach interventions, as compared to simply talking about its importance. The impediments for engaging in more prevention and outreach interventions were explored, ranging from some of the features of health care payment policies to counseling psychologists' own predilections for the predictable comforts of one-to-one counseling and therapy.

While the amount of research evidence on prevention and outreach is significantly smaller in quantity than that on individual counseling and therapy, the evidence has been strongly supportive of the effectiveness of many of these interventions, especially given their cost-effectiveness when addressing problems for which a large part of the population is at risk. A major challenge for the coming decade is for counseling psychologists to develop a better research base for understanding both the unique contributions of and comparative cost-effectiveness of remedial vs. prevention and outreach interventions.

References

Albee, G. W., Bloom, B. L., Broussard, E., Cowen, E. L., Erlenmeyer, Kinmling, L., Gomez, E., Klein, D. C., Menninger, R., Pastor, V. S., Reilly, J., & Rubinger, V. (1978). Report of the task force on primary prevention. *President's commission on mental health.* Washington, DC: U.S. Government Printing Office.

Baker, S., Swisher, P., Nadenichek, P., & Popowitz, C. (1984). Primary effects of primary prevention strategies. *Personnel and Guidance Journal, 62,* 459–464.

Bandura, A. (1977). *Social learning theory.* Englewood Cliffs, NJ: Prentice-Hall.

Banikiotes, P. G. (1977). The training of counseling psychologists. *The Counseling Psychologist,* 7(2), 23–26.

Binder, A., & Binder, V. L. (1983). Juvenile diversion. *The Counseling Psychologist, 11*(2), 69–77.

Black, C. (1985). *Repeat after me.* Denver, CO: M. A. C. Printing and Publications.

Blocher, D. H., & Biggs, D. A. (1983). *Counseling psychology in community settings.* New York: Springer.

Brown, S. D. (1980). Coping skills training: An evaluation of a psychoeducational program in a community mental health setting. *Journal of Counseling Psychology, 27,* 340–345.

Burnette, C., Williams, R. L., & Law, J. G. (1987). Therapeutic and lifestyle reduction of aggressiveness in Vietnam veterans, *Group, 11*(1), 3–14.

Caplan, G. (1964). *Principles of preventive psychiatry.* New York: Basic Books.

Cecil, H. F. (1988). Stress: Country-style: Illinois' response to farm stress. *Journal of World Community Psychology, 9,* 51–60.

Craighead, L. W., McNamara, K., & Horan, J. J. (1984). Perspectives on self-help and bibliotherapy: You are what you read. In S. D. Brown & R. W. Lent (Eds.), *Handbook of counseling psychology* (pp. 878–929). New York: Wiley.

Danish, S. J., D'Augelli, A. R., & Ginsberg, M. R. (1984). Life development intervention: Promotion of mental health through the development of competence. In S. D. Brown & R. W. Lent (Eds.), *Handbook of Counseling Psychology* (pp. 520–544). New York: Wiley

Danish, S. J., Howard, C. W., & Farrell, A. (1990). The ACT (Athletes Coaching Teens) drug prevention program. *High School Psychology Teacher News, 21*(1), 2–3, 8.

Deffenbacher, J. L. (1988). The practice of four cognitive-behavioral approaches to anxiety reduction. *The Counseling Psychologist, 16,* 3–8.

Deffenbacher, J. L., Story, D. A., Stark, R. S., Hogg, J. A., & Brandon, A. D. (1987). Cognitive relaxation and social skills interventions in the treatment of general anger. *Journal of Counseling Psychology, 34,* 171–176.

Drum, D. J., & Figler, H. E. (1973). *Outreach in counseling.* New York: Intext.

Drum, D. J., & Knott, J. E. (1977). *Structured groups for facilitating development.* New York: Human Sciences Press.

Duncan, D. E., Scott, R. B., & Castro, O. (1982). A mobile unit as an adjunct to a community outreach program of education, screening and counseling for sickle cell disease, nutritional anemia, and hypertension. *Journal of the National Medical Association, 74,* 969–977.

Dustin, D., & Blocher, D. H. (1984). Theories and models of consultation. In S. D. Brown & R. W. Lent (Eds.), *Handbook of Counseling Psychology* (pp. 751–784). New York: Wiley.

Fitzgerald, L. M., & Osipow, S. H. (1986). An occupational analysis of counseling psychology. *American Psychologist, 41,* 535–544.

Friedman, M., Thoresen, C. E., Gill, J. J., Powell, L. H., Ulmer, D., Thompson, L., Price, V. A., Rabin, D. D., Breall, W. S., Dixon, T., Levy, R., & Bourg, E. (1984). Alteration of Type A behavior and reduction of cardiac recurrence in post-myocardial infarction subjects. *American Heart Journal, 108,* 237–248.

Gebhardt, D. L., & Crump, C. E. (1990). Employee fitness and wellness programs in the workplace. *American Psychologist, 45,* 262–272.

Hansen, F. K. (1981). Primary prevention in counseling psychology: Rhetoric or reality? *The Counseling Psychologist, 9*(2), 57–60.

Ivancevich, J. M., Matteson, M. T., Freedman, S. M., & Phillips, J. S. (1990). Worksite stress management interventions. *American Psychologist, 45,* 252–261.

Joint Commission on Mental Illness and Health (1961). *Action for mental health.* New York: Basic Books.

Kagan, N. I., & Kagan, H. (1990). IPR—A validated model for the 1990s and beyond. *The Counseling Psychologist, 18,* 435–439.

Kandell, J. (1988). *Availability and desirability of candidates skills for doctoral level counseling center positions: Ten year comparison.* Unpublished master's thesis, University of Maryland, College Park, MD.

Kessler, D. A., & Albee, G. W. (1975). Primary prevention. *Annual Review of Psychology, 26,* 557–591.

Kritsberg, W. (1985). *The adult children of alcoholics syndrome.* New York: Bantam Books.

Krumboltz, J. D., Becker-Haven, J. F., & Burnett, A. F. (1979). Counseling Psychology. *Annual Review of Psychology, 30,* 555–602.

Levant, R. F. (1983). Toward a counseling psychology of the family: Psychological-educational and skills-training programs for treatment, prevention and development. *The Counseling Psychologist, 11*(3), 5–28.

McNeill, B. W., & Ingram, J. C. (1983). Prevention and counseling psychology: A survey of training practices. *The Counseling Psychologist, 11*(4), 95–96.

Magoon, T., & McDermott, M. (1979). Availability and desirability of various skills and candidates for positions in counseling centers: A replication. *Journal of Counseling Psychology, 26,* 169–172.

Marciniak, D. (1984). A stress management training program for low-income women. *Women and Therapy, 3*(4), 163–168.

Matheny, K. B., Aycock, D. W., Pugh, J. L., Kurlete, W. L., & Silva-Cannella, K. A. (1986). Stress coping: A qualitative and quantitative synthesis with implications for treatment. *The Counseling Psychologist, 14,* 499–549.

Minatoya, L. Y. (1982). Comments on counseling psychology. *The Counseling Psychologist 10*(3), 27–28.

Morrill, W. H., Oetting, E. R., & Hurst, J. C. (1974). Dimensions of counselor functioning. *Personnel and Guidance Journal, 52,* 354–359.

Mosher, R. L., & Sprinthall, N. A. (1971). Psychological education: A means to promote personal development during adolescence. *The Counseling Psychologist, 2*(4), 3–82.

Osipow, S. H. (1977). Will the real counseling psychologist please stand up? *The Counseling Psychologist, 7*(2), 93–94.

Perone, J. (1989). *Adult children of alcoholics* (manual). College Park, MD: University of Maryland Counseling Center.

Richards, R. L., Burlingame, G. M., & Fuhriman, A. (1990). Theme-oriented group therapy. *The Counseling Psychologist, 18,* 80–92.

Rodin, J., & Stone, G. C. (1987). Historical highlights in the emergence of the field. In G. C. Stone (Ed.), *Health psychology: A discipline and a profession* (pp. 16–26). Chicago: University of Chicago Press.

Rosen, J. C., & Solomon, L. J. (Eds.) (1985). *Prevention in health psychology.* Hanover, NH: University Press of New England.

Schlossberg, M. K. (1989). *Overwhelmed: Coping with life's ups and downs.* Lexington, MA: Lexington Books.

Sprinthall, N. A. (1990). Counseling psychology from Greyston to Atlanta: On the road to Armageddon? *The Counseling Psychologist, 18,* 454–462.

Sprinthall, N. A., & Scott, J. R. (1989). Promoting psychological development, math achievement, and success attributions of female students through deliberate psychological education. *Journal of Counseling Psychology, 36,* 440–446.

Taylor, S. E., Falke, R. L., Shapton, S. J., & Lichtman, R. R. (1986). Social support, support groups, and the cancer patient. *Journal of Consulting and Clinical Psychology, 54,* 608–615.

Thoresen, C. E., Hosford, R. E., & Krumboltz, J. D. (1970). Determining effective models for counseling clients of varying competencies. *Journal of Counseling Psychology, 17,* 369–375.

Toomer, J. P. (1982). Counseling psychologists in business and industry. *The Counseling Psychologist, 10*(3), 9–18.

Watkins, C. E., Jr. (1985). Psychoeducational training in counseling psychology programs: Some thoughts on a training curriculum. *The Counseling Psychologist, 13,* 295–302.

Warnath, C. F. (1971). *New myths and old realities: College counseling in transition.* San Francisco: Jossey-Bass.

Whitfield, C. (1987). *Healing the child within.* Dearfield Beach, FL: Health Communications.

Woititz, J. G. (1983). *Adult children of alcoholics.* Dearfield Beach, FL: Health Communications.

Wood, B. L. (1987). *Children of alcoholism: The struggle for self and intimacy in adult life.* New York: New York University Press.

Yalom, I. D., & Vinogradov, S. (1988). Bereavement groups: Techniques and themes. *International Journal of Group Psychotherapy, 38,* 419–446.

Chapter 17

Consultation: An Evolving Perspective

What do the following four situations have in common?

> A staff psychologist in a university counseling center notes that 60 percent of the freshmen students seen in this past semester came from just one of the eight residence halls on campus.
>
> A counseling psychologist in independent practice was often asked to interview students who had been suspended or expelled from the school system for disruptive behavior. Four of the seven students referred to her in the past year were suspended because of creating serious disruptions in Mr. Watson's history classes.
>
> A counseling psychologist in an Employee Assistance Program of a manufacturing company provided career counseling for workers who wished to consider transfers, promotions, or alternative careers. His records for the past year indicate that 75 percent of the requests for career counseling came from workers in just one of six work groups of relatively equal size in the plant.
>
> A department chairwoman in a large university noted that most of the complaints she received were from graduate students in one of the four graduate programs in the department and that the withdrawal rate in that program had been about 70 percent for the past five years, whereas in the other three programs the withdrawal rate was approximately 25 percent.

In all of these examples one part of an organization is generating a lot more problems than the others. Counseling psychologists can simply keep counseling all of the referrals (the steady flow of clients is "good for business"). On the other hand, one may begin to wonder whether there is something that can be done to prevent so many "casualties." The ultimate goal of consultation is typically that of prevention and/or development as defined in the previous chapter. In contrast to some of the services discussed in that chapter, consultation achieves these goals by working with *other persons who have responsibilities for students, clients, and workers.* Exploring and illustrating the broad range of such work is the goal of this chapter.

CONSULTATION DEFINED

We define consultation as a professional service that uses knowledge of human behavior, interpersonal relationships, and group and organizational processes to help others become more effective in their roles. Thus, consultation may encompass an extremely broad range of interventions, from consulting with parents having difficulty managing their children or teachers managing their students, to assisting in the design of staff development for a 12-person staff of a day-treatment center who are experiencing low morale and high turnover, to helping a university design an entirely new program of student services and campus living arrangements. As Dustin and Blocher (1984) note, "Often, the term [consultation] is apparently used to describe almost any kind of meeting among practitioners or agencies aimed at improving the quality of services" (p. 752). While such breadth makes it extremely difficult to specify the techniques of consultation, it does provide the opportunity to explore the diverse ways in which counseling psychologists can assist others in improving the quality of their services and organizations.

It is important to contrast consultation with both traditional counseling and the kinds of prevention and outreach activities described in the previous chapter. The concept that probably provides the greatest contrast is that of *indirect service,* which means, for example, helping the resident director, the history teacher, the supervisor, and the faculty of a program with high attrition become more skilled in their professional roles so that fewer of the persons they work with develop problems needing the help of counselors and/or that their program or organization will function more effectively. While the consultant does not directly see the employees, students, and so forth, in any of these situations, these persons benefit from the consultation services to the extent that the consultee (e.g., the resident director, teacher, supervisor, department chair) acquire new perspectives on working with their constituencies. Obviously, consultation provides some direct services to the directors, leaders or supervisors, but the primary beneficiaries are the much larger number of students, employees, and so forth, in these organizations.

As the values of consultation are explored in the next section, it will also become increasingly clear that counseling psychologists' roles as consultants have a high degree of overlap with both I/O psychologists and community psychologists. In fact, as further described in the section on training, the content of both of these disciplines is important background knowledge for effective consultation. That same section will also show how training as counseling psychologists provides some very special skills that make counseling psychologists uniquely well prepared to be consultants.

THE VALUE OF CONSULTATION

One can view consultation as directed primarily toward the improvement of the way in which human beings relate to one another. In that perspective, the value of consultation is to make the world a better place to live. Philosophers in all ages, and most especially during the Enlightenment, noted the importance of human relationships in the functioning of society. Some readers may have experienced, in a college residence hall, the painful consequences of uncaring and abusive interpersonal relationships. In the presence of such relationships, without appropriate interventions, both the physical and psychological quality of life spirals downward, making the environment an increasingly undesirable place to be.

Furthermore, in studies of mental health in the 1950s (Joint Commission on Mental Illness and Health, 1961), it became clear that individual therapy was an inadequate tool for addressing the extensiveness and complexity of all the problems brought to psychologists. Can the quantity and magnitude of such problems be reduced by our psychological understanding of human behavior? In perhaps the most seminal article for both outreach and consultation, Morrill, Oetting, and Hurst (1974) clearly articulated the value of indirect service if counseling psychologists are to prevent as well as remediate problems. Consultants must be able to intervene at the environmental level, helping the organization become more interpersonally healthy and supportive. In such environments individuals experience less stress and, ideally, can be more helpful to one another. Such relationships can, in turn, make it less likely that group members develop problems so serious that they need the help of a professional counselor.

From this more practical viewpoint, then, consultation can be highly cost-effective. In many cases, consultants work with a pyramidal model; that is, an individual consultant works with only an individual consultee or a small staff, such as residence hall directors, or a small group of supervisors, each of whom is responsible for many students or employees. Spending 20 hours in consultant activities could result in perhaps a savings of hundreds of hours of individual counseling both in the current year and subsequent years.

COUNSELING PSYCHOLOGISTS AS CONSULTANTS

In the past 15 years, there has been increasing recognition by counseling psychologists of the importance of specialized preparation for the role of consultant. Gallessich and Watterson (1984) found that more than two-thirds of the APA-accredited programs offered consultation courses, with 30 percent of these programs requiring them. Fitzgerald and Osipow (1986) found approximately half of all counseling psychologists involved in some sort of consultation activity. Younger counseling psychologists were twice as often involved in consultation as a full-time practice. On the other hand, most psychologists have spent much less time on consultation activities than on counseling, research, supervision, or even administration. Gallessich (1985) also feels that ambivalence about consultation is evidenced in the relative lack of convention programs and research studies on consultation in counseling psychology conferences and publications. In this section, we first explore the natural affinity of counseling and consultation, then examine what we believe to be some of the impediments to greater involvement of counseling psychologists in consultation and why consultation remains, among college counseling center directors, one of the skills they most often look for but do not find in sufficient number (Magoon & McDermott, 1979; Kandell, 1988).

The examples of consultation at the beginning of this chapter may have made some readers wonder how a counseling psychologist is suitable for such roles. Despite the diversity of types and locations in which consultation takes place, there are a number of generic steps in consultation that can be identified. It is in looking at these steps that one can most clearly see how basic counseling skills can be readily transferred to consultation.

Brown (1985) describes five stages, or steps, in consultation. While other authors have proposed variations of and subdivisions to these stages, Brown's five are fairly representative of those through which consultation evolves: establishing a relationship (or entry), assessment (or problem identification), goal setting, choosing and implementing intervention strategies, and evaluation/termination. The connections between counseling and consultation become obvious in each stage. Just as it is essential in an individual counseling relationship to establish a working relationship before trying to solve a problem presented by the client, the relationship or entry phase in consultation also requires time to develop an atmosphere of trust and effective communication. The consultee will be all too ready to jump into problem-solving; however, just as in individual counseling, if the move into problem solving is made before a relationship is established, there will be much resistance to any problem-solving suggestions. Moreover, just as counselor self-confidence is important in communicating expertness and attractiveness to individual clients, the same attributes are equally if not more important for the consultant who is often working with a high-level professional who may indeed have considerably more status and/or rank than the consultant, for instance, a vice-president, a dean, a chief of staff. (Although this concept of working with such high-placed persons is frightening to many graduate students in consultation practica, they are often amazed that, within a few weeks of beginning their project, they feel they are being regarded as important professionals.)

The second step, problem identification, "relies on skillful interviewing, the ability to conceptualize the information once it is gathered, and the ability to state the problem in a clear and straightforward manner" (Brown, 1985, p. 419). This statement was written regarding consultation, but it applies equally well to making a diagnosis with an individual client. While problem identification is usually more complicated in the consulting situation, the basic skills are identical to individual diagnosis. Stum (1982) has outlined a number of interviewing strategies that are particularly appropriate for the problem identification stage.

One area of expertise needed in this stage is not met by usual training in counseling psychology. Critically important, especially when working outside the triadic model described in this chapter, is an understanding of organizational functioning. A brief chapter by Gallessich (1982) outlines some of the essential key concepts such as open systems theory, management concepts, and human relations concepts. For the counseling psychologist who wants to be involved in consulting with organizations, more extensive knowledge about organization structure would be essential. A classic and valuable text for this background is that by Katz and Kahn (1978) on the social psychology of organizations. Graduate students in counseling psychology often may have the opportunity to take courses in industrial/organizational psychology or in organizational behavior in a college of business as a way of gaining some of this critical background.

The third stage of consultation, goal setting, is again almost a direct transfer of learning from goal setting in individual counseling. Brown (1985) suggests that this area poses the least difficulty as students move from the counselor to the consultant role. One problem area in goal setting, in both counseling and consultation, is resistance encountered from the client or consultee as an attempt is made to determine specific goals. The experienced counselor and the experienced consultant are both used to hearing "Well, that's not quite it" when goals are first stated specifically. While there may be some times when the goal has not been stated properly, just as often the statement of the goal is appropriate for the situation as described; however, its clear formulation makes the client or consultee suddenly and painfully aware of the magnitude of the changes that have to be undertaken. In brief, the goal-setting stage may involve dealing as much with resistance as it does with redefinition of goals. Counseling psychologists' basic skills in concreteness, immediacy, and confrontation, all as used in individual counseling, are the best resources for coping with such resistance.

The next step of choosing and implementing strategies may be perhaps the most difficult stage for consultants even though it is again not unlike the implementation of the working alliance as previously described in this text. If consultation is viewed as a collaborative activity, it is especially important that time be given at this stage to explore a variety of alternative ways of achieving the goals that have been agreed on. Having the consultee become aware of various alternatives and the advantages and disadvantages of each and *then* having the consultee choose which one to implement, albeit with the consultant's advice and counsel, is the best way of ensuring that the necessary steps will be taken to translate the plan into action.

A related issue concerns the power of the consultee in the organization and the commitment to change by other members. It is in addressing these concerns that a knowledge of group processes and developmental group interventions is an essential part of the consultant's background and training. As almost all consultation interventions require the involvement and commitment of persons under the direction of the consultee, understanding interpersonal and group processes for change is a *sine qua non* of consultation. Many counseling psychologists are already trained in these processes by virtue of their preparation as group counselors. On the other hand, for students in programs where such group training is not a routine part of counselor training, it would be important to elect appropriate courses in group dynamics, social psychology, or sociology of organizations.

Regarding the evaluation and termination stages of consultation, all too often consultation activities are not evaluated in any systematic way. Gallessich (1982) has a number of suggestions and forms that can be readily adapted to evaluating a broad variety of consultation situations. As in individual counseling, termination problems often occur when it is apparent that the goals cannot be achieved. Also, even when goals have been achieved, as a consultation project comes to an end, the consultee may seem to have a "relapse" and try to get the consultant to stay "just a little longer" or "take just a little bit more time to work on this problem as well." Such requests often reflect some insecurity on the part of the consultee about his or her ability to carry on the changes that have been implemented. Understanding this dynamic and helping the consultee feel ready to manage on his or her own is just as important in consultation as in individual counseling.

In addition to the transferable knowledge and skills we have described for the five generic stages of consultation, it is critically important to understand the importance of the concepts of cultural diversity as they affect consultation. It is important to realize that all of the phases, such as entry, problem identification, and goalsetting, may be greatly affected by cultural differences. Establishing trusting relationships with consultees from cultural backgrounds different from the consultant's may present the same challenges as developing a working alliance with a culturally different client as described in the chapter on cross-cultural counseling. Gibbs (1985) notes that the power-authority dimension may take on "added significance when one of the participants in the dyad is a majority person and the other a minority person, primarily because it is a microcosm of the larger social context in which majority-minority relationships have evolved. . . . the dynamics of power and powerlessness in interpersonal helping encounters should be acknowledged and analyzed so that the consultant can deal effectively with the variety of adaptive strategies that lower-status consultees may employ in an attempt to reduce the power differential" (p. 430).

TYPES OF CONSULTATION

The relatively generic steps in consultation are implemented in very diverse ways given that there are many different types of consultation that can be identified. Despite several major reviews of models of consultation (Gallessich, 1982, 1985; Dustin & Blocher, 1984) it is far more difficult to delineate distinctive types of consultation than types of counseling (e.g., client-centered, psychodynamic). We have chosen four illustrations of the most common kinds of consultation in which counseling psychologists engage. We use the labels "triadic" (two examples) and "process" consultation (two examples). Two points need to be made. First, the different types illustrated are not rigidly distinctive and mutually exclusive. As will be shown, one type can easily "evolve" into another type. Secondly, other consultants might use slightly different labels because there is not a clearly agreed-upon set of types of consultation. Various writers have described consultation according to one, two, or even three dimensions with multiple adaptations of the dimensions of counselor functions described in the previous chapter. Dustin and Blocher review several of these overlapping complex models and conclude that the frameworks have not been particularly useful in generating an understanding of either the processes or outcomes of consultation. We have tried to choose distinctive examples that can illustrate at least some meaningful differences.

The first two illustrations are based on what Dustin and Blocher (1984), among others, have identified as triadic consultation. In this particular approach, the counseling psychologist as consultant works with another person, such as a teacher, supervisor, parent, physician, or other professional, to assist them with one of their students, employees, patients, and so forth (in the clearest form of this model). The triad then consists of the consultant, the consultee, and the "client" the consultee is working with. Much more typically, the "client" is a class or group of employees or type of client or patient; thus, the client part of the triad might be multiple.

The final two examples in this chapter are drawn from what is more typically known as process consultation. While some authors make distinctions between process consultation, organizational development, program development, and program-centered consultation, we believe that the basic assumptions about process consultation underlie effective consultation of all these types. In contrast to the kind of "expert advice" given in the triadic type of consultation,

> process consultation puts the emphasis on helping others to help themselves, not on solving their problems for them or giving them expert advice. The reasons for advocating the relevance of process consultation are both theoretical and practical. On the practical level, we have all had our share of disastrous experiences where our 'expert' advice was refused, misunderstood or actually sabotaged. On the theoretical level, process consultation is more developmental. If the person being helped just accepts expert advice he may solve his immediate problem but he may not learn anything about how to solve problems of this nature, skills that would enable him to solve a similar problem in the future. (Schein, 1987, pp. 8–9)

Schein's two small books on process consultation (1969, 1987) provide both an excellent review of the concepts and illustrations of process consultation in the business world.

All of our examples have been drawn from our own and colleagues' experiences—with appropriate modifications to protect confidentiality of the consultees.

Triadic Behavioral Consultation

Our first example of triadic consultation is based on the theoretical contributions of behavioral psychology, specifically the study of learning processes known as experimental analysis of behavior. While the work of B.F. Skinner (1938) is best known to the general public, the basic concepts underlying this type of response-contingent learning theory go back to Thorndike (1911). In the last two decades, several excellent books have been published on the application of these principles to human problems (Kanfer & Goldstein, 1986; Rimm & Masters, 1979). Both of those books focus on the psychologist as the direct service provider; that is, the psychologist goes into the setting and works directly with the clients, students, or employees to change their behavior. In the behavioral consultation model, however, working with the triadic model, as noted above, the consultants work with teachers or supervisors or managers, as consultees, to help them understand the basic behavioral principles pertinent to their situation and to help them design appropriate interventions and evaluations. An outstanding text for the behavioral consultant is that by Bergan (1977).

The Pizza Reading Project. A teacher assigned to teach a class of seventh-grade "slow learners" contacted the counseling psychology consultant for whatever help she could give him with his unruly class. For the first time, he had been assigned to teach the slow learners, and was finding them disruptive, uncooperative, and stubborn. In addition, the students were performing poorly in all academic areas. The teacher had heard from a colleague how the consultant had assisted another teacher in getting her students to be more attentive in class. This kind of request for consultation is fairly typical in that the consultee (the teacher) describes the problems in terms of internal states of the students; that is, they are stubborn, lazy, unruly, and so forth. The first task of the behavioral consultant is to help the consultee define the problem in terms of actions that can easily be seen and readily measured. Further, as explained in the study of experimental analysis of behavior, it is often easier to begin behavioral consultation projects designed to increase rather than decrease behaviors. Therefore, to help this teacher, the consultant's first interest was in helping the teacher define behaviors that he wanted to see increase in the classroom. The teacher named many such behaviors. However, when he was asked to decide which one was most important to begin with, he readily chose reading. The class's average reading level was at the fourth-grade level and reading was one of the most difficult tasks for many of these students to do for more than a couple of minutes at any one time. The teacher's own creativity had helped him find some other tasks and problem sets he could get the students to work on for as much as 15 to 20 minutes, but in his words, "On a good day, I might be able to have the class read five minutes before there are so many disruptions and conversations that further reading is impossible."

Unwittingly, the teacher had given the consultant important information for the next step in a behavioral consultation: identifying measures of behavior. He had standardized measures of the current reading level of each of the students, and, although he had not recorded the actual time spent reading, his primary goal was an increase in the number of minutes spent reading. It was easily possible during the following weeks to have the teacher record, for each of the students, how many minutes they spent on a reading assignment before they became distracted and stopped. Such measures, taken at the very beginning of the project, served as baselines against which students' subsequent progress could be evaluated.

The third step for a behavioral consultation project involves establishing contingencies, that is, tying a behavior to a specific outcome that, hopefully, will change the behavior. The teacher needed to choose some reinforcement that the students would want to work for and that could be offered frequently enough; students should not have to work many days or weeks to earn the reinforcement. The teacher had the misfortune of having the students for the last period of the day. Therefore, his immediate thought was to provide early dismissal as a very potent reinforcement, but he quickly realized that this would create problems for other classes if his students were running around the halls. Early dismissal also was logically unacceptable—he wanted the students to be spending more time working in class, not getting out of class. The teacher felt that the other most powerful reinforcement would be some sort of snack food, noting that it had been a couple of hours since lunch and many of the students could not wait to get out of class to head for the school snack bar. Wanting to avoid the worst of junk foods, the teacher decided that making pizza available (the home economics teacher was willing to loan the microwave oven to the teacher) could meet the requirements of a readily available reinforcer.

For the beginning stages of the project, the plan was kept as simple as possible. The students were informed that for each 5-minute segment of the 15-minute reading period spent reading (or at least staying at their desks and engaging in no side conversations or distractions) they could receive a small sliver of pizza. The teacher could easily record, each day, the number of minutes each student read. Moreover, the plan benefited from those students that were especially hungry and did not want to be disrupted by other students. Thus, for the first time since the beginning of the year the teacher had some of the students themselves interested in discouraging other students from disruptive behaviors.

While the project continued for several months and the contingencies were changed to help "phase in" other valuable reinforcers, such as feedback from improvement on tests and more smiles and verbal approval from the teacher, the principles that have been reviewed were not in any way changed. Time spent reading was tied to a specific contingency. By the end of the semester, the teacher was feeling much better about his skills in managing the class. Relative quiet was maintained for the full 20-minute reading period he now included. The students varied immensely, however, as to how much they actually read and understood. Some showed significant gains in reading, others did not but were at least not disrupting other students.

Several observations can be made about both the effectiveness and generalizability of these kinds of approaches. As Rimm and Masters (1979) found in their review, contingency management approaches to reading have frequently been investigated and found quite effective, though the results vary somewhat according to the ability level of the students. Moreover, as in this project, a typical side effect of these interventions is that classroom disruption significantly declines. This approach is best implemented in a situation where someone is in control of reinforcements, such as the teacher or, in a business setting, the supervisor or manager. O'Brien, Dickenson, and Rosow (1982) have described a large number of industrial settings where this kind of behavioral approach is directly applicable. Further, Glenwick and Jason (1980) show how this approach can also be useful in community settings, where, although no supervisors may be present to observe behavior, outcomes such as saving money or responding to important social issues such as saving energy can be sufficient reinforcers for changing behaviors.

Looking at the project from the perspective of the consultant, it can be seen that the consultant in this situation functioned primarily as an expert, teaching the consultee the principles of behavior management. The consultee then, in turn, used these principles to enhance his performance in his role. It is probably clear that our example could have focused simply on one individual child in the classroom, which would have been the purest case of the triadic model: consultant, consultee, student. In our example, the third part of the triad was a class. It could have been a particular division of a production company, a sports team, or a nursing home staff. In all of these latter cases, one gains the cost-benefit effects of the pyramid nature of the triad. The consultee, with the expert help of the consultant, is able to affect many other persons in the performance of their roles.

Triadic Mental Health Consultation

Our second example of triadic consultation represents a setting more than a theoretical basis like the behavioral example just reviewed. Before getting into our example in a mental health setting, however, it must be noted that both the legal and medical professions have frequently used the term *psychological consultation* or *mental health consultation* in a manner that does *not* meet our stipulation of consultation as indirect service. For example, an attorney employed one of the authors as a consultant to make assessments of some individuals who had been mandatorily retired to determine whether or not their mental health had been significantly impaired, as was stipulated in a legal case. Physicians often ask psychologists for assessments of a person's psychological status, especially if there is insufficient organic evidence to explain the patient's symptoms.

Surgeons and physicians also frequently ask psychologists to provide counseling to clients before or after surgery or after heart attacks, regarding adjustments and needed changes in lifestyles. In the examples just cited, the psychologist is providing direct assessment or direct service to the client and the other professional person learns nothing about how to provide services that would prevent future occurrences of such a need.

We firmly agree with Gallessich (1982) that "the goal of the mental health model [of consultation] is to expand consultees' knowledge and skill in preventing and remediating mental illness and promoting mental health" (p. 149). Consultees may be lacking in information, skill, or confidence in meeting the professional demands of their everyday life. Physicians, ministers, dormitory counselors, police officers, and teachers are all examples of groups that can benefit tremendously from having a better understanding of some of the mental health aspects of both the typical and atypical psychological problems faced by their patients, parishioners, clients, students, and so forth. In fact, mental health consultation developed primarily out of the recognition of the need for considering the mental health implications of various stress points in life. Ever since Lindemann's (1944) early work on natural disasters, psychologists have been more aware of many of the psychological problems associated with various life stresses. Caplan (1970) provides extensive descriptions of a wide range of mental health consultation activities that have been developed since that time.

The "What will happen to me?" Project. To illustrate the mental health consultation approach, we have chosen a project that took place in a pediatric surgical unit of a major hospital. The problem for this consultation began with a surgeon's concern over how distraught she repeatedly found her young patients before they underwent what she considered relatively routine surgery such as tonsillectomies and appendectomies.

The pediatric surgeon sought out one of the hospital psychologists to find out if there were something she, as the surgeon, could do to reduce the children's anxiety. She was asking for a simple, brief "prescription" that she could obtain by spending five minutes with a psychologist and then go back to the wards and never have an anxious patient again! Fortunately, the psychologist was knowledgeable about a number of pertinent areas, including separation effects (Bowlby, 1973) and some of the fears and the threats of the unknown that both children and adults experience when facing surgical procedures. He was also aware that many parents deliberately tried to keep the children from thinking about the surgery and the hospital and gave them lots of reassurances without much information.

In an initial discussion with the psychologist, the surgeon quickly saw that there was no simple answer, and readily realized the psychologist was talking about a lot of behaviors and issues she had seen in her patients. She invited the psychologist to join with her in meeting with some of her patients and becoming familiar with the services on the pediatric ward. In the following weeks, the psychologist spent an increasing amount of time observing both preoperative and postoperative contacts between the surgeon and the patients as well as their families. The psychologist also came to realize the critical role of the nurses in these cases and spent some time getting acquainted with their roles. (The consultant was even invited to observe a surgical procedure but, remembering why he chose psychology rather than medicine, declined!)

Although the many hours the psychologist spent in this "observation phase" are somewhat atypical of mental health consultation, the fact that he did so allowed him to become readily accepted by the surgeon and nurses as a concerned and trustworthy person who saw what their harried professional lives were like. It is absolutely essential that a relationship be established between consultant and consultees whereby they believe the consultant understands the nature of their work if the eventual goal is to have the consultees change something about their styles.

The consultant recommended to the surgeon that the two of them needed to review a variety of possible procedural changes they might make to address the children's anxieties. Given that many of these interventions involved changes in the nurses' routines, he also suggested a subsequent meeting with the nurses to explore the range of possibilities and identify which ones they felt could most readily be incorporated into the hospital procedures. By including the nurses in the remaining steps, this consultation shifted from a consultee-centered mental health consultation project (with the surgeon as the consultee) to a more program-centered administrative mental health consultation project focused on the pediatric service.

To provide a quick overview of the eventual decisions, the surgeon, interns, residents and nurses seemed to readily understand how both separation anxiety and lack of information contributed to the children's inordinate anxiety. With the strong leadership of the surgeon, some changes were made in procedures that would allow parents to be with their children for far greater periods of time than before in both the presurgical and recovery periods. The consultant also became involved in preparing a videotape regarding a number of routine surgical procedures, appropriate parts of which could be viewed by children with their families. From the consultant's viewpoint, the most important outcome of his intervention was not those changes in procedures or the videotape but rather the fact that the surgical team and the nurses were all now aware of the need to provide answers to the children's questions, as much as they could, when they asked questions. Often they found the children did not really want many details; they were pleased just to have someone willing to give them some information rather than just dismiss their question with vague reassurances.

Because of a surgeon's request for assistance in dealing with anxious children, a whole team of medical personnel had developed skills in reducing the stress of surgery and helping patients become more involved in their own recovery. Similar kinds of mental health consultants can be used to help police officers deal with rape victims or to help teachers understand how to deal with the effects of a student suicide on the victim's classmates. In all of these examples, counseling psychologists as consultants can make significant contributions to both the professional well-being of the consultees and, perhaps most importantly, to the well-being of the students, clients, patients, and citizens with whom their consultees interact.

Process Consultation: Basic Form

As shown earlier, process consultation has a more interpersonal focus as compared to the task focus of the previously described kinds of triadic consultation. The basic assumption of process consultation is that the consultee, usually the manager (or director, vice-president, or other executive officer) has clearly acknowledged that the organization is "hurting somehow but does not know the source of the pain or what to do about it" (Schein, 1987, p. 32). "Process consultation is designed to help a client or group understand how it sets goals, gathers information, solves problems, makes decisions, and allocates work roles" (p. 53). This description makes clear that any group of persons in an organization can benefit from process consultation; usually, however, consultants are invited in only when at least some part of the staff is feeling pain.

He's a Nice Guy, BUT . . . . The young director of a small, residential center for disturbed children contacted us about some morale problems his staff was having. He had heard from one of his employees that we had helped a nursing home staff that had experienced similar problems. First, a bit of agency description. As a residential facility it had three shifts of personnel, largest for the daytime, smallest for night. Night-duty workers were typically college students with the primary responsibility of keeping things quiet between 11 P.M. and 7 A.M. The day shift consisted of one teacher, one social worker, and one recreational therapist, each of whom had help from one or two trainees in related university programs. The evening shift had no teachers but had one social worker and a counselor to coordinate various programs run by college student employees who typically were enrolled in majors like special education, recreation, and psychology. A long-standing problem, from the director's perspective, was that each shift felt it was left with residual problems that the previous shift should have handled, ranging from the evening shift faulting the teachers for lack of clarity in homework assignments, to the night shift saying that the evening shift did not have the kids settled down by 11 P.M. "as they were supposed to," to the day shift saying the night shift "didn't control" some of the most obstreperous kids. Recently, these disagreements had escalated and several threats were being made between employees about getting them fired, filing charges about unethical behavior, and so forth. Over the past six months, 60 percent of the college student employees had quit, one of them saying he did not need "this kind of crap for what you're paying me." The director felt things were getting out of control.

We thought we needed a great deal more information about staff relationships, information we could get only by observing some of the staff at work. We explored the possibilities of having a consulting team member spend a couple of hours on each shift over a period of four weeks during which she would also have an opportunity to interview each employee for about 20 minutes. We also asked about whether staff meetings were held and about the opportunity for our team member to sit in on these meetings. Obviously, this kind of preparation for consulting is very expensive, timewise. However, we believed it to be essential before we could know how to proceed to accomplish Schein's first stage of "unfreezing," that is, providing an atmosphere in which staff would feel psychologically safe enough to receive feedback about their own roles and how they might be changed. From the consultant's observation of staff roles and interviews, two things became clear. First, there was no sense of teamwork within or among the three shifts; within each shift all individuals described certain duties they had and those duties constituted the beginning and end of their jobs. Secondly, the director was seen as a "nice guy," but one who knew little about how to manage. Staff members were never sure where they stood with him and felt it useless to bring up staff problems since he usually ignored them or said, "Well, we'll have to work on that," and then nothing would happen. Staff meetings were rarely held and usually included only the daytime staff and one or two people from the evening staff. The director would make announcements, tell staff about some problems he knew about and how he thought they should be handled. Memos were passed on to evening shift and night shift people as the director thought appropriate.

We proposed to the director a "staff development project" in which there would be late afternoon weekly staff meetings involving the consultant plus most of the staff from all three shifts. A minimum number of staff, plus perhaps some temporary volunteers, could be assigned to cover the residents' programs for the 90 minutes that staff would meet each week. Workers from the day and night shifts would each receive comp time since the meeting was to be held outside of their regular work hours. A total of 16 persons would be at each staff meeting. The consultant outlined a program of problem exploration strategies, including how to establish group goals and resolve conflicts as well as other team-building exercises (see Johnson & Johnson, 1987). The consultant would act as a "facilitator" for these staff development meetings. By this time in the project, employees had come to know the consultant and felt that she was "really a good listener" and that the proposed plan would probably work. In short, the consultant had established a working relationship that allowed the unfreezing process to occur.

Despite the consultant's worries about the first joint staff meeting being potentially explosive, the combination of team-building exercises and a chance for each staff member to describe "some problems that affect all the work shifts" ended with much positive feeling on the part of the staff. They became aware that more of their problems were shared than they realized (mostly as a result of the consultant asking them to focus on problems that concerned all their work shifts). Once a greater sense of teamwork was established, the staff members felt that they could begin to air some of their more individual concerns without alienating other staff members. Serendipitously, a few staff members also found they had interests and friends in common with other shift employees yet had not previously known this since they had had so little interaction.

Although not all subsequent staff meetings went so well, the eventual outcomes were quite positive. By the end of the six weeks of staff meetings, the staff had begun to make plans with the director to hold two staff meetings a month, using the same kind of arrangement they had had during the consultation, so that everyone could attend. Thirty minutes was to be given to a "case presentation" dealing with one of the current residents. Staff could then discuss some management issues as well as try to understand better the causes of the child's behavioral problems. Remaining meeting time would be spent discussing the issues that had been put on the agenda during staff development meetings (a long list from "establishing goals" to "keeping the kitchen clean"). Task forces were to be set up, including representatives from two or more shifts, to address those problems that needed more discussion and planning time than was available at staff meetings. The director's lack of personnel management skills became less problematic as staff assumed responsibility for both identifying and working on problems. The director was also quite pleased because the arrangement freed him to do better what he already did well, that is, keep on top of finances, maintenance, and day-to-day operation details. Thus, Schein's second step of changing through "cognitive restructuring" had occurred from the very first through the very last of the six weeks of meetings. Staff members had found it helpful to look at their roles and the work environment in different, more constructive ways.

As an interesting follow-up note, a year later the agency expanded their staff meeting agenda to include in-service training topics, bringing in specialists from the university and community to talk on relevant topics such as diagnosing dyslexia, building self-esteem, and managing self-destructive behavior. The group was also working on ways to have some staff rotate to different shifts so they could get a better feel for what some of the problems were in each shift. At this stage, it can be seen that the process consultation had accomplished Schein's third stage of "refreezing"—that is, integrating the new point of view into the consultees' view of their own roles and their relationships with significant others.

Process Consultation: Organizational Development

As the primary goal of the consultation in our next illustration is to develop multiple changes in programs and policy rather than to focus on interpersonal relationships (even though these will be a necessary part of the consultation project), the term *organizational development* is often used for this kind of consultation. Our distinction is perhaps an overly fine point—many consultants see all process consultation as part of organizational development. Also, as seen in the last example, the process consultation that focused on staff relationships also resulted in policy changes. The distinction, at best, may be a matter of initial emphases. Moreover, it should be noted that organizational development (O.D.) is a broad term that encompasses much more than consultation. O.D. specialists are increasingly full-time employees of large organizations.

Our example also illustrates the conception that the best beginning for O.D. is a diagnosis based on data collection from various members representing *all* parts of the organization (Baker & Gorman, 1976). To achieve this kind of data-based diagnosis we utilized the concepts of environmental assessment. As Huebner and Corazzini (1984) explicate, the person-environment interaction focus of environmental assessment is most congruent with the emphases of counseling psychology. From this perspective, to make improvements in human functioning in any setting, one must assess not only the characteristics of individuals but also their perceptions of the environment in which they find themselves. The results of the environmental assessment are then shared with all parts of the organization as a basis for planning possible changes in policies. Our illustration has a surprise ending—more on that later.

The Hospital Career Development Project. We were contacted by the personnel director of a large city hospital, which specializes in some of the most difficult kinds of surgery and health care. The director was concerned about the high degree of employee turnover at the entry level in a lot of technical fields, such as radiology, as well as in most of the service positions, for example, kitchen and custodial workers. Employees had complained about lack of advancement opportunities. The personnel director wanted us, as experts in the area of career development, to tell him how to help employees see more opportunity for advancement within the hospital system. The director spoke of the possibilities for creating a "career development center" to help advise employees as well as establishing some clear "mechanism" within their hiring policies to make clear that there were opportunities for career changes and advancement.

In our first phone discussions with the consultee, we described our need for a better understanding of the 1,000+ employees' concerns about their career development opportunities as well as other aspects of their work that were related to high rates of turnover. (As a side point, it is important to note that we had done some quick, even if crude, comparisons of their turnover rate with some other major hospitals to find out they did, indeed, have a slightly higher turnover rate. This factor is an important one to check, for often an organization will talk about its high turnover rate when, because of the nature of the positions or setting, it may actually have a low turnover rate. For example, a nursing home with a yearly turnover rate of 40 percent would have a good record—many nursing homes have 80–100 percent turnovers in staff in a given year!)

The director wanted to go with whatever would work best. We asked to meet with representatives of the workers' groups. The employee representatives were particularly enthusiastic about this strategy and helped us obtain random samples of the employees in each work category to complete the brief questionnaire we designed. The questionnaire focused on the employees' perceptions about opportunities for transfer and promotion within the hospital setting. We also utilized standardized measures of the work environment (Work Environment Scale: Moos, 1981) and job satisfaction (Job Description Index: Smith, Kendall, & Hulin, 1969). Therefore, we were able to provide the consultee with not only a fairly extensive report of employee concerns with limited opportunity for promotion or transfer but also a description of the employees' perception of an extremely rigid and authoritarian command structure from the top down, that is, from the hospital director through ward and section administration. While there was respect for the management's emphasis on efficiency and competency in this highly specialized hospital, these emphases seemed to preclude any attention to or caring for human needs, for example, some variation in job roles, occasional flexibility of workshifts, and inviting employee input on how to improve the environment. "Show up on time, never question the orders, and get out of here as soon as possible" was an employee description typical of their attitude toward the hospital.

As is our usual style, we sent our written statement to the consultee and set up a time to meet with him and the various employee group representatives after they had had a chance to read the report (a procedure we had all agreed to in the initial phase). The project then came to an abrupt end! After the consultee, that is, the personnel director, had read the report, he shared it with the hospital director. He informed him about our planned meeting in which we intended to look at what the results of the environmental assessment could tell us about possible policy changes that would address employee concerns. The hospital director was infuriated on two counts: one, it was his understanding that the personnel office was working with us to explore "the possibility of setting up a career development office, not to make a survey of employee morale." He did not want anyone in the hospital to know of the report's findings regarding morale. Second, the hospital director made clear—for the first time, in the view of the personnel director—that the two of them had very different views about potential possibilities for change in the organization. While the personnel director was familiar with concepts such as job enrichment and the importance of opportunities for horizontal or vertical mobility, the hospital director's view was that this was a highly technical agency that required much specialized training; therefore, there would be few if any opportunities for horizontal mobility and "there [would be] ample opportunity for *good* people to move up within their own specialties." If high turnover was the price that had to be paid to have appropriately trained people, then so be it.

The personnel director had gotten caught in the same problem that many of the employees had—he was trying to do something beyond his immediate job description of simply keeping the personnel office running. In retrospect, we wondered whether we might be faulted for not having included contact with someone higher up in the administrative structure from the beginning of the project. However, we reminded ourselves that in the large organization we were working with, the director of the personnel office was only one step removed from the top and that (1) he genuinely believed that he had support of the director to proceed as we were and, (2) in large organizations it is unusual for consultants to work directly with the very top executive. While our project failed in "organizational development," that is, no changes were made in formal policy, we include it for its usefulness in identifying both the public (in this case, concerns over lack of career mobility) and hidden (in this case, authoritarian structure and poor morale) agenda with which an organization must deal. Schein (1987) provides other examples where consultation results in information about the organization that is unanticipated and most uncomfortable. Organizational development, as Schein uses the term, can take place only when administrators are open to recognizing both positive and negative aspects of their organization.

Environmental assessment approaches to organizational development can have successful conclusions. In one example particularly relevant for counseling psychologists, Daher, Corazzini, and McKinnon (1977) were consultants to a residence hall where a large number of students had made complaints about the living conditions to the resident assistant, who in turn described the students as frustrating and belligerent. Using both standardized and specially developed environmental assessment measures, the consultants found significant concerns raised over the issues of privacy, noise, involvement, support, intellectuality, organization, and order. After the results were reported to the residents, there was a greater acknowledgment by them of some of these difficulties. They agreed among themselves to appoint committees to develop quiet hours and other programs to develop mutual respect. When the residents took part in completing questionnaires at a later time, significant improvements were noted on resident involvement, academic achievement, and support.

Some Observations on Types of Consultation

It is important to note that each of the situations just described might have been approached through any one of the four consultation interventions illustrated. Triadic models could certainly have been used to address at least parts of the process consultation examples working with the residential center director or personnel manager. Conversely, the process consultation approach might have been used in either of the triadic examples if a whole staff of teachers or medical personnel had been interested in the problem area instead of just a single individual. The choice of kind of consultation will not always depend on what is asked for by the consultee. It will also depend on the skills of the counseling psychologist as a consultant in addressing the true nature of the problem. For example, is the teacher identified as "the problem" the only teacher with a problem or simply the one with the most visible problem? Is the problem of staff morale really a problem of all staff interpersonal relationships or is it a problem of staff versus supervisor? Depending on which "diagnosis" is made, the choice of approaches may vary. More individual-centered problems are typically approached by triadic models; more systemwide ones with process consultation. Such assessments are necessary so that the most appropriate approaches are utilized. As Gallessich (1982) laments, too many "consultants tend to follow the 'law of the hammer,' which holds that professionals tend to interpret problems in terms of their particular tools or skills: to the person with a hammer, everything looks like a nail. Consultants trained in conflict management are likely to diagnose problems in terms of staff conflicts. Health professionals are likely to diagnose problems in terms of their particular treatment specialty" (p. 105).

IMPEDIMENTS TO CONSULTING

We noted earlier that despite employers and training directors increasingly valuing consultation and numerous opportunities to be a consultant on a university campus (Hamilton & Meade, 1979), counseling psychologists' activities in the area remain relatively minimal compared to other activities such as teaching and counseling. One could easily make the argument that, because of its preventive nature, more attention should be spent on consultation than on actual counseling. Conyne (1982), noting the profession's lack of systematic attention to consultation theory, research, and application, suggests that consultation is "undernourished, if not starving" (p. 53).

We can identify at least four impediments to counseling psychologists' greater use of consultation. The first of these impediments is also encountered as counselors move from personal counseling to career counseling or group counseling. Learning a new kind of counseling clearly rearouses all the threats to one's self-competence that were experienced when first beginning counseling. Our consultation supervisees tell us that in consultation these threats to sense of competence are more pervasive and longer lasting than in either career counseling or group counseling. There are greater differences in both environment and skills called for. Group counseling and career counseling are usually done on the same "turf" as individual counseling; consultation usually is not.

A second impediment is the lack of feedback one gets from consultation as compared to counseling. First of all, many of the persons the consultant hopes to affect in some way through the consultee are never seen. Moreover, because each consultation project is usually of several months' duration, one builds up an "experiential repertoire" very slowly in contrast to other kinds of counseling. In the same time span in which one completes four consultation projects, literally dozens of career or personal clients may have been seen.

A third impediment has to do with perceived failure. Somewhat like marriage counseling with couples seeking a divorce, consulting sometimes ends prematurely with an agreement not to proceed. In most of these situations, it is often difficult for a counselor to get past the concept of "failure" even though it can be acknowledged, intellectually, on the basis of considerable data, that the costs of some marriages outweigh the benefits of continuing. Similarly, in a variety of consulting situations, when the project terminates prematurely, the clearest message is that the consultee has seen the cost of change and is not willing to undertake it relative to the cost of the present situation. Such a premature termination, then, is not a failure as much as it is a reasoned choice. Finally, the consultant may often feel like an outsider. Either the consultee, or those working for him or her may indirectly or even directly communicate to the consultant, "Keep out of my territory." The consultant can then feel his or her services are not really wanted even if the consultee has clearly acknowledged that a problem exists and that some help is needed. This kind of ambivalence communicated by a consultee can make a consulting counseling psychologist long for the more predictable security of individual counseling!

UNIQUE ETHICAL PROBLEMS IN CONSULTING

While both Gallessich (1982) and Robinson and Gross (1985) have outlined a large number of ethical concerns regarding consultation activities, we agree with Lowman (1985) that, with a few exceptions, these issues are largely extensions of many of the ethical issues already reviewed in Chapter 3. The consultation situation, by virtue of the number of people involved and the complexities of the interactions with so many different levels of the organization, may increase the *probability* of ethical conflicts but most are not substantively different. For example, in both individual counseling and consultation, the counseling psychologist may be forced to deal with issues of radically different value orientations. In individual counseling, how does the counselor proceed in working with a client who has radically different views about abortion than the counselor; analogously, how does the consultant proceed when asked to work with an organization where the management is seen as far more coercive and authoritarian than the consultant believes essential or with an organization that has a long record of being insensitive to minorities? A consultant may become aware of ethical or illegal activities on the part of some of the employees or perhaps even the consultee. Again, the choices and issues are essentially no different than when learning about illegal or unethical behavior on the part of a client in individual counseling. Similarly, consultants may receive inappropriate requests from a consultee to "shade" the data to support a particular viewpoint; individual counselors have certainly had clients ask for similar "shadings" when written reports have to be prepared to be sent to an agency administrator.

There are, however, at least two issues that are arguably qualitatively different in consulting. Even beginning consultants should be aware of these unique ethical dilemmas so that the potential problems they present can be prevented or at least minimized. The first of these is most succinctly worded as "Who is the client?" This question needs to be asked in terms of ethical principles regarding rights of the client, including confidentiality. While the easy immediate answer is that the consultee is the client, the problem quickly becomes evident when two related questions are considered. Who has to give consent for providing interviews or completing questionnaires or surveys as part of the data collection? An individual client responds only for himself or herself and can give full consent. However, in consultation, is it appropriate for the consultee to give consent for his or her students or employees or supervisees to allow the consultant access to employee or student records? How do laws regarding invasion of privacy affect the relationship between the consultant and the employees or students? Relatedly, who owns the information and data that are collected? The consultee, who is paying the consultant, may often feel that he or she has the right to ask for either any questionnaires or surveys that employees filled out or for any notes taken in interviews with them. How does the consultant protect the confidentiality of the people interviewed or surveyed even though they are not clients? Obviously these are issues that need to be addressed as part of the contract negotiation for consultation; unfortunately, unless consultants are aware of such issues, they may not address them in initial negotiations and later find themselves in difficult dilemmas in trying to protect the "hidden clients" in the consultation situation.

A second ethical concern seems somewhat less significant but can be equally troublesome and deserves careful thought. In the examples at the beginning of this chapter, certain teachers or supervisors or residence halls were generating a significant number of problems. It seems obvious that one might suggest that they invite a consultant to help them. Unlike most counseling where the clients request services, in suggesting a consultation project to a person or agency, it can be construed as solicitation, that is, trying to get them to buy services. Clearly, in the interest of developing prevention as compared to remedial services, counseling psychologists want to *inform* persons of the possibilities of some relevant consultation activities; however, care must be taken to ensure that presentations stay more on the informing side than on the solicitation side no matter how strongly one feels about the appropriateness and importance of a consultation intervention.

Given the impediments and ethical issues just explored, the role of training and mentoring for consultation services appears critical. A major purpose of this chapter has been to illustrate not only what counseling psychologists do as consultants but also what kinds of background and experience they need to fulfill these roles. It should not be surprising that Gallessich (1982) and Crego (1985) both argue for specific improvements in both the conceptual and practicum aspects of training counseling psychologists for consultation.

RESEARCH ON CONSULTATION

In the final section of this chapter, we will briefly review the difficulties that have been encountered in evaluating the effectiveness of consultation. Three major reviewers of research on consultation (Mannimo &

Shore, 1975; Medway, 1982; Dustin & Blocher, 1984) have made extensive criticisms of the quality of research in consultation, similar, in many ways, to the criticisms of research on counseling and psychotherapy that were made in the 1950s and 1960s. A major concern in many of the studies in consultation is the lack of specification about exactly what the consultation involved; therefore, it is impossible to understand sometimes conflicting results given that it is not clear what "treatment" was provided in many of the studies. Moreover, in many of the studies cited, consultation included not only the kind of indirect service we have defined as consultation but also direct service kinds of consultation where the consultant is an "expert" actually seeing the client. Most studies of consultation do not include adequate control groups, if any control groups are included at all!

Conducting research on consultation is extremely difficult. It includes not only the majority of the problems of conducting research on counseling and psychotherapy but many additional ones as well. Consider only the difficulty in developing a sizeable number of consultation cases to study. Where it may be possible, in a given semester, to accumulate 50 to 100 individual cases or perhaps eight or ten groups to study, it would take years to accumulate that many consultation projects unless one were working with an extremely large consultation staff.

With these important limitations in mind, it can be noted that studies of the consultation process, like early studies in psychotherapy, have yielded their most consistent results in terms of satisfaction of consumers. Most consultees report being quite satisfied with both the process and the result of the consultation activities. Far more difficult to find are examples of changes in the clients, students, or employees supervised by those consultees, or even changes in behavior of the consultees themselves.

It is, of course, not difficult to imagine the problems that are encountered in collecting data on the changes in behavior of the persons responsible to the consultee. In many cases, while the consultee may be significantly committed to the project, the person supervised by the consultee may have little investment in the project. In some cases, employees, students, and so forth, are not even aware that their supervisor is receiving consultation.

Notwithstanding these many difficulties, a variety of positive behavioral changes have been found that indicate that consultation clearly can be effective beyond the consultee's level of satisfaction with his or her performance. As noted earlier, the environmental intervention consultation of Daher, Corazzini, and McKinnon (1977) resulted in significant changes in the college students' behavior in the dormitory. As one other example, Jaffe, Thompson, and Paquin (1978) were able to show that their development of a family consultation program for an urban police department resulted in an increased number of families accepting referral appointments and, in subsequent months, in decreased number of calls to the police.

As noted at the beginning of the chapter, there is very little theory to guide consultation and there are definitional issues regarding what is included in consultation. These conditions make traditional research designs extremely difficult to implement; the "discovery-oriented" research approach of Mahrer (1988) may be a far better alternative to consider. Such an approach could result in improvement in the kinds of data collection which, in turn, would help clarify what is being done in the intervention. Then, more appropriate process and outcome questions could be formulated. Dustin and Blocher (1984) make further specific suggestions about how systematic and intensive case studies also hold considerable promise. They appropriately call for drawing on some of the similarities we noted above between counseling and consultation. Relationship conditions, social influence processes, cognitive change, social modeling, classical conditioning, and related processes may help tie together diverse consultation approaches just as they have helped identify commonalities in counseling processes.

SUMMARY

Consultation is one of counseling psychology's most cost-effective strategies for implementing preventive, remedial, and developmental services. With a focus on helping others become more effective in their service roles in all types of organizations from families to hospitals to businesses, consultants assist not only their consultees but, more importantly, potentially all those for whom the consultees have responsibility. Consultation is most congruent with counseling psychology's theme of working with intact persons' assets and strengths with special attention to person-environment interactions.

From among the numerous kinds of consultation that have been described, two major types were illustrated in this chapter. Triadic models involving a consultant, consultee, and "client" were illustrated by one based on behavioral principles and another based on mental health consultation. In both illustrations, instead of one person as a client, the "client" was a group of individuals (i.e., a class or pediatric surgery patients), illustrating the unique cost-benefit aspects of consultation.

Two examples of process consultation were described, one focused on staff relationships, the other on the possibility of developing new organizational policies. Contrasted to the triadic model, where the consultant works primarily with one individual, in process consultation the consultant works mostly with a group of persons, possibly staff members but, nearly as often, with representatives of all parts of the organization—whether it be a residence hall, school, or business. Other examples of each of these kinds of consultation may be found in the literature cited in the chapter.

Counseling skills can be extended to the generic steps of consulting roles, though additional kinds of knowledge and skills are needed for consultation that are not typically covered by counseling psychologists' training. Graduate students typically have opportunities to take courses that address many of these needed fundamentals, for example, organizational behavior and group processes.

The final sections of the chapter reviewed (1) four "normal" impediments to consultation to help explain counseling psychologists' tendency to prefer the known comforts of counseling interview rooms to the less predictable vicissitudes but stimulating challenges of consultation; (2) special ethical concerns regarding the question of "Who is the client?" in consulting as well as the need to be especially sensitive about "solicitation" when suggesting consultation projects; and (3) some of the data from, and difficulties of, conducting research on consultation. Most investigators now view more qualitative approaches to research on consultation as the more promising way to make significant advances in understanding the processes and outcomes of consultation.

References

Baker, H. K., & Gorman, R. H. (1976). Diagnosis: Key to O.D. effectiveness. *Personnel Journal, 55,* 506–510.

Bergan, J. R. (1977). *Behavioral consultation.* Columbus, OH: Merrill.

Bowley, J. (1973). *Attachment and loss: Vol. 2. Separation, anxiety and anger.* New York: Basic Books.

Brown, D. (1985). The pre-service training and supervision of consultants. *The Counseling Psychologist, 13,* 410–425.

Caplan, G. (1970). *The theory and practice of mental health consultation.* New York: Basic Books.

Conyne, R. K. (1982). Reaction to Meade, Hamilton, and Yuen: The time is yesterday. *The Counseling Psychologist, 10*(4), 53–55.

Crego, C. A. (1985). Ethics: The need for improved consultation training. *The Counseling Psychologist, 13,* 473–476.

Daher, D. M., Corazzini, J. G., & McKinnon, R. D. (1977). An environmental redesign for residence halls. *Journal of College Student Personnel, 18*(1), 11–15.

Dustin, D., & Blocher, D. H. (1984). Theories and models of consultation. In S. D. Brown & R. W. Lent (Eds.), *Handbook of Counseling Psychology* (pp. 751–781). New York: Wiley.

Fitzgerald, L. F., & Osipow, S. H. (1986). An occupational analysis of counseling psychology. *American Psychologist, 41,* 535–544.

Gallessich, J. (1982). *The profession and practice of consultation.* San Francisco: Jossey-Bass.

Gallessich, J. (1985). Toward a meta-theory of consultation. *The Counseling Psychologist, 13,* 336–354.

Gallessich, J., & Watterson, J. (1984). Consultative education and training in APA-accredited settings: An overview. Paper presented at the 92nd Annual Meeting of the American Psychological Association, Toronto, Canada.

Gibbs, J. T. (1985). Can we continue to be color-blind and class-bound? *The Counseling Psychologist, 13,* 426–435.

Glenwick, D., & Jason, L. (Eds.) (1980). *Behavioral community psychology.* New York: Praeger.

Hamilton, M. K., & Meade, C. J. (1979). *Consulting on campus.* San Francisco: Jossey-Bass.

Huebner, L. A., & Corazzini, J. G. (1984). Environmental assessment and intervention: In S. D. Brown & R. W. Lent (Eds.), *Handbook of Counseling Psychology* (pp. 579–621). New York: Wiley.

Jaffe, P. G., Thompson, J. K., & Paquin, M. J. (1978). Immediate family crisis intervention as preventive mental health: The family consultation service. *Professional Psychology, 9,* 551–560.

Johnson, D. W., & Johnson, F. P. (1987). *Joining together* (3rd ed.). Englewood Cliffs, NJ: Prentice-Hall.

Joint Commission on Mental Illness and Health. (1961). *Action for mental health.* New York: Basic Books.

Kandell, J. (1988). *Availability and desirability of candidates' skills for doctoral level counseling center positions: Ten year comparison.* Unpublished master's thesis, University of Maryland, College Park, MD.

Kanfer, F. H., & Goldstein, A. P. (Eds.). (1986). *Helping people change* (3rd ed.). New York: Pergamon.

Katz, D., & Kahn, R. L. (1978). *The social psychology of organizations.* New York: Wiley, 1978.

Lindemann, E. (1944). Symptomatology and management of acute grief. *American Journal of Psychology, 101,* 141–149.

Lowman, R. L. (1985). Ethical practice of psychological consultation. *The Counseling Psychologist, 13,* 466–472.

Magoon, T., & McDermott, M. (1979). Availability and desirability of various skills and candidates for positions in counseling centers: A replication. *Journal of Counseling Psychology, 26,* 169–172.

Mahrer, A. R. (1988). Discovery oriented psychotherapy research: Rationale, aims and methods. *The American Psychologist, 43,* 694–702.

Mannimo, F. P., & Shore, M. F. (1975). The effects of consultation: A review of empirical studies. *American Journal of Community Psychology, 3,* 1–21.

Medway, F. J. (1982). School consultation research: Past trends and future direction. *Professional Psychology, 13,* 422–430.

Moos, R. H. (1981). Work Environment Scale. Palo Alto, CA: Counseling Psychologists Press.

Morrill, W. H., Oetting, O. R., & Hurst, J. C. (1974). Dimensions of counselor functioning. *Personnel and Guidance Journal, 52,* 354–359.

O'Brien, R. M., Dickenson, A. M., & Rosow, M. (Eds.) (1982). *Industrial modification: A learning based approach to industrial organization problems.* New York: Pergamon.

Rimm, D. C., & Masters, J. C. (1979). *Behavior therapy.* New York: Academic Press.

Robinson, S. E., & Gross, D. R. (1985). Ethics of consultation: The Canterville Ghost. *The Counseling Psychologist, 13,* 444–465.

Schein, E. H. (1969). *Process consultation: Its role in organizational development.* Reading, MA: Addison-Wesley.

Schein, E. H. (1987). *Process consultation* (Vol. 2). Reading, MA: Addison-Wesley.

Skinner, B. F. (1938). *The behavior of organisms: An experimental analysis.* New York: Appleton.

Smith, P. C., Kendall, L. M., & Hulin, C. I. (1969). *The measurement of satisfaction in work and retirement.* Chicago: Rand McNally.

Stum, D. L. (1982). DIRECT: A consultation skills training model. *Personnel and Guidance Journal, 60,* 296–301.

Thorndike, E. L. (1911). *Animal intelligence.* New York: Macmillan.

Part IV

Professional Development

Chapter 18

On Becoming a Counseling Psychologist: Professional Development in Graduate School and Beyond

This chapter is intended primarily for those in graduate programs preparing to become counseling psychologists. (The one exception is the first section, which is for those readers not yet in graduate programs but who have decided they would like to become counseling psychologists.) Graduate training in counseling psychology can be much more than academic study; ideally it is a challenging and stimulating time for both professional and personal growth, in which the first steps are made in becoming a lifetime member of a rewarding profession. Our selection of perspectives and topics presented is derived, for the most part, from more than 20 years of personal observations and discussions about what factors facilitate the career development of young counseling psychologists. While we are able to cite a number of pertinent references, only a few of the topics we discuss have been empirically investigated. Advisors, faculty, advanced-level graduate students, and recent alumni of a program are all good sources of viewpoints to consider, especially since each counseling psychology program has its own unique characteristics that may affect the attractiveness of various professional development opportunities.

There are three major parts to this chapter. The first, and briefest, is for aspiring counseling psychologists concerning selection of a graduate program. The second, and longest, concerns professional development during graduate school. In that part we first review six perspectives we believe essential to becoming an effective manager of one's own professional development beginning with graduate school years. This is then followed by a description of six opportunities that are part of almost every graduate program but are often overlooked, mostly because students are thinking more about surviving graduate school than professional development. The third part focuses on professional development in the years following the doctoral degree. Again, there are two sections: first, we review the implications of initial career choices and transitions; second, we describe the essential steps for establishing a career (e.g., obtaining licensing and other credentials, considering independent practice, and planning for continuing professional development).

FOR ASPIRING COUNSELING PSYCHOLOGISTS

Selecting a Graduate Program

We assume that readers of this section have liked what they have learned about counseling psychology and have decided to learn more about graduate training programs in this professional specialty. The first difficult decision to make is whether to consider master's degree programs, typically requiring two years of full-time study (or several more years of part-time study), or doctoral degree programs, typically requiring five or six years of full-time study, including the internship. (Only a few doctoral programs allow much part-time study; part-time doctoral degrees often require ten years or more.) As we elaborated in Chapter 3, psychology has, since the 1940s, viewed the doctoral degree as the only degree appropriate for fully independent practice. Completion of only a master's degree in psychology will impose significant limits to career opportunities. On the other hand, as also noted in Chapter 3, there are more practice opportunities for one with a master's degree in counseling, as compared to a master's degree in psychology. Readers interested primarily in a practitioner's master's degree in counseling should consider the variety of counseling programs such as mental health counseling, marriage and family counseling, rehabilitation counseling, and community counseling. Hollis and Wantz (1990) list over 400 such programs. It must be emphasized, however, that the vast majority of these programs prepare one for a career as a counselor; to use the title *psychologist* for practice requires a doctoral degree in almost every state now.

For those considering pursuing the doctoral degree in counseling psychology, there may be a number of reasons to complete a master's degree. First, the shorter time period required allows a more reasonable test of whether one is really interested in and likes making the kinds of academic and professional commitments needed for the several years it takes to become a counseling psychologist. Some students decide that the opportunities available as a professional counselor at the master's degree level are sufficient, especially since the doctoral degree would require another three (minimally) and possibly four or five years of study and internships.

Second, many students interested in doctoral programs do not have the academic credentials needed to gain acceptance directly into a doctoral program (often a 3.5 grade point average in extensive psychology coursework and Graduate Record Exam scores of 1100 or more), yet do have the 3.0 grade point average in general undergraduate coursework typically needed for entering a master's degree program. Those who enter and complete a quality master's degree program at a high level of academic performance, especially if a research thesis is included, may increase their opportunities to gain subsequent acceptance into a doctoral program. The choice to pursue a master's degree as a way to improve one's credentials for applying to doctoral programs typically adds a year or two to graduate study but does have the advantage of increasing chances for entry into doctoral study if desired. There are, of course, no guarantees; however, each year a number of master's graduates are able to achieve the option of going on to doctoral studies.

For those considering doctoral programs in counseling psychology, there are several major resource books that are important to consult. The first and most basic is *Graduate Study in Psychology and Associated Fields,* which is updated annually by the American Psychological Association (APA). This book lists all programs that are offering degrees of all types of psychology in regionally accredited universities. Doctoral-level counseling, clinical, and school programs that are accredited by the APA are clearly indicated. (In Chapter 3 we described the process of accreditation and noted some of the career implications of choosing nonaccredited as compared to accredited doctoral programs.) Each program is briefly described in terms of the kinds of degrees it offers, the required grade point averages and various kinds of exams required for admission to the program (e.g., Graduate Record Examination), the number of applicants versus the number accepted, amount of financial support available, and so forth. In short, the book provides a great deal of statistical information about almost every program in psychology.

A second major resource includes two "how-to" books on the process of applying to graduate school: *The Complete Guide to Graduate School Admission* (Keith-Spiegel, 1990) and *Preparing for Graduate Study in Psychology: Not for Seniors Only* (Fretz & Stang, 1980). These books describe not only time lines and procedures for applications but also how to prepare oneself both academically and experientially to become a competitive applicant for doctoral-level programs. For example, they describe how the kinds of courses one takes as an undergraduate may be even more important than simply obtaining high grades. Other sections describe the steps that may be taken to increase the possibilities for attending graduate programs in psychology for those who lack outstanding grades or high Graduate Record Exam scores.

In a situation somewhat peculiar to counseling psychology, over half of the applicants for any given program may have an undergraduate background in a major other than psychology. Counseling psychology programs vary greatly as to how many credit hours and what specific psychology courses must be taken before becoming an applicant for the program. Those readers who do not have an undergraduate degree in psychology are well advised to inquire at schools which interest them as to the specific prerequisite courses.

Types of Doctoral Degrees

For students who are now in or expecting to be in a master's degree program and will subsequently be considering various doctoral degree programs, it is important to become aware of some actual differences and, more importantly, some perceptions about differences in types of doctoral degrees in terms of the opportunities they provide for both short-range and long-range professional development goals. Doctoral programs in counseling psychology most frequently offer the Ph.D. (Doctor of Philosophy) degree; others offer an Ed.D. (Doctor of Education) degree; some programs offer a choice of either degree. It is possible that some Psy.D. (Doctor of Psychology) programs may soon be offering degrees in counseling psychology. Because the Ph.D. degree has long been the primary recognized research degree from universities, it is not surprising that counseling psychology, with a scientist-practitioner emphasis, has most often offered the Ph.D. degree. However, since many APA-approved counseling psychology programs have long been housed in colleges and schools of education, some of those programs offer primarily the Ed.D. degree. In earlier times, that degree choice may have indicated less stringent research training and dissertation requirements than in other parts of a university, but that is rarely true in today's colleges of education. It is the Psy.D. degree that most often today represents a greater emphasis on professional practice with a sometimes correspondingly lesser emphasis on research training and dissertation requirements. Even here, however, there is considerable overlap; the most stringent Psy.D. programs may have research training demands as rigorous as some of the less demanding Ph.D. programs. Those who prefer their graduate training to have a stronger emphasis on practice than on research may want to explore Psy.D. programs.

One issue to consider in choosing the type of degree is that there can sometimes be a *temporary* handicap in obtaining jobs or qualifying for insurance payments when holding other than the Ph.D. degree. In recent years there have been instances where legislation has been written for reimbursement that specifically refers to a Ph.D. degree. In such cases special appeals may need to be made to gain appropriate recognition when holding other doctoral degrees. On the other hand, type of degree is *not* a major issue for obtaining credentials like licensing, listing in the National Register of Health Service Providers in Psychology, and the diplomate from the American Board of Professional Psychology. It is the content and the official recognition of the program as a psychology program which is most important for those credentials. In fact, one of the major reasons for the existence of the National Register of Health Service Providers in Psychology is to provide insurance companies and other sanctioners with information regarding those persons who hold various degrees but have met all of the basic training and experiential requirements to be considered health service providers in psychology.

There is also the larger issue of perceptions about differences in the degrees. Persons outside the profession of counseling psychology may not be familiar with the Ed.D. as a legitimate degree, since in other than counseling and school psychology it is relatively rare. Psychologists unfamiliar with the degree may make certain assumptions about a lack of substantive content and/or research training of such degree recipients. Similar perceptions affect the Psy.D. degree. Fox (1990) notes the continuing "deeply held prejudice against professional training" (p. 4) held by many psychologists who argue that the scientist-practitioner model is the only viable training model. While those holding any type of degree from an APA-approved program can usually provide assurances of the quality of the training necessary for licensing and other credentials, they may have to defend their credentials more often than those with a Ph.D.

Nevertheless, students who find an Ed.D. degree or a Psy.D. degree program offering the kind of training they find most attractive are encouraged to look at the above comments as simply indicating possible inconveniences that could be encountered. There are currently nationally recognized scholars and practitioners in psychology holding all three types of degrees. *Any program that meets one's needs and interests should be considered.*

GRADUATE SCHOOL AS PROFESSIONAL DEVELOPMENT

Ideally, graduate school in counseling psychology is a time of significant professional and personal growth as well as the attainment of knowledge. We have noted throughout the book the emphasis of counseling psychology on person–environment interactions. In the next two sections of this chapter we look at the interactions of graduate students (persons) and graduate schools (environments) that are essential to attaining the ideal. Graduate school environments, like most environments, tend to elicit certain feelings and behaviors. Many of these feelings and behaviors help students achieve their goals. However, others may also frequently be elicited that limit the range of goals and/or make attainment of goals more difficult and frustrating than necessary. The next section identifies six perspectives that greatly facilitate satisfaction and productivity during the graduate school years in terms of both professional and personal development. Unfortunately, many of these perspectives are poorly cultivated in the graduate school environment. In fact, there are a variety of factors in our educational system that press toward the antithesis of these perspectives. Understanding both the needs of persons developing as counseling psychologists and the environmental presses of graduate school is, therefore, an essential part of the next section.

Six Challenging Perspectives

Changing the Means-to-an-End Attitude into Professional Development. We find many graduate students begin graduate school with what we call a means-to-an-end perspective, one that served them well in high school and college. In high school, one tries to do well to have the opportunity to go to a good college; in college, one tries to do well to get into graduate school; then one focuses on surviving graduate school in order to earn the doctoral degree. Then life begins! We would like to interrupt this means-to-an-end course of study. *The end is here! You are now part of counseling psychology.* (We shift here to the second-person "you" form for the remainder of the chapter, feeling the need for a more personal frame of reference for this largely advisory material.)

We recommend your looking at graduate school as the beginning of your professional development. Such a change will require you to adopt an activist position as you encounter a variety of challenges. Essentially, you must ask how you can get the most out of each experience instead of doing just enough to get by or over the "hurdle." Taking a professional-development rather than a means-to-an-end perspective is best accomplished by understanding the five other challenging perspectives in this section: (2) changing self-preservation into self-actualization, (3) balancing dependence and independence, (4) finding a mentor, (5) actively coping with disappointments, and (6) finding personal development in professional development. For these five perspectives we examine some typical problem areas and frustrations you may encounter as a graduate student, then suggest ways of mastering the challenge of growing professionally and personally.

Changing Self-Preservation into Self-Actualization. For students just beginning graduate study, turning self-preservation into self-actualization may be the most salient challenge. Graduate study in counseling psychology may bring numerous threats to one's sense of self-efficacy. We define *self-efficacy* as the "expectation that one can master the problems that one faces in a given situation." (The concept of self-efficacy has become a central one in the social learning perspective on personality development and in cognitive-behavioral therapy. See Bandura, 1977.)

The quantity and quality of the requirements of graduate courses will probably exceed those you had in undergraduate courses. Moreover, other students in the class are usually as academically talented as you (or perhaps seemingly more so). Seeing "first clients," even if only role-playing, may leave you tongue-tied. The thought of completing a dissertation ("Did you hear her dissertation was 210 pages long?") may simply be beyond your hopes of anything you could do. In the absence of some of the psychological supports we talk about later in this chapter, any student facing all these threats might well consider a different career.

The major concern we need to address about these threats to self-efficacy is the possibility that they will lead to self-doubts and avoidant behaviors—the latter in the service of a felt need for self-preservation. We are not concerned that you experience some self-doubts; you will probably not be stretched enough to reach your full potential without them. We want to "certify" that it is all right to have such doubts. What you do in reaction to them is the critical factor to be discussed here. All too often, the way any of us cope is to minimize or avoid contact with the difficult situation. At the extreme, such avoidance may mean withdrawal from graduate school and termination of a long-planned career objective. At a lesser extreme, it results in students minimizing their work in the threatening area and considering the requirement as simply a hurdle to get over. "Get by with as little as possible and get out as soon as possible" is the creed of the self-preservation specialist.

Such a strategy, however, may lead to many unfortunate disappointments for both you and your program faculty. If course demands are the threat and one responds by avoiding much material related to that course, one is engaging in a self-defeating behavior that leads to the self-fulfilling prophecy of not doing well. Relatedly, graduate students sometimes deal with the threat of research by avoiding any research activities until absolutely compelled to confront them—until they must start their dissertation.

What should you do when confronted by threats to self-efficacy? First, as we have already said, simply recognize what is happening to you. Initial feelings of acute anxiety, dread, or the need to "get away from it all" may simply be the result of these challenges—they are not necessarily indicating more serious psychological problems and/or unsuitability for the profession of counseling psychology. Second, at the risk of oversimplifying, we urge you to think of reframing threats to self-efficacy as a problem-solving task. The literature on personal problem solving and counseling (Heppner & Krauskopf, 1987) describes many of the strategies for appraisal of problems, goal setting, and problem-solving actions. There are many steps you can take on your own; also, as we discuss later, if your doubts seem overwhelming, they may be a good catalyst for considering the benefits of personal counseling for yourself. In response to demands from academic courses, you may want to consider new methods of reading, studying, or time management. For threats from initial counseling experiences, you may want to consult additional skill-building workbooks (e.g., Egan, 1975), study casebook materials, observe peers counsel, and so forth. For research, you might seek out a research team project, where you would have much smaller and more defined activities than planning and conducting a full study.

In summary, we simply suggest that, after experiencing threats to self-efficacy, you must ask yourself what you need to do to make this an area in which you grow and develop, that is, actualize your potential. Easier said than done, we agree. (One advisee said, "I'd like to self-actualize, but I have this horrible exam next week.") If you find yourself at any time in the future looking at your own avoidant tendencies, generated by self-doubts, say, "Stop! I need to look at what I can *do* rather than what I can *avoid.*" If you do, we will have accomplished our goal for this brief section of the chapter.

We do recognize that striving for self-actualization in the face of the many demands of graduate work will test your ability to set limits. There are indeed only 24 hours in a day and we all do need some sleep. If you are being challenged simultaneously in many areas, it may be important to decide upon your priorities. Which challenges will you work on at this time vs. some future time? If you entered graduate school right out of undergraduate school, you may still be working on the assumption that you will be able to reach a reasonable level of mastery on most of the tasks and demands that come with each semester. Part of the process of becoming a professional, and dealing with tasks that are often vague and extensive, is learning to live with the feeling that one is never truly completely "on top" and "caught up." Feelings of completeness and mastery that sometimes came at the end of semesters may be ones you have to file in long-term memory. Being a professional is not defined in terms of number of tasks for a given semester. Part of self-management as a professional is deciding, throughout your entire career, which tasks can be accomplished in the near future and which will have to wait for coming months and even later times. The bottom line for this kind of setting of limits is to remember that you are *deferring* rather than avoiding work that you cannot manage at the present time.

Our final point related to changing self-preservation into self-actualization concerns the role of competition in our society, sometimes most blatantly evident in our system of higher education (e.g., curving exam scores). Such procedures obviously foster individual competitiveness, meaning that students may almost studiously avoid any collaborative work and mutual assistance. Much has been written about how such procedures are inimical to higher-level thinking and creativity. Because students in graduate programs in counseling psychology are already a very select group, there is little if any need for students to feel in competition with each other. We genuinely believe that a well-functioning graduate program will include some aspects in which students work together, for example, studying in groups for the most demanding courses, assisting each other in research projects, providing constructive peer supervision in counseling practica.

Balancing Dependence and Independence. Balancing dependence and independence and the next two perspectives, finding a mentor and actively coping with disappointments, are, in our view, inextricably bound together. Indeed, they also are, in a sense, integral to the challenge just discussed regarding self-actualization. However, we believe that there are some points that are best made by considering the perspectives separately. Both graduate studies and undergraduate studies exert some strong environmental press toward dependence; that is, they elicit dependent behaviors from students. Relatively clear requirements are laid out; students then perceive hurdles they must get over to obtain the coveted degree. Moreover, the threats to self-efficacy reviewed in the preceding paragraphs may also stimulate dependence on any available experts (e.g., faculty and supervisors) to tell you explicitly and specifically what to do. You may also find yourself wanting more specific feedback from your faculty and supervisors. Are you adequately following the rules? Trying to do things differently, even if something different seems better to you, may seem to risk abandonment by your advisor.

One related aspect of dependence—if you have returned to graduate school after working relatively independently in another career, the structure and hurdles of graduate school, as well as the traditional roles of faculty power over students, may make you feel like you are being treated like a child. Your sense of lost independence will anger you just as much as if you were to visit your home and have your parents tell you what time to go to bed. In our view, the push toward dependency found in many graduate programs can stimulate both passivity and rage.

On the other hand, it is also true that much effective learning can take place by depending on available program structures and resources. The challenge is to be sure that you do not limit your professional development to a passive dependence on what is routinely given to you. To the extent that you enjoy the comfort of this structure, you will probably take less initiative to find and follow other options that will enrich your graduate study. Just as living at home during your undergraduate years may limit the development of your autonomous independent living (Mendelson, 1987), being dependent on the structure of your graduate program for all of your professional development will similarly limit the range of your professional development. Thus, the challenge is *balancing* dependence and independence. What steps do you need to take to ensure some independent action for your professional development?

Just as with the threats to self-efficacy, the antidote begins with recognition that the push toward dependency in graduate school must be met by some counteraction on your part. First, you must ask what you *want* from your graduate program, as compared to asking "What will my graduate program provide for me?" We advise students to continually think about both long-term (e.g., five-year) goals as well as shorter-term (e.g., coming year) ones. What specific kinds of practice and research experiences would you like to have during the coming year? What roles would you like to be prepared to fill in five years? Do you have any styles of personal interaction that you want to try to modify in the near future?

Relatedly, what arrangements have you made to have some balance, so that graduate school does not fill up your entire life? The demands of graduate school can be totally absorbing. Professors are skilled in making demands of both themselves and students that will fill all available waking hours. To have any kind of avocational or recreational interests, the somewhat clichéd saying is all too appropriate: One doesn't *find* time, one *makes* time.

Finding a Mentor. During the 1970s and '80s, the concept of the mentor received increasing attention in career development for all professions (Hall & Sandler, 1983; Levinson, 1980). While its definition has varied widely, the most useful definition for our purposes has been presented by Bova and Phillips (1982): "Mentors are those who practice most of the following principles: 1. Try to understand, shape, and encourage the dreams of the protégés, 2. Often give their blessing on the dreams and goals of their protégés, 3. Provide opportunities for their protégés to observe and participate in their work by inviting their protégés to work with them, 4. Teach protégés the politics of 'getting ahead' in the organization. A mentor is usually a person of high organizational or specific career status who by mutual consent takes an active interest in the career development of another person" (p. 7). Bogat and Redner (1985) were one of the first to call attention to the role of the mentor in graduate school as it subsequently affects one's professional development in psychology. Rawles (1980) had previously noted that the majority of scientists of all types who reported having a significant mentor indicated that 85 percent of the mentors were their former teachers and professors. Ironically, despite this perceived importance, faculty-student relationships in many programs seem to keep the mentor-protégé relationship from happening naturally and spontaneously. Cronan-Hillix, Gensheimer, Cronan-Hillix and Davidson (1986) found only 53 percent of psychology students they surveyed reported having mentors. They further concluded, "Our study provides some reason to doubt that a true mentor can be 'assigned' to a student. Most students entered into such relationships as a result of seeking out a faculty member who had similar interests. Students thought that faculty less often sought out students with a view to becoming their mentors" (Cronan-Hillix et al., 1986, p. 126).

To the extent that students have a "means-to-an-end" perspective, they may not view faculty as people with whom they will continue to have relationships in subsequent years and therefore do not look for mentors among the faculty. Moreover, faculty and student roles in courses might sometimes seem almost adversarial—faculty seem to hold all the power and may be making course and/or program demands that students find neither valuable nor interesting—obviously not the conditions to promote mentoring. A further irony is that graduate students often feel they can relate most closely to younger junior faculty; however, the research on mentors suggests that those identified as valuable mentors have been among the more senior faculty (Bogat & Redner, 1985).

Given that the climate is often not conducive to mentor-protégé relationships, you may need to think carefully about how to initiate finding a mentor among the faculty and supervisors in your graduate program. This statement reveals one of our assumptions—that is, that career development of counseling psychologists is indeed facilitated by having a mentor. While we clearly know of many outstanding counseling psychologists who have developed rewarding and significant careers without having mentors, it is our own view that progress in the early stages of one's career—from the internship through first positions—is greatly accelerated by their assistance. We urge you to go back and reread the definition provided by Bova and Phillips (1982) and begin thinking about your current or possible future advisors as suitable to this kind of role. In short, we urge you to think about advisors as more than a signature on your course requests at the beginning of each semester!

Actively Coping with Disappointments. No matter how carefully you have researched your choice of programs, you are likely to find, at some point, a course or professor, a practicum or requirement that does not meet your own view of what you expected from graduate school.

> Any system imposes limitations on you. The challenge is to learn how to work creatively within that system to obtain your key goals without sacrificing your integrity by "selling out." We often hear both students in college and professionals in a human services system argue that the "system" won't allow them to be themselves, that they feel stifled, and that they could be creative and productive "if it weren't for . . . so much reading and so many papers to write, leaving me with no time to be concerned with what I am learning . . . the silly requirements and the grading game . . . the unrealistic pressures placed on me by the professors." (Corey & Corey, 1989, p. 19)

Again, a means-to-an-end perspective leads to a passive accommodation to such disappointments. We encourage you to think about a more activist self-management response on at least two levels. First, explore any of your disappointments with your fellow students both at your own beginning level and those at more advanced levels in the program. In this way you may (1) gain some perspective on whether the concern is widely shared or one unique to you, and (2) discover ways other students have actively dealt with that disappointment. If your concern is widely shared, then those who share it may want to bring it to the attention of the faculty or program director through student representatives, grievance procedures or other mechanisms. In one sense, such procedures are a way of learning to cope with the system, a skill that will be needed even after you leave graduate school. "There are reviews and evaluation practices on all levels in the professional world. In a business, for example, your supervisors rate you and determine whether you get a promotion or a raise. If you are a professional, your clients rate you by the business they bring to you or take away from you" (Corey & Corey, 1989, p. 21).

When the problem is one that is not shared by others, the courses of action may seem less evident. Just as we discussed in the earlier section on changing self-preservation into self-actualization, the primary need is to reframe the concern as a problem to be solved. What, in more behavioral concrete terms, is the problem? What kinds of possible solutions can you envision? What kinds of alternatives are available? What are the costs and benefits of some of the various solutions in terms of how much they involve changes in you and changes from others? In short, the challenge is for you to be sensitive to any of your own complaining reactions to disappointments—usually a counterproductive activity for both your present mental health and your future professional development. Instead, consider how to take an activist role in reaching alternative solutions through changing something about "the system" and/or yourself—the focus of the final perspective we discuss.

Finding Personal Development in Professional Development. Graduate study in counseling psychology is qualitatively different from that in, for example, history, physics, or music. Becoming an effective counselor happens only by learning a great deal about yourself. It is not simply a matter of applying a set of techniques. *You* are the major tool—one that must be highly adaptable to be effective with a wide range of clients and interventions. To become that adaptable, many of your values, assumptions, and personal styles will have to be examined. As a counselor you might experience value conflicts with clients, for example, in matters of religion, abortion, gender roles, perceived responsibilities for family members, and so forth. Other clients may be part of a culture that has a very different value system than you do, leading them to close out options that you would consider viable and effective choices for them. Even less obvious to most counselors are the assumptions we all make about various cultures. As we explored in Chapter 11, counselors make many assumptions and attributions about non-verbal behavior, lack of assertiveness, levels of self-disclosure, and observing promptness for appointments that may make it particularly difficult to establish a working alliance with clients from various cultural backgrounds. These assumptions and attributions may be the primary signal for areas of knowledge, skills, and attitudes that you need to make part of your professional development program.

Understanding how your own personality and style of interacting affect clients is also a critical part of your learning. Relatedly, some areas of your own personal struggle may be the source of significant countertransference issues (see Chapter 7) that block progress in a counseling relationship. All of these areas can often be addressed by personal counseling for yourself, a topic that has long been debated as to whether or not it should be a required part of training in counseling psychology.

You may be aware that psychoanalysis has, from its beginning, essentially required that trainees complete their own psychoanalysis before being fully certified as psychoanalytic practitioners. Psychologists of other theoretical orientations have been much less explicit and more varied in their opinions about the value of personal counseling as part of the training of therapists. Only a few programs take official positions in their written materials regarding whether students should consider personal counseling. A few programs regularly provide students with lists of recommended psychotherapists to consult for personal counseling.

Despite this relative lack of explicit discussion of the value of personal counseling as part of the training of counseling psychologists, Kestenbaum (1986) found two-thirds of his sample of 147 graduates from five different APA-approved counseling psychology programs had sought some personal counseling during their training. The majority of these students entered psychotherapy in order to seek help with relationship issues with family, friends, or significant others. Few of them indicated that the stresses of graduate training were the primary source for seeking counseling, but rather indicated that their graduate training did give them a new perspective about the value of seeking professional help for their personal problems. Approximately 60 percent of the students who sought personal counseling during graduate training had also been in therapy before coming to graduate school, a trend that apparently continues after receiving the doctorate as well. Guy, Stark, and Poelstra (1988) found that those who seek personal therapy after entering professional practice are more likely to be those who sought counseling during graduate school. Kestenbaum (1986), like Ralph (1980), found that the overwhelming majority of students had very favorable responses to their participating in therapy while in graduate school. They felt that their counseling skills had been helped primarily through their being able to make more effective use of their feelings in their own counseling. They were able to more quickly develop an empathy with clients' difficulties. On the other hand, Kestenbaum also found that 21 percent of the students felt that their counseling experience created a number of multiple role complexities for them which subsequently affected their own work with clients. More specifically, when the counselors felt that their therapy was at an impasse, they found themselves having more difficulties working with their own clients. Clark (1986) reviewed the few studies available as to whether or not personal therapy of the counselor would benefit client outcome and concluded that "at present, it has not been empirically demonstrated that personal therapy is beneficial to client outcome" (p. 542).

Like much of the research we cited in earlier chapters on the effects of counseling itself, the self-reports of participants, in this case, graduate students in personal therapy, are far more positive than the evidence we can collect for how it affects performance. For those who are experiencing personal distress during the graduate school years, counseling offers a way not only of dealing with that stress but also improves one's sense of skills and techniques for relating to clients. Clearly, from a professional development point of view, engaging in personal counseling while in graduate school may be a highly valuable option to consider.

We have now described six perspectives that we believe will help you become an effective manager of your own professional development. We turn now to some special opportunities for you to consider in planning your professional development during graduate school years.

GRADUATE SCHOOL YEARS: PROFESSIONAL DEVELOPMENT OPPORTUNITIES

We describe six opportunities we believe merit some special consideration in your plans for the graduate school years. These opportunities are often not made explicit in formal coursework, yet are almost always available as part of the elective aspects of counseling psychology programs.

Elective Courses

Your graduate program probably offers a number of elective courses beyond the required ones. Undergraduates often consider electives primarily in terms of immediate interests and the demands they make on one's time—they try to find "an easy course." We encourage you to think about electives in graduate school not only in terms of any immediate interests, but also in terms of what those courses can contribute to your professional development, especially by expanding your future internship and career options. At the present time, there are three specific suggestions we can make. You might consult faculty, interns, and alumni from your program for other suggestions to consider.

As we noted in Chapter 10, various authors have pointed out that assessment training in counseling psychology is sometimes viewed as inadequate for the broad variety of roles in which counseling psychologists sometimes find themselves. Many hospital internships, and some community mental health center internships, expect applicants to have a considerable amount of experience in using a variety of objective and projective individualized assessment batteries. Many counseling psychology programs, and some clinical psychology programs, require very minimal levels of formal assessment experience. If you want to consider an internship and/or part of your career in a hospital setting, you should examine the extent of your program's assessment training relative to what would be expected in those settings. Looking at the application forms of hospital internship settings may give you a picture of the kinds of assessment experiences they expect. Some of the applications ask for how many specific batteries of each type you have given and may in fact ask you to submit a report you have prepared from using a variety of assessment techniques with one of your clients.

Substance abuse treatment is a second area that is typically elective in most programs but is increasingly a fundamental part of services provided in various managed care and employee assistance programs. In fact, the single most universally offered service in EAPs is some form of substance abuse counseling. Coursework and practica that address this area will have a significant positive impact on your marketability for early career placements.

A final area to suggest is consultation, as described in the previous chapter. As we noted there, counseling center directors have indicated for over a decade, that they find far too few people trained in this area for their needs. If you are considering an internship or a career in a counseling center, and if consultation training is not a requirement of your program, then this is clearly an elective you may want to consider.

Your specific professional goals, changing times, and strengths of your program may all lead to other suggestions more pertinent than these three. The fundamental point is to include consideration of your long-range professional goals when choosing electives.

Professional Readings

You may feel almost overwhelmed with the amount of reading already required in your graduate courses and cannot imagine taking on any more reading. Yet, if you are to become an effective manager of your own professional development, the time to start some elective professional reading is right now. Courses, by design, have limited breadth; moreover, professors or instructors teaching these courses do not know everything (at least the ones we know!). As a way to stay abreast of current developments in psychology in general, we highly recommend a regular perusal of the *APA Monitor,* the monthly newspaper of the American Psychological Association, and the *American Psychologist,* the primary journal of the association. The articles in the journal cover the entire gamut of psychology, and you may wish to read only an occasional article; however, the "Comments" section is one of the quickest ways to become acquainted with some of the most controversial issues in professional practice and scientific research in contemporary psychology.

For counseling psychology specifically, we recommend a similar perusal of the tables of contents of each issue of the *Journal of Counseling Psychology,* the primary empirical research journal of the field; *The Counseling Psychologist,* the primary conceptual journal of the field; and *Professional Psychology: Research and Practice,* the major journal about professional practice issues. Granted, few if any of us read any of the journals from cover to cover, yet by taking time to skim the contents of these journals, we get a feel for the current issues and topics of greatest concern, and can take note of articles that we do specifically want to read or consult as time permits.

We also urge you to think about some elective reading in your own area of special interest. That may be a topic such as women's issues, multicultural counseling, or service delivery techniques such as behavior modification or career counseling. Almost every different population of clients, treatment technique, theoretical orientation, and scientific research problem has a specialized journal that is probably worth consulting with some frequency, again if only to review the table of contents and identify articles of specific interest. A handy way to keep up-to-date on recent books in your specialized area of interest is to order them directly from a publisher if you notice that several of them are published by the same house. The publisher will put your name on a mailing list; you will then receive bi-yearly if not quarterly catalogues listing many current publications in your particular area of interest.

As we close this section, we recognize that we have spent all of our time telling you what to read, not when to read it. As we noted in one of the earlier sections of this chapter, a continual task of professional life is learning how to *make* time for what we think is valuable; if you wait to *find* time to read, your accumulation of newsletters and books will soon be as high as the Empire State Building.

Another value of regularly reading these journals is that you will soon realize that some of your own work in classes and research may be of the same caliber as that being published. Thus, you can begin to see yourself as a contributor to journals, not only a reader of them. With some editorial suggestions from an advisor or faculty member, many research projects or conceptual papers of graduate students can become suitable for publications in these journals.

All of the journals mentioned, and many other specialized ones, are available at reduced rates through student memberships in various professional organizations. In the last decade, the American Psychological Association and many of its more than 40 divisions have developed student memberships; for a fraction of the cost of professional membership, students can receive special newsletters, news of the division's current activities, and reduced rates on the journals. The address for the APA is found in Chapter 3; the address of the Student Affiliate Group of the Division of Counseling Psychology appears on the inside cover of each issue of *The Counseling Psychologist.* Many counseling psychology students are also interested in the American Association of Counseling and Development and its 16 divisions, for example, American Mental Health Counselors Association, National Career Development Association, and Association for Multicultural Counseling and Development. Information on student membership and journals is available from AACD Student Membership, 5999 Stevenson Ave., Alexandria, VA 22304-3303.

Professional Conventions

We could not have written wisely about professional conventions ourselves until we had been in the profession many years and slowly began to realize the many unexpected ways in which these conventions can affect graduate students' professional development. If you were to stop reading at this point and rush off to a professional convention, you might well be overwhelmingly disappointed. Regional and national psychology conventions are large and complex affairs, often with thousands of participants and many paper sessions and symposia scheduled for almost every hour. Simply attending some of these sessions and then returning to your home or hotel room is *not* how a convention contributes to your professional development.

The greatest benefits of professional conventions occur for graduate students, as we have observed them, from their presenting a paper or participating in a symposium at a convention. How can you have such an opportunity? You might expect conventions to be primarily for well-established professionals with active research programs. On the contrary, it is much easier to present a paper at a professional convention than to have a paper published. While many professional journals are able to accept fewer than half or even a quarter of the papers submitted for publication, most conventions accept for presentation nearly half or more of all the papers that are submitted. Most master's thesis research projects completed in counseling psychology programs have a good chance of acceptance for presentation at a regional or national convention poster session. Poster sessions refer to times when a large number of papers are posted on bulletin boards, with accompanying illustrative tables. The authors remain standing by for the selected time period so that interested persons can come by and discuss the papers with authors. In contrast to poster sessions, symposia are often made up of several brief research presentations from various research team members followed by comments from a knowledgeable discussant or two. Having the opportunity to present at a symposium is most often related to being part of a research team or having a mentor. At every convention, there are symposia which include several graduate students from the same program or from different universities but working on similar projects known to the symposium organizer—typically, an established researcher from a practice setting or from a faculty.

We have gradually become aware of the immense benefits of such participation by graduate students. Those who do take part in such presentations, although initially very frightened about the prospects, typically come away with a greatly increased sense of self-efficacy and feeling connected to the field of counseling psychology. Suddenly they have found a number of people (in addition to their advisor!) quite interested in the details of their work and have indeed found themselves to be the expert in that particular area. That submitting a relatively brief abstract of one's ongoing work to a convention takes such a small amount of effort yet can lead to such gratifying experiences is, obviously, a very cost-effective investment for professional development.

It is also important to note that presenting at a convention is something that is listed on your resume. Such a listing strongly marks your professional commitment. Most employers in both practitioner and academic settings want to be sure that they are considering someone not only competently skilled in psychological services but also involved in broader professional aspects. Such involvement is not only a promise of remaining a vitalized professional but also brings credit to an agency when staff participate in national conventions. Studies of the reputations of agencies and academic programs sometimes include tallies of the places of employment of convention presenters (Skovholt, Stone, & Hill, 1984).

There are other aspects of convention participation that are also very important for professional development. All conventions run a number of social hours, times when the participants meet very informally. These times are especially significant for the networking experience of graduate students. This is a time to meet many other counseling psychologists of widely varying levels of experience but all with strong commitments to professional development. You can meet the most well-known practitioners and researchers as well as those who, like yourself, may just be beginning a career. Making such contacts may well lead to further correspondence that will help you with your own research and career opportunities. Osberg and Rollin (1989) have provided further elaborations on how attending conventions is a primary networking technique for young professionals. Most importantly, those social activities can greatly enhance your sense of being part of a profession—establishing your personal professional identity as a counseling psychologist.

You can most easily learn about opportunities for presenting at conventions by being a student member of the various professional organizations described in the previous section. Additionally, your advisor and/or mentor may be able to tell you about other regional and state conventions where you have opportunities to present conceptual or research papers you complete as part of your graduate study.

"Externships"

This section describes some of the potential benefits of participating in "externships." The term *externship* is one that has come into use mostly since the 1970s. Up until that time, the term *internship* was used much more broadly than it is today and applied to almost any experience outside of formal practica in one's doctoral program. Internships were made up of a variety of part-time or full-time experiences spread over a number of years. Many other disciplines, in both the mental-health and non-mental-health fields, may use the term *internship* in this broader way and use it to refer to any field experience, even during the undergraduate years. However, as a part of the more standardized regulations for the content and training of programs developed in the 1970s, the psychology internship became defined as a one-year full-time or a two-year half-time experience completed only after all doctoral practicum requirements had been met (APA, 1979).

The term *externship* then emerged to refer to practical experiences in agencies outside of program practica but prior to the internship year. Externship experiences may range from relatively formal training programs involving the student in 20 hours a week of training and service to more informally arranged training experiences for as little as a half-day a week for one semester. There is no official definition of externship;

there may be significant variations from program to program in how this term is used if it is used at all.

Externships have several very specific values for subsequent internship and career opportunities for many graduate students. First of all, most internship programs are looking for persons who have had at least some prior significant experience in that particular kind of setting. Hospitals may be reluctant to consider an applicant who, despite a strong transcript and outstanding supervisor recommendations, has never worked in a hospital setting. Similarly, a university counseling center may be a bit reluctant to consider an intern whose total experience in practica and employment has been in in-patient psychiatric facilities. Thus, if you are planning to apply for internships or for career positions that are in settings different from where you have completed your practica and any employment, you may well want to consider an externship of at least one semester or more in whatever setting to which you plan to apply.

Second, students in traditional scientist-practitioner programs may often have fairly intensive but not very extensive practicum experience in terms of number of hours of practical experience. The accreditation standards for APA-approved programs require only 400 hours of practicum experience of which 150 hours must be direct service (APA, 1979). Graduate students in Psy.D. doctoral programs and other more practice-oriented programs may be assigned to work 20 hours a week in an agency throughout their doctoral training and therefore have literally thousands of hours of accumulated experience prior to the internship. Consequently, graduate students who have not held employment as a mental health professional (for example, after the master's degree but before entering the doctoral program) may want to consider an externship as a way of increasing the number of hours of experience. Veterans Administration hospitals sometimes provide intensive summer externships of 500 hours; a variety of counseling centers and community mental health agencies provide 20-hour-a-week externships for students who are in their final years of training before going on internship.

A third value of externships is similar to one noted in the section on elective courses—students in counseling psychology may want to increase their amount of assessment experience especially if they are considering internships and careers in hospital settings. Externships specifically focused on assessment may sometimes be arranged in various hospitals and agencies.

Finally, externships may be valuable for providing some more specialized experience than your program provides, even if only to expose you to an area you may not choose to pursue further. Such areas might include those mentioned in the elective course areas such as assessment or substance abuse. They might also include special populations such as working with the elderly, with an ethnic minority population, with

AIDS patients, and so forth. In summary, externship choices may be a way of preparing yourself for specific internships or careers; other times they may be chosen simply because you want the breadth of exposure available at the externship level but do not intend to pursue further such experiences at the intern or career level. There are no formal directories of externships and, in fact, information about them is often difficult to obtain. Your best sources are typically your advisor, program director, and advanced-level graduate students who have taken advantage of these opportunities.

Internships

"Managing the internship application experience: advice from an exhausted but content survivor . . . Having gone through it, I now believe preparation should begin in the first year of graduate school" (Jacob, 1987, p. 146). There is more published advice for prospective and current interns than exists on any other topic discussed in this chapter. A few of the titles of these articles indicate the range of available advice beyond that provided by Jacob. "Strategies for selecting and securing the pre-doctoral internship of choice" (Brill, Wolkin, & McKeel, 1985); "Survival guide for intern applicants" (Belar & Orgel, 1980); "Transition from graduate school to internship: A potential crisis" (Solway, 1985); "The quality and process of the internship experience" (Cole, Kolko, & Craddick, 1981).

Choosing from well over 300 recognized internship sites may seem a daunting process; moreover, since internship application is, like entry into graduate school, a competitive process, students have considerable anxiety about the process. The combination of these two features no doubt accounts for the plethora of articles on this topic. Unfortunately, most of the literature is focused on the application process and managing potential difficulties in the transition to the internship rather than looking at the longer-term professional development aspects regarding the choice of internships. Therefore, our primary focus will be on those aspects and we will leave to you, the reader, the task of consulting the literature for the many useful pieces of advice regarding the application process itself.

First, consider the purpose of an internship. "Internships should provide the trainee with the responsibility to take substantial opportunity for carrying out major professional functions in the context of appropriate supervisory support, professional role modeling, and awareness of administrative structures. The internship is taken after completion of relevant, didactic and practicum work and precedes the granting of the doctoral degree" (APA, 1979).

Each internship provides a somewhat different set of intensive training experiences. The primary question for you, when considering the choice of internships, is which kinds of experiences you would want to have to enhance and complement your current doctoral training. Students readily think about some of the choices regarding settings, such as hospitals, counseling centers, and community mental health centers, but are less likely to think about what the internship will offer them in terms of experience with other theoretical orientations, such as behavioral, psychodynamic, and opportunities with various client populations, whether by diagnostic category (e.g., eating disorders, career dissatisfaction, and posttraumatic stress syndrome) or demographic characteristics (e.g., gender, age, and ethnicity).

Your choice of an internship has both direct and indirect career implications. The direct implications come from the more obvious connection between your gaining experience with a particular kind of setting or service to your marketability for that kind of career for your first job. Obviously, persons with internships completed in hospital settings will be in a stronger position when applying for psychology positions in hospitals; similarly, someone completing an internship in a university counseling center will be more competitive for a career position in a counseling center than a candidate that has completed only one practicum in a counseling center.

The more indirect career implications from choice of internship relate to the previously discussed concept of networking. Typically, the persons with whom you work in your internship setting most likely know other professionals in that kind of setting and will therefore be able to tell you more about job opportunities in that setting than any other. Thus, your informal network for potential jobs will be shaped in part by your choice of internship setting.

There are also some important aspects to consider about internships and their effect on your qualifications for licensure, other professional credentials, and employment. There are several hundred internships listed in the directory of the Association of Psychology Internship Centers (APIC), issued each fall, providing brief descriptions of the kinds of training available in each internship, the prerequisite qualifications for candidates, and application procedures. For licensing and other credentials as professional psychologists, internships that are APA-approved are typically fully accepted, without further questions or documentation, as meeting requirements for internship-level training. Other internships listed in the APIC directory are usually acceptable, after providing some documentation from the agency, to many licensing boards and some employers (the Veterans Administration and some states require that the internship be completed in an APA-approved program).

It is possible to complete a specially arranged internship in an agency that does not officially list its program in the APIC directory to gain some specialized experience (e.g., working with AIDS patients in a hospital without an internship program). While a graduate from an APA-approved doctoral training program is permitted to complete an internship that is not APA-approved but that provides appropriate supervised experience and training, the lack of formal recognition as an internship has significant licensing and career implications. Some students who know that the state in which they want to practice will admit them for licensure without having a formally recognized internship sometimes choose this route. However, we feel that this is such a high-risk choice, in case there is ever a decision to change one's employer or the state in which one practices, that we require the occasional student who chooses this route to sign a statement indicating that he or she realizes the potential limits of such an internship choice to one's licensing eligibility and career opportunities.

It is preferable that you give primary attention to the above considerations in your choice of internships before looking at the other factors that seem so tempting to graduate students—location, cost of living, distance from significant others. While all of these personal factors may be very useful secondary considerations, when they are used as primary considerations, they may lead to choices of internships that, in the short range, are gratifying but result in significant missed opportunities in terms of long-range career development. You might best serve your long-term career development when you are able to adopt the attitude "I can live anyplace for just one year."

As we discussed in Chapter 3, as of this writing, there is increasing attention being given to the possibility of extending the internship requirement to two years with the second year being a postdoctoral stint in a more specialized internship setting. Because of the tremendous number of logistical issues in being able to offer the hundreds of necessary postdoctoral internships that such a new requirement would entail, it is unlikely that it will be a firmly stated requirement in the immediate future. However, there will probably be a steadily increasing number of specialized postdoctoral traineeships available for those who wish to gain intensive experience in a particular kind of treatment, for instance, neuropsychological, geropsychological, forensic, and so forth. If this requirement is introduced, then there will be even greater importance to looking at the predoctoral internship as the source of breadth of training.

In the process of choosing an internship, there is one special factor for counseling psychology graduate students to consider. A fairly large number of the internships listed in the APIC directory indicate that they limit their applicants to those who graduate from clinical psychology programs. While that qualification does almost always indicate that these internships want their applicants to have fairly extensive assessment training and considerable experience with clients with significant degrees of psychopathology, each year there are a number of counseling psychology students whose training includes such factors and who make the case for their appropriate suitability to be an applicant to the internship. In short, if there is an internship listed as open only to clinical psychology students that you very much want to consider and you believe you have the kinds of training described in the eligibility requirements, we encourage you to submit an application. In many cases, the staff is simply unaware of differences between counseling psychology and more generic counseling and has made some misattributions about limits to the nature of an applicant's training.

In summary, the choice of internship is a major component in long-range professional development and provides an opportunity for both depth and breadth that will complement training experiences gained in your program and any previous employment experiences as you make the transition to your first career.

The Dissertation

The final section of considerations for program development during graduate school applies to one of the final requirements for obtaining a doctoral degree—the dissertation. The primary purpose of this section is to help you plan the dissertation in the context of your professional development. This purpose may be a challenging one to fulfill.

The history of students' views toward and work on dissertations is replete with means-to-an-end perspectives. Ironically, in such a view the dissertation then gains more importance in the life of the student than it ever should. Whatever ambivalence about your program is still keeping you only partially engaged in the program and whatever threats to self-esteem have been leading you toward avoidance may all become fixated on this "final hurdle." Thus, it is not surprising that Garcia, Malott, and Brethower (1988) report that nearly a quarter of those students who drop out of graduate school do so after they have completed all the course work save the dissertation.

You may rightfully say the preceding paragraph sounds like blaming the victim, as the failure to complete the dissertation is explained in terms of the students' perspectives or neuroses. Ever since the 1960s, there has been an increasing amount of literature indicating that part of this failure to complete theses is also related to a lack of supervision and effective incentives (see Garcia, Malott, & Brethower, 1988). More recently, other environmental aspects have been suggested by the work of Mallinckrodt, Gelso, and Royalty (1990), who found that Holland personality types were not only significantly related to research interests in counseling psychology but also to delays in the completion of research requirements. "Investigative and investigative-artistic students have the highest interest in research. Enterprising interests were related to lower levels of research interest and a delay in completing training" (p. 26).

Thus, both individual and environmental factors can work against the dissertation being a positive professional developmental experience.

We first attempt to address the environmental factors. One of the logical interventions that is increasingly promoted is the development of structured courses or supervisory systems that provide for a higher level of supervision of the dissertation. In one such program that has been formally evaluated, Garcia, Malott, and Brethower (1988) found that students who participated in a system including weekly meetings, task specification, feedback, and incentives, completed significantly more tasks than those in a control group. Interestingly, though, there was no judged difference in the quality of the projects that were completed in either of the two groups.

If you encounter significant problems in making progress on the dissertation, you may indeed want to look into more structured opportunities for supervision and support available in your own university. If there is no structured program in your program or department, you may be able to find similar kinds of help from a writing center that is part of campus services. Although such centers are geared primarily for undergraduates, the writing counselors often look forward to working with the higher-level challenges that graduate students provide in contrast to those of beginning freshmen, who may still be struggling with writing coherent paragraphs.

In picking your dissertation advisor, you may want to be sure that you pick an advisor not only for expertise in a topical area but also one who fits with your own style of functioning, who can assist you with relatively undefined tasks like deciding on a topic for a dissertation and then executing it. Though there may seldom be more than one faculty member with expertise in your area of interest, wherever there can be congruence between your style and the advisor's, your progress will be facilitated. If you have difficulty choosing an advisor who seems to naturally fit your style, it is not unreasonable to explore the possibility of asking your advisor to work with you in a way that might be different from his or her usual style.

There are two other bits of useful advice that come from the Mallinckrodt, Gelso, and Royalty (1990) study of supportive environments for research. They noted that positive change in research interests is related to a program's conveying "to students that all experiments are flawed and that a particular study need not make a great contribution to knowledge to be worth doing and . . . 'wedding science to practice'—that is, teaching students to use their clinical experience as a source of research ideas" (p. 30).

From the professional development perspective, one can also look at the dissertation in its environmental context as one of the transitions, along with the internship, between your graduate school years and the beginnings of your establishment in a career as a counseling psychologist. Your choice of topic for the dissertation could well be the beginning of a program of research that you plan to continue in either a service setting or academic position. Your dissertation topic may also be one with special implications for your subsequent practice, for example, conducting research with abused spouses attending a community clinic, or with "plateaued" employees as part of an EAP. In short, rather than simply looking for a dissertation topic that is feasible, you should think about the topics that will have practical use for you as well. Obviously, this is a major way to provide yourself with both intrinsic and extrinsic incentives for working on the dissertation. Topics that are supposedly feasible but are unrewarding sometimes make for the least feasible dissertations!

PROFESSIONAL DEVELOPMENT IN INITIAL POSTDOCTORAL CHOICES

The moment for which you have worked so hard finally comes. You receive the doctoral degree in psychology. The first postdoctoral requirement is that you celebrate appropriately—whatever that is for you.

In this section, we explore the professional development issues and implications in three areas of planning for your initial postdoctoral year. The first set of issues concerns the type of position you will enter. Despite counseling psychology's long major involvement in the study of career development, ironically, there is little formal consideration given in counseling psychology programs to either the short-range or long-range implications of the type of first position one chooses. As a graduate of a counseling psychology program, you will have a diverse range of opportunities, from, for example, hospital staff psychologist, to assistant professor of psychology, to supervised independent practitioner, to full-time research psychologist, to a formal postdoctoral training or research fellowship. Are there differential career implications for choosing one of these paths over another? Speaking more pragmatically, how easy is it to change from one type of position to another after a year or two? Are some career paths more satisfying than others, especially for long-range goals? Do different career choices affect how difficult it will be to maintain a sense of being part of a profession, that is, not feeling isolated?

The second set of issues is related to the rapidly changing social patterns regarding men's and women's careers and child rearing. We see an increasing number of new professionals who begin their families and careers almost at the same time. (One graduate bought her first home, defended her dissertation, and had her first child all in the same month.) Simply managing the issues involved in two professionals sharing a life together entails numerous career implications even when both have positions they like—a tall order in itself. The addition of children exponentially increases multiple-role demands and implications. In this area there is a burgeoning literature to which we can only allude as we describe what we believe the most salient considerations of multiple roles for postdoctoral career planning.

The third set of issues relates to managing the transition to your first job. In this area there is a reasonable amount of literature on actually searching for positions as a psychologist and some very relevant articles about this transition from graduate school to professional roles. We highlight some of the recommendations in these articles as well as add some of our own.

Career Choices and Their Implications

If you are certain about what type of position you intend to enter and do not plan a change in later years, then this section will be relatively unimportant for you. If you are, however, like most counseling psychology students about to graduate, you suddenly realize that you are faced with making choices among what seem to be very different career paths. In fact, these choices *can* lead to very different career paths and lifestyles—workload, flexibility, security, income, and satisfaction. Notice that we emphasize the word *can.* We like to think of the choice of an initial career position like the choice of major for undergraduates who have some idea of interests and even a general career goal but are not sure which major to choose to get there. Just as there are several majors that can lead to any one career goal, there are several initial postdoctoral position choices that can lead to any given professional objective.

In keeping with the majors analogy, however, it is also clear that some majors lead more directly to a career goal; for example, a zoology major may provide much more extensive preparation for a career in medicine than would a political science major; to become a civil engineer one will have to take a rather extensive set of specific courses essentially equivalent to the major even if one does not major in civil engineering. In this section, we identify factors that facilitate changes in types of counseling psychology careers.

There is very little pertinent published information about how to decide among specific career choices within counseling psychology. For many decades, a majority of counseling psychologists worked in campus settings either as staff psychologists in counseling centers or as professors; therefore, few options were considered by most counseling psychologists. Most studies of new counseling psychologists adapting to their first careers are in one of these settings (e.g., Simono & Wachowiak, 1983; Ponterotto & Furlong, 1986). The need for attention to issues in other career patterns has been noted and is scheduled to be addressed in several articles for new professionals, during the 1990s, in *The Counseling Psychologist.* These articles will encompass the special considerations inherent in choices of positions such as independent practice, mental health centers, and hospital/medical settings.

As a way of introducing possible and pertinent implications of career choices, consider Simono and Wachowiak's (1983) study of counseling center psychologists' career patterns. They found a majority of these counseling psychologists relatively satisfied with their positions, with the majority of those who changed to other type positions doing so for reasons of advancement or family reasons. Only 9 percent moved to different types of positions because of dissatisfaction with counseling center positions. Of those who had long-term careers in counseling centers, most had a counseling center position as their first postdoctoral position; however, there were some persons who entered careers as counseling center psychologists at many points in the postdoctoral years. Some entered such a position as a midcareer change, that is, after many years in another type of counseling psychology position. We share this summary about those counseling center positions because we believe that such patterns hold for most types of positions that counseling psychologists choose. The majority find reasonable levels of satisfaction with their first choice; a slight majority stay with something close to that type of position throughout their careers. At the same time, changes between types of positions occur throughout the career life span. Hospital psychologists or independent practitioners can be found starting out at age 50+. Thus, there is always the possibility for change.

There are a few noteworthy points to note about this kind of flexibility. First, moving to any type of position is greatly facilitated by having had some prior type of work experience in a particular setting. At any point in one's career, it would be difficult to obtain employment as a hospital psychologist or a counseling center psychologist without ever having had formal training experience or work experience in one of those settings, either as part of predoctoral or postdoctoral training and experience. This on-site experience requirement is a little less important for independent practice and community mental health centers where the most important question is whether or not you have the skills to work with the kinds of client populations to be served.

Perhaps the greatest limits regarding flexibility concern academic positions in highly rated universities. Such positions are always related to evidence of one's scholarly work as reflected in publications. The newer the counseling psychologist, the fewer the publications necessary. In fact, Ponterotto and Furlong (1986) were able to show that the more one had specialized training in what were then priority areas such as group counseling and multicultural counseling, the less critical was an extensive publication record. However, the more time that elapses since the doctoral degree, no matter what type of position one holds, the more publications that are expected of one who wishes to enter academia. Consequently, should you choose to move into a service position for the first years of your career and then plan to move to academia, unless you are able to publish articles while you are in that service position, you would be unlikely to be able to make the move into such an academic position in a counseling psychology program in a major research university. In one sense, it is usually easiest to enter an academic career straight out of graduate school. If you found yourself not suited for an academic career, it would be easier to move into a service position, assuming you had a reasonable range of service experience through practica and predoctoral internship, than it would be to move from a service position to an academic one.

Finally, there are the longer-range considerations of advancement and salary related to type of position. While beginning positions in diverse settings may have quite similar salaries and all have some room for advancement in the first few years, the picture rapidly changes. Opportunities for advancement and increases in salary seem most limited in institutional settings such as counseling centers and community mental health centers. The salary scales may be relatively compressed and the only way to advance may be to move into an administrative position, of which there may be relatively few. While such factors may be comparatively unimportant for initial choices, they may have significance for your longer-range career goals. In academia, the speed with which one gets promoted and has salary increases is very directly related to scholarly publications. Thus, it would be possible to find two counseling psychologists both 15 years after their Ph.D., with one being a modestly paid associate professor earning less than a counseling center psychologist but the other a full professor earning more than all but the most successful independent practitioners.

In independent practice, the opportunities for advancement and income are almost totally a function of your own initiative and time invested. Note that one does not have a salary when in independent practice; one can speak only of net income after paying office expenses. While the average income of practitioners is generally only slightly more than the average salary of those in service positions in hospitals, clinics, and counseling centers, the range and standard deviation of income in independent practice is immense. Some persons prefer to see relatively few clients simply to generate a modest income and have considerable time for other activities; others find fulfillment in investing a great deal of time and energy into a very extensive counseling practice, spending many hours of their own each week in direct service as well as supervising others, perhaps even organizing and managing a group practice for which one receives part of the fees of each participating practitioner. In the latter case, the income level would easily double or triple the salary of the typical psychologist working in a hospital or clinic setting. Also in contrast to other settings, in independent practice there is no built-in career ladder. The day-to-day responsibilities of the professional practitioner with 25 years of experience are essentially the same as the new professional practitioner. Consequently, professional development opportunities become all the more critical for maintaining a sense of being part of a dynamic profession.

Once having decided on the type of position to seek, you can find a wide range of published advice. Most articles have been written regarding finding and interviewing for academic positions (Heppner & Downing, 1982; Ponterotto & Furlong, 1986), but there is a reasonable degree of generalizability for many positions. The major difference between academic positions and service positions is how one finds out about them. As Ponterotto and Furlong (1986) have made clear, personal contact networks are a major factor in candidates obtaining academic positions. (Personal contacts are defined as an affirmative answer to the question "Did your graduate advisor, or any of the individuals who wrote letters of recommendation on your behalf, personally know any of the faculty in the program which hired you?") For more service-oriented positions, especially outside one's own geographic area, the most extensive information can be found in the classified-ad section of the monthly APA newspaper, the *Monitor.* Many counseling center positions are also listed in the *Chronicle of Higher Education,* a weekly newspaper that is available in almost all colleges and universities.

In summary, we have described the possibilities for considerable flexibility in terms of movement from one type of position or another *given the appropriate experiential background and accomplishments.* Thus, when considering first postdoctoral positions, you need to look at what other types of positions you might want to consider later in your career and determine whether or not you should be obtaining any particular kind of experience from your initial career position.

Multiple-Role Considerations

As recently as a decade ago, this section might have been addressed only to women. Now we are also seeing a significant number of men who allow many of their career decisions to be affected by their roles and responsibilities as partners and parents. In this section, we use the term *multiple roles* to refer to roles you might fill outside of specific career-related ones but which have an impact upon career-related choices and behavior, thus affecting professional development. Counseling psychologists have been among the primary researchers on the issues that multiple roles present for psychological adjustment as well as for career adjustment. As O'Neil,

Fishman, and Kinsella-Shaw (1987) indicate, career decisions for dual-career couples may entail a whole range of gender-role and marriage-family dilemmas. Gilbert and Rachlin (1987) point out that in "dual-career families" (that is, where both partners have careers in which they wish to advance) there are many sources of conflict that arise in relation to "allocation of family work; feelings of confidence, entitlement and power; decisions concerning career placement and advancement; and the integration of career and family priorities" (p. 33).

We noted early in this chapter that part of the role of being a professional is the realization that you have to set your own priorities and limits. When you have a significant relationship with another professional person, then setting those priorities and limits is exponentially more complex, especially to the extent that there may be some significant differences in the values of partners, ranging from importance of a career to importance of a clean bathroom! Ideally, both parties of a professional couple can find positions that are satisfying and fulfilling in the same location. Unfortunately, that is a rare find; and even if you would be lucky enough to be in such a situation initially, jobs and expectations change so that over time one partner usually becomes more satisfied than the other. It is our observation that most couples deal with these "satisfaction differentials" in one of two ways. In one strategy, one partner stays in a satisfying career while the other one takes his or her turn in a less satisfying one with the understanding that at some later point in time, priority will be given to his or her being in a satisfying career. Alternatively, and sometimes as part of the first strategy, the less satisfied partner moves from job to job in an attempt to find a more satisfying one. There are any number of other less often used strategies, all of which rely for their effectiveness on explicit understandings of both members of the couple as to what is equitable and, if equity is not being experienced now, when there will be the opportunity to work toward a more equitable situation. (Dual career issues are lifelong—the quality of a marriage and well-being in retirement are directly related to the very kinds of factors that Gilbert and Rachlin noted above for dual-career marriages.)

Changing times have also meant a greater number of women and men receiving doctoral degrees in counseling psychology and also maintaining active roles as a parent. One quickly learns that effective parenting is a very time- and energy-demanding task. Managing the stress of adding the parenting role to other professional and life roles can be greatly facilitated by understanding two factors that are directly related to career planning. The more flexibility that one has in terms of time periods (flex-time) when the job can be done, the less stress there will be in managing child-care responsibilities. Secondly, contrary to the expectations of yet-to-be parents, child-care responsibilities are not limited to the first few years.

While the nature of the responsibilities change radically over the years, demands on time and energy will exist at least until children are of college age (and may not slow down much even then). At every age there are unexpected emotions that both fathers and mothers feel in relationship to their children that will affect how much time and energy they will want to put into their work. The work of Lee (1984) on the counseling concerns of women who are first-time mothers, after having established careers, is just one example of an article that could be written for the mothers or fathers of children or adolescents of almost any age.

Because of the relative recency of many of these social changes involving both men and women, the data on the effects of these multiple roles on personal well-being and professional development are only now beginning to appear. McBride (1990) has provided a succinct summary of the studies that have been finding that the multiple-role experience has affected women far more than men. She outlines a variety of factors that seem to affect the amount of stress in handling multiple roles but most of all describes the need for better research to understand their mental health effects. Clearly, a pertinent research agenda for many counseling psychologists for the decade of the nineties would be continued study of both the mental health and career effects of multiple roles on both men and women.

In summary, we believe that the career choices for a counseling psychologist who is a parent and/or partner of another career person need to include not only specific position responsibilities but also a careful and explicit exploration of how time, energy, and location demands of each position would affect outside-of-work responsibilities and quality time in these relationships.

The Transition: From Graduate School to First Position

"Graduate programs in psychology typically do not provide their students with anticipatory socialization concerning entry into a professional setting, the role demands of professional life, and the personal adjustments needed for professional development" (Olson, Downing, Heppner, & Pinkney, 1986, p. 415). No matter what your career choice, your preparation for this critical transition should begin with a reading of the Olson et al. article. We list below their six myths; in the article the authors describe the realities that render these statements myths and suggest what new professionals need to do to cope with the realities. The authors suggest, and we concur, that being prepared to deal with these transitions is the greatest service you can do for yourself. Here are their myths, or what might alternatively be called "Six Irrational Beliefs of New Professionals":

Myth (1) As soon as I unpack my bags, I will be settled;
Myth (2) My new associates will welcome me enthusiastically and accept me as one of them;

Myth (3) I will never be an apprentice again;
Myth (4) I will easily master the varied demands of my job;
Myth (5) I must perform perfectly, lest someone discover that I am a fraud;
Myth (6) Because I worked so hard to get here, I will love my job. (Olson et al., 1986, pp. 416–418)

In addition to some of the factors that they point out in dealing with the realities behind these myths, we believe that there are other key surprises. As you read these, they will probably strike you as just common sense; however, again and again we find new professionals feeling they were unprepared for what, with hindsight, seems so obvious. Let us provide a few examples.

In a new setting you will have to learn the norms of that setting. What are the behaviors that are rewarded; who interacts with whom, what are the taboos, for example, topics of discussion, behaviors, theoretical positions, research areas, political activities, that are deemed unacceptable or at least second class? How can you establish your own role and identity within that local culture? You will be expected, in most positions, to be able to handle the multiple roles of being a subordinate in some cases, a peer in most cases, and a superior (supervisor) in others. Each of these positions has implications for how you will interact with others, ranging from how you address each other to what kinds of information, concerns, and issues you share with one another. Just as we discuss some of the avoidant behaviors that went with self-preservation in graduate school, you may experience similar avoidant tendencies in your professional position if you find some aspects of your position disappointing. Most especially, if you believe there is little that can be done about those disappointments, you will find yourself increasingly cynical, possibly withdrawing and even undermining others (Civikly, 1979).

Schlossberg (1981, 1989), a counseling psychologist, has written extensively about the factors that determine how stressful a transition can be. In her latest (1989) book she describes practical strategies for coping with those changes. The skills of any counseling psychologist in assessing the strengths and limitations of both persons and environments are the fundamentals needed for implementing her recommended steps of taking stock of your situation, taking stock of yourself and supports, and taking stock of your strategies as a prerequisite for taking charge of your transitions so that they become part of, rather than an impediment to, your professional development.

Baron, Sekel, and Stott (1984) described a variety of specific tasks that they believe help the counseling center psychologist cope with the excitement and stress of the first year. They give very specific recommendations for (1) correcting unrealistic expectations, (2) making an accurate organizational assessment, (3) developing networks of support, (4) preventing overcommitment, (5) continuing professional growth, and

(6) assessing future goals and needs. In the next, and last, section of this chapter, we provide some specific recommendations to address the latter four components of these six tasks.

ESTABLISHING A CAREER

After you have chosen your first position and begun managing the transition phase described above, there are four remaining areas that need your attention in order to give yourself a maximum amount of flexibility and satisfaction as your career develops. The first two areas of concern are: (1) obtaining licensing as a psychologist and (2) considering other useful credentials, such as listing yourself in the National Register of Health Service Providers in Psychology and obtaining the Diplomate from the American Board of Professional Psychology. The third area relates to the kind of information you need if you want to consider a part-time or full-time independent practice. As noted in earlier chapters, an increasing number of new graduates in counseling psychology programs are entering such practice. Moreover, Watkins, Lopez, Campbell, and Himmell (1986) found that over one-half (57.1%) of all counseling psychologists engage in some independent practice even while holding full-time positions as counseling center psychologists, hospital psychologists, professors, and so forth. Because material concerning issues about independent practice is rarely contained in training programs, we identify a few major issues to consider and some current pertinent publications. We then come to the fourth and final area—professional development as most professional psychologists think of it. Considering the wide variety of professional programs and activities, which ones should you choose to keep feeling renewed and fulfilled as a counseling psychologist?

Licensing

In Chapter 3 we discussed some of the controversies about licensing. Fretz and Mills (1980) provided an extensive description of the numerous challenges to and changes in licensing laws during the 1970s. For the 1990s, any psychologist who expects to provide psychological services to the public needs to consider becoming licensed as a psychologist. In every state, offering psychological services for a fee requires licensing; many state agencies and all Veterans Administration hospitals require that psychologists be licensed, or in the case of new psychologists, that they be license-eligible and eventually become licensed. Thus, many of your professional career appointments will be affected by licensing.

Most critically, you need to be aware that each state has slightly different requirements for determining eligibility for licensure. Most of these requirements address courses taken as part of the doctoral program, the type of program (is it officially designated a psychology program?), and the kinds of supervised experience you have had at both predoctoral and postdoctoral levels. Completion of an APA-approved training program and an APA-approved internship are generally the most acceptable ways of meeting predoctoral training requirements for eligibility for licensing. However, a major issue of which you should be aware is that an applicant needs to be able to demonstrate that not only did he or she graduate from such a program but that he or she took the courses and had the experiences that are required to be part of an APA-approved program or internship. For example, your transcript could well be examined to see whether or not you did indeed have a course in the biological bases of behavior or that your internship did include formal one-to-one supervision. Any requirements of an approved program that are *not* evident in your own personal record will result in difficulty in becoming eligible for licensing. In some cases the questions raised can be addressed by documentation from your program or internship directors explaining why a given requirement is not reflected on your transcript or in a description of the internship. Nevertheless, even if the explanation is acceptable to the licensing board, it may mean as much as a six-month to one-year delay in your eligibility.

Postdoctoral supervision requirements for licensure are even more variable across states. In some states, you might need only a letter from the chief psychologist of an agency where you are working to indicate that you are a supervised employee, with no further definition of what supervision means. In other states, you may be required to provide evidence that you have had individual supervision in some specific ratio to direct services provided. It is extremely important that once you are established in a position in a state where you intend to get licensed, you find out the specific requirements of that state's law requiring postdoctoral supervised experience and begin to keep appropriate records of psychological services you provide and supervision you receive.

Once eligible for licensure, you will be required to take some type of examination. Most states use the Examination for Professional Practice in Psychology (EPPP), a comprehensive multiple-choice exam covering all areas of psychology. The examination is continually revised with input from a panel of psychologists from many experimental and applied areas. Students who completed undergraduate majors in psychology and who have had fairly comprehensive psychology courses at the graduate level seldom have difficulty with the exam. If, however, you have a more limited psychology background and/or have difficulty taking multiple-choice exams, you may want to consider taking one of the many examination preparation courses that are advertised each month in the APA *Monitor.* There are also a variety of self-help materials available; if you found in the past that you were disciplined enough to use those self-help materials getting ready for exams like the Graduate Record Exam, such materials may again be all that you would need. One of our favorite suggestions for persons who already have an extensive background in psychology is to review the glossary of a comprehensive introductory psychology textbook. Simply becoming reacquainted with all those terms will stimulate many associations to a variety of psychobiological functions, basics of learning, and so forth, that you once knew but have since forgotten.

In addition to the EPPP, an additional essay and/or oral exam may be required. In many states, this portion of the exam gives further attention to ethics, research, and the specifics of the state law. It is important for you to determine the content of any additional part of the licensing exam. It is very useful to talk to persons who have recently taken the exam to find out what kinds of questions were asked. For most of these examinations it is important to have a fairly specific understanding of both the APA Ethical Principles and the state's law regarding the practice of psychology, especially the reasons for which a person could lose his or her license. A few states have procedures for identifying specialty areas (e.g., counseling, clinical, etc.). Such states may require some additional specialized written or oral examination.

After being licensed in one state, if you should move to another state, there may be some degree of reciprocity such that you may not have to complete all parts of the new state's exam. However, there is tremendous variation from state to state and the reciprocity rules change periodically. Contrary to the hopes of many graduate students, there is no single step or set of steps you can take to guarantee your eligibility for licensing or reciprocity in all states. Following the suggestions in the earlier parts of this section regarding eligibility is the best protection you can give yourself.

Other Credentials

After you have obtained licensure, there are at least two other types of credentials worth considering for enhancing your career opportunities. Becoming listed in the National Register of Health Service Providers in Psychology provides evidence that you have had appropriate predoctoral training and supervised experience to qualify as a health service provider. The primary advantage for listing in the register is that this list is widely used by insurance companies and a number of licensing boards as recognizing that the candidate meets the requirements for providing reimbursable health services. Because of the number of times that legislation is written with the generic term *clinical psychology,* meaning those who are approved for providing health services, counseling and school psychologists, as well as Ed.D. and Psy.D. degree holders, are all particularly well served by the register. Once listed in the register, one does not need to continually provide further documentation regarding the adequacies of your preparation as a health-service-providing psychologist.

The other major credential you may want to consider is the Diplomate from the American Board of Professional Psychology (ABPP). This board was established at approximately the same time as the specialty of counseling psychology, that is, the late 1940s, to provide recognition of the most competent applied psychologists. The board originally awarded diplomates in school, counseling, clinical, and I/O psychology. It now also offers diplomates in clinical neuropsychology, family psychology, and forensic psychology. While the board was established to provide the equivalent of board certification in many medical specialties, it has never been used as widely in psychology as it is in medicine. There are a slowly increasing number of tangible advantages, for example, higher pay levels possible in the Veterans Administration, higher fees for assessment services provided in various states, more extensive reciprocity in licensure when moving from state to state. However, the primary motivation for many candidates who apply for the diplomate remains the attainment of this recognition of excellence.

To earn the diplomate, one has first to provide evidence of appropriate doctoral degree training and five years' experience, including the internship, in counseling psychology (or other specialties as listed above). Applicants who meet the eligibility requirements submit an extensive work sample focused on assessment and intervention and then have an on-site examination by several diplomates. These examiners directly observe an applicant's work such as an assessment interview of a client and also conduct an extensive oral examination on professional theory, research, practice, and ethical issues. As with the licensing exams, talking to someone who has recently undergone the ABPP examination may be one of the most useful ways to learn about the process. In the January issue of each year's *The Counseling Psychologist* there is a listing of those persons who have been awarded the diplomate in counseling psychology in the past year.

There are a number of other registers, diplomates, and specialty certifications available, many of them advertised in the APA *Monitor* and/or the American Association of Counseling and Development monthly newsletter. It is probably fair to say that each of these others is less widely recognized in psychology than the National Register or the ABPP Diplomate; however, they may each have some networking value; that is, the listing identifies a variety of persons around the country who have the specialized interests indicated by the type of register or certification—for example, treating sexual dysfunction, group therapy, career counseling, or rehabilitation counseling. For any psychologist with a significant amount of fee-for-practice service, certificates from these specialized agencies may also have some value for assuring clients of your specialized training, just as you may find, for example, reassurance by seeing various kinds of certificates recognizing specialized training in your physician's or dentist's office.

Independent Practice Considerations

When examining the best strategies for beginning and maintaining an independent practice a recent panel of experts "suggested that competence could be built by means of thorough and diversified training at the graduate level, postgraduate therapy training, and a lot of therapy experience in an institutional setting *before* [italics added] one establishes a practice. Through practical experience, the neophyte clinicians will then be able to accept clients for who they are and to develop enough faith in themselves and their skills as clinicians. Last, the panel noted that it takes a personal commitment of time and energy to build a practice. The need to examine one's conscience about this commitment and the need to create a flexible schedule for important things outside of work (e.g., family, friends, recreation, exercise) are viewed as important considerations in making this career decision" (Walfish & Coovert, 1989, p. 55).

The statements from this panel clearly indicate the importance of having a strong base of experience before moving into independent practice settings. The panel also noted the complexity of other issues that one encounters in making the move from an institutional-based practice, with its regular work hours, steady supply of clients, and so forth, to the independent practice arena. In the latter, one clearly must attend to a variety of marketplace issues such as finding clients, record keeping, and billing. An increasing number of publications are available for those in independent practice. Each year various books are published primarily for the practitioner (e.g., Stromberg, 1988; Woody, 1989). More attention is being given in periodical publications as well, including a variety of articles in *Professional Psychology* and in the "Register Report," the newsletter of the Council of the National Register of Health Service Providers in Psychology. There is also the *Journal of Practice Building Strategies: Psychotherapy.* All of these references deal with topics such as marketing, computer software for record keeping, malpractice, and other professional liability considerations. Some practitioners have also recommended looking at journals from other disciplines, especially when concerned with the larger issues of establishing partnerships in group practices. *Legal Economics* is a journal for lawyers that some psychology colleagues have suggested as one that is applicable to psychology practice for dealing with major issues such as how to market a practice, how much to spend on overhead, whether or not to have branch offices, and so forth.

Maintaining professional development when in independent practice may be most challenging yet all the more critical. How can you avoid the feeling of isolation, loss of professional identity, and burnout, especially if you are in solo practice and not in regular contact with other psychologists on a day-to-day basis? Independent practice psychologists have found a variety of ways to cope with those feelings, including teaching courses at local colleges or universities, or holding a part-time position in a clinic or agency. When such possibilities are not easily available or otherwise attractive you might want to consider peer consultation groups. Greenburg, Lewis, and Johnson (1985) and their colleagues have conducted and written about the usefulness of peer consultation groups for practitioners. The majority of practitioners they studied expressed a desire to belong to such a group if available; those who had already participated in such groups indicated a high degree of satisfaction. Finally, independent practitioners find participation in conventions and workshops one of the most essential components of maintaining a sense of connectedness with other professionals.

Continuing Professional Development

So now to our final area—the commencement of your own totally self-directed professional development. We focus our suggestions here on how to meet your own personal needs for maintaining a vitalized and satisfying career as a counseling psychologist.

You may now believe that you will learn more than you will ever need to know in all the courses that are required in your program. You will soon find, however, that the old adage "The more I learn, the less I know" will apply to your own professional development as a counseling psychologist. By the time you finish graduate school you will probably have a list of things you *really* want to learn—without the presence of requirements. Many of the goals that both new and experienced psychologists have for such new learning can be met by what are called continuing education programs. Fortunately, the profession of psychology maintains nationally, through the American Psychological Association, and often locally through state associations, a large variety of programs. They are regularly listed in the APA *Monitor.* They may range from a two-hour workshop to week-long programs focused on various psychological disorders, new assessment technologies, new treatment techniques, and new settings for practice.

These programs can also meet other needs than just further training. If you were to find yourself the only counseling psychologist in a practice, research, or teaching setting, you might experience a growing sense of isolation, and perhaps a lack of professional identity. Participating in continuing educational programs is particularly valuable for touching base and networking with colleagues with similar interests, values, and concerns. A few states have requirements for participating in continuing education for renewing one's license to practice. Thus continuing education courses may meet extrinsic as well as intrinsic needs.

Another way to maintain collegial connections and gain fresh perspectives is by becoming an active participant in various psychological associations. State psychology associations may be the easiest to become involved in without feeling overwhelmed by huge numbers of colleagues. Most of the members of state psychological associations are involved in some sort of professional practice; an increasing number of state associations have special interest groups for practitioners in areas like, for example, geropsychology and forensic psychology. In such groups you can quickly become known to many fellow professionals and find colleagues with similar interests.

The Division of Counseling Psychology (Division 17) of APA provides the primary route for counseling psychologists to maintain colleagueship with other counseling psychologists. We wrote earlier about the ways for becoming a member of the student affiliate group of counseling psychology; once you have your doctoral degree you can then become a full member of APA and then a full member of Division 17. The division has an extremely active role in the national APA convention program each year. Because it has such a large number of its members participating in the convention, it is able to offer a large amount of programming at the convention. Currently there are over 40 hours of programming at each APA convention, specifically for programs involving Division 17 members. These programs cover a variety of practice and research interests. An increasing number of them are sponsored by the division's special interest groups and its various committees, for example, the Committee on Women, the Professional Affairs Committee, the Education and Training Committee, the Scientific Affairs Committee, the Private Practice Committee. A program of regional conferences for counseling psychology was developed under the leadership of then President James Hurst during 1988. Some regional conventions are periodically recurring. As suggested by its name, the division's New Professionals Committee tries to attend specifically to the concerns of those beginning their careers as counseling psychologists.

Still less formal arrangements sometimes occur in areas where there are several psychologists living close together. They may form clubs to bring psychologists of similar interests together to read the same books or journal articles and meet regularly (e.g., monthly) to talk about those readings. As you might expect, the value of such groups extends far beyond the content found in the book or article; this is truly a time for colleagueship, providing participants with an opportunity to explore any other current specific questions or concerns as well as enhance one's sense of professional identity.

As a way of bringing to a close this journey through the many facets of professional development we encourage you to keep a record of the kinds of experiences which you find most valuable and meaningful during your graduate training. Once that formal training ends, you may want to use your list as a guide in finding the activities and experiences that will be most stimulating and gratifying for you. With that accomplished, you will be well on your way to a long, productive, and satisfying career as a counseling psychologist.

SUMMARY

The primary purpose of this final chapter is to help the reader to develop a perspective on graduate education that marks it as the beginning of lifelong professional development. Different types of programs and graduate degrees in counseling psychology must first be considered by those who have not yet begun graduate school. Then six challenging perspectives help to explore the ramifications of a professional development view of graduate school: (1) changing the means-to-an-end attitude into professional development, (2) changing self-preservation into self-actualization, (3) balancing dependence and independence, (4) finding a mentor, (5) actively coping with disappointments, and (6) finding personal development in professional development.

First, because graduate school has a number of environmental presses that do not serve students well in terms of managing their own career development, an alternative to a means-to-an-end perspective is realized by looking at graduate school as the first phase of *being* a counseling psychologist rather than how to *become* a counseling psychologist. Next, one must take an active role in response to perceived threats to self-efficacy, environmental presses toward dependency, and the inevitable disappointments in any program. Of great value to the graduate student is mentoring. Finally, one must recognize the challenges to values and assumptions that come with graduate training and how personal counseling may be a significant asset in coping with such challenges as well as in learning effective counseling skills.

The next major section reviewed a variety of opportunities for professional development and enrichment available in most counseling psychology programs. These opportunities are often not made explicit and therefore are overlooked. Opportunities for professional development can be obtained through elective courses, professional readings, professional conventions, externships, internships, and the dissertation. The final parts of the chapter focused on the initial postdoctoral years and establishing a career as a counseling psychologist. Special considerations, options, and resources can be identified for considering types of career choices, the implications of multiple roles in making career choices, and then managing the transition to a full-time career. In the last section, attention was given to issues in and advice for obtaining licensing as a psychologist, obtaining other valuable professional credentials, considering and establishing an independent practice, and, finally, continuing strategies for lifelong professional development.

References

American Psychological Association (1979). *Criteria for accreditation of doctoral training programs and internships in professional psychology.* Washington, DC.

American Psychological Association (1990). *Graduate study in psychology and associated fields.* Washington, DC.

Bandura, A. (1977). Self-efficacy: Toward a unifying theory of behavioral change. *Psychological Review, 84,* 191–215.

Baron, A., Jr., Sekel, A. C., & Stott, F. W. (1984). Early career issues for counseling center psychologists: The first six years. *The Counseling Psychologist, 12*(1), 121–125.

Belar, C. D., & Orgel, S. A. (1980). Survival guide for intern applicants. *Professional Psychology, 11,* 672–675.

Bogat, G. A., & Redner, R. L. (1985). How mentoring affects the professional development of women in psychology. *Professional Psychology: Research and Practice, 16,* 851–859.

Bova, B. M., & Phillips, R. R. (1982, November). The mentoring relationship as an educational experience. Paper presented at the National Conference of the Adult Education Association of the United States of America, San Antonio, TX (Eric Document Reproduction Service, No. ED224 944).

Brill, R., Wolkin, J., & McKeel, N. (1985). Strategies for selecting and securing predoctoral clinical internships of choice. *Professional Psychology: Research and Practice, 16,* 3–6.

Civikly, J. M. (1989, November). Developing a professional identity. Paper presented at the Second National Conference on the Teaching and Employment of Graduate Teaching Assistants, Seattle, WA.

Clark, M. M. (1986). Personal therapy: A review of empirical research. *Professional Psychology: Research and Practice, 17,* 541–543.

Cole, M. A., Kolko, D. J., & Craddick, R. A. (1981). The quality and process of the internship experience. *Professional Psychology: Research and Practice, 12,* 570–577.

Corey, M. S., & Corey, G. (1989). *Becoming a helper.* Belmont, CA: Wadsworth.

Cronan-Hillix, T. C., Gensheimer, L. K., Cronan-Hillix, W. A., & Davidson, W. S. (1986). Students' views of mentors in psychology graduate training. *Teaching of Psychology, 13,* 123–127.

Egan, G. (1975). *Exercises in helping skills.* Monterey, CA: Brooks/Cole.

Fox, R. E. (1990, Winter). NCSPP: A political sleeping giant. *National Council of Schools of Professional Psychology Newsletter,* p. 4.

Fretz, B. R., & Stang, D. J. (1980). *Preparing for graduate study in psychology: Not for seniors only.* Washington, DC: American Psychological Association.

Fretz, B. R., & Mills, D. H. (1980). *Licensing and certification of psychologists and counselors.* San Francisco: Jossey-Bass.

Garcia, M. E., Malott, R. W., & Brethower, D. (1988). A system of thesis and dissertation supervision: Helping graduate students succeed. *Teaching of Psychology, 15,* 186–191.

Gilbert, L. A., & Rachlin, V. (1987). Mental health and psychological functioning of dual-career families. *The Counseling Psychologist, 15,* 7–49.

Greenburg, S. L., Lewis, G. J., & Johnson, N. (1985). Peer consultation groups for private practitioners. *Professional Psychology: Research and Practice, 16,* 437–447.

Guy, J. D., Stark, M. J., Poelstra, P. L. (1988). Personal therapy for psychotherapists before and after entering professional practice. *Professional Psychology: Research and Practice, 19,* 474–476.

Hall, R. M., & Sandler, B. R. (1983). *Academic mentoring for women students and faculty: A new look at an old way to get ahead.* Washington, DC: Association of American Colleges.

Heppner, P., & Downing, N. E. (1982). Job interviewing for new psychologists: Riding the emotional roller-coaster. *Professional Psychology: Research and Practice, 13,* 334–341.

Heppner, P., & Krauskopf, C. J. (1987). An information-process approach to personal problem solving. *The Counseling Psychologist, 15,* 371–447.

Hollis, J. W., & Wantz, R. A. (1990). *Counselor Preparation, 1990–92: Programs, personnel, trends* (7th ed.). Muncie, IN: Accelerated Development.

Jacob, N. C. (1987). Managing the internship application experience: Advice from an exhausted but contented survivor. *The Counseling Psychologist, 15,* 146–155.

Keith-Spiegel, P. (1990). *The complete guide to graduate school admission.* Hillsdale, NJ: Erlbaum.

Kestenbaum, J. D. (1986). Perceived impact of personal counseling by counseling psychology graduate students. *Dissertation Abstracts International, 48/01B,* 266 (University Microfilms No. AAC8709088).

Lee, R. E. (1964). When mid-career mothers first return to work: Counseling concerns. *Journal of Counseling and Development, 63,* 39.

Levinson, D. J. (1980). The mentoring relationship. In M. Morgan (Ed.), *Managing career development* (pp. 117–119). New York: Van Nostrand.

Mallinckrodt, B., Gelso, C. J., & Royalty, G. M. (1990). Impact of the research training environment and counseling psychology students' Holland personality type on interest in research. *Professional Psychology: Research and Practice, 21,* 26–32.

McBride, A. B. (1990). Mental health effects of women's multiple roles. *American Psychologist, 45,* 381–384.

Mendelson, C. (1987). Adjustment to college: The role of perception of childhood interactions with parents, autonomy, and social support. *Dissertation Abstracts International, 48/01B,* 3406 (University Microfilms No. AAC8725534).

Olson, S. K., Downing, N. E., Heppner, P. P., & Pinkney, J. (1986). Is there life after graduate school? Coping with the transitions to postdoctoral employment. *Professional Psychology: Research and Practice, 17,* 415–419.

O'Neil, J. M., Fishman, D. M., & Kinsella-Shaw, M. (1987). Dual-career couples' career transitions and normative dilemmas. *The Counseling Psychologist, 15,* 50–96.

Osberg, T. M., & Rallin, N. L. (1989). Networking as a tool for career advancement among academic psychologists. *Teaching of Psychology, 16,* 26–28.

Ponterotto, J. G., & Furlong, M. J. (1986). A profile of recently employed academicians in APA-approved and nonapproved counseling psychology programs. *Professional Psychology: Research and Practice, 17,* 65–68.

Ralph, N. (1980). Learning psychotherapy: A developmental perspective. *Psychiatry, 43,* 243–250.

Rawles, B. A. (1980). The influence of a mentor on the level of self-actualization of American scientists. *Dissertation Abstracts International, 41,* 134AA (University Microfilms No. 80-22,331).

Schlossberg, N. K. (1981). A model for analyzing human adaptation to transition. *The Counseling Psychologist, 9*(2), 2–18.

Schlossberg, N. K. (1989). *Overwhelmed: Coping with life's ups and downs.* Lexington, MA: Lexington Books.

Simono, R. B., & Wachowiak, D. (1983). Career patterns in counseling centers: Counseling psychologists review their past, present, and future. *Professional Psychology: Research and Practice, 14,* 142–148.

Skovholt, T. M., Stone, G. L., & Hill, C. E. (1984). Institutional affiliations of contributors to scholarly and professional activities in counseling psychology: 1980–1983. *Journal of Counseling Psychology, 31,* 394–397.

Solway, K. S. (1985). Transitions from graduate school to internship: A potential crisis. *Professional Psychology: Research and Practice, 16,* 50–54.

Stromberg, C. (1988). *The psychologist's legal handbook.* Washington, DC: The Council for the National Register of Health Service Providers in Psychology.

Walfish, S., & Coovert, D. L. (1989). Beginning and maintaining an independent practice: A Delphi Poll. *Professional Psychology: Research and Practice, 20,* 54–55.

Watkins, C. E., Jr., Lopez, F. G., Campbell, V. L., & Himmell, C. D. (1986). Contemporary counseling psychology: Results of a national survey. *Journal of Counseling Psychology, 33,* 301–309.

Woody, R. H. (1989). *Business success in mental health practice: Modern marketing, management and legal strategies.* San Francisco, CA: Jossey-Bass.

Name Index

Subject Index

Permissions and Acknowledgments

Chapter 1

Tables 1-1 and 1-3 (pp. 14, 18) from Watkins, C.E., Lopez, F.G., Campbell, V.L., & Himmell, C.D. (1986), "Contemporary Counseling Psychology: Results of a National Survey," in *Journal of Counseling Psychology, 33,* pp. 301–309. Copyright 1986 by the American Psychological Association. Reprinted by permission. Table 1-2 (p. 17) adapted from Fitzgerald, Louise F., & Osipow, S.H. (1986), "An Occupational Analysis of Counseling Psychology: How Special Is the Specialty?," in *American Psychologist, 41;* adapted from Table 3, pp. 538–539. Copyright 1986 by the American Psychological Association.

Chapter 4

Table 4-1 (p. 90) from Gelso, C.J. (1979), "Research in Counseling: Methodological and Professional Issues," in *The Counseling Psychologist, 8(3),* pp. 7–35; adapted from Table 1, p. 13; copyright © 1979 and reprinted by permission of Sage Publications, Inc.

Chapter 6

Table 6-1 (pp. 181–182) from Hill, C.E., & O'Grady, K.E. (1985), "List of Therapist Intentions Illustrated in a Case Study and With Therapists of Varying Theoretical Orientations," in *Journal of Counseling Psychology, 32,* pp. 3–22. Copyright 1985 by the American Psychological Association. Reprinted by permission.

Chapter 10

Table 10-1 (p. 299) from American Psychiatric Association: *Diagnostic and Statistical Manual of Mental Disorders, Third Edition, Revised.* Washington, D.C., American Psychiatric Association, 1987. Reprinted by permission.

Chapter 11

Table 11-1 (pp. 348–349) from *The Counseling Psychologist,* Vol. 8, No. 1, 1979; Table 11-2 (p. 349) from Sue, D.W., Bernier, J.E., Durran, A., Feinberg, L., Pedersen, P., Smith, E.J., & Vasquez-Nuttall, E. (1982), "Position Paper: Cross-Cultural Counseling Competencies," in *The Counseling Psychologist, 10(2),* pp. 45–52; tables copyright © 1979 and 1982 and reprinted by permission of Sage Publications, Inc.

Chapter 12

Figure 12-1 (p. 370) from John L. Holland, *Making Vocational Choices: A Theory of Vocational Personalities & Work Environments,* 2/e, © 1985, p. 29. Reprinted by permission of Prentice Hall, Englewood Cliffs, New Jersey.

Chapter 16

Figure 16-1 (p. 494) from Morrill, W.H., Oetting, E.R., & Hurst, J.C. (1974), "Dimensions of Counselor Functioning," in *Personnel and Guidance Journal, 52,* pp. 354–359, by the courtesy of Weston H. Morrill, Ph.D.

About the Authors

About the Authors

CHARLES J. GELSO received his Ph.D. in counseling psychology from Ohio State University in 1970. Since that time he has been affiliated with the University of Maryland, College Park. From 1970 to 1982, he was a psychologist at the University Counseling Center and an affiliate professor in the Department of Psychology; since 1982 he has been a full-time faculty member in the department.

Dr. Gelso has taught a variety of undergraduate and graduate courses in the counseling psychology program at the University of Maryland. The course most influential in his work on *Counseling Psychology* has been an introductory course on the topic which is taught to upper-level graduate students, many of whom are considering advanced training and careers in the helping professions. Dr. Gelso has been involved in teaching, research, and counseling practice throughout his career. His current research interests include the role of the therapist-client relationship, with special emphasis on such concepts as working alliance, transference, and countertransference. He is also interested in how the graduate-school experience turns counseling psychology students toward or away from science and scholarly research.

Dr. Gelso has been published widely in journals of counseling psychology, and is the author (with Deborah Hazel Johnson) of *Explorations in Time-Limited Counseling and Psychotherapy,* a book studying the process and effects of therapy in which limits have been set in advance on the number of sessions. He was associate editor and then editor of the *Journal of Counseling Psychology* from 1980 through 1987, and continues to actively review for several professional journals. Dr. Gelso is a Fellow of both the American Psychological Association and the American Psychological Society.

BRUCE R. FRETZ received his Ph.D. in counseling psychology from Ohio State University in 1965. Since that time he has been a faculty member in the Department of Psychology at the University of Maryland, College Park. He has taught more than 20 courses, including introductory, developmental, personality, and testing courses at the undergraduate level, and nearly every course in the counseling psychology doctoral program. He regularly teaches graduate courses in assessment, career counseling, and professional issues.

Dr. Fretz's current research interests include the process and outcomes of career counseling for clients who are experiencing significant psychological stress which they attribute to their career situations. Another current research interest focuses upon psychological issues in the effective management of life transitions among persons over 65. Dr. Fretz has been program director of a geropsychology training program funded by the National Institute of Mental Health.

Bruce R. Fretz served as editor of *The Counseling Psychologist* from 1985 to 1990, and continues to serve as consulting editor for several journals devoted to counseling and applied psychology. His other books include (with David H. Mills) *Licensing and Certification of Psychologists and Counselors* and (with D. Stang) *Preparing for Graduate Study in Psychology: Not for Seniors Only.* He has been a consultant to more than 20 universities developing counseling psychology programs, and is also a consultant to numerous government agencies and private businesses in the development of pre-retirement programs.

Dr. Fretz currently serves on the board of directors of the National Register of Health Service Providers in Psychology. He holds a diplomate in counseling psychology from the American Board of Professional Psychology. He is a Fellow of the American Psychological Association in the divisions of Counseling Psychology and Teaching of Psychology, and served as president of the Division of Counseling Psychology in 1991–1992.